MW00337118

Residential Property Management

Principles and Practice

David Kuperberg, *RAM, CPM*

N. Mike Patellis, *RAM, CPM*

Barbara Dershowitz, *Editor*

BuilderBooks™

National Association of Home Builders
1201 15th Street, NW
Washington, DC 20005-2800
www.builderbooks.com

Residential Property Management: Principals and Practices
David Kuperberg, RAM, CPM
Mike Patellis, RAM, CPM

Theresa Minch	Executive Editor
Jessica Poppe	Assistant Editor
Barbara Dershowitz	Copyeditor
Armen Kojoyian	Cover Designer

BuilderBooks at the National Association of Home Builders

ERIC JOHNSON	**Publisher**
THERESA MINCH	**Executive Editor**
DORIS TENNYSON	**Senior Acquisitions Editor**
JESSICA POPPE	**Assistant Editor**
JENNY LAMBERT	**Assistant Editor**
BRENDA ANDERSON	**Director of Fulfillment**
GILL WALKER	**Marketing Manager**
JACQUELINE BARNES	**Marketing Manager**
GERALD HOWARD	NAHB Executive Vice President and CEO
MARK PURSELL	Executive Vice President Marketing & Sales
GREG FRENCH	Staff Vice President, Publications and Non-dues Revenue

ISBN 0–86718–573-2

Printed in the United States of America

Cataloging-in-Publication Data available at the Library of Congress

Patellis, Mike, 1938–
Residential property management : principals and practices / Mike Patellis, David Kuperberg.
p. cm.
Includes index.
ISBN 0-86718-573-2 (hardback)
1. Real estate management—United States. I. Kuperberg, David, 1956– II. Title.
HD1394.5.U6P38 2003
333.33′8—dc21

2003006496

Disclaimer
This publication is designed to provide accurate and authoritative information in regard to the subject matter covered. It is sold with the understanding that the publisher is not engaged in rendering legal, accounting, or other professional service. If legal advice or other expert assistance is required, the services of a competent professional person should be sought.

—From a Declaration of Principles jointly adopted by a Committee of the American Bar Association and a Committee of Publishers and Associations.

For further information, please contact:
BuilderBooks™
National Association of Home Builders
1201 15th Street, NW
Washington, DC 20005-2800
(800) 223–2665
Check us out online at: www.builderbooks.com

8/03 [SLR Production]/[SLR Production]/[Data Reproductions Corp.] 2000

FOREWORD

Responsible, dedicated, educated multifamily property management professionals are a lynchpin in the success of any multifamily development endeavor. Ideally, the relationship between the property owner and the property management staff should be synergetic. If you will, visualize the functioning of a successful multifamily property thusly: the property developer/owner and the property management staff share the same goal—to attract residents and ensure the financial viability and stability of the property.

In essence, property managers are tasked with the enormous responsibility of managing the daily operations of multi-million dollar companies. Whether you manage high-end luxury apartment homes or affordable apartment homes, your role is vital. Those property managers, who have gone above and beyond and availed themselves to furthering their careers by seeking the Registered in Apartment Management (RAM) designation are among the best in the business.

As you now begin your quest for the widely-recognized RAM designation, this textbook, will serve as an invaluable guide. In addition to the authors N. Mike Patellis and David Kuperberg, many industry experts and NAHB staff persons have lent their expertise to this publication. I would hope you use this book as a reference guide. As I, and many of my fellow RAMs know to be true, by the time you reach the pinnacle of your success, this book will serve as a dog-eared testament of your in-depth knowledge of the property management industry.

Andrew M. Chaban, RAM
CEO, Princeton Properties
Lowell, MA

PREFACE

CHARLES E. SCHUMER
NEW YORK

COMMITTEES:
BANKING
ENERGY
JUDICIARY
RULES

United States Senate
WASHINGTON, DC 20510

December 16, 2002

David Kuperberg
President
Cooper Square Realty, Inc.
6 East 43rd Street
New York, NY 10017

Dear David:

The field of multi-housing management has matured considerably over the past several decades. Likewise, so have the daily demands that are made of the professional multi-housing manager. To be up to the task, you must possess the qualities of intelligence, insightfulness, stick-to-itiveness, and integrity. And you must be thoroughly educated in the fundamentals of this rapidly evolving profession.

By becoming a multi-housing manager, you have committed to make a positive difference in the lives of thousands of people. Not only will you be responsible for protecting the investments of the property owners who will engage your services, but you also will be responsible for ensuring the residential quality of life of the individuals and families whose homes you will manage. By enrolling in the RAM course of study, you have committed to become the best-educated, most qualified multihousing manager you can be.

I take this opportunity to congratulate the authors and the editor of this formidable text. If you will heed their wisdom, I assure you that it will guide you well. I also wish to congratulate the National Association of Home Builders for its leadership position in ensuring quality housing throughout the United States and the world, and for allocating so many resources of time, energy, and funding to the education and professionalization of the multihousing management profession.

Finally, I congratulate you. By all indicators, the demand for knowledgeable, competent, and ethical multi-housing managers will only continue to grow. You have truly chosen an outstanding career, and I wish you success.

On behalf of those whom you will serve, I also thank you for your commitment to excellence.

Sincerely,

Charles E. Schumer
U.S. Senator

PLEASE RESPOND TO THE FOLLOWING OFFICE:

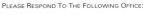

☐ ALBANY: Leo O'Brien Building, Room 420, Albany, NY 12207, (518) 431-4070

☐ BINGHAMTON: Federal Office Building, 15 Henry Street, Room B6, Binghamton, NY 13901, (607) 772-8109

☐ BUFFALO: 111 West Huron, Room 620, Buffalo, NY 14202, (716) 846-4111

☐ HUDSON VALLEY: P.O. Box A, Red Hook, NY 12571, (914) 285-9741, (845) 569-0923

☐ LONG ISLAND: Two Greenway Plaza, 145 Pine Lawn Road, Room 300N, Melville, NY 11747, (631) 753-0978

☐ NEW YORK CITY: 757 Third Avenue, Suite 1702, New York, NY 10017, (212) 486-4430, TDD: (212) 486-7661

☐ ROCHESTER: 100 State Street, Room 3040, Rochester, NY 14614, (716) 263-5866

☐ SYRACUSE: 100 South Clinton, Room 841, Syracuse, NY 13261, (315) 423-5471

☐ WASHINGTON: 313 Hart Senate Office Building, Washington, DC 20510, (202) 224-6542, TDD: (202) 224-0420

 http://schumer.senate.gov

ABOUT THE AUTHORS

David Kuperberg, CPM, Adv. RAM

An acknowledged leader and innovator in the field of multihousing management, and a vocal advocate of industry training and certification, David Kuperberg is President of Cooper Square Realty, Inc., one of the New York metropolitan area's most successful and highly respected residential management organizations.

Mr. Kuperberg began his multihousing career in 1978, when he assumed the management of a small family-owned portfolio of distressed New York City properties. Working from a storefront in the lower east side of Manhattan, repairing locks and windows in the back to make ends meet, Mr. Kuperberg started buying and syndicating properties in the early 1980s, and cultivated a reputation as a capable and ethical self-managed developer. Soon after, Mr. Kuperberg recognized the opportunity in sponsoring cooperative and condominium conversions, and he mastered the management of shared-interest associations. He established Cooper Square Realty, Inc., in 1984 and has since expanded the company to employ more than 1,000 building service workers and 80 in-house employees, all working for the benefit of the more than 100 properties with an aggregate of 16,000+ units and more than 1-million square feet of commercial space that have entrusted their management to Mr. Kuperberg and his firm. In addition, Cooper Square Realty, Inc., is now a full-service real estate organization, providing asset management, sales and brokerage, and mortgage brokerage to an expanding cadre of clients. Calling upon his degree in civil engineering and his training with the national engineering and architecture firm of Lockwood-Greene, Mr. Kuperberg also has introduced professional construction industry standards to capital and construction projects in the properties under his management.

Celebrated both within and outside the multihousing arena, Mr. Kuperberg and Cooper Square Realty, Inc., have been honored with such awards as Management Company of the Year from the Associated Builders and Owners of Greater New York, Inc., (ABO), two Leadership in Management awards from *The Cooperator* magazine, and numerous management awards from *Habitat* magazine. Under Mr. Kuperberg's stewardship, two Cooper Square Realty, Inc., managers have been named New York RAM of the Year, and Mr. Kuperberg himself was recognized as National RAM of the Year at the National Association of Home Builders' 30th Anniversary Pillars of the Industry event. He is the recipient of the prestigious Access-Ability Award, which was conferred by Community Access, a program that provides housing for the homeless mentally ill, and in 2002 he was named Humanitarian of the Year by the Greater New York Chapter of IREM (the Institute for Real Estate Management), and was the honoree of the Harold J. Kalikow Camp for Boy Scouts with Disabilities.

A frequent speaker at industry events, Mr. Kuperberg has appeared on *Court TV* and *Fox News* as a residential real estate expert. He has written numerous articles for such publications as *Real Estate Weekly, The Cooperator,* and *Habitat* magazine, and has been quoted in *The New York Times* and elsewhere.

Past Chair of the RAM Board of Governors, Mr. Kuperberg also chaired the State Licensing of Property Managers Subcommittee of the National Association of Home Builders, during which time he authored *Licensing of Residential Property Managers: A Study of State Licensing Requirements* (published by NAHB). Mr. Kuperberg is the 2003 President of the New York Chapter of IREM, and serves as a Life Governor of the National Board of Governors of RAM, Vice President of the ABO, member of the Residential Management Committee of the Real Estate Board of New York, member of the Building Owners and Managers Association of Greater New York (BOMA), board member of Community Access, and board member of several cooperatives and condominiums. He is also Captain of his local volunteer fire company.

Mr. Kuperberg has earned the multihousing management industry's highest designations of CPM (Certified Property Manager) and Advanced RAM (Registered in Apartment Management), and the coveted AMO certification for Cooper Square Realty, Inc.

Mr. Kuperberg may be reached c/o Cooper Square Realty, Inc., 6 East 43rd Street, New York, New York 10017-4609; by phone at (212) 682–7373; by fax at (212) 682–5441; and via e-mail at dkuperberg@coopersquare.com.

N. Mike Patellis, CPM, Adv. RAM

An entrepreneur and visionary in the multihousing arena, N. Mike Patellis is founder and President of Marietta, Georgia-based Patellis Property Management Company, specializing in property management education, training, and consultation, and the management of single family housing for individual owners and corporate entities. Mr. Patellis also has served as the primary Contract Instructor to the United States Departments of the Navy, Air Force, and Marine Corps for the *Registered in Apartment Management* (RAM) curriculum in conjunction with the Congressional mandate to privatize all military housing within the United States.

Highly decorated and today retired from active duty with a distinguished combat service record, Mr. Patellis served in the United States Army, achieving the rank of Lieutenant Colonel and earning a degree in Commerce/Economics from Bellarmine College in Louisville, Kentucky, while assigned as a Senior U.S. Army advisor to the Kentucky Army National Guard and Army Reserve. Upon leaving the military in 1979, Mr. Patellis entered the field of property management and cultivated his expertise in a variety of industry positions, including Regional Vice President of an Atlanta-based residential management firm; District Manager of National Housing Partnership—Atlanta Regional Office; Deputy Executive Director of the City of Atlanta Housing Authority; National Director of Public Sector Housing for a national management firm; and Regional Manager of 16 multi-family Class A communities in two states.

Mr. Patellis's career accomplishments include the management administration of thousands of dwelling units in several multi-state territories and the simultaneous supervision of more than 1,000 multifamily housing maintenance and other staff members; the development and implementation of administrative and operational procedures for public and Section 42 (LIHTC) housing; consistent rent-up in advance of projections; consistent reduction of bad debt; and consistent expansion of portfolio occupancy and net operating income for owners.

A recognized authority in the multihousing management industry and within such areas as conventional Class A multifamily housing, tax credits, public and subsidized housing, and commercial and industrial space, Mr. Patellis is engaged by apartment associations, private management companies, and national organizations to teach, lecture, and consult on property management techniques and organization. In addition to teaching the RAM course worldwide to civilian and military personnel of the United States Armed Forces, Mr. Patellis also has conducted executive workshops at such industry events as Multi-Housing World, the National Home Builders Show, and the National Apartment Association. He has been engaged as Property Management Training Contractor for notable real estate concerns throughout the United States, including but not limited to the Associated Builders and Owners of Greater New York and the Harrisburg, Pennsylvania Home Builders Association, among many others, and he participates often in conferences between the Department of Defense and the private sector. A sought-after public speaker, Mr. Patellis communicates the philosophy, "If it can't be done, let's do it." This philosophy, combined with real-life, hands-on management experience and expertise, has placed Mr. Patellis among the "Who's Who" of property management.

A licensed and active Georgia real estate broker, Mr. Patellis is an Advanced RAM Dean, CPM (Certified Property Manager), and NAHP (National Assisted Housing Professional). At the writing of this book, Mr. Patellis was awarded the prestigious honor of Life Governor of the NAHB RAM Board of Governors.

Mr. Patellis may be contacted c/o Patellis Property Management Co., 283 Indian Hills Trail, Marietta, Georgia 30068-4050; by phone at (770) 973–2181; by fax at (770) 973–0883; and via e-mail at mbpatellis@mindspring.com.

Barbara Dershowitz, Editor

An award-winning writer/editor/publisher, public speaker, business development coach, and long-time multihousing communications authority, Barbara Dershowitz is founder and President of the Long Island, New York-based Business Communications Workshop, and B. Dershowitz Communications, Inc. (bdci).

Past Contributing Editor of *Real Estate Forum, Better Buildings, Real Estate New York,* and *The Cooperator* magazines, Ms. Dershowitz has authored or edited more than 1,000 published articles on every aspect of the multihousing industry. She is co-author and publisher of the book, *How To Choose The Right Management Company For Your Residential Property: A Decision-Maker's Guide,* and served as head researcher and editor to Mr. Kuperberg during the production of *Licensing of Residential Property Managers: A Study of State Licensing Requirements* (published by NAHB).

Through her companies, Ms. Dershowitz provides every type of communications service to the residential community, including but not limited to marketing and informational brochures, booklets, books, and collateral materials, websites, newsletters, house rules handbooks, and employee and property staff manuals. She has provided recordkeeping and corporate documentation services to management companies, property owners, and co-op and condo boards, and has served as a privately contracted management overseer. Outside the multifamily industry, Ms. Dershowitz and her companies serve an impressive roster of for-profit and nonprofit clients with the full range of communication and creative services.

A professional speaker, Ms. Dershowitz has created and facilitated executive communication and corporate organization seminars for such groups as the American Association of Architectural Administrators, the Council of New York Cooperatives and Condominiums, and *Habitat* magazine, among others. She is also author/editor of a series of educational skillbooks, was researcher and host of the television pilot of *Women's Views,* and produced and hosted the popular public affairs radio program, *Long Island Success.*

Ms. Dershowitz may be contacted c/o Business Communications Workshop, 136 Seaman Road, Jericho, New York 11753-1608; by phone at (516) 938–0323; by fax at (516) 938–0210; and via e-mail at bd@i-2000.com.

About Multifamily

The 850 state and local home builder associations that comprise the 206,000 members of the National Association of Home Builders includes a network of Multifamily Councils that protect the interests of apartment developers and owners at the state and local level and provide the grassroots support for the federation's national multifamily agenda. At-large Multifamily Council membership is available to multifamily builders, owners, managers and lenders who operate in a state where a Multifamily Council does not yet exist. Council members receive a variety of benefits targeted specifically to their needs, including publications and educational programs, and have access to all association benefits and services. For more information, or to receive a membership package, contact NAHB Multifamily at 1–800-368–5242, ext. 8215 or multifamily@nahb.com.

About RAM

The NAHB Multifamily Registered in Apartment Management (RAM) program is a comprehensive 40-hour training program specifically designed to train property managers of multifamily rental, condominium, and cooperative housing, both market rate and subsidized. The 30+-year-old RAM certification is the only national certification program. The curriculum includes office/financial management, marketing, all aspects of tenant processing and maintenance and security issues. Upon successful completion of the examination, participants can complete an experience profile and application for certification. If all of the criteria have been successfully met, the candidate is awarded the RAM certification. This certification is the standard in our industry, and is widely accepted and endorsed outside of our organization by other related trade associations.

ACKNOWLEDGMENTS

The following individuals and organizations were instrumental in developing Residential Property Management. Without their guidance, support, and assistance this project would not have been possible:

The RAM Board of Governors; Mr. Frank Basile, RAM, CPM, and Mr. George C. Caruso, RAM, CPM, authors of the Fourth Edition of this text; Ms. LaVonne Rhoda, Vice President of Compliance, CED/Concord Management, Maitland, Florida; Ms. Patty Landry, Chair, RAM Board of Governors and Executive Assistant/Councils Coordinator/MFC Director, Home Builders Association of Greater New Orleans, Metairie, Louisiana; Ms. Jacqueline Bruchi, Shadowlake Management Company, Gretna, Louisiana ; Mr. David Buchwalter, AdCar Associates, Inc., Bayside, New York; Mr. Henry A. Dubro, JASA Housing Management and Development; Mr. Tracy Hill, former RAM Board of Governors, Rowling Meadows, IL; Ms. Brenda Hays (McClain), Brenda McClain & Associates; Ms. Sharon Dworkin Bell, Senior Staff Vice President, Multifamily, National Association of Home Builders, Washington, D.C.; Ms. Courtenay Smith Brown, Director, Professional Development, Multifamily, National Association of Home Builders, Washington, D.C.; Ms. Theresa Minch, Executive Editor, BuilderBooks, National Association of Home Builders, Washington, D.C.; Ms. Jessica Poppe, Assistant Editor, BuilderBooks, National Association of Home Builders, Washington, D.C.; Ms. Daria Jakubowski, past Education Programs Director, National Association of Home Builders, Washington, D.C; Ms. Claire Collins, Princeton Properties, Lowell, MA; Mr. Terry Allan Johnson, Abbitt Management Inc., Newport News, VA; Mr. Henry A. Dubro, JASA Housing Management and Development, Far Rockaway, NY; Mr. Greg Carlson, Carlson Realty, Inc., Forest Hills, New York; Mr. Nicholas LaPorte Jr., Executive Director, Associated Builders and Owners of New York, Inc., New York, NY; Wilfred N. Cooper, Sr. WNC & Associates, Inc., Costa Mesa, CA; Ms. Gail Badger-Morgan, Marion Scott Real Estate, New York, NY; Ms. Shirley Stanley, Stanley Properties, Jacksonville, FL; and Senator Charles "Chuck" Schumer, (D), New York.

The authors especially wish to recognize and thank Ms. Barbara Dershowitz, President of Business Communications Workshop and B. Dershowitz Communications, Inc./bdci, Jericho, New York, editor, researcher, writer, and multihousing communications professional extraordinaire, for her expert oversight, coordination, and enhancement of this book.

David Kuperberg particularly wishes to acknowledge and thank Mr. Jerome Belson, Chair of the Associated Builders and Owners of Greater New York, Inc., "my local New York RAM affiliate, who has been a great supporter of mine throughout my professional career"; and Mr. Herb Warshavsky, former Executive Director of the Association Builders and Owners of Greater New York, Inc., and Life Governor of the RAM Board of Governors, "for introducing me to RAM and for his guidance throughout my career. I also wish to deeply thank my personal assistant Ms. Ann Glaser, who tirelessly and flawlessly coordinates my days and all my RAM work; and Cooper Square Realty Inc., HR Director Ms. Melissa Leahy for her outstanding work on the figures in this textbook. Finally, I wish to express my undying love and appreciation to my wife Jeanne and our children Danielle and Russell, who give meaning to everything I do."

N. Mike Patellis particularly wishes to acknowledge and thank the following individuals and organizations for their support, editorial enhancements, and contributions to the professionalization of the multifamily management industry: Mr. Sidney L. Malkin, CPM, Principal, Sid Malkin & Associates, Roswell, Georgia; Ms. Carol Donovan, Adv. RAM, Vice President of Operations, HSI Management, Inc., Atlanta, Georgia; Ms. Susan Chapel-White, Executive Director, and Ms. Diane J. Miller, Associate Executive Director, Southern Affordable Housing Management Association, Atlanta Georgia; and Atlanta Multifamily HUD (this acknowledgment does not constitute an endorsement). "I also wish to express my complete love and gratitude to my wife Becky, without whose love and encouragement my portion of this text would most likely still be in draft."

CONTENTS

FIGURES

INTRODUCTION

Not so long ago, the field of multifamily management was still in its formative stage, a profession working diligently to define its primary principles and practices. Today, however, multifamily property management is recognized as an essential service industry, the ultimate response to owners who seek not only day-to-day oversight for their properties but also knowledgeable, expert management to ensure the long-term stability and viability of their investments. The practitioners of this vital and noble calling—multifamily property managers—are now respected as well, and are acknowledged as highly skilled professionals with a constantly expanding array of competencies.

This book, *Residential Property Management Principles and Practices,* is the single most comprehensive reference guide for those who are serious about multifamily management. Founded on the rich history of its predecessor, *Multihousing Management 1,* the core text of the Registered in Apartment Management (RAM) program, (the longest-running and best respected residential property management education and credentialing program in the industry), *Residential Property Management Principles and Practices* offers an enhanced level of professional information and insight.

For example, among the many features that identify this text as the next evolution in the articulation of residential property management is the inclusion of definitive information about the management of shared-interest associations (home owners associations, condominiums, cooperatives, etc.), along with updated information about the management of government-assisted properties and military bases. This book also provides expanded outlines and samples of management plans, property staff manuals, and resident handbooks, and it addresses the all-too-critical issues of risk management in the new light of environmental hazards and terrorism. Moreover, *Residential Property Management Principles and Practices* updates and explores the legal issues faced by the industry, speaks more clearly and deliberately to the professionalization of the industry, and provides an industry glossary and carefully plotted index to facilitate easy reference.

It is exactly because of this enhanced level of presentation, a more cogent organizational structure, and the fact that the residential property management industry has come so far, that the decision was made to rename this book, *Residential Property Management Principles and Practices.* While this text will continue to be used as the primary text for the RAM Program, it is intended to be used by all property management professionals, from leasing agents to asset managers to property management executives staff, as a guide for the successful management of every type of multiple-unit residential dwelling.

Indeed, the services of the professional multifamily manager are in demand wherever people live. And the charge of the professional multifamily manager is a formidable one. It is a charge that demands the best educated, best prepared professionals the industry can produce.

It is the hope of the authors and of NAHB that *Residential Property Management Principles and Practice*s will provide both the inspiration and the information necessary for its readers to attain the highest level of achievement in the outstanding endeavor of residential property management.

1

The Expanding Role of Professional Multihousing Management

WHY MULTIHOUSING PROPERTY OWNERS HIRE PROFESSIONAL MANAGEMENT

Whether it's a high-rise apartment building in the city, a development of attached townhouses or garden apartments in suburbia, a multi-acre homeowners association, a senior community, a military installation, a boarding school or college dormitory, or any other form of multiple-unit housing, the contemporary multihousing industry throughout the United States—indeed, throughout the world—demands the services of professional management. Just as the nature, structure, and requirements of the multihousing industry as a whole have grown in scope and complexity—most rapidly and significantly over the past four decades—so the practice of multihousing management also has evolved to address those complexities and produce today's multihousing managers: professionals uniquely qualified to meet and master every multihousing challenge.

The history of multihousing communities and the practice of multihousing management is almost as old as history itself, with evidence suggesting the existence of residential condominiums as long ago as 2000 BC. In the Dark Ages, along with most of the other major elements of civilization, multihousing fell into disuse but re-emerged during the feudal period of medieval Europe when local lords and dukes began to sharecrop their landholdings. At that time, retainers or stewards, most of whom were mercenary soldiers in the lord's private armies, "managed" property for their feudal lords. This early form of "management" consisted mostly of collecting the rent. (Because high ethical standards were usually not a priority for these mercenaries, the multihousing management profession has had to work hard over the decades to cast off the shadow of a questionable reputation deriving from that period.) Hundreds of years later, in the early 18th century the first known residential cooperative was established in France and a new set of multihousing management challenges was born.

In America, the history of multihousing communities and multihousing management began in earnest in the late 1800s and early 1900s as the country underwent industrialization and large concentrations of laborers moved to the cities to work in factories. The need to house these workers and their families, combined with improvements in structural engineering technology, brought about fundamental changes in the way cities were organized and how people lived.

For example, in many cities in the eastern United States, tenement buildings were developed to house lower-paid factory workers and new immigrants who had made their way to America in search of the Great American Dream. In the industrial Midwest, the first engineered towns such as Pullman, Illinois, and Gary, Indiana, included apartments and townhouses for workers at Pullman and U.S. Steel, respectively. The management of these company towns, the precursors of today's mixed-use developments, was performed by the companies that built and owned them and extended far into many other aspects of workers' lives. Although company towns eventually faded from importance, they served as a source of substantial strife in their heyday in the early years of organized labor.

Immediately after World War I, major cities sprouted apartment buildings aimed at middle-income families. The management of these buildings (which seldom exceeded 150 units) was made easy by the housing shortage, which kept occupancy rates high and turnover rates low. Although most of these buildings were managed by their owners, property management firms began to emerge in some of the larger cities, often as extensions of general real estate brokerage firms.

The moderate-income buildings of the time generally were owner-operated with a resident caretaker, or "super" (superintendent), to assist. Rent collection problems were almost nonexistent because few residents dared to risk eviction. But it was in the luxury buildings of such urban centers as New York, Chicago, and Boston that professional management first made significant headway.

The rental construction boom of that era contributed greatly to the evolution of property management. With owners becoming more affluent, investing in more properties, and rewarding themselves with longer vacations, their absentee ownership fostered increased management by agents or tenants. These agents or tenants would collect the rent, pay the property's bills, forward the net proceeds, report any unusual circumstances to the owner, and act as a buffer between the owner and the residents. Usually not authorized to spend money without the owner's prior approval, these early managers functioned primarily as caretakers, looking after the building during the day and/or when the owner was not present. In exchange for their services, these agents typically received a small salary or a reduction in rent if they happened to live in the building they managed. Those real estate agents who managed properties did so at first as an accommodation to the owners and with the expectation that the owners would favor them with additional business. But soon real estate agents realized the profit potential in apartment management and began studying the business and developing operating procedures. Even so, in this nascent stage of the industry, professional managers were rare.

It was the Great Depression of the early 1930s that marked the beginning of modern multihousing management as we know it today. With numerous apartment building owners forced to default to banks, insurance companies, savings institutions, and other large financial organizations, these institutions began to establish their own in-house management staffs or to contract for outside management. Property management became a necessity as more and more properties came under the same ownership.

This period in American history was an especially difficult one. Occupancy plunged as families doubled and tripled up to conserve what limited funds were available. The situation began to stabilize during the late 1930s, but the difficulties did not end entirely until World War II in 1940.

During and immediately after World War II, America experienced a critical housing shortage in all cities and in some other nonurban areas. Because rent controls curtailed profits and forced owners to cut expenses, because many repair and maintenance materials (such as copper pipe, lead drain and vent pipe, and petroleum-based shingles and linoleum) were almost unattainable owing to their use in the war effort, and also because the low turnover caused by the housing shortage eliminated the normal general maintenance required when turnovers occurred, owners had little incentive to do more than minimally maintain their properties and deal with dire emergencies. In an effort to cut costs, and with little trouble renting properties and the low turnover rates, many owners terminated their outside management contracts. This situation eased somewhat between 1947 and 1949 but recurred with the outbreak of the Korean Conflict.

A sustained nationwide postwar housing boom occurred after rent controls were lifted in 1953. (Rent controls were not lifted in New York and New Jersey.) Throughout the country, larger and more complex apartment buildings were designed and constructed, and, for the first time, many were built in new suburban areas surrounding the cities. This housing boom was fueled by the baby boom from 1949 to 1962 as family formations and births reached unprecedented levels. Indeed, the whine of circular saws and the crash of hammers were some of the sounds most familiar to children growing up in this period as houses, apartment buildings, schools, and commercial developments were constructed at a record pace.

The new multihousing developments that were being constructed were larger and costlier than ever before, reaching as high as $50 million. The first mega-developments, such as Peter Cooper Village/Stuyvesant Town in New York City (one of the largest single developments in the United States, today housing more than 25,000 residents), were built and managed directly by large banks and life insurance companies that had previously limited their housing activities to lending. The field of professional residential management developed rapidly as these large institutions moved into the housing industry directly.

Prior to this time, managers had few leasing responsibilities, almost no responsibility for maintenance, and none for preventive maintenance. But by the early 1960s, with an increase in vacancies caused by the building boom, managers began learning how to market rental units for owners. As rent collection became a problem and more money had to be spent on maintenance, especially where this expense had been deferred in prior years, managers were dealing with these issues as well.

Up to this point, management skills had not kept pace with the change in the housing industry. And certainly no one thought about who would manage a new property until after it was built, at which point the task was often assigned to someone's relative or friend. But as the size and demands of residential developments increased, the manager's status changed from rent collector and caretaker to professional, and the provision and quality of management services improved as procedures and technologies were developed for rent collection, preventive maintenance, and overall property management.

Aided by government programs, the construction boom continued through the mid-1970s. These programs, coupled with liberal tax and capital gains rules, provided substantial incentives for building and owning apartment buildings. Corporations also began to see the opportunities in real estate investment, but with only certain notable exceptions, the stock of rental housing built by the private sector has not grown significantly since the late 1970s.

The multifamily housing industry reached a stage of overbuilding in the 1980s, probably as a result of the unusually favorable tax treatment of rental real estate under the Economic Recovery Act of 1981. From 1983 through 1986, there were well over half a million starts every year in buildings with five or more apartments. But when the Tax Reform Act of 1986 temporarily eliminated many of the incentives to invest in rental housing, multifamily housing production entered a period of persistent decline. Exacerbated by a credit crunch and by the recession of the early 1990s, building starts with five-plus units fell to under 140,000 units per year from 1991 through 1993.

In 1994, the 1986 Section 42 Act was made permanent, states were authorized to create agencies to oversee affordable housing, and a recovery began, with five-plus starts hovering at slightly below 300,000 during the period of 1997 to 2000. This was more than double the rate of production of the early 1990s but still substantially below the peaks of the 1970s and 1980s.

Most of the special incentives, liberal tax rules, and subsidized mortgage programs that provided the core of housing for lower-income families were phased out in the late 1970s when the federal government costs for these programs began to soar. Increasing the supply of affordable rental units became one of the real challenges of the 1980s. Rental housing development had been hard hit by a number of factors, including the near total curtailment of federally subsidized and tax-advantaged development programs; inflation of land, construction, and operating costs; overbuilding and severe economic recession in the southwest oil-producing states; rental control and development restrictions in congested urban areas from New York to Los Angeles; the return to low inflation and moderate interest rates, which assist many first-time home buyers in moving out of the rental housing market; and a tapering off of family formations and fewer young people moving into the workforce.

Today, successful rental housing development depends on careful analysis of spot markets and targeted rental populations. Superior management is essential to reduce operating costs and attract residents with the appropriate renter profile.

Until 1981, government-assisted housing accounted for an increasingly large percentage of total rental housing produced in the United States. In 1980, this share was more than 50 percent for the first time. Since then, direct government subsidies to private developers for the construction of low- and moderate-income rental housing have been greatly reduced. In addition, changes to the tax laws have ended the short-lived boom in rental housing construction financed by syndications.

Today, the tools available to help private developers seeking to build affordable rental housing include the:

- Low Income Housing Tax Credit program, which may be used for both new construction and rehab
- State and local housing finance agency programs, such as tax-exempt and taxable bonds
- Federal HOME program and, to a lesser extent, the Community Development Block Grant (CDBG) program (most often these two programs provide gap financing, which is used in conjunction with the tax credit program, tax-exempt bond financing, and several additional programs in individual states such as Georgia, among others, that offer an additional tax write-off)
- Federal Home Loan Bank's Affordable Housing Program (AHPO) (also used as a source of gap financing)

Although the record boom of the late 1970s has yet to be matched, the professional multihousing management arena has continued to develop and evolve, especially but not only in and around urban areas where numerous conversions of rental buildings to condominium or cooperative status have occurred.

In direct contrast to the mercenary and often unethical soldiers hired by Europe's feudal lords to collect rent, and mere shadows of the early caretakers engaged by landlords for minimal maintenance services, today's multihousing management professionals must be experts in every aspect that impacts the multihousing industry in general and the properties they manage in particular. From construction, finance, law, insurance, and structural, mechanical, and aesthetic maintenance to purchasing, marketing, computer technology, staff supervision, and human relations, today's multihousing managers must be masters of many trades because property owners are depending on them for the operational and financial viability of their investments.

HOUSING STOCK AND TYPES OF MULTIHOUSING OWNERSHIP

Since 1984, the nature of ownership and the types of owners of multifamily housing in the United States have changed dramatically. According to the 1999 American Housing Survey (U.S. Census Bureau and the Department of Housing), of the 112,292,000 occupied housing units in the United States, 37,401,000 (36.4 percent) are rental or condominium residences. Although 30.6 percent of the occupied rental housing stock in urban areas is single family residences, overall approximately 29 percent of the occupied rental housing stock (9,858,000 units) is in buildings with 10 or more units. It is these rental units that form the heart of the housing stock that is professionally managed.

Although a significant number of the smallest apartment properties are operated by their owners, much of the housing stock with four or fewer units per building is also professionally managed. And the bulk of residential properties of all types with more than 50 units (including shared-interest associations such as cooperative corporations and homeowners associations) is professionally managed by paid staff working directly for the owner (in-house management) or by independent professional management companies (fee-based management).

Because the professional multihousing manager acts as the agent of the owners whose properties they manage, and to satisfy owners' expectations and requirements, the manager must understand and be familiar with the various types of multihousing ownership. Managers must also understand that often an owner will choose a form of ownership based on its tax treatment at the time and that the tax treatments of real estate have a tendency to shift over time.

In general, multihousing properties are owned by three types of owners:

- Profit-motivated entities
- Nonprofit entities
- Publicly owned entities

The most common types of multihousing ownership are as follows (Fig. 1–1).

INDIVIDUAL OWNERS/INVESTORS

A great many small multihousing properties, as well as a fair number of older, larger properties, are owned and/or invested in by individuals.

MULTIPLE OWNERSHIP

Under multiple ownership, two or more individuals own a multihousing property together and at the same time. In many states, multiple ownership takes the form of either joint tenancy or tenancy in common. Under joint tenancy with the right of survivorship, it is difficult to transfer or sell shares because the single title to the property cannot be divided and those owners who survive after one or more of the other owners die have the right of survivorship, which guarantees their right to the decedent's interest. Under tenancy in common, the title is drawn in each owner's name and may be designated in unequal shares. Hence, each owner has the right to do whatever he/she wants to do with his/her shares, including selling, mortgaging, or giving them away. There is no right of survivorship under tenancy in common, so the shares of the deceased owner pass to that owner's beneficiary(ies) with the owner's estate and/or according to the terms of the owner's will.

FIGURE 1-1. Most Common Types of Multihousing Ownership

Individual owners/investors
Multiple ownership
Partnerships
Joint ventures
Syndicates
Corporate ownership
Ownership by financial institutions
REITs
Pension funds
Shared-interest associations
Limited dividend and nonprofit owners
Public housing
Military
Educational
Foreign ownership

PARTNERSHIPS (GENERAL AND LIMITED)

Partnerships are a common form of ownership for multihousing properties of all sizes. In partnerships, two or more individuals are co-owners of a legal for-profit business. The two most common types of partnerships are general and limited. In a general partnership, all partners have an active interest in the partnership and usually are all liable for the activities of the partnership. Limited partnerships, which are a popular ownership structure for large multihousing developments, typically have two classes of partners: general and limited. The general partner(s), of which there must be at least one, manages and operates the partnership and has unlimited liability for it. The limited partners are passive investors whose risk is limited to the interest that they have invested in the operation; therefore, they have limited liability. Under most normal circumstances, the limited partners cannot be involved in the day-to-day operation of the partnership and have other limits on their investment. However, should the general partner(s) fail in his/her performance on behalf of the property, the limited partners, although under no legal obligation to do so, may choose to assume responsibility. Limited partnerships are a popular ownership structure for large multihousing properties.

JOINT VENTURES

Joint ventures have become increasingly common for large multihousing properties. A joint venture frequently involves two firms, one with experience in multihousing management and the operation of income properties and one with experience in financial markets. With the deregulation of banks and savings and loan associations, financial institutions have become more active as joint venture partners. The structure of joint ventures varies from deal to deal; however, the agreement usually provides for a specified holding period for the property and division of the profits at sale.

SYNDICATES

Syndicates, which offer the opportunity for large groups to invest, can be partnerships, limited liability corporations, or corporations and can involve either public or private security offerings. If public, the syndicate will be regulated by the Securities and Exchange Commission (SEC) and by the state(s), as appropriate. If private, the state's individual "Blue Sky" laws apply. ("Blue Sky" laws are regulations governing the sale of securities and mutual funds designed to protect investors from being taken by fraudulent or unscrupulous deals.) Prior to 1986, syndications were extremely popular because of the favorable tax treatment that allowed many people to become involved in real estate transactions. After the 1986 tax law changed, however, the ability for passive investors to profit from favorable tax treatment was significantly limited. Hence, syndications based on tax shelters are less prevalent today than they once were.

CORPORATE OWNERSHIP

Corporations are legal entities that operate under a charter granted by the state in which they were formed. They may be general corporations or close corporations (C corporations), which are the most common corporate structures, or they may be subchapter-S (S corporations), which have the same advantages of general and close corporations except that sub-S corporations eliminate federal corporate income tax and allow all profits to pass though to the shareholders' personal tax return. As independent legal entities, corporations may sue and be sued, their existence must be terminated through legal action, and shareholders hold their stock. Corporate shareholders have limited liability to creditors and are insulated from corporate obligations. The affairs of the corporation are administered by directors who are elected by the shareholders. In certain cases, corporations whose primary business is not real estate purchase multihousing properties to diversify their holdings.

OWNERSHIP BY FINANCIAL INSTITUTIONS

Insurance companies, banks, and other institutions that are the primary lenders of the capital required to finance multihousing construction typically participate in real estate ownership for two reasons: default and to produce investment income. Previously, ownership by a financial institution occurred by default as the result of foreclosing on delinquent accounts, with the institution serving as interim caretaker until such time as the property could be resold. Although this ownership by default still occurs, insurance companies, lending institutions, and other such institutions also purchase multihousing properties as income-producing investments that also appreciate in value.

REAL ESTATE INVESTMENT TRUSTS

Real estate investment trusts (REITs) were popular in the early 1970s but faded from the scene in the middle of that decade after several of the funds had widely publicized problems resulting from poor investments. REITs invest their assets in real estate holdings, which may include apartments, office buildings, and shopping centers. REITs may own and operate the real estate held in the portfolio, and some REITs also finance real estate. The REITs sell ownership shares to investors, who get a share of the earnings and depreciation from the portfolio held by the REIT. In this way, REITs are similar to mutual funds because an investor can purchase shares in a multihousing property or group of properties. REIT shares are traded on the stock exchange and also over the counter. For potential customers, REITs issue prospectuses that provide detailed descriptions of the structure and the management operation of the funds, and they are regulated like similar securities.

PENSION FUNDS

Pension and retirements funds have been purchasing all types of income-producing real estate for many years. In some markets, pension funds are quite active. The administrator of the fund, acting in the capacity of fiduciary for the fund, purchases property both for current return and for capital appreciation in later years.

SHARED-INTEREST ASSOCIATIONS

Cooperatives, condominiums, homeowners associations, and planned unit developments are four types of ownership structures that involve groups of owners of multifamily attached, semi-attached, or single-family housing. These groups own and operate some common property and provide varying levels of service to the residents of the property. In general, shared-interest associations require that each owner accept and abide by a set of legal agreements, usually referred to as covenants, as part of the purchase of the unit. These agreements provide for the operation and maintenance of the property. A board of directors or managers is elected by all owners in the shared-interest association, and it is this board's responsibility to make decisions on behalf of the association; however, some of their decisions may be subject to approval by the full body of owners. The cooperative is only slightly different from a condominium, homeowners association, or planned unit development in that in a cooperative, a corporation (generally nonprofit) owns the real property, and the corporation issues shares of stock to the shareholders who then are entitled to enter into a proprietary lease for a unit in the building. Under the terms of the lease, the lessee can live in the property as long as she/he owns stock in the cooperative. Operating expenses are covered by the proprietary lease payments. Unlike the other forms of ownership, shared-interest associations such as co-ops, condos, homeowners associations, and planned unit developments generally have an unlimited life and usually are not sold or dissolved. Individual owners will buy and sell, but the overall structure of the association will not change appreciably.

LIMITED DIVIDEND AND NONPROFIT OWNERS

Several housing programs initiated by the federal government in the late 1960s and 1970s enabled nonprofit or limited-profit groups and developers to provide housing for low-income residents. The ownership structure of these properties provided for mortgage loans at rates as low as 1 percent and terms of 40 years, in exchange for certain limits on income and cash distribution to owners, rents, and resale of the property and operations.

PUBLIC HOUSING

Since the initial enactment of the Housing Act of 1937, public housing authorities have built, owned, and, in many cases, operated housing owned by the federal, state, or local governments. While more than 1,362,000 such units were built over a 50-year period, fewer than that number still exist because of demolition or disuse owing to lack of renovation funds and other problems.

MILITARY

Military housing is the responsibility of the Office of the Under Secretary of Defense and provides residential shelter to individuals in the various branches of the Armed Forces. A unique set of protocols govern the operation and management of military housing, which, nevertheless, requires professional management in the same way as all other multifamily housing.

EDUCATIONAL

Many public and private educational institutions own multihousing properties to house students and faculty and for other reasons. The management of educational housing, including but not limited to boarding schools and dormitories, is an active part of professional multihousing management.

FOREIGN OWNERSHIP

More and more foreign dollars are invested in American real estate with each passing year. Although foreign investors typically favor commercial and industrial properties, some are either constructing or purchasing multihousing properties in the United States.

GOALS OF MULTIHOUSING PROPERTY OWNERS

Multihousing property owners typically have one or more of the following goals, which may or may not be mutually exclusive (Fig. 1-2).

FIGURE 1-2. Reasons and Goals for Multihousing Property Ownership

Periodic income
Capital appreciation
Speculation
Control of investment
Financing leverage
Tax shelter
Inflation hedge
Use by owner
Estate building
Pride of ownership

PERIODIC INCOME

Owners who invest in residential real estate typically expect a profitable return on their investment. This return may come in the form of periodic income, such as monthly, quarterly, or annual dividends or profits, which are derived when the property generates surplus revenue.

CAPITAL APPRECIATION

Owners who invest in residential real estate also typically expect their investment to appreciate, or increase, in value at a rate faster than the rate of inflation.

SPECULATION

Owners who participate in real estate speculation typically take large risks based on what they predict will be very fast, very formidable gains.

CONTROL OF INVESTMENT

Compared with many other types of investments, the ownership of real estate provides measurably greater control over how the investment is managed to achieve profitability and to remain profitable.

FINANCING LEVERAGE

Unlike many other types of investments, real estate allows interested investors to borrow funds from outside sources to finance the investment. In addition, once a property is owned, it can also serve as collateral to finance other investments.

TAX SHELTER

Depending on the prevailing tax laws, real estate can provide an outstanding tax shelter for those who own it.

INFLATION HEDGE

Residential real estate has historically been an excellent hedge against inflation. This is especially true of rental properties for two reasons. First, it is generally expected that rent rates will keep pace with inflation. Second, when inflation causes the cost of private homes to spiral beyond the ability of many people to afford them, the most common alternative is renting. Hence, inflation actually increases the value of rental units for their owners.

USE BY OWNER

A residential real estate owner sometimes will choose to live in the multihousing property she/he owns. This is an understandable choice given the fact that the revenue generated by the other units in the property may allow the owner to live there for free.

ESTATE BUILDING

Considering that real estate has demonstrated an historically consistent increase in value, often in the short term but virtually without exception in the long term, real estate ownership allows investors to build sizable personal estates with relatively little risk compared with other types of investments.

PRIDE OF OWNERSHIP

For many people, the ownership of real estate represents a personal achievement. Many multihousing property owners feel this way and derive great pride from the ownership of their properties.

Income, capital appreciation, speculation, control, financing leverage, tax shelter, inflation hedge, personal use, estate building, and pride of ownership are all valid reasons and goals for the ownership of multihousing properties.

VALUE AND ROLE OF PROFESSIONAL RESIDENTIAL PROPERTY MANAGEMENT

The primary job of the professional residential manager is to help the property's owner meet her/his unique goals and objectives for the property. Although the owner's individual requirements and expectations will determine how the manager accomplishes this task in specifics, the professional multihousing manager has four overarching obligations to every owner under any circumstances (Fig. 1–3):

- To perform as a fiduciary (an individual, corporation, or association that holds assets for another party and has the legal authority and duty to make decisions regarding financial matters on behalf of that other party)
- To preserve and, if possible, increase the value of the property
- To produce a profit for the owner(s)
- To provide the highest quality living environment while preserving the property's value and producing a profit for the owner(s)

FIGURE 1-3. Professional Multihousing Manager's Four Primary Obligations to Property Owner(s)

To perform as a fiduciary
To preserve and, if possible, increase the value of the property
To produce a profit for the owner(s)
To provide the highest quality living environment while preserving the property's value and producing a profit for the owner(s)

These four fundamental obligations of the professional multihousing manager apply no matter what the owner's reasons are for owning the property and regardless of what the owner's unique goals and objectives are for the property. These obligations also directly define the essential value of professional residential property management.

In turn, multifamily housing owners recognize the value and role of professional residential property management, which helps owners to manage and operate their multihousing holdings more responsively, more cost-efficiently, and more profitably than the overwhelming majority of owners could do on their own; keeps owners' multifamily properties better maintained, safer and more secure, and in greater compliance with local, state, and federal regulations and requirements; increases the quality of life for residents and the actual dollar value of the property as measured by lenders, potential investors, and other financial influencers better than owners could do on their own; and may allow the owner to secure a better rate for new construction based on the demonstration of professional management.

That said, the professional multihousing manager will perform best for the owner/client if he/she knows the owner's unique and individual goals for the property. For example, the manager must be aware if the owner's "profit" is not necessarily a monetary one. While it is true that most multihousing properties are expected to provide a monetary profit, some types of developments, such as those built under government-assisted, low-income housing programs, provide a benefit to the residents who live in them and to the owner in the form of income tax advantages.

Due to the complex nature of real estate investment and its tax implications for owners and investors, it is incumbent upon the professional multihousing manager to know what the owner's goals and objectives are for the property and what the property's financial condition is, at any given moment. The manager must be aware at all times of the most current developments in the factors that can impact and affect the owner's goals and objectives. These factors may include (Fig. 1–4):

- Owner's need for personal cash flow and/or the cash flow requirements of the property
- Cash returns on cash invested
- Long- and short-term capital gains
- Owner's income tax position and the profit or loss produced by the property for tax purposes (The profit or loss may need to be managed to ensure that it fits within the constraints planned initially or adopted later.)
- Sale or syndication requirements
- Any regulatory requirements imposed by lenders or government programs
- Holding period for the property (The number of years an investor plans to continue holding a property will

FIGURE 1-4. Factors That Affect an Owner's Goals for the Property

Cash flow
Cash returns
Capital gains
Income tax position and profit or loss
Sale or syndication requirements
Regulatory requirements
Holding period for the property
End use of property upon sale or disposition
Special requirements of government housing program or nonprofit ownership structure

have an impact on what repairs and improvements investors may decide to make.)

- End use of the property upon sale or disposition (If the property will be either rehabilitated or demolished at the time of sale or disposition, management decisions will vary from those made when the present use is to be continued.)

- Special requirements of a government housing program or of a nonprofit ownership structure

Clearly, knowing the owner's unique goals and objectives for the property and being aware of the property's current financial condition are crucial to the manager who intends to perform well. But just knowing what the owner requires and expects is far from enough. To be considered even just competent, the manager also must fulfill a variety of professional roles on behalf of the owner and the property.

Whereas once upon a time multihousing managers were nothing more than glorified maintenance workers and rent collectors, today's professional multihousing managers have evolved into experts with proficiency in a growing catalogue of diverse knowledge and function areas. These areas include:

- Finance
- Law
- Sales and marketing
- Insurance
- Construction
- Structural and mechanical engineering
- Plant maintenance
- Leasing
- Purchasing
- Computer technology
- Human resources and personnel management
- Interpersonal relations

When the owner of a multihousing property communicates her/his goals to the manager—who is the owner's agent in the management of the property—the manager becomes informed of the standards the owner will use to evaluate management's performance and value. If the manager fails in the fulfillment of her/his obligations to the owner—that is, if the manager does not act with competence and integrity as the owner's fiduciary, does not preserve and increase the value of the property, does not produce a profit for the owner, does not provide an acceptable living environment for residents, does not address the owner's unique individual expectations and requirements, and does not demonstrate mastery in the areas of specialization that are required of professional multihousing managers—then the manager has not performed in her/his professional role. The manager's value to the owner is therefore diminished, and the relationship between the manager and the owner is jeopardized.

Conversely, if the manager's efforts do indeed help the owner meet her/his objectives, and if the manager consistently performs with the level of professionalism appropriate to her/his position, then the owner will deem the manager to have great value and the relationship between the owner and the manager will be strong.

TITLES AND ROLES OF PROFESSIONAL MULTIHOUSING MANAGERS

Professional multihousing managers manage residential properties, which also may be correctly referred to as "sites" or, for larger properties, "developments." For the purposes of this text, the word "property" will be used to mean any multihousing building, complex, community, site, or development.

Similarly, in terms of the title and role of the professional multihousing manager, it is correct to refer to both the management company and the manager as the "managing agent." However, at the writing of this text, the multihousing management industry does not maintain definitive titles and job descriptions for the various duties, responsibilities, and levels of multihousing management. To address this void and contribute further to the standardization and professionalization of the multihousing management industry, the authors here submit the following descriptions and criteria for the various roles and titles of multihousing managing agents.

EXECUTIVE PROPERTY MANAGER

The most experienced property management professional, the executive property manager is an expert not only in residential property management per se but also in the management, administration, and supervision of the management organization and its staff. Almost without exception, the executive property manager holds the highest or nearly the highest credentials, authority, and responsibility in a management organization and may be the founder, chief executive officer, president, or executive vice president of the firm. In any case, while the number and level of middle management personnel between the executive property manager and the property manager (see below) depends on the size of the company, its geographic location, and the number of properties in the company's portfolio, the hierarchy of a management organization typically fans downward from the executive property manager's position, and all management team members, whether they are employees or outside vendors, are ultimately accountable to her/him.

SENIOR MANAGER (VICE PRESIDENT OF MANAGEMENT, DIRECTOR OF MANAGEMENT, OR REGIONAL PROPERTY MANAGER)

The senior manager is the professional directly responsible for the management operations of the properties in the company's client portfolio. Unlike the executive property manager, who is also concerned with and responsible for the operations of the management company, the senior manager is focused directly on the delivery of management services to clients. She or he supervises the management firm's management staff and reports directly and personally to the executive property manager only. The senior manager's responsibilities usually include:

- Supervising the management of each client property by the property manager (see below) to ensure the accomplishment of the owner's goals and objectives
- Achieving a satisfactory cash flow for each client property and ensuring that each client property is managed and operates in an efficient, cost-effective manner
- Preparing the annual operating budget for each client property
- Reviewing and analyzing the monthly financial statements of each client property, including income and expenses
- Ensuring that each client property is operated and maintained in accordance with the standards and procedures established by the owner and/or the management company as set forth in the operations manual
- Negotiating service contacts for each client property
- Ensuring that maintenance and rental standards are upheld
- Making periodic scheduled and unscheduled inspections of each client property
- Defining, projecting, planning, and overseeing major capital improvements to each client property, as required
- Recommending and implementing marketing programs, rental rates, maintenance programs, and other innovative ideas for each client property
- With the property manager, recruiting, hiring, training, compensating, supervising, evaluating, and motivating property employees
- Communicating regularly with the owners of client properties

PROPERTY MANAGER (SITE MANAGER, DEVELOPMENT MANAGER, ON-SITE MANAGER, OR RESIDENT MANAGER)

The property manager is arguably the most important professional in the management of a multihousing property. It is the property manager who is physically at the site day in and day out, interacting with the property's staff and employees, with the owners and residents, and with the senior manager to whom the property manager reports. In some cases, the property manager may report directly to the property owner, but it is more likely that she/he will report to the senior manager or, if the management company does not have a senior manager, directly to the executive property manager.

The property manager is responsible for the day-to-day, front-line operation of the property as follows:

- Ensuring that the owner's goals and objectives are communicated to and understood by the property staff
- Ensuring that the property operates in a cost-efficient manner while providing satisfactory housing to the residents
- Ensuring that the property is maintained according to the standards established by the management company and/or the owner by coordinating property maintenance activities
- Under the guidance of the senior manager, training all property personnel under her/his supervision
- Accounting to the senior manager for all moneys pertaining to the property
- Learning and implementing the standard operating procedures prescribed by the management company and/or the owner
- Performing property inspections
- Processing service requests
- Purchasing
- Record-keeping
- Maintaining positive resident relations
- Compiling and submitting all required reports

The decision of whether to have the property manager live on- or off-site depends on the management company's operating philosophy, the owner's requirements and expectations, the size of the property, the cost of providing a free apartment to the manager, and whether the manager wishes to live on-site. Proponents of property managers living on-site contend that by doing so, the manager is able to maintain 24-hour control of the property and gain insights about the property that would not be available otherwise. Conversely, opponents of property managers living on-site believe that such an arrangement can cause managers to get too close to their properties and/or become too friendly with certain residents and thereby distort their impartiality or give other residents the impression that impartiality is lost, even if that is not so. Living on-site also allows all residents easy access to the property manager for nonemergency requests during off hours, a situation that can become problematic under certain circumstances and for certain managers. Finally, those who advocate that property managers live away from the properties they manage believe that these managers can be more objective because they can take a fresher look at the property each day.

In any case, if a maintenance supervisor or other property personnel live at the property, it may not be necessary for the manager to live on-site as well. The decision rests ultimately with the management company that employs the manager and/or with the property owner who employs the management company.

ASSISTANT MANAGER

Larger properties may have an assistant manager who works side by side with, and reports to, the property manager. In the property manager's absence, it is the assistant manager who performs most of the same responsibilities as the property manager but without the same degree of expertise and/or authority. Competent, ambitious assistant managers are easily groomed for property manager positions.

ASSET MANAGER

The role of the asset manager is relatively new in the field of multihousing management. The asset manager is generally most adept at the financial end of property management, including financial planning, analysis, and investment. Asset managers are typically found where owners, such as financial institutions or property owners with considerable holdings, require a professional to gather and report financial information with a deliberate focus on profitability. It is therefore not unusual to find an asset manager working hand-in-hand with the owner and with the management company's executive property manager to ensure the financial viability of the property.

WHY PROFESSIONAL MULTIHOUSING MANAGEMENT IS AN OUTSTANDING CAREER

As previously noted, the roles, responsibilities, and public perception of the multihousing management industry have evolved dramatically, almost since the dawn of humanity. Once regarded and paid as just a caretaker and rent collector, and then as little more than a glorified maintenance worker, today's multihousing manager is increasingly recognized and compensated as a respected professional with a broad range of specialized knowledge and expertise.

Multihousing management certainly has come a long way, and the role of the professional multihousing manager continues to expand as the multihousing industry itself evolves in sophistication and complexity. Now and into the foreseeable future, the professional residential manager must possess and demonstrate a wide and varied range of personal characteristics and professional competencies and must stay current and well-trained in a remarkably extensive scope of disciplines to provide the level and quality of service and professionalism that management companies require, that multihousing property owners expect, and that multihousing residents demand. These characteristics and competencies include (Fig. 1–5):

- Industry-specific expertise, including mastery of:
  - Accounting and financial management skills
  - Law (including but not limited to Fair Housing)
  - Marketing and sales
  - Insurance
  - Construction
  - Structural and mechanical engineering
  - Plant maintenance, including structural, mechanical, and aesthetic maintenance

FIGURE 1-5. Required Expertise for the Professional Multihousing Manager

Mastery of industry-specific:
- Accounting and financial management
- Law
- Marketing and sales
- Insurance
- Construction
- Structural and mechanical engineering
- Plant maintenance, including structural, mechanical, and aesthetic maintenance

English literacy (and possibly literacy in one or more other languages)
Computer technology
Leasing
Purchasing
Negotiating
Organization, planning, and execution
Administration
Human resources and interpersonal management and communication
Time management
Stress and anger management
Attention to detail
Decisiveness
Assertiveness
Integrity
Commitment to ongoing professional education
Entrepreneurial attitude

- English literacy (and possibly literacy in one or more other languages)
- Computer technology skills
- Leasing knowledge
- Purchasing knowledge
- Negotiating skills
- Organization, planning, and execution skills
- Administrative skills
- Human resources and interpersonal management and communication skills for dealing with:
    - Management company staff, including superiors and subordinates
    - Property owners
    - Property staff
    - Existing and prospective property residents
    - Property-related service professionals such as attorneys, accountants, engineers, architects, and others
    - Property-related vendors and contractors
    - Government agencies, social service programs, and their representatives
    - Inspectors
    - The media
- Time management skills
- Stress and anger management skills
- Attention to detail
- Decisiveness
- Assertiveness
- Integrity
- Commitment to on-going professional education
- Entrepreneurial attitude to benefit:
    - Management company
    - Property owner
    - Manager

Indeed, few careers offer the levels of personal and professional demand, challenge, opportunity, and reward that multihousing management offers. And considering the facts that people will always need a place to live, that multihousing communities respond to that need, and that technology, law, and all the other areas attendant to the multihousing industry continue to evolve, professional multihousing management also will continue to evolve as a necessary, noble, and outstanding career path and profession.

INTEGRITY, PROFESSIONALISM, AND CREDENTIALING IN THE MULTIHOUSING MANAGEMENT PROFESSION

There are few fields of endeavor that touch the personal, domestic lives of so many individuals and families in the way that multihousing management does. Because multihousing management is all about people and the homes in which they live, it is incumbent upon the multihousing management professional to execute her/his work with integrity and professionalism. Much that is unpleasant and destructive can happen when multihousing professionals fail to perform to the highest ethical standards.

For example, in 1994 and then again in 1999, New York City's multifamily housing community was rocked by two waves of a residential management scandal that continue to have repercussions to this day. In this two-part scandal, a formidable complement of management companies, management professionals, condominium and cooperative board members, building maintenance workers, service professionals, vendors, and contractors were arrested, indicted, and convicted of corruption that included bribe-taking, bid-rigging, grand larceny, racketeering, and other acts of financial malfeasance. The victims of all these criminal acts were the hundreds of residential properties and their thousands of owners and residents who had entrusted the financial and operational management of their investments and homes to the wrongdoers who defrauded them.

It is for the protection of the industry as a whole, the ethical professionals who overwhelmingly populate it, and the clients who are served by it, that the multihousing management field is today taking a very serious look at its licensing and credentialing requirements. Several credentialing organizations are actively lobbying for uniform standards and performance criteria within the industry, and most have developed stringent internal codes of ethics and rigorous, on-going certification and re-certification programs for their members. (See Chapter 13, The Law and Multihousing Management for information about professional requirements and certifications for multihousing managers throughout the United States.)

Let there be no mistake. Honesty, integrity, and ethical behavior are the hallmarks of the true multihousing management professional who wishes to bring honor to her/himself, to her/his profession, and to her/his client portfolio. Such a professional will do nothing to sully her/his reputation or the reputation of the profession she/he represents.

Moreover, the true professional will take deliberate, on-going steps to remain as knowledgeable as possible in the field of multihousing property management. To that end, the true professional will most certainly attain the credential of RAM and Advanced RAM offered by NAHB, the National Association of Home Builders.

ABOUT THE NATIONAL ASSOCIATION OF HOME BUILDERS RAM AND ADVANCED RAM PROGRAMS

BACKGROUND

The National Association of Home Builders (NAHB), parent organization of the Registered in Apartment Management (RAM) Program, is a national trade association representing the housing industry with over 203,000 members in more than 800 state and local associations nationwide. The multifamily housing industry is represented by the NAHB Multifamily Council. NAHB established the Multifamily Council in 1982 to direct programs and services to its increasingly diverse multifamily membership and to serve as the voice of the multifamily builder-owner.

Multifamily members are organized in state and local multifamily councils representing builders, developers, owners, and managers, as well as related professionals such as investors, lenders, and architects. NAHB's professional staff develops training programs, seminars, and workshops; follows multifamily housing legislation; researches and writes special reports on industry trends; and manages the RAM certification program.

The Registered in Apartment Management Program was developed in 1971 by the National Association of Home Builders and is the oldest residential property management certification in the United States. The RAM program provides training to property managers of multifamily rental, condominium, cooperative, subsidized, market-rate, and military housing throughout the country. In 1980, the United States Department of Housing and Urban Development (HUD) designated NAHB as an approved certifying organization for managers and assistant managers of federally assisted and public housing.

RAM is a competency-based credential. The goal of the RAM Program is to set professional competency standards and to service the needs of the multifamily management industry by offering high-quality professional training (Fig. 1–6). Pride in belonging to a professional group is a vital part of RAM certification. The RAM Program is administered by a 13-member RAM Board of Governors. The basic RAM course is a 40-hour, entry-level property management training program based on this textbook.

RAM CERTIFICATION AND RAM CANDIDACY

Becoming a RAM means meeting the high standards of education, experience, and ethics established by the RAM Board of Governors. Eligible candidates must agree to abide by the RAM Code of Ethics and must be of exemplary character and reputation. Certification requirements also include:

- Two years of multihousing management experience
- Successful completion of the RAM Professional Profile
- Successful completion of the national RAM examination

Application for candidacy can be made at any time by submitting a completed RAM Professional Profile and application fee. In the event all three certification requirements are not met at the time of application, RAM candidacy status will be granted. RAM candidates have up to two years to meet the certification requirements. Completion of the basic RAM school is not necessary for full certification; however, it is the best preparation for the exam. The course also counts for 125 points on the Professional Profile.

All RAMs and RAM candidates receive the quarterly *Professional Management* newsletter and other publications. For more information, contact NAHB at (800) 368-5242, extension 8338.

BENEFITS OF THE RAM PROGRAM

In addition to the benefits of the RAM Program listed in Figure 1–7, interaction with other RAMs leading to added practical knowledge to apply on the job is one of the most beneficial aspects of the RAM Program.

FIGURE 1-6. RAM Program Objectives

To raise the professional standards and improve the practice of housing management by recognizing managers who demonstrate a high level of competence and ethical fitness for their jobs

To provide eligibility to managers and assistant managers who wish to qualify for employment in housing developments subject to HUD certification requirements

To identify persons with acceptable knowledge of the principles and practices of housing management, related disciplines, and laws governing and affecting the industry

To encourage multihousing managers to pursue continuing education programs for their professional development

To assure multihousing owners and residents of competent management service

FIGURE 1-7. Benefits of the RAM Program

Certification as a Registered Apartment Manager (RAM)
Industry recognition as a multihousing management professional
Certification for employment with housing developments subject to HUD certification requirements
RAM certificate, lapel pin, and identification card
Subscription to quarterly *Professional Management* newsletter and other multifamily publications
Annual Awards Banquet
Annual *RAM Membership Directory*
Affiliation with the National Association of Home Builders (NAHB) and Multifamily Council
Interaction with NAHB housing specialists

RAM CODE OF ETHICS

The RAM Code of Ethics (Fig. 1–8) helps to promote and maintain the highest standards in management and personal conduct within the multihousing industry. The code is rigorously enforced by the RAM Program and truly sets the RAM apart from every other residential manager. Adherence to the RAM Code of Ethics is required for RAM certification.

COURSE CONTENT, TESTING, AND SCHEDULE

This book is the official text for the RAM course. Additional assignments may be given by the various instructors. The sponsoring organization will administer the national RAM exam at the end of the course. That exam is developed by the RAM Board of Governors.

The schedule and location for each RAM course are determined by the sponsoring local home builders association, the multifamily council, or the local community college. You can find RAM schools by going to the NAHB web site, www.nahb.org and choosing the Education drop down list to do a search. For information on the RAM course in your area, contact NAHB at (800) 368-5242, extension 8338.

RE-CERTIFICATION

Education for a RAM does not stop with initial certification. RAMs must re-certify every three years by earning at least 75 re-certification points during that time. Each eight hours of continuing education is worth 25 points. Seminars of fewer than eight hours are worth 3.5 points per hour of instruction. Potential methods of earning points for RAM certification are listed in Figure 1–9.

FIGURE 1-8. RAM Code of Ethics

As a Registered Apartment Manager, I pledge to —

1. Maintain loyalty to the ownership of the properties I represent and pursue their goals and objectives and to accept no management assignments that would pose a conflict of interest on my part.
2. Obtain and maintain in force all licenses required by the state or local governments having jurisdiction over my activities.
3. Hold inviolate the confidential and fiduciary relationship with my employer and the confidential information entrusted to me by employees and residents.
4. Serve all employees and residents impartially and neither provide nor accept any special compensation, commissions, or payments without the prior knowledge or consent to such payment by my employer and the property owner.
5. Allow no exploitation of my position, industry, or profession.
6. Uphold all laws and regulations providing for fair access to housing opportunities, housing purchase, and accommodations. This includes but is not limited to all federal, state, and local Fair Housing Laws, the Rehabilitation Act of 1973, the Americans with Disabilities Act of 1992, and related acts and regulations.
7. Exercise sound business principles in managing properties.
8. Use only legal and ethical means to influence legislation or regulation.
9. Issue no false or misleading statements to the public.
10. Refrain from disseminating any malicious information concerning any property or person.
11. Utilize every opportunity to improve public understanding of the Registered in Apartment Management Program.

FIGURE 1-9. How to Earn RAM Re-certification Points

ATTEND MULTIHOUSING MANAGEMENT-RELATED COURSES AND PROFESSIONAL DEVELOPMENT PROGRAMS

Luncheons, dinners, or meetings (with speakers) sponsored by state and local home builders associations and/or multifamily councils
Work-related courses at local community colleges, universities, and junior colleges
Industry-related conventions or trade/home shows
NAHB Convention education programs
In-house training programs and other industry-related seminars
Seminars presented by U.S. Department of Housing and Urban Development
Educational events of related trade associations (such as the Institute of Real Estate Management [IREM] or National Assisted Housing Management Association [NAHMA])

PARTICIPATE IN OTHER ACTIVITIES

Write articles to be published in *Professional Management* newsletter, other NAHB publications, or other trade publications related to multihousing management and development.
Speak at industry-related programs such as RAM seminars or other industry-related workshops.
Take a leadership role in the industry by serving as an officer or on a working committee of an industry-related trade group.

The re-certification program is designed to keep each holder of the RAM designation at the forefront of the multifamily housing industry and to maintain the standards of the industry.

ADVANCED RAM (ADV. RAM)

The Advanced RAM (Adv. RAM) Program is designed for the career-conscious multifamily residential manager who aspires to the next level of property management. It offers a more advanced education and credential. The Advanced RAM program is based on six all-day advanced modules covering legal issues and fair housing for property managers, financial management, marketing and leasing, administrative operations and management skills for property managers, advanced maintenance, and personnel.

To become certified as an Advanced RAM, a RAM must be in good standing with the national program, have at least five years of experience, and have successfully completed the six modules.

The re-certification requirements and membership renewal procedures in effect for the certified RAM also apply to Advanced RAM candidates.

CONCLUSION

No matter where they live, people have always needed homes to live in. From the earliest time, people have recognized this need and the profit potential in providing residential shelter to others. As the complexities of owning residential property have developed with advances in technology and in all other areas of human existence, so too the challenges of owning and operating multiple-unit dwellings have expanded in scope and sophistication.

The advent and evolution of the multihousing management profession reflects the history of human residential evolution coupled with the requirements and expectations of multihousing property owners. Today, a wide and diverse range of individuals and groups own and operate multihousing properties for an equally wide and diverse range of reasons and goals. But despite the scope of owners and their ownership objectives, all multihousing property owners desire to have their properties managed in such a way as to preserve and increase the value of the property and to provide a reasonable living environment while producing a profit. It is the fulfillment of these fundamental owner requirements and expectations that the professional multihousing manager—the owner's managing agent—must accept as her/his primary obligation.

Beyond the acceptance of this obligation, the multihousing management professional who intends to perform competently also will focus on the individual and unique requirements and expectations of the owners of each property she/he manages. She/he will be aware of, support, and work to manifest the owner's goals for the property.

The multihousing management professional who intends to perform competently also will deliberately master a growing catalogue of proficiencies and skills to be able to deliver the highest caliber of service to the owners and resident of the properties she/he manages. These proficiencies embrace the areas of finance, law, marketing, insurance, construction, structural and mechanical engineering, plant maintenance, leasing, purchasing, computer technology, human resources, interpersonal relations, and a host of other capabilities that continue to evolve as the multihousing management profession evolves.

Multihousing properties are known by a variety of names, such as "sites" and "developments." Similarly, professional multihousing managing agents are known by a variety of titles. These titles may reflect the professional's level of experience and expertise and/or the geographic area in which the professional works. Such titles as executive property manager, senior manager, property manager, site manager, development manager, on-site manager, resident manager, assistant manager, and asset manager are common in the industry. But regardless of what title the manager holds, and no matter whether the manager is assigned to a property, a site, or a development, she/he is a member of an outstanding profession that offers unparalleled challenges and rewards to those who practice it.

The National Association of Home Builders (NAHB) is the premier professional organization for multihousing management professionals. Through NAHB's RAM and Advanced RAM Certification Programs, multihousing management professionals are educated, trained, and encouraged to be the most competent—the most superior—professionals in the multihousing management arena. This book is the primary text for the RAM Certification Program and the definitive text for the multihousing management profession.

2

Planning for Multihousing Management Success

PLANNING: THE PRIMARY FACTOR IN MANAGEMENT SUCCESS

It is an unfortunate but undeniable fact in all professional arenas that most people do not consciously and deliberately plan for the success of their employer, for the success of the clients or customers they serve, and, by obvious extension, for their own success. Instead of taking the long view and realizing that they must first invest some time and energy to create a roadmap that will help them arrive at their own desired destination as quickly and efficiently as possible, most people work each day waiting for the clock to strike five and each week waiting for Friday. Then they wonder why they have so few accomplishments and why accolades and promotions mysteriously elude them.

The truly professional multihousing manager is set apart from the masses. The professional multihousing manager knows that there is no mystery to achieving success. The professional multihousing manager knows that planning is the fundamental element that will yield the success she/he desires for the management company that employs her/him, for the owners whose properties he/she manages, and ultimately for herself/himself.

What follows is a discussion of those areas in which the professional multihousing manager regularly plans to achieve superior multihousing management success.

UNDERSTANDING A MANAGEMENT COMPANY'S INTERNAL STRUCTURE

Chapter 1, The Expanding Role of Professional Multihousing Management provided an introduction to the multihousing management profession, including a brief overview of its history. At the time of this textbook's publication early in the first decade of the 21st century, professional multihousing management is becoming more highly respected with each passing year for providing a necessary and valued service. The multihousing management industry is evolving at a remarkable pace, for those organizations that perform in-house management for their own portfolio of properties and for those fee-based management companies that serve independent client properties. (Although the bulk of this text references fee-based management companies, all of the information contained in these pages is pertinent and applicable to in-house management operations as well.)

Today there are thousands of multihousing management companies operating in the United States, with client portfolios ranging from less than a hundred units in one location to 100,000 or more units nationwide. All of these companies generate revenue by providing some lesser or greater range of management service to the owners of the properties that engage them. Many also provide ancillary services that generate additional revenue, such as sales and brokerage, capital improvement and construction consulting, and other such services. But the fundamental purpose of a multihousing management organization is and always will be to perform as the owner's managing agent.

Although the internal organization of individual management firms may appear to be somewhat different at first glance, the reality is that most are structured along similar lines. And all share the same two objectives: first, to provide professional management services to the owners of residential properties who either cannot or do not wish to manage their properties themselves and second, to be profitable and remain in business.

As a member of a management team, it is essential that the professional multihousing manager know and understand how her/his management company is structured in order to accomplish these objectives.

LINE AND STAFF POSITIONS WITHIN THE MANAGEMENT COMPANY

Unlike product businesses, which depend on the quality of tangible goods for profitability and success, multihousing management is a service business. It therefore depends on the quality of the service it delivers for profitability and success.

The services delivered by professional multihousing management companies are rendered by people. Hence, the grandeur or sparsity of a management company's offices is not as important to the company's reputation and productivity as are the technologies that help the company achieve its goals, the company's hierarchical organization, and, especially, the caliber and performance of the individuals who work there. Of course, this is not to say that the physical appearance, comfort, and image of the management company are unimportant. They are vitally important, especially with regard to communicating professionalism to prospective and existing clients and attracting and retaining the highest quality professionals. Typically, though, management companies that take pride in themselves, in their employees, and in their services will naturally create an atmosphere that communicates these qualities. The point is that, in the end, as in all service businesses, it is the people who make or break a management company.

In examining the hierarchical organization of a management firm, the first important distinction is between line and staff positions. Line positions are held by those people who have direct responsibility for managing one or more multihousing properties. Depending on the size of the management company, some or all of the following typical line positions may be present:

- Assistant property manager
- Property manager
- Asset manager
- Senior manager
- District manager
- Division manager
- Vice president
- Senior vice president
- Executive vice president
- Chief operating officer
- President

Although the line personnel are most visible because they interact most frequently with the outside world, the management company could not function without the staff personnel who work inside the company offices. Classic staff positions include the managers or directors and department employees of:

- Human resources
- Marketing
- Accounting
- Legal services
- Compliance services
- MIS (management of information services or systems/computer operations)

The people in these staff positions do not bear day-to-day responsibility for the management of the company's portfolio properties. Instead, they are essential to the ongoing operation of the management company itself and are vital to the line personnel for the support that they provide.

Regardless of the size of the management company, as long as there are two or more people employed, the line/staff relationship must be handled carefully and should have clear-cut lines of authority and communication so that conflicts do not develop. For example, a marketing director who provides the executive property manager with recommendations concerning how a property should be marketed may come in conflict with the property manager who has direct line responsibility for renting that property. In situations like this, it is the executive property manager's job to ensure that all line and staff personnel understand their respective roles and to mediate any conflicts among personnel.

The philosophy regarding the use of line and staff personnel varies from firm to firm, depending on the operating philosophy of the company's owner/chief executive officer/president and/or the executive property manager and on the personalities and capabilities of company personnel. Where line personnel lack expertise in certain areas such as marketing or training, staff personnel may be retained to fill that gap or the firm may outsource to outside contractors. Smaller firms typically contract for staff functions such as legal services and advertising, for example, while larger firms may keep all functions in-house. In the end, the executive property manager must communicate to all of the management company's workers their responsibility to operate as a team to accomplish common objectives.

To better understand where the property manager's position falls within the organizational structure, Figure 2–1 illustrates the typical on-site staffing and organization for a 200-unit conventional property with a turnover rate of 100 units per year. Although the organization may vary somewhat from firm to firm and market to market, this on-site property organization is typical of most management operations in suburban low-rise markets. It will be used as the typical on-site property organization in the discussions of management company staffing that follow.

Figures 2–2 through 2–4 illustrate sample organizational structures for small (typically managing under 1,000 units), medium (typically managing 1,000 to 5,000 units), and large (typically managing more than 5,000 units) management companies. (These ranges may vary to lesser or greater degrees, as may the positioning of personnel in the organiza-

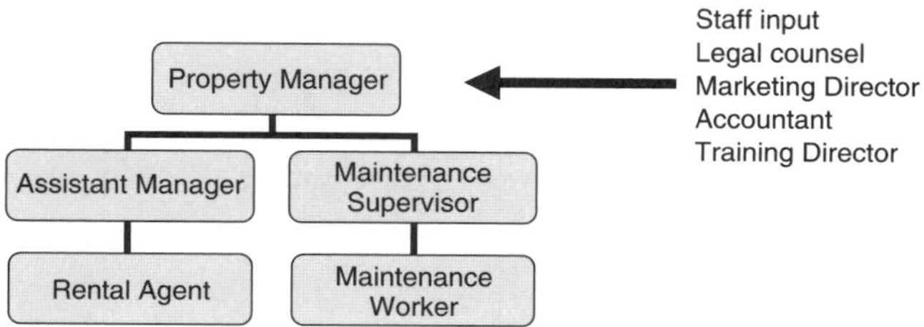

Figure 2–1 Typical on-site management organization.

tional charts. Nevertheless, these ranges and charts may be considered representative.)

In examining the organizational charts, note that as the size of a firm increases, so does the number of middle management positions. These middle managers are added to keep each executive's span of control at two to five subordinate managers. The principle of span of control reflects the fact that, for maximum effectiveness and efficiency, no individual manager can direct and control more than five or six subordinate managers over a long period of time.

Understanding how the management company is organized is especially critical for the property manager with more than one property to manage. The manager must know the philosophy of the management company relative to how many properties each manager may be assigned. This is true because the manager's workload combined with the level of in-house staff support will determine how productive the manager can be and ultimately how successful both the manager and the management company will be at meeting clients' expectations.

When considering a multihousing manager's portfolio of management assignments, bear in mind the level of attention each property requires. The property manager may need to be on-premises for one property once a week for several hours whereas another property in the same manager's portfolio needs contact every day. The actual amount of time a manager spends at a given property depends on several factors, including but not limited to the condition of the property, the travel time involved, and the number of properties in the manager's portfolio (Fig. 2–5).

Determining the unit and property load for a multihousing manager is a delicate balance at times. The executive property manager, who usually makes the assignments, must consider both the quality of the effort and the number of hours the manager spends in the performance of her/his job. The executive property manager must realize, for example, that the assignments may be completed but the properties may deteriorate because the manager's workload is too heavy. Or the job may be accomplished at the expense of a 16-hour workday. Either situation is undesirable and should be remedied for optimal performance and productivity on the manager's part.

For the multihousing manager, knowing the true scope of her/his own workload and how the management company supports the workload will enable her/him to plan the most productive work schedule.

OFF-SITE STAFF POSITIONS

The property manager generally relies heavily on the following individuals, who typically perform their functions away from the property itself, either in the offices of the management company or, if the professional is a consulting contractor to the management company, in the consultant's own offices.

Marketing Director

Depending on the size of the management company and on the marketing challenges facing either the management firm and/or its clients, this professional may be an internal employee or a contractor. In either case, the marketing director

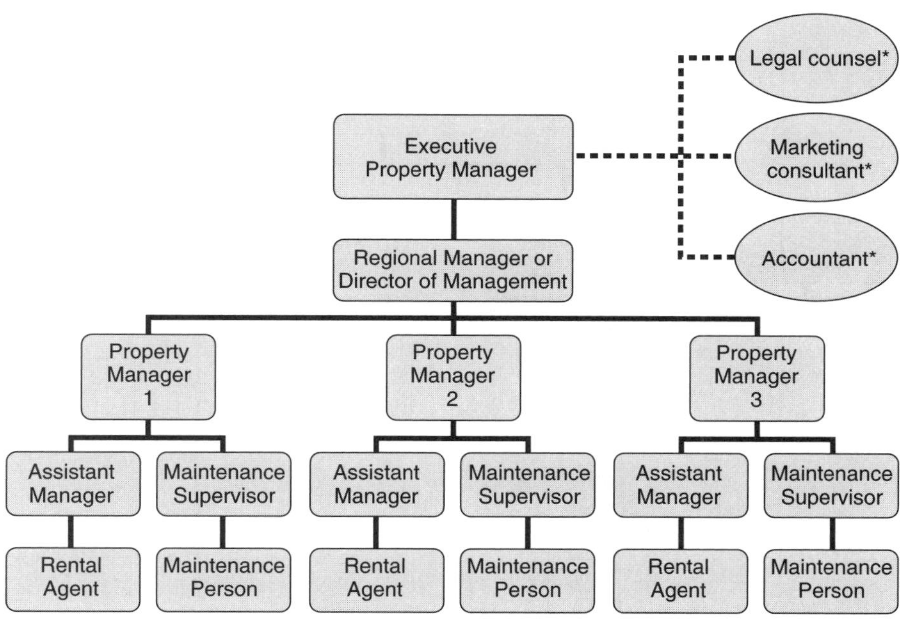

Figure 2–2 Organization chart for a small management firm.

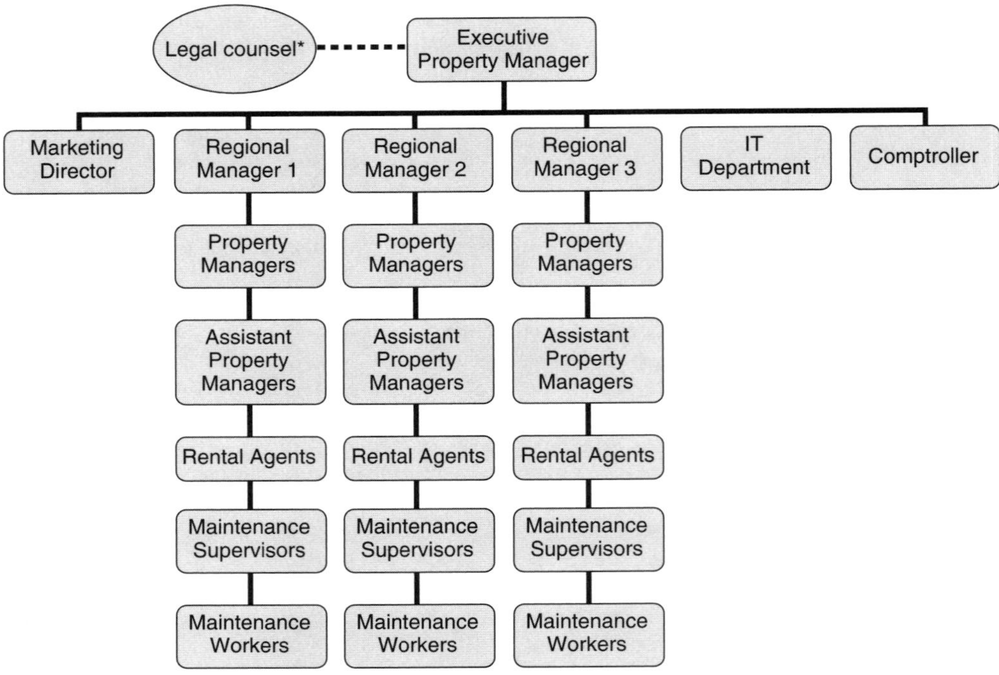

Figure 2–3 Organization chart for a medium management firm.

is generally responsible for establishing and implementing both the management company's own internal marketing program and the marketing programs for properties within the management company's client portfolio. As a staff member, the marketing director is usually found within larger management operations, especially when the company handles properties with high resident turnover, many new properties, a large number of conventional developments, and/or properties with marketing problems. The marketing director usually reports to either the executive property manager or the senior manager.

Training Director

Like the marketing director, the training director may be either an internal employee or a contractor. In either case, this professional is usually found in larger management operations and is responsible for developing and coordinating the

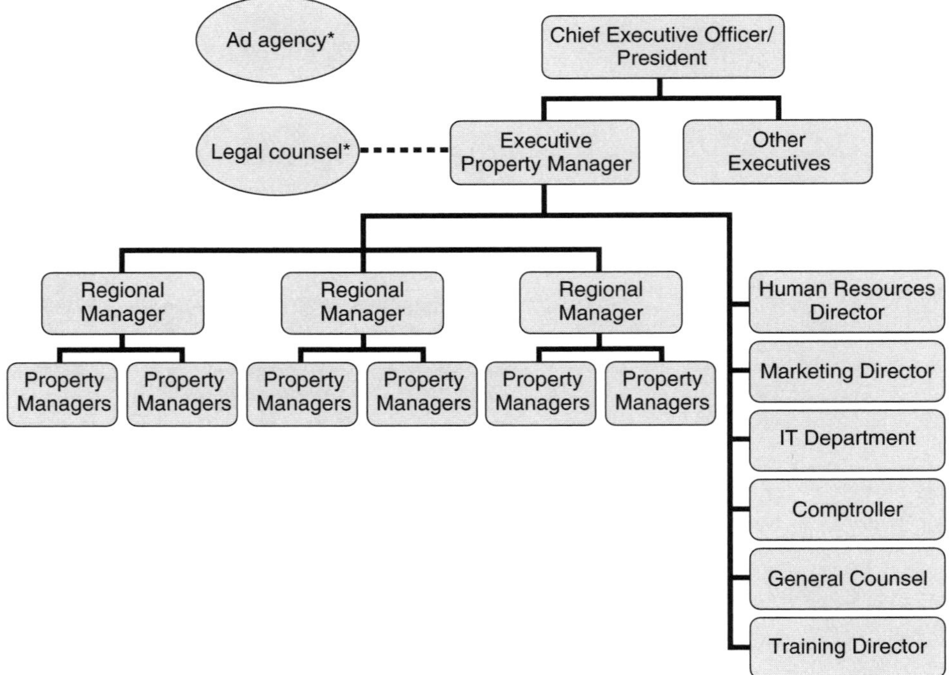

Figure 2–4 Organization chart for a large management firm.

FIGURE 2-5. Factors That Affect the Number of Properties One Person Can Manage

- Age of the properties
- Condition of the properties
- Number of units in each property, the number of residents in each property, and the total number of units and residents for which the manager is responsible
- Number of property locations and the location of the properties relative to the management company office and relative to each other because of travel time
- Regional geographic location of the properties and the effects, if any, of the region on the properties (e.g., extensive snow removal, pool maintenance, etc.)
- Whether any of the properties are in the rent-up stage
- Whether the properties are subsidized or conventional
- Any special problems with finances, resident profile, deferred maintenance, delinquencies, or other matters in one or more of the properties in the manager's portfolio
- Economic profile of the residents of the properties
- Age profile of the residents of the properties (e.g., senior residents requiring additional specialized services)
- Experience and proficiency of the manager
- Experience and proficiency of the individuals working under the manager's supervision
- Functions assigned to the manager by the management company, and the quality, quantity, and type of staff support available to the manager from the management company's home office
- Owner's management expectations and goals for each property in the manager's portfolio

management company's training program. The training director is generally responsible for training workers both within the management company itself and within the management firm's portfolio properties, and he/she reports to the executive property manager.

Fair Housing Director and Equal Employment Director/Compliance Director

Generally found in medium- and large-sized management firms, the responsibilities of the Fair Housing director and Equal Employment director/compliance director may fall to the same individual and/or may be combined with the position of marketing or training director. The Fair Housing director is responsible for answering any Fair Housing issues directed to the management firm, developing and reviewing marketing plans relative to Fair Housing, and administering all Fair Housing compliance activities. The Equal Employment director is responsible for administering the Equal Employment Opportunity requirements of the management firm. The compliance director is responsible for ensuring that the management company and all of the properties it manages comply with all applicable aspects of the law.

Maintenance Manager

Typically found in medium- and large-sized management companies that handle many large properties and/or employ or oversee many property maintenance workers and/or are involved in new construction or rehab projects, the maintenance manager is responsible for supervising new construction/rehab; serving in an advisory capacity to the property manager, who has direct line responsibility for hiring; training on-site maintenance staff; establishing the management company's overall client property maintenance policies; establishing maintenance procedures for individual client properties; providing technical advice to the executive property manager, senior manager, property manager, and property maintenance staff members; conducting inspections for routine and preventive maintenance at the management company's client properties; and negotiating contracts and purchases relative to maintenance issues. The maintenance manager usually also has some staff maintenance responsibilities for properties within the management company's portfolio. She/he may report directly to the executive property manager or the senior manager rather than to the property manager because the responsibilities of this position span more than one property.

Purchasing Agent

The purchasing agent usually either directly purchases materials, services, and supplies for the management company's portfolio properties or serves in an advisory capacity to the line personnel who perform this function. The purchasing agent reports directly to the executive property manager or the senior manager.

Bookkeeper Or Accountant

The bookkeeper or accountant is responsible for keeping the books of the management company and the properties managed by the management company. In larger management companies, there may be an individual who holds the title of chief financial officer, vice president of finance, or comptroller and who participates with and/or supervises the bookkeeper(s) and/or accountant(s). In any case, this individual reports directly to the executive property manager.

MIS Director/Computer Personnel

Regardless of size, virtually all management firms utilize computer systems and the wide and growing library of specialized industry software for such purposes as accounting, data maintenance, and report generation. Some management firms develop their own proprietary software to custom-tailor client services. When a management company has a designated individual responsible for overseeing computer operations, that individual is the MIS (management information services or systems) director. MIS directors typically report to the executive property manager or chief financial officer, vice president of finance, or comptroller. In smaller companies, the person responsible for computer operations may report to the accounting department supervisor.

Administrative Assistants and Clerical Support Staff

Administrative assistants and other clerical support staff are subordinate to the individuals above them in the management company hierarchy and take instruction from those individuals to perform administrative, clerical, and secretarial tasks.

Even though the multifamily housing manager may be assigned to one or more properties outside the physical location of the management company and therefore have limited contact with the individuals listed above, it is incumbent upon the manager to become acquainted with and to cultivate these individuals to best plan for the success of the properties in her/his portfolio and for her/his own success.

SITE-BASED POSITIONS

The property manager assigned to one or more properties will find that she/he must quickly learn to work productively with several individuals who are also on-site. Again depending on the size of the management company and on the specific property, the property manager may share the on-site management office and resources not only with the management assistant but also with the positions outlined below.

Rental/Leasing Agent

The rental/leasing agent is the primary individual responsible for renting units (apartments, townhouses) in the property. The rental/leasing agent typically reports to the property manager.

Property Bookkeeper

Although the management company may have one or more in-house bookkeepers and/or accountants responsible for keeping the books of the company and overseeing the books of client properties, some properties are large enough to warrant one or more on-site bookkeepers. When this is the case, these bookkeepers must be in constant communication with, and report to, both the property manager and the management company's central bookkeeping/accounting department and the bookkeeping/accounting director, comptroller, vice president of finance, and/or chief financial officer.

Maintenance Supervisor (or Superintendent)

In smaller properties, the property manager may hire and directly supervise technicians, grounds people, and other maintenance personnel. In larger properties, the maintenance supervisor is typically responsible for operating an effective maintenance program, including training maintenance staff and maintaining the property according to the standards established by the owner and/or management company; establishing work schedules and assigning work orders as required to maintain efficient use of staff time and of contractor services to maintain the property's condition and appearance ("curb appeal"); refurbishing vacancies within the time limit prescribed by the management company and reducing turnaround time on vacated units; handling resident service requests within the timetable prescribed by the management company; implementing the company's preventive maintenance program; controlling maintenance expenditures within budgetary guidelines; taking appropriate action in response to property inspection reports submitted by the senior manager and/or the property manager or owner, including any corrective action recommended in these reports; and properly maintaining and using the property's trucks and other maintenance vehicles and equipment belonging to the property.

When a skilled maintenance person, such as the maintenance supervisor or the maintenance technician, is required to report to a property manager who is less than knowledgeable about the technical aspects of property maintenance, problems can occur. (The situation is complicated when the maintenance supervisor earns more than the property manager, as is sometimes the case.) Such conflicts can be avoided when both the property manager and the maintenance supervisor recognize that their cooperation with and respect for each other contribute to the welfare of the property and its residents.

Maintenance Technician (or Handyman)

The maintenance technician performs skilled maintenance work and may also handle service requests and operate the property maintenance office if there is no maintenance supervisor or when the maintenance supervisor is not present. The maintenance technician should therefore be familiar with all policies and procedures of the property and should know how to write work orders, schedule maintenance work, and make move-in and move-out inspections. In larger properties, the maintenance technician reports to the maintenance supervisor and may also be called a maintenance assistant. In smaller properties without a maintenance supervisor, the maintenance technician reports directly to the property manager.

General Maintenance Worker

The general maintenance worker position exists in properties of all sizes and may includes duties such as maintaining overall property cleanliness, trash collection and removal, general landscape maintenance, general repair functions, and other similar tasks. This employee should follow the work schedule prepared by the maintenance supervisor or, if there is no maintenance supervisor, by the property manager, and should be able to take orders from a supervisor and perform the work as instructed.

Housekeeping Employees

Housekeeping employees are responsible for apartment clean-up under the supervision of the property manager or maintenance supervisor.

Grounds Workers

Grounds workers are responsible for taking care of the grounds, including the lawns, shrubs, and trees. Depending on the geographic location and requirements of the property, they may be full-time or seasonal. Because of the skill required in certain types of landscape maintenance, some properties also use contractors for this service.

Security Personnel (Including Concierges, Door Staff, and Safety Personnel)

Some properties have some form of grounds and/or lobby presence or patrol to help keep the property secure. In upscale properties, a concierge stationed in the lobby or other designated location may serve this purpose, in addition to performing other service duties for residents. In high-rise buildings, a doorman stationed in the lobby may perform this function in addition to other services for residents. In other types of properties, other workers may be hired for this type of work. For liability reasons, the workers who patrol the grounds and/or monitor lobby doors may not be called security guards. A full-time safety officer or compliance manager, as they are now called, could be a full-time property employee or could be hired from an outside firm to perform security-related duties. This service is often provided under a contractual arrangement with a firm that performs similar services for other properties in the area. Whether they are employed by the property or contracted from an outside firm, security personnel are accountable directly to the property manager.

Part-Time and/or Seasonal Workers

Part-time or seasonal workers include swimming pool lifeguards, summer lawn workers, and other temporary or seasonal employees.

Clearly, many, if not all, of the on-site personnel listed above are essential to property management success. For this reason, the property manager will want to cultivate these workers and design a plan to help them be as productive as possible.

CHAIN OF COMMAND

Chain of command refers to the hierarchy of various supervisory, reporting, and accountability relationships within an organization. For example, when a management company has been engaged, all property personnel, including the maintenance supervisor, usually report to the property manager, who in turn reports to the senior manager. The senior manager and any other supporting staff report to the executive property manager. And the executive property manager reports to the management company's clients, who are the owners of the properties that the company manages. In properties in which the manager works directly for the owner without a full management organization to support her/him, the manager must report directly to the owner or to an employee or contractor of the owner who is responsible for the property's management activities.

Regardless of whether or not the property manager's chain of command is long, as when a management company is involved, or short, as when the property is being managed in-house by the owner, the chain of command must be respected to maximize organizational and communication efficiency. By the same token, provisions should exist in all chains of command for persons at any level to bypass the level in the chain immediately above their position if they believe that a matter requires special attention (such as when a supervisor sexually harasses an employee, for example).

An appeals route to the personnel department is usually provided in management companies with personnel departments. But under normal circumstances, bypassing the standard chain of command creates a chaotic situation, and shortcuts that circumvent the normal chain of command cause confusion and negatively impact morale. For example, the senior manager who gives an order directly to a property's employees without going through the property manager tends to undermine the property manager's authority and encourages the property staff to do likewise. The senior manager suffers also because she/he then has too many people reporting directly to her/him. Similarly, an owner should not go directly to the property manager when that manager reports to a senior manager. By doing so, the owner reduces the senior manager's effectiveness and hence the ability of the entire management team to manage the property effectively.

For a property manager to function optimally, she/he must understand, respect, and plan to function productively within the chain of command under which she/he works.

PROFESSIONAL CONTRACT SERVICES

Sometimes management companies contract for, or outsource, professional services such as accounting and auditing, data processing, and delinquent rent collection from former residents. This type of service is frequently used when a management company believes it will get better service at a lower cost by going outside its own organization. As the company grows, it may be in a position to hire in-house specialists to provide one or more of these services, for both the properties it manages and the management company itself.

Management companies in growth modes should periodically perform a cost/benefit analysis and re-evaluate their positions to determine whether switching from a contracted service to an in-house service is advisable. Factors to be considered include the quality of service available from a contractor compared with the quality of in-house service, the relative costs involved, the dependability and on-going availability of the outside service, and whether a staff specialist can be fully utilized.

Although such internal business evaluations and decisions are not part of the property manager's job description, the manager who wishes to make herself/himself as knowledgeable as possible about the multihousing management business and as valuable as possible to the company that employs her/him will go the extra mile and offer after-hours assistance to the senior manager and/or executive property manager who is working on these projects. Including such value-added performance in a personal plan for success will go a long way toward helping the property manager accelerate her/his career.

UNDERSTANDING THE OWNER'S MANAGEMENT OBJECTIVES AND EXPECTATIONS

Chapter 1, The Expanding Role of Professional Multihousing Management indicated that every residential property owner harbors one or more unique and personal reasons for owning her/his property. These reasons may include periodic income, capital appreciation, speculation, control of investment, financing leverage, tax shelter, inflation hedge, use by owner, estate building, and/or pride of ownership.

Chapter 1 also noted that the professional multihousing manager has four primary obligations to every owner, which are to:

- Perform as a fiduciary
- Preserve and, if possible, increase the value of the property
- Produce a profit for the owner
- Provide the highest quality living environment to residents while preserving the property's value and producing a profit for the owner

To fulfill these obligations and meet the owner's individual expectations and requirements, the manager must take the time necessary to understand the owner's unique and personal ownership objectives and keep herself/himself updated as the owner's objectives change. Only in this way can the truly professional multihousing manager develop a viable management plan for the property and meet and exceed the expectations and requirements of the owner, the management company, and the manager.

COMMUNICATING WITH AND REPORTING TO OWNERS

The property manager and/or senior manager and/or executive property manager should have ongoing contact with the owners of the properties under their management. To be effective, both the manager and the owner need to know who will be making what decisions, who will be reporting to whom and how. Clearly establishing the chain of command and channels of communication is critical to smooth management, and the owner and the appropriate management company personnel should establish a firm reporting structure at the outset of their business relationship.

Documented communication (i.e., communication that is committed to paper and is logged and maintained in appropriate files) is the most effective way for the owner and the manager to express expectations, requirements, responses, and activities and to have a recorded history of their interactions. For the protection of all involved parties, the minimum reporting requirements that the manager and/or management company will fulfill for the owner, and the timing, level of detail, and level of management discretion should be determined at the beginning of the management assignment and stipulated in the management agreement. (See the discussion on the management agreement below.)

Management reporting requirements usually stipulate that routine reports will be provided to the owner on a monthly basis and will include a summary of activities; monthly financial reports, including current receivables and payables, budget and year-to-date income and expense reports, and reconciled bank, investment, and other accounts; a discussion of the rationale for unbudgeted expenses during the last month; a discussion of the rationale for contracts entered into or terminated during the last month; a discussion of the property's staffing situation during the last month and any staff-related actions taken by the manager/management company; a discussion of occupancy, moves into and out of the property, and resident-related issues during the last month; a discussion of any legal action pending and/or initiated during the last month; and all other issues that impact the property, the owner's interest in the property, and the manager/management company's oversight of the property.

Efficient long-term management depends on this kind of regular and clear communication between management and the owner. Management will be most effective and owners will be most satisfied when the reports and information flowing between the manager/management company and owners are timely, correct, and in sufficient detail.

Should the property manager be excluded for any reason from direct contact with and/or reporting responsibility to the owner, the manager should make it her/his business to be as informed as possible about what the owner communicates to the senior manager and/or executive property manager. The property manager can do this by requesting periodic meetings with her/his management company supervisors to keep current about the owner's end goals and level of satisfaction. In this way, the property manager will always know the owner's expectations and requirements and can plan to meet and then exceed them.

KNOWING THE PROPERTY

The superior property manager approaches each new assignment as a challenge to make the property a desirable habitat while generating the greatest possible return for the owner. To accomplish this, the manager must be thoroughly familiar with every aspect of the property and design a management plan that takes into account every nuance of information about the property.

Figure 2–6 is a comprehensive checklist of property characteristics that have a direct bearing on the value of the property to its owner and to its residents and that have a direct impact on—and are directly impacted by—professional management. The property manager should respond to the checklist with all available current information, updating and referring often to the checklist and the information it generates as a guide for management activity.

STRUCTURAL, PHYSICAL, AND MECHANICAL FEATURES, MAINTENANCE REQUIREMENTS, AND CONSERVATION NEEDS

Expanding the property manager's knowledge of the property from the general information contained in the checklist in Figure 2–6 to the specifics of the property's structural, physical, and mechanical features, its maintenance requirements, and energy and water conservation needs will stand the property manager in very good stead throughout her/his tenure at the property. Doing so will enable the manager to plan appropriately for routine custodial maintenance work and staffing to address the day-to-day maintenance of the property; for preventive maintenance work and staffing to prevent potential problems before they occur and prolong the life of the property and its elements; for corrective maintenance work and staffing to address maintenance issues that require repair or replacement; for property staff performance and competency assessments; for budget projections; and for marketing strategies and activities.

To best become familiar with the property's structural, physical, and mechanical features, maintenance requirements, and conservation needs, the property manager should tour and inspect the property using a checklist like the one shown in Figure 2–7 as a guide. While inspecting the property, the manager should examine not only the technical aspects of its structural and mechanical features but also its aesthetic elements.

If the property manager is unsure of what to look for while filling out the checklist, she/he should ask another expert, such as the executive property manager, the senior manager, the property's maintenance supervisor or technician, or the property's engineer, architect, or building contractor, to accompany her/him on the first go-round. Once the manager is shown what to look for, she/he will be able to complete the checklist alone on subsequent inspections.

In addition to completing the maintenance checklist, the property manager should plan regular and surprise property inspections during both day and night hours. These inspections will help the manager to create and implement a property-wide maintenance program that includes routine, preventive, and corrective maintenance programs and addresses all structural, mechanical, and aesthetic elements. The property manager should perform these inspections eagerly and thoroughly. "Walking the property" is one of the most important and valuable teaching tools and learning experiences for property managers of all experience levels.

To design and facilitate the most effective maintenance plan, the property manager must determine the property's immediate, medium-range, and long-range maintenance needs and how the property's personnel and equipment can meet those needs; anticipate possible maintenance emergencies, how the property's personnel and equipment can respond to each emergency and what to do if the personnel and/or equipment are insufficient to respond to the emergency; and be aware of, and know how to make the best use of, all resources and information necessary to ensure maintenance of the property (e.g., building plans, equipment manuals, locations of valves, standpipes, copies of building codes and safety standards, etc.).

The property manager's maintenance program should contain clear descriptions of the tasks to be performed and clear assignments of which property personnel are to perform the tasks, when, and how they must document what they have done. The manager must distribute this program in the form of a written maintenance plan to every member of the property's staff so there are no misunderstandings and everyone knows what is expected of her/him.

With regard to conservation of resources, including electricity, fuel, and water, the property manager must be acutely aware of consumption levels and ways to reduce these levels and must include conservation in the property-wide maintenance plan. Conservation represents more than just a cost saving, as more and more residents are becoming socially and environmentally conscious and seeking residential locations that are likewise socially and environmentally conscious. (For more information on maintenance and conservation management, see Chapter 5, Property Maintenance and Energy and Water Conservation.)

PROPERTY FINANCES AND BUDGETING AND FINANCIAL REPORTING CONSIDERATIONS

There are two interconnected reasons why the property manager needs to understand the finances, budgeting, and financial reporting considerations of the property she/he manages. The first reason is that the financial structure of a property dictates to a great degree the manner in which it will be operated. After all, virtually everything that occurs in a residential property is connected in some way to either collecting or spending money according to the owner's instructions. The second reason is because management companies depend on the fees they collect from the properties they manage to stay in business. That's why one of the property manager's most important duties is to make regular reports on the financial condition of the property she/he manages to the executive property manager, senior manager, and/or appropriate finance and accounting professional of the management firm and to assist in the preparation of annual operating and financial budgets for the property, a critical element in planning for management success. (See Chapter 4, Multihousing Management Economics and Finances for a discussion of financial considerations, budget preparation, and other matters related to the economics and finances of property management.)

To get the clearest picture of the finances, budgeting, and financial reporting considerations of the property she/he manages, the manager must understand the property's financing and established financial structure. That is, the manager needs to know how the owner has financed and/or is financing the purchase or construction and ongoing operation of the property and what financial structure the owner has put in place for the present and future viability of the property. Having this understanding will allow the manager to incorporate the special requirements of that financing into the property's management plan.

The types of financial structures possible for residential properties are nearly as numerous as the types of residential property ownership. The owner's objectives often determine

FIGURE 2-6. Comprehensive Checklist of Property Characteristics

Name of Property ____________________

Address of Property ____________________

____

- ☐ Legal Record of Property *(block & lot, etc.)* ____________________
- ☐ Assessed Valuation ____________________
- ☐ Date of Last Assessment ____________________
- ☐ Status of Appeals ____________________

Ownership Data

- ☐ Owner of Property ____________________
- ☐ Owner Objectives ____________________

Description of Surrounding Area

- ☐ Immediate ____________________
- ☐ Local ____________________
- ☐ Extended ____________________

Property Type

- ☐ Townhouse, High-rise, etc., and Conventional or Subsidized ____________________
- ☐ Year of Construction ____________________
- ☐ Materials of Construction ____________________

Overall Size of the Property

- ☐ Unit Size, Area & Lay-Out ____________________
- ☐ Unit Mix ____________________
- ☐ Rent Rates for Various Units ____________________
- ☐ Non-yield Space ____________________
- ☐ Comparison with Substantially Similar Properties in the Area ____________________

Overall Condition of the Property

Curb Appeal/Presence of/Condition of:

- ☐ Exteriors ____________________
- ☐ Landscaping ____________________
- ☐ Parking ____________________

Exterior Recreational Facilities/ Amenities ____________________

Interior Areas/Presence of/ Condition of:

- ☐ Interior Common Areas ____________________
- ☐ Interior of Units ____________________
- ☐ Interior Recreational Facilities ____________________

continued

FIGURE 2-6. Comprehensive Checklist of Property Characteristics (*Continued*)

Supporting Amenities/Presence of/ Condition of:

- ☐ Laundry Room ____
- ☐ Storage Facilities ____
- ☐ Clubhouse or Party Room ____
- ☐ Parking ____
- ☐ Vending Machines ____
- ☐ Pay Phones ____
- ☐ Other ____

Signs of Deferred Maintenance/ Deterioration ____

Financial Condition of the Property

- ☐ Present ____
- ☐ Projected ____
- ☐ Primary/Major Sources of Income ____
- ☐ Primary/Major Sources of Expense ____

Present Staff Situation

- ☐ Property Staff
  Attach a list of all property employees and their positions, and a copy of the property employee handbook and/or hiring, training, and firing policies and procedures.
- ☐ Management Office Staff
  Attach a list of all property employees and their positions, and a copy of the management company employee handbook and/or hiring, training, and firing policies and procedures.

Tenancy Information

Attach the following to checklist for reference:

- ☐ Most Current Lease Form
- ☐ Tenant Rent Roll
- ☐ Copy of Tenant/Resident Handbook
- ☐ Demographics of Current Resident Population ____
- ☐ Economic Level of Current Resident Population ____
- ☐ Present Occupancy Rate ____
- ☐ Reasons for Vacancies ____
- ☐ Present Marketing Plan (*description of*) ____
- ☐ Present Management Situation and Procedures (*description of*) ____
- ☐ Present Management Plan (*description of*) ____
- ☐ Discussion of any recent or pending lawsuits involving the property ____

continued

FIGURE 2-7. Structural/Physical/Mechanical Maintenance Checklist (*Continued*)

Name of Property ____________________

Address of Property ____________________

- ☐ Legal Record of Property *(block & lot, etc.)* ____________________
- ☐ Owner of Property ____________________
- ☐ Description of Property
  Including zoning and degree of conformity, significant location or site factors, and soil and drainage conditions
- ☐ Description of Property Layout
  Attach outdoor and indoor blueprints and floor plans, and layout and finishes of all facilities amenities, dwelling units, etc.

Property Amenities
(attach list of amenities and respond to the following for each)

- ☐ *current operation condition* __________
- ☐ *usefulness to the property* __________
- ☐ *remaining useful life* __________
- ☐ *ease of maintenance* __________
- ☐ *efficiency of operation* __________
- ☐ *recommendation for repair, replacement or other* __________

Curb Appeal and Appearance

- ☐ *current operating condition* __________
- ☐ *usefulness to the property* __________
- ☐ *remaining useful life* __________
- ☐ *ease of maintenance* __________
- ☐ *efficiency of operation* __________
- ☐ *recommendation for repair, replacement or other* __________

Electrical Systems

- ☐ *current operating condition* __________
- ☐ *usefulness to the property* __________
- ☐ *remaining useful life* __________
- ☐ *ease of maintenance* __________
- ☐ *efficiency of operation* __________
- ☐ *recommendation for repair, replacement or other* __________

Elevators

- ☐ *current operating condition* __________
- ☐ *usefulness to the property* __________
- ☐ *remaining useful life* __________
- ☐ *ease of maintenance* __________
- ☐ *efficiency of operation* __________
- ☐ *recommendation for repair, replacement or other* __________

continued

FIGURE 2-7. Structural/Physical/Mechanical Maintenance Checklist (*Continued*)

Fire Prevention Systems

- ☐ *current operating condition* ______
- ☐ *usefulness to the property* ______
- ☐ *remaining useful life* ______
- ☐ *ease of maintenance* ______
- ☐ *efficiency of operation* ______
- ☐ *recommendation for repair, replacement or other* ______

Grounds and Landscaping

- ☐ *current operating condition* ______
- ☐ *usefulness to the property* ______
- ☐ *remaining useful life* ______
- ☐ *ease of maintenance* ______
- ☐ *efficiency of operation* ______
- ☐ *recommendation for repair, replacement or other* ______

Heating, Ventilation, Air Conditioning (HVAC)

- ☐ *current operating condition* ______
- ☐ *usefulness to the property* ______
- ☐ *remaining useful life* ______
- ☐ *ease of maintenance* ______
- ☐ *efficiency of operation* ______
- ☐ *recommendation for repair, replacement or other* ______

Internal Dwelling Units

- ☐ *current operating condition* ______
- ☐ *usefulness to the property* ______
- ☐ *remaining useful life* ______
- ☐ *ease of maintenance* ______
- ☐ *efficiency of operation* ______
- ☐ *recommendation for repair, replacement or other* ______

Laundry Room

- ☐ *current operating condition* ______
- ☐ *usefulness to the property* ______
- ☐ *remaining useful life* ______
- ☐ *ease of maintenance* ______
- ☐ *efficiency of operation* ______
- ☐ *recommendation for repair, replacement or other* ______

Parking Areas

- ☐ *current operating condition* ______
- ☐ *usefulness to the property* ______
- ☐ *remaining useful life* ______
- ☐ *ease of maintenance* ______
- ☐ *efficiency of operation* ______
- ☐ *recommendation for repair, replacement or other* ______

continued

FIGURE 2-7. Structural/Physical/Mechanical Maintenance Checklist (*Continued*)

Plumbing Systems

- ☐ *current operating condition* __________
- ☐ *usefulness to the property* __________
- ☐ *remaining useful life* __________
- ☐ *ease of maintenance* __________
- ☐ *efficiency of operation* __________
- ☐ *recommendation for repair, replacement or other* __________

Refuse Disposal and Removal Areas

- ☐ *current operating condition* __________
- ☐ *usefulness to the property* __________
- ☐ *remaining useful life* __________
- ☐ *ease of maintenance* __________
- ☐ *efficiency of operation* __________
- ☐ *recommendation for repair, replacement or other* __________

Roof

- ☐ *current operating condition* __________
- ☐ *usefulness to the property* __________
- ☐ *remaining useful life* __________
- ☐ *ease of maintenance* __________
- ☐ *efficiency of operation* __________
- ☐ *recommendation for repair, replacement or other* __________

Safety Features

- ☐ *current operating condition* __________
- ☐ *usefulness to the property* __________
- ☐ *remaining useful life* __________
- ☐ *ease of maintenance* __________
- ☐ *efficiency of operation* __________
- ☐ *recommendation for repair, replacement or other* __________

Security

- ☐ *current operating condition* __________
- ☐ *usefulness to the property* __________
- ☐ *remaining useful life* __________
- ☐ *ease of maintenance* __________
- ☐ *efficiency of operation* __________
- ☐ *recommendation for repair, replacement or other* __________

Signage

- ☐ *current operating condition* __________
- ☐ *usefulness to the property* __________
- ☐ *remaining useful life* __________
- ☐ *ease of maintenance* __________
- ☐ *efficiency of operation* __________
- ☐ *recommendation for repair, replacement or other* __________

continued

FIGURE 2-7. Structural/Physical/Mechanical Maintenance Checklist (*Continued*)

Stairways

- ☐ *current operating condition* ____________
- ☐ *usefulness to the property* ____________
- ☐ *remaining useful life* ____________
- ☐ *ease of maintenance* ____________
- ☐ *efficiency of operation* ____________
- ☐ *recommendation for repair, replacement or other* ____________

Structural Defects

- ☐ *current operating condition* ____________
- ☐ *usefulness to the property* ____________
- ☐ *remaining useful life* ____________
- ☐ *ease of maintenance* ____________
- ☐ *efficiency of operation* ____________
- ☐ *recommendation for repair, replacement or other* ____________

Other

- ☐ *current operating condition* ____________
- ☐ *usefulness to the property* ____________
- ☐ *remaining useful life* ____________
- ☐ *ease of maintenance* ____________
- ☐ *efficiency of operation* ____________
- ☐ *recommendation for repair, replacement or other* ____________

Condition of and degree of optimal space utilization in:

- ☐ *Storage Rooms* ____________
- ☐ *Maintenance Garage(s)* ____________
- ☐ *Maintenance Workshop(s)* ____________

Inventory
Attach inventories of:

- ☐ All current property furnishings owned by owner
- ☐ Equipment, tools, supplies, etc.

Maintenance Data
Attach

- ☐ Purchasing Data & Policies/Procedures
- ☐ Maintenance Contracts & Warrantees
- ☐ Full Account Information About:
  - *Utilities*
  - *Insurance*
  - *Current Contacts with Vendors, Suppliers, Contractors, etc.*

the type of ownership and the structure of the financing package for a particular property. Generally speaking, the financial structure of the great majority of properties combines both debt and equity.

Leveraging (using borrowed funds) is an accepted way of increasing the financial returns to the owners of a property. Leveraging has the effect of increasing the return on a property when the overall rate of return is greater than the rate of interest on the debt. Conversely, however, if the return on the property is less than the interest rate on the debt, the effect of leverage is just the opposite: it increases the loss.

Frequently, the higher the leverage or overall proportion of debt, the greater the opportunity for higher yields and the greater the possibility of losses. A property with high leverage is much more sensitive to small variations in income than one with a low overall leverage.

The financial structure of multihousing properties has become much more complex in recent years. The traditional financial structure for most properties has been a fully amortizing mortgage at a fixed interest rate for either 20 or 30 years. Some properties financed by the U.S. Department of Housing and Urban Development (HUD) have carried mortgages with 40-year terms. In the late 1970s, when fully amortizing mortgages at attractive fixed interest rates became difficult to obtain, alternative types of financing flourished, and balloon mortgages, variable rate mortgages, and other mortgage derivatives became common, as did other types of financing instruments. Many of these instruments fit into a large category known as mortgage-backed securities, such as a mortgage pass-through (where investors buy instruments that represent a pro rata interest in the principal and interest payment on a mortgage or pool of mortgages) and a mortgage pay-through bond (similar to a pass-through security, but the investors in the pay-through bond do not have an ownership interest in the mortgage(s) that back the security; rather, the mortgage(s) serve as collateral for repayment of principal and interest on the instrument).

The changes created by the Tax Reform Act of 1986 substantially lessened the advantages of high leverage in real estate developments. Consequently, the financial structure of many then-new developments changed once again, with some properties developed with higher than traditional proportions of equity.

Obviously, management companies want the properties they manage and the owners of those properties to be solvent. The property manager therefore needs to have current knowledge of how various properties are financed and especially how the properties she/he manages are financed and are faring so that she/he can plan and perform optimally for the owner.

PROPERTY RESIDENTS

Residential properties are defined by many factors. Of course, location, physical structure, size, type, number and layout of dwelling units, amenities, and quality of management all play significant roles. So, too, does the resident profile. The occupants of a rental property may be called residents, renters, or tenants (in legal contexts, they must always be referred to as tenants), and the occupants of a shared-interest association may be referred to as shareholders, unit owners, or homeowners, but without exception the type of person who is attracted to and who chooses to live in a specific property will have a marked impact on how the property is perceived, how it is marketed, and how it is managed.

From an economic perspective, residents of rental properties fall into four categories: low income, moderate income, middle income, and high income. These categories are easily verified by simply reviewing the location, construction, and amenities of existing rental properties and multifamily communities. Although a resident's selection of a place to live may have been determined by choice or by circumstances combined with level of income, nevertheless everyone needs a place to live. It is therefore the responsibility of the property manager to market the properties they manage to those persons who are best qualified to live in them.

RECOGNIZING AND MANAGING RISK

The property manager has two primary obligations when it comes to risk management. The first is to provide a reasonably safe and secure living environment for residents and guests and a reasonably safe and secure working environment for individuals who work in the property. The second is to protect the owner's investment.

The property manager who wishes to create an effective risk management program will do everything possible to prevent emergencies, have a clearly defined plan of action in the event of an emergency, and ensure that the property is protected with adequate and appropriate insurance coverage. In our litigious society, where even the smallest issue becomes grist for a lawsuit, it is imperative that the property manager recognize and manage risk as thoroughly and professionally as possible.

Fire safety, personal injury, and property damage have traditionally been the three most common types of risk in a multifamily property. It is the manager's responsibility to familiarize herself/himself with the property to recognize and remedy those conditions that could contribute to increased risk. The manager may respond to a perceived risk in one of four ways:

- Avoidance (eliminating risk)
- Prevention (minimizing risk)
- Transfer (transferring risk to someone else)
- Retention (recognizing and assuming the risk)

Knowing how to recognize and manage risk is a critical element in planning for successful multihousing management. The entire topic of risk management—insurance coverage, how the property manager should plan for and handle losses, and how to maximize life, safety, and security within the property—is explored in great detail in Chapter 6, Risk Management and Management Maintenance Plans.

FAIR MANAGEMENT AGREEMENT AND FEE

The typical residential property management contract is an agreement between the property owner and the management company. It is generally negotiated between the property owner and the executive property manager, and it establishes the responsibilities and obligations of both the owner and the management company for the property's management. Although the property manager usually is not involved at all in the negotiation of the management agreement, it is important to know the terms of the agreement so that she/he can plan to fulfill them.

To minimize any misunderstandings between the parties, the management agreement should always be committed to writing with the help of an attorney who specializes in real estate law. The sample agreement in Figure 2–8 is a simple agreement in common use today for single-owner, conventional rental properties. (The agreement would be more complex in situations involving a federal or state subsidy or tax-exempt bond financing and would involve as a third party the regulatory body that issued the financing or the bonds. Such agreements are quite complex and carry substantial legal commitments.)

In the typical management agreement, the management company is usually responsible for the day-to-day operation of the property, including renting apartments, signing leases, collecting rents, supervising maintenance, and paying expenses. The owner is responsible for providing the funds to operate and manage the property and for setting the overall goals for the property and its management and the parameters in which the management company is to perform.

The management fee is the owner's monthly payment to the management company for managing the property. The amount of the fee is typically computed in one of three ways:

- A flat monthly fee
- A percentage of the rents collected
- A percentage of net operating income achieved

The standard rental management agreement includes the following:

- Name(s) of the owner(s) and all other legal information about the form of ownership
- Full legal name of the management company
- Term of the agreement (commencement and termination dates)
- Cancellation provisions
- Description of the property
- Management's obligations and/or authority to:
    - Initiate and participate in rental activities, including marketing
    - Establish and collect rents and security deposits
    - Establish and access bank accounts for the property
    - Obtain fidelity bonds
    - Pay operating expenses
    - Provide financial and other reports to the owner(s)
    - Disburse net proceeds to the owner(s)
    - Perform and/or arrange for property maintenance
    - Respond to property emergencies
    - Respond to violations
    - Supervise property employees
- Insurance coverages for the property, the owner(s), and the management company
- The management fee and any additional fees

The written management plan should serve as part of the agreement between the owner and the management company.

CULTIVATING A STRONG PROPERTY MANAGEMENT TEAM

As shown in Figures 2–2 through 2–4, the larger the management company, the more layers there are between the property manager and the executive property manager. This makes sense since larger management operations typically offer a wider menu of services, have more supervisory positions, and employ more people with specific areas of specialization.

However, away from the management company home office, in the confines of the property, the property manager actually operates in a somewhat autonomous environment. And while the property manager is supported by the same professionals in the management company, generally it is the responsibility of the property manager to staff the property itself and supervise the property's staff. It is therefore important for the manager to plan for property staffing success. This means knowing what the property's staffing needs are and how to meet those needs as effectively and efficiently as possible, which means hiring the best, most qualified workers and supervising them properly so that they perform optimally. This is the way to cultivate a strong property management team.

Besides her/his assistant manager, who is usually a direct employee of the management company hired specifically to support the property manager, the manager is typically responsible for hiring and supervising staff in two specific performance areas: maintenance and leasing.

FIGURE 2-8. Sample Management Agreement*

This agreement is made on ____(Date)____ between ____(Insert development name)____ ("Owner"), ____(a partnership/an individual/a corporation)____ organized and existing under the laws of the State of ________, and ____(Management company name)____, ("Agent"), ____(a partnership/an individual/a corporation)____ organized and existing under the laws of the State of ____________________.

WITNESSETH:

In consideration of the terms, conditions, and covenants set forth in this agreement, the Owner and Agent mutually agree as follows:

Appointment

1. The Owner appoints the Agent, and the Agents accepts appointment, on the terms and conditions hereinafter provided, as exclusive managing agent of ____(Name of Development)____ comprising ________ dwelling units, together with the land on which such dwellings are erected, referred to as the "Development."

General

2. In order to facilitate efficient operation, the Owner shall inform the Agent of the standards to be kept and furnish the Agent with a set of community or house rules and a complete set of the plans and specifications of the Development. With the aid of these documents and inspection made by competent personnel, the Agent will inform itself with respect to the layout, construction, location, character, plan, and operation of the lighting, heating, plumbing, and ventilation systems, and other mechanical equipment in the Development. Copies of guarantees and warranties pertinent to the construction of the Development and in force at the time of the execution of this Agreement shall be furnished to the Agent.

Bonding

3. After consultation with the Owner, the Agent shall hire, at a salary approved by the Owner, all management personnel, including the Development manager where necessary for the efficient discharge of the duties of the Agent hereunder. Compensation for the services of such employees shall be the responsibility of the Owner. The Agent and those employees who handle or are responsible for the handling of the Owner's moneys shall, at the request of the Owner and at the expense of the Owner, be bonded by a fidelity bond acceptable both to the Agent and the Owner, in an amount and by a company acceptable to the Agent and the Owner. The Owner shall be the obligee under such bond.*

Services and Duties

4. Under the personal and direct supervision of one of its principal officers, the Agent shall render services and perform duties as follows:

(a) The Agent shall be responsible for obtaining all rental applications, income information, credit reports as required by the Owner, and such other information as may be requested by the Owner. The Agent shall be responsible for obtaining a lease from each Resident ("Lessee") prior to occupancy and collecting the rental payment and security deposit required prior to occupancy. The Agent shall execute the lease for and on behalf of the Owner ("Lessor") in the name of the Owner.

(b) If requested by the Owner and on the basis of an operating schedule, job standards, and wage rates previously approved by the Owner on the recommendation of the Agent or resulting from wage negotiations, investigate, hire, pay, supervise, and discharge the personnel necessary to be employed in order to maintain and operate the Development properly. Such personnel shall in every instance be in the Owner's and not in the Agent's employ.

(c) Immediately ascertain the general condition of the property and cause an inventory to be taken of all furniture, office equipment, maintenance tools and supplies, including a determination as to the amount of fuel on hand.

continued

FIGURE 2-8. Sample Management Agreement* (*Continued*)

(d) Coordinate the plans of Residents for moving their personal effects into the Development or out of it, with a view towards scheduling such moves so that the inconvenience to other Residents is kept to a minimum.

(e) Maintain businesslike relations with Residents whose service requests shall be received, considered, and recorded in systematic fashion in order to show the action taken with respect to each. Complaints of a serious nature shall, after thorough investigation, be reported to the Owner with appropriate recommendations. As part of a continuing program to secure full performance by the Residents of all items and maintenance for which they are responsible, the Agent shall make an annual inspection or an inspection whenever a Resident vacates, whichever occurs first, of all dwelling units and reports its findings to the Owner and to the consenting parties.

(f) Collect all monthly rents due from Residents, all rents due from users or lessees of nondwelling facilities in the Development, and all sums due from concessionaires. The Owner authorizes and directs the Agent to request, demand, collect, receive, and provide receipt for any and all rents that may any time become due to the Owner, and to take such legal action as necessary to evict Residents.

(g) Cause the building, appurtenances, and grounds on the Development to be maintained according to standards acceptable to the Owner, including but not limited to interior and exterior cleaning, painting, decorating, plumbing, steam fitting, carpentry, and such other normal maintenance and repair work as may be necessary, subject to any limitations imposed by the Owner in addition to those contained herein. With the exception of payments required under the mortgage, taxes, insurance, utilities, and Owner-approved contractual obligations, no disbursement shall be made in excess of $500 unless specifically authorized by the Owner; excepting, however, that emergency repairs, involving manifest danger to life or property, or immediately necessary for the preservation and safety of the property, or for the safety of the Residents, or required to avoid the suspension of any necessary service to the Development, may be made by the Agent irrespective of the cost limitation imposed by this paragraph. Notwithstanding this authority as to emergency repairs, it is understood and agreed that the Agent will, if at all possible, confer immediately with the Owner regarding every such expenditure and its effect on the budget. The Agent shall not incur liabilities (direct or contingent) that will at any time exceed the aggregate of $________ or any liability maturing more than one (1) year from the creation thereof, without first obtaining the approval of the Owner.

(h) Take such action as may be necessary to comply promptly with any and all orders or requirements affecting the Development placed thereon by any federal, state, county, or municipal authority having jurisdiction over the Development, subject to the same limitation contained in Paragraph (g) of this Article in connection with the making of repairs and alterations. The Agent, however, shall not take any action under this Paragraph (h) so long as the Owner is contesting, or has affirmed its intention to contest, any such order or requirement. The Agent shall act promptly, and in no event later than 72 hours from the time of their receipt, notify the Owner in writing of all such orders and notices of requirements.

(i) Subject to approval by the Owner, make contracts for water, electricity, gas, fuel oil, telephone, vermin extermination, and other necessary services, or such of them as the Owner shall deem advisable. Also, place purchase orders for such equipment, tools, appliances, materials, and supplies as are necessary properly to maintain the Development. All such contracts and orders shall be made in the name of the Owner and shall be subject to the limitations set forth in Paragraph (g) of this Article. When taking bids or issuing purchase orders, the Agent shall act at all times under the direction of the Owner, and shall be under a duty to secure fore and credit to the latter any discounts, commissions, or rebates obtainable as a result of such purchases.

(j) With the approval of the Owner, cause to be placed and kept in force all forms of insurance needed to adequately protect the Owner (or as required by law), including, where appropriate, Workers Compensation Insurance, public liability insurance, boiler insurance, fire and extended coverage insurance, and burglary and theft insurance. All of the various types of insurance coverage required for the benefit of the Owner shall be placed with such companies, in such amounts, and with such beneficial interests therein as shall be acceptable to the Owner and the Agent, and otherwise be in conformity with the requirements of the mortgage. The Agent shall promptly investigate and make a full written report as to all accidents or claims for damage relating to the ownership and maintenance of the Development, including any damage or destruction to the Development, the estimated cost of repair, and shall cooperate and make any and all reports required by any insurance company in connection therewith.

continued

FIGURE 2-8. Sample Management Agreement* (*Continued*)

(k) From the funds collected and deposited in the account provided in this agreement under Article 6, if requested by the Owner, cause to be disbursed regularly and punctually (1) salaries and any other compensation due and payable to the employees of the Owner, including the resident manager, and the taxes payable under Paragraph (l) of this Article; (2) the payment required to be made monthly to the mortgages; (3) real estate taxes when due; (4) fire and other hazard insurance premiums; and (5) sums otherwise due and payable by the Owner as operating expenses authorized to be incurred under the terms of this Agreement, including the Agent's commission.

(l) Working in conjunction with an accountant, prepare for execution and filing by the Owner all forms, reports, and returns required by law in connection with unemployment insurance, Workers Compensation Insurance, disability benefits, Social Security, and other similar taxes now in effect or hereafter imposed, and also requirements relating to the employment of personnel.

(m) If requested by the owner, maintain a comprehensive system of office records, books, and accounts in a manager satisfactory to the owner, which records shall be subject to examination by the owner's authorized agents at all reasonable hours. As a standard practice, the Agent shall render to the owner not later than the 25th of each succeeding month a statement of receipts and disbursements, a schedule of accounts receivable and payable, and a reconciled bank statement as of the end of the preceding month. It shall render a quarterly comparison of income and expense to the budget.

(n) See that each unit is placed in rental order after being vacated by a Resident and that any chargeable damage is collected from the vacating Resident by charging the security deposit or otherwise. The Agent shall be responsible for the reletting of each unit to qualified persons and, in this regard, to obtain the same documents as set forth in paragraph (a) of this Article. The Agent shall maintain a current list of prospective Residents to facilitate re-rental.

(o) It shall be the duty of the Agent at all times during the term of this Agreement to operate and maintain the Development according to the highest standards achievable consistent with the overall plan of the owner. Full compliance by the Residents with the terms and conditions of their respective Leases shall be secured, and to this end the Agent shall see that all Residents are informed with respect to such rules, regulations, and notices as may be promulgated by the Owner from time to time. The Agent shall be expected to perform such other acts and deeds as are reasonable, necessary, and proper in the discharge of its duties under this Agreement.

Agent

5. Everything done by the Agent under the provisions of Article 4 shall be done as the Agent of the Owner, and all obligations or expense incurred under Article 4 shall be for the account, on behalf, and at the expense of the Owner, except that the Owner shall not be obligated to pay the overhead expenses of the Agent's office. Any payments to be made by the Agent under this agreement shall be made out of such sums as may be provided by the Owner. The Agent shall not be obliged to make any advance to or for the account of the Owner or to pay any sum, except out of funds provided, nor shall the Agent be obliged to incur any liability or obligations for the account of the Owner without assurance that necessary funds for the discharge thereof will be provided.

Bank Account

6. The Owner has established and maintains a bank account in its name. All funds collected by the Agent shall be deposited in said bank account in the name of the Owner. The Owner shall designate from time to time the persons authorized to withdraw funds from said bank account, including the signing of checks thereon, and in the event the Owner requests the Agent to make various payments as set forth in this Agreement, then such payments shall be made by the Agent from such bank account, but such payments shall be subject to the limitations set forth in this Agreement.

Compensation

7. (a) Except as set forth, the sole compensation which the Agent shall be entitled to receive for all services performed under this Agreement shall be a fee computed and paid monthly or at such longer interval as shall be mutually agreed by the parties in an amount equivalent to ______ percent of gross collections, exclusive of all surcharges.

continued

FIGURE 2-8. Sample Management Agreement* (*Continued*)

(b) Owner shall pay for all advertising, including but not limited to brochures, newspapers, radio, television, and circulars during the initial rent-up period and thereafter. All advertising, whether placed by the Owner or Agent, shall be subject to the approval of the Owner and in the event advertising is placed by the Agent with the consent and approval of the Owner, it shall be placed in the name of the Owner and shall be billed to the Owner. In the event any advertising is placed with the consent and approval of the Owner and is billed to the Agent, the Owner shall reimburse the Agent without any profit or markup of any type made by the Agent to the Owner.

Duration of Agreement

8. (a) Unless cancelled pursuant to Sections (b) or (c) of this Article, this Agreement shall be in effect from the date of execution for a period of three (3) years.

(b) In the event a petition in bankruptcy is filed by or against either Owner or Agent, or in the event that either shall make an assignment for the benefit of creditors or take advantage of any insolvency act, either party may terminate this Agreement without notice to the other, but prompt advice of such action shall be given to either party by the other.

Definitions

9. As used in this Agreement:

(a) The term *development manager* shall mean a person engaged in managerial supervision on behalf of the Agent, whether residing on the premises or not, and shall not be construed to mean a maintenance supervisor, caretaker, or other maintenance employee of the Owner.

(b) The term *resident* shall mean the lessee.

(c) The term *lease* shall mean that certain form of agreement between the Owner and its Residents (and any renewals thereof) under the terms of which said Residents are entitled to enjoy possession of their respective dwelling units.

(d) The term *rent* shall mean those monthly charges that Residents are bound to pay to the Owner pursuant to the terms of their respective Leases.

(e) The term *gross collections* shall mean all amounts actually collected by the Agent, either as rents, late charges, laundry equipment rentals, or similar receipts from Residents, lessees, and concessionaires (but not including security deposits).

Summary

10. (a) This Agreement shall inure to the benefit of and constitute a binding obligation upon the contracting parties, their respective successors, and assigns.

(b) This Agreement shall constitute the entire Agreement between the contracting parties, and no variance or modification thereof shall valid and enforceable, except by supplemental Agreement in writing, executed and approved in the same manner as this Agreement.

OWNER: ______________________________

By ______________________________

AGENT: ______________________________

By ______________________________

(Vice President)

(Corporate Seal)

*Readers should consult a local attorney to determine legal requirements for such an agreement in their local jurisdiction.

PROPERTY MAINTENANCE STAFFING

A property can be situated in an outstanding location and be overstocked with attractive amenities such as pools and tennis courts and a health club and a clubhouse. But if the property is poorly maintained—if it looks dirty and run-down, if its structural and physical features are shabby and its mechanical elements are broken—it will quickly develop a negative reputation, existing residents will vacate, and no one will want to move in. In short, a poorly maintained property will fail.

Hiring and working with competent maintenance personnel is therefore one of the property manager's most critical responsibilities. When determining and planning property maintenance staffing requirements, the manager must take the following factors into consideration:

- The size and defining features of the property, specifically the number of residential buildings and residential units in the property

- The physical and structural elements of the residential units and buildings, the common areas inside the buildings, and the outdoor and other common buildings and grounds areas; the current condition of these elements; and the plans of the owner, if there are any, to alter or upgrade these elements (e.g., including but not limited to the physical and structural integrity of the property's buildings and units, the entranceways and/or lobbies, stairwells, roofs, basements, sidewalks/walkways, gutters, etc.)

- The mechanical elements of the residential units and building(s), the common areas inside the building(s), and the outdoor and other common building and grounds areas; the current condition of these elements; and the plans of the owner, if any, to alter or upgrade these elements (e.g., HVAC [heating/ventilation/air conditioning units, including boilers/burners, hot water heaters, air conditioners, etc.], elevators, plumbing, electricity, etc.)

- The amenities and aesthetic elements of the residential units and building(s), the common areas outside the building(s), and the outdoor and other common buildings and grounds areas; the current condition of these elements; and the plans of the owner, if any, to alter or upgrade these elements (e.g., landscaping, garages/parking lots, recreational facilities such as pools, tennis courts, etc.)

- Resident profile (demographic information about residents, such as economic level, age, etc.)

- Resident turnover (the frequency with which residents move into and out of the property)

- Days and hours of maintenance operation in the property

- The number and type of contractual services required for maintenance of the property

- Any legal and/or union requirements concerning the property's maintenance staffing

- The requirements and expectations of the owner relative to the maintenance of the physical, structural, mechanical, amenities, and aesthetic elements of the property

Generally, the maintenance supervisor (or superintendent in some properties and locations) is in charge of the property's maintenance. Other maintenance personnel might include a maintenance assistant; maintenance technicians who handle service requests and other jobs requiring special skills; general maintenance workers who do cleaning, pick-up, and other closely supervised work; grounds people; housekeeping employees; and seasonal or part-time maintenance workers. It is the property manager's responsibility—sometimes with the maintenance supervisor, depending on the size of the property—to hire these workers, to supervise their work, and to ensure that their performance enhances the quality of life for residents and the value of the owner's investment.

PROPERTY RENTAL STAFFING

The viability of a multihousing property depends on many factors, including and especially the ability of the property to attract and retain the most desirable residents. Typically, the management company is responsible for this function and engages one or more rental agents to accomplish this usually on-going task.

The property manager planning to hire one or more rental agents for her/his property should take the following factors about the property into consideration:

- The amount of traffic in and around the property and the rental office

- Current residency rate

- Resident turnover rate

- Resident profile

- Vacancy problems

- Whether the property is subsidized or conventional

- Required documentation

- Hours and days of rental office operation

- Available supervision

- Experience level of existing and candidate rental personnel

Both the maintenance and the rental office personnel are vital to a property's success. The property manager responsible for staffing the property with these workers, and sometimes also with bookkeeping and/or security personnel, must clearly understand the responsibilities to be carried out at the property, the competency and experience levels of existing and candidate staff, and the support that each staff member can expect from the manager, from the management company, and from the owner.

COMPLYING WITH GENERAL AND SPECIFIC LEGAL EMPLOYMENT ISSUES

As this text emphasizes, the professional multihousing manager must be a master of many disciplines. In the case of the property manager who is hiring and supervising property staff, this mastery must include knowledge of, and compliance with, general and specific employment law.

The field of employment law/labor relations is complex and constantly changing. It includes but is not limited to such issues as recruiting, screening, and hiring practices; compliance with Equal Employment Opportunity and sexual harassment and other discrimination regulations; Americans With Disabilities Act (ADA) and Federal Family and Medical Leave Act (FMLA) requirements; other federal, state, and local employment regulations; and union contract terms and conditions as appropriate to the property. The property manager must be familiar with all of these legal employment issues and must ensure that all of the property's job descriptions, employee handbooks, and employment policies comply.

DEVELOPING OPERATIONS, EMPLOYEE, AND RESIDENT MANUALS

It's been said that if one fails to plan, then one plans to fail. Nowhere is this adage more true than in the field of multihousing management. As demonstrated throughout this text, competent multihousing management demands meticulous and on-going planning for and attention to the immediate, short-, medium-, and long-range goals and objectives of the property's owner(s).

It is not possible for any property manager, no matter how naturally intelligent or well-organized, to remember, let alone accomplish, everything that needs to be done today, tomorrow, and into the future, without the benefit of a cogent, comprehensive written plan. The written plan, the purpose of which is to provide a process guide and an achievement barometer, is a fundamental tool for all property management tasks, responsibilities, and activities. Similarly, the codified handbook of policies, procedures, and protocols is an invaluable reference source without which the manager would find herself/himself re-inventing the wheel—and the rules governing the use of the wheel—each time a question or issue arises.

The multihousing manager committed to performance success will therefore invest the necessary time and effort to either secure or create the following written plans and handbooks:

- Operations manual
- Management maintenance plan (including a risk management plan)
- Marketing plan
- Employee handbook
- Resident handbook

OPERATIONS MANUAL

Like the owner's manual of an automobile, the management operations manual should present the features and equipment that define the overall management entity through which the property manager is expected to perform, how those features and equipment work and interact with each other, and how the manager should use or operate those features and that equipment for maximum benefit. Typically, the management entity is an independent management company of one size or another, but it could also be the owner's own management entity, the management entity of a third party engaged by the owner to arrange for the management of the owner's property, or a management entity unique to one particular property. In any case, the purpose of the operations manual is to codify the management policies, procedures, and protocols that govern the manager's activities and to provide the manager with a how-to guide that anticipates issues and challenges and supplies the solutions and responses for dealing with them in advance.

The operations manual helps both the management company and the individual property manager operate more effectively, more efficiently, and more fairly because it articulates exactly how things get done and what is expected of everyone. In this way, an operations manual helps management staff make many decisions independently, allowing supervisory staff members to delegate more freely and make more productive use of their own time. Not insignificant to overall management success, the operations manual also contributes greatly to continuity of service by allowing anyone to step in at any time and know precisely how to proceed with what needs to be accomplished. This is especially valuable when new management staff members are being trained and when any staff member, including the property manager, is absent for any period of time. For this reason alone, but also for all the reasons above, all management companies and professionally managed properties, regardless of size, should have an operations manual and should update the operations manual periodically as revisions and/or new information needs to be included.

To be the most valuable and effective resource, the operations manual should be bound in such a way as to allow it to be a living document. A living document is one that can be updated and revised periodically without having to reprint the entire document. This is achieved by binding the document in a three-ring binder so that pages with revisions can be easily inserted and removed. All pages and entries should be dated to inform the user that she/he is reading the most recent information.

The operations manual should be organized into three distinct parts: policies, procedures, and forms. Policies are the rules governing action in a given situation. Procedures are the steps for implementing the policies. Forms are the tangible documentation used for demonstrating and evaluating policies and procedures and, if properly designed, are among the most efficient ways to transmit information.

The complete management operations manual will contain specific information about how the management company operates and how its operations support the management of its client portfolio. The following topics should be included in the operations manual, which should be organized into separate sections for easiest reference:

- History of the management company or entity
- Statement of the management company's or entity's corporate philosophy
- Organizational chart
- Discussion of job positions and functions within the company
- Company's personnel policies (including staffing, firing, hiring, training, promotions, compensation, benefits)
- Management-specific policies, procedures, and forms, including:
    - Leasing and application procedures and processing
    - Collecting and recording rents
    - Occupancy, including move-in, move-out, and eviction
    - Budget and record-keeping
    - Purchasing and disbursement
    - Maintenance
    - Security
    - Risk management
    - Marketing

The operations manual should be written in simple, concise language, ideally by someone who understands the purpose of the document and its contents. For example, when writing a job description for the manual, the individual actually working in that particular position could be asked to write the job description. The draft could then be reviewed by the supervisor and/or the person responsible for compiling the manual. The same applies when writing a specific procedure. The staff member most familiar with the procedure could be asked to compose the section on the procedure's rationale, usefulness, and step-by-step instructions and to submit the draft to her/his supervisor and/or the person responsible for putting the manual together.

Clearly, the operations manual is an essential tool for effective management. As indicated in the section above on management agreements, the operations manual should serve as part of the agreement between the owner and the management company. Once the property manager is in possession of an operations manual that supports her/his functions as an agent of the management entity, her/his attention can be turned to the creation and implementation of a management maintenance plan designed specifically for the individual property. (Also see the discussion of operations manuals in Chapter 9, Managing the Site Office and the Operations Manual.)

MANAGEMENT MAINTENANCE PLAN (INCLUDING A RISK MANAGEMENT PLAN)

If the operations manual provides a how-to for the property manager, then the management maintenance plan provides a what-to. For the property manager, the purpose of creating a management maintenance plan—which should have a risk management plan as a major component—is to deliberately and succinctly set forth the objectives the manager intends to achieve within the property and the steps she/he will take to achieve them.

Hence, the organization and table of contents of a management maintenance plan for an individual property will appear similar to the organization and table of contents for an operations manual. But the actual contents will go further than that of the operations manual. Each entry in the management maintenance plan will express management objectives for that specific topic and then incorporate the contents of the operations manual as a tool for accomplishing those objectives. The organization and table of contents of a management maintenance plan will look something like this:

- A description of the property
- An organizational chart of the property management/maintenance staff
- A discussion of job positions and functions within the property staff
- A statement of the owner's and hence the manager's goals and objectives for:
- Cultivating property personnel (including such personnel policies as staffing, hiring, firing, training, promotion, compensation, benefits, etc.)
    - Maximizing leasing and optimizing application procedures
    - Collecting and recording rents
    - Addressing occupancy issues, including move-ins, move-outs, and evictions
    - Budget and record-keeping
    - Purchasing and disbursement
    - Maintenance and improvements
    - Security
    - Risk management
    - Marketing

Like the operations manual, the management maintenance plan should serve as part of the agreement between the owner and the management company.

MARKET ANALYSIS, INCOME AND EXPENSES ANALYSIS AND RENT PROJECTIONS, LONG-TERM FINANCIAL ANALYSIS, AND MANAGEMENT VARIABLES AS THEY AFFECT THE MANAGEMENT MAINTENANCE PLAN

To produce the most useful management maintenance plan, the property manager must be conversant with the necessary data and information. Figure 2–6 provides an excellent starting point for the property manager to determine the information that should be included in the management maintenance plan and the actions that need to be taken.

Market Analysis

The information culled from this comprehensive checklist of property characteristics will support the manager in the creation of a market analysis of the region, the neighborhood, and the property. Such an analysis will enable the manager to determine the rent being charged for comparable housing and the anticipated demand for property units. Competitive rates and demand are the two main factors generally considered in establishing rental rates. Of course, adjustments should be made to competitive rent levels to compensate for differences between the property in question and competitive properties. (The method of determining rents is discussed in Chapter 4, Multihousing Management Economics and Finances.)

The first step in preparing a market analysis is to analyze the region in which the property is located. This analysis identifies the general economic and demographic conditions in the region, the physical aspects of the area surrounding the property, and the trends that affect the property. It should include an analysis of the city or metropolitan area having a direct economic impact on the property in question.

The next step is an in-depth study of the immediate neighborhood, an area with common characteristics of population and land use. After defining the boundaries of the neighborhood, information should be gathered regarding the neighborhood's population and trends. This information should be analyzed to determine its impact on the property.

Finally, a three-part property analysis should be made by preparing a complete description of the property's building(s) by physically walking through the property to inspect its accommodations, basic architectural design, and overall physical condition; by examining the property's total operation, including but not limited to an analysis of the physical condition of the property, including any deferred maintenance and a plan for corrective action; by an analysis of the financial condition based on the most recent financial statements; and by an operations analysis evaluating the policies, personnel, and procedures in effect at the property.

Income and Expense Analysis and Rent Projections

An effective management maintenance plan must include an income and expense analysis to assist in the projection of rent. Rent levels are determined in large part by the surrounding properties and their rent levels. Recent changes in rent-setting by HUD attempt to tie rent for government-assisted developments to the market. Although real estate economics may dictate rent levels higher than the market, maintaining rents at above-market levels is difficult. As vacancy levels go up, rent levels either hold even or decline because competition for residents forces prices down.

The income and expense analysis informs the owner of what the management company expects in terms of gross income, expenses, and resulting net income. The analysis also projects anticipated rental income and rates over a period of time and relates these to anticipated expenditures.

Long-term Financial Analysis

The management maintenance plan should contain a long-term financial analysis. Important components of this analysis are property valuation, financing/refinancing, capital improvements, and a 5-year or 10-year cash flow analysis.

These items, which are beyond the normal scope of the property manager's responsibilities, are typically researched, prepared, and presented by the executive property manager to the owner. However, the property manager should be aware of their existence and importance.

Type of Ownership

Obviously, the type of ownership of the property to be managed influences management planning. (For example, profit/loss is not necessarily a consideration in condominium associations.) Property managers should be aware of how each type of ownership impacts property management, even if they do not manage properties under different types of ownership at the present time. (See Chapter 1, The Expanding Role of Professional Multihousing Management for a discussion of the housing stock and types of multihousing ownership.)

Target Market

In developing a target market, the manager must be careful to develop criteria that do not violate the Fair Housing Act and/or other applicable laws. The manager cannot use criteria that result in limiting access to housing to persons or families on the basis of race, color, national origin, religion, sex, familial status, handicap, or any other discriminatory criteria established by the federal, state, or local government. (For a more complete discussion of the Fair Housing Act, see the Code of Federal Regulations, Volume 24, commonly called 24 CFR. Local and state departments of labor or human resources also can supply information pertaining to additional protected categories.)

Property Location

Management challenges addressed in the management maintenance plan will vary according to the property's rural, suburban, urban, or resort location.

Property Size

Management challenges and procedures also will vary according to the size of the property. The impact of property size on the policies and procedures for dealing with various areas of management (e.g., staffing, leasing, maintenance resident selection, resident relations) is discussed throughout this text. However, no matter the size of a multihousing project, the management company should have a set of operating procedures to manage it and someone with management responsibility and accountability in charge of its management.

MAINTENANCE AND RISK MANAGEMENT PLANS IN THE LARGER MANAGEMENT MAINTENANCE PLAN

Both maintenance and risk management are topics so significant to the successful management of a property that each requires a comprehensive plan unto itself. The plan may be incorporated into the overall management maintenance plan for the property as a whole, but specific attention must be paid individually to the maintenance and risk management factors of each property.

Maintenance refers to the upkeep of the property's structural, physical, mechanical, and aesthetic elements. The considerations that should be included in an effective maintenance plan are discussed in Chapter 5, Property Maintenance and Energy and Water Conservation.

Risk management refers to the owner's obligation and, by extension, the manager's responsibility to provide a reasonably safe and secure living environment to all residents and guests. The issues that should be included in an effective risk management plan are discussed in detail in Chapter 6, Risk Management and Management Maintenance Plans.

MARKETING PLAN

As with all other commodities that must be marketed to the appropriate target consumer to generate revenue and profitability to the seller/owner, residential communities also must be properly marketed. A unique, standalone marketing plan that may be incorporated later into the overall operations manual should therefore be developed for each individual property. The topics that should be included in the effective marketing plan are discussed in detail in Chapter 7, Marketing Rental Housing and the Marketing Plan.

EMPLOYEE HANDBOOK

The employee handbook is a vital instrument for managing both the management company and the property. Because the property manager's responsibilities include supervising the property staff, it is important to the manager's success to have a codified employee handbook that explains all aspects of working for the management company and/or at the property. A detailed discussion of how the property manager should assemble an effective employee handbook appears in Chapter 3, On the Front Line: The Property Manager.

RESIDENT HANDBOOK

Regardless of the size of the property managed, every property manager quickly comes to recognize the benefits of distributing a codified, concise, and clear resident handbook to residents. Such a handbook serves as a reference guide to the property's rules, policies, and procedures and the lease stipulations and informs residents that management decisions are fair and uniform, not arbitrary. The property manager is therefore well advised to put some time and energy into creating a single, codified document that clearly defines the rules, regulations, policies, procedures, and protocols of residency in the property and to disseminate the handbook to all property residents. The topics to be included in a residents handbook are discussed in Chapter 8, Processing Applications, Move-in and Move-out Procedures, and Resident Relations and the Resident Handbook.

Like the "stars" of every profession, the multihousing management industry's most effective, efficient managers all know that the secret to success is to first plan your work and then work your plan. With so many tasks to accomplish every day and so many people to be accountable to, the superior multihousing manager will recognize the value and benefits of developing and maintaining a written operations manual, a management maintenance plan, a marketing plan, an employee handbook, and a resident handbook.

CONCLUSION

Planning is essential for multihousing management success. As a service business, the management company, regardless of size, has two primary objectives: to provide management services to owners who either cannot or do not wish to manage their properties themselves and to be profitable and remain in business. For the property manager to plan effectively for the success of the company she/he works for, for the owners who engage the company, and for herself/himself, the property manager must first be thoroughly familiar with how the management company operates.

Within the management company, line positions are held by those people who have direct responsibility for managing one or more multihousing properties. The property manager occupies a line position, as does the management company's senior manager, executive property manager, and executive vice president, president, and/or chief executive officer. Staff personnel are those who work inside the company offices and support the line personnel. Staff personnel include the managers or directors and department workers of human resources, marketing, accounting, legal services, and MIS/computer operations.

Note that as the size of a firm increases, so does the number of middle management positions. These middle managers are added to keep each executive's span of control at two to five subordinate managers. The principle of span of control reflects the fact that, for maximum effectiveness and efficiency, no individual manager can direct and control more than five or six subordinate managers over a long period of time.

Similarly, it is important for the manager with a portfolio of more than one property to know the philosophy of the management company relative to how many properties each manager may be assigned. This is true because the manager's workload combined with the level of in-house staff will determine how productive the manager can be and ultimately how successful both the manager and the management company will be at meeting the owner's expectations.

When considering a multihousing manager's portfolio of management assignments, bear in mind the level of attention each property requires. The actual amount of time a manager spends at a given site depends on several factors, including but not limited to the condition of the property, the travel time to and from the property, and the number, types, and circumstances of all of the other properties in the manager's portfolio.

The property manager typically relies on the following off-site staff who usually work in the management company office: marketing director, training director, Fair Housing director/Equal Employment director/compliance director, maintenance manager, purchasing agent, bookkeeper or accountant, MIS director/computer personnel, and the administrative assistant/clerical support staff.

The property manager typically supervises and relies on the following on-site staff members with whom she/he works at the property: management assistant, rental/leasing agent, property bookkeeper, maintenance supervisor, maintenance technician, general maintenance workers, housekeeping employees, grounds employees, security personnel, and part-time and/or seasonal employees.

The property manager will want to cultivate both off-site and on-site workers and design a plan to help them be as productive as possible on behalf of the client property.

Chain of command refers to the hierarchy of supervisory, reporting, and accountability relationships within an organization. For a property manager to function optimally, she/he must understand, respect, and plan to function productively within the chain of command under which she/he works. The manager who wishes to make herself/himself as knowledgeable as possible about the multifamily housing management business and as valuable as possible to the company that employs her/him will go the extra mile and offer after-hours assistance to the senior and/or executive property manager. Planning to do this will go a long way toward helping the property manager accelerate her/his career.

The property manager planning for success also will take the time necessary to understand the property owner's unique and personal ownership objectives and keep her/himself updated as the owner's objectives change. The manager will document all activities on behalf of the owner and will comply with all owner reporting requirements.

To plan effectively, the manager will get to know the property thoroughly. She/he will use a comprehensive checklist of property characteristics and a structural/physical/mechanical maintenance checklist to become familiar with all aspects of the property and as guides for management activity. She/he will become an expert in the property's financing, budgeting, and financial reporting considerations. Having this understanding will allow the manager to incorporate the special requirements of that financing into planning for management success.

The property manager planning for success will know and cultivate the property's residents by identifying the type of renter who constitutes the greatest existing or target population of the property and fulfilling the wants and expectations of those individuals to the greatest possible extent.

The manager also will recognize and manage risk by taking deliberate action to prevent emergencies, having a clearly defined plan of action in the event of an emergency, and ensuring that the property is protected with adequate and appropriate insurance coverage. Knowing how to recognize and manage risk is a critical element in planning for property management success.

The property manager planning for success will become familiar with the terms and conditions of the management agreement between the management company and the property owner. She/he will cultivate a strong property management team by planning to staff the property with the most qualified workers and supervising them properly.

Finally, the property manager who is committed to success will either secure or create a written operations manual, a management maintenance plan (including a risk management plan), a marketing plan, an employee handbook, and a resident handbook. These documents will guide the manager in her/his quest to be an outstanding multihousing management professional.

3

On the Front Line: The Property Manager

RESPONSIBILITIES AND CHARACTERISTICS OF THE SUCCESSFUL PROPERTY MANAGER

To reiterate a critical statement, the property manager—who may also be called the development manager, the site manager, the on-site manager, or the resident manager—is arguably the most important professional in the management of a property. It is the property manager who is physically at the property day in and day out, interacting with the property staff and employees, with the owners and residents, and with the senior manager to whom the property manager reports.

The responsibilities of the property manager are many, varied, and formidable. And just as certain personal and professional characteristics and skill sets are not only helpful but also necessary to be truly successful in any other field of endeavor, so there are specific personal and professional characteristics and skill sets that are essential to the property manager's successful fulfillment of her/his myriad responsibilities. These personal and professional characteristics and skill sets include:

- Math, communication, and language literacy skills
- Management and organizational skills
- Administrative and supervisory skills
- Interpersonal skills
- Personal qualities and skills:
  - Maturity
  - Sociability
  - Initiative

This part of the text explores and defines these characteristics and skill sets and encourages the professional property manager to acquire and cultivate them for herself/himself.

MATH, COMMUNICATION, AND LANGUAGE LITERACY SKILLS

There can be no exception to the fact that the ability to perform mathematical operations, communicate effectively, and exhibit language literacy (the ability to read and write in English and in whatever other language would be most helpful in managing the homes of certain populations) are absolute prerequisites for the successful property manager.

Daily, the property manager is confronted with mathematical calculations. On at least a monthly basis, she/he must provide a balanced accounting to both the management supervisor and the property owner. And over the course of her/his tenure in the property, the property manager will be called on often to participate in budget and finance-related activities and decisions that impact the property. For these reasons, the ability to figure and calculate numbers is essential to the property manager's ability to perform her/his job.

The property manager also must be able to communicate effectively. In a service business such as multihousing management, the ability to make a verbal statement in such a manner as to be understood and respected is critical to professional success.

Most importantly, the property manager must be literate. In an increasingly technical environment and at a site office where frequent reference to manuals is necessary and written documentation is required, the property manager absolutely must be able to read and write on a reasonably advanced level.

MANAGEMENT AND ORGANIZATIONAL SKILLS

After math and language proficiency, the most important skills for the property manager to possess are the abilities to manage and organize effectively. Management skill includes the competencies to:

- Recognize the property's requirements and what must be done to succeed
- Plan
- Organize the workloads of self and others
- Make decisions
- Delegate to others
- Motivate others
- Meet deadlines promptly
- Identify financial, action, and staffing priorities
- Set, accomplish, and follow up daily, weekly, and monthly goals for self and others

The experienced property manager recognizes that, while the basics remain the same in all properties, each property assignment has its own unique set of identifying traits and challenges. To navigate the situations that arise and to meet the daily challenges of property management, the property manager must master the art and craft of management.

Organization, the ability to evaluate priorities, and the capacity to make swift, well-reasoned decisions are the hallmarks of the skilled property manager. To cultivate these skills, managers sometimes need a change of venue from the management office. Often, "getting away" constructively by walking the property, talking with residents, meeting with staff personnel, and observing property conditions helps the manager to gain perspective. In any case, walking the property at least once a day is an important management practice.

ADMINISTRATIVE AND SUPERVISORY SKILLS

Administration is the act of running an organization. Supervision is the act of directing the personnel within the organization. Property managers need to hone both administrative and supervisory skills to accomplish the following tasks successfully:

- Master paperwork and detail with good organization skills
- Hire, train, motivate, direct, and evaluate staff with the skills needed to do the job
- Direct and work well with property staff
- Access crucial information via manual methods and via computer

When it comes to administration, the ability to listen well is one of the most important skills a manager can possess. The manager must be able to listen carefully to both residents and the other staff personnel and hear what these two groups are communicating. This is true because both residents and the property personnel are in a position to provide valuable information and insight from different but important perspectives.

Because they cannot perform all of the functions required to run a property by themselves and because they are responsible for the activities of other property personnel, property managers also must be able to supervise effectively. They must operate through their employees and subordinates, and doing so requires keen supervisory and human resource management skills.

Listening, communicating, and giving clear instructions are valuable skills for both the administration and supervision of the property. In spite of work pressures and deadlines, the property manager must always be able to communicate instructions and information clearly and to discuss with residents and other property personnel the reasons and rationale for those instructions and that information. People respond best to instructions and information when they understand "why." What's more, when people understand why they are hearing what they are hearing and/or doing what they are doing, they may be able to suggest a better way of accomplishing the objective. And what property manager couldn't use a better way?

INTERPERSONAL SKILLS

A discussion of interpersonal skills is a logical extension of the discussion directly above. Because multihousing management is a business dedicated to serving people, the property manager must be able to relate to and work well with people. Dealing effectively with others, especially with property residents and personnel, requires strong interpersonal skills.

In his classic book, *How To Win Friends and Influence People,* people manager extraordinaire Dale Carnegie emphasizes empathy—the ability to understand and share the feelings of others—as one of the key principles in effective interpersonal relationships. Applying the principle of empathy to the property manager's responsibilities, it is clear that, to be effective, the property manager must think and respond in terms of the other person's interests and desires.

When dealing with the owner, for example, the property manager must empathize by making the owner's priorities her/his own priorities. When dealing with residents, the manager must be able to respond to requests and complaints from a position of empathy and be able to clearly articulate that the property's policies and procedures are for the residents' benefit—to enable them to enjoy the multihousing lifestyle—in such a way that the resident feels that the property manager has empathized and dealt effectively with her/him. And when dealing with property staff, the property manager must be mindful to take into consideration the employee's feelings and responses and to explain how a request made of a staff member fits in with the overall objectives of the property so that the employee is made to feel that she/he is making a valuable contribution. In short, the successful property manager must become adept at speaking in terms of the other person's interests.

In general, when dealing with other people, the property manager must be able to:

Relate effectively to, and demonstrate concern for, the resident population and the property staff—As mentioned above, the property manager must be able to listen and respond empathetically and effectively to the resident population and to the property's staff. Property managers do not need to become personal friends with each resident or every staff member in a property. Nor should they assume the responsibility of making everyone happy. But if the property manager performs her/his responsibilities in a professionally courteous and empathetic manner, the result will be an environment conducive to maximum enjoyment of the multihousing lifestyle for residents and maximum productivity for property personnel.

Be firm in carrying out policy—Some property managers think that they will anger residents by being firm in enforcing property policies and that the personnel they supervise will resent them if they require a certain level of performance. In fact, the reverse is true. Residents typically lose respect for management when property policies are not fairly, impartially, and consistently enforced. And workers lose respect for supervisors who are wishy-washy, indecisive, and who do not give straight answers or apply the same standards to all workers. Of course, a policy should not be carried out blindly if it does not make sense in a particular situation. The rule of reason must always prevail in spite of procedures to the contrary. But policies and procedures that are based on sound business practice will be reasonable under most circumstances and will serve the property manager in good stead if she/he will enforce them uniformly, decisively, and impartially.

Give and receive instructions in a professional manner—The property manager must be careful to clearly explain the reasons for a particular request of a resident or staff member and the rationale for a negative response to a resident's or staff member's inquiry or request. When a property manager communicates clearly and directly, the resident or staff member is encouraged to take the information or rejection in stride and not have her/his morale damaged in the process. Under no circumstances should a manager create, incite, or be party to a confrontation with either a resident or a staff member, especially in front of an audience.

Demonstrate integrity, consistency, respect, responsibility, and patience in dealing with the owner, with residents, and with staff—The qualities of integrity, consistency, respect, responsibility, and patience will carry the property manager a long way in her/his dealings with all people. On the job, the property manager must maintain a professional relationship with the owner, with residents, and with staff, even though they may be personal friends during nonworking hours. Above all, the property manager must avoid an appearance of favoritism that could compromise her/his ability to deal effectively with residents and/or staff. Like all people, owners, residents, and staff learn to respect the property manager who respects them. But respect is one of the most elusive of commodities. It cannot be conferred or demanded but must be earned, usually over a considerable period of time. It is for this reason that consistency in interpersonal dealings is so important.

Although consistency in dealing with all people is critical to the property manager's success, she/he may choose to project a different image or attitude depending on the situation. For example, a property manager's image to an applicant may be different from the one projected to a resident who is chronically delinquent in his/her rent payments. The key is for the property manager to adopt the appropriate attitude in dealing with all people in different situations and to project that attitude consistently whenever the same or similar situations arise.

That said, the property manager should, of course, maintain a positive image and attitude with everyone, especially with a resident who is moving out. A person who has lived in a property helps to create the impression others have of that property. That person can produce either favorable or unfavorable word-of-mouth publicity. The property manager should do everything possible to ensure that the person leaves with a favorable attitude. Unhappy former residents usually communicate their feelings to a large number of people.

And when dealing with difficult residents, the property manager must always remember to be both patient and determined. To think that a problem with a resident can be overcome by being aggressive and demanding is a fallacy. The most effective property managers employ equal measures of empathy and firmness when dealing with difficult residents.

PERSONAL QUALITIES AND SKILLS

Maturity

People who possess the quality of maturity are those who are in control of themselves and their relationships with other people and with circumstances. Mature people demonstrate integrity even when it is inconvenient, and eschew procrastination in favor of prompt, thorough, and meticulous action even when it takes more time than they'd like. Mature individuals are willing to accept responsibility and know how to handle authority, and they do what needs to be done in the interest of the greater good even when they don't feel like doing it. The successful property manager is an inherently mature individual.

Sociability

The milieu (social environment) of multifamily properties requires that a property manager be genuinely interested in people. If a property manager or any other staff member lacks the desire to interact with people, she/he will ultimately fail in this service business that has interaction with residents at its core. Although sociability is not the only measure of residential management success, it is an especially important contributor to it.

Initiative and the Ability to Take Control of Situations

For the property manager, initiative and the ability to take control of situations is like a double-edged sword. Although the property manager's position requires initiative—the ability to act independently, to plan and carry out work assignments with only intermittent supervision—and the ability to take control of rather difficult situations on occasion, it also requires conformity and acquiescence to company procedures and supervisory personnel. The mid-range of these skills, wherein the property manager is motivated to do her/his best at whatever is assigned and undertaken and has high expectations for her/his own performance and the performance of subordinates and does what is in her/his power to elicit that performance, is therefore the ideal target.

This, then, has been a discussion of the characteristics that identify the truly professional, truly successful property manager. The manager at every level of experience, from the novice to the most jaded, would do well to adopt these characteristics and cultivate them for her/his own success and the success of the property she/he manages.

PROPERTY MANAGER AS SUPERVISOR

MANAGING PROPERTY STAFF

Companies do not grow and succeed unless their employees grow and succeed. This theory applies especially to the multihousing management industry.

How people perform and interact within a company determines to a large extent the company's success. At the heart of the challenge is getting employees to use the knowledge and skills they possess. Many companies send employees to school to acquire new knowledge and skills, such as how to close sales and how to prospect. When the employees return, sometimes their productivity is enhanced, but more often it reverts to approximately where it was prior to the schooling. What happens is that these people are exposed to new knowledge and techniques but their attitudes do not change. Unless they are motivated to change, they will use only a small percentage of the new knowledge and skills they obtain. Goals are the ideal way to motivate employees.

Individuals who perform effectively and utilize their knowledge and skills have measurable, specific, written goals and a plan for the accomplishment of these goals. Unless employees establish goals and objectives and a plan of action and become committed to them, attending courses may be of little benefit.

Goals give direction to vision and help to channel energy and resources. One useful definition of management is the organization and coordination of resources for the accomplishment of specific goals and objectives. Companies without specific goals and objectives are not maximizing their resources.

Goal setting assists an organization because time is not wasted on activities unrelated to the goals. Motion and progress are different commodities, and motion is not necessarily progress. The effective organization is one that stays focused on progress. And progress is measured by whether or not the company is making advances to a specific goal.

Management by objective and management by exception are two popular management styles. Management by objective requires the establishment of a set of goals that reflect the values and priorities of the management company and property owners. Progress toward these goals is assessed periodically. In management by exception, it is rental and inspection reports and other forms of feedback, rather than progress toward specific goals, that tell management where specific management action is needed.

The goals established under management by objective must be identified in meaningful terms for each employee. They might include:

- Occupancy numbers and resident retention targets
- Rent collection dollars
- Net operating income
- Handling service requests
- Property employee retention

The property manager's management maintenance plan that was discussed in Chapter 2 should become a guide for accomplishing these goals. The plan should include:

- Budgets
- Standard operating procedures
- An operations manual
- Job descriptions
- Proper scheduling

Management by objective lets the company know both its accomplishments and areas that require improvement and makes this business more exciting. By the same token, feedback, such as rental and inspection reports, lets management know if it is on track. These reports and other feedback allow the company to know where specific management action is needed. This process is known as management by exception, the corollary of management by objective.

In terms of managing and motivating employees, it is important to remember that to endure and be effective, relationships must be based on a value-for-value principle, understanding that people do things for their own reasons and that employees are internally motivated to help accomplish company goals when they recognize they can reach their own goals at the same time.

These principles are the key to employee motivation. The property manager should therefore show employees how to identify their own personal goals and how these personal goals tie in with the goals of the management company and/or the property owner.

Goals help employees eliminate wasted motion, time, and resources. Goals also eliminate doubt as to what employees should do to accomplish their specific objectives. Sometimes goals and objectives are made more meaningful by tying in a bonus based on accomplishment of the company's objectives.

ESTABLISHING GOALS FOR EMPLOYEES

The goal of everyone seeking to hire workers should be to hire people who are suited for the positions they will occupy and then to ensure that these employees are well trained, adequately compensated, properly directed, motivated, and reviewed periodically according to a regular schedule. The procedures described below are designed to help accomplish these overall company goals.

SOURCES OF APPLICANTS FOR PROPERTY POSITIONS

Those people within the property and the management company who have hiring authority should always be on the alert for candidates who possess the qualifications required for success in any given employment position. Typically, the property manager is interested in qualified applicants for the positions of assistant manager, leasing agent, bookkeeper, maintenance supervisor, maintenance technician, and grounds person. Because employees who are already in place should be given every opportunity to achieve their maximum potential and to make the maximum contribution for the benefit of the property, the property manager should look within the organization first for those who are qualified as a result of technical knowledge, experience, and interests.

However, the property manager should not limit her/his employee search to existing employees only. Instead, the property manager should review the qualifications of interested persons within the organization and also take advantage of outside sources. These sources include newspaper and Internet advertising, private employment agencies, referrals from present employees, well-managed and well-maintained competitive properties, the state employment agency, business or technical colleges within the community, and any minority recruitment sources listed in the management firm's affirmative action plan, if applicable. Figure 3–1 contains a list of information that the property manager should be able to provide to all prospective employees.

When placing classified print ads, remember that the ads that stand out get the most attention. Therefore, a double-column ad with a border and/or extra-large print will catch the eye of prospective employees faster than will other ads. Also, many newspapers charge for classified ads by the line, so ask the ad representative how to maximize the information in the ad while minimizing the number of lines.

Figure 3–2 shows two classified ads that contain the appropriate information as they might appear in a newspaper or other similar print medium with and without abbreviations. Notice how much space is saved by abbreviating while still communicating the necessary information.

FIGURE 3-1. EMPLOYMENT INFORMATION (FOR ADS AND APPLICANTS)

- Position title
- Type of property
- Duties and responsibilities of the position
- Specific professional skills required
- Type of professional experience required
- Number of years of same or related experience required
- Other requirements (e.g., must have own tools; valid driver's license, etc.)
- Availability of the position
- Must be bonded (if applicable)
- Training offered in position
- Advancement opportunities
- Salary range (may be commensurate with experience)
- Benefits (e.g., health and hospital coverage, vacation, paid holidays, sick leave, disability insurance, profit-sharing, pension and retirement plans, etc.)
- Other benefits (e.g., apartment and parking space on premises, residential phone and utilities, etc.)
- How to apply for the position (e.g., fax, email or mail resume, or applications accepted in person – include time, dates and location)

SCREENING PROSPECTIVE EMPLOYEES

Under the supervision of the senior manager, the property manager is responsible for ensuring that job applicants are adequately screened before being hired. This step is vital because no amount of training can overcome poor employee selection and placement. The steps for properly and adequately screening prospective employees are discussed in Figure 3–3.

No matter what job a property manager is interviewing prospective employees for, the manager must observe definite rules about the types of questions that can be asked on the application and/or other forms that applicants are asked to fill out and during the in-person interview. Many questions and courtesies that seem appropriate to the interviewer can appear discriminatory to the applicant and may create trouble for the interviewer with the EEOC (Equal Employment Opportunity Commission) or other agencies that enforce employment laws. For example, an interviewer can be sued for:

- Offering coffee to nonminority applicants only
- Discussing the applicant's age
- Not hiring a woman because the job involves travel with men or because the interviewer believes the working conditions or hours are unsuitable for a woman

The sample interview questions in Figure 3–4 are adapted from those used by a California management company. The questions comply with both federal and the slightly more stringent California statutes. The property manager should review the interviewing and hiring practices of the management com-

FIGURE 3-2. SAMPLE CLASSIFIED ADS

Property Manager
Manage xxx-unit residential property with x- member maintenance and management office staff. Must be computer literate, able to work independently, and have good speaking, writing, basic math skills. Minimum two years in similar position required. Salary commensurate with experience. Benefits include on-premise two- bedroom apartment with phone and all utilities and one parking spot, plus all health/retirement/ vacation. Available September 1. EOE. Fax resume in confidence to xxx-xxx-xxxx.

Leasing Agent
For large residential management firm. At least five years experience required. Must know word processing. Opportunity to advance to leasing manager after six months. Salary plus benefits. EOE. Interviewing Friday, April 7. Call for appointment Monday - Thursday April 3-6, 9 AM to 4 PM, (xxx) xxx-xxxx.

Property Manager
Manage xxx-unit resdntl. dvlpmnt. w/x-member maint. & mngmt. office staff. Must be computer literate, able to work independently, w/good speaking, writing, basic math skls. Min. 2 yrs. in similar position req. Salary commens. w/exp. Benefits include on-premises 2 br. apt. w/phone & all util., 1 prkg. spot + all health/ retirement/vacation. Avail. 9/1. EOE. Fax res. in confidence xxx-xxx-xxxx.

Leasing Agent
For lge. res. mgmt. firm. 5+ yrs. exp. + wd. processing req. Oppty. advance to leasing mngr. after 6 mos. Sal. + bnfts. EOE. Interviewing Fri. 4/7; call for appt. Mon.-Thurs. 4/3-6, 9 AM - 4 PM (xxx) xxx-xxxx.

pany she/he works for and consult an experienced local labor/employment attorney to determine what, if any, additional local laws are involved in the interviewing and hiring process.

Every interviewer must remember that federal laws have coverage requirements that may exclude certain types or sizes of businesses; that federal contractors are subject to many additional requirements (such as affirmative action); and that properties operated under federal contracts are subject to extensive additional requirements. Where appropriate, property managers with federal contracts should review their contract documents for these requirements and consult an affirmative action specialist for advice on compliance.

State laws, which vary widely from state to state, determine many aspects of the employment relationship, such as wrongful discharge, employment contract, and employment at will. These laws may expand or extend federal requirements, such as nondiscrimination, beyond the definition in federal law. Even local laws, such as city ordinances prohibiting certain types of discrimination, may apply.

In all interviewing and employment situations, the individual and/or organization responsible for interviewing, hiring, and employing should consult with an experienced labor/employment attorney when setting up a personnel program or making personnel decisions.

During the interview, the property manager should have the application in hand and make notes as the prospective employee talks. The manager should be as accurate as possible in taking notes and avoid subjective comments. For example, "Nervous, ill at ease, unresponsive," is a valid observation. "Would not fit in" is not a valid observation. Interviewers must be careful not to commit to writing any note that may be construed as prejudiced or discriminatory. Conversely, notes that provide objective information are invaluable in making the final employment decision.

Overall, the interviewer's objective is to identify employment candidates whose skills are most likely to produce success in a specific job function. This matching maximizes the job comfort level of an employee and increases productivity for the property.

EMPLOYEE TESTING

Some firms use both skill testing and psychological testing in the hiring process. Used properly, testing can be a powerful tool to help determine the best suited candidates for employment. To be effective, testing methods and types of tests must be carefully designed and selected, and they should be compared and comply with the EEOC testing guidelines, if applicable.

The executive property manager usually establishes policies on testing and determines the specific tests to be used. Industrial psychologists are one valuable resource for developing tests and for training staff in their use.

Testing for physical ability may be done only after the employer offers an applicant a job. The employer can make the job offer conditional on the outcome of a physical examination provided that the employer requires a physical examination of all entering employees in that particular job category. An applicant may not be denied a job based on a physical examination unless specific physical requirements are included in the job description.

COMPLYING WITH THE IMMIGRATION CONTROL AND REFORM ACT OF 1986

Because all employers in the United States are required to verify that every new employee is either a citizen of the United States or an alien possessing the required authorization for employment in the United States, employers must retain written records to document that verification. In addition, the law:

- Prohibits hiring or continuation of employment of any alien who is not legally authorized for employment in the United States
- Prohibits discrimination against properly documented aliens seeking employment
- Authorizes inspections to check on compliance and penalties for violations of the law

FIGURE 3–3. STEPS IN SCREENING PROSPECTIVE EMPLOYEES

1. Ask the candidate to fill out an official company employment application.
   This application should be reviewed by a local attorney to ensure it does not ask discriminatory questions.

2. The property manager, or an appropriate individual designated by the property manager, reviews the application.
   The candidate should complete the entire application. Check for the candidate's signature; it makes the application an official legal document.

3. Ensure that all of the applicant's employment time spans are properly accounted for and verified where verification appears appropriate.
   Be alert to large gaps between jobs as well as "job hopping."

4. Obtain a background check and require bonding for all prospective employees who will be handling cash and/or who will have access to the property's residential units.
   The application and offer letter should state that hiring and continued employment are contingent upon being bondable, and that any false or misleading statement on the application will be grounds for immediate termination.

5. Check that all prospective employees who will be operating vehicles while on duty are appropriately licensed and that they have no outstanding convictions for driving under the influence of either alcohol or drugs or in an unsafe manner.*
   An alternative is to include the statement that hiring and continued employment are contingent on bonding, and to ask if the applicant knows of any reason why s/he could not be bonded or insured.

6. Contact at least two employment or business references and one personal reference to verify the candidate's work record and personal habits.
   Be aware that accurate information – especially if it reflects negatively on the applicant – is more likely to be given over the phone since people often hesitate to commit derogatory statements to writing.

7. Make sure that all pertinent information about the applicant is noted and kept with the application.
   The application should remain as submitted for the files.

8. Administer all appropriate pre-employment tests, including those testing typing, clerical, and maintenance skills.
   Make sure that the tests fit the testing guidelines of the Equal Employment Opportunity Commission (EEOC).

9. Conduct an in-depth personal interview. This is the most important part of the screening process and should be conducted by the person who will supervise the candidate. The interviewer should make use of the information gathered from the application and should question the candidate in order to make an informed determination about whether or not s/he will be successful in the position
   Figure 3-4 contains guidance on interview questions to ensure that the questions asked comply with federal, state, and local laws and regulations. Also see Immigration Control and Reform Act of 1986 later in this chapter for verification of right to work after screening is complete and the job is offered to the best candidate.

*An employer could be accused of discrimination if an arrest record was requested rather than a conviction record. The exception to this general rule are charges that have been filed but have not yet come to trial or otherwise been adjudicated. These charges, particularly for DWI/DUI, can have an extremely adverse impact on the property's insurability. For that reason, the property manager can inquire into pending charges that have not been disposed of when s/he has a valid job-related reason for needing that information.

FIGURE 3–4. INTERVIEWING JOB APPLICANTS: QUESTIONS AND COMMENTS TO USE AND TO AVOID

Subject	Nondiscriminatory Questions or Comments	Discriminatory Questions Comments to Avoid
Race or color	None	All references to or inquiry into an applicant's race, complexion, or color of skin.
Religion or creed	None	All references to or inquiry into an applicant's religious denomination, religious affiliations, church, parish, religious leader, or religious holidays observed. Applicant may not be told, "This is a [Catholic, Protestant, Jewish, or ____] organization."
Disability		"Do you have a handicap?" "Have you ever been treated for any of the following diseases. . .?"
Arrest records	"Have you ever been convicted of a crime? If so, please give details."	"Have you ever been arrested?"
Name	"Have you ever worked for this company under a different name?" "Is any additional information relative to a change of name, use of an assumed name or nickname necessary to obtain a check on your work record? If yes, explain."	All questions or comments about the origin or name of a person whose name was changed by court order or other means including marriage.
Address or duration	"What is your present address?" "How long have you been a resident of this city?"	
Birthplace, birth date, and citizenship	Employers now legally must require a prospective employee to produce a birth certificate, naturalization, or baptismal record because they are required by the Immigration Control Act of 1986 to check the citizenship of all new employees. Not to do so is to be subject to heavy penalties.	"Where were you born?" "What is your birth date?" "Are you or your spouse's parents naturalized or native-born citizens of the United States?" "What date were your or your spouse's parents granted citizenship?"

*An applicant may not be denied employment because of a conviction record unless a direct relationship exists between the offense and the job or unless hiring would be an unreasonable risk. An exoffender denied employment is entitled to a statement of the reasons for such denial (Correction Law, Article 23-A, 6754).

continued

FIGURE 3–4. INTERVIEWING JOB APPLICANTS: QUESTIONS AND COMMENTS TO USE AND TO AVOID

Subject	Nondiscriminatory Questions or Comments	Discriminatory Questions Comments to Avoid
Birthplace, birth date, and citizenship (continued)	"If you are not a U.S. citizen, we require that you have the legal right to remain and work in the United States." People on student visas (up to 6 or 8 years) usually can not work, but some students with green cards do have a work permit. Some temporary visas also allow work.	
Language	Questions about what languages an applicant speaks and writes fluently.	"What is your native language?" Inquiry into how an applicant learned to read, write or speak a foreign language.
Photograph	At the time of hiring, the Immigration Control and Reform Act of 1986 requires the employer to obtain and review a photo identification.	Employers may not require an applicant to submit a photograph at any time before hiring.
Education	Questions about an applicant's academic, vocational, or professional education and the public and private schools attended.	
Experience	Questions about an applicant's work experience.	
Relatives	Requests for names of applicant's relative other than spouse or other relative already employed by the company by which the applicant is being interviewed (depending on company policy). After hiring, Requests for names of applicant's dependents eligible for insurance coverage partly or wholly provided by the firm.	Requests for names, addresses, ages, number, or other information concerning applicant's spouse, children, or other relatives not employed by the company by which the applicant is being interviewed. National origin.
None	Questions or comments about an applicant's lineage, ancestry, national origin, descent, parentage, or nationality or that of an applicant's relatives or spouse.	

continued

FIGURE 3–4. INTERVIEWING JOB APPLICANTS: QUESTIONS AND COMMENTS TO USE AND TO AVOID

Subject	Nondiscriminatory Questions or Comments	Discriminatory Questions Comments to Avoid
Age	None. Upon hiring, employer must require that employee provide proof of citizenship and a photo identification to comply with the immigration laws. A birth certificate and driver's license may be used to provide this proof, and they would reveal age.	How old are you?
Sex or marital status	None. After hiring, questions about age, sex, and marital status could be appropriate if the employer provides benefits such as insurance that require that information.	Questions or comments about an applicant's sex prior to hiring. "Please indicate whether you are single, separated, or divorced." Requests for names of or other information about an applicant's spouse or relatives. "Where does your spouse work?" "What are the ages of your children, if any?" "Who will care for your children while you work?"
Birth control	None	Inquiries about capacity to reproduce.
Military experience	Questions about an applicant's military experience in the Armed Forces of the United States or service in a particular branch of the Armed Services such as the Army or the Navy.	Questions about an applicant's general military experience.
Organizations	Do you belong to any organizations that will contribute to your ability to perform the job for which you are applying?"	

Warning - If the answer to an interview question indirectly reveals an applicant's race, creed, color, national origin, sex, marital status, handicap, age, or arrest record, it may be considered evidence of discrimination. Even if the question eventually passes muster with the court, going through the process of defending a claim of discrimination is expensive and burdensome. Some applicants are especially sensitive, and on such short acquaintance the interviewer cannot know who he/she is dealing with. In most cases, the information sought can be lawfully obtained by a more direct question. For example, if the interviewer is worried about travel or overtime requirements, instead of asking, "How old are your children?" he/she can ask, "Is there any reason you would not be willing to or able to travel extensively or work overtime on short notice?" However, some of this information will be required when the offer to hire is made and the applicant must then meet the requirements of the Immigration Control Act of 1986. Some companies are required to tabulate some of this information to the EEOC-1 report to prove they are acting legally and for their affirmative action record keeping.

To comply with the Act, multihousing management companies and other employers must require every applicant to whom a job is offered to provide proof of work eligibility and U.S. citizenship or lawful residence. The law prohibits employers from hiring applicants who cannot produce the necessary documents. All employers are subject to inspections to check on compliance with the law. Employers who do not comply face stiff fines for each hiring or violation of the verification requirement.

Although the prospective employee is responsible for providing the documents needed, multihousing managers can give advice and assistance. For example, they could provide references to services that can help a prospective employee obtain a copy of a birth certificate quickly.

The Immigration Control and Reform Act of 1986 does not affect employees who were already on the payroll on or before November 6, 1986. Managers who have questions about the law or about whether a particular document is acceptable should consult either their legal counsel or the Immigration and Naturalization Service (INS). A property manager could ask a new employee to sign an employee information form (Fig. 3–5) to comply with record-keeping requirements applicable to some employees. Signing this form must be voluntary, and it should be reviewed by local counsel before use. This document should be kept in a file separate from the employee's personnel file, and the personnel file should not reflect the information in the form.

Each new employee should sign an employment eligibility verification (Fig. 3–6) to comply with the Immigration Reform and Control Act of 1986. Managers are required to have one of these signed forms for each person hired since November 6, 1986. The fines for violation of this law are substantial.

Multihousing management companies should inform all job applicants about these legal requirements. Supervisors interviewing for vacancies should brief applicants about their responsibility for providing the necessary documents. Letters offering employment should instruct the recipients to bring their documents with them when they report for work because the employer has only three days to obtain and verify them. The federal government requires the employer to exercise "due care" in making sure the documents presented are legitimate. The INS offers a free employers handbook that details the types of documents that will commonly be presented. The handbook provides extensive information that will enable a property manager to review documents with greater accuracy.

Conditions of employment (Fig. 3–7) could be signed by each new employee. This agreement may help to establish "employment at will" and eliminate the possibility of court cases brought by discharged employees who allege that they had lifetime tenure based on various representations or letters they had received prior to being employed or while employed.

COMPLYING WITH THE AMERICANS WITH DISABILITIES ACT

The Americans with Disabilities Act (ADA) was signed into law on July 26, 1990 and became effective on July 26, 1992. The Act is one of the most significant pieces of social legislation passed in recent years, and the delay in implementation was provided to allow employers and regulators sufficient time to prepare for this change. The ADA was preceded by the Rehabilitation Act of 1973, which prohibited discrimination against handicapped individuals but only for contractors with the federal government. Many of the concepts and provisions included in the 1973 Act were carried over to the ADA.

The main thrust of the ADA is to guarantee fair and equitable access to employment opportunities for qualified disabled applicants and employees. The ADA is based on the basic premise that many qualified people are excluded from job opportunities because of unnecessary barriers to entry and the perception that a disabled individual cannot perform a job. Employers and their agents are subject to significant financial penalties for failure to follow the ADA's guidelines.

According to the Act, an individual is considered to be disabled if she/he has a physical or mental impairment that substantially limits one or more of the major life activities or if she/he has a record of such an impairment. The individual may also be covered by the Act if she/he is being regarded as having such an impairment. Recent court cases also have been defining "disability" and have found alcoholism, for example, to be a disability in some instances.

Disabled individuals are not automatically protected by the Act. The individual must have an impairment that "substantially limits" one or more major life activities. Further, to be protected under the ADA, an individual must be qualified as defined by the Act. The term "qualified individual with a disability" means an individual with a disability who, with or without reasonable accommodation, can perform the essential functions of the position.

The most controversial aspect of the ADA is the requirement on the part of the employer to provide "reasonable accommodation" to disabled applicants and employees. Reasonable accommodation is a key provision of the ADA because of the special nature of the discrimination that it addresses. Under the concept of reasonable accommodation, an employer is not required to lower quality or quantity standards or create a new job. Nor is the employer required to provide devices that the individual normally uses in her/his personal life. However, an employer may be required to modify the structure of a job, modify the physical work environment, or provide special devices necessary for the applicant or employee to perform the job.

COMPLYING WITH THE FAMILY AND MEDICAL LEAVE ACT OF 1993

The Family and Medical Leave Act of 1993 (FMLA) is one of several pieces of legislation resulting from the many demographic changes that have occurred in the American workplace. As the traditional workforce gives way to a more diverse group of workers, new laws have been and will be enacted to protect their rights, provide for their special needs, and ensure fair and adequate access to the economic opportunities offered in the workplace. FMLA was enacted to provide workers with time off to adjust to a new child in the home or to deal with a serious illness in the family unit without fear of losing their jobs.

FIGURE 3–5. EMPLOYEE INFORMATION

*This form is to be completed by the newly hired employee and is to accompany the notice to payroll. It should not be given to anyone who is still in the application phase of employment.**

Employee Name ______________________________

Date of Hire ____________ **Department** ______________

Decisions affecting employment are made without regard to race, color, religion, sex, national origin, handicap, or age. To assist the company in complying with government reporting requirements, please supply us with the following information. Your submission of this information is entirely voluntary and will be kept in a confidential file separate from other employee information. If you do not wish to provide this information, check the appropriate box and sign below:

☐ ***I do not want to supply this information.***

Birth date ____________

Check One in Each of the Following Groups:

Sex: ☐ Male ☐ Female

Race/Ethnic Group:

☐ White
☐ Black
☐ Hispanic
☐ American Indian/Alaskan native
☐ Asian/Pacific Islander
☐ Other

Check if any of the following are applicable:

☐ Vietnam era veteran
☐ Handicapped individual
☐ Disabled veteran

____
Employee Signature

* Properties required to keep applicant statistics for affirmative action programs can adapt this form to those purposes. This form should be reviewed by a local attorney before use for any purpose.

FIGURE 3–6. EMPLOYMENT ELIGIBILITY VERIFICATION

U.S. Department of Justice
Immigration and Naturalization Service

OMB No. 1115-0136

Employment Eligibility Verification

Please read instructions carefully before completing this form. The instructions must be available during completion of this form. ANTI-DISCRIMINATION NOTICE: It is illegal to discriminate against work eligible individuals. Employers CANNOT specify which document(s) they will accept from an employee. The refusal to hire an individual because of a future expiration date may also constitute illegal discrimination.

Section 1. Employee Information and Verification. To be completed and signed by employee at the time employment begins.

Print Name: Last	First	Middle Initial	Maiden Name
Address *(Street Name and Number)*		Apt. #	Date of Birth *(month/day/year)*
City	State	Zip Code	Social Security #

I am aware that federal law provides for imprisonment and/or fines for false statements or use of false documents in connection with the completion of this form.

I attest, under penalty of perjury, that I am (check one of the following):
- ☐ A citizen or national of the United States
- ☐ A Lawful Permanent Resident (Alien # A__________)
- ☐ An alien authorized to work until ___/___/___
  (Alien # or Admission #) __________

Employee's Signature	Date *(month/day/year)*

Preparer and/or Translator Certification. *(To be completed and signed if Section 1 is prepared by a person other than the employee.) I attest, under penalty of perjury, that I have assisted in the completion of this form and that to the best of my knowledge the information is true and correct.*

Preparer's/Translator's Signature	Print Name
Address *(Street Name and Number, City, State, Zip Code)*	Date *(month/day/year)*

Section 2. Employer Review and Verification. To be completed and signed by employer. Examine one document from List A OR examine one document from List B and one from List C, as listed on the reverse of this form, and record the title, number and expiration date, if any, of the document(s)

List A	OR	List B	AND	List C
Document title: __________		__________		__________
Issuing authority: __________		__________		__________
Document #: __________		__________		__________
Expiration Date *(if any)*: ___/___/___		___/___/___		___/___/___
Document #: __________				
Expiration Date *(if any)*: ___/___/___				

CERTIFICATION - I attest, under penalty of perjury, that I have examined the document(s) presented by the above-named employee, that the above-listed document(s) appear to be genuine and to relate to the employee named, that the employee began employment on *(month/day/year)* ___/___/___ **and that to the best of my knowledge the employee is eligible to work in the United States. (State employment agencies may omit the date the employee began employment.)**

Signature of Employer or Authorized Representative	Print Name	Title
Business or Organization Name	Address *(Street Name and Number, City, State, Zip Code)*	Date *(month/day/year)*

Section 3. Updating and Reverification. To be completed and signed by employer.

A. New Name *(if applicable)*	B. Date of rehire *(month/day/year) (if applicable)*

C. If employee's previous grant of work authorization has expired, provide the information below for the document that establishes current employment eligibility.

Document Title:__________ Document #: __________ Expiration Date (if any): ___/___/___

I attest, under penalty of perjury, that to the best of my knowledge, this employee is eligible to work in the United States, and if the employee presented document(s), the document(s) I have examined appear to be genuine and to relate to the individual.

Signature of Employer or Authorized Representative	Date *(month/day/year)*

Form I-9 (Rev. 11-21-91)N Page 2

FIGURE 3–7. CONDITIONS OF EMPLOYMENT*

BECAUSE OF THE INHERENT UNCERTAINTY OF BUSINESS CONDITIONS, THE ____(NAME OF PROPERTY)____ CANNOT GUARANTEE OR PROMISE EMPLOYMENT ON ANY FIXED TERM, SPECIFIED DURATION, PERMANENT, OR LIFETIME BASIS. RATHER, ALL EMPLOYEES OF THE COMPANY ARE EMPLOYED ON AN AT-WILL BASIS FOR AN INDEFINITE DURATION BASED UPON THE CONTINUED MUTUAL CONSENT OF BOTH THE COMPANY AND THE EMPLOYEES.

THIS MEMORANDUM REFLECTS THE FINAL, COMPLETE, AND EXCLUSIVE AGREEMENT BETWEEN ____(NAME OF PROPERTY)____ AND ITS EMPLOYEES CONCERNING THEIR DURATION AND TENURE OF EMPLOYMENT, AND ALL PRIOR AGREEMENTS, REPRESENTATIONS, AND PROMISES, IF ANY, ARE MERGED HEREIN. NO SUPERVISOR, OFFICER, OR AGENT OF THE COMPANY HAS ANY AUTHORITY TO ALTER, MODIFY, WAIVE, OR MAKE ANY EXCEPTION IN ANY WAY TO THIS AGREEMENT EXCEPT IN WRITING DULY AUTHORIZED.

____________	____________	____________
EMPLOYEE	DATE	TIME
____________	____________	____________
WITNESS	DATE	TIME

* ***STATE AND LOCAL REGULATIONS VARY CONSIDERABLY. THIS FORM SHOULD BE CLEARED BY LEGAL COUNSEL TO BE SURE IT CONFORMS TO FEDERAL, STATE, AND LOCAL LAWS.***

The Family and Medical Leave Act was signed into law by then-President Clinton on February 5, 1993. Employees covered by a collective bargaining agreement are not required to be covered until the expiration of the agreement. The Act covers all employers with 50 or more employees within a 75-mile radius.

According to FMLA, employers must offer eligible employees up to 12 weeks of unpaid leave per year to use in the event of a birth, adoption, or placement of a child in the employee's home. The leave must also be available in the event of a serious medical condition for the employee, her/his spouse, her/his child, or her/his parent. The leave is to be available for either spouse. To be eligible for this leave, the employee must have been employed for 12 months and worked at least 1,250 hours during the year.

Also according to FMLA, the employee must be allowed to return to her/his former position or an equivalent position with equal pay and benefits. The employer must maintain the employee's benefits while she/he is on leave. In the event the employee does not return from the leave, the employer may recover health premiums paid by the employer. An employer providing paid family leave may offset such leave against the 12 weeks of unpaid leave.

COMPLYING WITH COLLECTIVE BARGAINING AND UNION CONTRACT REQUIREMENTS

Depending on the location and circumstance of the property, collective bargaining and union contracts may govern some or all of the property's employees. Where this is the case, the property manager must become well versed in the applicable requirements and must develop an on-going relationship with a labor attorney who can advise her/him regarding the property's obligations to these employees and vice versa.

COMPENSATION

Under the supervision of the senior manager, the property manager is responsible for supervising the compensation of property employees. Normally, employee compensation is agreed upon during preparation of the property's annual budget. If the property manager wishes to deviate from the budget, she/he must secure the prior approval of the senior manager. A form, such as the Salary Increase Exception Form (Fig. 3–8), could be used to request an increase that exceeds payroll guidelines and/or budget. The form provides blanks for the information required to make an intelligent decision.

In terms of compensation, the goal is to be competitive within each market to ensure that the company hires and keeps qualified personnel. Comparisons of compensation by other management companies and/or properties should include all items to enable a fair comparison, including such factors as incentives and bonuses, and benefits as well as such intangible factors as the stability of the organization and available career opportunities within the organization.

The property manager must exercise deliberate judgment in the initial compensation offered to a new employee and in granting raises. With regard to hiring a new employee, the manager may want to hire an individual on a trial basis with the commitment that the person's performance will be reviewed in six months, at which time a decision will be made about converting the person to regular employee status and adjusting compensation. (The term "permanent employee" should be avoided because it implies that the person referred to has permanent employment as opposed to being employed at will.)

This type of probationary employment is a common practice. To avoid confusion later, the terms and conditions of the probationary period should be presented to the prospective employee in writing and accepted by the prospective

FIGURE 3–8. SALARY INCREASE EXCEPTION FORM

CONFIDENTIAL

EMPLOYEE NAME ______________________ **JOB TITLE**____________________________

PROPERTY _____________________________ **LOCATION** ___________________________

NUMBER OF UNITS ______________________

DATE OF HIRE ____________________ **SALARY AT HIRE** _______________________

CURRENT SALARY _____________________

REASON FOR INCREASE ____

APPLICABLE PAY RANGE $ ___________ **TO $** __________ ______________

EFFECTIVE DATE ________________________________ ___________

RENT-FREE APARTMENT OR TOWNHOUSE PROVIDED? ☐ YES ☐ NO
STANDARD WORK HOURS PER WEEK: _________ _________________________

PRIOR SALARY INCREASE INFORMATION

EFFECTIVE DATE ____________ PERCENT INCREASE ___________ AMOUNT OF INCREASE $ _______
EFFECTIVE DATE ____________ PERCENT INCREASE ___________ AMOUNT OF INCREASE $ _______
DATE OF MOST RECENT PERFORMANCE TEST ______________________ SCORE: _______________
DATE OF MOST RECENT PERFORMANCE TEST ______________________ SCORE: _______________

PROPOSED SALARY INCREASE

PROPOSED NEW SALARY: $__________________ EFFECTIVE DATE: _____________________

PERCENT INCREASE: __________ CHANGE AMOUNT: $___________ NEXT REVIEW DATE_______

STAFFING

PRESENT STAFFING: RENTAL ____________________ MAINTENANCE __________________
PROPOSED STAFFING: RENTAL ____________________ MAINTENANCE __________________

COMMENTS

____
____
____
____
____

REQUESTED BY _____________________ **DATE** ____________________
PROPERTY MANAGER

APPROVED BY _____________________ **DATE** ____________________
REGIONAL MANAGER

APPROVED BY _________________________ **DATE** ____________________
EXECUTIVE PROPERTY MANAGER

employee in writing, before hiring takes place. The employee must acknowledge her/his understanding of employment at will status both before and after the trial period. As for the property manager's part, any commitment about performance and compensation reviews must be honored at the time agreed upon.

With regard to raises, under normal circumstances a raise should be considered on an annual basis, preferably during a regular annual review during a specific month of the year. An annual salary review ensures that each employee receives a review at least once a year and that no one is overlooked.

The annual review should take into consideration the employee's overall productivity, contribution, and attitude, as well as any changes in the employee's responsibilities since the last review. Any inconsistencies or deviations from what is expected in the review should be documented to avoid potential claims of unfairness or discrimination. Both the property manager and all employees must be aware that a salary review does not automatically equal a raise, nor does it mean that an employee cannot receive a raise between reviews if job performance and/or additional responsibilities warrant, and/or if, in the case of a new employee, the initial trial period has ended satisfactorily and an interim increase is due.

INCENTIVES, BONUSES, AND THE BONUS PLAN

To increase employee productivity, companies are well advised to create a closer link between pay and individual performance. Straight hourly wages generally lead to job dissatisfaction and greater turnover, and across-the-board wage increases at the same levels for all employees tend to breed mediocrity. This is true because when everyone is paid the same, there is no encouragement to strive for excellence, and overall performance and productivity tend to decline to the lowest level. The fact is, people resent being paid the same and getting the same percentage increase as others who are not putting out the same level of effort or achieving the same desirable results. Their initiative and drive tend to recede as they see that they get no benefit commensurate with their output.

Conversely, not only does incentive pay—pay increases based on productivity and performance, also sometime called merit pay—encourage people to produce more, but employees also usually feel more satisfied with their work. This is generally true because people tend to be more satisfied when they are productive. Time passes faster, they enjoy their work more (as long as it is not inherently repetitious and/or boring), and they earn more.

To illustrate how incentives work, assume that a company has computed that it could provide an average 8 percent increase to its employees based on company profits. In a compensation system granting a straight percent wage increase, a high achiever could only earn the same 8 percent increase as the lower performers in the company. However, under the incentive or merit increase policy, higher producers might be granted a 12 percent increase while lower producers would get a significantly lower percentage increase, no increase, or perhaps be replaced altogether.

Similar to but different from an incentive increase, the bonus is another common type of performance and productivity incentive. A bonus is a compensation payment above and beyond an employee's standard compensation. An employee receiving a bonus should understand how it is calculated and the direct impact her/his job efforts have on the amount of the bonus. Ideally, the employee may even be responsible for calculating the amount of her/his bonus, with the calculation verified by the senior manager or property manager. There is no limit on the amount of a bonus, and while many firms may pay bonuses ranging from 5 to 50 percent of base pay, in some cases the amount of a bonus can actually exceed base pay.

With the senior property manager's approval, the property manager may consider implementing short-term interim bonuses, contests, or award programs to encourage the fastest possible accomplishment of immediate or short-term objectives, such as occupancy, for example. For maximum motivational impact, bonuses must be paid by the committed date, and short-term bonuses should be paid immediately after accomplishment of the assigned objective. The property manager should personally deliver bonus checks to those earning them and should accompany the delivery of the check with a compliment, which provides further positive reinforcement. In this way, the employee receiving the bonus can be made to clearly understand the direct relationship between the amount of the bonus and her/his performance on the job. From both the employer's and the employee's perspectives, bonuses are treated like regular income for tax purposes and are included in the regular rate to determine a person's overtime rate.

Although incentives such as bonuses can serve as powerful motivators, bonuses are not universally accepted as being positive. If they are not equitably established and properly administered, they can have an adverse effect upon morale and performance. Therefore, adherence to established guidelines for bonuses is essential. A description of a sample maintenance bonus and recognition program appears in Figure 3–9.

It is up to the property maintenance supervisor to complete the form for the property maintenance supervisor bonus and recognition program (Fig. 3–10), which determines what bonus she/he has earned for the quarter. All of the numbers can be taken from existing reports and in effect constitute the supervisor's report award. It is made more meaningful to the employee by the fact that a portion of her/his compensation depends on the results.

The property manager must bear in mind that collective bargaining and union agreements may obviate the possibility of merit-based incentives. In general, as with all matters relating to personnel employment, compensation, and benefits, any incentive pay and/or bonus system should be carefully reviewed by appropriate legal counsel for compliance with wage-and-hour and other applicable laws, and the basis for any increases must be carefully documented to avoid charges of discrimination.

ACCOMPLISHING OBJECTIVES

Each portion of the bonus plan depends on accomplishment of one of the primary objectives of a property maintenance program discussed in the paragraphs below.

FIGURE 3-9. Maintenance Bonus and Recognition Program

Each quarter the property maintenance supervisor will receive a bonus if s/he achieves 15 points for that quarter. Points are awarded on the following basis:

CASH FLOW

If the property's cash flow objective for the quarter is achieved, two points are awarded. If the goal is not achieved, but no out-of-pocket loss occurs, one point is awarded.

OPERATING & MAINTENANCE BUDGET VARIANCE

If a favorable variance occurs for the quarter, two points are awarded. One point is awarded for an unfavorable variance under 5 percent.

SERVICE REQUESTS

At the end of the quarter, one point is awarded for each of the following conditions:

- A minimum of 50 percent of the cards are returned
- An excellent rating on a minimum of 80 percent of the returned cards
- No poor nor below-average ratings

TURNOVER UNITS

Two points are awarded if all units are made ready for occupancy to company standards within the 5-work-day goal.

HUD INSPECTION

Three points are awarded for a satisfactory rating.

CURB APPEAL

If the property manager's quarterly rating of curb appeal is superior, three points are awarded, two points for above average and one for satisfactory.

SENIOR MANAGER INSPECTION

Three points are awarded for an excellent rating and two points for satisfactory.

ANNUAL PROCEDURES TEST

For the most recent test, two points are earned for a 95-percent score and one point for a score between 90 and 95 percent

PROPERTY AGE HANDICAP

To equalize the handicap of property age, three points are awarded to the point total for properties that are over 15 years old, two points for those between 10 and 15 years old, and one point for those between 5 and 9 years of age.

OTHER BONUSES & RECOGNITION

NUMBER ONE SUPERVISOR

An additional bonus is paid twice yearly to each property maintenance supervisor who is ranked number one within her/his region, and annually to the property maintenance supervisor who is ranked number one within her/his division. This bonus is based upon percent of accomplishment of the point objective. In the case of ties, the division manager determines the winners based on property improvement.

REGIONAL & DIVISIONAL

The management firm recognizes the regional and division winners in the company newsletter as well as the property maintenance supervisors who achieved their objectives each quarter. In addition, the regional and division winners each receive a special plaque and a letter from the president of the company. This program is designed to enable a person to achieve a bonus and recognition if s/he accomplishes a pre-determined objective. This program puts her/him in competition with her/himself.

RANKING

Another bonus and additional recognition are based upon the employee's ranking among all maintenance supervisors in her/his region and division. Therefore, s/he earns a bonus for excellent performance regardless of how other employees perform. S/He controls the major portion of the bonus. Yet s/he can compete for an additional bonus amount and more recognition. This system is the best of both worlds. It provides monetary rewards and recognition.

Figure 3–10. Bonus and Recognition Report

Project ____________ Phase ____________ Location ____________

Quarter ____________ Year ____________ PMS ____________

Cash Flow **Points**

Month	Objective	Actual
	$	$
	$	$
	$	$
	$	$
	$	$

_____ % _____

Service Requests

Month	Percent Returned	Percent Excellent	No. Below Avg or Poor	

_____

Turnover Units

No. not ready within 5 days: _____

No. not to standards: _____ _____

HUD Inspection Rating _____ _____

RPM Curb Appeal Rating _____ _____

DM Inspection Rating _____ _____

Test Score _____ _____

Age Handicap _____ _____

Total Points: _____

Point Objective: _____

Maintenance Signature ____________

Bonus payment due: _____

Date ____________

Achieving a Certain Net Operating Income (NOI)

Because the state of a property's net operating income mirrors the property's overall financial health, all on-site personnel carry a responsibility for net operating income. Making net operating income a factor in an employee's compensation program ensures that the person takes an interest in the stability and enhancement of the property's net operating income and does not act as if it is only the property manager's responsibility. Because maintenance accounts for a large controllable expense item, the maintenance supervisor strongly influences the bottom line.

Adhering to the Budget

To further reinforce and focus the supervisor's attention on her/his financial involvement, the maintenance supervisor is also paid based on how well she/he adheres to the budget. Of course, using the budget as a performance criterion assumes that the supervisor had input into the budget numbers in the first place and is aware of them in their final form. If so, the supervisor is more likely to believe that the budget does indeed represent an achievable and realistic guideline and also one that reflects an efficient budget. If the property staff has no input into the budget, then the budget is not a viable yardstick by which to measure performance.

Satisfactorily Handling All Service Requests Within a Specified Period of Time

The property manager must constantly monitor employee performance when it comes to handling service requests. When a service request is completed, the maintenance worker should leave the last copy of the service request form with the resident. In some management companies, the last copy is a self-addressed, stamped postcard that is graded by the resident and returned directly to the home office. These cards are tabulated and the results are included in a monthly report that goes to all management personnel, including all maintenance supervisors. This report focuses primarily on the percentage of cards returned compared with those left with residents and the percentage of returned cards in each rating category (e.g., excellent, above average, average, below average, and poor).

Satisfactorily Refurbishing All Units Within a Specific Period of Time

If the manager's objective is achieved on every vacant unit for the quarter, bonus points are awarded. (The manager of a down unit [also called an 'off line' unit and referring to a unit identified as being unrentable because of a physical deficiency] may or may not be accountable for the unit when being considered for a performance type bonus. Accountability of down units varies from organization to organization.)

Maintaining the Property in Accordance with Management Company Standards

Periodic inspections by the property manager are used to award points for maintaining company standards.

Achieving Excellent Curb Appeal At All Times

Curb appeal is measured on a monthly or quarterly basis by the property manager's report and rating.

Satisfactorily Completing a Procedure Test

This test is administered annually to each supervisory level property staff member to ensure that she/he keeps current with the company's procedures and is familiar with all updates issued since the last test.

Not only does the incentive plan described above ensure that a person's compensation is commensurate with performance, it also provides an excellent vehicle for recognizing those employees with outstanding performance. People are especially sensitive and receptive to recognition and credit for the work they do. This incentive plan provides a highly motivational method of recognizing performance.

ESTABLISHING PERSONNEL POLICIES AND PRACTICES

IMPORTANCE OF THE EMPLOYEE HANDBOOK

Personnel policies are the standardized, uniformly enforced programs and actions that apply to all employees' employment. Personnel policies include but may not be limited to such issues as terms and conditions of employment, appropriate and inappropriate workplace conduct (especially as such conduct relates to sexual and other forms of harassment), dress code, performance evaluation, salary increases, working hours and conditions, vacations, sick leave, and employment termination. Both management company and property employees should clearly understand all of the personnel policies that impact their own employment and the employment of the workers they supervise.

Many misunderstandings between employees and the management company can arise when the company does not have clearly written personnel policies and/or when the company fails to provide written personnel policies to workers. The employee handbook is an effective instrument to communicate personnel policies and to greatly reduce the chances of any employment-related misunderstandings. Generally, the creation of such an employee handbook is the responsibility of the executive property manager, but the property manager should consider initiating, overseeing, and participating in the creation of such a handbook specifically for the property staff she/he personally supervises as well.

The sample table of contents presented in Figure 3–11 shows many of the topics that should be included in a comprehensive employee handbook. It also serves as an outline for the creation of such a handbook for companies that do not already have one and for companies that wish to update their existing handbook to include the most current employment issues.

FIGURE 3-11. Sample Employee Handbook Table of Contents*

Part One: About the Company
Letter from the President
Company History
Human Resource Philosophy
Organizational Chart and Chain of Command
Handbook Disclaimer

Part Two: Equal Employment Opportunity (EEO) and Affirmative Action (AA) Statements
Equal Employment Opportunity
Affirmative Action [if applicable]
General
Handicapped
Veterans
Standards of Conduct
Sexual Harassment Policy

Part Three: Employment Policies
Employment Status Definitions
Position Classification System
Recruitment and Hiring
Immigration Reform Act
Promotions and Transfers
Temporary Promotions
Performance Evaluation
Initial Evaluation Period
Separations
Resignations
Terminations
Reduction in Workforce (RIF)
Retirement
Reemployment of Former Employees
Reference Checks on Former Employees

Part Four: Standards of Conduct and Disciplinary Action
Acceptable and Unacceptable Standards of Conduct
Discipline Procedures
Actions that Warrant a Warning Prior to Discharge
Actions that Warrant Discharge

Part Five: Employee Grievance Procedures
Grievance Procedure
Role of the Supervisor
Role of Employee Grievance Committee

Part Six: Compensation
Compensation Philosophy and Policy
Work hours, Timecards, and Pay Periods
Delivery of Paychecks
Salary Administration
Salary Advances
Social Security
Overtime and Compensatory Time
Incentives and Bonuses
Separation Pay
Workers' Compensation
Garnishment
Gratuities, Outside Employment, and Conflict of Interest

Part Seven: Time and Attendance
Attendance
Tardiness
Holidays
Vacation Leave
Sick Leave
Bereavement Leave
Personal Days
Unpaid Leaves of Absence
Short-Term Disability Leave
Long-Term Disability Leave
Family Medical Leave
Military, Jury, and Voting Leave
Emergency Leave
Inclement Weather Leave

Part Eight: Employee Insurance Benefits
Workers' Compensation Insurance
Business Travel Insurance
Group Life Insurance
Accident Insurance
Long-Term Disability Insurance
Dental and Basic and Major Medical Insurance
Eligibility
How to Apply
Coverage
Enrollment
Filing a Claim
Conversion Privilege (COBRA Law)
Termination of Insurance
Retirement and Insurance
ERISA Rights

continued

FIGURE 3-11. Sample Employee Handbook Table of Contents* (*Continued*)

Part Nine: Safety and Security
Security
Housekeeping and Accident Prevention
Accident Reporting Procedures
Fire Emergencies
Fire Extinguishers
Evacuation Procedures
Emergency Oxygen Equipment

Part Ten: Miscellaneous
Changes of Name, Address, or Insurance Beneficiaries
Employee Personnel Files
Smoking Policy
Personal Mail and Telephone Calls
Travel and Expense Account
Service Awards
Extracurricular Activities
Training Program
Tuition Assistance
Solicitation
Dress Code

* Adapted from the Contents page of the *NAHB Employees Handbook.*
This sample Table of Contents has been provided as a guideline. Not every item contained in this sample Table of Contents will apply to every firm, and some firms will have topics that have not been included here.
Because the courts of some states have held that an employee handbook constitutes an employment contract, the handbook should always contain the following disclaimer:
"This handbook is not a contract and is not intended to create contractual obligations binding on the employee and the company or to alter the employment relationship from an at-will relationship that may be terminated by either party or any time for any reason that is not unlawful. The policies set forth in this handbook may be modified from time to time without advance notice."

Typically, the employee handbook provides some background information about the company and its founder and current executives. The handbook should discuss items such as:

- The company's hiring policies, including those mandated by law
- The company's employment policies, including those mandated by law
- The company's standards of conduct and code of discipline
- The company's employee grievance procedure
- Employment compensation, including benefits mandated by law
- Employee time and attendance policies
- Employee benefits
- Workplace safety and security
- Miscellaneous policies and procedures unique to the company

Because the courts of some states have held that an employee handbook constitutes an employment contract, the handbook should always contain the following disclaimer:

> "This handbook is not a contract and is not intended to create contractual obligations binding on the employee and the company or to alter the employment relationship from an at-will relationship that may be terminated by either party at any time for any reason that is not unlawful. The policies set forth in this handbook may be modified from time to time without advance notice."

TRAINING NEW EMPLOYEES

Because the operations manual contains the information and procedures that guide employees in the performance of their jobs, a section-by-section review of the manual is an efficient way for a property manager to begin training a new employee and to institute a formal training program if the management company does not have one or to supplement the management company's program. The new employee might be required to read one section of the handbook at a time and then to discuss and ask questions about the information contained in that section during specifically scheduled training meetings with the manager. Ideally, part of the training for a new employee should take place away from the constant interruptions of the rental office or maintenance garage.

The second portion of the training should be on the job, with close supervision by the manager or other responsible person designated by the manager. During this on-the-job training, another employee who is proficient in a given task should demonstrate for the new employee how the task should be done. Then the new employee's supervisor should ascertain that the employee understands and is capable of performing the task.

Throughout the training period, the supervisor should make certain that the new employee understands each item and task covered in a particular section of the operations manual before going to the next section. The manager should encourage the new employee to ask questions freely about any information that may not be clear; the manager should respond immediately, clearly, and completely to each question; and both the manager and the trainee should understand that no questions are stupid or irrelevant.

INDIVIDUAL TRAINING ACTION PLAN

In addition to structured training in company procedures, it is helpful to develop a training action plan (Fig. 3–12) for each employee. This plan should outline and track supplemental training that may enhance an employee's performance and possible advancement. Such a training program could include, but would not be limited to, attending specific company-sponsored training programs as well as those sponsored by industry associations such as the National Association of Home Builders and its affiliates. These programs could include general industry courses, such as the Registered in Apartment Management Certification Program, or more specialized technical courses, such as those for heating and air conditioning equipment repair.

An employee's individual training plan should be updated as the employee completes various courses, seminars, and training sessions. Because training is an on-going activity, the plan also should be reviewed at least annually—ideally, simultaneous with the employee's annual evaluation—to ensure that it addresses current training needs. The training plan should be modified as appropriate each time it is reviewed to include any necessary additional training.

Employees attending training programs, whether they are employer-sponsored or presented by outside organizations, should submit an evaluation of the training to the property manager or the training director, if the company has one. The employee should indicate on the course/seminar evaluation (Fig. 3–13) whether the training was successful in addressing the needs it promised to address and also whether other personnel within the organization would benefit from attending the course or seminar.

PARTIAL AND FULL STAFF TRAINING

Whether it is the training of the entire property or management company staff or the specific training of staff members from individual departments or who share similar job responsibilities and/or tasks, the training and education of staff is an on-going process that should include:

- Regularly scheduled management company and property staff meetings
- Regularly scheduled and "surprise" property walk-throughs and employee interviews performed by the property manager
- Periodic participation by all employees in whole staff and partial staff educational and training courses
- Periodic attendance by all employees in whole staff and partial staff activities and functions sponsored by various industry associations

Although a combination of in-house and outside training is highly recommended, training through outside organizations is meant to supplement, not replace, in-house training. In-house training emphasizes the duties and responsibilities specific to the management company or to the property. Outside training helps to cover issues that in-house training may not cover, helps to support in-house training with reinforcement from an outside source, provides a wider perspective than just that of the specific company or property, and helps to create and reinforce a professional attitude on the part of those who participate.

EMPLOYEE TESTING

Testing New Employees

When testing a new employee, it is a good business practice to administer a test that includes representative questions from each area of responsibility of the new employee's job. A properly designed test has a pre-designated passing grade to assure the manager that the employee has a grasp of the procedures necessary to accomplish the job. The passing grade should be established after the test has been administered to a representative sample group. The minimum score is usually between 70 and 80 percent but under any circumstances no lower than 65 percent. Testing of new hires must be done carefully under the guidelines of applicable employment law to ensure that there is no disparate impact. Tests that require reading comprehension should be scrutinized especially carefully.

The test may or may not require absolute knowledge of specific parts of the operations manual. The employee's ability to gain immediate access to the information needed may be sufficient. However, the test should be timed because anyone is able to locate an answer if given unlimited time, and this luxury often does not exist in the daily rush of business activities.

Testing of new hires should be done immediately after the training period and before the person assumes full, relatively unsupervised responsibility for her/his position. The purpose of testing at this time is to verify that the person has the knowledge to perform the job adequately and to identify where the new employee may need additional training. The test also serves as an additional inducement for learning procedures. The results of the test should assure the manager that the job is in the hands of a person knowledgeable about company procedures and about her/his responsibilities. In this way, testing new employees can help to prevent the costly and sometimes personally devastating mistakes that often occur when a person begins performing a job without adequate training.

The practice of testing new hires should be part of the evaluation process, but passing it should not be an absolute condition of continued employment because such a personnel policy must be administered uniformly and without exception.

Figure 3–12. Training Action Plan

Name ______________________ Designations (indicate date received)

Job title ______________________ RAM ________ CAM ________ CPM ________

Property ______________________ ARM ________ CAMT ________ Other ________

Location (City, state) ______________________ Procedural test scores

Hire date ____________ 90-day review date____________

Annual Review Dates Year ____________ Review date ____________
Year ____________ Review date ____________
Year ____________ Review date ____________
Year ____________ Review date ____________

List RAM school, training schools, technical schools, apartment association training, etc.

Training Needs	Est. Date To Commence	Employee Initial	RPM Initial	Date	Number of Hours	Date Completed

Achievements
List property achievements and dates (suggestion awards, offices held, honors, certificate or plaque awarded, served as speaker, etc.)

Achievement	Date

Figure 3–13. Course/Seminar Evaluation

Name of course/seminar ______________________________

Sponsored by ______________________________

Course date ______________ Numbers of hours ______________

1. Do you think this course/seminar will help you in the performance of your job? Yes or No
2. In what way(s) will it help you? ______________________________

____

____

3. How would this course/seminar benefit other personnel in the company, if at all?

____

____

____

4. What did you like best about this course/seminar? ______________________________

____

____

5. What did you like least about this course/seminar? ______________________________

____

____

6. Did this course/seminar deliver what its promotion material promised? If not, why not?

____

____

7. General comments: ______________________________

____

____

____

8. How long have you been employed in your present position? ______________
9. How long have you been with the company? ______________

Property name ______________________________

Your name ______________________________

Your present title ______________________________

Date ______________________________

Annual Testing of All Employees

Some management organizations require that employees be tested on an annual basis to ensure that they have not forgotten the procedures, to help to reinforce those procedures (because people learn through repetition), and to ensure that they have read and understand all updates issued since the last test.

Annual tests can be used as a training and evaluation device. They provide an excellent opportunity for the manager to counsel personnel in their areas of weakness. Annual testing also ensures that employees will "bone up" on all procedures at least once a year. Also, the willingness to be tested is one mark of a professional. Many professions, including law, accounting, architecture, and real estate brokerage, require testing of some type to achieve certification and often to maintain that certification. It is not inappropriate for multihousing management to do likewise.

To provide the employees with the information they need to perform their duties and to do well on the annual test, the property manager should see that the property's operations manual is kept up-to-date and that new common issues that arise are adequately addressed by the manual. Where no annual testing policy exists, this should not be an excuse for lack of on-going training.

Personality Tests

The tests discussed above are tests of job performance proficiency. In addition to those types of tests, personality testing and an understanding of personality styles can also be useful in many aspects of multihousing management, including interpersonal relations, hiring and placement, managing and motivating, management development, team building, renting, and complaint handling. When people understand personality types, they get along better with one another because they are able to identify potential interpersonal conflict and minimize or avoid it entirely. Problems usually arise because people lack awareness of the differences in other people. But when employees understand the differences, they can better adapt their styles to facilitate an effective and trouble-free interaction.

Personality testing is a sensitive legal area and must be done carefully. Any test used must be carefully designed and evaluated so that it will be regarded by a court as job related; certain personality tests may not meet that criterion. Even if it is job related, any personality test or instrument should be validated to ensure that it is nondiscriminatory, accurate, and reliable. It should accurately measure the characteristics it purports to measure, and those characteristics should be relevant to job performance. Before a manager implements such a test or instrument, she/he should have it reviewed by legal counsel experienced in employment discrimination cases.

Personality test should not be considered absolute and final predictors of performance. The results of personality tests are only indicators of certain characteristics and do not measure a person's degree of motivation or technical competence. Decisions about applicants for employment therefore cannot legally be based solely on results from such tests or instruments. Unless the personality test is job related, such tests should not be used.

The results of legal personality tests are merely one of many measurement tools used to evaluate people during the employment selection process. The results of such tests should be available to the interviewer and to the person for whom the applicant will work (if the interviewer and the direct supervisor are not the same person) prior to the in-depth personal interview and may provide the basis for some of the interview questions. When such questions are to be incorporated into the interview, they need to be carefully reviewed prior to the interview for possible legal implications.

If a personality test is to be administered to an employee, the manager needs to carefully explain the test and its purpose to the employee beforehand. The manager should emphasize that the test is not to judge performance but rather to provide an opportunity for the employee and the manager to learn more about the employee so that together, the employee and the manager can plan how to improve the employee's effectiveness and productivity. The manager must then be careful not to use the test to judge performance. This temptation is one reason personality tests may be inadvisable.

Conversely, although personality measuring instruments are generally called "tests"—which implies a judgment or a pass-fail situation—there are no right or wrong answers or results on these tests. Each employee is a unique human being and each can make a valuable contribution to the organization provided she/he is in a job position that is appropriate for her/his personality. No one personality type is good for all positions, and no position is right for every personality type. Personality instruments provide a means of creating balance in an organization and help to prevent managers from hiring only people like themselves. Indeed, it is the wise manager who recognizes the need to hire individuals with strengths other than the manager's own. It is very sound business practice to bring into the workplace a mix of personalities, abilities, and skills, and managers who are well informed about personality types are motivated and able to do just that.

CULTIVATING PROFESSIONAL AND PERSONAL STAFF DEVELOPMENT

Professional development includes not only knowing how to perform specific job functions but also personal development and growth, which includes setting goals, self-motivation, determination, enthusiasm, time management, interpersonal relation skills, and self-confidence. Personal development should be an integral part of any hiring and training program.

When making a hiring decision, a property manager should look first at the personal skills a candidate possesses and then at the technical knowledge that the individual may possess. Technical skills can be learned by almost anyone, but the right attitude toward personal and professional development often outweighs technical ability.

THE VALUE OF PERSONAL DEVELOPMENT TRAINING

Property managers typically spend a great deal of time training their property staff in technical areas but not much time training staff in personal development. Yet studies consistently show that only 20 percent of a person's success results from knowledge about the job and the industry; the majority of a person's success results from personal qualities such as self-understanding, motivation, time-management skills, self-esteem, image, and appearance. These personal skills help a person to more effectively apply her/his technical skills.

Also significant is the fact that providing personal development training demonstrates to employees that the management company cares about the people who work for it.

MANAGING STRESS

At a one-day property management workshop presented under the auspices of the Cincinnati Management Association, each attendee who participated in the session on stress was asked to list the three events that cause the most stress. The responses were compiled to determine the overall group rating of the most stress-producing events for property managers.

In order from first to last, the following events were identified as producing the most stress for property managers: vacancies, late rent and angry residents (tied for second place), and living on-site (many said that occupying an apartment in the property they manage is stressful because they never get any relief from the pressure). Managers also identified ringing telephones, pets, and problems with staff members as among the major stress producers in their jobs.

The best professionals, and certainly the best managers, know how to manage stress in their lives. Here are some actions managers can take to minimize or alleviate the inevitable stress that occurs in multihousing management:

- Practice effective time management, both on and off the job
- Avoid taking work home on a regular basis
- Take regular vacations
- Elicit personal support from family and friends
- Actively pursue a hobby or interest outside of work
- Exercise regularly
- Practice relaxation techniques regularly
- Follow sound sleep and nutritional guidelines
- Stay within five pounds of ideal weight
- Quit smoking
- Quit or avoid addictive substances such as alcohol, sleep and relaxation medications (prescription and over-the-counter), and illegal drugs

To improve time management, successful professional managers eliminate or cut down on low-priority activities and concentrate on those that are most responsible for helping them accomplish the job. Too often people spend 80 percent of their time on activities that accomplish only 20 percent of the job. But when managers focus and direct their efforts, they use a higher percentage of their abilities and talents and they are therefore more likely to accomplish their personal and professional objectives. At the same time they reduce stress by eliminating nonproductive activities. Other time management techniques include:

- Padding "extra time" in advance of meetings to ensure punctuality and as much as 15 minute between appointments for personal "breathing space"
- Setting aside one or two specific times during the day to respond to e-mails instead of feeling pressured to respond to them as soon as they come in
- Working at a clear desk rather than at a cluttered one
- Mastering the fine art of delegation

Even with all these stress and time management techniques, managers must remember that not all stress is bad. In fact, everyone needs a certain amount of stress for normal stimulation. Most managers would prefer to suffer temporarily from burn-out than from rust-out, which generally occurs if she/he never extends herself/himself in the performance of either work or play.

In summary, property managers who take care of themselves and their health by getting enough sleep, eating properly, exercising regularly, engaging in relaxing activities, and practicing time management techniques can cope productively with nearly any kind of normal stress.

MEETINGS OF ON-SITE PERSONNEL

On-site employees typically enjoy the opportunity to get together and to know that they are a vital part of a larger organization. As shown in Figure 3–14, regular meetings of on-site rental and maintenance personnel can provide many benefits.

Staff meetings should be scheduled on a weekly basis and generally should last no more than half an hour. Meetings should follow a deliberate agenda to be most productive and to avoid degenerating into bull and/or grievance sessions.

The meeting should begin with a review of what has been accomplished since the last meeting. A discussion of what needs to be done should then follow, with agenda items addressed in priority order. The manager should then summarize the conclusions reached as a result of the meeting and who is scheduled to do what job by what date. In this way each person knows what she/he is responsible for accomplishing before the next meeting. The senior manager should attend these meetings from time to time and as required to provide insight into specific issues, to review proposed actions that may require her/his approval for implementation, to observe the property manager's effectiveness in meeting and supervisory situations, and to generally contribute to positive morale building.

The site for the meeting can vary from the rental office to the clubhouse to the maintenance office. The subject matter of the meeting may dictate the proper location. For example, if the main agenda topic deals with the care, maintenance, and use of the clubhouse, the clubhouse would be the ideal location. Figure 3–15 provides guidelines for running optimally efficient and productive on-site meetings.

FIGURE 3-14. Benefits of Staff Meetings

- Give employees a sense of belonging and help them to believe that they are "in" on things, which provides a big morale boost, improves attitude, and generates enthusiasm.
- Provide an opportunity for employees to discuss their common problems and to share ideas for solving them at the earliest possible moment. Meetings permit the use of the team approach to problem solving.
- Enable employees to provide feedback to management in a formal, organized way. Otherwise, they may not bother to make recommendations. Meetings help to tap the creativity and ideas in employees.
- Provide recognition in a group setting. Recognition of a particular outstanding achievement announced in a large group meeting has a much greater impact that the same words uttered in a small group in the office or one-on-one.
- Present management with opportunities to obtain field input prior to finalizing new procedures or revising old ones.
- Conserve time by more effectively and consistently covering information in one well-planned presentation in a group setting rather than many informal explanations. A meeting can conserve time and ensure a more effective, consistent presentation. Management can also use group dynamics to more effectively make a point or to reinforce a particular message, and everyone benefits by hearing the answers to questions asked by others.
- Keep employees better informed.

FIGURE 3-15. Guidelines for Effective Meetings

- Solicit participants' ideas prior to the meeting for items to include on the agenda.
- Prepare a format, written agenda and provide a copy to each participant.
- Ensure that everyone understands the purpose of the meeting and that all items on the agenda support that purpose.
- Ensure that any needed equipment is at the meeting site and in good working order, and that any visuals are available and in order.
- Start and end the meeting on time.
- Effectively use group dynamics, including questions and answers, in conducting the meeting. Involve each person.
- Effectively use interpersonal skills to ensure that each person feels free to make contributions, ask questions, and provide other input. In such an atmosphere, employees are more likely to believe that their contributions are worthwhile and that they have a significant part in the meeting.
- Keep the group discussion moving toward the objectives. Diplomatically stop anyone who is not speaking on the subject or who is starting to dominate the discussion.
- Prepare a written summary of the discussion and conclusions reached immediately after the meeting, and provide copies to the appropriate levels of management and the participants.
- Ensure that follow-up occurs after the meeting concerning recommendations and plans developed, and that each person understands her/his assignment(s) and timetable.
- Advise the participants and others of the actions taken as a result of the meeting or the reasons why action will not be taken. Participants must receive feedback as result of the meeting.

PERSONNEL EVALUATIONS

Evaluating all employees on an on-going basis is a sound business practice because employees function more effectively when they receive regular feedback on how they are performing. Performance evaluation is a day-to-day, two-way communication process. If it is carried out properly, neither the evaluator nor the employee being evaluated experiences any surprises at the annual evaluation meeting.

Like the on-going process of evaluation, the annual evaluation meeting provides an opportunity for dialogue concerning the employee's performance, strengths and weaknesses, and plans for improvement. Employees should be encouraged to state their thoughts and ask questions concerning:

- Their own performance
- The supervision and guidance they receive
- What, if any, additional assistance they need from their supervisor and/or the company
- Their goals and opportunities for advancement within the organization

To be most productive and to be happiest in their jobs, employees should clearly understand their job functions and the vital part these functions play in the overall goals of the company and/or property. The senior manager and/or property manager should encourage employees to set personal and professional goals and should explain to them how they can achieve these goals by helping the company accomplish its goals.

The evaluation meeting should be used not only for evaluation but also for one-on-one training, communication, motivation, and planning. The evaluation process should ensure that the individual does not get lost in the corporate shuffle. The day-to-day rush of activities may not present the opportunity to have this kind of discussion with an employee on an on-going basis, but when it is needed at some time other than during the annual review, the daily schedule should be adjusted to allow for such a discussion.

A regular schedule for each person's evaluation ensures that the supervisor and the employee take the opportunity to have this meaningful two-way communication that is of immense benefit to both the company and the individual. Rental and maintenance personnel should be evaluated at least annually, preferably semi-annually. The procedure could call for the senior manager to evaluate the property manager and make appropriate recommendations for improvement. The property manager then reviews the other property personnel in the same manner. The evaluation conference should be person-to-person and never by phone, mail, or e-mail.

The legal pitfall in any personnel evaluation system is that managers may fail to document negative as well as positive aspects of performance. Too often a troublesome aspect grows worse to the point that discharge is warranted, but last year's glowing evaluation provides the employee with evidence of unfair discharge. Property managers should develop the habit of documenting negative performance even if they focus on the positive. A sample evaluation form for a maintenance supervisor or maintenance assistant appears in Figure 3–16.

The senior manager and/or property manager should be constantly aware of the factors that indicate a problem or potential problem with personnel. Clues that a problem may be developing include:

- Low and/or declining occupancy/rentals within the property
- High and/or increasing move-outs and cancellations within the property
- Low and/or declining closing rates or rentals as a percent of traffic within the property
- High and/or increasing rent delinquencies within the property
- Lack of timely and accurate submission of reports to the home office, such as turnover reports, delinquent reports, and inspection reports
- High and/or increasing number of errors in paperwork submitted to the home office

No one individual sign may be sufficient to trigger a review. However, two or more signs reflect a possible underlying problem in the property office requiring immediate action to head off a crisis. Senior managers and property managers should be on the alert for these red flags. Much information can be gleaned by a careful and thoughtful analysis of reports submitted. However, these reports can only convey signals of a potential problem; a thorough on-site analysis must be made to determine whether a problem exists and if so, what to do about it.

EMPLOYEE SUGGESTION AWARDS

The employee suggestion award is an excellent way to encourage each employee to be on the alert for new ideas and ways to improve procedures, reduce expenses, and/or increase income for the property and/or management company. Figure 3–17 describes how to write an employee suggestion awards procedure for the operations manual. An employee suggestion form appears in Figure 3–18 and an employee suggestion awards certificate in Figure 3–19.

DIRECTING EMPLOYEES

When a property manager is giving employees directions, sound management practice calls for the manager to give the employees the purpose of and rationale for the directions. An explanation permits employees to carry out the directions better and may encourage them to suggest a better way to accomplish the job. If a property manager states that a procedure must be performed because someone else (presumably higher up in the company) says so, the property manager may seem ineffective and the directive may not be carried out well. Property managers should involve employees in the decision-making process as much as possible and encourage them to participate in solving problems. The employee at the scene may provide valuable input and probably will be more receptive to the solution if she/he is part of determining that solution. In addition, the involved employee has a vested interest in ensuring the success of the solution.

When it comes to cultivating professional and personnel staff development, all employers—including the multihousing management industry—should bear in mind that excellent people like to work for excellent companies. The employer—in this case, the property manager—therefore should set the standard for excellence to attract and retain the best people.

PROPERTY MANAGER AND RESIDENT RELATIONS

Just as it is vital for the property manager to cultivate a positive and productive working relationship with property personnel, so it is equally critical for the property manager to establish and maintain relations with the property's residents that are as professional, as positive, and as productive as possible.

RECOMMENDED APPROACHES FOR DEALING WITH RESIDENTS

Responding to Reasonable Resident Requests

The property manager should demonstrate genuine concern over the resident's problem and a desire to solve it as quickly as possible. One of the items a resident pays for with her/his monthly rent check is service. The manager must reflect an attitude of service in all dealings with the resident.

Responding to Unreasonable Resident Requests

The property manager should explain that management cannot resolve all of the resident's problems but that she/he will try to take care of this particular one, if possible. If the problem cannot be handled, the manager should explain clearly why and perhaps offer an alternative solution. The manager's patience and understanding about problems that management cannot resolve go a long way toward neutralizing resident ill will. It also may prompt the resident to find alternate solutions. The resident is more content if the manager is tactful.

Discussing Violations of Rules

Violations should be discussed in a businesslike, straightforward fashion, without unpleasantness but with firmness. Again, rules in writing—preferably in a resident handbook—reinforce what the property manager says. In this way, the resident understands that the manager is not making policy on the spot to frustrate a particular resident but is carrying out a policy designed to improve the multihousing lifestyle for all concerned.

Reacting to Family Problems and Hardships

These situations occur most frequently in senior citizen developments, assisted developments, and in conventional properties, especially during poor economic cycles. The property manager should refer the family to a professional social agency for specific advice or assistance. The rule is not to become personally involved by giving advice or helping to resolve a problem. Instead, the manager should be knowledgeable about available social and neighborhood agencies that can assist in its resolution. The manager should help the family or person tap into available community resources.

Dealing with Unruly and Abusive Residents

The property manager should meet personally with these residents, talk in a calm, firm manner, and tell them what is expected of them if they want to remain in occupancy. The manager should stick with what she/he has said. If the behavior does not improve, the manager should ask them to move or commence the promised action, usually eviction. Unpunished abusive behavior is a signal to other residents that they can do likewise. The situation may soon become uncontrollable.

HANDLING RESIDENT COMPLAINTS

The property's operations manual should have procedures for handling different types of resident problems or complaints, such as disturbances by neighbors or the quality of work performed by maintenance. In developing those procedures, the property manager must consider many issues.

The manager and the staff must differentiate between a complaint and a service request. In this business, most dealings are with the latter. Management should be pleased that a resident has taken time to report a problem needing correction. In the long run, time and money are saved, especially if a problem is reported in the early stages. Preventive maintenance is much more cost-effective than maintenance by crisis. In addition, satisfactory and timely handling of service requests is one of the benefits residents pay for with their monthly rent check.

When a resident becomes angry and registers a complaint, whether or not it arose originally though a service request, the manager should be especially careful to use diplomacy. Tempers are likely to flare, and the situation has the potential to get out of hand and perhaps result in a dissatisfied resident, a move-out, and unfavorable word-of-mouth advertising.

Conversely, complaints are not necessarily bad. They bring to light potential problems. If someone is upset with the management company, the property, and/or its policies, the manager should know about it before a move-out results. The manager then has the option to do something about the problem. Too often people do not register their complaints but move instead.

The objective is to handle the complaint while ensuring a happy, satisfied resident. Instead of considering a resident complaint as a nuisance, the manager should consider it as an opportunity to solve a problem. A complaint offers a challenge.

The following guidelines should be considered in handling resident complaints:

Let the resident speak—The property manager should afford as many avenues of communication as possible to

Figure 3–16. Maintenance and Supervisor/Assistant Evaluation

______________________________ (Property)

______________________________ (Employee Name)

(Employee's Name and Job Title)

Responsibility	Maximum points	Actual points	Criteria/documentation
Service requests—24-handling	15	_____	Percent of requests handled within 24 hours and reasons for those not handled and ratings on the returned cards.
Refurbishment of vacancies—5 days	15	_____	Determine percentage of cases in which the objective was not accomplished and reasons why the objective was not accomplished in the other cases.
Property appearance—curb appeal	5	_____	Based on property inspections and other observations
Mechanical ability	15	_____	Number subcontractor calls and opinion of property manager and property manager
Resident and personnel relations	10	_____	Based on observation and contacts with residents by the property manager and property manager and observation of general rapport with other property employees
Expense controls and cash flow	10	_____	Actual expenses v. budget, cash flow v. objective
Maintenance test	10	_____	Score
Garage and office appearance	5	_____	Periodic inspection by management compared with standards

Reports	5	____	Timeliness, adequacy, and accuracy
Total points	100	____	

______________________________ ____________
(Employee Signature) (Date)

______________________________ ____________
(Property Manager Signature) (Date)

Overall rating:
Excellent: 90-100 Good: 80-89
Average: 70-79 Poor: Below 70

Period covered: ______________________________

Comments: ______________________________

Strengths

Weaknesses

Recommendations

FIGURE 3-17. Employee Suggestion Award Program

- The objective is to operate the property and/or the management company in the most efficient manner possible.
- To achieve this objective, the company has established an employee suggestion award program to encourage each employee to be constantly on the alert for new ideas and ways to improve procedures, reduce expenses, and/or increase income for the property and/or the management company.
- Any employee who has an idea that s/he believes will accomplish those objectives should submit it on the form included in this packet or in a memo.
- Property employees should submit proposals to their property managers. Property managers should submit their proposals to their senior managers. Central office personnel should submit their proposals to their immediate supervisors. Senior managers and central office supervisors should submit their proposals directly to the executive property manager.
- The senior manager or central office supervisor will perform a cost/benefit analysis to determine whether the suggestion is viable. After the analysis, if the senior manager or central office supervisor concurs with the proposal, he/she will submit it in writing to the executive property manager.
- The executive property manager will review each proposal received and make a final decision regarding implementation and appropriate award.
- The amount awarded for an implemented proposal is to be based upon a percentage of the estimated first year's potential savings and/or increased income to the property and/or management company, with a minimum award of $xx. Persons who receive an award will be recognized in the company newsletter.
- An employee who makes a suggestion that is submitted to the executive property manager for further consideration will receive a framed certificate of appreciation.
- An employee submitting a proposal will be notified within 45 days concerning the action taken on that proposal.

residents. This means being able and available to receive resident communications in person during office hours, over the phone (with messages promptly returned), and via fax, letter, and e-mail. However the communication comes to the property manager, she/he should "listen" carefully to what the resident is saying. If the communication is made in person, the manager should observe body language as well as what the resident is saying so that she/he can clearly understand how the resident feels. The manager should not offer excuses or become defensive; the resident does not care about the manager's problems and defensiveness only causes an argument. Above all, the property manager should not interrupt even if the natural impulse is to offer an explanation or remedy immediately. Letting the person get the problem off her/his chest without criticism, without exchanging anger for anger, and without interruption is the best course. If shown respect, understanding, and patience, most people are more than reasonable, and, in many cases, all the resident really wants is to have someone listen. Often, hearing the resident out permits her/him to cool off. Sometimes that is enough to prompt the resident to realize that the problem is not really serious and that arrangements can be made to handle it.

Clarify and restate the problem—After the resident has had an opportunity to tell her/his story in full, the manager may want to ask questions to ensure that the resident has fully explained what the problem is or what she/he perceives it to be. The manager then should briefly restate the problem to ensure that she/he understands what the resident is trying to communicate. The manager should express regret that the problem occurred. This expression of regret is not an apology but merely a way of showing empathy with the person who is upset. The manager might begin, "You probably felt really upset when . . . ," and then conclude with a restatement of the complaint. The manager's comments should not assert the other person is wrong but should show respect for the other person's opinion. If possible, some point of agreement should be found.

Ignore irrelevancies—The manager should recognize the irrelevancy of such verbal plays as personal attacks, sarcasm, and exaggerations and not reply if the resident resorts to using one or more of them.

Control behavior—The manager should speak or write to the resident in even, calm tones to set an appropriate pattern for the exchange.

Figure 3–18. Employee Suggestion Form

To ________________________ Date ________________________

From ________________________ Department/Property ________________________

Suggestion ____

____

____

____

____

____

____

____

Enclose any samples that might be helpful.

____

Original and 1 copy: Property Manager
1 copy: File

____

____

Date ________________________
To ________________________
From ________________________

____

____

Your above suggestion is ☐ approved ☐ disapproved

Reason____

____

____

____

____

____

____

Thank you for participating in the Suggestion Award Program. We hope you will continue to submit suggestions on ways to improve the company operations.

____
(Executive property manager)

____

Original: Person making suggestion
1 copy: Property manager
1 copy: Senior manager

Figure 3–19. Employee Suggestion Award Certificate

Employee Suggestion Award

Presented To

____

(Name of Employee)

In appreciation of a significant contribution to the

efficiency of ________________________________ ***and its client properties.***

____

Executive Property Manager

____________________ ____________________

Property Manager ***Senior Manager***

____

(Date)

Apologize when the resident is right—The manager may decide that the resident is right. In this case and when legal liability is not in question, the manager should say, "We made a mistake. It is embarrassing. I am really sorry. Here's what we're going to do to fix the situation."

Take action—Sometimes the only thing the manager can do at the moment is to write something down. The appearance of action is often as effective as the real thing. Follow-up to resolve the problem should be done as soon as possible.

Document the exchange and follow-up—Under all circumstances, when a resident communicates with management, the property manager should document the exchange and place copies of the documentation in the appropriate files (including and especially the resident's file) for future reference.

RESIDENT ORGANIZATIONS

Resident organizations can be desirable if they permit property managers to operate more effectively. The U.S. Department of Housing and Urban Development (HUD) requires support of resident organizations at assisted developments. In conventional developments, the property manager should make it her/his business to find out why a group is being formed. If it is a group that will reflect positively on the development and its management, then the property manager should maintain a positive working relationship with the organization.

Sometimes, however, resident organizations are started by so-called trouble-makers whose personal goals may not coincide with the best interests of the other residents. In this case, the manager should gather information and judge whether the proposed purpose of the organization and its intended means of accomplishing the purpose will benefit the development. In some cases, the property manager may need to seek the counsel of the senior manager.

If the determination is made that the organization is not in the best interest of the property and the residents, the property manager should attempt to avoid contact with the organization. An example of this type of resident organization might be one started by a resident who is upset because of a rent increase and is encouraging a rent strike.

PROPERTY MANAGER'S RELATIONSHIP WITH THE COMMUNITY AT LARGE

In addition to dealing positively and productively with property staff members and residents, the property manager often will be called on to interact with a variety of individuals and entities from the larger community. These include:

Local government—Local government officials can either help or hinder property management. Therefore, managers of both assisted and conventional housing should become involved and maintain rapport with the local government and other regulatory agencies that have jurisdiction over any aspect of how the property functions.

Inspectors—A professional and businesslike relationship should be maintained with local government inspectors. All staff members dealing with these people must be beyond reproach, without even the hint or possibility of any wrongdoing. Staff need to take the honest approach in dealing with inspectors, providing the information the inspectors request without attempting to hide anything. Inspectors are only doing their jobs, and property managers who are doing their jobs properly have nothing to hide because they are operating within all local laws and codes. It is the property manager's responsibility to notify the senior manager and/or owner and assist in correcting any code violations or other problems. In any case, the property manager should remember that it is less costly to comply with regulations than to fail to comply and deal with the result afterwards should a disaster occur.

The media—The relationship between the property manager, the property, and the media does not require that the manager get her/his picture in the newspaper or on television. It does mean that the property manager should cultivate a positive relationship with the local media to promote the positive aspects of the property and its residents. This is accomplished through frequent coverage and stories in the news about events at the property that create and convey a desirable image for the property, thus producing happier residents and more applicants. Such a relationship with the media also helps to offset any negative stories about unfavorable incidents at the property. A word to the wise: When media representatives contact a property manager for specific information about a complaint registered by a resident or some other potentially embarrassing situation, the manager should refer the representative to the senior manager and should not release any information without prior permission from the owner and/or the appropriate management company decision maker.

Social services programs—Residents' social services programs are the concern of management. Although management is not responsible for solving the social problems of residents, the property manager should be able to refer residents to local agencies equipped to deal with these problems. This referral service is more important in assisted developments in which low-income residents may need financial, legal, or other assistance. Seniors may need assistance in tapping into various government programs such as the hot meal program. The property manager should know whom to contact about specific programs, who might qualify for assistance, and how to apply.

CASE STUDY

The following story of a hypothetical but possible incident reviews the various ways the property manager could consider handling a resident problem.

A young boy and his teenage sister consistently pick on other children in their building. These bullies do not vandalize property or severely injure anyone. In other words, they leave no physical evidence of their actions. When the manager approaches the parents about the problem, they claim that their children would never do something like that. However, the accusations come from more than one family.

Unless the children are causing a resident relations problem, this situation is essentially a personal situation that should be dealt with by the accusing parents without involvement of management personnel. However, if the parents are unable to settle the problem among themselves and it appears to be causing a resident relations problem, the property manager should become involved. She/he should begin by simply using interpersonal skills in asking the parents of the offending children to help in moderating their behavior.

If this soft approach does not work and the situation is creating strong ill will or causing residents to move, the manager will have to take stronger action. The ultimate action, of course, is eviction for lease violation. However, the manager can try the following other approaches before taking this drastic step.

Because the parents are denying the accusations, the property manager should ask that the complaints be put in writing before taking any action other than a simple comment to the parents regarding the complaints and a request that they control their children. The complaints could be vindictive and untrue. However, people will generally be reluctant to put a false accusation in writing. Assuming that the complaining parents do comply with the request, the manager will be on firmer ground in confronting the parent of the offenders.

The property manager could call a meeting of the children involved—those who are making the accusations as well as the accused—and their parents to discuss the situation and the charges. At that point, the positions usually will be moderated and the facts (which generally lie somewhere in between) will come to light. Generally, an agreement can be reached. With this approach, the property manager does not have to deal one-to-one with each parent nor have to referee. The property manager's role is simply to facilitate direct communication and to get the disagreeing parties together so that they can settle their dispute themselves without direct intervention.

The property manager could set up a subtle surveillance of the children involved by assigning someone to wash, caulk, or paint part of the building, trim the bushes, or check the playground equipment for safety. The person observing would have to be careful to avoid any semblance of harassment. The children are less likely to carry out such acts in the presence of a uniformed grounds patrol person, so an unobtrusive maintenance worker serves this surveillance role better.

Another approach would be to appoint the parents of the offending children as part of a "kid watch," similar to the "crime watch" program. Their responsibility would include keeping the peace.

If the problem seems to be a general one or one that is increasing throughout the property, the property manager could include comment on the situation in the property's newsletter and ask that parents monitor their children's conduct more closely. In this way the property manager is not accusing any particular child.

If the aggressor is caught in the act or visible physical damage appears on the complaining child, contacting the police may be necessary. Regular personal contact with a police officer (especially one in juvenile services) can be invaluable in situations such as this.

If the offending child has undergone a drastic personality change that resulted in violence toward others, that change could be indicative of drug use or abuse, and that is a matter for the police and other professionals.

HOW TO BE A GREAT PROPERTY MANAGER

Several common traits are possessed by great management firms and great managers. These traits are listed in Figure 3–20 and include:

- Focusing on making life at the property a positive experience for residents
- Cultivating good listening as well as speaking skills
- Spending time "walking the property" and observing what is going on in the property in every way
- Being receptive to new ideas from staff and residents
- Working deliberately to become the best possible multifamily housing management professional

Successful management companies and professionals also have a strong people orientation. They understand the importance of their employees and take time to recognize and reward them in proportion to their contributions. They provide abundant opportunities for their employees to do meaningful work and to be involved in the decision-making process.

They are also accessible to their employees in order to:

- Personally see how the property looks and how it is functioning
- Allow employees to provide information directly to them
- Provide the morale boost that occurs when the senior manager takes the time to visit and show interest in how the employees are doing, and when the property manager takes the time to have a substantive one-on-one conversation with an employee

These companies and professionals have a high intensity of measurement and feedback. Their employees understand their responsibilities, and they are given feedback on how they are performing compared with those responsibilities. They understand their objectives and they are recognized and paid in accordance with the accomplishment of those objectives and their achievement. This approach provides the key to motivation.

The best make sure that each of their employees feels like a winner by making their success possible through proper hiring, training, and supervision. As the objectives are systematically raised, people become even more successful, have a greater feeling of self-esteem, and earn additional income.

These successful organizations and professionals stay close to their customers, who are both the property owner and the property residents in multihousing management.

FIGURE 3-20. Traits of Great Property Managers

Great property managers:

- Remember who pays the bills, namely the residents. The focus of their efforts is to ensure that residents find living in the property to be a positive experience.
- Understand why they have two ears and only one mouth. They listen well and understand what residents and staff want. Good listening skills are paramount.
- Spend time walking the property, listening, and observing. The difficulty in managing multifamily properties can be expressed as a mathematical formula:

$$DM = D^2$$

- DM is the difficult of management, and D is the distance from the property manager's desk to the site. Simply put, no one can manage well from an office. A property manager must spend time looking at the property through the resident's eyes and remember that the two areas the resident sees most often are the mailbox and the garbage dumpster.
- Remember that the best ideas come from staff and/or residents, and understand that all great successes are team efforts. Creating a team is vitally important, and teams need attention, nurturing, and support.
- Recognize that excellence does not come easily, overnight, or maintain itself without work. Managing and motivating are acts that get better only with practice.

"The customer is king" is true for the exceptional manager who must ensure that owners are satisfied with the services provided and residents are pleased with the property so that they will continue to live there for a long time and to refer other potential residents to the property. Although some property managers tend to treat residents as an interruption to the business, the fact is residents are the purpose of this business. Without residents, management would have no business and the property manager would have no job.

Successful companies and professionals are also better listeners. They listen to their customers, suppliers, and employees. They are alert to benefit from any suggestion that could improve the operation.

Excellent companies and professionals do not allow things to become overly complicated. One of their guiding philosophies is "Keep it simple." They keep staffs small. They insist on one-page memos. They focus on a few key values and objectives, and they let their people know what is important. This policy cuts down on the need for daily instructions and voluminous manuals.

These companies and professionals have a commitment to quality. All multihousing management companies and professionals must do the same to assure that:

- Properties are immaculately maintained with excellent curb appeal
- Residents receive consistent high-quality service
- Service is truly the foundation of the business

Other common characteristics of successful companies with obvious application to property management include:

- Treating employees as the most important resource and key to productivity
- Managers who love the product and have a hands-on knowledge of their company's technology, customers, and suppliers
- Flexible rules and policies so employees can exercise individuality within certain guidelines
- A tolerance for mistakes and the realization that progress often results from experimentation
- The ability not only to analyze and plan but also to make decisions, take the initiative, and act
- A level of expertise that recognizes the wisdom of "gut feeling" instinct and intuition and encourages the use of intuition in its employees

Finally, the most successful people in the world enjoy what they do, not because it's fun all the time but because it fulfills them personally, gives them a sense of purpose, and helps them to feel that they are making a real and valuable contribution to someone else's life. The practice of multifamily housing management can provide all of this to the professional who actively seeks it.

CONCLUSION

Just as certain personal and professional characteristics and skill sets are necessary for success in any field, so math, communication, and language literacy skills; management and organizational skills; administrative and supervisory skills; interpersonal skills; and maturity, sociability, and initiative are essential to the success of the property manager. Arguably the most important professional in the management of a property, the property manager is out there on the front line every day, with the owner, the management company, the property staff, and the property residents watching and judging her/his performance.

Because the property manager relies so strongly on the property staff, she/he must know how to manage and cultivate the staff for maximum productivity. The property manager can do this by establishing measurable, specific, written goals and a plan for their accomplishment. To most effectively motivate property staff members, the property manager should show employees how to identify their own personal objectives and how these tie in with the objectives of the management company and/or the property owner.

In turn, it is the property manager's responsibility to ensure that the property staff are well trained, adequately compensated, properly directed, motivated, and reviewed periodically according to a regular schedule.

When hiring, the property manager should look for candidates both inside and outside the property and the management organizations. She/he should use such resources as newspaper and Internet advertising, employment agencies, referrals from present employees, competitive properties, state employment agencies, business and technical colleges, and other recruitment sources to find the workers needed. She/he must be careful to stay within the bounds of the law in terms of both the interview procedure and hiring practices and must be sure to offer compensation that is competitive with the market.

The property manager is also responsible for training and testing property employees and for meeting with them periodically to keep them up-to-date about happenings within the management company and the property. The manager should create and distribute an employee handbook, which is an effective instrument to communicate personnel policies and to greatly reduce the chances of any employment-related misunderstandings.

Just as it is vital for the property manager to cultivate a positive and productive working relationship with property personnel, so it is equally important to establish and maintain professional, positive, and productive relations with the property's residents. Here, the value of a resident handbook becomes apparent.

The property manager also must know how to work productively with the community at large, including the local government, inspectors, the media, and social services.

The superior property manager also enjoys her/his job. On the front line every day, visible and accountable to the property owner, the management company supervisors, the property's staff, and the residents who live there, the property manager who embraces all of the guidelines offered in this textbook will be elevated above the crowd and will move confidently toward success as a multihousing management professional.

4

Multihousing Management Economics and Finances

- Economic and Financial Basics
- Conventional properties and subsidized developments, net operating income, cash flow and cash-on-cash return, and valuation techniques
- Establishing rent levels
- Changes in rent
- Rent collection
- Lease agreement
- Security deposit
- Financial management of the property
- Establishing the financial management system
- Chart of accounts
- Budgets and budgeting
- Developing the operating budget
- Developing the capital budget
- Budget review and approval
- Financial reporting and monitoring
- Variance analysis
- Cash management
- Financial audits
- The computer in financial management
- Conclusion

ECONOMIC AND FINANCIAL BASICS

As discussed in Chapter 3, the multihousing property manager, as the owner's agent, is responsible for:

- Ensuring that the owner's goals and objectives are communicated to and understood by the property staff
- Ensuring that the property operates in a cost-efficient manner while providing satisfactory housing to residents
- Ensuring that the property is maintained according to the standards established by the management company and/or the owner
- Under the guidance of the senior manager, training all property personnel under her/his supervision
- Accounting to the senior manager for all moneys pertaining to the property
- Learning and implementing the standard operating procedures prescribed by the management company and/or the owner for tasks such as:
  - Renting apartments
  - Resident selection and processing
  - Processing applicable forms
  - Rent collection
  - Coordinating property maintenance activities, including housekeeping and grounds care
  - Performing property inspections
  - Processing service requests

- Purchasing
- Record-keeping
- Resident relations
- Timely submission of all required reports

To fulfill each of these obligations optimally, the property manager must have a basic working understanding of the economics and finances of multihousing management and of the owner's perspective with regard to the financial investment she/he has made in the property.

CONVENTIONAL PROPERTIES AND SUBSIDIZED DEVELOPMENTS, NET OPERATING INCOME, CASH FLOW AND CASH-ON-CASH RETURN, AND VALUATION TECHNIQUES

UNDERSTANDING THE DIFFERENCE BETWEEN CONVENTIONAL PROPERTIES AND SUBSIDIZED DEVELOPMENTS

When an owner either does not have the cash required to purchase a property outright or to fund new construction or does not want to participate in an all-cash transaction, she/he must seek outside financing. When an owner secures a mortgage loan that is not insured or guaranteed by a government agency (e.g., the Federal Housing Administration [FHA]), that mortgage is a conventional mortgage. When financing is secured through a government agency, special regulations apply that do not apply to conventionally financed, privately owned properties. The government also sponsors its own housing projects, including subsidized and assisted housing, which is federal housing based on grants that reduce the cost of housing and allow for lower rent levels. All of these types of multihousing properties require professional management and an understanding of the economic and financial issues that impact them.

UNDERSTANDING NET OPERATING INCOME

Net operating income (NOI) is the difference between all of a property's operating revenue for a given period of time (such as rent received, late fees, NSF [insufficient funds] charges, ancillary income from laundry and vending, cable TV, parking or storage charges, and any other revenue that the property might have) and the property's operating expenses for the same period of time (such as office expenses, property staff payroll, management fees, utility expenses, and all maintenance and upkeep expenses that don't involve capital expenditures) before subtracting income taxes, debt service, capital items, and interest. Basically, it is the money remaining in the property's operating account at the end of the subject time period. Most property owners wish to maximize their NOI.

UNDERSTANDING CASH FLOW AND CASH-ON-CASH RETURN

Cash flow is the money that is left after the nonoperating expenses of a given period of time (such as income taxes, debt service, capital items, and interest) are subtracted from the NOI for the same period of time.

Cash-on-cash return is the annual dollar income divided by the total dollar investment, with the quotient expressed as a percentage. To achieve a positive cash-on-cash return, some owners choose to sell their property at a profit. Others hold on to their investment, operating the property and collecting rents that cover the operating costs of the property and also provide a profit.

UNDERSTANDING VALUATION TECHNIQUES

Knowing the current value of a property at any point in time is critical to multihousing owners. Real estate appraisers are the professionals who provide this valuation information, and they may use one of three techniques to calculate it: the cost approach, the market approach, or the income/economic analysis approach.

The cost approach calculates the value of the property relative to what it cost to construct. The market approach compares the value of the owner's property with the current value of other substantially similar properties. The income/economic analysis approach values the property based on the financial return the property provides to the owner.

ESTABLISHING RENT LEVELS

NEW AND EXISTING CONVENTIONALLY FINANCED PROPERTIES

In multihousing ownership, rent is the most common mechanism owners have to provide income. Although supplemental, or ancillary, income may be generated by such methods as on-premises laundry facilities or the rental of storage rooms within the property, it is the collection of rent that provides the mainstay income for multihousing owners. Thus setting the appropriate level of rent and collecting the rent on time and in full are critical to the owner's objectives and hence to the property manager's performance.

In conventionally financed properties, the considerations that go into establishing rent levels generally include the rental target market profile (i.e., low, middle, or high income); the desirability and status appeal of the property (as measured by location, age of the property, amenities, curb appeal, and maintenance); the individual unit being rented (its size, amenities, and other features); the costs to operate the property; comparable or competitive rents (the rents charged by competing comparable neighboring properties); and market conditions and what the marketplace will bear.

Figure 4–1 provides a chart to determine comparable rent values. The basic idea of the chart is that it allows for a comparison of rental rates by using a value assigned to each fea-

Figure 4–1. Estimates of Market Rental by Comparison

Anticipated start of occupancy ______________ **Date** ______________ **Initial** ______________

Property name Address	**Subject Property**									
		Adjustments*			**Adjustments***			**Adjustments***		
	Data	**Data**	**-**	**+**	**Data**	**-**	**+**	**Data**	**-**	**+**
Units in category										
Unit type										
Square feet										
Bedrooms										
Baths										
Balcony										
Bsmt/garage/carport										
Patio										
Dishwasher										
Washer/dryer										
Carpet/drapes										
Air-conditioning										
Other										
Utilities Incl.										
Gas, heat, A-C, appl.										
Electricity, lights, heat, A-C, appliances										
Amenities										
Age/Obsol./Cond.										
Management										
Quality construction										
Pool/clubhouse										
Misc. Rec. Facilities										
Location										
Other										
Sauna										
Exercise Room										
Tennis Court										
Playground										
Trend										
Rental rate										
Total plus adjustments										
Total minus adjustments										

* In the adjustments column, enter dollar amounts by which subject development varies from comparable development. If subject's consideration is better, enter the amount in the plus column. If subject is inferior, enter amount in the minus column. The net adjustment is added to or subtracted from rental of competitive property to determine market rental of subject property.

ture of each apartment being compared. For example, a dollar value is assigned to the presence of a balcony in the subject apartment. A comparable apartment that does not have a balcony would get a minus of that amount in the balcony category. The subject apartment's comparative value is arrived at by assigning values to each feature and then putting those values into the plus or minus category depending on whether the subject apartment has or does not have that feature. The net adjustment is then added to or subtracted from the rental of the competitive property to determine the market rental of the subject property.

A combination of all of the considerations that go into establishing rent levels (i.e., target market profile, property desirability and status, the individual unit, operating costs, comparable rents, and the market conditions) constitutes a thorough market analysis that will allow the owner and the manager to come up with rents that will attract prospective renters while allowing the manager to maintain the property and the owner to make a profit. The attitudes and policies of the owner toward the maintenance of the property, the people who rent there, and the profit the owner desires to make also play important roles in how rent levels are established.

FEDERALLY-ASSISTED AND PUBLIC HOUSING DEVELOPMENTS

In federally assisted and public housing developments, low-income residents are usually required to pay a certain percent of their income for rent in accordance with the latest approved rent schedule for that particular type of development. These schedules are based on comparable market analyses and the individual development's needs. The amount of rent charged in these types of developments generally has nothing to do with the condition of the property or the size of the apartment being rented and is established without exception by the government agency that owns the development.

CHANGES IN RENT

Market conditions do change, and it does happen that even the most carefully calculated rent pricing is mistaken. For example, during the rent-up phase when apartments are being rented for the first time in a newly constructed or newly renovated property, the owner or the manager may assume that a certain line of apartments is renting quickly because that line is particularly desirable. However, the reality may be that the rent being charged for those apartments is below market rate. When units are underpriced, it is important to raise the rent at least to market value as quickly as possible. This must be done carefully so as not to cross the line and wind up overpricing the units.

Conversely, if a particular line of apartments is difficult to fill during rent-up, it may mean that the rent is higher than market rate. In this case, the owner and the manager should first do what they can to increase the value of the apartment until its value equals the rent being charged. A decrease in rent should be considered only after it is determined that no improvements to the apartment can be made to bring it in line with the rent being charged. Residents will rarely complain if the people who move in after them pay more than they do for the same or for a substantially similar unit. But it's certain they will balk if the people who move in after them pay less. Should a rent reduction become necessary, the manager may therefore also want to consider some type of refund or concession arrangement with existing residents in that line.

In existing conventionally financed properties, inflation and higher operating costs, a high percentage of vacancies in apartments that are ready and available to be rented, a high percentage of delinquencies in rent payments, the amounts of the last rent increase or decrease in the property, and the availability of equal or similar accommodations for more or less rent in neighboring properties are all factors in determining possible upward or downward adjustments in rent levels. The analysis of appropriate rental rates should be an on-going practice, especially in response to significant changes in market conditions. That said, for best resident relations, rent adjustments should be made only once a year on the resident's move-in anniversary, and residents should be given at least two months' advance written notice of the adjustment.

APPROVAL OF CHANGES IN RENT IN VARIOUS TYPES OF PROPERTIES

Owner Approval

The need for the owner to approve any change in a rent schedule depends on the wording of the management agreement. The agreement requirements must be followed exactly.

Government Approval in Government-assisted Developments

HUD (the U.S. Department of Housing and Urban Development) and FmHA (Farmer's Home Administration) handbooks provide instructions for the preparation, submission, and approval of rent increases at assisted developments. Most assistance programs use the government's annual adjustment factor (AAF) system for determining rent increases, and most require approval from the HUD area office to increase rents more than the annual adjustment factor guidelines. In all cases, notice of a rent increase must be posted in the development 30 days in advance of the increase's proposed effective date. Should rents decrease, which sometimes happens, the decrease must go into effect immediately (there is no 30-day notice period), and residents will pay the lower amount when the rent is due.

Bond-financed Developments

The regulatory agreement for the development defines any restrictions on changes in rent rates in developments that have been financed with bonds.

Rent Regulation

Rent regulation (rent control and rent stabilization) programs were put into effect in certain markets during eras of negative economic conditions. The purpose of rent regulation was to help people afford rental housing and to champion the position of renters at a time when most leases favored the owner/landlord. Where rent regulation is still in place, it continues to limit the amount of rent an owner can charge and may provide occupancy succession rights and other renter rights that do not apply to deregulated and unregulated properties. In most instances, rent regulation has been shown to be counterproductive in that it provides disincentives for property maintenance and for new construction. Changes in rent-regulated properties are administered by local governing bodies on an annual basis. Managers of rent-regulated apartments and/or buildings should consult legal counsel for the specifics of the regulations with which they must comply.

NOTIFYING PROPERTY STAFF OF A REVISED RENT SCHEDULE

The property staff should be notified as soon as a rent schedule is revised because the staff members bear responsibility for implementing the increase in accordance with the established timetable. Increases normally occur when new residents sign their leases and existing residents sign lease renewals. In some cases, the lease may contain a provision that allows an interim increase prior to the expiration of the lease. In these cases, the additional rent increase can be effective for all residents after giving proper notice, usually 60 days.

The property manager should notify the staff of a rent change in writing and include an explanation of why the change is necessary. The property staff are more likely to explain an increase to residents in a positive way if they understand the rationale for the increase themselves.

The staff notification of rent change (Fig. 4–2) can provide this documented information for a rent increase or decrease. The form requires that the new gross potential rent (GPR) be computed and compared with the previous GPR. This comparison ensures that the new rent figures are correct.

The property manager must be able to calculate the property's GPR to determine how efficiently the property is operating. GPR is calculated by adding the current rent of all apartments in the property. For example, take an apartment community with 150 two-bedroom units. Say that 90 of the units are priced at $1,000 per month, and the remaining 60 are priced at $900 per month. To find the monthly GPR, the manager would multiply 90 by $1,000 ($9,000), and then multiply 60 by $900 ($54,000), and then add for a grand total monthly GRP of $144,000. This GPR informs the owner and the manager of the maximum potential rent if the property were 100 percent occupied and every resident paid on time and in full.

The "special provisions" section of the staff notification of rent change form can advise the staff of any special conditions concerning the increase (e.g., that it is effective for new residents only or effective for lease renewals at some future date, etc.).

The approved HUD or FmHA rent schedule (Form 92458) is used to convey rent change information to assist property personnel.

FORMAL NOTICE TO RESIDENTS OF RENT INCREASE AND EFFECTIVE DATE

Usually, a resident is entitled to notice of rent increase 60 days before the rent due date on which the increase becomes effective. The effective date is generally the lease expiration date. The 60-day notice (Fig. 4–3) should provide a resident with sufficient time to look elsewhere and to decide whether she/he intends to move. The resident should sign a new lease at the new rate if she/he remains.

Sending a 30-day reminder of the lease renewal (Fig. 4–4) is a service to the resident and sound management practice. The rent increase notices normally do not have to be sent by certified mail, but the property manager should check with a local attorney to be sure that the property's practices and procedures meet local legal requirements for notice.

Some management organizations discuss rent increases with existing residents personally and at the same time encourage them to sign a new lease. Policy differs with each management organization. In any case, the rent increase policy of the property should be spelled out in the property's operations manual.

Residents who live in a conventional property that is not subject to rent regulation and who are not satisfied with their rent increases may appeal to the management company and the owner and threaten to move. This threat is the ultimate weapon possessed by a resident, and it can be quite effective in overbuilt markets.

In assisted developments there are two categories of rent increases: annual adjustment, which is dictated by the agency governing the development, and budget based. A budget-based increase must be requested by the owner (and may be requested more than annually if circumstances justify). The procedure for a budget-based rent increase application requires that the application be posted in a conspicuous place in the development. The application to HUD must state that the application has been posted. Upon receipt of the application, HUD will take no action for 30 days, during which time residents may refute the rent increase request.

LARGE RENT INCREASES

Management company procedures may require that the property manager personally contact residents whenever a rent increase exceeds a certain dollar amount or percent of current rent. The purpose of these contacts is to explain carefully the reason for the increase and to influence each resident to renew her/his lease. The property manager should discuss these reasons with the senior manager prior to the contacts.

The property manager or senior manager should prepare an expense analysis form (Figure 4–5 shows a sample for a hypothetical property) for the property manager's use during these personal contacts if she/he believes it will help to explain the reasons for the increase. Even if it is not used for this purpose, the expense analysis reinforces the need for the increase for the manager.

The expense analysis includes a table that shows a breakdown of a rent dollar by expense category and the percent change in each of these categories. The pie chart (Fig. 4–6) shows what percentage of each dollar goes to each of the various expense categories. Often the form shows that rents are increasing by a smaller percentage than the increases in other expenses. It also shows the small amount that goes to reserves and profit and thus helps to combat the usual beliefs about landlord profiteering.

Figure 4–2. Staff Notification of Rent Change

To: Property Manager and Staff ____________ Date: ____________

From: Senior Property Manager ____________ Copies to: Accounting Department

Subject: Rent Increase (Decrease) ____________

This memo is to advise you and the staff of the following rent increases (decreases), effective ____________

Unit type	No. of units	Current monthly rent	Current monthly GPR	New monthly rent	New monthly GPR	Monthly Increase in GPR
1 BR UP						
1 BR DN						
2 BR UP						
2 BR DN						
2 TH						
3 TH						
4 TH						
Total						

Per unit average monthly increase ____________

Special provisions ____________

____

(Senior Property Manager signature)

FIGURE 4-3. Sixty-day Lease Renewal and Rent Increase Notice

(Date)

(Name)
(Address)
(City, State, Zip)

Dear ______________________________:

We want to remind you of the approaching expiration of your lease and invite you to continue to make your home with us by signing a new one-year lease. We have set aside ________(Date)________ for lease signing.

To conserve your time, we will be happy to arrange a specific appointment on that date. Please call us to arrange one at your earliest convenience.

As you know, individuals and businesses alike have been plauged with a high rate of inflation. We make every effort to control costs while continually striving to provide high-quality service. However, we have felt the impact of rising costs and find it necessary to adjust our rental rates accordingly. The new rent for your apartment is $ ____________.

We appreciate having you as a resident and look forward to seeing you on ______(Date)______ to process the necessary paperwork.

Sincerely,

____
(Property Manager Signature)

FIGURE 4-4. Sixty-day Lease Renewal and Rent Increase Notice

(Date)

(Name)
(Address)
(City, State, Zip)

Dear ______________________________:

Recently, we notified you of the approaching expiration of your lease and the scheduled date for signing a new lease. To date, you have not signed your new lease.

If for some reason you have decided not to renew your residency, please contact me directly. Remember that one of the requirements for a full refund of your security deposit is a 30-day written notice of your intent to vacate.

As mentioned in our previous letter, we appreciate having you as a resident and look forward to having you remain with us. However, we must have a newly signed lease on file. Please come in or contact us by phone immediately so we can process the necessary paperwork.

Sincerely,

____
(Property Manager Signature)

Figure 4–5. Expense Analysis

CLYDE ESTATES

	Annual Budget	Dollars per unit	Percent	Percent change from previous year
Income				
Rents	$1,285,240	4342	97.187	150.000
Charges and other	28,680	97	2.183	-0.300
Expenses				
Management fees	52,557	178	4.000	0.000
Administrative	44,369	150	3.377	2.500
Advertising	49,680	168	3.781	7.500
Payroll	115,645	391	8.802	4.250
Building maintenance	51,060	173	3.886	6.000
Common area maintenance	58,425	197	4.447	2.000
Utilities	65,548	221	4.989	3.688
Insurance	30,044	102	2.287	0.000
Taxes	107,000	361	8.144	12.500
Mortgages	580,464	1,961	44,178	0.100
Owner's distributions	159,128	538	12.111	-2.500

FIGURE 4-6. Expense Breakdown

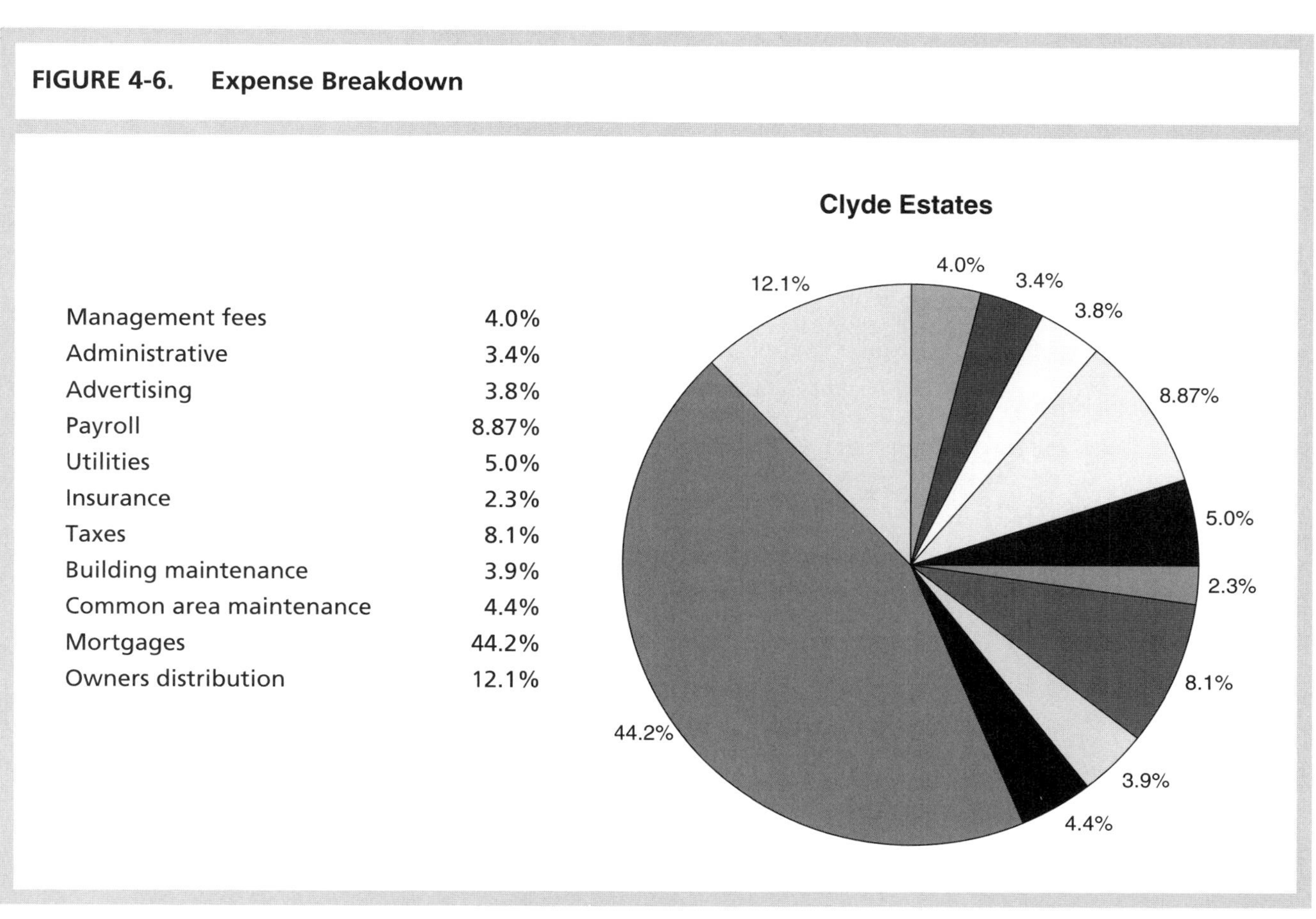

In addition to the specific reasons for the increase, the property manager could explain to the renter that management appreciates the resident and wants her/him to remain at the property, that management is eager to maintain its excellent service and high standards for the property's appearance, and that specific actions (examples should be cited) have been taken recently to improve the appearance of the property and/or the service rendered to residents.

This contact presents an excellent opportunity to determine the resident's degree of satisfaction with the property, to correct any problem discovered, and to restore any lost good will. The property manager must take immediate action on any legitimate complaints discovered during this visit.

The personal contact in either the resident's apartment or townhouse or in the rental office should not replace the written notice of increase but should supplement it. According to the terms of many leases, a 30- or 60-day written notice is required before raising rents. The written notice can be given to the resident at the time of the manager's visit to explain the increase.

The property manager should immediately report to the senior manager any problems encountered when residents learn of this increase. The property manager also should send a personalized letter to any resident who objects to the rent increase (Fig. 4–7).

How long to follow the personal contact procedure depends on the renewal rate. If a high percentage of the leases are renewed, management policy may call for a reversion to the less time-consuming mail notification route. If lease renewal is slow, additional follow-up with residents, with the owner, and with the central management office is called for. The manager can record her/his experience in her/his lease renewal efforts on the lease conversion report (Fig. 4–8).

In addition to the renewals, the close rate on new leases also indicates the acceptability of a rent increase. The close rate is calculated by dividing the number of rentals for a given period—a week, for instance—by the traffic for that period. A declining close rate after a rent increase indicates its impact. Some impact is expected, but it should not be drastic enough to cause a serious vacancy problem. The property manager must determine the seriousness of the problem and whether the property is better off charging higher rents at a somewhat lower occupancy level.

CALCULATING OCCUPANCY/VACANCY RATES AND DETERMINING RENT INCREASE PERCENTAGES

Under all circumstances in which a rent increase is being considered, it is important to bear in mind that properties can sometimes fare better economically and produce a higher net operating income with higher rents at a lower occupancy rate than with lower rents at 100 percent occupancy. Conversely, sometimes the opposite will be true. To know which will be the case, the property manager should first calculate the occupancy/vacancy rate, and then calculate the effective gross income generated by a range of rent/vacancy permutations.

Occupancy/vacancy percentages are figures used in every level of property management. These percentages form the basis for determining many operational and budgeting factors and are among the factors considered in the property's refinancing or sale value.

Occupancy/vacancy are always expressed as percentages (or a part of 100). As an example, say an apartment community has 350 units, of which 320 are currently occupied. The occupancy rate is calculated by dividing the number of occupied apartment (320 in this case) by the number of total apartments (350 in this case), yielding a quotient of 0.92. To express this quotient as a percentage, multiply by 100 for an occupancy rate of 92 percent. The vacancy rate is then calculated by subtracting the occupancy rate from 100 percent (for a vacancy rate of 8 percent in this case).

Many property management companies also will want to determine future occupancy percentages. This is an important percentage to know as it provides an indication of where the property is likely to be heading in terms of occupancy. Arriving at this future occupancy percentage will require additional data, such as the number of apartments that are expected to be vacant by move-out or evictions in a given period of time and the number of apartments where new move-in have been scheduled for the same period of time. The formula for calculating future occupancy is as follows:

> Current number of occupied apartments MINUS the number of apartments scheduled to become vacant in a given period of time PLUS the number of apartments that are pre-leased for the same period of time EQUALS total future occupied apartments DIVIDED BY the total number of apartments MULTIPLIED BY 100 EQUALS future occupied percentage.

As an example of this formula, take the 350-unit community in which 320 units are occupied. There are now 12 residents on notice, 3 in legal, and 8 units are pre-leased. Plugging in this data to the formula above produces the following equation:

$$320 - 15 + 8 = 313 \div 350 = 0.90 \times 100 = 90\%$$

Based on this calculation, the future anticipated occupancy rate is 90 percent and the future anticipated vacancy rate is 10 percent.

To use occupancy/vacancy rate information to help determine whether, and how much, to increase rent, follow this logic. Say a 100-unit property has a current 90 percent occupancy with a rent of $500. (For the sake of this example, it is assumed that all of the 100 units rent for the same $500 each.) Based on projected occupancy/vacancy rates, market information, and knowledge of competing neighboring properties, the manager projects that if the rent were to go to $525, occupancy would decrease to 87 percent. And if rent increased to $550, occupancy would further decrease to 85 percent. To know if and how to adjust rent levels for maximum income, the following calculations should be made based on 12 months of rent payments:

$$\$500 \times 100 \times 12 = \$600{,}000 \times .90 = \$540{,}000$$

$$\$525 \times 100 \times 12 = \$630{,}000 \times .87 = \$548{,}100$$

$$\$550 \times 100 \times 12 = \$660{,}000 \times .85 = \$561{,}000.$$

In the case above, increasing the rent by $50 a month with a simultaneous 5 percent increase in vacancy actually produces greater income than the lower rent at a higher occupancy rate.

FIGURE 4-7. Letter Explaining Rent Increase

(Date)

(Name)
(Address)
(City, State, Zip)

Dear ______________________________:

Thank you for your letter dated ______________ regarding the rent increase. I can understand your concern. (Name of Property) has experienced a continuing increase in our operating expenses.

We have absorbed some of the increase in the past two years, but we must increase rents to maintain the quality of service we believe is important for every resident. This decision was reached with great reluctance on our part, but the increase is necessary.

To control expenses and reduce the amount of any necessary rent increase, property managers must continually look for more efficient methods of operation, including quantity purchasing. We pride ourselves on the service that we provide to our residents and on the pleasant appearance of our apartment communities. The only way to continue to maintain these standards is to increase rents.

We thank you for your long-term residency, and we want to continue serving you. Our 12-month lease policy assures you of no interim rent increases. As a long-term resident, you receive a $______________ discount compared with the monthly rents charged to newer residents.

Sincerely,

____
(Property Manager Signature)

Figure 4–8. Lease Conversion Report

Week ending ______________________________

Development ______________________________ Location ______________________________

This report covers the results of personal contacts with residents whose leases will expire and whose rents will be increased in excess of a certain percentage. Refer to the procedures manual for specific details.

	Unit Type	Rent		Resident Reaction				
Name		Old	New	Yes	No	Maybe*	Resident Comments	

Summary Total Contacts ______________ yes ______________ no ______________ maybe______________

____________________ (Date)

______________________________ (Property Manager Signature)

* Carry "maybes" forward to the next report.

However, in another scenario based on the same hypothetical building, if rent were to increase to $525 and occupancy were to decrease by a full 5 percent to 85 percent, rental income would be reduced to $535,500 ($525 × 100 × 12 × .85 = $535,500). And if rent were further to increase to $550 with another 5 percent decrease in occupancy, rental income would be even lower at $528,000 ($550 × 100 × 12 = $660,000 × .80 = $528,000). In these cases, keeping the rent at $500 is the most profitable course of action.

By using these calculation techniques, the owner and manager can determine if and how to adjust rent rates to produce the greatest possible effective gross income.

RENT INCREASE/DECREASE GUIDELINES

Initial rents during rent-up for a conventional property should be determined by reviewing rents charged at competitive properties, making appropriate adjustments, and then considering any existing vacancies.

The rent-up procedures might call for considering a possible rent increase and/or decrease by unit type when the property is approximately 33 percent rented, again at 66 percent, and finally at 95 percent. Considering rent increases and/or decreases at specific periods allows a review of the rent-up rate by each unit type. The review highlights possible out-of-line conditions and where rent adjustments are needed. Generally, this action is taken by the senior manager, perhaps after consultation with the property manager.

When conventional properties have an apparent excess of units that are not generating rent (i.e., vacant/not assigned units that are vacant and have not been assigned to an incoming renter, and vacant/assigned units in which the current renter has expressed the intention to vacate and the unit has not yet been assigned to an incoming renter), the property manager should perform an analysis of rental rates and a market comparative analysis to maximize NOI with a particular emphasis on gross effective income. The rent increase review form (Fig. 4–9) and the apartment rent comparables form discussed below (Fig. 4–10) will be helpful in these analyses and calculations.

Rent adjustment guidelines include any special rent concessions based on resident longevity, for example, giving a $10 discount from the rent in effect when a resident signs a fourth-year lease renewal. In markets that have major military installations, special rents and lease provisions may cater to the needs of military residents. Military residents are general short-term renters because the average assignment at any one post is 18 to 36 months. However, those communities that do well in serving their needs can benefit greatly from referrals. (For a discussion about military housing, see Chapter 11, Government Assisted and Insured Housing and Military Housing.)

Rent increase review (Fig. 4–9)—The rent increase review is completed whenever consideration is given to increasing rents at a conventional property. The review includes a recap of the last three rent increases, the present status of units that are vacant and becoming vacant, these units as a percentage of their unit type, competitive rent levels, and vacancy information. The review also contains financial information to help determine how much of an increase is necessary to achieve cash flow and profit objectives.

Apartment rent comparables (Fig. 4–10)—This form is a convenient device for recording all of the pertinent information on competitive properties so that the appropriate adjustments can be made in comparing their rents with the rents for the subject property. The information on this form includes square footage and rental rate per square footage, age of the property, appliances, amenities, who pays utilities, and comments regarding the landscaping, overall appearance, and physical condition of the property. The data from the apartment rent comparables should be entered in the estimates of market rental by comparison form shown in Figure 4–1, and that form should then be completed for each type of apartment in the subject property (studio, one-bedroom, two-bedroom, etc.).

Calculating rental rate per square foot—Knowing how to calculate rental rate per square foot is important in making valid comparisons between apartments and also because many financial institutions use price per square foot of an apartment or of the total community as an indicator of the value of the property in comparison with other comparable properties. To calculate the rental rate per square foot in a given apartment, first find the total square footage of the apartment. This is done by multiplying the width of each room by its length (which provides the room's square footage) and then adding the square footage of all the rooms together. The apartment's rental rate is then divided by the apartment's total square footage for an answer in dollars and cents, as shown in the example below.

Take an apartment with a price of $1,200 per month and square footage of 900 square feet.

$1200.00\900 = $1.21 per square foot

IMPLEMENTING RENT INCREASES

When a decision is made to increase rent at conventional properties, the increase should be implemented immediately for new residents and as leases expire for existing residents. When the decision is not to increase rents, regular rent rate reviews should be conducted in the future to determine if circumstances have changed.

At conventional properties where rent-up is completed, the rent increase review should commence about nine months after the effective date of the last increase. The lead time might be less than nine months for some management companies; it depends upon the length of time necessary for the review process. The process might require 30 days prior to expiration. Therefore, the increase must be decided no longer than 10 months after the last increase to ensure its implementation before any leases are renewed.

Managers at assisted developments should consider rent increases during preparation of the annual budget. If the budget reflects that the cash flow objectives for limited dividend developments will not be accomplished, an analysis based on HUD or FmHA guidelines should determine if a rent increase is justified. As part of the routine, the senior manager and the property manager should discuss the financial statements each month to determine if a rent increase should be considered. (See the discussions of financial reporting and monitoring and budgets below.)

Figure 4–9. Rent Increase Review

	1 Up	1 Dn	2 Up	2 Dn	2 TH	3 TH	Total
Adjusted on 7-00 to	$400	$410	$460	$470	$520	$600	
Adjusted on 7-01 to	$420	$430	$430	$485	$550	$635	
Proposed Rents	$440	$440	$495	$510	$575	$665	
Vacant Not Assigned	0	1	2	0	0	0	3
Intents Not Assigned	0	2	1	0	0	0	3
Total VNA and INA	0	3	3	0	0	0	6
Total Units	58	58	42	42	58	28	286
INA/VNA as % of Total		6%	7%				3%
Other Charges							
Woods	$20	Lake	$20		Fireplace	$20	
End Unit	$10	Pet	$10		Carport	$15	

Competition (Details on attached apartment rent comparable form)

Development	1 Up	1 Dn	2 Up	2 Dn	2 TH	3 Br	Vacancy 2 Br un
A							6
B Loft	$400	$400	$485	$495	$570	$645	5-6
							4

Information on competition provided by ______________________ Date ______________

Budget Deficit	(8,416)	Deficit most recent month*	($1,240) Feb.
Number of Units	286	Deficit last month*	(644) Jan.
Deficit per Unit	29	Deficit current year*	(1,884)

*Out of Pocket Losses

Rental manager's recommendation and comments:
She thinks an increase would be acceptable at this time.

Regional manager's recommendation and comments
Recommended we proceed.

Prepared by: ______________________

Figure 4–10. Apartment Rent Comparables

Name ______________________________ Address ____________________________________

Type of unit: ☐ Garden ☐ Club ☐ High-rise ☐ Townhouse

Management or owner _____________________________ Phone _______________________

Year completed 1st phase __________ 2nd phase __________ 3rd phase __________

No. Units	No. Bedrooms	No. Baths	Vacancies	Sq. Ft.	Monthly Rent Unfurnished	Rent per Sq./Ft.	Avg. Absorp./wk

Total units ________________ Type utilities included All Gas Electric

Included in rent

☐ Range and oven
☐ Refrigerator, size _________
☐ Dishwasher
☐ Garbage disposal
☐ Washer connection

☐ Air-conditioning
☐ Carpet
☐ Fireplace
☐ Drapes or rods
☐ Patio/balcony
☐ Additonal storage
☐ Parking space unit

☐ Garage/carport
☐ Laundry room
☐ Clubhouse
☐ Pool
☐ Play area
☐ Sauna baths
☐ Other __________________

Occupancy Date _____________ Percent occupied _______________

Amount of extra charge

Pets _______ Children _______ Fireplace ______ Extra den _______

Other _______

Comments

Landscaping ____

____

Overall appearance ____

____

Physical-locational utility ____

____

Condition ____

____

A rent increase should be considered whenever an assisted or conventional property is not earning satisfactory cash flow and/or not covering expenses. In addition, the property manager should conduct interim rent increase reviews as expenses or conditions change, such as a substantial increase in the cost of utilities or in taxes. Early management awareness of significant increases in expenses allows appropriate action to be taken to secure a rent increase if that appears necessary.

Ordinarily, no increase or decrease should be implemented at any property without prior approval from the senior manager and sometimes the owner, depending on the degree of authority included in the management agreement.

The exact procedure for requesting a rent increase from HUD or FmHA for assisted developments varies with the type of program and is detailed in the appropriate HUD or FmHA handbook. This procedure should be clearly spelled out step by step in the property's operations manual and kept up to date.

Whenever a property manager is initiating a rent increase request or preparing a budget at an assisted development, she/he should consider increasing the monthly amount deposited into the reserve for replacement account. The purpose of this deposit increase is to compensate for inflationary factors and to replenish any deficiency from use of the funds. The local HUD or FmHA offices have authority to permit these increases.

Prior to the implementation of any rent increase, the property manager should be sure that the property is operating in an efficient, professional manner and that everything possible is being done to control expenses in line with maintenance standards. Several checkpoints can be used to challenge expenses and ensure that they represent an efficient operation. One such checkpoint is a comparison of expenses with those provided by various industry associations.

IMPLEMENTING RENT DECREASES

If the vacant units not assigned and intents not assigned within a property appear to be excessive, the property manager should consider performing another market analysis to maximize NOI. A temporary reduction in the rent for these units could serve as an unadvertised closing tool. A later decision may be to use the reduction as an advertised special to build traffic but may backfire because broadcasting rent reductions may alert prospects that the property is having vacancy problems. (See Chapter 7, Marketing Rental Housing and the Marketing Plan for additional marketing information.)

If a rent reduction is decided upon, the property manager should contact those who have given an intent to vacate in units where the rents have been reduced to determine if they would stay at the lower rents. Persons who have visited the rental office within the last few weeks and who have not yet rented should also be contacted. Every effort should be made to rent the affected units.

Whenever existing residents inquire at a conventional property about whether a reduction applies to their rent, the property manager has two choices. She/he can either renegotiate the existing lease or tell them that their rent must remain as agreed on in their lease. The more market-oriented approach is to void the existing lease and renegotiate a new lease for a new period of six months or a year. This approach follows from the philosophy that an existing resident should have the "best" deal available. However, if the company's philosophy is to take all leases to term, the property manager can provide a form letter for these residents to sign (Fig. 4–11) entitling them to the same reduction in rent when they sign the new lease.

The property manager should sign the letter entitling the resident to the discount, and the resident also should immediately sign the letter. A manager should hold this offer open to the resident only for a limited time. This letter allows the property to benefit from any increases between the present time and lease renewal time. Generally, present residents should not be notified specifically of any rent reduction. This policy usually should be implemented only when the rental person is approached by existing residents concerning a rent reduction and only in unassisted properties.

RENT COLLECTION

THE PROPERTY MANAGER AND RENT COLLECTION

Some properties bill their renters monthly while others adopt the policy that the rent is the same amount and due on the same day throughout the term of the lease so a bill is unnecessary. Some properties allow renters to pay rent at the on-site management office while others require that rent checks be mailed to the central management office or a designated bank lockbox, and still others provide for direct or electronic transfer of funds for rent payment. Some properties accept all forms of payment, including personal checks, bank checks, third-party checks, money orders, credit cards, and even cash, while others have strict policies governing the type of payment they will accept. Some properties offer discounts for rent paid in advance while others neither accept advance rent nor offer any kind of rent consideration.

Whatever the rent payment policy of the individual property, collecting the rent is the most fundamental task a property manager performs. Rent is the income stream for the property. Assuming it is sufficient to do so, rent pays all of the property's operating expenses; most, if not all, of its debt service and related expenses; and provides a profit to the owner. Without effective rent collection, nothing else matters because nothing else can get done. The property manager must therefore have an efficient and accurate method of monitoring rent collection, and the manager's approach to the collection of rent must be a firm, positive attitude that makes clear that the rent must be paid on time and in full when it is due. The property manager also must bear in mind that failure to implement an effective rent payment monitoring and rent collection policy is often the catalyst for owners to seek new management.

The rent collection effort should begin long before the first sign of delinquency. It should begin at the time of initial application, and it should continue throughout new resident processing. In every step of the process the leasing and management staff should consistently remind the potential resident of the property's rent collection policy. Emphasis should

FIGURE 4-11. Rent Reduction Agreement

As a resident of ___(Name of Property),___ I agree to renew my lease upon its expiration date on ___(Date)___. I understand that my rent will be $__________ less than the rent being charged new residents at the time of my lease renewal.

____
(Resident Signature)

____
____
____
(Address)

____
(Property Manager Signature)

____
(Date)

Copy to: Resident
Resident on file

be give to the due date and the necessity for prompt payment. This policy also should be clearly stated in the lease and in the resident handbook. Most managers find that proper applicant screening and strong rent payment orientation eliminate most rent collection problems. (See Chapter 8, Processing Applications, Move-in and Move-out Procedures, and Resident Relations and the Resident Handbook.)

To further reinforce the rent collection process, some management companies post their rent collection policy in a prominent location in the rental office (Fig. 4–12). HUD recommends this posting in all its assisted developments.

Many multihousing management software programs make monitoring rent payments and delinquencies as easy as typing in a command. (See the discussions on computers in financial management, below, and computers in the management office in Chapter 9, Managing the Site Office and the Operations Manual.)

PAYING RENT ON TIME AND IN FULL AND LATE RENT PAYMENT

Paying rent on time and in full is a habit just like any other and, once formed, tends to be self-perpetuating. Residents can be influenced to pay rent on time and in full when the property manager establishes mutual respect and applies collection techniques consistently and in a professional manner. Most managers find that renters whose first rent payments are on time and in full will be regular, dependable rent payers, while those who make late and/or incomplete initial payments will be chronically delinquent in the payment of their rent.

When a renter falls behind in the timing and/or total of rent payments that are due, the manager should immediately inaugurate a campaign of formal written notices and frequent contact in person and by telephone. The most effective collection work is done face-to-face by the property manager directly with the resident. The manager should initiate contact no later than five days after the rent is due and ask pleasantly but forcefully for payment. Formal written notices should be issued as part of the manager's conversations to permit expedient legal action if the rent payment is not forthcoming.

The property's operations manual should contain specific details regarding delinquent rent collection procedures. For example, it may state that the resident must pay a $50 late charge if rent is not paid by the third of the month. Between the third and the tenth of the month, the procedure may call for personal, telephone, and mail notices. No later than the tenth of the month, the manager would prepare and serve the necessary papers to initiate eviction proceedings and follow up with the property's attorney to ensure a speedy eviction. Most management companies require senior manager approval for exceptions to the rent collection policy. This rule makes the property manager less susceptible to residents' nonpayment excuses.

SPECIFIC RENT COLLECTION FUNCTIONS

The property manager must clearly understand that rent collection is an integral part of her/his job responsibilities, and rent collection responsibilities should be written into the manager's job description and performance evaluations. Further enforcement of this responsibility can result if the manager's bonus is at least partially based upon collections, provided that the bonus is structured properly. (See Chapter 3, On the Front Line: The Property Manager for a discussion of the property manager's responsibilities and structuring bonus incentives.)

As indicated above, the property manager's rent collection function begins at the time a prospect applies to rent a unit in the property. There is a direct relationship between the processing of the application and the eventual collection of rent. Done properly, a thorough screening at the time of

FIGURE 4-12. Sample Rent Collection Policy*

- All rent is due and payable on the first day of each month.
- You will receive a rent statement and a self-addressed envelope on or around the 25th of the month for the rent that is due on the 1st of the following month.
- Make your payment payable to the property and return your payment in the self-addressed envelope provided with the rent statement.
- A late charge will be assessed if your rent is not received in the home office by the 5th of the month. If the rent is not paid by the 10th if the month, the eviction process will be started.
- If your check is returned for insufficient funds or any other reason, you must immediately pay to the rental office the amount of the check plus any related bank fees and the late charge. Payment must be made by certified check or money order, and all payments to the property for the next six months also must be by one of these forms of certified funds.
- Managers of HUD-assisted developments should consult HUD procedures for rent collection policies.

application will eliminate most rent collection problems. For example, the property manager should be alert to the warning signs of poor rent payment history at prior addresses, insufficient income (rent more than 30 percent of gross income), and a marginal or poor credit rating. Each of these may signal that the prospect is a bad risk.

Once the selection and screening process has been completed and the resident is accepted for occupancy, the resident must be educated yet again about the property's rent payment policy and still again when the lease is signed.

After carefully screening applicants and educating new residents about the rent payment policy, the property manager must carry out sound policies and procedures for collecting rent that is not paid by its due date. These policies must be specific and applied fairly, consistently, and firmly. The system should not allow for excuses, problems, or deals. The truth is, many managers know each month who will be late with the rent. But without exception, immediate action must be taken when the rent becomes delinquent. This action is taken to protect the owner's interest and also because in a number of states, if a property manager allows consistent late payments, she/he is taken to have modified the term of the lease agreement by practice to allow late payment and cannot later collect the rent on time.

When a renter is permitted to delay payment of rent, the results are all negative:

- Other residents find out and eventually the nonpayment or slow payment can mushroom and spread throughout the property
- Collection and cash flow deteriorate
- The resident suffers because she/he owes more than can ever be repaid
- The residents who pay promptly suffer because the property eventually has to raise everyone's rent to compensate for those who do not pay at all or do not pay on time
- The manager is not performing her/his job in a satisfactory manner

The manager must therefore understand that long-term trouble begins the first time a resident is allowed to fall behind in paying rent. For many renters, once they slip behind in their rent, catching up is difficult if not impossible. So when a resident gives a hard-luck story about why she/he cannot pay the rent, the property manager should suggest borrowing the amount due from a bank, a loan company, a family member, or a friend. The manager must remember that her/his job is not to finance residents but to collect rent when it is due and that collecting rent from some residents is a contest of pressure. Always, the creditor who exerts the greatest pressure on the resident is the one who is going to get paid. If the resident absolutely cannot or will not pay, the manager must then remove that resident from the unit because a habitable unit waiting and ready for someone who can pay for it is far better than one occupied by somebody who cannot.

Residents often use poor maintenance as a reason for not paying rent. But much of the time, this excuse is merely a smoke screen for an inability to pay. Many of these complaints are heard for the first time only after the rent is past due. If the request for maintenance is a long-standing one, the manager is in the best position to know the seriousness of the request and whether it was a problem before the renter became a delinquent nonpayer.

In summary, the enforcement of sound rent collection procedures is absolutely vital to the management and long-term viability of a property. If the property is managed in an honest manner, the manager should not be afraid or embarrassed to demand the rent due to the owner. Rather, the manager should be confident that one of two things eventually will occur if the rent collection procedures discussed above are followed: either the resident will pay all the rent due or the resident will vacate the premises voluntarily or by eviction. Either is preferable to harboring a nonpaying renter.

RETURNED CHECKS

A check returned for insufficient funds puts the property manager in the same position as if the rent had not been paid at all. Immediately upon notification of a returned check, the property manager must institute standard collection proceedings against the resident. The manager also should be in contact with the resident to arrange for payment of the rent, any additional charges levied against the property by its bank for processing the returned item, and late charges.

As a general practice, the resident should be notified that from that payment forward, rent will only be accepted in the form of certified funds, money orders, or certified checks, for a minimum of six months. Moreover, a number of states have adopted statutes that make the passing of bad checks a crime. The manager should consider whether to avail herself/himself of these laws to assist in rent collection.

PAYMENT AGREEMENTS

Some management companies and/or owners allow property managers to make payment agreements with residents who are delinquent in their rent payments. This type of agreement should not be encouraged, but if it does take place it should be entered into only after the property manager has received express approval from the senior manager and/or owner on a case-by-case basis. Unfortunately, although some renters do truly intend to bring their accounts whole and are willing to promise that they will do so, such a promissory agreement is more often a stalling tactic that allows the delinquent renter to fall even further behind until there is no chance of ever catching up. The truth is, renters who cannot pay the rent should move to accommodations where they can.

That said, if the property manager does enter into a payment agreement with a renter, the manager should keep a written record of all contacts and promised payment dates so that she/he can follow up on whatever promises are made and take immediate action if the commitment is not honored. The delinquent rent collection status form (Fig. 4–13) has columns to record various follow-up actions. This form allows the manager to record the specific actions taken and promises made. It also allows the senior manager to review the collection efforts and provide appropriate counsel. Ideally, at the time a payment promise is made, the manager

Figure 4–13. Delinquent Rent Collection Status

____
Month of Report

____
Name of Development

T.C: Telephone Call
P.C.: Personal Contact
L.M.D.: Left Message on Door

Name	Address	Date Contacted Prior 10th	Date Contacted After 10th	Date Final Notice Was Posted	Money Offered to Move	Dates to Attorney or JP	Court Date	Court Results	Comments
	4121 Shady Oak Dr	T.C. 4/29 T.C. 5/11							4/29 - to pay 5/10 5/11 - to pay 5/12 Paid 5/12
	10159 Ellis Dr.	T.C. 4/29							4/29 to pay 5/2 Paid 5/2
	10111 E. 42nd St	T.C. 4/29 T.C. 5/6 T.C. 5/8	T.C.: 5/11 can't pay until 5/25			5/15 J.P.	5/30	Eviction	4/29 - to pay 5/5 5/6 - to pay 5/7 5/8 - to pay 5/10
	4236 Shady Oak	T.C. 4/29	T.C. 5/11						4/29 - to pay 5/10 5/11 - to pay 5/11 Paid 5/11
	1061 Ellis Dr.	T.C. 5/4							5/4 - NSF check to make good 5/6 Paid 5/6

should write and send a memo to the renter reiterating the renter's payment promise and the consequences for failing to keep it. In this way, the manager has a paper trail and the resident cannot say she/he did not have the same understanding of the promise as the manager.

At lease renewal time in a conventional property, the manager should consider residents' payment records before making a decision about whether to renew their leases. Any resident with more than two instances of late rent payment in the past year should be carefully reviewed prior to being offered a renewal lease. However, managers must remembers that all lease renewal practices must comply with state and local laws. Curious but true, some state laws do not recognize late payment as just cause for refusal to renew a lease. (See the discussion on leases below.)

Lease renewal procedures for federally assisted developments are discussed in HUD handbook 4350.3.

EVICTION

The property manager should begin the eviction process as a last resort but should not hesitate to initiate the eviction if all other rent collection procedures have failed. Having a vacant unit available for rent to a paying resident is better than having one occupied by a nonpaying resident.

Procedures for the eviction of residents for nonpayment of rent vary from state to state and may be determined by the lease or the law. The property manager should know the specific requirements in her/his state. This information, which is usually obtained with the assistance of the senior manager, should be confirmed and documented by a knowledgeable attorney.

Eviction proceedings normally should commence regardless of the reason why the rent has not been paid. Trouble begins when exceptions are made because word spreads quickly throughout the property that exceptions are made to the rent collection procedures.

EVICTION GUIDELINES

Ordinarily, the property and/or landlord/owner may not terminate a tenancy except for the reasons listed below. However, because termination of a lease is governed by law, these reasons may vary from state to state.

- Material noncompliance with the lease. This includes:
- One or more substantial violations of the lease, including subleasing without the owner's consent, nonpayment of rent or any other financial obligation specified in the lease beyond any grace period (Accepting or not accepting a rent payment after a demand for possession notice or a legal eviction process for nonpayment of rent has been filed with the local authorities may or may not negate the eviction and lease termination process. Individual state landlord/tenant laws should be consulted in such matters.)
- Repeated minor violations of the lease that disrupt the livability of the property, adversely affect the health or safety of any person or the right of any resident to quiet enjoyment of the lease premises and related property facilities, or interference with the management of the property. This includes payment of rent or other financial obligation under the lease after the due date but within the grace period. Repeated minor violations might include payment of rent after the due date but within the grace period enough times to have an adverse effect on the property.
- Material failure to carry out obligations under any state landlord and tenant act.

Tenancy may not be terminated for other good cause unless the owner has given the resident prior notice that such cause constitutes a basis for termination of occupancy. The termination notice must be in writing and must be set forth in the following way:

- The termination notice must state that the tenancy is terminated on a specific date
- The termination notice must state the reasons for the action with enough specificity to enable the resident to prepare a defense (If the tenancy is terminated because of the failure to pay rent, a notice stating the dollar amount of the balance due on the rent account and the date of such computation satisfies the requirement of specificity.)
- The termination notice must advise the resident that if a judicial proceeding for eviction is instituted, the resident may present a defense

In any judicial action instituted to evict residents, properties (the landlord/owner) can use only the grounds that are set forth in the termination notices. However, they can rely on grounds of which they had no knowledge at the time the termination notice was sent.

The required notice to a resident should be given in one of three ways:

- By sending a letter by both first class mail and certified mail (return receipt requested), properly stamped and addressed to the resident at her/his property address along with a proper return address. Sending the notice by both first class and certified mail helps to ensure that the resident receives at least one copy of the notice. Delivery by certified mail is required in a number of locations and is advisable everywhere. However, many residents will avoid picking up certified mail when they suspect what the contents are. Should that be the case, the fact that the first class letter was not returned is some proof to present to the judge that one copy was delivered.
- By serving a copy of the notice on any adult person opening the door at the leased dwelling.
- By posting a copy of the notice on the main door of the residence. Posting is generally allowed only in closely defined circumstances and is not allowed in some jurisdictions. The property manager should consult legal counsel for the specific local requirements.

The most common reasons for eviction cases to be dismissed are improper notice and improper service of the notice. The property manager should be well briefed by the property's attorney in proper use of notices and proper service before beginning the eviction process.

When termination of the tenancy is based on other causes, the termination notice should be in accordance with the termination provisions of the lease, but in no case can termination of the tenancy be earlier than allowable by applicable law. When the termination notice is based on material noncompliance with the lease or material failure to carry out obligations under a state landlord/tenant act, the time of service should be in accordance with the lease and state law. An attorney should be consulted throughout the eviction process to ensure the property's compliance with all applicable regulations and laws.

With regard to legal and allowable eviction procedures in assisted developments, the property manager must consult with a local attorney and the HUD or FmHA handbook for the most current eviction guidelines. In nonstandard or extraordinary eviction circumstances, HUD or FmHA also should be advised of the situation in writing.

As soon as the decision is made to evict or a resident is referred to an attorney for eviction, the property manager should not accept any additional payment from that resident and should so advise the home office if rent is collected centrally. In some states, acceptance of payment after eviction proceedings have commenced can nullify the proceedings. In other states, property managers may and do accept cash, and the judge deducts the amount from the amount to be paid. In yet other states, eviction proceedings can be nullified by full payment of the rent, late payment charge, bank fees, and attorney's fees. Property managers must know and follow the laws applicable to their properties.

POST-OCCUPANCY COLLECTIONS

When a resident moves out owing rent and/or other moneys for such items as damages, the property manager is normally expected to obtain the former resident's new address and send that information to the central office with the move-out paperwork. The management company generally employs a collection agency for post-occupancy collections; however, the procedures of the management company may call for two in-house collection efforts prior to turning the account over to a collection agency.

One such in-house collection method is to send an initial settlement letter such as the one shown in Figure 4–14 requesting payment and a follow-up letter in two weeks if payment is not received as a result of the initial letter. If payment is not received within two weeks of the second letter or within 30 days of the move-out, the account is then turned over to a collection agency.

In all cases in which a resident moves, is evicted, or "skips" (moves out without prior notice) owing the property money, the property manager should prepare the appropriate report and file it with the credit bureau that the property is using. Filing credit information can become quite useful in collecting money later. Nearly all former residents will want to purchase a car or home at some later date. When they do, they usually need to correct any blemishes on their credit record, and the property manager will be able to collect all or part of the debt. Reporting to the credit bureau the names of departing residents who owe the property money should be part of the usual move-out processing. The property manager should, of course, consult with an attorney before taking any action against residents who move, are evicted, or skip owing the property money. (See also Chapter 8, Processing Applications, Move-in and Move-out Procedures, and Resident Relations and the Resident Handbook.)

FAIR DEBT COLLECTION PRACTICES ACT

In 1996, the U.S. Consumer Credit Protection Act was amended to prohibit abusive practices by debt collectors. The amendment, entitled Fair Debt Collection Practices Act, requires that debt collectors treat debtors fairly and prohibits certain methods of debt collection but does not erase any legitimate debt owed. In all cases of collection, the property manager should be familiar with the methods used for collection and with the Fair Debt Collection Practices Act and what is and isn't allowed. Ideally, an attorney versed in credit and collection should be consulted.

Information about the Fair Debt Collection Practices Act can be accessed at www.ftc.gov/bcp/conline/pubs/credit/fdc.htm.

THE LEASE AGREEMENT

PURPOSE AND FORM OF THE LEASE AGREEMENT

Also called an occupancy agreement, the lease agreement is the single most important document used in property management. It is a legal contract the purpose of which is to clearly communicate agreement between the property owner and/or the owner's agent and the renter about:

- The dwelling unit
- The amount of the rent
- The lessor (landlord/owner) and lessee (tenant/renter)
- The effective date and term of the lease
- Responsibilities of the lessor (landlord/owner)
- Responsibilities of the lessee (tenant/renter)

Usually, the property management executive, with the guidance of a local attorney, decides what form of lease to use. The options include:

- A model form, provided either by a multihousing industry trade association or a legal forms company
- The management company's standard lease used throughout the organization
- A lease form custom developed by an attorney for the particular property

The design of the lease form should take into consideration the types of tenancy the property has, state and local

FIGURE 4-14. In-house Management Company Collections Letter to Residents Who Move, Are Evicted, or "Skip"

(Date)

(Name)
(Address)
(City, State, Zip)

Dear ______________(Name)______________:

Your account with (Name of Property) with reference to the apartment/townhouse listed below is outstanding:

____
(Unit number)

____
(Address)

____
(City, State, Zip)

Please forward a certified check or money order in the amount of $ __________ to:

____
(Property Manager's Name)

____
(Property Name)

____
(Address)

____
(City, State, Zip)

If payment is not received within 5 days of the date of this letter, we will have no alternative but to turn your account over to our attorney.

If your check has already been sent, please disregard this notice.

Sincerely,

____
(Property Manager Signature)

laws, and prevailing local landlord/tenant practices. Under any circumstances, the lease a property manager intends to use should be reviewed by an attorney prior to use. Each state has different laws and regulations concerning the lease of real property, and these laws may require that certain provisions be either included or excluded from a lease. Additionally, the lease should be reviewed and revised every 24 to 36 months to keep in compliance with the laws, regulations, and court practices in the area in which it is used.

The sample lease (Fig. 4–15) is a commonly used residential lease that is enforceable in a number of states. For other states, it would need modification. For example, the late fee provision is legal in a number of states, but a $35 charge may be over the permitted maximum. Some states impose additional legal requirements. For instance, in some states a lease is considered a consumer contract and as such must be submitted to the attorney general's office for approval to be sure it complies with that state's plain language law.

Regardless of the kind of lease drawn up for a property, the lease should contain the following provisions, also known as the terms of occupancy:

- The name of the owner and/or the owner's agent
- The names of all adults who will occupy the apartment
- The names of any guarantors or cosigners
- Identification of the dwelling unit
- The term of the lease (in specific dates and years)
- The terms of rent, including how often and when it is to be paid (e.g., monthly on the first of the month), and the periodic and aggregate amounts of the rent (i.e., the amount of each payment and the total of all payments for the term of the lease)
- Any escalator clauses that stipulate increases in rent at certain specified times during the term of the lease
- Security deposit provisions
- Any special stipulations (e.g., pet policies, renewal options, abandonments)

Of course, all parties should sign the lease for it to be a legally binding agreement.

HUD and FmHA have standard lease forms for their developments. These forms can be modified or a custom form can be used, but the language of the lease must be reviewed and approved by HUD and FmHA. Tax-exempt, bond-financed developments often are required to use either a custom-tailored lease or certain lease riders to comply with the provisions of the bonds.

RULES FOR LEASE EXECUTION

The property manager must complete the following items on the lease form when preparing it for signature:

- Property name
- Resident's name
- Apartment address and number
- Annual rent
- Monthly rent and when due
- Late charge policy and amount
- Pet deposits or fees
- Effective date and term
- Date signed
- Manager's signature

The property manager is responsible for ensuring that all persons who will occupy the unit are listed on the lease and that all individuals of legal age sign the lease. The manager should clearly explain the following items to the resident before the lease is signed:

- The terms of the lease
- Rent due dates including possible consequences for late payment or nonpayment
- That no adult can reside in the apartment unless her/his name is on the lease
- That the apartment must be kept neat and clean
- Any lease provisions regarding modifications to the unit, including painting and wallpapering of walls
- That renter's insurance should be purchased (a number of jurisdictions now have provisions relating to disclaimers and insurance coverage that must be included in the lease or in a rider)
- That the security deposit cannot be used for the final month's rent and that certain conditions must prevail for return of the deposit

Two or more copies of the lease agreement should be signed. The original is placed in the resident's file folder in the rental office, a copy is given to the resident at the lease signing, and a copy may also be placed in the separate file maintained for the unit if such a file exists. Large management companies may need additional copies for the accounting department and perhaps one for the property management home office. The operations manual should contain lease distribution information.

KEEPING THE LEASE DOCUMENTS SAFE

For the renter, the lease is the legal agreement that entitles her/him to reside in the apartment. For the owner and manager, the lease is the legal agreement that guarantees income to the property. To say the least, the lease document itself is a critical document. Leases are also costly and time-consuming to duplicate if they are lost or damaged. Therefore, all lease files should be stored in a locked and secure environment. Many properties purchase a fireproof file for storing original leases and other related documents or maintain a duplicate file at an off-site location. However they are main-

Figure 4–15. Residential Lease

APARTMENT LEASE

1. PARTIES: THIS LEASE made this ________ day of _________, 20____ between ______________________________ (hereinafter referred to as Lessor) and ______________________________ (hereinafter referred to as Lessee).

WITNESSETH:

That in consideration of the representation made in the application filed by the Lessee and the conditions and covenants herein set forth, the Lessor hereby leases to the Lessee the following described property:

2. PREMISES: Apartment No. __________ at Address ____________________ in City ________________State__________ Zip Code ________ for use by Lessee as a private residence only.

3. TERM: This lease is for a term of _____________ commencing on the __________ day of _______, 20______ and ending in the last calendar day of _______, 20______.

4. RENT: The Lessee agrees to pay to the Lessor a rental of ___________________ ($_______________) Dollars, payable as follows:

5. RENTAL PAYMENTS: In monthly installments of _________________ ($____________) Dollars each to be due and payable respectively on the first day of ___________, 20____, and on the first day of each month thereafter. All rental payments are to be paid at the Resident Manager's Office or at such place as Lessor may designate. Such rental payment is to be made by check, money order or bank cashier's check. CASH IS NOT ACCEPTABLE FOR ANY PAYMENTS DUE.

6. PRO-RATED RENT: It is understood and agreed that Lessee is taking possession of the premises on the ______ day of ______________, 20____, and is to pay the sum of ___________ ($__________) Dollars, as rent from that date through the first day of ___________, 20_____.

7. LATE CHARGES AND RETURNED CHECKS: The Lessee agrees to pay a late charge of THIRTY-FIVE AND NO/100 ($35) DOLLARS in the event that the monthly installments are not received by the first (1st) day of each month. REGARDLESS OF THE DAY OF THE WEEK ON WHICH THE FIRST (1st) MAY OCCUR AND REGARDLESS IF WHETHER THE FIRST (1st) IS A HOLIDAY OR OTHER NON-BUSINESS DAY. RENT WILL BE CONSIDERED DELINQUENT IF RECEIVED AFTER THE FIRST (1st) DAY OF THE MONTH.

If the Lessor is given a check and said check is not honored on presentation for any reason whatsoever, Lessee agrees to pay a bad check charge of FIFTEEN AND NO/100 ($15) DOLLARS in addition to any late charge.

8. DEPOSITS: At the time of execution of this Lessee has deposited with Lessor, the receipt of which is hereby acknowledged, the sum of _______________ ($_________) Dollars Security Deposit which is to be held by the Lessor as a guarantee for the full and faithful performance of all the terms and conditions of the Lease by the Lessee. THIS DEPOSIT IS NOT RENT AND SHALL NEVER BE APPLIED BY THE LESSEE AS PAYMENT IN WHOLE OR IN PART OF ANY RENTAL PAYMENTS DUE UNDER THIS LEASE. In the event of any violation of the terms of this lease by the Lessee, this security deposit, or a portion thereof, may be retained by the Lessor as partial damages.

continued

Figure 4–15. Residential Lease (*Continued*)

9. SECURITY DEPOSIT RETURN:

The Lessor shall not be obligated to release the Security Deposit unless the following conditions are met:

1. Full term of the lease has expired.
2. Thirty days written notice given by the Lessee to the Lessor.
3. No damage to property beyond fair wear and tear.
4. Entire apartment, including range, exhaust fan, refrigerator, bathroom, closets and cabinets are clean. Refrigerator to be defrosted.
5. No stickers or scratches or holes on walls.
6. No damage to carpet beyond wear and tear.
7. No unpaid charges or rent.
8. All keys are returned.
9. All debris and rubbish and discards placed in proper rubbish containers.
10. Forwarding address left with management.

____
(Initials)

10. CHARGES AGAINST DEPOSITS:

At the expiration of the term of this lease the balance, if any, of said security deposit will be returned to Lessee after deducting there from any unpaid rent and/or the following charges or damages, if in the discretion of Lessor such charges are necessary in order to put the leased premises in suitable condition for occupancy by a subsequent lessee:

(a) Apartment cleaning charge of THIRTY-FIVE AND NO /100 ($35) DOLLARS.
(b) A stove cleaning charge of TWENTY-FIVE AND NO/100 ($25) DOLLARS.
(c) A refrigerator cleaning charge of TWENTY-FIVE AND NO/100 ($25) DOLLARS.
(d) The reasonable cost of repairing any damage to the premises, furnishing, or equipment, or the cost of the replacement or any furnishing or equipment removed from the premises or damaged beyond repair.
(e) Missing fire extinguisher charge of THIRTY AND NO/100 ($30) DOLLARS.
(f) Expended fire extinguisher charge of FIFTEEN AND NO/100 ($15) DOLLARS.
(g) Apartment keys not returned – FIFTEEN AND NO/100 ($15) DOLLARS.

In the event the above deductions exceed the amount of the security deposit the excess shall promptly become due and payable from the Lessee.

11. OCCUPANTS:

The Lessee agrees that the premises are to be occupied by those persons specifically named in the Lessee's application. If any other person resides with the Lessee without prior written authorization form the Lessor, the Lessor has the right to declare the lease in default. The Lessee further agrees that the above-demised premises cannot be assigned or sublet by said Lessee either in whole or in part. The Lessee recognizes that the Lessor must be in a direct Lessor-Lessee relationship and that a subletting or an assignment would complicate the Lessor's dealings. The Lessee shall not have the right to request subletting or assignment; however, if the Lessee does, the Lessee agrees that the Lessor's decision (not to assign or sublet) need not be made in accordance with any particular commercial criteria or standards (including "reasonable commercial standards") and that the Lessor's decision, for whatever reason, shall be conclusive and binding on the Lease.

12. OCCUPANCY:

Should the Lessee be unable to obtain possession on the date of the lease term because of delays of the Lessee, or by reason of the holding over of any previous occupants of said premises, or if a building is to be constructed and workmen or contractors have not brought the building to a condition

continued

Figure 4–15. Residential Lease (*Continued*)

permitting occupancy, or should there be any other delay in granting possession, the Lessor shall not be liable in damages to the Lessee.

13. STRUCTURAL DAMAGE:

If the leased premises are destroyed by fire, and such fire is due to the Lessee's fault or negligence, then in that event the monthly installments shall not abate.

If the leased premises or the building of which it is or may be a part shall be damaged by fire or by other unforeseen event, without fault of the Lessee, then, and in the event, the Lessor shall have the option to decide whether the Lessor shall or shall not repair and restore said building or leased premises to their original shape; and if the Lessor decides to repair and restore the building or the rented premises as aforesaid, then, from the time such damage occurs until the repairs are completed, an equitable abatement of the monthly installments will be allowed. It is agreed, however, that if the damage is such as not to render the leased premises untenable for the purpose for which they are rented, then there shall be no abatement of the rent while the repairs are being made.

Except for the normal hanging of pictures and wall decorations that do not deface wood, masonry or sheetrock surfaces, the Lessee shall not drive any nails or tracks or set any screws into any part of the apartment or building, or make any structural change, whatsoever without first obtaining the written consent of Lessor.

14. DEFAULT:

Should the Lessee fail to pay rents as they fall due as aforesaid or violate any of the conditions of this lease, or should there be any misstatement or untruth in the application made by the Lessee, the Lessor shall have the right at the Lessor's option to re-enter said premises and annul this lease. Such re-entry shall not bar the recovery of rents or damages for breach of the lease contract nor shall the receipt of rent after conditions broken be deemed a waiver of forfeiture. And in order to entitle the Lessor to re-enter it shall not be necessary to give notice of rent being due and unpaid, nor to make demand for rent the execution of this lease, signed by the parties thereto, which signing is hereby acknowledged, being sufficient notice of the rents being due and a demand for the same and shall be so construed, any law, usage, or custom to the contrary, notwithstanding.

And the Lessee further covenants and agrees that should the Lessee violate any conditions of this lease, then in such case, the whole rent for the whole term of the lease shall at once become due and payable at the option of the Lessor, and the Lessor may proceed by attachment, suit, or otherwise, to collect, the whole in the same manner, as if by the terms of this lease the whole rent or the entire term were payable in advance.

15. TERMINATING LEASE:

If either the Lessee or the Lessor desires that this lease terminate at the expiration of its item, including month to month, one must give to the other WRITTEN NOTICE TO BE RECEIVED NOT LESS THAN THIRTY (30) DAYS PRIOR TO THE EXPIRATION OF THE LEASE TERM. If the written notice is given less than thirty (30) days prior to the expiration date, the Lessee's obligation to pay rent shall extend to the number of days required to fulfill the thirty (30) day notice period.

16. AUTOMATIC RENEWAL:

Failure of either party to give prior termination notice will automatically renew this lease for an additional term on a MONTH-TO-MONTH basis, and under such circumstances either the Lessor or the Lessee shall be required to give thirty (30) days written notice in order to terminate the lease. This notice may be given at any time and if the notice period does not correspond with a full calendar month the Lessee's final rent payment will be prorated in accordance

continued

Figure 4–15. Residential Lease (*Continued*)

with the number of days required to fulfill the notice period or the number of days the Lessee occupies the apartment until, whichever is the longer.

17. CHANGES IN LEASE PROVISIONS:

The Lessee further agrees that, unless otherwise provided herein, upon the termination of the initial term of the lease, the Lessor can make changes in the lease provisions after the initial term and during the period in which the lease is on a month-to-month basis by notifying the Lessee of such changes to the Lessee by regular mail, personal delivery or positing at least 30 days prior to the date of the change. Failure of the Lessee to object to said changes in writing within seven (7) days from the date of postmark, delivery or posting of the notice of changes shall be deemed approval of such changes. Such changes will be binding upon the Lessee as long as the Lessee remains a tenant of the Lessor. This provision is a continuous one and will apply at the expiration of the original term and during each subsequent monthly term.

18. ABANDONMENT:

The Lessee's absence from the premises for seven (7) consecutive days without prior written notice, during which time rent or other charges are delinquent, shall be deemed abandonment of the premises. Such abandonment will be deemed cause for immediate termination without notice, and the Lessor at its option may cancel the lease or –re-enter and let the premises for such terms as may be immediately obtainable, and apply the net amount collected to the amount due hereunder by the Lessee. Re-entering and letting shall not relieve the Lessee of its obligation to pay amounts due under this lease.

19. WARRANTY AND INDEMNITY:

It is further understood and agreed that the Lessor shall not be liable for any injury to person or damage to property which may occur on account for any defect in said premises or the premises of the apartment complex of which the leased premises are a part, for any damages caused by rain, wind, broken pipes, failure of air conditioning or heating or other causes. The Lessee agrees and does hereby indemnify protect and save harmless the Lessor from any loss cost, damage or expense caused by or resulting from injuries to persons or property, while in, on, or about the premises herein leased and any and all property of said Lessee which may be located or stored either in the demised premises or the apartment complex of which the demised premises from a part shall be at the sole risk of the Lessee. The Lessee waives any right of subrogation against the Lessor under any insurance policy and shall cause the Lessee's insurance carriers to Lessee waives any right of subrogation against the Lessor under any insurance policy and shale cause the Lessee's insurance carriers to waive the same. The Lessee hereby acknowledges the good condition of the leased premises and his acceptance of this lease is conclusive evidence that said premises are in good and satisfactory order and repair unless otherwise specified herein, and he agrees that no misrepresentation as to the condition of the premises has been made and no promise made to decorate, alter, repair, or improve the premises unless otherwise specified in writing. The Lessor reserves the right to visit and inspect said premises at any reasonable time to show the same to intended Lessees; and to display "FOR RENT" signs on said buildings or premises.

20. LIABILITY:

It is understood that no employee of the Lessor is furnished to provide any personal services to the Lessees, his family, employees or guests, and the Lessee agrees to relieve the Lessor and hold the Lessor harmless from any and all liability in connection with such service. By way of illustration, but not by way of limitation, no employee of the Lessor is authorized to perform any errand, porter, cleanup, valet, maid, babysitting, carpentry, handyman, garbage removal, trash removal or other services; and, in the event any such services are rendered, the Lessor shall not be liable in connection therewith, and the Lessee shall fully indemnify and save the Lessor harmless.

continued

Figure 4–15. Residential Lease (*Continued*)

21. TAXES, INSURANCE AND UTILITIES:

Lessee shall pay the public utility bills for said leased premises when and as the same severally become due, making all required deposits with public utility companies, unless specifically included in the rent. The Lessor shall not be liable for any injury or damage whatsoever which may arise or accrue either upon its furnishings or its failure to furnish hot or cold water or heat or air conditioning or other utilities to the leased premises regardless of the cause or on account of any defect in the building or premises. The monthly rental figure contained hereinabove is based in part upon ad valorem tax rates, rental taxes, and public utility service rates existing at the time of the execution of this lease, and being paid by the Lessor. In the event of any increase or increases in the existing rates during the term of this lease the Lessor may, at its option, assess all of the Lessees in this apartment complex with a pro rata share of such increases. The tenants pro rata share shall be that portion of such increase equal to the product obtained by multiplying said excess by a fraction, the numerator of which shall be the number of apartment units covered by this lease and the denominator of which shall be the total number of apartment units in the development. The Lessee agrees to pay his or her pro rata share of such increase in monthly installments as additional rent hereunder commencing with the month following the date the Lessor must pay said increase. The Lessee agrees that if any taxing authority enacts a tax, which is computed on the rent, then this tax shall be paused onto the Lessee as additional rent and the monthly rent shall be increased by the amount enacted by the taxing authority.

22. EXCULPATORY AND RELEASE PROVISION:
This provision was specifically called to my attention. I understand the provision was bargained for before the lease was signed, and I agree that the provision is valid and binding.

____
(Initials of each Lessee)

The Lessor (including its managing and leasing agents and its other agents, servants and employees) shall not be liable or responsible in any manner to the Lessee, or to any of the Lessee's spouse, children, dependents, guests, invitees, heirs, personal representatives, assigns, or to any persons having interests in any property located on the premises or the complex of which the premises are a part, for personal the injury (including death), property damage, property loss (including decrease in value of property), or any other type of loss or damage giving rise to any claim for damages or to any other type of claim whatsoever, which results from negligence and/or other fault, except willful I agree misconduct, and which arises in whole or in part from any condition, accident or occurrence relating to the premises or the complex of which the premises are a part, including: any defective or other condition in buildings, equipment, improvements, appurtenances, storage areas, swimming pools facilities, other facilities, and common areas, and including latent and patent conditions, whether known or unknown and whether now existing or later developing; conditions relating to plumbing, heating, air-conditioning, and equipment, appliances, facilities or machinery, whether in proper working order resulting from acts of God and the elements including rain, hail, snow, storms, floods and earthquakes; conditions relating to repair, alteration or replacement work performed by or on behalf of the Lessor, or relating to circumstances delaying or preventing such work from being performed; conditions relating to theft, burglary, vandalism, acts of violence other acts of third-parties, acts of other Lessees of the complex, and any acts or matters relating to security; and any conditions or circumstances relating to any services or undertaking provided by the Lessor or by anyone acting on behalf of the Lessor.

AND THE LESSEE ACKNOWLEDGES THAT THE PROVISIONS F THE PRIOR PARAGRAPH, WHICH LIMIT THE LIABILITY OF THE LESSOR (INCLUDING ITS MANAGING AND LEASING AGENTS AND ITS OTHER AGENTS, SERVANTS AND EMPLOYEES), WERE BARGAINED FOR BETWEEN THE LESSEE AND THE LESSOR.

23. ATTORNEY'S FEE:

In the event of employment of an attorney for the collection of any amount due hereunder, or for the institution of any suit for the possession of said property, the Lessee shall pay and shall be taxes with the reasonable attorney's fee, which shall be a part of the debt evidenced and secured by this lease.

continued

Figure 4–15. Residential Lease (*Continued*)

24. RULES AND REGULATIONS:

The Lessee agrees to comply with and to cause the Lessee's guest and family members to comply with the rules and regulations for the project that may exist from time to time and the Lessee agrees that the rules and regulations may be amended from time to time by the Lessor and notice of such amended rules and regulations shall be sufficiently given by posting a copy thereof on the door of the leased premises. IT IS AGREED THAT THE VIOLATION OF ANY SUCH RULES AND REGULATIONS BY THE LESSEE OR ANY OF THE LESSEES GUESTS OR FAMILY MEMBERS SHALL CONSTITUTE A DEFAULT IN THE TERMS OF THIS LEASE. The Lessee hereby agrees to be bound by the following:

1. Notices: All complaints and requests shall be made to the Manager. The Lessee shall also give immediate notice to the Manager of any accident, property damage or injury.
2. Moving: Moving of furniture and other bulky articles other than within the Lessee's own apartment shall be conducted on the premises only after the consent of the Lessor is first obtained. Any damage done to the building or any property of the Lessor or to the person or any property of anyone else by the moving of articles in or out of the premises by the Lessee shall be paid for by the Lessee causing such damage.
3. Pets: Pets will not be permitted in the leased apartments UNLESS EXPRESS WRITTEN CONSENT OF THE LESSOR IS GIVEN as provided in paragraph #31 of this apartment lease.
4. Aerials: The Lessee agrees that no radio wires, or television aerials, or the appurtenances shall be placed on any building without the express written consent of the Lessor.
5. Guests: Each guest shall be the responsibility of the Lessee so visited, including any damage done to the premises by any such guest. Children shall not play in the halls or stairways of the leased premises or be allowed to create disturbances of any nature.
6. Noises: No Lessee shall make, or permit to be made by his family or guest, any disturbing noises or interfere in any way with rights of other residents or the operation of the property by the Lessor or its Agents. It is further agreed that the apartment shall not be used to give instructions in music or singing.
7. Inflammables and Explosives: Storage of kerosene, gasoline, butane or other inflammable or explosive agencies is prohibited inside the premises.
8. Sales: No yard or auction sales of any nature shall be permitted under any circumstances.
9. Waterbeds: Waterbeds are only permitted in downstairs apartments and ONLY WITH WRITTEN PERMISSION OF THE LESSOR. Such permission will be contingent upon the Lessee's providing proof of adequate damage protection under apartment dweller's insurance coverage.
10. Locks and Keys: The Lessor may retain the pass key to each apartment. No Lessee shall alter any lock or install a new lock on any door leading into his apartment without the prior written permission of the Lessor. If such approval is given, the Lessee shall provide the Lessor with a key for the Lessor's use.
11. Sweeping: No Lease shall sweep or throw or permit to be swept or thrown from the leased premises including porches, windows, and doorways, any dirt or other substances into any of the corridors, halls, or into the yard area or on the porch area of any other Lease.

continued

Figure 4–15. Residential Lease (*Continued*)

12. Repairs: The Lessor, his agent, his janitor, watchmen, and employees may enter the leased premises at any reasonable time to examine the same or make needed repairs to the premises, or to install or repair pipes, wires, and other appliances and items deemed by the Lessor essential to the use and occupation of other parts of the building.

13. Windows: Cleaning and maintenance of windows and glass doors are the Lessee's obligation. Foil on windows and glass doors is forbidden.

14. Appearance: The hanging of rugs, laundry, towels, mops, or articles of clothing over the window sills or balcony rails is forbidden. Outside garbage containers other than those provided by the Lessor are forbidden on the demised premises.

15. Light Bulbs: The Lessee agrees to replace all burned out light bulbs in his apartment.

16. Drapes/Blinds: Drapes or blinds, which are furnished by the Lessor, must be used. Should you desire to use your own drapes/blinds, written permission of the Lessor is required. Personal drapes must have plain off white linings. Personal blinds must be ivory or off-white in color.

17. Fire Extinguisher: The fire extinguisher is to be used in the event of a fire in the apartment, the building or on the grounds of the complex. The extinguisher is not to be removed from the premises. If the fire extinguisher is not to be removed from the premises. If the fire extinguisher is used at any time, it should be immediately reported to Lessor so that the device can be "recharged" to assure continued protection. The Lessee should periodically check the gauge of the fire extinguisher to assure that it remains 'charged' and ready for use. If the gauge should indicate that the device needs to be 'recharged', or if the Lessee is uncertain as to condition, the situation should immediately be reported to the Lessor. Should the device need to be 'recharged', it will be done AT NO COST TO THE LESSEE if the discharge is due to leakage or other malfunction. Discharge for unauthorized reasons will be charges to the Lessee.

18. Smoke Detector: All apartments are equipped with smoke detectors for the protection of the Lessee. These detectors should be tested monthly to assure their working condition and any problems immediately reported to the manager. In the case of battery operated smoke detectors, it is the responsibility of the Lessee to replace inoperable batteries.

25. SWIMMING POOL:

The Lessee hereby releases, relieves, and holds the Lessor blameless for any damage or injury to persons or property caused as a result of the use of the swimming pool by the Lessee or any persons making use of said pool through the use, permission, or consent of the Lessee. No children under the age of ten (10) years of age will be allowed in or about the swimming pool area unless accompanied by an adult, and no child in diapers will be allowed use of the pool. Children are prohibited from using pool designated by the Lessor as "all adult" except as provided for under current published regulations for individual properties.

The complex pool is a private pool for the use of the Lessees only; the hours of operation shall be as posted. Guests of Lessees must be limited to two (2) persons per apartment at any one time and they must be accompanied by a Lessee unless express written permission to the contrary is given by the

continued

Figure 4–15. Residential Lease (*Continued*)

Manager. In those properties where "pool tag" systems is used, the current published regulations must be observed as to use of pool by residents and guests. The Lessee further agrees that only a greaseless type sun-tan lotion may be used and not oil base suntan lotion; and further that no ball playing, running or wrestling will be allowed in the pool or pool area unless specifically designated by the Lessor.

Beverages brought to the pool area should be in containers other than glass. NO GLASSES, BOTTLES, GLASS CONTAINERS OR FOOD ARE ALLOWED IN THE POOL AREA. Other pool rules are to be observed as posted from time to time by the Lessor.

26. VEHICLES: Motorcycles including motorbikes and minibikes shall not be parked in the breezeways, hallways, patios, grass or lawn area. These will be parked in other areas specifically provided by the Lessor with care taken to protect the asphalt from damage caused by kick-stand or oil leakage. Riding of same on sidewalks or lawns is prohibited. In those communities where specific areas are designated for the parking of boats, trailers and RV's such designation must be observed by the Lessee.

All vehicles parked in the parking lot by the Lessee, his guests, agents or invites shall be operable and shall bear a current license plate. Vehicles shall be parked only in the paved areas provided for parking. THE LESSOR SHALL GIVE TO THE LESSEE THREE DAYS NOTICE TO REMOVE ANY INOPERABLE VEHICLE, IF THE LESSEE FAILS TO REMOVE THE VEHICLE, THE LESSOR SHALL REMOVE IT AT THE LESSEE'S EXPENSE.

IT IS EXPRESSLY PROHIBITED TO WORK ON OR REPAIR AN AUTOMOBILE OR MOTORCYCLE OR ANY OTHER TYPE VEHICLE ANYWHERE ON THE PREMISES. LIKEWISE, THE WASHING OF AUTOMOBILES OR MOTORCYCLES ON THE PREMISES IS NOT PERMITTED.

27. NUISANCES: The Lessee to comply with all the laws and ordinance of the City in regard to nuisances insofar as the leased premises and the streets, alleys and premises of the Lessor around the same are concerned, and that the Lessee will by no act or omission render the Lessor liable for any violation of such City law or ordinance. Should the Lessee, his family or guests, fail to maintain a standard of behavior consistent with the consideration necessary to provide reasonable peace and quiet to other tenants, such as by being boisterous or disorderly, creating undue noise, disturbance or nuisance of any nature or kind, then at the option of the Lessor, the rent for the whole expired term of the lease shall at once become due and payable, and the Lessor shall have the further option to cancel this lease, and recover possession of the premises.

28. ENTIRE AGREEMENT: This lease and the amendments, if any attached hereto and forming a pert hereof, set forth all covenants, promises, conditions, and understandings between the Lessor and the Lessee concerning the leased premises, and there are no covenants, promises, agreements, conditions, or understandings, either oral or written between them other than herein set forth. No modification or limitation or extension of any condition of this lease will be binding unless in writing and signed by the Lessor and the Lessee. The Lessor's failure to take advantage of any default on the part of the Lessee shall not be constructed as a waiver thereof, nor shall any custom or practice that may grow up between the parties in the course of administering this instrument be constructed to waive or to lessen the right of the Lessor to insist upon the provisions hereof.

continued

Figure 4–15. Residential Lease (*Continued*)

It is understood that the terms "Lessor" and "Lessee" are used in this agreement and they shall include the plural and shall apply to persons both male and female. All obligations of the Lessee are to be jointly and severally. This lease, whether or not recorded, shall be junior and subordinate to any mortgage hereafter placed by the Lessor in the entire property of which the leased premises form a part.

29. LESSOR'S CONSENT:

Whenever any action or any condition is prohibited or restricted under this lease unless the Lessor's consent is secured, or the Lessor's consent is required under this lease either expressly or by implication, the Lessee agrees that the Lessor's decision to consent or not need not be made in accordance with any particular criteria or commercial standards (including "reasonable commercial standards") that the Lessor may make its decision on the basis of any factors which seem relevant to the Lessor's decision, for whatever reason, shall be conclusive and binding on the Lessee. The Lessor may condition the giving of its consent upon whatever requirements and conditions seem desirable to the Lessor regardless of whether the Lessor's position and/or the particular requirements and conditions accord with any particular criteria or commercial standards, including reasonable commercial standards.

30. PARTIAL INVALIDITY:

If any section, clause, sentence, word or provisions of this lease or the application thereof to any party or circumstances shall to any extent, be or become invalid or illegal, and such provision shall thereby become null and void, the remainder of this lease shall no be affected thereby, and each remaining provision of this lease shall not be affected thereby, and each remaining provision of this lease shall be valid ad enforceable to the fullest extent permitted by law.

31. PET PROVISIONS:

(1) THE LESSEE AGREES THAT ONLY THE PET DESCRIBED AND NAMED BELOW AND WHICH HAS BEEN APPROVED BY THE MANAGER CAN OCCUPY THE PREMISES. NO ADDITIONAL OR DIFFERENT PET IS AUTHORIZED UNDER THIS AGREEMENT.

(2) The Lessee aggress that pet will be kept inside apartment at all times except when on a leash and accompanied by the Lessee.

(3) The Lessee agrees that if pet becomes annoying, bothersome, or in any way a nuisance to other Lessee or to the apartment operation, the Lessee will immediately upon notice from the Lessor remove pet from the premises or vacate the apartment.

(4) The Lessee agrees to pay the Lessor a non-refundable pet fee in the amount of $ ______________________. Type of Pet: __________________
Weight:_____________ Breed:________________ Color: _______________
Tag No. __________________

____
(Initials if applicable)

32. TRANSFER PROVISION:

It is hereby agreed that in the event of a business transfer of the Lessee to a location more than fifty (50) miles distant from the leased premises, this lease may be cancelled at any time provided:

(1) The Lessee gives the Lessor written notice to be received not less than thirty (30) days prior to the intended date of transfer. If written notice is given less than thirty (30) days prior to the intended date of transfer, the Lessee's obligation to pay rent shall extend to the number of days required to fulfill the notice period or the number of days the Lessee continues to occupy the apartment unit, whichever is the longer. Said notice shall state the address to which the Lessee is to move.

continued

Figure 4–15. Residential Lease (*Continued*)

(2) THE LESSEE PRESENTS A NOTARIZED LETTER FROM HIS EMPLOYER STATING THE LOCATION TO WHICH THE LESSEE IS BEING TRANSFERRED AND EFFECTIVE DATE OF THE TRANSFER. If proved at a later date that the Lessee did not transfer more than 50 miles from his apartment, then the rent for the unexpired term of the lease will become due and payable.

(3) The Lessee agrees to allow parties authorized by the Lessor and prospective tenants to visit the premises during the thirty (30) days prior to the date of cancellation between the hours of 10:00 a.m and 7:00 p.m.

_______________ (Initial)

(4) THE LESSEE AGREES TO FORFEIT ALL HIS DEPOSIT AND CONSIDERATION FOR THE EXERCISE OF THIS RIGHT OF CANCELLATION, whether or not the effective date of transfer is during the original term or any subsequent term of the lease.

READ YOUR LEASE BEFORE SIGNING

_______________________ Lessor

_______________________ Lessee

By: _______________________ Agent of Lessor

_______________________ Lessee

33. REITERATION: The Lessee further agrees and acknowledges that Article 19 (WARRANTY AND INDEMNITY) Article 20 (LIABILITY) and Article 22 (EXCULPATORY AND RELEASE PROVISION) were specifically called to the Lessee's attention by the Lessor and were bargained for before the lease was signed and that the Lessee was informed and understood the meaning of these provisions and their legal effect prior to signing this lease.

_______________________ Lessee

_______________________ Lessee

Warning—This pro-landlord lease is known to be good in several states. It is not guaranteed to be legal in all states. Any lease should be reviewed by a local attorney before it is used.

tained, lease files should be protected from fire and water damage, break-in, vandalism, and all other possible damage.

REVISING THE LEASE AND AMENDMENTS TO AN EXISTING LEASE

A revised lease should be prepared when any one of the following conditions occur:

- The name of one or more of the parties signing the lease changes her/his name (whether by marriage, divorce, or other legal action)
- The resident moves into a different dwelling unit
- The original lease is lost or destroyed (If all copies of the lease agreement are lost, the property manager should make immediate arrangements with the resident to sign a new one. If the resident's copy is lost, another copy of the original can be provided.)

An amendment to the lease should be prepared when an additional occupant is approved to reside in an apartment or townhouse. An existing resident may take a roommate who, after approval by management, signs the amended lease and is liable individually and along with the present resident for the rent payment, any damage caused to the unit, as well as other lease provisions. However, executing an entirely new lease is preferable to modifying an existing one.

GUARANTY OF LEASE

The guaranty of lease form (Fig. 4–16) is used for a guarantor or co-signer. A guarantor is an individual who is liable on the lease for payment of the rent and any damages to the unit but who does not have rights to live in the unit. A co-signer has the same obligations as a guarantor but is also considered a co-tenant with all the rights and obligations of the tenant, including the right to live in the unit. Generally, a guarantor or co-signer is advisable in situations in which the prospective renter has marginal or insufficient credit. The wording of the guaranty of lease form may vary from state to state. The property manager therefore should consult an attorney prior to using a guaranty of lease form.

SECURITY DEPOSIT

The security deposit and first month's rent, and sometimes the last month's rent as well, are normally collected in the rental office at the time of lease signing, definitely prior to move-in, and preferably in the form of a money order or certified check.

SECURITY DEPOSIT HANDLING

Lease provisions and landlord/tenant legislation govern the collection, use, disposition of interest earned, and return of security deposits. Normally, the management company cannot use the resident's security deposit to cover delinquent rent or damages while the resident resides at the property. The security deposit may be used to reimburse the owner for uncollected rent or damages after the resident has moved.

To help reduce misunderstanding in this sensitive area, information regarding the collection, use, disposition of interest earned, and return of the security deposit should be thoroughly covered during new resident processing, and a policy statement such as the one shown in Figure 4–17 should be included in the resident handbook and other written documents provided to the resident at the time of move-in. (See also Chapter 8, Processing Applications, Move-in and Move-out Procedures, and Resident Relations and the Resident Handbook.) The lease signed by the resident should indicate her/his specific knowledge of this information, and this agreement should state clearly the conditions for the return of the deposit.

SECURITY DEPOSIT ACCOUNT

Usually an interest-bearing account is established for security deposits. Many states require that residents be paid the interest received on their security deposits.

Sound accounting principles and some state laws require that security deposit accounts be kept separate from the property's operating account and not used to pay expenses or in any way be co-mingled with other moneys. Having insufficient funds to cover outstanding security deposit balances for all residents is a breach of fiduciary responsibility.

RECOMMENDED GUIDELINES FOR A SECURITY DEPOSIT REFUND POLICY

The property's operations manual should provide a policy for administering the refund of security deposits to residents. Some states and local jurisdictions have regulations governing the prompt return of security deposits with fines specified for failure to comply.

If a resident fulfills her/his lease according to its terms, the policy should state that only charges for any damages are deducted from the security deposit. Fulfillment of the lease depends on the items included in the lease, and usually occurs when a specific set of actions such as those shown in Figure 4–18 have been completed.

A lease also can be fulfilled by completing an approved transfer of a resident either within the property or to another affiliated property of the management company, or if the management company decides not to renew the lease for another term and submits a written notice signed and dated by an agent of the company that the management company will not renew the lease. In each instance, the resident is entitled to her/his security deposit refund.

If a resident does not fulfill her/his lease, additional rent should be charged in accordance with lease provisions and in addition to charges for damages and previous unpaid items. This amount could include rent for the remaining term of the lease or until the unit is occupied, whichever comes

FIGURE 4-16. Unconditional Guaranty of Lease

Date ____________________

To Whom It May Concern:

I (We) ____ of ________________________ will be responsible for any financial obligation for rent or related services or damage incurred by __________________________________, unit no.____________ at ________________.

In consideration of the making of the attached lease by the Lessor with the Lessee, at the request of the undersigned Insuror and in reliance on this guaranty, the Insuror hereby guaranties payment of the rent to be paid by the Lessee and the performance by the Lessee of all of the terms and conditions of the Lease, and the Insuror promises to pay all of the Lessor's expenses, including reasonable attorney fees incurred by the Lessor in enforcing all obligations of the Lessee under the Lease or incurred by the Lessor in enforcing this guaranty.

The Insuror understands that the Lessor will obtain an investigative credit report in connection with the Insuror's application to become a resident/co-signer of ______________.
(Property)

This report may include information about the Insuror's character, general reputation, personal characteristics and/or mode of living, and credit standing.

The Insuror understands that the Lessor will provide the name of the reporting agency obtaining this information.

IN WITNESS WHEREOF, the undersigned has caused this Guaranty to be executed in this ________ day of ______________ 20____.

____
(Property manager)

____
(Guarantor) (Social Security no.)

____
(Driver's license no.)

____
(Military ID no.)

____
(Guarantor) (Social Security no.)

State of ____________________

____
(Driver's license no.)

County of ____________________

SS:______________________________
(Military ID no.)

continued

FIGURE 4-16. Unconditional Guaranty of Lease (*Continued*)

Subscribed and sworn to before me, a Notary Public in and for said County and State, this the ______________ day of __________________ 20________.

____

(Notary Public)

____

(Type name)

My commission expires:

____

Information on party signing this affidavit

Address and phone number of Insuror: ______________________
____
____

Relationship to resident: ______________________________

Employer's name: ______________________________________

Credit references: ______________________________________
____
____
____
____
____
____
____
____
____
____
____
____
____
____

first. However, in no case can a management company collect rent from two persons on the same apartment for the same period of time.

The final account settlement letter with refund check or balance due statement should be mailed to the resident's forwarding address within 7 to 30 days after move-out depending on the requirements of the state in which the property is located. This matter should be cleared with legal counsel. The property manager should constantly monitor the security deposit refunds to make sure they are mailed promptly to former residents. This sensitive area gives rise to an occasional landlord abuse and has caused a significant amount of legislation.

Some firms have determined that collecting and administering security deposits are not worthwhile activities because of the time consumed in handling and administering deposits, particularly in those states that require annual interest be paid on deposits. As alternatives, they have gone to "bonds," escrow accounts, or eliminated deposits altogether.

Any one of these approaches makes sense in the correct circumstances. The bond is an arrangement whereby an insurance or bonding company guarantees the amount of the security deposit, in the event it is required, and charges the resident a premium to guaranty the security deposit. If the resident damages the unit, the property manager collects from the insurance company rather than the resident. Because no deposit is posted, the management firm has no obligation to pay interest and no obligation to issue an annual statement in those locations that require both interest and an annual statement.

The final alternative is to eliminate the security deposit altogether. This approach is somewhat risky and should be adopted only after careful review of the property's past history on security deposit refunds. If the property is regularly returning in excess of 95 percent of the deposits collected and has a stable tenancy, a no-deposit policy will probably work successfully, but it must be carefully monitored. The property manager evaluates potential residents on carefully designed criteria and requires the resident to sign an agreement to reimburse the property for any damage. This approach is particularly applicable for luxury apartments because those residents have substantial incomes and well-established credit.

The property manager is permitted to vary the security deposit required only on the basis of well-established credit. The deposit policy should be uniform for all residents. Any exceptions would have to be approved by the property management executive.

FINANCIAL MANAGEMENT OF THE PROPERTY

Up to this point, the various elements that define and impact the economics of property management have been explored. It has been determined that the property manager must become familiar with both the owner's economic focus for her/his investment and with those economic considerations that affect the owner's focus and the operation of the property (e.g., NOI, cash flow and cash-on-cash return, and valuation techniques).

Establishing rent levels and rent collection have been established as the two most fundamental and most crucial finance-related activities in which a property manager can participate. And the lease agreement has been examined as the legal instrument that documents the financial and other obligations of the renter to the owner and the owner's agent (the property manager), and vice versa.

Indeed, the property manager's main responsibility is to ensure that the property operates according to sound financial principles and that it produces a profit for the owner. It is therefore easy to understand why, in the absence of a financial management system, the executive property manager, the senior manager, and the property manager would have difficulty renting, maintaining, or administering a property and why a deliberate financial management system is essential to the success of both the property and the property manager. (Note: Throughout the discussion that follows, references to the manager apply equally to both senior managers and property managers.)

ESTABLISHING THE FINANCIAL MANAGEMENT SYSTEM

The numbers and analyses provided by a sound financial management system are essential to the functioning of any property. The well-designed financial management system has four basic interrelated elements:

- Budgeting
- Collections and disbursements
- Monthly financial reporting
- Financial operations

As part of its design, a financial management system provides the planning and control tools that permit the property to function. Some elements of the system look backward and show what has happened in the past. Other elements of the system look forward, project into the future, and provide a plan of action. Both views are important to a sound operation.

No two properties are designed or operated exactly alike. However, a sound financial management system should be designed to accommodate a number of different properties within the same overall design scheme. The design needs to be flexible enough to handle large and small properties and even different types of properties—such as rental properties and shared-interest associations like condominiums, for example—all within the same system.

Ideally, a management firm's financial management system will be the same for all of the firm's management accounts. The benefits of standardization are many. For example, it allows staff members to move from one property to another with a minimum of retraining. It allows for easy comparison between properties. And it provides one formalized, all-encompassing perspective to the management company's most important decision-makers (its owner, the exec-

FIGURE 4-17. Security Deposit Policy

The security deposit is not rent but a deposit to ensure the fulfillment of lease conditions and to serve as contingency against any damages to the apartment or townhouse. Security deposits are never applied to the final month's rent. If a lease is fulfilled according to its terms, charges for damages only – excluding normal wear and tear – are deducted from the security deposit. The following conditions must be met for return of security deposits:

- The terms and conditions of the lease must be fulfilled and no money owed to the property.
- Resident must give 30 days' written notice of intent to vacate by completing the appropriate form at the rental office.
- Apartments and townhouses must be left clean with no damage beyond normal wear and tear.
- After belongings are removed from an apartment, the former resident and a management representative inspect the unit to complete the inspection report, and both sign it. The Management company representative clearly indicates on this form any items for which the resident is to be charged.
- Departing residents must give the office a valid forwarding address.
- They must turn all keys into the office. Residents are not considered officially vacated until they have turned in their keys.

utive property manager, and the chief financial officer/vice president of finance/comptroller/director of accounting) and to its front line workers (senior managers, property managers, in-house staff members, and on-site staff members).

In designing a financial management system, the management company comptroller and/or senior manager must consider the following factors:

- What members of the management staff will be using the financial information the system produces?
- What information will they need?
- Where outside the management firm will the accounting department be sending the financial information?
- Do any of the people outside the firm who will be receiving the information need special formulas?
- What level of detail is needed in both internal and external information and financial reporting?

FIGURE 4-18. Lease Fulfillment Requirements

- A written notice of intention to vacate is signed and dated by the resident and is submitted at least 30 days prior to the expiration date of the lease; the full term of the lease has expired; and all provisions of the lease have been fulfilled. Some states may not require written notice when move-out occurs at the end of the term of the lease. Property managers should check with local legal counsel.
- All rent, late charges, and returned check charges are paid to the date of move-out
- Move-out is defined as follows:
    - Resident has moved all of his/her furnishings and clothes from the apartment.
    - Entire apartment, including range, oven, refrigerator, bathroom, closets, cabinets, and storage locker are clean. All debris, rubbish, and discards are placed in proper containers.
    - Forwarding address has been left with the property manager.
    - All keys are returned to the manager

- Can the system's reports be easily understood by those who are using them?
- Do the information and reports lend themselves to easy reference?
- Will anyone require information more often than monthly, and, if so, on what basis?
- Will special reports be needed for regulatory purposes, and do the reports need to be in a special format?
- What will be the initial and on-going operating costs of the system?
- How complex is the system, and is it easy to maintain?
- Can the confidential information contained in the system be kept secure?
- Who will be entering data into the system?
- How much training is needed to learn to use the system?

The executive property manager and management company comptroller should carefully design the overall flow of information within the financial reporting system and then review the options for implementing that design. Flexibility and ease of use should be the hallmarks of the system. A system that is easy to use and that produces results that are easy to understand, usually in the form of documented reports, provides the following benefits:

- Clear data for making decisions
- Easy interim reports
- Quick turnaround of data
- Flexibility in producing special reports

CHART OF ACCOUNTS

The chart of accounts forms the basic architecture of the financial management system. This chart consist of a series of numbers, each of which represents a different asset, liability, equity, income, or expense item. The structure of the financial management system will be dictated by the arrangement of the chart. Depending on the needs of the property and the degree of detail desired, the chart can be simple or quite complex.

Figure 4–19 is a sample page from a chart of accounts used for the sample budgets and financial statements in this part of the book. For developments financed or insured by HUD, financial reporting that is submitted to HUD must be based on the standard HUD chart of accounts and account definitions contained in HUD handbook 4370.2, *Financial Operations and Accounting Procedures for Insured Multifamily Projects*. One page of the chart of accounts section of this book is reproduced in Figure 4–20.

Managers and financial executives alike often are reluctant to review and revise the chart of accounts. But over time, conditions change or the nature of the properties being managed changes, older accounts are seldom deleted, and a chart of accounts can grow in size as accounts are added to accommodate special needs. A simple 100-account system may grow to 500 or more accounts over a five-year period or sooner. Therefore, the chart should be reviewed regularly, and accounts not being used should be deleted from the active file and stored elsewhere or removed entirely. Most properties can operate quite well with full detail and clarity using no more than about 150 accounts. Beyond that range, the detailed financial statements become unwieldy and the summary statements are difficult to consolidate in an orderly manner.

BUDGETS AND BUDGETING

Although many residential management firms augment their revenue stream with ancillary services such as landscaping, pool maintenance, and other related services, every management firm's main income is derived from the fees generated by managing residential properties. The internal budgets of residential management firms are developed by the companies' owners and highest level property management executives.

Similarly, although many property owners augment their revenue with ancillary services such as on-premises coin-operated laundries or rentable social or storage spaces, every residential property's main income is derived from the rents paid by residents. Preparing the operating and capital budgets of residential properties is generally a joint effort between the senior manager, the property manager, the assistant manager, the management company's chief financial staff member, the property owner, the owner's asset manager (if appropriate), and the owner's accountant.

Establishing an accurate and practical operating budget and a realistic capital budget are the first steps in the effective financial management of a property. The operating budget is the basic document for planning the financial operation of the property for the coming year. The capital budget anticipates the property's financial needs over time, usually the upcoming three to five years. Operating within the property's budgets is the joint responsibility of the senior manager and the property manager. Property employees, from the maintenance supervisor to the property office staff, also must cooperate in keeping the property within the prescribed budgetary guidelines.

Two truths apply to the budgets of residential properties. First, the budget process of estimating and planning requires time and care to produce solid results. Second, the budget and the process of arriving at a budget are essential management tools, and no property should operate without them. In truth, the property manager should view the budget process, the operating budget, and the capital budget as a comprehensive opportunity to implement ideas and plans for the property that will enhance its value and hence the management company's value to the owner.

BUDGET DESIGN

The format and contents of budgets vary from property to property according to the size of the property, the needs of

Figure 4–19. Chart of Accounts

Income	
Rent	4111
Free units	5119
Vacancy losses	5120
Pro rated rent	5121
Rent concessions	5122
Laundry income	6001
Miscellaneous income	6002
Bad debt recoveries	6003
Interest income	6004
Storage fees	6100
Collection fees	6101
Security deposit forfeits	6102
Pet Fees	6103
Lease cancellation fees	6104
NSF and bank fees	6105
Expenses	
Advertising	
Advertising – periodicals	7061
Advertising – signs/graphics	7062
Administration	
Temporary help	7200
Credit reports	7221
Donations	7222
Dues and subscriptions	7225
General expenses	7226
Leasing expenses	7231
Leasing referrals	7233
Legal	7234
Office supplies and postage	7240
Accounting and audit	7241
Professional development	7241
Public relations	7242
Local phone	7244
Long distance	7245
Answering services	7246
Pagers and radio	7247
Building Repairs	
Drapes, blinds	7804
Electrical	7805
Plumbing	7807
Roof	7808
Floor covering replacement	7810
Floor covering repair	7811
Exterior painting labor	7815
Exterior painting supplies	7816
Exterior repairs	7817
Janitorial supplies	7821
Keys and locks	7822
Light bulbs	7823
Interior paint labor	7830
Interior paint supplies	7831
Interior repairs	7832
HVAC replacements	7835
HVAC supplies and services	7836
Appliance replacement	7840
Appliance repair	7841
Interior contract cleaning	7845
Exterior cleaning	7846
Fire and Safety System	7847
Temporary help	7200
Common Area Repairs	
Cable Television	7901
Electrical	7902
Parking lot repair	7903
Equipment	7905
Pool repair	7910
Pool supplies	7911
Grounds maintenance	7915
Landscape repair	7916
Extermination	7921
Garbage hauling	7922
General cleaning	7923
Security	7924
Management Fees	8500
Payroll and Related Expenses	
Manager	8701
Assistant Manager	8702
Clerical	8703
Leasing	8704
Maintenance staff	8705
Grounds staff	8706
Recreation	8708
Leasing bonuses	8741
Other bonuses	8799
Employee benefits	8800
Employee FICA	8801
Employee FUTA	8802
State unemployment	8803
Workers' Compensation Ins	8804
Travel allowances	8861
Travel-other	8863
Utilities	
Electricity	9101
Occupied unit electricity	9102
Vacant unit electricity	9103
Model electricity	9104
Water	9121
Occupied unit water	9122
Sprinkler	9123
Gas	9141
Sewer	9161
Debt Service, Insurance, and taxes	9600
Mortgage principal and interest	9601
Replacement reserves	9602
Mortgage insurance	9800
Property and casualty insurance	9900
Property taxes	

Figure 4–20. HUD Chart of Accounts

FINANCIAL OPERATIONS AND ACCOUNTING PROCEDURES FOR INSURED MULTIFAMILY PROJECTS CHAPTER 4

5200 **Vacancies – Accounts 5220 through 5290:**
These accounts record rental income lost through vacancy of an apartment unit or otherwise revenue-producing space or equipment. Agents normally debit the accounts monthly from the Rent Roll. At the end of the accounting period, the balance of these accounts are closed to Account 3250, Profit and Loss.

5300 **Elderly and Congregate Services Income:**
Accounts in this Series are used primarily by Section 202 projects and other projects designed for the elderly. The accounts record revenues received other than rents for services provided to tenants (e.g., meal services, housekeeping and nursing care services). Service-related expenses are charged to accounts in the 6900 Series.

5400 **Financial Revenue:**
These accounts record interest income received or accrued from invested project cash and Funded Reserves. The account is credited from the Cash receipts Journal or by a general journal entry prepared at the end of the accounting period.

5900 **Other Revenue:**

5910 – **Laundry and Vending Revenue:** This account records project revenues received from laundry and vending machines owned or leased by the project.

5920 – **NSF and late Charges:** This account records charges assessed to tenants for rent checks returned for insufficient funds and for late payment of rents.

5930 – **Damages and Cleaning Fees:** This account records charges collected from tenants for damages to apartment units and for fees paid by tenants for cleaning of an apartment unit (other than regular housekeeping services).

5940 – **Forfeited Tenant Security Deposit:** This account records any security deposit forfeited by tenants moving out of the project. The account is credited only when the tenant security deposit is deposited to the project operating account.

the resident population, the conditions of the management contract (including the management fee), and the owner's policies and objectives for the property. Under any circumstances, to be most useful the budget format should mirror the structure of the property's monthly and annual financial reports, reflecting the same income and expense accounts.

Depending on the policies and practices of the management firm or owner, the budget either stops at NOI or extends through debt service, ownership transactions, and capital improvements to net cash flow. In either event, the budget always extends at least through NOI.

The annual operating budget may be broken down into monthly segments. All revenue and expenses would be allocated to the months in which they are likely to occur. Figures 4–21 through 4–24 contain a full sample operating budget for Clyde Estates, a hypothetical garden apartment community.

SEASONALIZATION

The budget process helps the property manager to anticipate income and expenses and manage the property's available cash. The manager who does not keep track of cash flow and cash available at the beginning of the year is much more likely to have month left at the end of the money than she/he is to have money left at the end of the month. All income and expenses estimated in the budget may be seasonalized so that the budget will reflect the actual receipt of income and expenses if such detail is desired. In most properties, substantial variances occur in both income and expenses from month to month.

For instance, the total operating expenses of Clyde Estates for the year (Fig. 4–25) reflect a variance of 33 percent. The variance in operating expenses has a substantial effect on the monthly income. Although the property makes an overall profit for the year, it sustained a loss in March. If the budget were determined simply by dividing all annual expenses by 12, the loss would not be anticipated and cash might not be available.

With regard to the monthly cash flow (Fig. 4–26) after payment of all expenses for the year, for properties with substantial seasonal changes in expenses—for example, a property that pays for heating and cooling in apartments—the variance in income will be greater. The number of months with losses also will increase even though the property makes a profit for the year.

BUDGET ASSUMPTIONS

When drafting the budget, the budget can be either a historically based budget or a zero-base budget. A historically based budget uses assumptions about the property's existing history of costs to project expenses into the future. When such historical performance is used to draft a budget moving forward, any deviations from the budgeted numbers must first be investigated before those numbers are repeated for the coming year. Following past performance without any consideration to the accuracy, appropriateness, adequacy, or usefulness of any cost may perpetuate overspending and present an inaccurate projection of the property's finances.

Conversely, building a budget exclusively by researching projected income and costs without any historical data (e.g., assuming income based on anticipated per-unit payments rather than actual payment history, and assuming expenses based on information provided by engineers, vendors, contractors, suppliers, etc., rather than on actual expense data) results in a zero-base budget. For most existing properties, a combination of historic costs and the zero-base system will yield the best results. For such a combination budget, a property manager would use historic costs to anticipate administrative and maintenance costs and a zero-base approach to payroll, benefits, and taxes.

New properties or those undergoing renovation must use a zero-base approach because there is no applicable historic record to use.

BUDGETING GUIDELINES

The property manager needs to ask the following two questions in every budgeting situation: Is it logical? and Is it reasonable?

If any of the work being done on the budget fails these tests, that failure is the signal to re-evaluate that step and as many prior steps as necessary until the work meets both tests. Too often as the budget is being developed these common sense tests are ignored. One of the most important tools a property manager uses in the budget process is common sense.

The budget should be as accurate as possible and somewhat conservative in its assumptions. As a planning and control tool, it must mirror reality. It should reflect the probable income and expenses.

Ordinarily, the budget for the coming period should not differ radically from the financial results of the previous year. If it does, the reasons for changing the assumptions should be sound. At the same time, the budget numbers must not be forced to fit some preconceived circumstance that is no longer justified.

The budget should be a realistic picture of the likely outcome of the property's financial operations for the year. The property manager may have to stretch a bit to reach the numbers, but they should be attainable by normal efforts.

CONTINGENCY FUNDS

Ideally, the property will go into the new fiscal year liquid, with sufficient cash to cover all anticipated expenses and enough additional cash to pay for any and all unanticipated expenses during the year. In virtually all situations, whether or not the property actually has such a cash reserve, the property manager will want to have some discretionary funds in the budget to cover unforeseen events. Depending on the condition of the property, its age, its access to capital, and on the owner's and manager's policies regarding contingency funds, these discretionary funds might be included in the budget either as a specifically identified reserve fund or as an additional percentage added to all estimates of expenses. In any event, it is critical to either have or budget for sufficient funds to cover unanticipated expenses.

Figure 4–21. Summary Budget

Sample Budget

FINAL BUDGET FOR 2002														296	As a %
INCOME:	January	February	March	April	May	June	July	August	September	October	November	December	TOTAL	Per Unit	of GPI
GROSS RENTS	$133,200.00	$133,200.00	$133,200.00	$133,200.00	$133,600.00	$134,000.00	$134,400.00	$134,800.00	$135,200.00	$135,600.00	$136,000.00	$136,400.00	$1,612,800.00	$5,449.00	122.747%
[Vacancies/Free Units/Etc.]	($31,747.00)	($33,135.00)	($33,247.00)	($30,402.00)	($29,175.00)	($27,947.00)	($26,720.00)	($25,492.00)	($24,265.00)	($21,810.00)	($21,810.00)	($21,810.00)	($327,560.00)	($1,107.00)	-24.930%
NET RENT INCOME	$101,453.00	$100,065.00	$99,953.00	$102,798.00	$104,425.00	$106,053.00	$107,680.00	$109,308.00	$110,935.00	$113,790.00	$114,190.00	$114,590.00	$1,285,240.00	$4,342.00	97.817%
CHARGES INCOME	$2,020.00	$2,020.00	$2,020.00	$2,020.00	$2,020.00	$2,020.00	$2,020.00	$2,020.00	$2,020.00	$2,020.00	$2,020.00	$2,020.00	$24,240.00	$82.00	1.845%
OTHER INCOME	$370.00	$370.00	$370.00	$370.00	$370.00	$370.00	$370.00	$370.00	$370.00	$370.00	$370.00	$370.00	$4,440.00	$15.00	33.800%
GROSS POSSIBLE INCOME (GPI)	$103,843.00	$102,455.00	$102,343.00	$105,188.00	$106,815.00	$108,443.00	$110,070.00	$111,698.00	$113,325.00	$116,180.00	$116,580.00	$116,980.00	$1,313,920.00	$4,439.00	100.000%
EXPENSES:															
MANAGEMENT FEES	$4,154.00	$4,098.00	$4,094.00	$4,208.00	$4,273.00	$4,338.00	$4,403.00	$4,468.00	$4,533.00	$4,647.00	$4,663.00	$4,679.00	$52,558.00	$178.00	4.000%
ADMINISTRATIVE	$2,568.00	$2,951.00	$13,686.00	$3,234.00	$2,568.00	$2,568.00	$2,868.00	$2,568.00	$2,868.00	$2,568.00	$2,868.00	$2,868.00	$44,183.00	$150.00	3.377%
ADVERTISING	$4,760.00	$3,500.00	$3,200.00	$3,200.00	$3,200.00	$6,760.00	$5,500.00	$6,760.00	$3,200.00	$3,200.00	$3,200.00	$3,200.00	$49,680.00	$168.00	3.781%
SALARIES	$6,957.00	$7,013.00	$7,033.00	$8,531.00	$9,175.00	$9,175.00	$9,175.00	$9,175.00	$8,560.00	$7,138.00	$7,179.00	$7,179.00	$96,290.00	$325.00	7.328%
BENEFITS & TAXES	$1,570.00	$1,572.00	$1,573.00	$1,634.00	$1,660.00	$1,660.00	$1,660.00	$1,660.00	$1,635.00	$1,577.00	$1,579.00	$1,579.00	$19,359.00	$65.00	1.473%
Sub Total Payroll	$8,527.00	$8,585.00	$8,606.00	$10,165.00	$10,835.00	$10,835.00	$10,835.00	$10,835.00	$10,195.00	$8,715.00	$8,758.00	$8,758.00	$115,649.00	$391.00	8.802%
BUILDING MAINTENANCE	$3,342.00	$3,342.00	$3,582.00	$3,842.00	$3,842.00	$9,582.00	$4,342.00	$4,342.00	$4,082.00	$3,842.00	$3,342.00	$3,582.00	$51,064.00	$173.00	3.886%
COMMON AREA EXPENSES	$4,108.00	$4,108.00	$5,908.00	$6,433.00	$8,808.00	$4,208.00	$4,208.00	$4,208.00	$4,108.00	$4,108.00	$4,108.00	$4,108.00	$58,421.00	$197.00	4.447%
UTILITIES	$11,291.00	$10,053.00	$4,861.00	$3,617.00	$3,685.00	$5,202.00	$5,529.00	$5,231.00	$4,275.00	$3,314.00	$3,721.00	$4,769.00	$65,548.00	$221.00	4.989%
TOTAL OPERATING EXPENSES	$38,750.00	$36,637.00	$43,937.00	$34,699.00	$37,211.00	$43,493.00	$37,685.00	$38,412.00	$33,261.00	$30,394.00	$30,660.00	$31,964.00	$437,103.00	$1,477.00	33.281%
INSURANCE	$2,504.00	$2,504.00	$2,504.00	$2,504.00	$2,504.00	$2,504.00	$2,504.00	$2,504.00	$2,504.00	$2,504.00	$2,504.00	$2,504.00	$30,048.00	$102.00	2.287%
TAXES	$8,917.00	$8,917.00	$8,917.00	$8,917.00	$8,917.00	$8,917.00	$8,917.00	$8,917.00	$8,917.00	$8,917.00	$8,917.00	$8,917.00	$107,004.00	$361.00	8.144%
TOTAL OTHER EXPENSES	$11,421.00	$11,421.00	$11,421.00	$11,421.00	$11,421.00	$11,421.00	$11,421.00	$11,421.00	$11,421.00	$11,421.00	$11,421.00	$11,421.00	$137,052.00	$463.00	10.430%
TOTAL ALL EXPENSES	$50,171.00	$48,058.00	$55,358.00	$46,120.00	$48,632.00	$54,914.00	$49,106.00	$49,833.00	$44,682.00	$41,815.00	$42,081.00	$43,385.00	$574,155.00	$1,940.00	43.711%
NET OPERATING INCOME (NOI)	$53,672.00	$54,397.00	$46,985.00	$59,068.00	$58,183.00	$53,529.00	$60,964.00	$61,865.00	$68,643.00	$74,365.00	$74,499.00	$73,595.00	$739,765.00	$2,499.00	56.289%
DEBT SERVICE:															
MORTGAGE PRIN & INTEREST	$46,872.00	$46,872.00	$46,872.00	$46,872.00	$46,872.00	$46,872.00	$46,872.00	$46,872.00	$46,872.00	$46,872.00	$46,872.00	$46,872.00	$562,464.00	$1,900.00	42.808%
MORTGAGE INSURANCE	$1,500.00	$1,500.00	$1,500.00	$1,500.00	$1,500.00	$1,500.00	$1,500.00	$1,500.00	$1,500.00	$1,500.00	$1,500.00	$1,500.00	$18,000.00	$61.00	1.370%
TOTAL DEBT SVC	$48,372.00	$48,372.00	$48,372.00	$48,372.00	$48,372.00	$48,372.00	$48,372.00	$48,372.00	$48,372.00	$48,372.00	$48,372.00	$48,372.00	$580,464.00	$1,961.00	44.178%
RESERVE CONTRIBUTIONS															
RESERVE REFUNDS															
CAPITAL ITEMS															
NET INSURANCE CLAIMS															
OTHER ITEMS															
Income After Debt & Capital	$5,300.00	$6,025.00	($1,387.00)	$10,696.00	$9,811.00	$5,157.00	$12,592.00	$13,493.00	$20,271.00	$25,993.00	$26,127.00	$25,223.00	$159,301.00	$538.00	12.111%

Figure 4–21. Summary Budget (*Continued*)

(with operating ratios)

FINAL BUDGET FOR 2002														296	As a %
INCOME:	January	February	March	April	May	June	July	August	September	October	November	December	TOTAL	Per Unit	of GPI
GROSS RENTS	$133,200.00	$133,200.00	$133,200.00	$133,200.00	$133,600.00	$134,000.00	$134,400.00	$134,800.00	$135,200.00	$135,600.00	$136,000.00	$136,400.00	$1,612,800.00	$5,449.00	122.747%
[Vacancies/Free Units/Etc.]	($31,747.00)	($33,135.00)	($33,247.00)	($30,402.00)	($29,175.00)	($27,947.00)	($26,720.00)	($25,492.00)	($24,265.00)	($21,810.00)	($21,810.00)	($21,810.00)	($327,560.00)	($1,107.00)	-24.930%
NET RENT INCOME	$101,453.00	$100,065.00	$99,953.00	$102,798.00	$104,425.00	$106,053.00	$107,680.00	$109,308.00	$110,935.00	$113,790.00	$114,190.00	$114,590.00	$1,285,240.00	$4,342.00	97.817%
CHARGES INCOME	$2,020.00	$2,020.00	$2,020.00	$2,020.00	$2,020.00	$2,020.00	$2,020.00	$2,020.00	$2,020.00	$2,020.00	$2,020.00	$2,020.00	$24,240.00	$82.00	1.845%
OTHER INCOME	$370.00	$370.00	$370.00	$370.00	$370.00	$370.00	$370.00	$370.00	$370.00	$370.00	$370.00	$370.00	$4,440.00	$15.00	33.800%
GROSS POSSIBLE INCOME (GPI)	$103,843.00	$102,455.00	$102,343.00	$105,188.00	$106,815.00	$108,443.00	$110,070.00	$111,698.00	$113,325.00	$116,180.00	$116,580.00	$116,980.00	$1,313,920.00	$4,439.00	100.000%
EXPENSES:															
MANAGEMENT FEES	$4,154.00	$4,098.00	$4,094.00	$4,208.00	$4,273.00	$4,338.00	$4,403.00	$4,468.00	$4,533.00	$4,647.00	$4,663.00	$4,679.00	$52,558.00	$178.00	4.000%
ADMINISTRATIVE	$2,568.00	$2,951.00	$13,686.00	$3,234.00	$2,568.00	$2,568.00	$2,868.00	$2,568.00	$2,868.00	$2,568.00	$2,868.00	$2,868.00	$44,183.00	$150.00	3.377%
ADVERTISING	$4,760.00	$3,500.00	$3,200.00	$3,200.00	$3,200.00	$6,760.00	$5,500.00	$6,760.00	$3,200.00	$3,200.00	$3,200.00	$3,200.00	$49,680.00	$168.00	3.781%
SALARIES	$6,957.00	$7,013.00	$7,033.00	$8,531.00	$9,175.00	$9,175.00	$9,175.00	$9,175.00	$8,560.00	$7,138.00	$7,179.00	$7,179.00	$96,290.00	$325.00	7.328%
BENEFITS & TAXES	$1,570.00	$1,572.00	$1,573.00	$1,634.00	$1,660.00	$1,660.00	$1,660.00	$1,660.00	$1,635.00	$1,577.00	$1,579.00	$1,579.00	$19,359.00	$65.00	1.473%
Sub Total Payroll	$8,527.00	$8,585.00	$8,606.00	$10,165.00	$10,835.00	$10,835.00	$10,835.00	$10,835.00	$10,195.00	$8,715.00	$8,758.00	$8,758.00	$115,649.00	$391.00	8.802%
BUILDING MAINTENANCE	$3,342.00	$3,342.00	$3,582.00	$3,842.00	$3,842.00	$9,582.00	$4,342.00	$4,342.00	$4,082.00	$3,842.00	$3,342.00	$3,582.00	$51,064.00	$173.00	3.886%
COMMON AREA EXPENSES	$4,108.00	$4,108.00	$5,908.00	$6,433.00	$8,808.00	$4,208.00	$4,208.00	$4,208.00	$4,108.00	$4,108.00	$4,108.00	$4,108.00	$58,421.00	$197.00	4.447%
UTILITIES	$11,291.00	$10,053.00	$4,861.00	$3,617.00	$3,685.00	$5,202.00	$5,529.00	$5,231.00	$4,275.00	$3,314.00	$3,721.00	$4,769.00	$65,548.00	$221.00	4.989%
TOTAL OPERATING EXPENSES	$38,750.00	$36,637.00	$43,937.00	$34,699.00	$37,211.00	$43,493.00	$37,685.00	$38,412.00	$33,261.00	$30,394.00	$30,660.00	$31,964.00	$437,103.00	$1,477.00	33.281%
INSURANCE	$2,504.00	$2,504.00	$2,504.00	$2,504.00	$2,504.00	$2,504.00	$2,504.00	$2,504.00	$2,504.00	$2,504.00	$2,504.00	$2,504.00	$30,048.00	$102.00	2.287%
TAXES	$8,917.00	$8,917.00	$8,917.00	$8,917.00	$8,917.00	$8,917.00	$8,917.00	$8,917.00	$8,917.00	$8,917.00	$8,917.00	$8,917.00	$107,004.00	$361.00	8.144%
TOTAL OTHER EXPENSES	$11,421.00	$11,421.00	$11,421.00	$11,421.00	$11,421.00	$11,421.00	$11,421.00	$11,421.00	$11,421.00	$11,421.00	$11,421.00	$11,421.00	$137,052.00	$463.00	10.430%
TOTAL ALL EXPENSES	$50,171.00	$48,058.00	$55,358.00	$46,120.00	$48,632.00	$54,914.00	$49,106.00	$49,833.00	$44,682.00	$41,815.00	$42,081.00	$43,385.00	$574,155.00	$1,940.00	43.711%
NET OPERATING INCOME (NOI)	$53,672.00	$54,397.00	$46,985.00	$59,068.00	$58,183.00	$53,529.00	$60,964.00	$61,865.00	$68,643.00	$74,365.00	$74,499.00	$73,595.00	$739,765.00	$2,499.00	56.289%

% of GPI in NonProd Concessions & Vacancy	22.75%
Salaries as % of GPI	8.80%

AS A % OF TOTAL EXPENSE	
Management	9.15%
Administrative	-7.73%
Advertising	8.65%
Salaries & Benefits	20.14%
Building Maint.	8.89%
Common Area	10.17%
Taxes	18.63%
Insurance	5.23%

% GPI in Other Income 2.18%

Average NOI Per Month	"$56,892.00

	Number	Average Per Person
Full Year Staff	6	$18,075.00
Seasonal Staff	3	$3,767.00

Figure 4–22. Detailed Budget

Property: Clyde Estates Units: 296

Date Marker / Time Marker	Account Number	January	February	March	April	May	June	July	August	September	October	November	December	TOTAL	296 Per Unit	As a % of GPI
POTENTIAL RENT	4111	$133,200.00	$133,200.00	$133,200.00	$133,200.00	$133,600.00	$134,000.00	$134,400.00	$134,800.00	$135,200.00	$135,600.00	$136,000.00	$136,400.00	$1,612,800.00	$5,449.00	122.747%
Less:																
FREE UNITS	4203	$1,325.00	$1,325.00	$1,325.00	$1,325.00	$1,325.00	$1,325.00	$1,325.00	$1,325.00	$1,325.00	$1,325.00	$1,325.00	$1,325.00	$1,590.00	$54.00	1.210%
VACANCY LOSSES	5120	$16,255.00	$17,643.00	$17,755.00	$14,910.00	$13,683.00	$12,455.00	$11,228.00	$10,000.00	$8,773.00	$6,318.00	$6,318.00	$6,318.00	$141,656.00	$479.00	10.781%
PRO RATED RENT	4111															
CONSESSIONS	4111	$14,167.00	$14,167.00	$14,167.00	$14,167.00	$14,167.00	$14,167.00	$14,167.00	$14,167.00	$14,167.00	$14,167.00	$14,167.00	$14,167.00	$170,004.00	$574.00	12.939%
NET RENT INCOME		$101,453.00	$100,065.00	$99,953.00	$102,798.00	$104,425.00	$106,053.00	$107,680.00	$109,308.00	$110,935.00	$113,780.00	$114,190.00	$114,590.00	$1,285,240.00	$4,342.00	97.817%
STORAGE FEES	4311															
COLLECTION FEES	4312	$300.00	$300.00	$300.00	$300.00	$300.00	$300.00	$300.00	$300.00	$300.00	$300.00	$300.00	$300.00	$3,600.00	$12.00	0.274%
SECURTIY DEP FORFEITS	5201	$1,000.00	$1,000.00	$1,000.00	$1,000.00	$1,000.00	$1,000.00	$1,000.00	$1,000.00	$1,000.00	$1,000.00	$1,000.00	$1,000.00	$12,000.00	$41.00	0.913%
PET FEES	5303	$250.00	$250.00	$250.00	$250.00	$250.00	$250.00	$250.00	$250.00	$250.00	$250.00	$250.00	$250.00	$3,000.00	$10.00	0.228%
LEASE CANCEL FEES	5304	$400.00	$400.00	$400.00	$400.00	$400.00	$400.00	$400.00	$400.00	$400.00	$400.00	$400.00	$400.00	$4,800.00	16	0.365%
NSF & BANK FEES	5305	$70.00	$70.00	$70.00	$70.00	$70.00	$70.00	$70.00	$70.00	$70.00	$70.00	$70.00	$70.00	$840.00	$3.00	0.064%
TOTAL CHARGES INCOME		$2,020.00	$2,020.00	$2,020.00	$2,020.00	$2,020.00	$2,020.00	$2,020.00	$2,020.00	$2,020.00	$2,020.00	$2,020.00	$2,020.00	$24,240.00	$82.00	1.845%
LAUNDRY INCOME	5202	$370.00	$370.00	$370.00	$370.00	$370.00	$370.00	$370.00	$370.00	$370.00	$370.00	$370.00	$370.00	$4,400.00	$15.00	0.338%
MISC INCOME	5203															
BAD DEBT RECOVERIES	5204															
INTEREST INCOME	6104															
TOTAL OTHER INCOME		$370.00	$370.00	$370.00	$370.00	$370.00	$370.00	$370.00	$370.00	$370.00	$370.00	$370.00	$370.00	$4,400.00	$15.00	0.338%
TOTAL INCOME		$103,843.00	$102,455.00	$102,343.00	$105,188.00	$106,815.00	$108,443.00	$110,070.00	$111,698.00	$113,325.00	$116,180.00	$116,580.00	$116,980.00	$1,313,920.00	$4,439.00	100.000%

Figure 4–22. Detailed Budget (*Continued*)

Professional Management Company
Real Estate Management Division

Property: Clyde Estates
Units: 296

Date Marker / Time Marker	Account Number	January	February	March	April	May	June	July	August	September	October	November	December	TOTAL	296 Per Unit	As a % of GPI
EXPENSES																
OPERATING EXPENSES																
MANAGEMENT FEES	8501	$4,154.00	$4,098.00	$4,094.00	$4,208.00	$4,273.00	$4,338.00	$4,403.00	$4,468.00	$4,533.00	$4,647.00	$4,663.00	$4,679.00	$52,557.00	$178.00	4.000%
ACCOUNTING & AUDIT	7041			$11,300.00										$11,300.00	$38.00	0.860%
CREDIT REPORTS	7221	$170.00	$170.00	$170.00	$170.00	$170.00	$170.00	$170.00	$170.00	$170.00	$170.00	$170.00	$170.00	$2,040.00	$7.00	0.155%
DONATIONS	7321															
DUES & SUBSCRIPTIONS	7361	$30.00	$113.00	$30.00	$396.00	$30.00	$30.00	$30.00	$30.00	$30.00	$30.00	$30.00	$30.00	$809.00	$3.00	0.062%
GENERAL EXPENSES	7501															
LEASING EXPENSES	7701	$1,083.00	$1,083.00	$1,083.00	$1,083.00	$1,083.00	$1,083.00	$1,083.00	$1,083.00	$1,083.00	$1,083.00	$1,083.00	$1,083.00	$12,996.00	$44.00	0.989%
LEASING REFERRALS	7703	$375.00	$375.00	$375.00	$375.00	$375.00	$375.00	$375.00	$375.00	$375.00	$375.00	$375.00	$375.00	$4,500.00	$15.00	0.342%
LEGAL	7721	$150.00	$150.00	$150.00	$150.00	$150.00	$150.00	$150.00	$150.00	$150.00	$150.00	$150.00	$150.00	$1,800.00	$6.00	0.137%
OFFICE SUPPLIES & POST	8301	$300.00	$300.00	$300.00	$300.00	$300.00	$300.00	$300.00	$300.00	$300.00	$300.00	$300.00	$300.00	$3,600.00	$12.00	0.274%
PROFESSIONAL DEVELOPMENT	8401															
PUBLIC RELATIONS	8421		$300.00		$300.00			$300.00		$300.00		$300.00	$300.00	$1,800.00	$6.00	0.137%
LOCAL PHONE	8841	$175.00	$175.00	$175.00	$175.00	$175.00	$175.00	$175.00	$175.00	$175.00	$175.00	$175.00	$175.00	$2,100.00	$7.00	0.160%
LONG DISTANCE	8842	$100.00	$100.00	$100.00	$100.00	$100.00	$100.00	$100.00	$100.00	$100.00	$100.00	$100.00	$100.00	$1,200.00	$4.00	0.091%
ANSWERING SERVICE	8843	$75.00	$75.00	$75.00	$75.00	$75.00	$75.00	$75.00	$75.00	$75.00	$75.00	$75.00	$75.00	$900.00	$3.00	0.068%
PAGERS & RADIO	8844	$30.00	$30.00	$30.00	$30.00	$30.00	$30.00	$30.00	$30.00	$30.00	$30.00	$30.00	$30.00	$360.00	$1.00	0.027%
TRAVEL ALLOWANCE	8861	$50.00	$50.00	$50.00	$50.00	$50.00	$50.00	$50.00	$50.00	$50.00	$50.00	$50.00	$50.00	$600.00	$2.00	0.046%
TRAVEL OTHER	8863	$30.00	$30.00	$30.00	$30.00	$30.00	$30.00	$30.00	$30.00	$30.00	$30.00	$30.00	$30.00	$360.00	$1.00	0.027%
TOTAL MANAGEMENT		$4,154.00	$4,098.00	$4,094.00	$4,208.00	$4,273.00	$4,338.00	$4,403.00	$4,468.00	$4,533.00	$4,647.00	$4,663.00	$4,679.00	$52,558.00	$178.00	4.000%
TOTAL ADMINISTRATIVE		$2,568.00	$2,951.00	$13,868.00	$3,234.00	$2,568.00	$2,568.00	$2,868.00	$2,568.00	$2,868.00	$2,568.00	$2,868.00	$2,868.00	$44,365.00	$150.00	3.377%
ADVERTISING/PERIODICALS	7061	$1,700.00	$1,700.00	$1,700.00	$1,700.00	$1,700.00	$3,700.00	$3,700.00	$3,700.00	$1,700.00	$1,700.00	$1,700.00	$1,700.00	$26,400.00	$89.00	2.209%
ADVERTISING SIGNS/GRAPHICS	7062	$3,060.00	$1,800.00	$1,500.00	$1,500.00	$1,500.00	$3,060.00	$1,800.00	$3,060.00	$1,500.00	$1,500.00	$1,500.00	$1,500.00	$23,280.00	$79.00	1.772%
TOTAL ADVERTISING		$4,760.00	$3,500.00	$3,200.00	$3,200.00	$3,200.00	$6,760.00	$5,500.00	$6,760.00	$3,200.00	$3,200.00	$3,200.00	$3,200.00	$49,680.00	$168.00	3.781%

Figure 4–22. Detailed Budget (*Continued*)

Professional Management Company
Real Estate Management Division

Property: Clyde Estates
Units: 296

Date Marker Time Marker	Account Number	January	February	March	April	May	June	July	August	September	October	November	December	TOTAL	296 Per Unit	As a % of GPI
SALARIES:																
MANAGER	8701	$1,000.00	$1,035.00	$1,035.00	$1,035.00	$1,035.00	$1,035.00	$1,036.00	$1,035.00	$1,035.00	$1,035.00	$1,035.00	$1,035.00	$12,385.00	$42.00	0.943%
ASST. MANAGER	8702	$823.00	$823.00	$823.00	$823.00	$852.00	$852.00	$852.00	$852.00	$852.00	$852.00	$852.00	$852.00	$10,110.00	$34.00	0.769%
CLERICAL	8702															
LEASING	8703	$1,248.00	$1,248.00	$1,267.00	$1,292.00	$1,292.00	$1,292.00	$1,292.00	$1,292.00	$1,292.00	$1,292.00	$1,292.00	$1,292.00	$15,388.00	$52.00	1.171%
MAINTENANCE STAFF	8704	$3,285.00	$3,307.00	$3,307.00	$3,307.00	$3,307.00	$3,307.00	$3,307.00	$3,307.00	$3,307.00	$3,359.00	$3,400.00	$3,400.00	$39,900.00	$135.00	3.037%
GROUNDS STAFF	8705				$1,474.00	$1,474.00	$1,474.00	$1,474.00	$1,474.00	$1,474.00				$8,844.00	$30.00	0.673%
RECREATION	8705					$615.00	$615.00	$615.00	$615.00					$2,460.00	$8.00	0.187%
TEMPORARY HELP	7200															
LEASING BONUSES	8741	$600.00	$600.00	$600.00	$600.00	$600.00	$600.00	$600.00	$600.00	$600.00	$600.00	$600.00	$600.00	$7,200.00	$24.00	0.548%
OTHER BONUSES	8787															
TOTAL SALARIES		$6,957.00	$7,013.00	$7,033.00	$8,531.00	$9,175.00	$9,175.00	$9,175.00	$9,175.00	$8,560.00	$7,138.00	$7,179.00	$7,179.00	$96,287.00	$325.00	7.328%
BENEFITS & TAXES																
EMPLOYEE BENEFITS	7401	$534.00	$534.00	$534.00	$534.00	$534.00	$534.00	$534.00	$534.00	$534.00	$534.00	$534.00	$534.00	$6,408.00	$22.00	0.488%
WORKER'S COMP. INSURANCE	7604	$284.00	$286.00	$287.00	$348.00	$374.00	$374.00	$374.00	$374.00	$349.00	$291.00	$293.00	$293.00	$3,929.00	$13.00	0.299%
EMPLOYERS FICA	8801	$531.00	$531.00	$531.00	$531.00	$531.00	$531.00	$531.00	$531.00	$531.00	$531.00	$531.00	$531.00	$6,370.00	$22.00	0.485%
EMPLOYERS FUTA	8802	$40.00	$40.00	$40.00	$40.00	$40.00	$40.00	$40.00	$40.00	$40.00	$40.00	$40.00	$40.00	$481.00	$2.00	0.037%
STATE UNEMPLOYMENT	8803	$181.00	$181.00	$181.00	$181.00	$181.00	$181.00	$181.00	$181.00	$181.00	$181.00	$181.00	$181.00	$2,170.00	$7.00	0.165%
TOTAL P/R TAXES/BENEFITS		$1,570.00	$1,572.00	$1,573.00	$1,634.00	$1,660.00	$1,660.00	$1,660.00	$1,660.00	$1,635.00	$1,577.00	$1,579.00	$1,579.00	$19,358.00	$65.00	1.473%

Figure 4–22. Detailed Budget (*Continued*)

Professional Management Company
Real Estate Management Division

Property: Clyde Estates
Units: 296

Date Marker Time Marker	Account Number	January	February	March	April	May	June	July	August	September	October	November	December	TOTAL	$296.00 Per Unit	As a % of GPI
BUILDING MAINTENANCE:																
DRAPES BLINDS	7804	$50.00	$50.00	$50.00	$50.00	$50.00	$50.00	$50.00	$50.00	$50.00	$50.00	$50.00	$50.00	$600.00	$2.00	0.046%
ELECTRICAL	7805	$150.00	$150.00	$150.00	$150.00	$150.00	$150.00	$150.00	$150.00	$150.00	$150.00	$150.00	$150.00	$1,800.00	$6.00	0.137%
PLUMBING	7807	$200.00	$200.00	$200.00	$200.00	$200.00	$200.00	$300.00	$200.00	$200.00	$200.00	$200.00	$200.00	$2,400.00	$8.00	0.183%
ROOF	7808			$90.00			$90.00			$90.00			$90.00	$360.00	$1.00	0.027%
FLOOR COVERING REPLACE	7810				$500.00	$500.00	$1,000.00	$1,000.00	$1,000.00	$500.00	$500.00			$5,000.00	$17.00	0.381%
FLOOR COVERING REPAIR	7811	$600.00	$600.00	$600.00	$600.00	$600.00	$600.00	$600.00	$600.00	$600.00	$600.00	$600.00	$600.00	$7,200.00	$24.00	0.548%
EXTERIOR PAINTING LABOR	7815													$4,000.00	$14.00	0.304%
EXTERIOR PAINTING SUPPLIES	7816													$1,000.00	$3.00	0.076%
EXTERIOR REPAIRS	7817	$17.00	$17.00	$17.00	$17.00	$17.00	$17.00	$17.00	$17.00	$17.00	$17.00	$17.00	$17.00	$200.00	$1.00	0.015%
JANITORIAL SUPPLIES	7821	$125.00	$125.00	$125.00	$125.00	$125.00	$125.00	$125.00	$125.00	$125.00	$125.00	$125.00	$125.00	$1,500.00	$5.00	0.114%
KEYS & LOCKS	7822	$50.00	$50.00	$50.00	$50.00	$50.00	$50.00	$50.00	$50.00	$50.00	$50.00	$50.00	$50.00	$600.00	$2.00	0.046%
LIGHT BULBS	7823	$150.00	$150.00	$150.00	$150.00	$150.00	$150.00	$150.00	$150.00	$150.00	$150.00	$150.00	$150.00	$1,800.00	$6.00	0.137%
INTERIOR PAINT LABOR	7830	$1,000.00	$1,000.00	$1,000.00	$1,000.00	$1,000.00	$1,000.00	$1,000.00	$1,000.00	$1,000.00	$1,000.00	$1,000.00	$1,000.00	$12,000.00	$41.00	0.913%
INTERIOR PAINT SUPPLIES	7831	$400.00	$400.00	$400.00	$400.00	$400.00	$400.00	$400.00	$400.00	$400.00	$400.00	$400.00	$400.00	$4,800.00	$16.00	0.365%
INTERIOR REPAIRS	7832	$200.00	$200.00	$200.00	$200.00	$200.00	$200.00	$200.00	$200.00	$200.00	$200.00	$200.00	$200.00	$2,400.00	$8.00	0.183%
HVAC REPLACEMENTS	7835			$150.00			$150.00			$150.00			$150.00	$600.00	$2.00	0.046%
HVAC SUPPLIES & SERVICE	7836	$150.00	$150.00	$150.00	$150.00	$150.00	$150.00	$150.00	$150.00	$150.00	$150.00	$150.00	$150.00	$1,800.00	$6.00	0.137%
APPLIANCE REPLACEMENT	7840	$150.00	$150.00	$150.00	$150.00	$150.00	$150.00	$150.00	$150.00	$150.00	$150.00	$150.00	$150.00	$1,800.00	$6.00	0.137%
APPLIANCE REPAIR	7841	$75.00	$75.00	$75.00	$75.00	$75.00	$75.00	$75.00	$75.00	$75.00	$75.00	$75.00	$75.00	$900.00	$3.00	0.068%
INTERIOR CONTRACT CLEANING	7845															
EXTERIOR CLEANING	7846															
FIRE & SAFETY SYSTEMS	7847	$25.00	$25.00	$25.00	$25.00	$25.00	$25.00	$25.00	$25.00	$25.00	$25.00	$25.00	$25.00	$300.00	$1.00	0.023%
TOTAL BUILDING EXPENSES		$3,342.00	$3,342.00	$3,582.00	$3,842.00	$3,842.00	$9,582.00	$4,342.00	$4,342.00	$4,082.00	$3,842.00	$3,342.00	$3,582.00	$51,060.00	$173.00	3.886%

Figure 4–22. Detailed Budget (*Continued*)

Professional Management Company
Real Estate Management Division

Property: Clyde Estates
Units: 296

Date Marker Time Marker	Account Number	January	February	March	April	May	June	July	August	September	October	November	December	TOTAL	296 Per Unit	As a % of GPI
COMMON AREA EXPENSES:																
CABLE TELEVISION	7901	$1,500.00	$1,500.00	$1,500.00	$1,500.00	$1,500.00	$1,500.00	$1,500.00	$1,500.00	$1,500.00	$1,500.00	$1,500.00	$1,500.00	$18,000.00	$61.00	1.370%
ELECTRICAL	7902	$125.00	$125.00	$125.00	$125.00	$125.00	$125.00	$125.00	$125.00	$125.00	$125.00	$125.00	$125.00	$1,500.00	$5.00	0.114%
PARKING LOT REPAIR	7903					$4,500.00								$4,500.00	$15.00	0.342%
EQUIPMENT	7905			$300.00	$400.00	$200.00	$100.00	$100.00	$100.00					$1,200.00	$4.00	0.091%
POOL REPAIR	7910			$1,500.00										$1,500.00	$5.00	0.114%
POOL SUPPLIES	7911															
GROUNDS MAINTENANCE	7915	$1,458.00	$1,458.00	$1,458.00	$1,458.00	$1,458.00	$1,458.00	$1,458.00	$1,458.00	$1,458.00	$1,458.00	$1,458.00	$1,458.00	$17,500.00	$59.00	1.332%
LANDSCAPE REPAIR	7916	$75.00	$75.00	$75.00	$75.00	$75.00	$75.00	$75.00	$75.00	$75.00	$75.00	$75.00	$75.00	$2,825.00	$10.00	0.215%
EXTERMINATION	7921	$475.00	$475.00	$475.00	$475.00	$475.00	$475.00	$475.00	$475.00	$475.00	$475.00	$475.00	$475.00	$5,700.00	$19.00	0.434%
GARBAGE HAULING	7922	$475.00	$475.00	$475.00	$475.00	$475.00	$475.00	$475.00	$475.00	$475.00	$475.00	$475.00	$475.00	$5,700.00	$19.00	0.434%
GENERAL CLEANING	7923															
SECURITY	7924															
TOTAL COMMON AREA		$4,108.00	$4,108.00	$5,908.00	$6,433.00	$8,808.00	$4,208.00	$4,208.00	$4,208.00	$4,108.00	$4,108.00	$4,108.00	$4,108.00	$58,425.00	$197.00	4.447%
UTILITIES																
ELECTRICITY	9101	$998.00	$998.00	$998.00	$977.00	$977.00	$1,901.00	$2,349.00	$2,031.00	$1,783.00	$977.00	$977.00	$977.00	$15,840.00	$54.00	1.206%
OCCUPIED UNIT ELEC.	9102															
VACANT UNIT ELEC.	9103	$30.00	$30.00	$30.00	$30.00	$30.00	$30.00	$30.00	$30.00	$30.00	$30.00	$30.00	$30.00	$360.00	$1.00	0.027%
MODEL ELECTRIC	9104	$225.00	$225.00	$225.00	$225.00	$225.00	$225.00	$225.00	$225.00	$225.00	$225.00	$225.00	$225.00	$2,700.00	$9.00	0.205%
WATER	9121	$1,170.00	$1,274.00	$1,220.00	$1,358.00	$1,377.00	$1,927.00	$2,007.00	$1,882.00	$1,197.00	$1,059.00	$1,213.00	$1,363.00	$17,047.00	$58.00	1.297%
OCCUPIED UNIT WATER	9122															
SPRINKLER	9123															
GAS	9141	$8,327.00	$6,984.00	$1,847.00	$486.00	$535.00	$577.00	$476.00	$521.00	$498.00	$482.00	$734.00	$1,633.00	$23,101.00	$78.00	1.758%
SEWER	9161	$542.00	$542.00	$542.00	$542.00	$542.00	$542.00	$542.00	$542.00	$542.00	$542.00	$542.00	$542.00	$6,500.00	$22.00	0.495%
TOTAL UTILITIES		$11,291.00	$10,053.00	$4,861.00	$3,617.00	$3,685.00	$5,202.00	$5,529.00	$5,231.00	$4,275.00	$3,314.00	$3,721.00	$4,769.00	$65,548.00	$221.00	4.989%
TOTAL OPERATING EXPENSES		$38,749.00	$36,637.00	$44,118.00	$34,699.00	$37,210.00	$43,493.00	$37,684.00	$38,412.00	$33,261.00	$30,395.00	$30,660.00	$31,964.00	$437,284.00	$1,477.00	33.281%

Date Marker Time Marker	Account Number	January	February	March	April	May	June	July	August	September	October	November	December	TOTAL	$296.00 Per Unit	As a % of GPI
INSURANCE	7601	$2,504.00	$2,504.00	$2,504.00	$2,504.00	$2,504.00	$2,504.00	$2,504.00	$2,504.00	$2,504.00	$2,504.00	$2,504.00	$2,504.00	$30,044.00	$102.00	2.287%
PROPERTY TAXES	8823	$8,917.00	$8,917.00	$8,917.00	$8,917.00	$8,917.00	$8,917.00	$8,917.00	$8,917.00	$8,917.00	$8,917.00	$8,917.00	$8,917.00	$107,000.00	$361.00	8.144%
TOTAL OTHER EXPENSES		$11,420.00	$11,420.00	$11,420.00	$11,420.00	$11,420.00	$11,420.00	$11,420.00	$11,420.00	$11,420.00	$11,420.00	$11,420.00	$11,420.00	$137,044.00	$463.00	10.430%
TOTAL ALL EXPENSES		$50,169.00	$48,058.00	$55,539.00	$46,119.00	$48,631.00	$54,913.00	$49,105.00	$49,832.00	$44,682.00	$41,815.00	$42,080.00	$43,385.00	$574,328.00	$1,940.00	43.711%
Net Operating Income (NOI)		$53,674.00	$54,397.00	$46,804.00	$59,069.00	$58,184.00	$53,530.00	$60,965.00	$61,866.00	$68,643.00	$74,365.00	$74,500.00	$73,595.00	$739,592.00	$2,499.00	56.289%

Figure 4–23. Payroll, payroll tax, and free units worksheets

Salary Budget

Payroll Tax Assumptions	
Social Security Rate	7.150%
Federal Unemployment Rate	0.800%
State Unemployment Rate	3.000%
Fed. Unemployment Ceiling	$7,000
State Unemployment Ceiling	$8,000

	AL:	FL:	LA:	MS:
Social Security Rate	7.150%	7.150%	7.150%	7.150%
Federal Unemployment Rate	0.800%	0.800%	0.800%	0.800%
State Unemployment Rate	3.300%	1.600%	5.310%	1.300%
Fed. Unemployment Ceiling	$7,000	$7,000	$7,000	$7,000
State Unemployment Ceiling	$8,000	$7,000	$7,000	$7,000

STAFFING RECAP	Number	
Full Time Staff	6	
Part Time Staff	1	
Seasonal Staff	3	
Average Cost per full yr employee		$18,075
Average Cost per seasonal employee		$3,767

HEALTH INSURANCE WILL COST AS FOLLOWS: EMPLOYEE ONLY @ $77.00/MO OR FAMILY @ $190.00/MO.

RAISE % 3.500%

Figure 4–23. Payroll, payroll tax, and free units worksheets (*Continued*)

Payroll and tax calculations for full-year staff

Name	Position	Wage Rate $/Hr - $/Mo	Raise Month	Unit Value Per Month	Health Ins. Per Month	Part Time Hrs Per Wk	Other Allow Per Mo	Old Monthly Base	New Monthly Base	ANNUAL GROSS	PAYROLL FICA	TAXES FUTA	STATE	Other	Total Units	Total Other	Health Insurance	TOTAL ANNUAL COST
Denise Russo	Manager	$1,000.00	2	$495	$190		$50	$1,000	$1,035	$12,385	$886	$56	$264		$5,940	$600	$2,280	$22,411
Maura Nestor	Asset Mgr	$4.75	5	$475	$77			$823	$852	$10,110	$723	$56	$264		$5,700		$924	$17,777
Marcy Anthony	Leasing	$4.00	4	$355	$77			$693	$718	$8,538	$610	$56	$264		$4,260		$924	$14,653
Susan O'Neil	Leasing	$4.00	3			32		$555	$574	$6,850	$490	$55	$226					$7,621
	Leasing																	
	Leasing																	
Bookkeeper																		
	Secretary																	
Doug Willits	Maint Super	$1,500.00	10		$190			$1,500	$1,553	$18,158	$1,298	$56	$264				$2,280	$22,056
	Maint Clerk																	
Paul Smith	Maintenance	$6.75	11					$1,170	$1,211	$14,222	$1,010	$56	$264					$15,451
	Maintenance																	
Barbara Johnson	Porter/Maid	$3.55	2					$615	$637	$7,621	$545	$56	$251					$8,473
	Porter/Maid																	
	Porter/Maid																	
	Grounds																	
	Pool																	
	TOTAL ADMIN.			$970.00			$50	$1,823	$1,887	$22,495	$1,608	$112	$528		$11,640	$600	$3,204	$40,188
	TOTAL MARKETING			$355.00				$1,248	$1,292	$15,388	$1,100	$111	$490		$4,260		$924	$22,273
	TOTAL MAINTENANCE							$3,285	$3,400	$39,900	$2,853	$168	$779				$2,280	$45,980
	TOTAL POOL																	
	TOTAL SEASONAL									$11,301	$808	$90	$373					$11,301
	TOTAL PROPERTY			$1,325.00			$50	$6,357	$6,579	$89,085	$6,370	$481	$2,170		$15,900	$600	$6,408	$108,441

TOTAL TAXES	$9,021

Figure 4–23. Payroll, payroll tax, and free units worksheets (*Continued*)

Payroll and tax calculations for seasonal staff

Name	Position	WAGE RATE $/Hr.	Months Worked	Health Ins. Per Month	Part Time Hrs Per Week	ANNUAL GROSS	PAYROLL FICA	TAXES FUTA	STATE	OTHER	Health Insuramce	MONTHLY COST	TOTAL ANNUAL COST
Moe Howard	Grounds	$4.25	6			$4,420	$316	$35	$146			$737	$4,917
Shemp Howard	Grounds	$4.25	6			$4,420	$316	$35	$146			$737	$4,917
	Grounds												
	Grounds												
Larry Fine	Pool	$3.55	4			$2,461	$176	$20	$81			$615	$2,738
	Pool												
	Pool												
	Pool												
	Pool												

		ANNUAL GROSS	PAYROLL FICA	TAXES FUTA	STATE	OTHER	Health Insuramce	MONTHLY COST	TOTAL ANNUAL COST
	SEASONAL MAINT.	$8,840	$632	$71	$292			$1,473	$9,834
	SEASONAL POOL	$2,461	$176	$20	$81			$615	$2,738
	TOTAL SEASONAL	$11,301	$808	$90	$373				$11,301

Name	Unit #	Market Rent on Unit	Rent Rec'd	Net OSD Per Month
1 B/R 1 Bath Model	127	$375	$0	$375
2 B/R 2 Bath Model	223	$495	$0	$495
3 B/R Townhouse Model	57	$525	$0	$525
Security Guard	43	$495	$50	$445
TOTAL		$1,890	$50	$1,840

	PERCENT	ANNUAL GROSS	PAYROLL TAXES FICA	FUTA	STATE	TOTAL UNIT	OTHER	HEALTH INSURANCE	TOTAL ANNUAL COST
PHASE 1	100.00%	$89,085	$6,370	$481	$2,170	$15,900	$600	$6,408	$108,441
PHASE 2									
PHASE 3									
PHASE 4									
PHASE 5									
PHASE 6									
TOTAL	100.00%	$89,085	$6,370	$481	$2,170	$15,900	$600	$6,408	$108,441

Figure 4–23. Payroll, payroll tax, and free units worksheets (*Continued*)

Monthly breakdowns of gross wages for seasonal staff

Name	Position	JAN	FEB	MAR	APR	MAY	JUN	JUL	AUG	SEP	OCT	NOV	DEC	TOTAL GROSS WAGES	CHECK TOTALS
Moe Howard	Grounds				$737	$737	$737	$737	$737	$737				$4,422	$4,420
Shemp Howard	Grounds				$737	$737	$737	$737	$737	$737				$4,422	$4,420
	Grounds														
	Grounds														
Larry Fine	Pool					$615	$615	$615	$615					$2,460	$2,458
	Pool														
	Pool														
	Pool														
	Pool														
	SEASONAL MAINT				$1,474	$1,474	$1,474	$1,474	$1,474	$1,474				$8,844	$8,840
	SEASONAL POOL				$615	$615	$615	$615	$615					$2,460	$2,458
	TOTAL SEASONAL														

If the last two columns don't agree your spreadsheet won't balance

Figure 4–24. Electricity Cost-Estimating Schedule and Cooling Degree-Days Table

Clyde Estates
296 Units

COST ESTIMATE BASE ON AVERAGE USE — Minium Bill Amount $50.00

	2002 Units of use	2001 Units of use	2000 Units of use	1999 Units of use	1998 Units of use	Average Use	Rate	Cost based on Avg
January	9500	9500	9500	9500	9500	9500	$0.1050	$998
February	9500	9500	9500	9500	9500	9500	$0.1050	$998
March	9500	9500	9500	9500	9500	9500	$0.1050	$998
April	9300	9300	9300	9300	9300	9300	$0.1050	$977
May	9300	9300	9300	9300	9300	9300	$0.1050	$977
June	16700	15000	14813	15518	13450	15096	$0.1230	$1,857
July	15800	17850	17627	18466	17850	17519	$0.1230	$2,155
August	22100	14000	13825	18000	14000	16385	$0.1230	$2,015
September	10800	12700	12541	15000	12700	12748	$0.1230	$1,568
October	9300	9300	9300	9300	9300	9300	$0.1050	$977
November	9300	9300	9300	9300	9300	9300	$0.1050	$977
December	9300	9300	9300	9300	9300	9300	$0.1050	$977
TOTAL	140400	134550	133806	141984	133000	136748		

COST ESTIMATE BASED ON USED MODIFIED TO MEAN DEGREE DAYS

	2002 Units of use	2001 Units of use	2000 Units of use	1999 Units of use	1998 Units of use	Average Use	Rate	Cost based on Deg Days
January	9500	9500	9500	9500	9500	9500	$0.1050	$998
February	9500	9500	9500	9500	9500	9500	$0.1050	$998
March	9500	9500	9500	9500	9500	9500	$0.1050	$998
April	87430	21855	2242	87420	43710	48529	$0.1050	$0
May	21237	14038	3895	12400	12197	12757	$0.1050	$0
June	18273	16903	11961	17751	12384	15454	$0.1230	$1,901
July	19160	17903	12084	22029	20057	18287	$0.1230	$2,249
August	24022	13519	13584	16667	14789	16516	$0.1230	$2,031
September	21473	12878	16733	8403	13008	14499	$0.1230	$1,783
October	7750	10333	93000	46500	3577	32232	$0.1050	$0
November	9300	9300	9300	9300	9300	9300	$0.1050	$977
December	9300	9300	9300	9300	9300	9300	$0.1050	$977
TOTAL	246445	154529	200599	258270	166822	205374		

COOLING
DEGREE DAY TABLE

	2002	2001	2000	1999	1998	Average
January	1	1	1	1	1	1
February	1	1	1	1	1	1
March	1	1	1	1	1	1
April	1	4	39	1	2	9
May	35	53	191	60	61	80
June	138	134	187	132	164	151
July	221	270	395	227	241	271
August	207	233	229	243	213	225
September	51	100	76	181	99	101
October	12	9	1	2	26	10
November	1	1	1	1	1	1
December	1	1	1	1	1	1
TOTAL	670	808	1123	851	811	852

(ERASE ALL CELLS WITH ZEROS REMAINING AFTER ALL DATA IN MODEL TO HAVE MODEL CALCULATE AVERAGES CORRECTLY)

NOTE: The model will yeild a $0.00 answer when the degree day solution is more than 130% of the average solution.

FIGURE 4-25. Operating Expenses: Clyde Estates

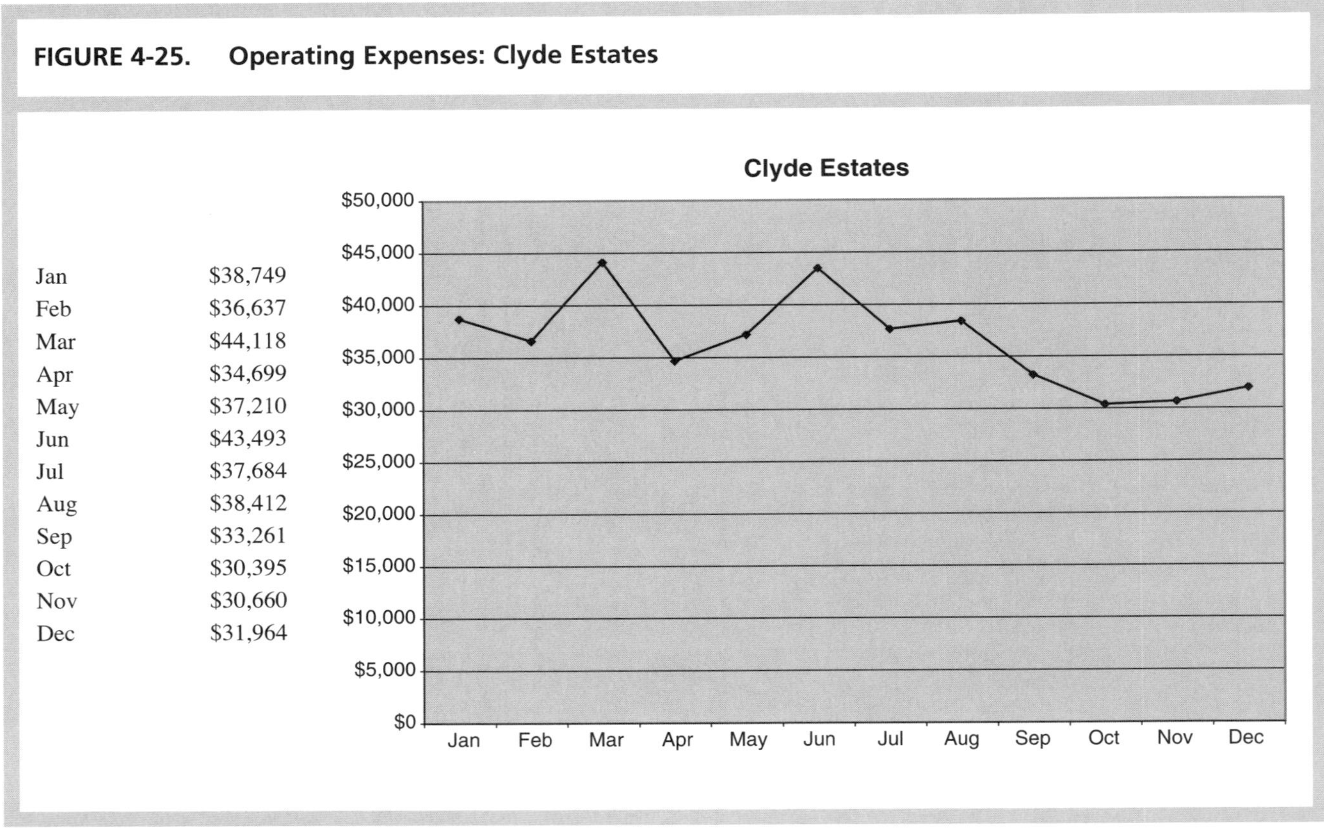

Jan	$38,749
Feb	$36,637
Mar	$44,118
Apr	$34,699
May	$37,210
Jun	$43,493
Jul	$37,684
Aug	$38,412
Sep	$33,261
Oct	$30,395
Nov	$30,660
Dec	$31,964

FIGURE 4-26. Cash Flow: Clyde Estates

Clyde Estates

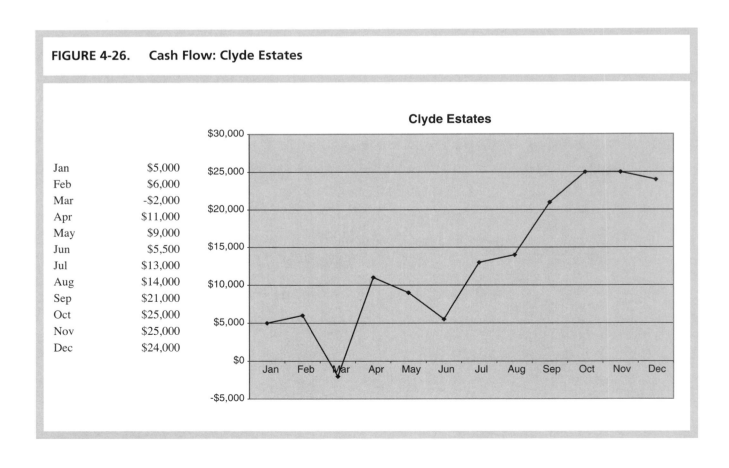

Jan	$5,000
Feb	$6,000
Mar	-$2,000
Apr	$11,000
May	$9,000
Jun	$5,500
Jul	$13,000
Aug	$14,000
Sep	$21,000
Oct	$25,000
Nov	$25,000
Dec	$24,000

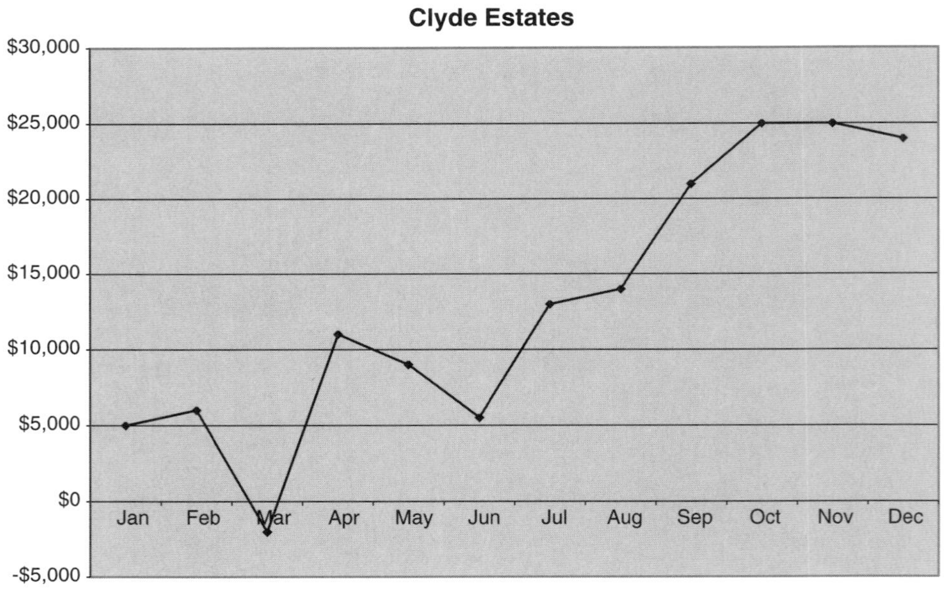

DEVELOPING THE OPERATING BUDGET

When putting together a property's operating budget, the first step is to do the necessary research. The research phase of the budget process will include the following activities:

- Assemble the income and expenses statements for the preceding three years, if they are available
- Obtain copies of the property's insurance policies
- Collect information on utility use, including historical costs, rates, and consumption, and present and projected rates for all utilities paid by the property
- Secure federal and state employer tax schedules and rates
- Research existing contracts for goods and services, particularly those that extend beyond the current year
- Investigate trends in the marketplace, including as much information as is available about competitive properties

Pending completion of this research, the actual budget process should begin in earnest at least three months prior to the end of the fiscal year. This starting date allows adequate time to fully develop the budget, research questions, and submit the final budget to the owner for approval. The property manager should have the final budget approved and distributed to the relevant staff members at least one month prior to the start of the fiscal year.

Property managers have only limited time to allocate to the budget process, so they must use that time efficiently. One method is to allocate effort in proportion to the total expense in each major expense category while taking into consideration the fact that certain expense items, such as real estate taxes, cannot ordinarily be controlled by the manager. The premise is to spend time first on those items of the budget that constitute the largest expenditures and continue through to those line items that represent the lease significant costs. In the case of Clyde Estates, for example, the pie chart in Figure 4–27 illustrates the breakdown of expenses by percentage of total expense.

The major expense categories are detailed below.

PROPERTY TAXES

The taxes levied on the property will be based on the value of the property and on the millage rates imposed by the various taxing bodies. (A mill is 1/10 of 1 percent [.001]. For example, a rate of 62 mills per $100 of assessed valuation would be $6.20 per $100, or $62 per $1,000 of value.) Depending on the policies of the management firm and on the preferences of the owner, the property manager may or may not be involved with the taxes. Regardless of who does it, however, the first step is to contact the local assessor's office and obtain copies of the assessment on the parcels the property contains and the tax levies for the most recent period.

The value of the property generally is set at some percentage of its true assessed valuation market value as of a specified date. If the taxpayer objects to that valuation, she/he must protest it with the assessor through a process called certiorari. If the administrative remedies fail with the assessor, the owner may take the matter to court for a trial and judicial determination of valuation. In some jurisdictions, the owner also has recourse to a review board.

Assessors most commonly use the income approach in valuing multihousing properties. The other two methods available are market value and replacement cost. The property manager should monitor the protest dates and check to see that the value placed on the property is appropriate prior to the expiration of the protest period each year. Commonly, owners will retain tax counsel to file a protest if that is necessary.

In many taxing jurisdictions, the final millage rate is not set until well into the year. In that event, a valid approach is to take the preceding three years' millage rates and calculate the annual rate of increase, then add this percentage to the last millage rate.

Because taxes comprise quite a large portion of the annual operating expenses, a property manager is well justified in researching and confirming the tax rates.

PAYROLL, TAXES, AND BENEFITS

Payroll may be the largest or second largest expenses in a property, especially if the property does not include heating and cooling in the rent. To obtain the payroll, taxes, and benefits figure, the property manager should use zero-base budgeting techniques every year.

The first step in determining payroll expenses for the coming year is to decide what functions the in-house staff will perform and which functions will be done by contractors. Tasks such as repainting apartments, landscape care, turnaround cleaning, snow removal, and extermination can typically be done by either in-house staff or contractors. In developing a budget, the property manager often will want to compare the costs of the alternatives before deciding on the payroll and contract costs for the coming year.

As any property manager knows, there are advantages and disadvantages to using both in-house staff and outsourcing to contractors. The advantages of employing staff include the closer supervision the property manager has over employees and the employee's dedication to one property and one task. The primary advantage of outsourcing is that the property does not have to pay for the services if it does not need them. Also, hiring, training, and supervising the staff in that particular area of expertise while the work is being done is the contractor's responsibility.

In starting the payroll worksheets, the property manager must determine the various tax and benefits costs for the coming year. These costs include:

- Federal social security (FICA) and federal unemployment (FUTA) taxes
- State unemployment taxes (SUT)
- Workers Compensation insurance premiums (WCOMP)

FIGURE 4-27. Operating Expenses: Clyde Estates

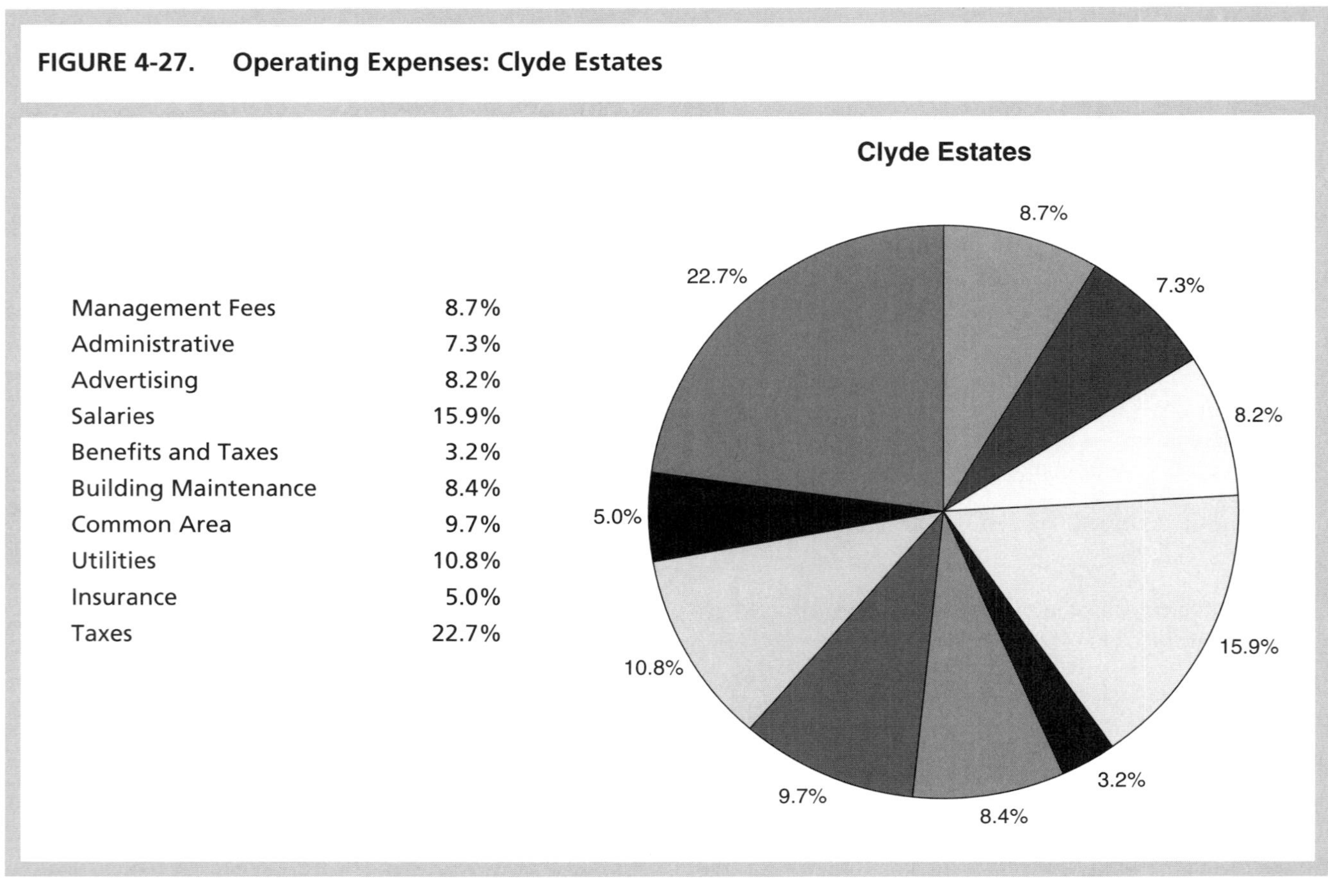

- Employee health insurance (if it is offered)
- Units provided free to staff
- Travel allowances
- All other benefits

These taxes and benefits will often total as much as 30 percent of the cash compensation paid to the staff, so careful research and estimating are essential. Figure 4–23 displays the basic tax assumptions and shows the payroll and tax calculation worksheets for full-year employees and for seasonal employees.

The payroll and tax calculations carry:

- All positions in their categories (full-year and seasonal)
- Their base wages
- The months of their annual salary reviews
- Taxes
- Allowances (e.g., travel, free unit)
- Cost of benefits (e.g., insurance)

The property manager can calculate the costs using a spreadsheet model or do it by hand. A spreadsheet template for figuring payroll enables the property manager to examine alternative staffing plans quickly and with the full costs attached.

With either method, once the annual costs have been calculated, they should be spread among the months, as illustrated in the monthly breakdowns of the gross wages in the payroll schedules (Fig. 4–23) for full-year staff and for seasonal staff, or presented on an annualized basis depending on the reporting requirements of the owner.

UTILITIES

Utility costs usually are one of the three largest operating expenses for a property. Considering the historic volatility of rates, they are increasingly significant. The estimate of utility costs depends on whether the property provides heating and/or cooling to the residents. If heating and/or cooling is provided, the volatile natures of both the energy market and the weather must be taken into account. The possible variance in costs is therefore considerably more than if the property provides only lighting, water, and sewerage. The property manager should be aware that methods may exist to secure fixed-priced contracts for energy. The advantages and disadvantages of this method of purchasing should be discussed with upper management and the owner before a decision is reached.

COMMON AREAS AND BUILDING MAINTENANCE

Expenses for maintenance of the buildings and common areas vary widely depending on the property's age, location, and design, the policies of the management company, and the instructions of the owner. The property manager should review previous spending experience in all the budget's maintenance subcategories, which appear under "Building maintenance," "Common area expenses," and "Utilities" in Figure 4–21. In budgeting for the coming year, the property manager should consider any required and discretionary changes in operations that she/he wants to make as well as changes from contract services to in-house service, or vice versa. These expenses should be budgeted for the months in which they are anticipated.

MANAGEMENT FEES

Management fees may be based on a flat monthly fee, a percentage of the rents collected, or a combination of a monthly fee and a percentage of rents collected. When the management fee is based on a flat monthly fee, factoring it into the budget is a simple matter. When it is dictated by contact as a percentage of gross revenues, the management fee can only be budgeted after the property manager has completed income projections for the year.

ADMINISTRATIVE EXPENSES

Administrative expenses include items such as legal, audit, telephone, office, computer. These items must be included in the costs because they are a normal part of operating expenses.

MARKETING/ADVERTISING

In competitive markets, marketing and advertising can be a considerable expense. The property manager must review the marketing and promotion program and the associated costs to determine that the anticipated expenses will be matched by the necessary and appropriate prospect traffic. The means of measuring advertising effectiveness as discussed in Chapter 7, Marketing Rental Housing and the Marketing Plan are useful in budget review. As part of the normal review process, the property manager should explore alternative promotion strategies and methods to see if the alternatives might be more cost effective.

INSURANCE

Although the property manager seldom is involved in the purchase of the property insurance for the property, she/he should work with the senior manager or owner to carefully review insurance costs to determine that the property's coverage is adequate and that costs are appropriate. All insurance coverages should be reviewed for both costs and adequacy each year. Scheduling this review in the third quarter of the fiscal year enables the property manager to incorporate changed costs into the pending budget.

DEBT SERVICE, MORTGAGE INSURANCE, RESERVES

If the operating budget includes debt services, the final step in developing the budget is to budget the principal and interest payments on the property mortgage(s) and other outstanding loans if there are any (e.g., lines of credit). Some mortgages are fixed and some are variable, and budget calculations must reflect this. In addition, some properties may have to pay mortgage insurance premiums that are set as a percentage of the mortgage amount or payment. These premiums are payable monthly with the mortgage. Often they are included as part of the mortgage payment.

All HUD-insured and some conventional mortgages require monthly payments to a reserve fund for replacements. The rules determining the amount and type of reserves required are set out in the agreement entered into at the time the mortgage was closed.

With regard to reserves, some properties also establish discretionary and self-imposed operating reserve accounts to cover unexpected operating expenses. These funds are generally calculated as a percentage of annual income as determined by the executive property manager and/or the owner.

INCOME AND EXPENSE ANALYSIS

The income and expense analysis is a critical by-product of the budgeting process. This analysis allows the owner and the manager to identify patterns and trends in income and expenses based on comparisons of past and present activity. Having an exact income and expense analysis helps considerably in establishing a practical and reasonable budget.

If the property is new and is preparing its first year's budget (the rent-up budget), all of the available elements that are included in the operating budget of an existing property should be included in the income and expense analysis. However, both owners and manager should be aware that expenses are generally higher and income is typically lower in the first year of operation than at any other time. This fact should be taken into consideration when preparing the first year rent-up budget.

DEVELOPING THE CAPITAL BUDGET

The day a property opens for business is the day it starts to deteriorate. The capital spending budget is a formal way of anticipating the property's capital repair and replacement needs over time. It informs the manager and the owner how much must be put into reserves for major repairs, replacements, and purchases throughout the property. Unless the owner and the manager are convinced that the income from the property will always be adequate to address any emergency or large capital expenditures that may occur, it is always wise to prepare a capital budget and to put aside the money necessary to fund it. Owners and managers must be mindful to factor in inflation and the rate of interest on the funds when calculating how much to set aside as a reserve for the capital budget.

As with the operating budget, the first task in structuring a capital spending budget is to list the needs of the property. In compiling this list, the property manager should examine the capital items, their remaining useful life, cost to repair, cost to replace, and anticipated date of replacement. All of the principles of budgeting mentioned earlier in connection with the operating budget also apply to capital budgets. However, because it projects farther into the future, the capital budget will have a longer time span, usually three to five years.

Because of the need for expertise in construction and mechanics, knowledge of tax considerations, and familiarity with the objectives of ownership in properly establishing the budgetary goals, capital budgets are often drawn up by the senior manager, asset manager, or owner of the property with the owner's accountant. Although the items on a capital budget may remain largely the same from one year to the next, each item should be examined and updated each year. A sample capital budget is shown in Figure 4–28.

LONG-RANGE BUDGETS

The third type of budget that a manager may be called on to help create is a long-range budget. This type of budget projects the property's income and expenses into the future, typically between three and five years. Long-range budgets are especially useful when coupled with capital budgets in the consideration of renovations, refinancing, or selling the property.

BUDGET REVIEW AND APPROVAL

Once the property manager has prepared the initial draft of the operating and capital budgets, the senior manager and other central office staff, including accounting and finance and the purchasing departments, if appropriate, should review them for content and accuracy. The budgets should then be reviewed by the owner. These revisions and approvals should be completed no later than 45 days prior to the commencement of the fiscal year. Upon approval, the budgets becomes the basic operating blueprint for the year.

However, neither the operating budget nor the capital budget is carved in stone. The property manager must review each budget quarterly to see that the operation of the property is proceeding along the projected lines and to determine any changes that may need to be made in the budget. The primary consideration behind changes in the budget is to ensure the continued accuracy of the cash flow projections. Budget changes should not be made merely to avoid variances. They should adjust for substantive differences in operating conditions. The variance analysis (see below) is the property manager's main tool for directing and redirecting spending so that the property is operated in the most effective and efficient manner.

FINANCIAL REPORTING AND MONITORING

Financial operations in a property include check writing, purchase order systems, inventory systems, banking relationships, and rent collection. (See Chapter 9, Managing the Site Office and the Operations Manual for more information on these financial operations.) Each of these functions is integrally tied to the financial management system and should be designed and used with that thought in mind.

The monthly income statement and balance sheet are two of the property manager's most important planning and control tools. The balance sheet reports the owner's assets, liabilities, and equity in the property. The monthly statements also comprise an integral part of financial reporting to the owner of the property. These reports show in capsule form how the fiscal affairs of the property are being managed and how closely the operation follows the operating budget.

The type and complexity of the monthly reports varies with the property and the accounting standards used for the property. Usually, the management company accounting department or comptroller issues a summary income statement and balance sheet to senior management staff, the senior manager, and the owner. A detailed monthly income statement (Fig. 4–29) is often also generated for internal use by the property staff and senior manager. It serves as the property manager's "scorecard," tracking income and expenses and comparing the actual results of the operation with the annual operating budget.

The summary income statement appears in Figure 4–30, and the summary balance sheet appears in Figure 4–31. It is important to note how the arrangement of the budget is mirrored both in format and in the detailed monthly income statement (Fig. 4–29) and in the summary of the detailed income statement (Fig. 4–30).

A few management companies also issue a statement of changes in financial position (sources and uses of cash report) for internal use. Properties operated on an accrual basis need this statement to tie the income statement to the ending cash position of the property. In accrual-based accounting, when charges are incurred but no invoice is received, these charges are referred to as accruals (because they "accrue," or increase, in value). These items, or an estimate of their value, are included in the financial statement, which is adjusted, if necessary, when the real invoice is received. Accruals also apply to the income side. In the accrual method of accounting, rents that are due and payable are treated as taxable on the date the rent bills are issued. Conversely, the same applies to bills received by the property.

Cash basis properties (an accounting method whereby only invoices and bills that have actually been paid are accounted for) do not require such a statement. The majority of firms use cash basis accounting for intermediate period reporting and convert to accrual for year-end reports only. This is true because cash flow is the basis of all calculations to determine NOI. By definition, cash-based accounting is based on cash flow: money in/money out.

The production of the monthly statements varies from property to property and management company to management company, but the two constants of the monthly reporting system should be speed and accuracy. For the statement to be of the most use to the manager, monthly statements must be available immediately after the end of the month, and they must be absolutely accurate.

Ideally, the reporting system should be geared to issue internal statements on the third or fourth business day after the

Figure 4–28. Sample Capital Budget

		1998	1999	2000	2001	2002
Parking lots Resurfacing 35,000 sq. feet per year, 1-1/2-inch new asphalt single lift over existing surface with all defects sawed out and repaired		138,000	138,000	162,000	162,000	162,000
Replace 900 linear feet curb and gutter			5,400	5,400		
Swimming pool Sandblast pool, refinish with chlorinated rubber paint, replace bad sections of gutter system, replace edge tiles on steps			18,000			
Replace filters, rebuild pumps rebuild heater				12,720		
Roofs Tear off and replace roof with new 3-ply 5#, 15#, 15#, hot-mopped build-up roof. Add Carey Tred to all equipment locations from roof hatches.	Bldgs. 3 & 7	43,200				
	Bldgs. 2 & 5		45,600			
	Bldg. 4			22,800		
	Bldgs. 1 & 6				45,600	
Carpets Replace unit carpets - 3,000 square yards per year		43,200	47,520	52,272	57,499	63,249
Replace hall carpets - 1,500 yards per year		24,000	26,400	29,040	31,944	35,128

Building Component Inventory

	Quantity	Installed	Condition	Replacement Expected
Parking lots and drives 3-inch asphalt over stone	210000 sq feet	1985	190,000 ft poor 35,000	Resurface 35,000ft per starting 2000
Curb and gutter	2800	1985	1,900 ft lightly spalled	900 ft in 1999 1990 900 feet rebar
			exposed	
Pool, gunite in ground rebuild	55000	1987	Gutter poor	Sandblast and
	1800		Linear peeling	2000
	1 10-horsepower pump	1987	Rebuilt 1978	Rebuild 2000
	2 rapid sand	1990	Badly corroded	Rebuild 2001
	1 750,000 Btu Lars Heater	1990	Needs tubes	Replace 2001
Roofs, 3-ply, built up asphalt	22,000 square feet per building			
	Building 1	1997	New	2002
	Building 2	1993	Fair	2000
	Building 3	1992	Poor	1999
	Building 4	1983	Good	2001
	Building 5	1993	Fair	2000
	Building 6	1997	New	2002
	Building 7	1992	Poor	1999
Carpets, Units		1990-92	10,000 yards obsolete colors	Rolling replacement 3,000 yards per year
Halls		1994	Poor	Rolling replacement 1,500 yards per year

end of the month, and the owner's reports no later than the tenth business day of the month.

When financial records and reports are prepared for the use of the owner and the manager, this is called managerial accounting. When records and reports are prepared for the use of outside accounting professionals, attorneys, or anyone else, this is called financial accounting.

VARIANCE ANALYSIS

Reviewing and analyzing the monthly and year-to-date variances between the budgeted figures and the actual results is a powerful management tool.

Although the format of the income statements can vary, all monthly income statements should carry both current month and year-to-date (YTD) variances. All variances should be labeled favorable or unfavorable. On the income side, a favorable variance occurs when income is greater than anticipated in the budget. On the expense side, a favorable variance occurs when expenses are less than were anticipated.

For the property manager, the variances highlight the spending projections that need revision. In addition to variances, other measures often are printed on the report for the manager to track. For example, our hypothetical property, Clyde Estates, also tracks expenses for the year to date in dollars per unit and dollars per square foot of rental space. Both of these measures are a convenient shorthand way for the property manager to track expenses and to compare the expenses of one property with those of another.

Finally, the system tracks income and expenses as a percent of the gross possible income (GPI) for the property. Percent of GPI is used in several of the expense comparisons published by management trade associations.

A monthly variance review permits the property manager to act quickly to offset or minimize financial impacts brought on by the market and/or the operation of the property.

CASH MANAGEMENT

The monthly statements help the property manager to manage the property's cash. The manager must look beyond the property's overall profitability or loss and ensure that its available cash is being managed and invested wisely. Cash management is more than just having money left at the end of the month. It involves timing the payment of bills, temporary or long-term investment of available funds, and monitoring all other management activities to ensure that the property's cash is used in the most efficient way.

The property manager normally would monitor the property's cash situation weekly and update projections monthly from the cash balances listed in the current asset section of the balance sheet (Fig. 4–31). The property manager should work closely with the senior manager and the owner to ensure that all available cash is invested to generate a maximum return to the property at all times. (See Chapter 9, Managing the Site Office and the Operations Manual for more on cash management.)

FINANCIAL AUDITS

The final step in the financial management system is the annual examination of the property's financial affairs. Often called an audit, this examination is an essential part of the accounting and internal control process. During the audit, the property's books and records as provided by the management company are reviewed and evaluated by a third party—an independent certified public accountant (CPA)—hired by the owner. The auditor hired by the owner also reports directly to the owner. Often, the CPA prepares the income tax returns as part of this process. Customarily, the auditor reports the results of the audit to the management firm at the same time she/he reports them to the owner. The type of examination, compilation, review, or audit that the auditor will perform will occasionally be specified in the mortgage, regulatory agreement, or management agreement for the property.

TYPES OF EXAMINATIONS

The American Institute of Certified Public Accountants (AICPA), the standards-setting body for CPAs, has defined three types of annual examinations: compilation, review, and audit. Each of these examinations has specific tests, standards, and rules associated with it.

COMPILATION

A compilation is the least extensive examination. In a compilation, the auditor assembles a balance sheet, income statement, and statement of changes in financial position for the property from the records maintained by the management company. The auditor works exclusively from management's records, does not test or verify any of the transactions, and gives no opinion as to the accuracy of the statements. This is the most limited type of examination and therefore the least expensive.

REVIEW

In a review, the auditor will examine the financial records, the way in which the records are kept, the internal controls in use, and occasionally test the accuracy of the statements in a limited way. The auditor will not render an opinion on the statements but will assemble them into the balance sheet, income statement, and statement of changes in financial position. The review is slightly more thorough than a compilation and is priced in the middle.

AUDIT

An audit is the most expensive and thorough examination of the three. It also is the only one in which the auditor expresses an opinion as to the accuracy of the statements and comments on the financial health of the company.

An audit, sometimes mistakenly referred to as a certified audit, is an examination that looks at how the records are

Figure 4–29. Detailed Monthly Income Statement

Professional Management Company
Real Estate Management Division

Month Ended: July 31, 2002
Property: Clyde Estates
Units: 296

Date Marker Time Marker	Account Number	Monthly Actual	Monthly Budget	Variance Favorable (unfavorable)	Year to Date Actual	Year to Date Budget	Variance Favorable (unfavorable)	Year To Date $ Per Unit	Year to Date $ Per Sq. Ft	Year to Date As a % of GPI
POTENTIAL RENT	4111	$134,400	$134,400		$934,800	$934,800		$3,158.11	$3.32	126.25%
FREE UNITS	5119	$1,325	$1,325		$9,275	$9,275		$31.33	$0.03	1.25%
VACANCY LOSSES	5120	$12,040	$11,228	($812)	$112,500	$103,929	($8,571)	$380.07	$0.40	15.19%
PRO RATED RENT	5121									
CONCESSIONS	5122	$5,700	$14,167	$8,467	$89,600.00	$99,169.00	$9,569.00	$302.70	$0.32	12.10%
NET RENT INCOME		$115,335	$107,680	$7,655	$723,425	$722,427	$998	$2,444.00	$2.57	97.71%
STORAGE FEES	6100	$250	$300	($50)	$2,210	$2,100	$110	$7.47	$0.01	0.30%
COLLECTION FEES	6101	$875	$1,000	($125)	$6,945	$7,000	($55)	$23.46	$0.02	0.94%
SECURITY DEP FORFEITS	6102	$500	$250	$250	$1,550	$1,750	($200)	$5.24	$0.01	0.21%
PET FEES	6103	$200	$400	($200)	$2,645	$2,800	($155)	$8.94	$0.01	0.36%
LEASE CANCEL FEES	6104	$300	$70	$230	$700	$490	$210	$2.36	$0.00	0.09%
NSF & BANK FEES	6105									
TOTAL CHARGES INCOME		$2,125	$2,020	$105	$14,050	$14,140	($90)	$47.47	$0.05	1.90%
LAUNDRY INCOME	6001	$370	$370		$2,590	$2,590		$8.75	$0.01	0.35%
MISC INCOME	6002									
BAD DEBT RECOVERIES	6003				$350		$350	$1.18	$0.00	0.05%
INTEREST INCOME	6004									
TOTAL OTHER INCOME		$370	$370		$2,940	$2,590	$350	$9.93	$0.01	0.40%
TOTAL INCOME (GPI)		$117,830	$110,070	$7,760	$740,415	$739,157	$1,258	$2,501.40	$2.63	100.00%

Figure 4–29. Detailed Monthly Income Statement (*Continued*)

Professional Management Company
Real Estate Management Division

Month Ended: July 31, 2002
Property: Clyde Estates
Units: 296

Date Marker Time Marker	Account Number	Monthly Actual	Monthly Budget	Variance Favorable (unfavorable)	Year to Date Actual	Year to Date Budget	Variance Favorable (unfavorable)	Year To Date $ Per Unit	Year to Date $ Per Sq. Ft	Year to Date As a % of GPI
EXPENSES										
OPERATING EXPENSES										
MANAGEMENT FEES	8500	$4,713	$4,403	($310)	$29,617	$29,566.00	($51)	$100.06	$0.11	4.00%
ACCOUNTING & AUDIT	7241				$11,300	$11,300.00		$38,318.00	$0.04	1.53%
CREDIT REPORTS	7221	$150	$170	$20	$975	$1,190.00	$215	$3.29	$0.00	0.13%
DONTATIONS	7222									
DUES & SUBSCRIPTIONS	7225		$30	$30	$645	$659.00	$14	$2.18	$0.00	0.09%
GENERAL EXPENSES	7226									
LEASING EXPENSES	7231	$996	$1,083	$87	$6,945	$7,583.00	$638	$23.46	$0.02	0.94%
LEASING REFERRALS	7233	$356	$375	$19	$2,782	$2,625.00	($157)	$9.40	$0.01	0.38%
LEGAL	7234	$161	$150	($11)	$1,035	$1,050.00	$15	$3.50	$0.00	0.14%
OFFICE SUPPLIES & POST	7240	$300	$300		$1,984	$2,100.00	$116	$6.70	$0.10	0.27%
PROFESSIONAL DEVELOPMENT	7241									
PUBLIC RELATIONS	7242	$210	$300	$90	$300	$900.00	$600	$1.01	$0.00	0.04%
LOCAL PHONE	7244	$175	$175		$1,250	$1,225.00	($25)	$4.22	$0.00	0.17%
LONG DISTANCE	7245	$120	$100	($20)	$670	$700.00	$30	$2.26	$0.00	0.09%
ANSWERING SERVICES	7246	$48	$75	$27	$500	$525.00	$25	$1.69	$0.00	0.07%
PAGERS & RADIO	7247	$12	$30	$18	$210	$210.00		$0.71	$0.00	0.03%
TRAVEL ALLOWANCES	8861	$50	$50		$350	$350.00		$1.18	$0.00	0.05%
TRAVEL OTHER	8863		$30	$30	$90	$210.00	$120	$0.30	$0.00	0.01%
TOTAL MANAGEMENT		$4,713	$4,403	($310)	$29,617	$29,566	($51)	$100.06	$0.11	4.00%
TOTAL ADMINISTRATIVE		$2,578	$2,868	$290	$29,036	$30,627	$1,591	$98.09	$0.10	3.92%
ADVERTISING/PERIODICALS	7061	$3,755	$3,700	($55)	$16,200	$15,900	($300)	$54.73	$0.06	2.19%
ADVERTISING SIGNS/GRAPHICS	7062	$1,650	$1,800	$150	$12,580	$14,220	$1,640	$42.50	$0.04	1.70%
TOTAL ADVERTISING		$5,405	$5,500	$95	$28,780	$30,120	$1,340	$97.23	$0.10	3.89%

Figure 4–29. Detailed Monthly Income Statement (*Continued*)

Professional Management Company
Real Estate Management Division

Month Ended: July 31, 2002
Property: Clyde Estates
Units: 296

Date Marker Time Marker	Account Number	Monthly Actual	Monthly Budget	Variance Favorable (unfavorable)	Year to Date Actual	Year to Date Budget	Variance Favorable (unfavorable)	Year To Date $ Per Unit	Year to Date $ Per Sq. Ft	Year to Date As a % of GPI
SALARIES:										
MANAGER	8701	$1,036	$1,035	($1)	$7,210	$7,210		$24.36	$0.03	0.97%
ASST. MANAGER	8702	$852	$852		$5,850	$5,850		$19.76	$0.02	0.79%
CLERICAL	8703									
LEASING	8704	$1,292	$1,292		$8,345	$8,930	$585	$28.19	$0.03	1.13%
MAINTENANCE STAFF	8705	$3,307	$3,307		$22,156	$23,126	$970	$74.85	$0.08	2.99%
GROUNDS STAFF	8706	$1,474	$1,474		$5,896	$5,896		$19.92	$0.02	0.80%
RECREATION	8708	$615	$615		$1,645	$1,845	$200	$5.56	$0.01	0.22%
TEMPORARY HELP	7200									
LEASING BONUSES	8741	$600	$600		$4,000	$4,200	$200	$13.51	$0.01	0.54%
OTHER BONUSES	8799									
TOTAL SALARIES		$9,176	$9,175	($1)	$55,102	$57,057	$1,955	$186.16	$0.20	7.44%
BENEFITS & TAXES										
EMPLOYEE BENEFITS	8800	$534	$534		$3,645	$3,738	$93	$12.31	$0.01	0.49%
WORKER'S COMPENSATION INS.	8804	$374	$374		$1,750	$2,328	$578	$5.91	$0.01	0.24%
EMPLOYERS FICA	8801	$531	$531		$3,690	$3,716	$26	$12.47	$0.01	0.50%
EMPLOYERS FUTA	8802	$40	$40		$270	$281	$11	$0.91	$0.00	0.04%
STATE UNEMPLOYMENT	8803	$181	$181		$1,200	$1,266	$66	$4.05	$0.00	0.16%
TOTAL P/R TAXES/BENEFITS		$1,660	$1,660		$10,555	$11,329	$774	$35.66	$0.04	1.43%

Figure 4–29. Detailed Monthly Income Statement (*Continued*)

Professional Management Company
Real Estate Management Division

Month Ended: July 31, 2002
Property: Clyde Estates
Units: 296

Date Marker Time Marker	Account Number	Monthly Actual	Monthly Budget	Variance Favorable (unfavorable)	Year to Date Actual	Year to Date Budget	Variance Favorable (unfavorable)	Year To Date $ Per Unit	Year to Date $ Per Sq. Ft	Year to Date As a % of GPI
BUILDING MAINTENANCE										
DRAPES BLINDS	7804		$50	$50	$300	$350	$50	$1.01	$0.00	0.04%
ELECTRICAL	7805	$120	$150	$30	$900	$1,050	$150	$3.04	$0.00	0.12%
PLUMBING	7807	$55	$200	$145	$845	$1,400	$555	$2.85	$0.00	0.11%
ROOF	7808					$180	$180			
FLOOR COVERING REPLACE	7810	$1,100	$1,000	($100)	$3,105	$3,000	($105)	$10.49	$0.01	0.42%
FLOOR COVERING REPAIR	7811	$352	$600	$248	$2,789	$4,200	$1,411	$9.42	$0.01	0.38%
EXTERIOR PAINTING LABOR	7815				$4,000	$4,000		$13.51	$0.01	0.54%
EXTERIOR PAINTING SUPPLIES	7816				$1,150	$1,000	($150)	$3.89	$0.00	0.16%
EXTERIOR REPAIRS	7817		$17	$17		$117	$117			
JANITORIAL SUPPLIES	7821	$98	$125	$27	$625	$875	$250	$2.11	$0.00	0.08%
KEYS & LOCKS	7822		$50	$50	$125	$350	$225	$0.42	$0.00	0.02%
LIGHT BULBS	7823		$150	$150	$345	$1,050	$705	$1.17	$0.00	0.05%
INTERIOR PAINT LABOR	7830	$945	$1,000	$55	$6,250	$7,000	$750	$21.11	$0.02	0.84%
INTERIOR PAINT SUPPLIES	7831	$190	$400	$210	$2,744	$2,800	$56	$9.27	$0.01	0.37%
INTERIOR REPAIRS	7832		$200	$200	$1,148	$1,400	$252	$3.88	$0.00	0.16%
HVAC REPLACEMENTS	7835	$98		($98)		$300	$300			
HVAC SUPPLIES & SERVICE	7836	$160	$150	($10)	$595	$1,050	$455	$2.01	$0.00	0.08%
APPLIANCE REPLACEMENT	7840		$150	$150	$845	$1,050	$205	$2.85	$0.00	0.11%
APPLIANCE REPAIR	7841	$85	$75	($10)	$955	$525	($430)	$3.23	$0.00	0.13%
INTERIOR CONTRACT CLEANING	7845									
EXTERIOR CLEANING	7846									
FIRE & SAFETY SYSTEMS	7847		$25	$25	$300	$175	($125)	$1.01	$0.00	0.04%
TOTAL BUILDING EXPENSES		$3,203	$4,342	$1,139	$27,021	$31,872	$4,851	$91.29	$0.10	3.65%

Figure 4–29. Detailed Monthly Income Statement (*Continued*)

Professional Management Company
Real Estate Management Division

Month Ended: July 31, 2002
Property: Clyde Estates
Units: 296

Date Marker Time Marker	Account Number	Monthly Actual	Monthly Budget	Variance Favorable (unfavorable)	Year to Date Actual	Year to Date Budget	Variance Favorable (unfavorable)	Year To Date $ Per Unit	Year to Date $ Per Sq. Ft	Year to Date As a % of GPI
COMMON AREA EXPENSE										
CABLE TELEVISION	7901	$1,500	$1,500		$10,500	$10,500		$35.47	$0.04	1.42%
ELECTRICAL	7902	$296	$125	($171)	$58	$875	$817	$0.20	$0.00	0.01%
PARKING LOT REPAIR	7903				$4,850	$4,500	($350)	$16.39	$0.02	0.66%
EQUIPMENT	7905		$100	$100	$645	$1,100	$455	$2.18	$0.00	0.09%
POOL REPAIR	7910				$1,350	$1,500	$150	$4.56	$0.00	0.18%
POOL SUPPLIES	7911									
GROUNDS MAINTENANCE	7915	$1,700	$1,458	($242)	$10,240	$10,206	($34)	$34.59	$0.04	1.38%
LANDSCAPE REPAIR	7916		$75	$75	$2,250	$2,450	$200	$7.60	$0.01	0.30%
EXTERMINATION	7921	$313	$475	$162	$3,325	$3,325		$11.23	$0.01	0.45%
GARBAGE HAULING	7922	$710	$475	($235)	$3,055	$3,325	$270	$10.32	$0.01	0.41%
GENERAL CLEANING	7923									
SECURITY	7924									
TOTAL COMMON AREA		$4,519	$4,208	($311)	$36,273	$37,781	$1,508	$122.54	$0.13	4.90%
UTILITIES										
ELECTRICITY	9101	$2,205	$2,249	$44	$8,050	$9,096	$1,046	$27.20	$0.03	1.09%
OCCUPIED UNIT ELEC.	9102									
VACANT UNIT ELEC.	9103		$30	$30	$50	$210	$160	$0.17	$0.00	0.01%
MODEL ELECTRIC	9104	$225	$225		$1,475	$1,575	$100	$4.98	$0.01	0.20%
WATER	9121	$1,983	$2,007	$24	$9,899	$10,333	$434	$33.44	$0.04	1.34%
OCCUPIED UNIT WATER	9122									
SPRINKLER	9123									
GAS	9141	$470	$476	$6	$17,925	$19,232	$1,307	$60.56	$0.06	2.42%
SEWER	9161	$542	$542		$4,212	$3,792	($420)	$14.23	$0.01	0.57%
TOTAL UTILITIES		$5,425	$5,529	$104	$41,611	$44,238	$2,627	$140.58	$0.15	5.63%
TOTAL OPERATING EXPENSES		$36,679	$37,685	$1,006	$257,995	$272,590	$14,595	$871.60	$0.92	34.84%

Figure 4–29. Detailed Monthly Income Statement (*Continued*)

Professional Management Company
Real Estate Management Division

Month Ended: July 31, 2002
Property: Clyde Estates
Units: 296

Date Marker Time Marker	Account Number	Monthly Actual	Monthly Budget	Variance Favorable (unfavorable)	Year to Date Actual	Year to Date Budget	Variance Favorable (unfavorable)	Year To Date $ Per Unit	Year to Date $ Per Sq. Ft	Year to Date As a % of GPI
INSURANCE	9800	$2,504	$2,504		$17,526	$17,526		$59.21	$0.06	2.37%
PROPERTY TAXES	9900	$8,917	$8,917		$62,417	$62,417		$210.87	$0.22	8.43%
TOTAL OTHER EXPENSES		$11,421	$11,421		$79,943	$79,943		$270.08	$0.28	10.80%
TOTAL ALL EXPENSES		$48,100	$49,106	$1,006	$337,938	$352,533	$14,595.00	$1,141.68	$1.20	45.64%
Net Operating Income (NOI)		$69,730	$60,964	$8,766	$402,477	$386,624	$15,853	$1,359.72	$1.43	54.36%

Figure 4–30. Summary Income Statement

Professional Management Company
Real Estate Management Division

Month Ended: July 31, 2002
Property: Clyde Estates
Units: 296

Date Marker Time Marker	Monthly Actual	Monthly Budget	Variance Favorable (unfavorable)	Year To Date Actual	Year to Date Budget	Variance Favorable (unfavorable)	Year to Date $ Per Unit	Year to Date $ Per Sq. Ft	Year to Date As a % of GPI
INCOME:									
GROSS RENTS	$134,400	$134,400	$0	$934,800	$934,800	$0.00	$3,158.11	$3.32	126.25%
[Vacancies/Free Units/Etc.]	$19,065	$26,720	($7,655)	$211,375	$212,373	($998.00)	$714.10	$0.75	28.55%
NET RENT INCOME	$115,335	$107,680	$7,655	$723,425	$722,427	$998.00	$2,444.00	$2.57	97.71%
CHARGES INCOME	$2,125	$2,020	$105	$14,050	$14,140	($90.00)	$47.47	$0.05	1.90%
OTHER INCOME	$0	$0	$0	$0	$0	$0.00	$0.00	$0.00	0.00%
GROSS POSSIBLE INCOME (GPI)	$117,830	$110,070	$7,760	$740,415	$739,157	$1,258.00	$2,501.40	$2.63	100.00%
EXPENSES:									
MANAGEMENT FEES	$4,713	$4,403	($310)	$29,617	$29,566	($51.00)	$100.06	$0.11	4.00%
ADMINISTRATIVE	$2,578	$2,868	$290	$29,036	$30,627	$1,591.00	$98.06	$0.10	3.92%
ADVERTISING	$5,405	$5,500	$95	$28,780	$30,120	$1,340.00	$97.23	$0.10	3.89%
SALARIES	$9,176	$9,175	($1)	$55,102	$57,057	$1,955.00	$186.16	$0.20	7.44%
BENEFITS & TAXES	$1,660	$1,660	$0	$10,555	$11,329	$774.00	$35.66	$0.04	1.43%
Sub Total Payroll	$10,836	$10,835	($1)	$65,657	$68,386	$2,729.00	$221.81	$0.23	8.87%
BUILDING MAINTENANCE	$3,203	$4,342	$1,139	$27,021	$31,872	$4,851.00	$91.29	$0.10	3.65%
COMMON AREA EXPENSES	$4,519	$4,208	($311)	$36,273	$37,781	$1,508.00	$122.54	$0.13	4.90%
UTILITIES	$5,425	$5,529	$104	$41,611	$44,238	$2,627.00	$140.58	$0.15	5.62%
TOTAL OPERATING EXPENSES	$36,679	$37,685	$1,006	$257,995	$272,590	$14,595.00	$871.60	$0.92	34.84%
INSURANCE	$2,504	$2,504	$0	$17,526	$17,526	$0.00	$59.21	$0.06	2.37%
TAXES	$8,917	$8,917	$0	$62,417	$62,417	$0.00	$210.87	$0.22	8.43%
TOTAL OTHER EXPENSES	$11,421	$11,421	$0	$79,943	$79,943	$0.00	$270.08	$0.28	10.80%
TOTAL ALL EXPENSES	$48,100	$49,106	$1,006	$337,938	$352,533	$14,595.00	$1,141.68	$1.20	45.64%
NET OPERATING INCOME (NOI)	$69,730	$60,964	$8,766	$402,477	$386,624	$15,853.00	$1,359.72	$1.43	54.36%

Figure 4–31. Summary Balance Sheet

Clyde Estates
Balance Sheet
July 31, 2002

Professional Management Company
Real Estate Management Division
296 Units

ASSETS	***G/L #***		***LIABILITIES***	***G/L#***	
Current			Current		
Petty Cash	1110	$100	Accounts Payable	2110	$56,000
Cash in Bank	1120	$123,584	Accrued Wages & Payroll Taxes	2120	$43,000
Sub-Total Cash		$123,684	Security Deposit Liability	2191	$108,950
			Sub-total Current Liab's		$169,250.00
Accounts Receivable	1140				
Investments	1170		Prepaid Rents	2210	$5,950.00
Security Deposit Fund	1190				
			Long Term Liabilities		
Prepaid Insurance	1240		Mortgages Payable	2320	3,530,000.00
			Other long term Liabilities	2390	85,000.00
Fixed Assets					
Land	1410	$455,000.00	TOTAL LIABILITIES		3,790,200.00
Buildings	1420	$5,013,000.00			
Furniture/Fixtures	1430	$98,850.00			
Tools & Equipment	1440	$45,700.00	***OWNERS EQUITY***		
Less Depreciation Allowances		($1,245,000.00)			
			Owners Capital	3120	$950,000.00
			Retained Earnnings from Operations	3120	$315,317.00
TOTAL ASSETS		$5,055,517.00	TOTAL LIABILITIES & EQUITY		$5,055,517.00

kept, the way in which accounting duties are divided, the internal controls, the accuracy of the books, the possibilities of fraud, and the on-going viability of the property. Essentially, the audit looks at every aspect of the operation during the year, verifies that it is correct in every material respect, and looks at financial prospects for the next year to ensure that the property will continue to be viable.

To carry out all of these duties, the auditor follows specific guidelines set out by the AICPA and the Financial Accounting Standards Board (FASB) on how to examine the books. The activities listed below are among those required by the guidelines:

- Test a statistically significant number of transactions to ensure that they are correctly reported in the books
- Verify all bank balances and debts
- Provide "reasonable assurance" that any significant errors and irregularities have been found
- Ensure that the internal controls are adequate to prevent errors or misstatements in the reports
- Inquire into potential liabilities
- Assure that the property has the ability to continue in business

Once the auditor examines all the records and does all of the testing, she/he drafts the balance sheet, income statement, and statement of changes in financial position and presents a written opinion of the statements taken as a whole. A sample auditor's opinion letter is presented in Figure 4–32. This letter is referred to as an unqualified, or "clean," opinion. Other formats for opinion letters are provided for properties that have significant problems or raise questions about their continuing viability.

In addition to providing an opinion, the auditor will also provide a management letter that delineates recommended changes in the financial management system to improve either its operation or its accuracy. The management letter provides the property manager with valuable suggestions for improving the financial management operations.

In all examinations, the property manager and staff should give the auditor access to all relevant records and as much assistance as is needed to get the job done. A meeting with the auditor prior to year end to clarify closing procedures and to begin setting up worksheets for the audit will ease the process and save both time and money.

REGULATORY REPORTING

In addition to reports to the owner, many developments financed with HUD mortgages and/or tax-exempt revenue bonds will require annual financial reports. The property manager should be familiar with those reporting requirements and ensure that they are met. In the case of bond financing, these requirements are especially important because failure to report could result in revocation of the bond's tax-exempt status. Such a change would result in serious tax consequences to the owner.

THE COMPUTER IN FINANCIAL MANAGEMENT

Computers make it possible to execute in mere hours or minutes those tasks that previously required hours, days, or weeks. They create accurate, professionally formatted reports and information, they make real-time, immediate data retrieval and communication possible, and they permit greater flexibility for customization.

Management companies and on-site management offices have a constantly growing catalogue of multihousing management accounting, budgeting, cash management, and database management software from which to choose. Prepackaged programs have become one of a multihousing management's most useful tools for financial analysis. These programs have a variety of uses:

- They produce special reports on the operation of the property not normally produced by the financial management system.
- Pro forma or template blanks are created for budgets, rent rolls, cash flow projections, initial rent-up calculations, and other types of financial situations. These template models are easy and quick to use so they allow the manager time to think about the issue rather than about grinding out the numbers.
- What-if models can show the various possible effects of financial changes such as rent increases.
- Models and automatic mathematic and printing functions enable a manager to perform projections and calculations that would require hours or days to complete manually. They help a manager to spot trends or problems and to fully examine them in a fraction of the time once required.
- Market surveys, rent analyses, occupancy reports, and a number of other regularly scheduled reports are produced faster and more accurately. Spreadsheets are especially appropriate for reports in which only a small portion of the information changes each time the report is done.
- The current generation of spreadsheets can display portions of the data contained in them in graphic form. This feature can be valuable for visualizing aspects of a multihousing property's operation.

A good example of the usefulness of electronic spreadsheets is provided in the model reproduced in Figures 4–21 through 4–24. The model consists of a three-module blank set up in a standard format for budgeting for garden apartment properties. The three modules—payroll, utilities, and

FIGURE 4-32. Independent Auditor's Report

We have audited the accompanying balance sheet of ______________________________ Company as of December 31, 20_____, and the related statements of income, retained earnings, and cash flows for the year then ended. These financial statements are the responsibility of the company's management. Our responsibility is to express an opinion on these financial statements based on our audit.

We conducted our audit in accordance with generally accepted auditing standards. Those standards require that we plan and perform the audit to obtain reasonable assurance about whether the financial statements are free of material misstatement. An audit includes examining, on a test basis, evidence supporting the amounts and disclosures in the financial statements. An audit also includes assessing the accounting principles used and significant estimates made by management, as well as evaluating the overall financial statement presentation. We believe that our audit provides a reasonable basis for our opinion.

In our opinion, the financial statements referred to above present fairly, in all material respects, the financial position of ______________________________ Company as of December 31, 20_____, and the results of its operations and its cash flows for the year then ended in conformity with generally accepted accounting principles.

detailed expenses—are all linked together so that the computer transfers the results of payroll and utility calculations automatically to the detailed analysis, and, finally, consolidates the entire budget in several automatic calculations.

In the payroll module, once the payroll, tax, and health insurance parameters are set, the module automatically calculates all payroll-related taxes and charges and puts them into the correct months of the year. Raises can be automatically calculated as well. This degree of automation greatly reduces the time required to work up a payroll and the possibility of errors.

However, as with every other business tool, spreadsheets have caveats as well. For example, one of the spreadsheet's most significant problems results when the person creating a model fails to completely test and verify its operation before using it. A model that produces defective results is more dangerous than having no information at all, and the complexity of the model requires thorough testing to reveal problems that are not immediately evident. Thorough testing and verification of a model is absolutely necessary when decisions involving hundreds of thousands, or millions, of dollars are made on the basis of the results. Fortunately, programs are also available to assist the manager in auditing and testing a model for programming errors before using it.

A final caution on the use of spreadsheet models involves making sure the underlying assumptions are accurate. If a manager begins with fundamentally defective assumptions in any financial analysis, the results derived will be convincing, professional looking, and absolutely wrong. All managers must avoid assuming that results produced by a computer program are necessarily right.

The only assurance a manager has about the results coming out of any model is that they will conform exactly to the assumptions used when the model was created. A manager should therefore view the results produced using a spreadsheet with the same degree of skepticism as a manually drawn analysis and perform the required due diligence by checking and double-checking all work produced.

SERVICE BUREAUS

Service bureaus provide either an alterative or a supplement to an in-house computer system. Using a service bureau essentially involves "renting" a computer and software system and the people to run them. When using a service bureau, the management company or property transmits its information to the bureau and the bureau does the calculating and paperwork.

Service bureaus have been around for many years and have some distinct advantages. Foremost among these advantages is the elimination of the capital investment in both hardware and software for certain applications. Other advantages include the elimination of the need for support personnel to operate the system and the availability of both training and assistance in the use of the system in the event of a problem.

However, service bureaus may not always be able to provide the level of customization requested, their turnaround time is somewhat longer than an internal system might be, and the cost may be somewhat higher because service bureaus are in a separate, profit-motivated industry.

In the end, deciding whether to use a service bureau depends on the needs and internal capabilities of the individual management company or property and on the manner in which technology is utilized to achieve the desired results.

CONCLUSION

To fulfill her/his professional obligations, the property manager must have a working understanding of the economics and finances of multihousing investment and management. This includes familiarity with the differences between conventional properties and subsidized developments and a grasp of the concepts of net operating income (NOI), cash flow and cash-on-cash return, and valuation techniques.

The property manager further must understand that rent payment and collection provide the mainstay cash flow for multihousing properties and that setting the appropriate level of rent and collecting the rent on time and in full are critical to the owner's objectives. Whether it is a conventional property or subsidized development, the property manager therefore must know and comply with the proper procedures for establishing rent levels, making adjustments in rent, notifying renters of rent adjustments, and collecting the rent, and she/he must act swiftly and confidently to remove residents who cannot or will not pay.

The property manager also must have full knowledge of the property's lease agreement and security deposit policies.

With regard to the financial management of the property, the property manager must participate knowledgeably in both historically based and zero-base operational and capital budgeting and in monthly financial reporting to both the senior manager and the owner. She/he also is responsible for the property's cash management, including timing the payment of bills, investment of funds, and monitoring all other management activities to ensure that the property's cash is used in the most efficient way.

The property manager must cooperate productively with the management company's financial decision makers, the owner(s), and outside professional auditors in the annual examination of the property's financial affairs. And she/he must be able to operate a computer and computer software to expedite the financial management of the property.

From the perspective of both the multihousing owner and the multihousing management company, the quality of a property manager's performance is reflected in an operation that functions smoothly and maintains a financially healthy bottom line. Understanding and participating in the economics and finances of multihousing management is fundamental to the property manager's professional success.

5

Property Maintenance and Energy and Water Conservation

The importance of proper maintenance

The six categories of multihousing property maintenance

Maintenance roles of staff and residents

Custodial or janitorial maintenance

Corrective or service maintenance

Preventive or planned maintenance

Emergency or crisis maintenance

Vacant unit maintenance and preparation

Outside contractors

Property-wide maintenance scheduling and inspections

Energy and water conservation

Resident relations in property maintenance

Maintenance logistics

The management maintenance plan (including a risk management plan)

Conclusion

THE IMPORTANCE OF PROPER MAINTENANCE

Maintenance refers to the preservation of assets through the upkeep of a residential property's structural, physical, mechanical, and aesthetic elements. The maintenance of a multihousing property is critical because maintenance equates to service, service is the defining feature that distinguishes all successful properties, and multihousing management is first and last a service business. In the end, it is the quality of the property's maintenance program and staff that can make the different between profit and loss for the property owner and success or failure for the management company and manager.

It is the property manager who is accountable to the property owner, the senior property manager, the executive property manager and the management company principal, and the property residents for the maintenance of the property. It is therefore the property manager's responsibility to:

- Be thoroughly familiar with the property
- Be aware of the property's maintenance history (even before the manager arrived)
- Inspect the property regularly
- Recommend and implement effective routine, service, and preventive maintenance programs
- Anticipate and respond to maintenance needs
- Train and supervise maintenance personnel
- Use the expertise of the property's maintenance manager or supervisor and the Scope of Work portion of any applicable contract to monitor the materials, workmanship, and work site of property contractors
- Ensure that maintenance standards are upheld
- Keep accurate maintenance records

- Know how to manage and resolve any maintenance-related situation that arises

This does not mean that the property manager must handle every maintenance situation herself/himself. What it does mean is that the manager must have an organized plan for every maintenance-related eventuality, must know which staff member or contractor to call on to perform the necessary work, must know how to evaluate the quality of the work performed, and must know what the fair market value is for the work so as to protect the property's financial position at all times.

The property manager also will find regularly scheduled staff meetings to be an invaluable management and maintenance tool. These meetings should be structured in advance by the manager, and they should be short and to the point. At the conclusion of each meeting, the entire property staff should know and understand their respective tasks/goals as established by the property manager.

The goals and benefits of an effective maintenance program and staff are detailed below.

INCREASED TRAFFIC THROUGH ENHANCED CURB APPEAL

The physical appearance of a property's buildings and grounds form that all-important first impression and account for most of the traffic that finds its way into a rental office. An unsightly property reveals a weak maintenance program, repels desirable prospective renters, and may in fact attract decidedly undesirable renters, but great curb appeal attracts more desirable residents, helps rental agents to close more deals faster, and can reduce the amount of money dedicated to advertising to build traffic. In short, excellent curb appeal is a primary goal and benefit of an effective maintenance program.

HIGHER CLOSING RATES FOR RENTAL AGENTS

Rental agents have a hard enough job without having to overcome the challenges of grounds that are ill-kept or not attractively landscaped, grass that is not cut, amenities that are dirty or out of order, and buildings and units that are in states of neglect and disrepair. Conversely, the rental agent who can take a prospective renter through a well-manicured landscape into an apartment or townhouse that is freshly painted, immaculate, and has all working appliances is likely to come out with a new resident. For many if not most prospects, the condition of the unit is the most important factor in their decision to rent. The second, but only slightly less important, factor is the condition of the property's common areas and its curb appeal. It is clear, then, that maintenance is essential to the successful renting of units.

SWIFT AND SATISFACTORY REFURBISHMENT OF VACANCIES

Refurbishing vacant units and readying them for marketing and for new resident move-in is a major function of property maintenance. When vacant units are refurbished within the established timetable, attractive units are available for marketing faster, move-ins are expedited, and the rent stream continues with minimal interruption.

REDUCED TURNOVER AND INCREASED RESIDENT RETENTION

When residents are pleased with the way the property's common areas are maintained and especially with the way their service maintenance requests are responded to, their reasons for leaving are significantly reduced. On-going routine and service maintenance and effective preventive and emergency maintenance are absolute musts for high resident retention.

MAINTAINING PHYSICAL VALUE

Nothing consumes cash faster than simultaneous multiple major capital expenditures. Conversely, an on-going dedication to maintaining a property's physical, structural, mechanical, and aesthetic elements through well-supervised routine and service maintenance programs and a well-planned preventive maintenance program allows the manager to maintain the property's value for the owner while providing a stable and attractive environment for existing and prospective renters.

IMPROVED CASH FLOW, EXPENSE CONTROLS, AND NET OPERATING INCOME

As discussed in Chapter 4, Multihousing Management Economics and Finances, because maintenance is the biggest controllable expense item, it is a key factor in determining the cash flow of a property. Although the policies of the management company and the owner's objectives for the property play a significant role in the level and quality of maintenance that is delivered, there can be no question that regularly scheduled routine and preventive maintenance and superior service maintenance response time and performance will preserve the long-term economic life of the property by decreasing expenses and making the best use of available manpower, equipment, and money.

ENHANCED REPUTATION FOR THE MANAGEMENT COMPANY

Prospects who are looking to rent in the most desirable property make it their business to learn about the reputations of various management companies. When a management company can point to a portfolio of exceptionally well-maintained properties, that reputation precedes the company, prospects are favorably disposed to the property even before they arrive on-site, and current residents are proud to call the community home.

THE SIX CATEGORIES OF MULTIHOUSING PROPERTY MAINTENANCE

Each maintenance activity in a multihousing property falls into one of six categories:

- Custodial or janitorial (routine maintenance)
- Corrective or service
- Preventive or planned
- Emergency or crisis
- Deferred
- Vacant unit maintenance and preparation

To maintain any property optimally, the property manager must be able to identify which category of maintenance a task falls into and then create a plan that details when each maintenance task is to be addressed, by whom, how long it should take to complete, and its cost and cost/benefit to the property. A brief introduction to each maintenance category appears below, and increasingly detailed discussions of custodial, service, preventive, emergency maintenance, and the maintenance and preparation of vacant units follow throughout this part of the text. Deferred maintenance is not expanded upon as widely because those items that require maintenance but don't get it will eventually wind up in the service or emergency maintenance category.

CUSTODIAL OR JANITORIAL MAINTENANCE

As its name suggests, custodial or janitorial maintenance is maintenance that is performed regularly, usually by the property staff, to best maintain the property's appearance. An effective custodial or janitorial maintenance program is the best way to help maximize net operating income (NOI) for the owner.

CORRECTIVE OR SERVICE MAINTENANCE

Corrective maintenance is work performed to repair an item or system. Service maintenance is a type of corrective maintenance that is almost always performed inside dwelling units. Whereas corrective maintenance includes repairs to a property's common areas and equipment (e.g., broken windows), service maintenance as a subcategory of corrective maintenance is typically performed at the request of a resident. Without a formal request for service maintenance, neither the property manager nor the maintenance staff would know that a repair or other maintenance service needs to be performed.

Although corrective maintenance of the items and systems that keep a property operational is essential, residents most often experience service maintenance and they most often judge the quality of an entire property's maintenance by the quality of service they receive in response to a request for maintenance. A smoothly running corrective/service maintenance response program is one of the best ways to ensure a well-maintained property and satisfied, long-term residents.

PREVENTIVE OR PLANNED MAINTENANCE

Preventive or planned maintenance anticipates likely problems and takes steps to prolong the useful life of various physical, structural, mechanical, and aesthetic elements before they have the chance to become costly problems. The philosophy behind preventive or planned maintenance is that it is the least expensive form of maintenance over the long run because properly maintained elements last longer and perform better than elements that are not maintained. An effective preventive or planned maintenance program contributes significantly to maximizing the owner's NOI.

EMERGENCY OR CRISIS MAINTENANCE

Situations that require emergency or crisis maintenance sometimes occur spontaneously and without warning but often are the result of a poor or absent custodial and/or preventive maintenance program, or of a deferred maintenance program that deferred for too long. In any case, emergency/crisis maintenance is always required after the fact, must be dealt with immediately or in very short order, and is almost always more costly than the custodial and/or preventive maintenance that would have prevented it in the first place.

DEFERRED MAINTENANCE

Deferred maintenance is maintenance that needs to be done but is put off for one reason or another. Such reasons may include a lack of finances or the decision to allocate available funds to a different priority, or the decision to wait for a more conducive time of year to address the maintenance issue (e.g., waiting until after the freeze/thaw season to address an area of cracked concrete). Although deferring maintenance is sometime strategically justifiable, in many instances deferring for too long can lead to a more costly, and even a dangerous, emergency or crisis situation. What's more, the worst thing for a prospective renter to experience is a property defined by visibly deferred maintenance. When it comes to deferred maintenance, the most important step for a property manager to take is to place the item on a maintenance schedule and then stick to the schedule.

VACANT UNIT MAINTENANCE AND PREPARATION

The swift maintenance and preparation of vacated units is one of the most important functions of a property's maintenance department. Vacant units must be refurbished for showing and occupancy as quickly as possible to minimize rent downtime and maximize the attractiveness of the property.

MAINTENANCE IN CONVENTIONAL AND ASSISTED PROPERTIES

Although priorities and programs may vary from property to property, the maintenance goals of both conventional and federally assisted development are the same: to preserve the property's assets and to maintain an attractive appearance and a safe, functioning living environment at a reasonable expense level. In both conventional and assisted properties, the objective of the property manager is to accomplish these goals to the greatest possible extent.

MAINTENANCE ROLES OF STAFF AND RESIDENTS

THE PROPERTY MANAGER'S ROLE IN PROPERTY MAINTENANCE

Property managers generally do not possess the skills necessary to perform the maintenance tasks that are required throughout the properties they manage, nor should they. Performing the tasks is not the job of the property manager. The property manager's job is to be sufficiently familiar with the property and what needs to be done throughout the property so that she/he can determine the maintenance work, assign the work to the maintenance staff, ensure that maintenance staff members have been adequately and appropriately trained to do the tasks that are assigned to them, establish measurable standards, and see that staff perform the required work to these standards.

To this end, the property manager will find it especially helpful to document specific job descriptions. These descriptions should include clear expectations, instructions, and all standard operating procedures (SOP) for maintenance and should be assembled and included in the operations manual and the management maintenance plan, organized by task, and cross-referenced by employee. Copies of the job descriptions, expectations, instructions, and procedures also should be given to the employees who are expected to perform them. This will guide maintenance employees in the performance of their job functions and help to reduce the amount of time the manager must spend supervising and scheduling tasks.

When it comes to maintenance, the property manager sometimes operates on a management by exception basis, whereby the she/he can assume that the procedures are operating satisfactorily when the objectives are accomplished. Additional involvement by the property manager is required only when the objectives are not accomplished and an exception occurs.

In addition to determining maintenance tasks and delegating their performance to maintenance staff members, the property manager also is expected to secure and have available the property's building plans and valve location chart, the operating manuals for all appliances and equipment installed in and/or used by the property, and all building code regulations and required safety standards. The property manager should keep a meticulous inventory of all maintenance equipment and all pertinent information relating to each appliance and piece of equipment, including the model and serial number, the manufacturer's manuals, manufacturers' and other warranties, insurance coverages, date purchased and date installed, a maintenance history, and necessary parts and parts on hand.

As indicated in Chapter 2, Planning for Multihousing Management Success, depending on its size, a property may employ a maintenance manager or maintenance supervisor in addition to the property manager. Although it would be reasonable to expect that the maintenance manager or supervisor would maintain the inventory described in the paragraph above, an important caveat must be inserted here with regard to property maintenance staff. It is this: In some organizations, the property manager and the property maintenance manager/supervisor are on the same level and both report to the senior property manager or owner. However, this arrangement is likely to produce conflict and reduce the effectiveness of the organization. One person alone must be accountable for the entire property to avoid the problems that inevitably arise when no one is in charge because two or more people are technically in charge. Therefore, for the best results, the chain of command should dictate that the maintenance manager/supervisor report to the property manager.

THE MAINTENANCE STAFF

The role of the property's maintenance staff is to perform most of the maintenance functions, including custodial, corrective/service, preventive, and emergency maintenance, maintenance and preparation of vacant units, and all additional maintenance work assigned by the property manager. In larger properties, a maintenance manager/supervisor may direct the rest of the maintenance staff but as stipulated above, she/he should always be subordinate to the property manager.

Depending on the size and requirements of the individual property, maintenance staff may also include one or more maintenance assistants, one or more maintenance technicians, general maintenance workers, housekeeping employees, grounds employees, and part-time and/or seasonal employees. It is the property manager's responsibility to ensure that each maintenance worker is assigned to tasks that she/he has been trained to do and that maintenance employees are productive and comfortable in their assigned roles. (See Chapter 2, Planning for Multihousing Management Success for information about property maintenance personnel and staffing techniques and Chapter 3, On The Front Line: The Property Manager for a discussion about evaluating and increasing maintenance staff morale and productivity.)

In some properties, especially smaller ones, varying levels of maintenance may be contracted to outside vendors. In these cases, the property manager is responsible for ensuring that the work is done properly and that the invoices for the work are reasonable and accurate.

THE ROLE OF RESIDENTS IN PROPERTY MAINTENANCE

Although they have the right to expect property staff to perform necessary and appropriate maintenance functions in the property's common areas and to respond to in-unit service maintenance requests promptly and professionally, residents are not simply passive observers when it comes to maintaining the property in which they live. On the contrary, residents are responsible for keeping their units reasonably clean, abiding by the rules and regulations established for the use and maintenance of the property's common areas and equipment, and alerting the property's management office as quickly and accurately as possible when maintenance needs to be performed either in the common areas or in their dwelling unit. Such notification is very helpful to management because problems are much less costly to fix at an early stage (e.g., an unreported leaky faucet not only increases water consumption and utility expense but may also cause other serious problems or indicate a rusted pipe that needs replacing). The role of residents in property maintenance is vital to the stability of the property and should be documented in the resident handbook.

CUSTODIAL OR JANITORIAL MAINTENANCE

Custodial maintenance is the backbone of every property's maintenance program. Custodial maintenance must be performed on an on-going basis if the property is to maintain a clean, well-cared-for appearance and be attractive to both existing and prospective residents. Typically, custodial maintenance is performed on the property grounds, the building exteriors and interiors, and the property's maintenance equipment. Such tasks as regular clean-up, grass cutting, checking for and replacing burned out light bulbs in common areas, and periodically changing the oil in the property vehicles all fall under the heading of custodial maintenance.

SCHEDULING CUSTODIAL MAINTENANCE

Because custodial maintenance is easy to overlook in the press of other tasks, it must be scheduled and the schedule must be adhered to to ensure that it is performed routinely. For example, a custodial maintenance schedule may call for cleaning hallways three times per week, with certain hallways cleaned on certain days. Without a deliberate schedule, the tendency of property staff is to neglect these tasks because they are not accompanied by an immediate request from a resident or order from the property manager. However, it is extremely important to respect and enforce the scheduling of such custodial maintenance tasks as grass cutting, garbage collection, snow removal, pest control, washing and waxing floors, and cleaning mailboxes because without them, the property's curb appeal and quality of life will quickly deteriorate. Figure 5–1 provides a list of typical items requiring custodial maintenance.

It is the property manager's responsibility to schedule custodial maintenance tasks or, when the maintenance manager/supervisor makes up the schedule, to review the schedule and make sure that the maintenance manager/supervisor is enforcing it. The maintenance schedule should be prepared in advance of each week and should be distributed to all maintenance personnel and posted in the management office and the maintenance office/workshop/garage so that everyone involved in the property's maintenance can refer to it.

A schedule of selected custodial maintenance duties (Fig. 5–2) shows how often custodial maintenance jobs should be done, the estimated time to perform the custodial work (Fig. 5–3), and a representative list of jobs that are done frequently by the maintenance staff. Of course, conditions and jobs change from day to day. However, this schedule gives some idea of how much time is needed from total weekly work hours to complete custodial work. This timetable, or one like it, should be used to improve overall efficiency.

A WORD ABOUT PEST CONTROL IN CUSTODIAL MAINTENANCE

Pest control is an important aspect of interior custodial maintenance. When scheduling exterminator visits, the property manager or maintenance manager/supervisor should remember to schedule as many units as possible for the same visit. Exterminating one unit at a time only causes unwanted visitors to relocate to somewhere else in the building, whereas making the entire building, or as much of it as possible, inhospitable to these intruders will help to encourage them to move out entirely. It is the property manager's responsibility to ensure that all extermination activities comply with environmental laws and regulations.

A WORD ABOUT LAWN AND PLANT MAINTENANCE

Almost universally, the grounds of a residential property form the first impression of the overall property. The units may be large and magnificently appointed, but existing residents will quickly revolt and few prospective renters will visit if even the most minimal landscaping is missing or ugly, grass is uncut, and what plants there are look like they wish they lived somewhere else.

Ultimately, the property manager, or the maintenance manager/supervisor who reports to the property manager, is responsible for determining the property's lawn and landscape maintenance requirements. However, most managers are not experts in botany, horticulture, lawn care, or decorative landscaping. For this reason, many properties engage the services of an outside landscape maintenance firm. This subcontracting maintenance resource helps the property manager and/or maintenance manager/supervisor establish appropriate routine mowing and pruning schedules for in-house staff while providing the year-round lawn, plant, tree, and soil care services that in-house staff do not perform.

Managers and/or maintenance managers/supervisors of properties that do perform all landscape maintenance functions in-house will want to consult with the local county extension/agricultural agent and/or the maintenance manager/supervisor at a local golf course for advice on fertilizing, weeding, spraying, and disease control. However, properties that wish to present the most attractive and best-maintained landscaping generally will opt for the services of paid professionals who have a vested interest in keeping the property's grass, plants, shrubs, trees, and landscape design healthy, well-manicured, and attractive.

A sample procedures checklist for lawn and plant maintenance appears in Figure 5–4. A landscape maintenance schedule that promotes year-round care appears in Figure 5–5. As with extermination, it is the property manager's responsibility to ensure that all lawn and plant maintenance activities comply with environmental laws and regulations.

FIGURE 5–1. Typical Items Requiring Custodial Maintenance

Grounds
- Fencing
- Grass
- Lighting
- Parking lots
- Playground areas, benches, and equipment
- Public telephones
- Signs
- Storm drainage system
- Swimming pools
- Trees and landscaping
- Walking paths

Building Exteriors
- Air-conditioning equipment
- Exterior masonry
- Exterior wood surfaces
- Foundations
- Gutters and downspouts
- Lighting
- Mailboxes
- Power lines
- Public utility equipment
- Roofing and stacks
- TV antennas
- Windows and window panes

Building Interiors
- Basements
- Circulating pumps
- Clubhouse/community center
- Models
- Elevators
- Heating and hot water systems
- Laundry areas
- Lobbies, halls, stairwells, common areas
- Maintenance facility
- Offices
- Mechanical rooms
- Storage areas

FIGURE 5–2. Schedule of Selected Custodial Maintenance Duties

Daily and as needed
- General cleanup
- Trash area
- Models
- Clubhouse/community center
- Pool in summer months
- Laundry areas
- Animal control

Three times weekly
- Trash pick-up
- Playground area, benches, and equipment
- Maintenance facility
- Rental office
- Basements

Weekly
- General inspection
- Signs
- Storage locker area
- All property lights should be checked one night per week to ensure that they are operative

Every 2 weeks
- Hallways
- Gas and electric area lights

Monthly
- Exterior painting

Every 2 months
- Basket-weave fence
- Downspouts and gutters
- Circulating pumps — oil
- Vehicle maintenance

Every 90 days
- Filter changing

FIGURE 5–3. Estimated Time to Perform Custodial Maintenance Work

Community building and laundry room, 1 hour daily
- Clean washing machines and dryers
- Sweep and mop tile floor
- Carry out trash
- Check and clean rest rooms as needed
- Check and clean rental office
- Clean community building entryway and hallways

Police property, 1 hour daily
- Walk property; pick up debris and toys
- Check and clean trash pads
- Check and clean all sidewalks and streets as needed

Entry halls, 15 to 20 minutes per hall
- Sweep steps and hallways
- Dust or damp wipe all handrails and baseboards
- Mop steps and tile areas
- Wash interior and exterior doors as needed
- Sweep stoop and walkway as needed

Grass cutting, approximately 1 hour per building
- Cut, trim grass, and clean building and shrub beds with push mower and trimmers
- Cut grass on grounds adjacent to building with tractor
- Sweep sidewalks free of grass cuttings

Replace furnace air filters, 10 minutes per furnace

Snow removal time is based on weather conditions

FIGURE 5–4. Lawn and Plant Maintenance Checklist

Warning

☐ Weed control chemicals are powerful toxins and must be used in accordance with label instructions for the type of problem being addressed. Many types of chemicals cannot be used where they will run off into local streams and rivers. Appropriate respirators should be used with these materials at all times. Maintenance supervisors should consult their local cooperative extension agents to determine appropriate materials and applications rates. Some commonly used chemicals have been either banned or severely restricted in their use in recent years. Prior to using any chemical, the maintenance supervisor should make sure the chemical is still legal. If it is not legal, he/she should contact the appropriate authorities to dispose of the remaining material.

Lawn Care

☐ Mowing lawns properly promotes healthy grass and discourages weeds and diseases. Cutting the grass at different heights is important. In early spring cut grass to 2 inches, in mid-summer to 2? inches, and in late fall from 1½ to 2 inches. Never cut off more than 1/3 pf the grass blade.

☐ Cut new sod to 2½ inches until it knits in approximately 40 days. Pay particular attention to the terrain to avoid scalping new sod. New sod should be watered frequently. Fertilize with a straight fertilizer after three mowings.

☐ Water lawns thoroughly when rainfall is insufficient.

☐ Seed lawns if required between September 10 and October.

Fertilization and Weed Control

☐ Fertilize lawns in the spring and fall with a weed-and-feed type fertilizer. As weather conditions allow, make spring application between April 1 and April 15, and the fall application between September 1 and September 15.

☐ For effective lawn care, the ground temperature must be a least 55 degrees. Generally, this condition is met when the air temperature is higher than 55 degrees for a minimum of 5 days. The lawn must be moderately wet from rain, watering, or morning dew. Water the grounds a section at a time. If application is made after the morning dew, the process should begin no later that 6a.m. and should be finished 2 to 3 hours later.

☐ To ensure timely arrival of materials, order fertilizer around January 20 for the spring application and July 10 for the fall application. The property manager is responsible for ensuring that these materials are ordered and distributed.

☐ Follow the fertilizer manufacturer's application directions explicitly, and apply only to the grass. Avoid fertilizing shrubs and other plants.

☐ Make frequent checks for grass and weeds growing around curbs, streets, stoops, and private walks. Use a chemical spray that kills weeds on contact.

Plant, Shrubbery, and Tree Care

☐ Water new plants on a daily basis until they are well established. Apply mulch to flower beds in the latter part of April.

☐ Hand prune shrubs (except for hedges) to retain their natural character. Hand prune yews and junipers between March 15 and April 15. Refer to the maintenance manual fir safety precautions. Prune shade trees only to eliminate limbs and too low, double crotches, and broken branches.

☐ Spray shrubs and trees with a federally approved chemical for bag worms, spiders, and other insects between June 1 and June 30.

☐ Replace shrubbery between September 10 and October 10.

____

(Date)

I have spot-checked the items initialed and found that the development summarization procedure
☐ is
☐ is not complete.

____

(Development Manager)

____

(Development name)

FIGURE 5–5. New Landscaping Checklist

Landscape architect has verified installation of the landscaping on

____
(Date of installation)

Landscape contractor cared for plants until

____
(30 days later)

The plants listed below have died:

____
____
____
____
____
____
____

Landscape contractor was notified.

____
(Date)

Landscape contractor replaced these plants

____
(Date)

New plants have been checked for size and tagged with planting date.

Contractor took care of plants until

____
(30 days later)

Replacement plants listed below died:

____
____
____
____
____
____
____

Landscape contractor replaced these

____
(Date)

New plants have been checked for size and tagged with planting date.

Contractor took care of plants until

____
(30 days later)

I certify that all new or replacement plants have survived for 1 year.

____
(Date)

____
(Maintenance supervisor)

____
(Development name)

FILTER CHANGES AND SMOKE ALARM TESTS, AND ENERGY AND WATER CONSERVATION INSPECTIONS

During all custodial maintenance calls to residential units, maintenance workers also should check and change filters as needed, test the unit's smoke alarm to be sure it is functioning, inspect kitchen and bathroom faucets for leaks and commodes for continuous running, and repair or schedule for repair as appropriate. The checklist for the filter change and smoke alarm test (Fig. 5–6) provides a sample guideline for making these tests. A control log (Fig. 5–7) helps to ensure that the tests are done regularly. (See the discussion on energy and water conservation below.) Inspections for peeling paint, the presence of window guards, and other federal, state, and local requirements also may be mandated in some jurisdictions.

CUSTODIAL MAINTENANCE OF PROPERTY EQUIPMENT

'The maintenance of property equipment also should be scheduled as part of custodial maintenance. This is to ensure that the manufacturers' recommended maintenance protocols are followed to prolong the useful life of the equipment and also because failure to follow the manufacturer's recommended maintenance protocols may void the warranty.

CORRECTIVE AND SERVICE MAINTENANCE

Corrective maintenance includes the maintenance and repair of the property's common areas. The scheduling of corrective maintenance may be the result of the property manager "walking the property" and observing a condition that requires maintenance attention or reports from property staff or residents. Service maintenance is corrective maintenance that is performed inside a dwelling unit in response to a resident's request. Examples of service maintenance include repairing leaking faucets, closet doors that have come off their tracks, and broken appliances that are the property's responsibility. To ensure that residents use the property's appliances properly, the resident handbook should include operating instructions for each appliance that comes with the unit. The resident handbook also should include specific instructions on how to request service maintenance, including the fact that all service maintenance requests must be in writing.

SCHEDULING AND RESPONDING TO SERVICE MAINTENANCE REQUESTS

As indicated, service requests should be in writing to avoid misunderstandings. To this end, service request forms like the one shown in Figure 5–8 should be available to all residents in the management and/or maintenance office. A copy of the form should be included in the resident handbook and should appear as a model in both the property's operations manual and management maintenance plan.

In properties wherein service maintenance requests are taken by phone, all staff taking maintenance requests should be trained in how to "talk through" a problem with the resident so that the proper diagnosis is made and the maintenance employee has a fairly good idea of what will be required to repair the problem. Office staff members who receive phoned service requests should be required to record the information on the service request form and the forms discussed below. To make sure this system works, the property manager might arrange for the maintenance manager/supervisor or some other articulate maintenance employee to conduct periodic seminars to explain the most common maintenance problems to the office staff so they are better equipped to write complete work orders.

Some properties allow residents to transmit service maintenance requests to the management and/or maintenance office via e-mail or other web-based systems. When this transmission is done via a form that is received electronically by the office, office staff should download the form and keep records of the information on the form as discussed below. When this transmission is done via a simple e-mail message that does not include a form, office staff should transfer the information to the appropriate form(s) as discussed below.

Regardless of how the service maintenance request is received, it is important for the maintenance staff to know if the resident has a pet in the unit and/or a dead bolt lock on the front door. The resident handbook should indicate that it is the resident's responsibility to inform management of such an animal and to either cage or remove the pet when maintenance workers are in the unit. The property manager and/or maintenance manager/supervisor also must make certain that the maintenance department has all keys necessary to gain access, including keys for dead bolt locks. Otherwise, much time is wasted traveling back and forth and not being able to gain access to the unit to make the repair. The service request form includes boxes for the resident to indicate the presence of an animal and a dead bolt in the unit. (In some jurisdictions, double key dead bolt locks are illegal because of the difficulty in escaping during a fire.)

Residents should be discouraged from communicating service maintenance requests directly to maintenance personnel because the property management and/or maintenance office must be aware of all requests so that they can follow up and control maintenance scheduling. Maintenance workers should be instructed that if a resident approaches them directly with a service request, they should politely inform the resident that they are not allowed to take such requests and that the proper procedure is for the resident to fill out a service request form. No member of the maintenance staff should promise a response or perform maintenance work unless and until the property manager or maintenance manager/supervisor has directed her/him to do so.

Except for emergency requests, service maintenance requests are normally responded to on a first-come, first-served basis. An exception may be when two or more requests are grouped because of convenience in location. In any case, a specific time should be set aside in every working day for the maintenance staff to respond to service maintenance requests. This time should be scheduled so as not to interfere with necessary custodial maintenance activities. It is the responsibility of the property manager, or the maintenance manager/supervisor reporting to the property man-

FIGURE 5–6. Filter Change and Smoke Alarm Test*

☐ Change filters four times a year on a quarterly basis. The second and fourth quarter changes are made during summarization and winterization of the development when maintenance personnel must enter each apartment to perform other functions. ________

☐ During these quarterly visits, test the smoke alarms by pressing the test buttons to make sure the alarms go off. Alarms that do not work should be repaired or replaced immediately. They can also be tested with a special "smoke" spray. _______

☐ Place a new battery in each smoke alarm at the fourth-quarter test every year. In addition, change filters and make smoke alarm test at unit turnover. __________

☐ The maintenance supervisor uses the filter and smoke alarm control log to schedule and control filter changes and smoke alarm test by building, week, and month. The time needed to change filters and make smoke alarm tests throughout the developments depends upon a number of factors, including other preventive maintenance actions, volume of service requests, and number of turnover units. It could vary from a week to months. In some seniors housing developments, smoke alarms are tested every month. __________

ager, to schedule service maintenance requests in as timely a manner as possible. Some properties have adopted the policy of responding to service maintenance requests within 24 hours. The individual responsible for scheduling service maintenance responses must always bear in mind that residential management is a service business, and even though the property may be managed very well, residents will often base their judgment of management on how quickly and professionally their own requests are responded to.

It cannot be emphasized strongly enough that no property employee, including maintenance workers, should enter any resident's unit without the resident's prior permission. The only exception to this rule is an emergency or custodial service where prior notice has been served (e.g., changing filters in a unit's furnace). When responding to a service maintenance request, maintenance employees should enter a resident's unit only with the resident's express permission. This permission may be granted in two ways. If the resident is home, the maintenance staff member should announce who she/he is and why she/he is there and should ask the resident if it is all right to enter the unit. Only after the resident opens the door and allows the maintenance worker in should the worker enter the unit. If the resident is not home, the maintenance worker should first check to see if the resident has given permission to enter the unit when the resident is not there. The service request form should include a box for the resident to check to give permission for the maintenance staff to enter the unit to perform service maintenance when the resident is not home. Whether or not the resident is home, whenever a maintenance worker is in a dwelling unit, the worker should place a door hanger on the outside doorknob of the front door stating that the property maintenance department is working in the unit. (A door hanger is a card designed to fit over the door knob similar to the "Do not disturb" signs in hotels.)

At the end of the maintenance visit, the maintenance staff should have the resident sign off on the service request form. The maintenance staff should give a copy of the form to the resident and retain a copy to be presented to the property manager or the maintenance manager/supervisor either immediately upon leaving the unit or at the end of the work day, depending on the established protocol. If the resident was not at home when the service call was completed, a service call notice card should be left for the resident on the kitchen table or in some other highly visible location. The service call notice card informs the resident of what work was done and whether it was completed or if staff will need access to the unit again to complete the work.

RESIDENT ABUSE OF DWELLING UNIT

Should it appear to the maintenance worker that the maintenance request is the result of a resident's abuse of the unit, this observation should be indicated on the service request form and the maintenance worker should be instructed to so inform the property manager before proceeding with the repair. The property manager should then speak with the resident about the conditions noted and, if appropriate, arrange for advance payment before the repair is performed.

SERVICE REQUEST SYSTEM

As noted above, the property manager's goal should be to have maintenance staff respond to each service maintenance request as quickly as possible, ideally within 24 hours. This goal should be stated in the property's operations manual, maintenance plan, and resident handbook. If meeting this goal is not possible for a particular service request, the property manager or maintenance manager/supervisor should notify the resident and provide a date on which the service can be performed. If a delay occurs, the resident should be informed immediately and a new date set. In every case, every effort should be made to complete the promised repairs within the time commitment, and follow-up should be maintained to ensure that the repair is made when promised. No service maintenance request, regardless of how small, should be allowed to linger or fall through the cracks.

When residents request service maintenance, all they see is the service request form and the maintenance personnel who perform the repair. But for the property manager, maintenance manager/supervisor, and maintenance staff, keeping track of service maintenance activities requires a clear

FIGURE 5–7. Filter and Smoke Alarm Control Log

(Development) (Year)

Building	First Quarter	Second Quarter	Third Quarter	Fourth Quarter	Comments

(Date) (Maintenance Superintendant signature)

FIGURE 5–8. Service Request

DEAD BOLT ____________
ANIMAL ______________

MAINTENANCE SERVICE RECORD
ENERGY CONSERVATION

PROJECT CODE ____________

NAME ______________________________ DATE ______________ TIME ____________

PHONE NO. ______________________________ CIRCLE APT. TYPE 1BR. 2BR. 2TH. 3TH. 4 BR.

ADDRESS ____ APT. # ____________

SERVICE NEEDED ____

TYPE OF SERVICE RENDERED ____

MATERIALS USED ____

LABOR CHARGE	MATERIAL CHARGE	TIME ON JOB	DATE	INITIAL

DEAD BOLT ____________
ANIMAL ______________

SERVICE REQUEST
ENERGY CONSERVATION

PROJECT CODE ____________

NAME ______________________________ DATE ______________ TIME ____________

PHONE NO. ______________________________ CIRCLE APT. TYPE 1BR. 2BR. 2TH. 3TH. 4 BR.

ADDRESS ____ APT. # ____________

SERVICE NEEDED ____

OUR GOAL IS TO PERFORM SERVICE REQUESTS TO THE SATISFACTION OF THE RESIDENT.

RENTAL MANAGER SIGNATURE ____

continued

FIGURE 5–8. Service Request (*Continued*)

DEAD BOLT ___________
ANIMAL ___________

RESIDENT COMMENT
ENERGY CONSERVATION

PROJECT CODE ___________

NAME ___________ DATE ___________ TIME ___________

PHONE NO. ___________ CIRCLE APT. TYPE 1BR. 2BR. 2TH. 3TH. 4 BR.

ADDRESS ___________ APT. # ___________

SERVICE NEEDED ___________

PLEASE HELP US ACHIEVE OUR GOAL BY RETURNING THIS POSTAGE-FREE INFORMATION CARD INDICATING HOW YOUR SERVICE REQUEST WAS HANDLED.

EXCELLENT_______ GOOD_______ AVERAGE_______ BELOW AVERAGE_______ POOR_______

COMMENTS: ___________

MAINTENANCE SIGNATURE ___________ RESIDENT SIGNATURE ___________

DEAD BOLT ___________
ANIMAL ___________

RENTAL OFFICE SERVICE RECORD
ENERGY CONSERVATION

PROJECT CODE ___________

NAME ___________ DATE ___________ TIME ___________

PHONE NO. ___________ CIRCLE APT. TYPE 1BR. 2BR. 2TH. 3TH. 4 BR.

ADDRESS ___________ APT. # ___________

SERVICE NEEDED ___________

TYPE OF SERVICE RENDERED ___________

MATERIALS USED ___________

LABOR CHARGE	MATERIAL CHARGE	TIME ON JOB	DATE	INITIAL

system to be most efficient. The service request form, service request record, parts order control form, and service procedures discussed below define a smooth service maintenance program and should be included as part of the property's operations manual and in the maintenance plan. For highest efficiency, these form and the information they contain should be computerized.

SERVICE MAINTENANCE DOCUMENTATION FORMS

Service Request Form

The service request form (Fig. 5–8) not only allows the resident to write the service maintenance request but also provides a means of recording the information pertaining to each request. When it is completed, a copy of the service request form should be given to the property manager and, if there is one, also to the maintenance manager/supervisor. A copy also should be left with the resident to allow the resident to grade the service, write comments, and return it to the management office or management company. If the resident response part of the form is to be mailed, it should be a stamped and self-addressed.

Service Request Record

The service request record (Fig. 5–9) is used to list each service maintenance request in the order it is received and to trace the status of each request until the work is completed. This document serves as the property manager's control to ensure that all follow-up on service requests is handled expeditiously and as a follow-up on service requests pending because parts have been ordered. This record should be maintained in the property management office along with the service request log discussed in the Property-wide Maintenance Scheduling and Inspections section below. It is the maintenance employee's responsibility to make an entry into the service request log each time a maintenance call is made.

Parts Order Control

The parts order control form (Fig. 5–10) monitors the status of any parts ordered for completion of a service request. The property manager or maintenance manager/supervisor should record the unit number, the name of the part ordered, the date it was ordered, the anticipated delivery date, and any other pertinent information. This form normally ties in with the service request record. It allows the property manager and the maintenance manager/supervisor to review the status of all parts ordered to determine if the property's existing inventory of parts is sufficient to fulfill normal service requests on a timely basis, and whether parts ordered are being delivered as promised. The property manager should coordinate with the owner and the management company's purchasing department or senior property manager regarding the maintenance of inventory and should establish a standard purchasing procedure so that parts and equipment can always be secured as quickly as possible.

SERVICE MAINTENANCE PROCEDURES

The following service maintenance procedures should be included in the property's operations manual and the maintenance plan.

Service Request

The property manager or maintenance manager/supervisor should assign each service request to a specific maintenance person for response.

Work Completed

The maintenance staff person should visit the unit and perform the necessary work. Using the service request form or computer-generated work order, the maintenance worker should record the actual work performed, the time spent, and the material used. As indicated above, if it appears that the maintenance request is the result of a resident's abuse of the unit, the maintenance worker should indicate this on the service request form and inform the property manager before proceeding with the repair. The maintenance worker should initial, date, and return the service request form to the property manager or maintenance manager/supervisor.

Service Call Notice

As mentioned above, if the resident is not at home when the service is performed, the maintenance person should leave a service call notice card on the kitchen table or in some other highly visible place to indicate that the unit was entered and the repair made. If the maintenance person is unable to gain access to the unit, she/he should place a note on the door requesting that the resident call the office to set up another time for the repair. The maintenance worker should make a record that a note was placed on the door and should alert the management or maintenance office that the resident needs to reschedule. If the resident does not contact the management or maintenance office within 24 hours, the property manager or maintenance manager/supervisor should dispatch the same maintenance worker to the unit to make sure that the note was taken off the door. (Notes left on doors for prolonged periods of time signal that the resident is away, which may constitute a security risk.) If the note has not been taken off the door after 24 hours, the maintenance worker should remove it, inform the management or maintenance office, and the management or maintenance office should try other means to contact the resident to reschedule the work.

Smoke Alarm Tests and Energy and Water Conservation Inspections in Service Maintenance Calls

As with the protocol for custodial maintenance, the property's procedures also may call for the maintenance person to test the smoke alarms in the unit (Figs. 5–6 and 5–7) and to perform an energy and water conservation inspection. An appropriate box on the service request form can be inserted to indicate that this conservation inspection is required and

FIGURE 5–9. Service Request Record

To: ______________________________

Property: ______________________________ From: ______________________________

Request No.	Name	Address and Phone no.	Date Service Requested	Date Comp.	Status

FIGURE 5–10. Parts Order Control

To: ____________________

Property: ____________________ From: ____________________

Part Ordered	Service Request Number	Order Placed By	Supplier	Date Ordered	Expected Delivery Date	Date Rec'd	Date Installed	Price	Status and Follow-up

was performed. The inspection might consist of checking all kitchen and bathroom faucets for leaks and commodes for continuous running and repairing or scheduling for repair as appropriate. This conservation inspection takes little extra time during a service call and can save large sums of money over time. (See the discussion of energy and water conservation below.)

Housekeeping Check

The service request form also might include a box for the maintenance person to check if she/he finds the unit in unsatisfactory condition. This may be defined as an unsanitary condition, appliances in a state of disrepair, or any other condition that reveals poor housekeeping. Should this be the case, the maintenance worker should indicate so on the form and call this information to the property manager's attention for further investigation. This additional action requires little extra time for the maintenance person and can benefit the property, but unless this item is included on the form no one will remember to make this check or to report the condition to the manager.

Completion

The staff person should record completion of the job on the service request form. After receiving the completed service request form from the maintenance staff, the property manager should record the completion on the service request record sheet or computer record to cancel additional follow-up on that request unless the resident complains.

Filing

Copies of the completed service request form and all associated documentation should be placed in the resident's file and in the separate file on the unit, if one exists. The maintenance department also may wish to retain a copy of all documentation.

MONITORING SERVICE MAINTENANCE PERFORMANCE

As a matter of good business policy, the property's operations manual and maintenance plan should require that the property manager make periodic spot checks and/or surveys of service maintenance request handling. This might include phone calls to random residents who have requested service within the past week. The manager might ask if the resident is pleased with the service and if the service was performed on a timely basis. This monitoring helps to ensure quality control and perhaps to keep a small problem from becoming a large one. Similarly, the resident's response on the returned service request form provides another tool for monitoring service maintenance performance. Whether they are communicated over the phone, on the service request form, or even when residents meet the property manager in passing, all problems that are brought to the attention of the property manager must be investigated and handled promptly before they become crises.

PREVENTIVE OR PLANNED MAINTENANCE

Regular preventive and planned maintenance, which is financially prudent and enhances operational efficiency, is designed to prevent corrective and emergency maintenance, which is expensive and inefficient, causes a disruption in scheduled staff work, and usually is an inconvenience to one or more residents. Through a carefully devised and enforced program of on-going preventive maintenance, the property's structural, physical, mechanical, and aesthetic elements, machinery, and equipment are maintained in good operating condition, thus reducing or preventing sudden, costly problems or breakdowns.

The following equipment and building elements typically benefit from regular preventive maintenance:

- Motor vehicle and other motorized equipment
- Heating and air conditioning systems
- Sewers
- Elevator systems
- Plumbing systems
- Simming pools
- Lawns and plants
- Shops, sheds, and storerooms

Every property, regardless of size, should enforce a program of preventive maintenance. Along with the property manager, an engineering inspector should make an annual inspection of the entire property to identify conditions that need preventive or remedial action to avoid major repairs. A checklist for this inspection appears in Figure 5–11.

SCHEDULING PREVENTIVE MAINTENANCE

Each property's specific conditions, geographic location, and other factors, including the results of an engineer's property survey as shown in Figure 5–11, will influence the items that should be included in its preventive maintenance program. But certain preventive maintenance jobs can be grouped logically during specific seasons of the year and scheduled for those times. For example, fall is the time of year to schedule actions designed to prevent winter freeze-ups, conserve energy in heating, close swimming pools, perform preventive maintenance on mechanical equipment, perform lawn and plant maintenance, and inspect and repair furnaces. These actions are more efficient if they can be accomplished under one umbrella procedure, requiring only one triggering mechanism and one follow-up to ensure accomplishment.

Below are two sample preventive maintenance programs: a fall program, "Winterization of the Property," and a spring program, "Summerization of the Property." The property's operations manual and maintenance plan should provide detailed outlines similar to these for the preventive maintenance actions to be taken and the time of year or month in which they should be performed and a checklist to record the accomplishment of each action so that the person responsible can verify the work.

FIGURE 5–11. Preventive Maintenance Inspection By Engineering

Engineers are to perform an annual inspection of each occupied development to identify conditions that need corrective action to avoid major repairs.

- Make an entry for all items; if an item does not relate to the development, or a problem does not exist, indicate with: "N/A" or "no problem noted."
- Log abnormal conditions; do not log normal housekeeping items.
- Recommend corrective action or further investigation in the section for recommendations and comments.
- Inspector should examine each item personally; rely upon interviews with maintenance personnel only if indicated.

____
(Development)

____
(Location)

____
(Date of Inspection)

____
(Maintenance personnel interviewed)

____
(Maintenance personnel interviewed)

____
(Maintenance personnel interviewed)

Site

Drainage

Erosion-Excessive erosion or slacking of banks, slopes, swales, or ditches? __________

Undermining-Washout beneath paved swales, roads, parking lots, curbs, sidewalks, transformer pads, or foundations? __________

Lack of Drainage-Areas draining slowly or holding water; ground grade around buildings not providing positive drainage? __________

Lakes and Ponds-Erosion of banks, condition of outlet or overflow? __________

Streets and parking lots

Asphalt or concrete payment-Broken or soft areas, areas of poor drainage, inlets above surface, unsealed cracks between pavement and adjoining structures?

Damaged Surface-Parking spaces deteriorating from gas and oil drippings? __________

Carport Damage-Needs structural repairs?

Utilities

Storm Sewers and Dry Wells-Check manholes, inlets and catch basins for accumulation of debris.

Private Lift Station-Note general condition and last services: determine from interview any significant problems. __________

Building Sewer Cleanouts-Check for accessibility.

Water Shutoff Valves-Check location on plans and determine if the valves are accessible (not covered with sod). __________

continued

FIGURE 5–11. Preventive Maintenance Inspection By Engineering (*Continued*)

Electric Transformers and Utility Pedestals-Inspect for damage. ____

Fire Hydrants-Check for proper grade and freedom from obstructions. ____

Area Lighting-Note condition of equipment and determine from interview if it is operational.

Hazards

Playground Equipment-Check for damage that may create a hazard. ____

Lakes and Ponds-Warning signs missing fencing (if installed) in good repair, banks undermined?

Traffic Control and Street Signs-Need repair, others needed, view obstructed? ____

Dead Trees

Covers-Broken or missing manhole, inlet, or outlet covers, or grills? ____

Walks and Steps-Broken or tilted walks or steps, missing or damaged handrails? ____

Needed Site Improvements

Sidewalks-Paths worn in grass indicate additional sidewalks? ____

Landscaping-Condition of trees and shrubs; need for fertilizing, trimming, and pruning? ____

Retaining Walls-Structural cracks, exposed reinforcing, breaks or improperly inclined walls? ____

Buildings

Shingle Roofs-Brittle, broken, curled, or missing shingles; loss of granular surface? ____

Built-Up Roofs-Dried, cracked, blistered top coat; failed joints around flashing, cants, and vents; low areas or lack of drainage; loss of granular surface?

Flashing-Broken, brittle, rusted, or missing? ____

Settlement-Cracks in masonry walls or veneers with general vertical direction and with companion relief cracks; cracks in foundation or basement walls; abnormal drywall cracks or binding windows or doors (determine from interview with maintenance personnel)

continued

FIGURE 5–11. Preventive Maintenance Inspection By Engineering (*Continued*)

Stucco or Siding-General condition; needs painting; cracks or checks, missing areas, evidence of water infiltration behind stucco or siding? ____________

Crawl Spaces-Damp or wet condition, evidence of mold or mildew on wood structural members of subfloor, lack of drainage or vapor barrier? ____________

Balconies-Walking surface damaged; buckling or soft spots in decking, deteriorating or missing flashing, evidence of water infiltration into adjacent walls or through deck? ____________

Elevators-Service procedures followed and license current? ____________

Fire Extinguishers and Alarms-Check for availability, accessibility and operation in required public spaces.

Exterior Windows, Doors, Trim-Need recaulking and/or repainting. ____________

Mechanical Equipment

(Determine from interview with maintenance personnel.)

Water System-Buildup of deposits in water heaters and water lines; evidence of staining of fixtures beneath faucets? ____________

Gas Furnace Systems-Soft spots or rusted out spots in heat exchanges or flues? ____________

Electrical Systems-Excessive amount of blown or popped circuit breakers or fuses, hot distribution panels

Recommendations and Comments

(Add attachments if necessary)

Winterization of the Property

The winterization procedures (Fig. 5–12) included in the winterization checklist were established as a result of an emergency situation at a Midwest multihousing property. The freeze-ups and other damage caused by a severe winter prompted an investigation into the reasons for the damage and into the preventive actions that could be taken to avoid a recurrence of that experience. Other appropriate actions for that time of the year were grouped with the activities designed to prevent winter freeze-ups. An addendum to the winterization checklist provides additional actions for properties with high-rise buildings.

The property manager, or maintenance manager/supervisor reporting to the property manager, should sign the property winterization report to certify that these steps have been taken and forward the report to the property manager for receipt no later than September 10 to November 10 each year, depending on the area of the country in which the property is located. Both the property manager and the property manager are responsible for spot-checking selected items. Property managers can develop their own checklists based on the samples provided in Figures 5–12 through 5–14, adding any other items appropriate to the specific property.

Summerization of the Property

Developing summerization procedures follows logically from the winterization procedures. The property manager or maintenance manager/supervisor should direct the maintenance staff to perform the jobs listed in the property summerization checklist (Fig. 5–15) between February 1 and June 1.

The property manager or maintenance manager/supervisor should sign the property summerization report to certify that these steps have been taken and should forward the report to the property manager no later than June 10. Both managers are responsible for spot-checking to ensure that all items have been accomplished. The summerization checklist is also designed to serve as a spot-check report from the property manager.

EMERGENCY OR CRISIS MAINTENANCE

Emergency or crisis maintenance service requests must be given top priority by property staff and resolved as quickly as possible. Examples of emergency or crisis maintenance situations include:

- A fire in the property
- The odor of gas
- A serious water leak
- Smoking or sparking electrical equipment
- Serious structural problem
- Sewer back-up
- Malfunctioning heating or air conditioning system
- An elevator stuck with someone in it
- Any other condition that could lead to personal injury or loss of property

Although it is obviously not possible to anticipate the occurrence of emergency or crisis situations requiring maintenance, the property maintenance staff can be prepared for all eventualities by including emergency procedures in the property operations manual and maintenance plan. The property manager along with the senior manager and maintenance manager/supervisor can compile these emergency procedures by consulting with the appropriate experts in each area (e.g., the gas company for what to do in the event of a gas leak until their emergency response team arrives at the property) and documenting this information as a set of protocols in the property operations manual and maintenance plan so that any maintenance worker will have standard response guidelines.

The property also must have arrangements for receiving after-hours emergency calls. The property's operations manual and maintenance plan must include this emergency procedures information, and the resident handbook should include emergency contact information. In addition to 911, this emergency contact information should include the phone number of the local police precinct, firehouse, and ambulance corps, and the management company's emergency after-hours response number. This after-hours emergency response number could be the number of an on-call maintenance person, a reliable subcontractor, an answering service that has emergency contact instructions, or the home or mobile number of the property manager or maintenance manager/supervisor. The emergency phone number should appear several times throughout the resident handbook along with the specific items that constitute emergencies and should also be posted on a sign at the entrance to the property office in case a resident goes to the office with an emergency after hours.

VACANT UNIT MAINTENANCE AND PREPARATION

As with the custodial, corrective, preventive, and emergency maintenance of a property, the property manager also is ultimately responsible for the maintenance and preparation of vacant dwelling units so that they can be shown and rented as quickly as possible. As with custodial, corrective, preventive, and emergency maintenance, the property manager is not the one to actually do the work, but it is her/his responsibility to see that the work gets done. The discussion that follows explains the various tasks and objectives of vacant unit maintenance and preparation.

VACANCY NOTIFICATION TO MAINTENANCE STAFF

As soon as an intention to vacate is received from a resident, the property manager's first step is to notify the maintenance staff so that the vacated unit can be refurbished as quickly as possible. The unit turnaround control form (Fig. 5–16) includes a formal intention to vacate for the resident to sign. This form, reproduced as a multiple-part form, can be the initial document used in the unit turnaround scheduling system. It can also be used as a transmittal document in costing

FIGURE 5–12. **Winterization Checklist*†**

To Prevent Freeze up

☐ Air blow or add antifreeze to swimming pool lines, drain swimming pool pumps, clean and store pool equipment such as chairs. Drain pool to recommended depth; this can range from full to empty depending on the design and construction of the pool. **Warning-**Always exercise great care when pumping more than 12 inches of water out of an in-ground pool; seek appropriate advice on proper depths to be maintained. Some pool designs will "float," or pop out of the ground if the proper weight of water is not kept in them.

☐ Clean, oil, and drain gasoline from lawn equipment. Ensure that vehicles and snow equipment are serviced and operational.

☐ Sweep gutters and clean gutters and downspouts with a hose. Check splash blocks and provide proper tilt to allow water to flow away from buildings.

☐ Remove hoses from outside sillcocks; drain, roll, and store them in a dry, heated area.

☐ Turn off the water to sillcocks in utility rooms, furnace rooms, and laundry rooms; drain them and remove handles. Place signs/tags on the indoor and outdoor shutoff valves stating that the lines are not to be used until spring.

☐ Drain lawn sprinkler system to prevent damage from freezing.

☐ Test and check the fire sprinkler system to make sure water lines will not freeze and burst.

To Conserve Energy

☐ In common areas, hallways, walkup basements, utility rooms, furnace rooms, and laundry rooms, set thermostats at a safe and economical level and remove handles/dials.

☐ At senior citizens developments, the lowest setting in walking areas should be approximately 65 degrees; in the sitting areas, it should be approximately 70 degrees at all times.

☐ Set hot water heaters in apartments, townhouses, and common areas at the lowest normal level consistent with winter operation.

☐ Ensure that pilot light assemblies, blowers, motors, pressure relief valves are clean and operational and that vent pipes and heat exchangers are not obstructed.

☐ Inspect laundry rooms, community buildings, and other common areas for air leaks around windows, doors, and any other place air leaks might occur; seal up leaks to conserve energy.

To Control Utility Expenses

☐ Adjust common lighting timers and photoelectric cells for winter month's operation.

* The development maintenance supervisor should oversee the actions described in this checklist between October 1 and November 1 of each year. The maintenance supervisor checks the box to the left of each task performed, and the development manager initials the box at the end of each item he/she has spot-checked.

†Refer to the high-rise addendum to the winterization checklist for items relating specifically to high-rise developments.

continued

FIGURE 5–12. Winterization Checklist*† (*Continued*)

Preventive Maintenance

☐ Inspect apartment unit furnaces to ensure that pilot light assemblies, blowers, and motors are operational and clean.

☐ Ensure that stack pipes and heat exchanges are not obstructed. Change filters.

☐ Check, date, and initial fire extinguisher tags. Ensure that extinguishers are operational; recharge or replace if required.

☐ Inspect each component of the fire alarm system and fire sprinkler system in accordance with the procedure outlined in the operations manual.

☐ Test smoke alarms in accordance with the procedure outlined in the operations manual. A special spray is available for doing a "smoke" test.

☐ Apply fertilizer, weed killer, and additional seed where required lawns. Perform other jobs in accordance with the lawn and plant maintenance procedure.

☐ Repair pot holes and cracks in asphalt and concrete to eliminate substantial deterioration of the stone base through the winter period. The maintenance supervisor should inspect asphalt and concrete parking areas and driveways to identify where pot hole repairs are necessary and make sure the repairs are made prior to the rains and freezing weather that cause seepage into the stone. Seepage causes expansion and requires substantial repair in the spring at a cost 3 to 5 times greater than the cost to repair pot holes in the fall.

☐ In cold climates remove, clean, and store tennis court nets in maintenance garage to increase the life of the nets and prevent rot from weathering. Shut down the tennis court lights for the winter.

☐ In cold climates dismantle and clean swing set chairs and seats, and store in maintenance garage.

☐ Inspect porch and balcony handrails and secure or replace those that are loose. Loose handrails are a potential safety hazard and liability.

☐ The maintenance supervisor should arrange for at least two persons who are able and willing to report at any hour to assist regular maintenance employees with emergency snow removal.

I have spot-checked the items initialed and found that the development winterization procedure

☐ is complete

☐ is not complete.

____

(Date)

____

(Development Manager)

____

(Development Name)

FIGURE 5-13. Winterization Sign/Tag

THIS LINE HAS
BEEN WINTERIZED
DO NOT USE

the unit preparation and for recording the ultimate disposition of the security deposit. In any case, a copy of it should be provided to the maintenance staff indicating the move-out inspection appointment date and, if the unit has been rerented, the date the new resident will be moving in. If the unit has not been rented, the property manager should note on the form if no other units of this type are available for showing. This will create a priority for refurbishing the unit.

Simultaneous with giving the maintenance staff a copy of the unit turnaround control form, the property manager also should give to the resident a move-out instruction form (Fig. 5–17) to use as a guide in preparing the unit for move-out inspection and to minimize any cleaning charges. Copies of the intention to vacate/unit turnaround control form and the move-out instructions form also should be included in the property's operations manual, maintenance plan, and resident handbook.

MOVE-OUT INSPECTION

The property manager and/or a qualified maintenance staff representative should perform the move-out inspection with the resident and should complete a move-in/move-out maintenance inspection report (Fig. 5–18) during this inspection. The report should be compared with the copy used for the move-in inspection to determine any charges.

The property manager should be sure to write a specific explanation next to each item requiring repair. If an item is to be charged to the vacating resident, the appropriate amount should be indicated next to that item on the form. The property manager can use a schedule of charges to estimate the cost to the resident. Both the property manager or other property representative and the resident should sign the inspection form to signify agreement about the condition of the unit.

The move-in/move-out maintenance inspection report also provides a checklist for developing the vacant unit preparation schedule (Fig. 5–19) and setting up the unit on the master unit preparation summary (Fig. 5–20).

With the maintenance staff at the ready, the property manager should notify the maintenance manager/supervisor or the appropriate housekeeping maintenance worker and subcontractor (e.g., painters) as soon as the unit has been vacated and the move-out inspection has been completed so that work can begin immediately. The property manager must remember to notify these parties if the move-out date changes so that schedules can be revised accordingly. (For more on move-out procedures, see Chapter 8, Processing Applications, Move-in and Move-out Procedures, and Resident Relations and the Resident Handbook.)

REFURBISHING THE UNIT

The property maintenance staff typically does most, if not all, of the unit refurbishment work. But depending on the size of the property, the capability of the maintenance staff, the philosophy and policy of the management firm, and the instructions of the owner, the staff could do all of the work or nearly none. The property management executive generally determines which services are done in-house and which are subcontracted. The cost/benefit analysis on contracting versus performing the work in-house is usually done in conjunction with the annual budget. (See Chapter 4, Multihousing Management Economics and Finances and the discussion below on outside contractors.)

FIGURE 5–14. High Rise Addendum to Winterization Checklist*

☐ Close stairwell, corridor, and storm windows.

☐ Close and weather seal roof tower doors.

☐ Check seal of roofing material around vents, pipes, exhaust ducts, and parapets. Leaks around these items become more severe in the winter because snow and ice accumulation on the roof prevent or slow the runoff of melted water.

☐ Ensure that the roof drains are free of debris and the drainage way is not obstructed.

☐ Add electric heat tape to wet sprinkler system pipes and standpipes.

☐ Check condition of through-the-wall heating and cooling units and repair seals where necessary.

☐ Drain cooling tower, service fan assemblies, lubricate valves, and blow out all lines or fill them with antifreeze. Clean baffle boards and repaint all rusted areas.

☐ Winterize chiller, change water, or add rust inhibitor and oxygen chase as appropriate.

☐ Check operation of heaters in elevator penthouse; check vent actuators.

☐ Check dry pipe sprinkler system in unheated areas, drain accumulated condensation, check and change lubricant in air compressor.

☐ Check operation of garage ventilation fans, timers, and thermostats; check operation of vent damper controls and motors.

☐ I have spot-checked the items initialed and found that the development winterization procedure

☐ is complete

☐ is not complete.

____
(Date)

____
(Development Manager)

____
(Development Name)

*The maintenance supervisor should check the box to the left of each item accomplished. The development manager initials the box at the end of item he/she has spot-checked.

FIGURE 5–15. **Summerization Checklist**

To Control Utility Expenses and Conserve Energy

- ☐ Adjust timers and prototype cells from common area lighting for summer months.
- ☐ Turn off thermostats in common area, hallway, walkup basement, utility room, furnace room, and laundry room.
- ☐ Set hot water heaters in apartments, townhouses, and common areas at lowest normal level.
- ☐ Ensure that pilot light assemblies, vent pipes, and pressure relief valves are operational.
- ☐ Set temperature in sitting and walking areas of senior citizen developments at 75 degrees during the day from 6 a.m. to 10 p.m., and 70 degrees at night 10 p.m. to 6 a.m.

Preventive Maintenance

- ☐ Test swimming pool filter system pumps, valves, and chlorinators; check for proper chemical content. Ensure that the person responsible for operation is qualified and familiar with all functions of the pool and pool area in order to provide a safe and efficient operation. Clean and repair poolside equipment, clean and store pool cover.
- ☐ Sweep gutter and clean gutters and downspots with hose; check splash blocks and replace where needed, providing proper tilt allow water to flow away from buildings.
- ☐ Clean, oil, and drain gasoline from motor driven snow equipment and store for the summer; ensure that summer vehicles and lawn equipment are serviced and operational. Use only safety type gas cans for storage of flammable materials.
- ☐ Turn on outside sillcocks and check hoses; turn on the water at sillcocks and replace handles in the utility rooms, furnace rooms, and laundry rooms; remove winterization signs/tags and store.
- ☐ Apply fertilizer, weed killer, and additional seed where required to lawns; perform other operations in accordance with the lawn and plant maintenance procedures.
- ☐ Sweep and/or vacuum coils of inside air conditioning units and change filters; hose down outside unit coils and remove weeds, grass, or other obstruction; check condenser motor for wear and lubricate; replace filters.
- ☐ Fill chuckholes and generally repair damage caused by winter weather. Spruce up vacant units to make them as attractive as possible for spring traffic. Monitor curb appeal closely in preparation for the usual increase in traffic in the spring.
- ☐ Act immediately to correct problems.
- ☐ Inspect balconies for leaks and tears in the flashing or wall deck surfaces; check for buckling and wood rotting underneath. If balconies need painting and sealing, perform immediately or schedule.
- ☐ Install tennis court nets; make tennis court lights operational.
- ☐ Install swing set chains and seats.
- ☐ Inspect each component of the fire alarm system, using the procedures outlined in the operations manual.

I have spot-checked the items initialed and found that the development summarization procedure

- ☐ is complete
- ☐ is not complete.

____
(Date)

____
(Development Manager)

____
(Development Name)

* The maintenance supervisor oversees the actions described in this checklist between March 1 and May 1 of each year. He/she checks the box to the left of each task performed, and the development manager initials the box at the end of each item he/she has spot-checked.

FIGURE 5–16. Unit Turnaround Control Form

Property ______________________ Date of notice ______________

Resident ______________________ Telephone no. ______________

Address ______________________

Bldg. no. __________ Apt. no. __________

You are herby advised that I will vacate my apartment on ______________ for the following reason:

____

____

____

____

The vacating date provided on this form is definite, and you are hereby authorized to show the premises to prospective tenants by appointment. I understand that this notice ☐ is ☐ is not in breach of my present lease and does not relieve me of any liability under my present lease.

My security deposit refund and/or final statement should be forwarded to:

____
(Print or type your name)

____
(Address)

____
(City) (State) (Zip code)

______________ ______________________
(Date) (Signature of resident)

To: Maintenance superintendent

1. * Appointment for move-out inspection date ______________ time __________
2. Date of move-out inspection ______________________
3. * Date of new resident move-in ______________________
4. Date ready for occupancy ______________ Initial __________
5. * Months unit occupied ______________________
6. * Date of manager's inspection ______________ Initial __________
7. * Items to be corrected within 24 hours ______________________
   ______________________ Date __________
8. Date items corrected ______________ Initial __________
9. * Date of manager's final acceptance ______________________

*To be filled in by property manager

____
(Property Manager's Signature)

FIGURE 5–17. Move-out Instructions for Resident

____
Resident

Kitchen

- Microwave oven cleaned inside and out.
- Refrigerator, including shelves, crisper, under crisper, and area under footguard cleaned.
- Cupboards, sink, faucet fixtures, tile, and exhaust fan cleaned.
- Stove, including burners, controls, burner rings, and drip pans cleaned.
- Oven cleaned, with no oven cleaner left in oven or dripped on floor.
- Floor cleaned.
- Air-conditioning and heating unit closet cleaned.

Living room, dinning room, and bedroom

- Baseboards cleaned.
- Finger marks and other marks cleaned off switches and walls.
- Traverse rods cleaned.
- Window sills cleaned, window washed, and screens washed or cleaned.
- Stick-on picture hangers removed by wetting first; do not rip off.
- Closets vacuumed and clothes hangers removed.

Bathroom

- Tub, toilet tank, vanity bowl, and cupboard cleaned.
- Chrome fixtures and exhaust fan cleaned.
- Medicine cabinet wiped and cleaned.
- Shower runners and floor cleaned.

Patio

- Patio swept and mopped or hosed.
- Grass cut, refuse carried away, and storage compartment cleaned.

Turn in apartment and mailbox keys at final inspection.

____
(Property manager's signature)

FIGURE 5–18. Move-in/Move-out Maintenance Inspection Report

____
(Apartment Community)

____
(Resident Name)

____
(Address, Apt. No.)

____
(Date)

KITCHEN	Move In	Move Out	Cost
Stove-Outside			$
Burners			
Drip Pan			
Vent			
Time-controls			
Oven & Racks			
Broiler Pan			
Light			
Floors			
HOOD FILTER			
Fan-light			
COUNTER AREA			
Counter top			
Sink/Faucets			
Drains/Disposal			
DISHWASHER			
Outside-controls			
Inside (all parts)			
CABINETS DOORS			
Shelves/Drawers			
Under Sink			
BATHROOM			
Windows			
Walls and Tile			
Floors			
Shelves			
Doors			
Mirror			
TUB & SHOWER			
Clean			
Shower Dr/Runners			
FIXTURES			
Basin			
Drains			
Faucets			
Counter Tops			
Exhaust Fan			
Bowl and Seal			
Towel Racks			
PATIO/BALCONY			
Clean			
Seal Deck			
Repair			
MECHANICAL			
Hot Water Heater			
Furnace Unit			
Air-conditioner			
Air-conditioner Filter			
Air-conditioner Case			

LIVING ROOM	Move In	Move Out	Cost
Floor Covering			$
Walls & Covering			
Windows			
Screens			
Drapes			
Other			
BEDROOM			
Floor Covering			
Walls & Covering			
Windows			
Screens			
Drapes			
Other			
BEDROOM			
Floor Covering			
Walls & Covering			
Windows			
Screens			
Drapes			
Other			
BEDROOM			
Floor Covering			
Walls & Covering			
Windows			
Screens			
Drapes			
Other			
FURNITURE			
Dining/Kitchen			
Living Room			
Bedroom(s)			
Other			

Total Costs $

continued

FIGURE 5–18. Move-in/Move-out Maintenance Inspection Report (*Continued*)

Additional Comments: ____

(If additional pages are needed, please attach, but remember that both parties should receive a copy)

I understand that all discrepancies other than those noted above will be the residents responsibility and will be deducted from the Security Deposit at the time of move out.

(Signature of Inspection Manager)	(Date Move In)
(Resident Signature)	(Move in)
(Signature of Inspection Manager)	(Date Move In)
(Resident Signature)	(Move in)

FIGURE 5–19. Vacant Unit Preparation Schedule

Unit ____________________ Type ____________________ Date Vacated ____________________

Development ____ Phase ____________________

UNIT REFURBISHMENT SCHEDULE

	Assigned To	Scheduled for (date)	Date Completed	By (Initials)
Trash Out				
Heavy Clean				
Appliance Test				
HVAC Test				
Turnover Maintenance				
Hard Floor Replace				
Repaint				
Blinds/Drapes				
Carpet Clean				
Wallpaper				
Carpet Replace				
Final Clean				
Quality Check				
Ok To Show				

FIGURE 5–20. **Master Unit Preparation Summary**

Property ______________________________ Phase ______________

Week of ______________________________ Page ________ of ________

Ready to Rent		Ready Units-Holding Deposits			Move-outs			Being Prepared		
UNIT	TYPE	UNIT	TYPE	MOVE IN	UNIT	TYPE	DATE	UNIT	TYPE	DATE DONE

In all cases, a work schedule must be developed so that the turnover work is done in the most efficient fashion. Supervision must be provided at all points to ensure both the quality and the timeliness of the work. These duties are the responsibility of the property manager or the property's maintenance manager/supervisor, who answers to the property manager. The refurbishment schedules of individual units should be coordinated into a master schedule to ensure that units are prepared as quickly as possible for showing and re-rental, that an appropriate assortment of units is always available to the marketing staff, and to be certain that maintenance staff time is allocated most efficiently.

The vacant unit preparation schedule (Fig. 5–19) should be used to schedule, control, and check the preparation of a unit. This form should be prepared by the property manager or the maintenance manager/supervisor after completing the move-out inspection. The schedule is divided into separate tasks that are performed in refurbishing the unit. The number and complexity of tasks vary with the type of unit involved and with the age of the property.

Each task in preparing the unit for reoccupancy should be assigned to a specific individual, and a target date for completion of the task should be set. Breaking the tasks out by individual and setting target completion dates is essential to an efficient system that is easy to supervise. Once the unit turnover has been scheduled in this way, copies of the schedule should be retained by the property manager, given to the maintenance manager/supervisor, and posted in the unit. The copy posted in the unit allows any property manager, staff member, or subcontractor to see at a glance the status of the unit refurbishment.

The procedure for readying units (Fig. 5–21) details the heavy and final cleaning processes in unit refurbishment. This list or one like it, along with any additional details on the unit preparation process, should be included in the property's operations manual and maintenance plan along with the unit turnaround control form, the move-out instructions for residents, and the move-in/move-out maintenance inspection report form so that a staff member new to a task will understand the unit refurbishment process and have definite direction and guidelines for the minimum quality standards expected.

The second part of the unit turnover scheduling system, the master unit preparation summary (Fig. 5–20), lists all units that are either vacant or scheduled to be vacated. It provides the property manager with an overall view of the units available to be marketed so the manager can adjust the refurbishment schedule if a shortage of one type of unit develops.

INSPECTION OF A REFURBISHED UNIT

Nothing can kill a potential rental faster than showing a poorly prepared or incomplete unit to a prospective resident. Therefore, as soon as the property manager receives the completed vacant unit preparation schedule, she/he should do a final quality check and inspection. The property manager must check every unit before it goes onto the ready-to-show list to ensure that the unit meets the property's quality standards.

If the refurbished unit still needs work, the property manager should specify the items to be corrected and return the form to maintenance for action within 24 hours. The manager should inspect the unit again after the remaining items are corrected, and the unit should not be placed on the ready list until the property manager has signed off that it is ready to show.

Only after the unit has received its final quality assurance check should it be placed on the ready list and marketed. Then, the unit should be inspected on a daily basis to ensure that it is still in perfect condition (clean, the light bulbs still work, the toilet seats are down, etc.).

TURNAROUND TIME

The property maintenance staff should complete the refurbishing of a vacated unit to mesh with the new resident's move-in schedule. The unit should be in perfect move-in condition on the day of move-in. To accomplish this, the maintenance staff should be notified as soon as a unit has been re-rented and a move-in date established.

The goal is to minimize the time between move-out and move-in. Recommended maximum downtime is no more than two to three working days unless substantial work is involved. The property manager and the maintenance staff should work together as a team to ensure a smooth turnaround.

MOVE-IN INSPECTION WITH THE NEW RESIDENT

The property manager or other management representative should greet the new resident on move-in day, present the resident handbook (if this has not already been done), ensure that the resident understands the operation of all unit appliances and equipment and how to make a service maintenance request, and, with the new resident, inspect the unit and complete the same move-in/move-out maintenance inspection report form that was used for the last occupant's move-out inspection (Fig. 5–18). When the inspection and report are complete, both the property manager/management representative and the resident should sign it.

Ideally, the move-in/move-out maintenance inspection report should indicate no need for corrective or remedial work if the prior inspections were performed and acted upon as necessary. However, in the event that the unit still has problems, these should be recorded on the report, called to the attention of the maintenance staff, and corrected within 24 hours at the maximum, preferably the same day. If a correction cannot be made immediately because parts are not available or for any other legitimate reason, the resident should be notified and given a date when the corrections will be made. Follow-up should be maintained to ensure that these commitments are honored. After the corrections are made, the resident should initial the notations on the move-in/move-out maintenance inspection report so that the form shows at the new resident's eventual move-out time that those items were not defective at move-in. (For more on move-in procedures, see Chapter 8, Processing Applications, Move-in and Move-out Procedures, and Resident Relations and the Resident Handbook.)

Managers at large properties with significant on-going move-in/move-out activity should use special forms like the

FIGURE 5–21. Procedure for Readying Apartments

KITCHEN
Work Area

- Clean counter tops, sink, inside and outside of cabinet doors, inside cabinets, and above and underneath cabinets; remove paint and stains; polish cabinets.

Stove

- Move stove away from wall.
- Remove grease and grime from wall behind stove and from back of stove.
- Scrub, mop, and wax floor where stove normally stands.
- Pull out and clean fan and filter; put back in place.
- Clean sides of stoves.
- Move stove back in place.
- Clean range top, front, and doors.
- Remove grease and grime from oven, including racks and broiler.

Microwave Oven

- Clean with warm water, mild detergent, and soft cloth or sponge. Rinse well. Do not use abrasive cleaners or steel wool pads as they can damage the control panel and the interior and exterior oven surfaces.

Refrigerator

- Move refrigerator away from wall.
- Remove grease and grime from wall behind refrigerator and from back of refrigerator.
- Scrub, mop, and wax floor where refrigerator normally stands.
- Clean sides of refrigerator.
- Move refrigerator back in place.
- Defrost freezer and clean.
- Remove and clean shelves and crisper.
- Clean inside of refrigerator before replacing shelves and crisper, remove grease and dirt from crevices and corners.

Light Fixtures

- Remove light fixtures, clean and replace.
- Remove switch plates from wall, clean, and put back in place.

Dishwasher

- Clean inside and outside, including agitator: remove water spots, soap erosion, and rust.

Baseboards

- Clean them unless they are freshly painted.

continued

FIGURE 5–21. Procedure for Readying Apartments (*Continued*)

FLOORS

- Scrub to remove accumulated grease, wax, and dirt from crevices and corners; mop; and wax.

BATHROOM

- Scour and remove rust stains from tub, tub fixtures, and shower rod.
- Clean and shine wall tile around tub area.
- Scour basin and soap holder, clean inside vanity cabinet, including doors; clean inside and outside of medicine cabinet and cabinet door, including mirror.
- Scour and remove rust stains from inside and outside stool; disinfect.
- Clean closet shelves and both sides of door.
- Remove light fixture, clean, and replace.
- Remove switch plates from wall, clean, and replace.
- Scrub and mop bathroom floor, making sure to remove dirt in corners and crevices; wax.

FURNACE AREA

Furnace

- Sweep and vacuum around furnace.
- Remove furnace vent cover, clean, and put back in place.
- Install new filter.
- Clean top, sides, and front of furnace, and tubing where accessible.
- Clean and polish both sides of bifold doors to furniture area.

Circuit Breakers or Fuse Box

- Vacuum exterior, paint or polish as necessary.

Cold Air Vent

- Remove from wall, clean, dry, and put back in place.

BEDROOMS, HALLWAYS, LIVING ROOM, AND DINING AREA

- Clean window sills, frames, tracks, casings, and both sides of glass.
- Clean closet shelves, rods, tracks, casings, and both sides of doors.
- Clean baseboard unless they are freshly painted.
- Clean and wax both sides of other doors; clean door casings.
- Remove light fixtures, clean, and replace.
- Remove switch plates from wall, clean and replace them.
- If necessary, remove and clean electrical wall outlets and replace.
- Vacuum and clean registers.
- Vacuum and shampoo carpet; strip, scrub, mop, and wax tile flooring.
- Notify development maintenance supervisor if any items need to be replaced.

one in Figure 5–22 to schedule move-in and move-out inspections on a weekly basis so that the maintenance staff can coordinate its workload with these inspections. Because the move-in and move-out schedule forms are identical except for their titles, the same form is used as a sample for both in this text. However, these schedules must be separate and distinct in a management operation.

OUTSIDE CONTRACTORS

WHEN TO USE OUTSIDE CONTRACTORS

The property's in-house maintenance staff should be used whenever possible to maximize the owner's NOI. However, when it is necessary to perform major repairs and/or work that in-house staff are not qualified to do, an outside expert should be retained to analyze the problem, recommend remedial action, and prepare specifications. Outside contractors should be used:

- For jobs requiring special licensing and/or skills that are not possessed by property personnel
- During peak workload periods
- When sufficient work in a specialty is not available to warrant a full-time staff position
- When a cost/benefit analysis shows that the work can be performed more efficiently and economically by a contractor than by in-house personnel
- When the work involves the use of dangerous materials that can either cause injury or involve significant insurance exposures

Examples of work for which an outside contractor may be more desirable than in-house staff include:

- Elevator maintenance, repair, and emergencies
- Heating and air conditioning service
- Special plumbing or electrical work
- Certain sewer issues
- Swimming pool maintenance and repair
- Certain lawn and landscape maintenance functions
- Cable and master antenna-related issues
- Extermination
- Trash, garbage, refuse, recyclables, and debris removal
- Exterior painting and sign painting
- Dwelling unit repainting and cleaning
- Outside window washing where special equipment is required
- Abandoned automobile removal
- Heavy snow removal (unless the property owns and operates a plow)
- Major renovation or rehabilitation
- Compliance with fire safety codes such as inspecting and recharging fire extinguishers
- Lead-based paint removal
- Asbestos abatement

CHECKING BEFORE ENGAGING CONTRACTORS

Once the decision has been made to use an outside contractor, the candidate contractors' credentials should be verified and their references should be checked before one is selected for the job. The property manager should request and receive from each candidate proof of all required and adequate licenses, insurances, (including employee liability and vehicle liability insurance), and Workers Compensation coverage; verification of experience; written guarantees and documented fees and overtime; and references that can be checked easily. If applicable to the project, the specifications provided by the candidate contractors should include the scope of the work and blueprints or drawings.

Pending receipt of all these items, the property manager should request bids from the candidate contractors according to the specifications provided to be able to make an apples-to-apples comparison. To secure these bids, the property manager or maintenance manager/supervisor under the property manager's supervision should send a request for bid form like the one shown in Figure 5–23, with specifications, to all contractors who are invited to bid. The contractor should be required to sign and return the form along with proof of insurance. The use of this form ensures that all contractors are provided with the same information, including specifications, and that they agree the bid is based on those specifications. This procedure precludes later disagreements. For larger projects, many management companies require that a sealed bid procedure be used.

In any case, the property manager should prepare a competitive bids form like the one in Figure 5–24, with the following documents attached:

- Request for bid
- Specifications
- Insurance certificate
- Vendors' proposal
- Checklist

The competitive bids form is a convenient means of assembling all information relative to the selection of a con-

FIGURE 5–22. Move-in/Move-out Inspection Schedule

Property ______________________ Week of ______________________

Address	Resident name	Date of Inspection	Resident Present	Maintenance Supt. Initial	Comments

______________________ (Property manager)

______________________ (Maintenance superintendent)

______________________ (Date submitted)

______________________ (Date returned)

FIGURE 5–23. Request for Bid*

Not an order

From ______________________________
(Development)
____
(Address)
____
(City, State, Zip)

Special instructions ______________________

Person requesting quotation ______________________

Date ______________________________

Delivery required by ______________________

Return quote on or before ______________________

Specifications attached ______________________
☐ Yes ☐ No

Phone No. ______________________________

Quantity	Description	Unit price	Total
		Grand total	

Terms	FOB	Shipping point	Approximate shipping date

Description of work to be done ______________________________________
____
____
____

To: ______________(Vendor)______________
Attn: ______________________________
____

Quotation date______________________
____
____
(Vendor signature)

Phone: ______________________ Fax: ______________________

*Source: Gene Glick Management Co., Indianapolis, Indiana

FIGURE 5–24. **Competitive Bids**

Development ______________________ Phase ____________ Location ________________

Job ____

____

Three bids were obtained from reputable subcontractors for the above work: ☐ Yes ☐ No

The following reputable companies submitted bids:

Name of company	Amount of bid	References checked by

The recommended bid is ________________ Why? ______________________________

____

Month work is budgeted for ______________________ Amount budgeted ______________

Work was not budgeted ______________ Why? ______________________________

Is this planned major expenditure? ______________________________________

Division manager recommends funding from:

☐ Cash flow ☐ Reserve for replacement Account balance $ ______________

☐ Residual receipts Account balance $ ______________

Other ______________________________

The recommended bid amount was verified for reasonableness by ______________________

The method used and amount determined was:

Dodge Manual $ ________________

Means Manual $ ________________

Other $ ________________

Explanation if three bids were not obtained ______________________________

____

____

______________________________ (Signature of development manager or other person soliciting the bid)

______________________________ (Approved signature)

______________________________ (Date)

______________________________ (Date)

______________________________ (Approved signature)

______________________________ (Approved signature)

______________________________ (Date)

______________________________ (Date)

*Attach current financial statement highlighting this line item for review.

tractor on one page to permit an orderly review by management and to ensure that all required procedures were followed. The form should include a brief description of the work to be performed, a statement that bids were obtained from an adequate number of reputable contractors or suppliers, the name of the low bidder, and the amount. In the event that fewer than three bids are received, an explanation should be provided.

The competitive bids form should also include the name of the person who verified the reasonableness of the bid. This verification can be accomplished by an outside or in-house expert and perhaps reference a source such as the *R.S. Means* manual (R. S. Means, Inc., Construction Plaza, 63 Smiths Lane, Kingston, MA 02364, 800-334-3509, www.rsmeans.com); *The Blue Book of Building and Construction* (Contractors Register, Inc., Jefferson Valley, NY 10535, 800-431-2584, www.thebluebook.com); or Dodge estimating manuals (Marshall And Swift Co., 911 Wilshire Boulevard, Los Angeles, CA 90017, 800-451-2367, www.marshallswift.com).

The management company and property manager should each keep a copy of the certificate of insurance for each contractor used on an on-going basis and for each one who has worked for the company in the past. A knowledgeable person in the management company should review each certificate prior to assigning a job to ensure that the coverage is adequate.

Contractors' insurance expiration dates should be logged to keep track of insurance coverage and to ensure that the coverage is renewed on a timely basis so that it does not expire. (See Chapter 6, Risk Management and Management Maintenance Plans for more on certificates of insurance.)

THE CONTRACTOR CONTRACT, PERFORMANCE MANAGEMENT, AND PAYMENT CONSIDERATIONS

The property's standard service work order contract may be used for most service jobs contracted with an outside provider. This service work order can state and authorize the work to be done, state the legal requirements placed on the contractor and the property (including the recommended minimum insurance coverage to be provided by the contractor), and serve as the contract for the work or service. It should incorporate by reference the specifications for all of the work bid along with the start and completion dates of the work. A sample service work order form appears in Figure 5–25. The contractor agreement is spelled out on the reverse of this service work order. It protects the interests of the management firm and the property. The service work order contract is signed by the property manager and the contractor. Property managers may wish to adopt this form after having it reviewed by a local attorney.

However, if the work is extensive and/or the requirements complex, and/or if the contractor has proposed his own contract, more sophisticated legal involvement may be in order. In such cases, no one representing the property should sign the contractor's proposed agreement until legal counsel has reviewed it. Many standard service contracts contain legal "boilerplate" language and stipulations that can be disadvantageous to the property and should be renegotiated where possible. When in doubt, the property manager should always consult with his/her supervisor before entering into a service contract.

Once the contractor has been selected and the contract has been signed, the property manager should arrange for a knowledgeable person to supervise the work on an on-going basis to ensure that it is satisfactorily completed in accordance with the specifications and the bid. The more extensive the work, the closer the supervision must be, and the person selected to supervise it must observe the work on a sufficiently frequent basis to ensure that it is done in compliance with the specifications. The number of inspections required and the qualifications of the person inspecting the work should be determined to a great extent by the estimated cost and complexity of the work and length of time required to complete it. The person supervising the work can use the major repairs inspection report shown in Figure 5–26 to keep track of the status of the work.

The property manager should constantly follow-up to ensure timely and satisfactory completion. After completion of the work, the property manager should perform a final inspection and obtain the contractor's signature on the service work order. The property manager also should obtain from the contractor a signed waiver of lien form to obtain reasonable assurance that everyone working on the job will be paid and to provide maximum protection against future liens against the property. The property manager should sign the work order and send it to accounting for payment in accordance with the property's purchase and payment procedures. Any discrepancy between the contracted amount and the contractor's invoice should be accompanied by a written explanation attached to the documents and approved by the property manager. Where work has not been satisfactorily completed or a punch list remains, the property should retain a certain percentage of payment until the contract has been completely fulfilled.

CONTRACTORS AND EMERGENCY WORK

Outside contractors engaged to perform emergency work, such as repair of a broken water main, should be required to follow the same procedures, paperwork, and approvals as described above. However, these may have to be processed after the emergency work has been completed.

PROPERTY-WIDE MAINTENANCE SCHEDULING AND INSPECTIONS

As demonstrated throughout this part of the text, many diverse maintenance activities are required in the typical property, and a high degree of organization and scheduling is necessary to ensure that the property reaps the maximum benefits of custodial, service, and preventive maintenance and vacant unit maintenance and preparation. This section provides a model procedure for effectively scheduling and monitoring property-wide maintenance activities. Property managers can adapt this model for their own use according

FIGURE 5–25. **Service Work Order**

Development Name

Important
invoice in duplicate and mail to:

Vendor

Work Order No.

THIS NUMBER MUST APPEAR ON ALL INVOICES AND STATEMENTS

Service Work Order

1. ☐ Cleaning ☐ Carpet-Reg ☐ Steam	4. ☐ Painting ☐ Drywall Repair
2. ☐ Exterminating	5. ☐ Repairs - DW ☐ Range ☐ Refrig
3. ☐ Lawn Service	6. ☐ Other repairs or service

Type of Service	Apartment Address	Apt No.	Bldg. No.	Dev. Phase #	Unit Size		Dollar Amount
					BR	TH	
*Noncontract work not to exceed $50.00 without RMS approval.							**Total Cost**

7. The above work is hereby authorized

(Superintendent Signature) ***(Date)***

8. Service has been completed with the following exceptions:

9. This service has been completed satisfactorily and payment is authorized.

(Superintendent Signature) ***(Date)***

10. Regional manager approval (if necessary)

(Signature) ***(Date)***

continued

FIGURE 5–25. Service Work Order (*Continued*)

VENDOR

Subcontractor agreement

The vendor is the subcontractor or supplier responsible for completing the work listed on the front of this form.

The maintenance supervisor is the person in charge of maintenance at the development at which the work is being done and the person responsible for approving the work to be done.

1. The Subcontractor/Supplier shall furnish Material or labor in strict accordance with plans and specifications if furnished as a supplement to this work order. The Subcontractor/Supplier shall be responsible for obtaining permits and approvals required for the work and shall fully comply with all applicable building codes and regulations.

2. The Subcontractor shall purchase and maintain insurance as set forth below and shall protect the Contractor and the Owner against claims as indicated therein which may arise out of or result from the Subcontractor's operation under this Contract, whether such operation be by the Subcontractor or any Subcontractor of the Subcontractor or by anyone directly employed by either of them, or by anyone for whose acts either of them may be liable:

   a. Claims under Workers' Compensation and occupational disease and any other similar employee benefit acts, with a minimum as required by the state statutory requirements.

   b. Comprehensive general liability or manufactures' and Contractor's Liability with limits of not less than $1 million per person and $1 million per occurrence for bodily injury and $500,000 property damage, or a combined single limit of $1 million per occurrence for bodily injury and $1 million property damage or a combined single limit of $1 million. The policy shall include complete operations insurance with the same minimum limits. Explosion, collapse, and underground exclusion shall be deleted from the policy on those classifications where applicable.

   c. Comprehensive automobile liability insurance with minimum limits of $300,000 per person and $500,000 per occurrence for bodily injury and $100,000 for property damage.

   d. The Subcontractor shall purchase such insurance as is required for his/her own tools and equipment which is to become a part of the building. The insurance referred to in subparagraph 2 shall not prohibit waiver of subrogation prior to loss.

3. The insurance required by subparagraph 2 (except to cover item d printed above) shall be written in no less than the amount set forth above and with such companies as shall be satisfactory to the Contractor, and in no event shall such insurance be less than the amount required by law. If required by the Contractor, certificates or a copy of the policies of insurance acceptable to the Contractor (except for d above) shall be filed prior to commencement of work with the division manager, at the address which follows:

____
Address

____
(City, State, Zip)

or other such person as the Contractor shall direct. These certificates or copies of the policies shall contain a provision that coverage afforded under the policies will not be cancelled until at least ten (10) days prior written notice has been given to the Contractor by certified mail at the Contractor's main office:

____
Address

____
(City, State, Zip)

4. The Subcontractor shall indemnify and hold the Owner and the Contractor harmless from and against all claims, damages, losses, and expenses, including attorneys' fees arising out of resulting

continued

FIGURE 5–25. Service Work Order (*Continued*)

from the performance of the work which are caused in whole or in part by any act or omission of the Subcontractor or anyone directly or indirectly employed by the Subcontractor or by anyone for whose acts any of them may be liable regardless of whether or not it is caused in part by a party indemnified hereunder. The Subcontractor shall waive all rights against the Contractor and the Owner for damages caused by fire or other perils to the extent covered by insurance, pursuant to the general conditions of the contract between the owner and the contractor, except such rights as the Subcontractor may have to the proceeds of such insurance held by the Owner as a trustee.

5. It is understood that if the basic contract by and between the Owner and the Contractor provides that all work is to be performed under a no-lien provision under the laws of the state, then all Subcontractors are bound thereby.

6. The Subcontractor agrees to comply with all of the provisions of the Occupational Safety and Health Act of 1970 and subsequent amendments, the Standards thereunder, and any State act in connection with providing every employee safe and healthful working conditions. The Subcontractor further agrees to comply with all record-keeping requirements concerning occupational injuries and illnesses incurred by employees of the Subcontractor as required by the Occupational Safety and Health Act of 1970 and subsequent amendments and Standards thereunder.

The Subcontractor shall indemnify and hold the Owner and the Contractor harmless from and against all claims, damages, losses, and expenses including attorneys' fees arising out of or resulting from their failure to comply with the Occupational Safety and Health Act of 1970, the standards thereunder, and any state act or standard.

The Subcontractor further agrees that all materials, supplies, and equipment provided by the Subcontractor hereunder shall meet the minimum standards and specifications set forth in the Occupational Safety and Health Act of 1970 and subsequent amendments, the standards thereunder, and any state act or standard.

7. The Subcontractor herewith guarantees all part of the work and materials for a period of one (1) year from the date of completion of work covered by the contract, or such longer period as may be applicable by virtue of a manufacturer's warranty against defects in workmanship, materials, construction, fair wear and tear excepted, and shall make good at his/her own expense any such defects that may appear within the period covered by the guarantee. The obligation of Subcontractor shall extend to all materials ordered and/or installed by the Subcontractor, whether payment therefore is made by the Subcontractor or is made directly by the Contractor to the Supplier.

8. The Subcontractor shall not be permitted to subcontract any or all of the work to be done, without the written consent of the Contractor.

9. This agreement and the work scope and specifications (if applicable) constitute the entire agreement between the parties, and no other agreements, promises, or undertakings, are expressed or implied, written or oral, that are not set forth herein.

10. All work stated on the other side of this agreement shall be completed within ____________ days from the date of this agreement.

FIGURE 5–26. Major Repair Inspection

Firm: ____________________ Contact: ____________________ Phone: ____________________

Address: ____

____

Project ____________________ Report #: ____________________

Location: ____________________ Project #: ____________________

Date: __________ Time: __________ Weather: ______________ Temp: ______________

Est. percentage of completion: ______________ Behind/On/Ahead of schedule: ______________

Present at site (other than subcontractor's crews:) ____

____

____

Work in Progress: ____

____

____

____

Noncompliance Items (number each item): ____

____

____

____

____

____

Discrepencies that have been corrected (refer to report and item numbers of write-up): ______________

____

____

____

Workmanship quality is ☐ Excellent ☐ Good ☐ Average ☐ Poor

Information or action required: ____

____

____

____

Signature of Inspection Supervisor

to the specific maintenance demands of the properties they manage.

SCHEDULING PROPERTY-WIDE MAINTENANCE ACTIVITIES

The maintenance schedule in Figure 5–27 shows a representative sampling of common custodial and preventive maintenance activities in a typical property. The property manager and/or maintenance manager/supervisor can adapt this form to the actual maintenance requirements of her/his property and then prepare this schedule on a weekly basis in advance of each week. The schedule should be reviewed daily to allow for any appropriate adjustments.

The estimated time column should show the best, most reasonable estimate of the amount of time required to perform each custodial and preventive maintenance activity according to the established standards of quality. Move-in/move-out inspections, service requests, and emergency work also need to be factored into the weekly schedule, although it is admittedly more difficult to estimate how much time to allocate for these maintenance activities. Nevertheless, as this text has stressed, infinitely more work is accomplished with a plan than without one.

Also as previously mentioned, this weekly maintenance schedule should be provided to each maintenance employee and also posted in the management office and in the maintenance office/workshop/garage. By distributing the schedule this way, the property manager and/or maintenance manager/supervisor will know immediately where each employee is supposed to be and what she/he is supposed to be doing. Moreover, employee downtime will be minimized since the employee can go on to the next item on her/his schedule after completing each task.

Each employee should be held accountable for indicating on the maintenance schedule form the actual time expended on each task and for providing this completed form to the property manager or maintenance manager/supervisor at the end of each day. At the end of the week, the property manager should review actual performance versus the schedule, including the actual versus estimated time for completion of each task, and the information contained on the service request record and the service request log (Fig. 5–28). This review permits an objective evaluation of both the maintenance program and the utilization of each maintenance employee based on the established standards. The manager can then use this historical performance to assist in future scheduling.

It is the property manager's obligation to provide a system that enables workers to perform as efficiently as their capabilities allow. A system as simple as a documented work schedule and service request log can create a win-win situation for everyone by improving the effectiveness of the property's maintenance operations, helping workers and the property to operate more professionally, and providing the best service to residents at the most economical cost. The principle is that work tends to improve when it can be shown to be measurable and that people tend to focus on that which is measured and reported. In turn, they become better workers. What's more, when managers know how to gauge performance and have an effective instrument to do it, they are not making judgments on appearances or fragmented, incomplete, inconsistent, or inaccurate evidence but instead on actual, verifiable facts, and they become more effective managers. The interested property manager should explore the existing software programs designed to help with preventive maintenance scheduling and tracking maintenance employee performance to further enhance the manager's own performance.

MAINTENANCE INSPECTIONS

The property manager should be inspecting the quality of maintenance in the property every time she/he walks out of the management office. Every trip across the property grounds, through the property parking lot, to the property pool area, or into the corridors and common areas of the residential buildings is an opportunity to inspect, observe, make note of, and improve the property's maintenance. The property manager should consider it Job One to be constantly aware of and vigilant about how well all aspects of the property are maintained, and "walking the property" should become a daily habit.

In addition to these frequent, informal inspections, the property manager must recognize that scheduled and unscheduled formal inspections of the property by the property manager herself/himself and also by the senior property manager are the cornerstones of managing the maintenance operation. These inspections should never be used to communicate a lack of trust in maintenance employees. Instead, they are indicative of sound business practices and are for the purposes of determining that directions are being carried out; that truthful feedback is being received; that company standards, property value, and traffic-building curb appeal are maintained; and to monitor the performance of programmed preventative maintenance activities. To this end, scheduled inspections should be conducted on a regular basis, and maintenance staff should be aware when they are to occur. Unscheduled inspections should be conducted once a month or so, at different times of the day, to give the property manager and senior manager a more candid overview of how maintenance employees are performing.

During maintenance inspections, the property and/or senior manager can use an interior inspection form like the sample in Figure 5–29 and an exterior inspection form like the sample in Figure 5–30 to spot-check maintenance work. Of course, each property manager must prepare checklists that meet the particular needs and climatic and weather conditions of his/her property. Committing observations to writing will pinpoint specific items requiring corrections, allow communication to the proper individuals, and ensure that action is taken after the inspections.

The completed maintenance inspection reports review, analyze, and provide information about:

- Condition of the grounds, common areas, models, office, and buildings
- Resident service and reasons for any past due requests
- General condition and rating of competitive properties
- Condition of and mileage on each property vehicle

FIGURE 5–27. Maintenance Schedule

Property ______________________

To ______________________

From ______________________

Date prepared ______________________

Maintenance superintendent initial ______________________

Job	Mon. Estimated time	Mon. Actual time	Tues. Estimated time	Tues. Actual time	Wed. Estimated time	Wed. Actual time	Thurs. Estimated time	Thurs. Actual time	Fri. Estimated time	Fri. Actual time	Sat. Estimated time	Sat. Actual time
1. Routine check of development												
2. Policing areas												
3. Trash areas, cleaning and pickup												
4. Clubhouse, cleaning												
5. Laundry area cleaning												
6. Rental office cleaning												
7. Hallway cleaning												
8. Carport identification												
9. Fence repair												
10. Downspout and gutter repair												
11. Check point lighting												
12. Street maintenance and cleaning												
13. Check playground area												
14. Vehicle maintenance												
15. Clean maintenance facilities												
16. Service request (see Service Request log)												
17. Administrative												

Figure 5–28. Service Request Log

Property ______________________

To ______________________

From ______________________

Address and Phone	Unit #	Service	Date of request	Date completed	Work order no.	Total time on job	Material used	Empl. Init.	Status

____

(Employee signature)

FIGURE 5–29. Interior Maintenance Inspection Report

Property: ______________________ Date: ______________

Inspected by: ______________________

Date of last inspection: ______________________

Areas to be re-inspected, Line item #: ______________________

Area	Condition Good	Condition Fair	Condition Poor	Line Item #	Maintenance Required	Action Taken
Entryway/Vestibule						
Ceilings				1		
Door Check				2		
Door Mats				3		
Floors / Carpets				4		
Hinges,Knobs,Locks				5		
& Hardware				6		
Glass				7		
Overall Cleanliness				8		
Walls				9		
Mailboxes						
Door / Locks				10		
Finish				11		
Name Plates				12		
Hallway(s)						
Ceilings				13		
Doors				14		
Floors				15		
Handrails				16		
Landings				17		
Overall Cleanliness				18		
Steps				19		
Walls				20		
Windows				21		
Elevators						
Cab Ceiling				22		
Cab Floor				23		
Cab Walls				24		
Doors				25		
Elevator Room				26		
Overall Cleanliness				27		
Ride				28		
Signal Buttons/Light				29		

Legend - Action Taken:

1 Reference to Building Staff #2 Reference to Board #3 Contractor Assistance/Repairs

continued

FIGURE 5–29. Interior Maintenance Inspection Report (*Continued*)

Property: ______________________ Date: ______________

Inspected by: ______________________

Date of last inspection: ______________________

Areas to be re-inspected, Line item #: ______________________

Area	Condition Good	Condition Fair	Condition Poor	Line Item #	Maintenance Required	Action Taken
Light Fixtures						
Entryway				30		
Bulbs				31		
Fixtures				32		
Entrance				33		
Bulbs				34		
Fixtures				35		
Hallways / Stairwell				36		
Bulbs				37		
Emergency Lights				38		
Fixtures				39		
Laundry						
Ceilings				40		
Drains				41		
Floors				42		
Overall Cleanliness				43		
Walls				44		
Washers / Dryers				45		
Stairwells						
Ceilings				46		
Floors				47		
Handrails				48		
Landings				49		
Overall Cleanliness				50		
Walls				51		
Windows				52		
Compactor						
Cleanliness				53		
Frames				54		
Hopper Doors				55		
Lighting				56		
Main Compactor				57		

Legend - Action Taken:

1 Reference to Building Staff #2 Reference to Board #3 Contractor Assistance/Repairs

continued

FIGURE 5–29. Interior Maintenance Inspection Report (*Continued*)

Property: ______________________ Date: ______________

Inspected by: ______________________

Date of last inspection: ______________________

Areas to be re-inspected, Line item #: ______________________

Area	Condition Good	Fair	Line Poor	Action Item #	Maintenance Required	Taken
Physical Plant / Mechanical Rooms						
Boiler & Burner				58		
Ceilings				59		
Fire Extinguisher				60		
Floors				61		
Permits & Certificates				62		
Maintenance Log				63		
Steam Room				64		
Ventilation				65		
Walls				66		
Water Storage						
Insulation				67		
Sump Pump				68		
Tank				69		
Various Piping & Valve				70		
Maintenance Shop / Superintendent's Office						
Cleanliness				71		
Organization				72		
Other Rooms						
Basements				73		
Store Rooms				74		
Sub-Basements				75		
Other						
				76		
				77		
				78		

COMMENTS: ______________________

Legend - Action Taken:

1 Reference to Building Staff #2 Reference to Board #3 Contractor Assistance/Repairs

FIGURE 5–30. Exterior Maintenance Inspection Report

Property: ______________________________

Reviewed by: ______________________________ Date: ____________________

Report Submitted by: ______________________________ Date: ____________________

Comments: ____

____

Exterior Items	Description	Action Needed	Estimated Time/Cost
GENERAL			
Overall Impression			
Overall Cleanliness			
FRONT			
Sidewalk			
Driveway			
Canopies			
Garbage Area			
Painting			
Trim			
Landscaping			
Facade-Lower			
Facade-Upper			
Caulking			
Fire Escapes/Balconies			
Stairs/Railings			
Outside Signs			
Outside Lights			
Timers			
YARDS			
Garbage Area			
Painting			
Trim			
Landscaping			
Facade-Lower			
Facade-Upper			
Caulking			
Fire Escapes/Balconies			
Stairs/Railings			
Outside Signs			
Outside Lights			
Timers			
Fencing			
WINDOWS			
Frames			
Glass			
Sills/Lintels			
Hardware/Locks			
Screens			
DOORS			
Frames			
Hinges			
Hardware/Locks			
ROOF			
Surface			
Flashing			
Gutters/Downspouts			
Roof Vents			
Chimneys			
Parapets			
Copings			
Cables			

- Vacant units, including date vacated, date ready for occupancy, date re-rented, anticipated move-in date, and condition of units reported as ready for occupancy

- Comments from at least five residents

- An overall rating for the property

- Actions required to bring the rating up to excellent if it is not rated excellent, including a timetable for these action and a follow-up date

The completed reports should be submitted to the next higher authority for review and necessary response. A full report on a property once each month is an excellent practice that will provide a measurable overview of how the property is maintained over time.

To ensure that the property inspection report is used, any unfinished work included on a prior report should be brought forward and listed on the most recent report. This inclusion is a red flag indicating that the report is not being utilized. The manager/inspector needs to find out why.

Through this system of checks and balances, employees knows that their work is to be inspected. Consequently, they are more likely to do the work correctly and consistently. In addition, this system encourages the senior manager and property manager to recognize employees when standards are maintained or exceeded. Such feedback is invaluable for creating and maintaining a motivational work environment.

Finally, to permit the most effective overall maintenance review by the senior manager or property manager, a maintenance contact report (Fig. 5–31) can be used on a monthly or quarterly basis. On the front, this report provides a comprehensive overview of the basic items that should be inspected and examined to ensure that the maintenance program is effective. On the reverse side, the maintenance contact report provides space for verification of the actual operation of most maintenance procedures.

These practices of maintenance inspection, documentation, and feedback are universally applicable. Inspecting and analyzing a property on a regular basis to monitor the accomplishment of established objectives is good business practice, no matter how small or large the property and/or management company.

ENERGY AND WATER CONSERVATION

Energy and water conservation produces benefits for the individual resident, for the property, and for the larger immediate and extended communities. The property manager will want to implement an effective program of energy and water conservation, which not only will pay for itself very quickly while helping to conserve rapidly diminishing natural resources but also will attract a better caliber of resident, that is, those who are interested in living in a socially conscious environment.

INITIATING AND IMPLEMENTING AN EFFECTIVE ENERGY AND WATER CONSERVATION PROGRAM

With regard to the conservation of resources, including electricity, fuel, and water, the property manager must be acutely aware of consumption levels and ways to reduce consumption levels and must include on-going conservation efforts in the property-wide maintenance plan.

To initiate an energy and water conservation program, the property manager can contact various utility companies that will perform free or low-cost audits to determine how resources can be conserved and money can be saved throughout the property. Some steps that a property manager can take to conserve energy and water are listed in Figure 5–32.

In addition, energy- and water-efficient replacements should be installed as appropriate, and new energy- and water-efficient appliances and fixtures should be installed whenever a unit is refurbished. The property manager also should consult with a knowledgeable local attorney about the types of energy and water conservation measures that are or soon will become required in the property's jurisdiction.

Also, whenever a maintenance worker responds to a resident service request, changes filters, or services a vacated unit, she/he should make an energy conservation inspection based on an energy conservation checklist like the one in Figure 5–33. The actions to be taken are listed under the appropriate headings and are to be carried out on an on-going basis.

Many properties also are finding that residents' conservation of energy and water increases significantly when consumption-based submeters are installed to replace the more common flat-rate billing systems for energy and water use. Submetering devices measure the individual use in each unit, allowing managers and owners to track and bill for actual usage and residents to pay for only what they use. Property managers in properties that have not yet investigated submetering may wish to do so and report their findings to the senior manager, the executive property manager, and the property owner for further consideration.

GETTING RESIDENTS TO 'BUY IN' TO THE PROPERTY'S ENERGY AND WATER CONSERVATION PROGRAM

To achieve the most successful results, the property manager should present the property's energy and water conservation program to residents in terms of the benefits they will derive from it. Specifically, residents should be made to understand that they must pay for energy and water whether it is directly to the utility company or through their rent, and that in either case, the property's energy and water conservation program reduces the overall cost of housing for the resident no matter who pays directly for the utilities.

Residents also need to understand that because of the increasing cost of increasingly scarce energy and water resources, control of consumption is vital to the economic survival of a property. Of course, if they are not already aware, residents also should be informed that conservation of energy and water is a major national goal. To this end, an energy conservation letter like the one in Figure 5–34 should be included in each new resident packet and in the property's resident handbook.

FIGURE 5–31. Maintenance Contact Report

(Phase)	(Phase)	(Date)

1. Property inspection report attached.
   Comments ______

2. Reviewed sampling of service requests for month with maintenance superintendent.
   Comments ______

3. Reviewed maintenance files. Comments on:
   Move-in inspections ______
   Move-out inspections ______
   Service requests ______

4. Reconciled petty cash fund.
   Comments ______

5. Maintenance staffing guide ______ Actual number of employees ______
   Comments ______

6. Is parts inventory adequate? ☐ yes ☐ no
   Comments ______

7.

Account	Budget YTD	Actual YTD	Variance	Explanation
Cleaning				
Grounds				
R&M				
Painting				
Truck				

8. Is trash pickup satisfactory? ☐ yes ☐ no

9. Is maintenance manual up-to-date? ☐ yes ☐ no

10. Comment on maintenance superintendent's attitude ______

11. Spot-checked quality of work being performed.
    Comments ______

12. Reviewed previous development inspection report.
    Comments ______

13. Air conditioning and heating equipment inspected in the following units (check equipment in same units where filters were checked for development inspection report):

Address	Apt. no.	Condition

continued

FIGURE 5–31. Maintenance Contact Report (*Continued*)

Review of documents and procedures

	Maint. Manual page	Mgmt. Manual page	Per proc.	Needs impr.	Date follow-up scheduled	Comments
Supplies and mat'ls. req. proc.	IV-28					
Energy actions program	V-23	H-67				
Lawn, plant maint. proc.	V-21	H-65				
Purchasing guidelines SOP	IV-66	H-9				
Move-in inspections	III-1	H-30				
Move-out inspections	III-11a	H-32				
Unit turnaround	III-10	H-34				
Maintenance scheduling proc.	IV-67	H-81				
Telephone log	VI-1					
Lease painting proc.	II-16					
Emergency service requests	II-13					
Service request proc.	II-1	A-9c				
Time cards	I-3					
Carport identification	VI-10					
Maintenance of motorized equipment	V-2	H-67				
Charges to tenant	II-8	III-17				
Construction punch out proc.	VI-28	E-5d				
Parts order control	IV-69	H-83				
Development visitation record	IV-1	H-40				
Development winterization/ summerization	V-11 H-61	V-15 H-63				
Warranties proc.	VIII-46	E-6				
Filter change proc.	V-18	H-67				
Purchase and payment proc.	IV-63	H-6				
Development inspection proc.	IV-20	C-5a				
Supplies and equipment inventory proc.	IV-31	H-86				

FIGURE 5-32. Energy and Water Conservation Measures

- Audits by local energy and water utility companies
- Property-wide energy and water usage and conservation inspections
- Posting signs promoting conservation
    - Next to thermostats
    - Next to light switches
    - Near doors and windows in common areas
    - On bulletin boards
    - In public areas of the management office
    - Over mailboxes in each building
    - In public bathrooms
- Insulation
- Locks on thermostats
- Seasonal newsletter reminders (As the seasons change, appropriate energy saving recommendations can be included)
- Resident education program
- Energy saving lectures
- Fliers
- Resident involvement (The property manager should involve the resident association in a joint effort to conserve energy because residents are more likely to participate in a program they have established and implemented.)
- Periodic property-wide energy inspections performed by the property manager, perhaps accompanied by an energy conservation expert and a representative of the resident association

RESIDENT RELATIONS IN PROPERTY MAINTENANCE

So far in this discussion of multihousing maintenance, the focus has been on "what" to do. This section focuses on "how" to do it—not the step-by-step mechanics of painting a wall or repairing a machine but the attitude that must back up every aspect of property maintenance. It is the attitude of "customer care"—the all-important attitude that expresses itself in the way the maintenance staff relate to their jobs and to the residents they serve. It is the attitude that defines a truly superior maintenance operation in a truly superior residential property.

ATTITUDE AND INTERPERSONAL RELATIONS: MAINTENANCE AS CUSTOMER CARE

It is a fact that residents typically see more of the maintenance staff than they do any other personnel associated with the management of their homes. So if the residents of a multihousing property are the "customers," then the property's maintenance operations represent "customer care" to a greater degree than any other facet of the property's operations. It follows logically that no area of property operations gives a greater opportunity to demonstrate superior customer care and public relations than maintenance, and in no area of property operations are productive interpersonal relations more important than maintenance.

The benefits of excellent customer care through maintenance are many. For example, the property manager will unfailingly find that residents react more positively and respectfully to maintenance persons who are knowledgeable and enthusiastic about their work and who communicate with residents using the proper levels of courtesy and professionalism. But perhaps more significant, a solid, courteous, productive, and professional rapport between a property's maintenance staff and its residents helps to ensure a well-maintained property and one in which turnovers are reduced and costs are correspondingly controlled.

THE PROPERTY MANAGER'S ROLE IN FOSTERING AN ATTITUDE OF SERVICE AND "CUSTOMER CARE" AMONG THE MAINTENANCE STAFF

To the maintenance staff of a residential property, including the maintenance manager/supervisor, the property manager is not only the boss and supervisor but also the model whose attitude and behavior inevitably filters down to every level of subordinate worker. If the property manager has a curt, unpleasant manner about her/him, that will have a markedly negative effect on employee attitude and productivity. Conversely, if the manager serves as a positive model for the subordinate workers she/he supervisors, then the property will run like a well-oiled, well-maintained machine, and all involved parties—from the owner and the management company's executive property manager and senior manager to the property's administrative and clerical office staff, the maintenance staff, and ulti-

FIGURE 5–33. Energy Conservation Checklist

Maintenance Service Calls

- ☐ Inspect kitchen and bathroom faucets for leaks, and repair or schedule for repair as appropriate.
- ☐ Inspect toilets for continuous running and repair or schedule for repair as appropriate.
- ☐ Check appropriate box on the service request form indicating that the inspection is made.

Quarterly Filter Changes

- ☐ Inspect kitchen and bathroom faucets for leaks and repair or schedule for repair as appropriate.
- ☐ Inspect toilets for continuous running and repair and schedule for repair as appropriate.
- ☐ Check hot water heater setting and adjust to 125 degrees in apartment without dishwashers and 130 to 165 degrees in apartments with dishwashers, depending on the type and age of the dishwasher. All temperature measurements should be made at the kitchen sink, not the heater outlet, as some developments experience a 10 to 12 degree drop from supply to outlet.
- ☐ Verify that the restrictor is still in the showerhead and install a new one if it has been removed.
- ☐ Check furnace to ensure that the pilot light assembly, blower, and motor are operational and clean and that the stack pipes are rust free.

Vacant Until Turnaround

- ☐ Clean refrigerator inside and outside, including the coils on the back; set dial at position number 1 and close door.
- ☐ During winter months – approximately October through April in most areas – set the heating thermostat at fifty five degrees.
- ☐ During the summer months – approximately May through September in most areas – shut off air-conditioning thermostat. The day prior to lease signing, the development manager is to turn the air-conditioning on to a setting of approximately eighty degrees.
- ☐ Keep lights turned off in vacant apartments when no one is working in them.
- ☐ Flush toilets and pour water into standpipes on a regular basis to replace what has evaporated to keep sewer gas from entering the unit.
- ☐ Include the energy conservation letter in each new resident's move-in packet. The development manager should call it to the resident's attention during the move-in inspection.

Routine and Preventive Maintenance

- ☐ Use 40-watt bulbs in outside carriage-type light fixtures.
- ☐ In walkup areas where lighting fixtures accommodate more than two bulbs, eliminate extra bulbs and use two 40-watt bulbs.
- ☐ Any new inside lighting is to be fluorescent.
- ☐ During the spring and summer months, the lights in the garage are to be turned off when the garage doors are open.
- ☐ Exercise judgment about lighting to ensure that life and property are not jeopardized. Energy conservation measures should never result in substandard illumination. In a specific situation with a conflict between following energy procedures and safety requirements, the latter always prevails. Lighting safety provides security and affects the aesthetics of the property. Avoid darkness that might result in resident injuries or fear and that makes the building unattractive.
- ☐ The development maintenance supervisor should ensure that timers and photocells are adjusted to the season of the year.

FIGURE 5–34. **Energy Conservation Letter to New Resident**

Dear Resident:

Energy conservation results in lower utility bills, a benefit to both you and the owner regardless of who actually pays the utility bills. Energy conservation is also consistent with the nation's energy goals. You can take the simple steps described in the list below to conserve energy.

Water

- When operating the garbage disposal, use cold water to solidify grease. This reduction in hot water usage saves energy and also prevents maintenance problems.
- Notify the development office immediately when you notice a leaking faucet in your bathroom or kitchen. A water faucet dripping 1 drop of water per second can waste as much as 650 gallons of water in 1 year.
- Take showers rather than tub baths because an average shower bath uses only 5 gallons of hot water compared to 10 gallons for a tub bath.

Heating and Air-conditioning

- Decide on a desired temperature and leave the thermostat at that setting rather than constantly adjusting it.
- Be sure obstacles do not block the return air grill that normally is located in the wall adjacent to the furnace room.
- During the cooling season maintain thermostat controls lower than 75 degrees. During the heating season keep the setting no higher than 68 degrees and (if you are away for an extended period of time) no lower than 55 degrees.
- If your apartment has a fireplace, close the damper tightly when the fireplace is not in use, so that the chimney does not draw heated or cooled air from the apartment.
- Drapes, blinds, and shades act as insulation. During the winter keep them open to let the sunlight warm the air and cut the heating system's load; during the summer close them on the sunny side to cut incoming heat.
- Keep the doors to the outside shut when either the air-conditioning or heat is on.
- Appliances give off heat that the cooling system has to counteract, so minimize their use during the hottest time of the day in the summer.
- After bathing, keep the bathroom door closed and turn on the exhaust fan or open the bathroom window to remove the moisture and prevent it from circulating throughout the apartment.

Kitchen

- Defrost the refrigerator when frost in the freezer compartment is about ¼ inch thick.
- When cooking on the range, use the vent fan to exhaust heated air directly to the outside and relieve the burden on the cooling system.
- The range cooks more efficiently if the diameter of pots and pans is matched to the diameter of the heating elements. This step also prevents heat escaping into the air.
- A refrigerator operates more economically when filled to capacity but not overloaded.
- Do not set the refrigerator or freezer to run at a colder temperature than necessary.
- Oven heat does not circulate efficiently so do not use the oven for quickly heating the kitchen.
- Glass and ceramic baking dishes transfer heat better than metal and generally can be used in an oven set 25 degrees lower than called for in cooking directions.
- When cooking, put lids on pots and pans; less heat escapes from them and lower heat settings can be used.
- Always make sure that the range is turned off after use.
- Whether cooked in the oven, broiler, or on top of the range, frozen foods use less energy if they are removed from the freezer and thawed in the refrigerator compartment first.
- Small appliances such as electric skillets, toasters, and crock pots are an economical way to prepare small meals since they use less electricity than the range.
- Be sure to use the correct amount of detergent in the dishwasher and load it properly for most efficient use. Dishwashers are most economical to use when filled to capacity.

Laundry

- As often as possible use the cold or warm water setting on the washing machines; hot water is the major cost item in washing clothes.

mately the residents—will be content and satisfied with the way the property is managed.

For the property manager to establish this positive tone, she/he must remember and communicate to the maintenance staff—indeed, to all of the property's workers—that the residents are the most important people in the property; that while filling out reports and attending meetings are important, they are purely secondary to servicing residents; that it is the residents who pay the salaries of everyone in the management and maintenance organization; that not only are residents *not* interruptions to the work of anyone who is employed by the property but are in fact the purpose of that work; and that it is the residents who can make or break the success of a management company and a property as a whole.

To establish this positive tone and create a motivational employment environment, the property manager should:

- Train maintenance and property staff in resident service principles through periodic full-staff training sessions and periodic one-on-one interactions
- Establish specific service goals (e.g., responding to service maintenance requests within 24 hours, refurbishing vacant units within two to three days)
- Establish mechanisms to measure the accomplishment of service goals
- Provide feedback to staff on the accomplishment of goals
- Evaluate employees on their accomplishment of specific goals
- Recognize staff accomplishments
- Arrange to compensate employees in accordance with their accomplishments

Some specific points for the property manager to emphasize to the maintenance staff are listed below.

Maintenance staff should always be clean and dressed neatly in appropriate attire. Coveralls should be made available to all maintenance staff, and maintenance workers should be encouraged to wear coveralls to protect clothes or uniforms when performing dirty or messy jobs. Maintenance workers also should have a clean set of clothes or uniforms available at the property to change into if necessary. The property is usually responsible for purchasing and providing coveralls and uniforms for maintenance staff.

Maintenance staff should maintain the appropriate "professional distance" with residents. Maintenance workers should not become too friendly with residents. Each resident should be addressed and treated with the same level of professional respect and courtesy, and no resident should receive preferential or favored treatment. Maintenance workers should be trained to disengage politely but firmly from lengthy conversations with residents who may be using the staff person as a personal sounding board, crying shoulder, or available ear. Maintenance workers also should not engage with residents in gossip about any other resident or property employee and should be cautioned about what they say when in the property, management, or maintenance office and/or speaking with the property manager and other staff members, since one can never be sure who else is in the room at the time.

Maintenance staff must perform their jobs professionally for all residents. Whether or not a maintenance worker likes a particular resident, all residents must receive the benefit of a job well done. Moreover, performing the work is the worker's primary responsibility. No amount of pleasant interaction will satisfy a resident if her/his roof continues to leak or plumbing continues to malfunction.

Maintenance staff must never become involved in verbal or physical altercations with residents. Any disagreement between a maintenance worker and a resident should be referred immediately by the worker to the property manager, who should attend to the matter immediately.

Maintenance staff should support and enforce the property's policies, especially in front of residents, even if they do not always agree with those policies. All property personnel should present a common front to the residents in support of company policies. Such policies include the required response to residents who request maintenance staff members to perform private work during off-duty hours, accepting tips from residents for custodial service and/or at holiday time, and all other policies that the property has established for its staff members. (These resident/staff policies also should be included in the operations manual, the maintenance plan, the staff handbook, and the resident handbook.)

Maintenance staff should be encouraged to be enthusiastic and positive about their work. The property manager should encourage all staff members to approach each day at work, and each task during the day, with an attitude of positive expectation and even enjoyment. The property manager also should encourage workers to find alternative employment if they do not enjoy their work, are not comfortable working according to the structure and expectations of property maintenance work, and/or cannot be convinced that their work contributes to the property and therefore matters.

The property manager is obligated to master and practice all the techniques and strategies for superior customer care discussed above and to work with the maintenance staff to cultivate the best possible maintenance department for the property. The techniques discussed above, and all techniques for providing excellent customer care to property residents through excellent maintenance performance, must be established as a philosophy, a policy, and a standard operating procedure. They should be included in the property's operations manual and maintenance plan and should become habits for the property manager and for the property's maintenance staff. In short, every aspect of customer care and service must become the way of life that defines the property.

MAINTENANCE LOGISTICS

Although the actual maintenance of a multihousing property is an on-going task with a constant ebb and flow of work, there are certain logistics about planning property maintenance that need only be devised once to serve productively over time. These logistics include the strategies and techniques for maintenance budgeting; planning the maintenance office/garage; the best techniques for maintenance staff communication; and management and maintenance during new construction.

BUDGETING FOR MAINTENANCE

The property manager is responsible for ensuring that sufficient funds are allocated to allow for on-going and emergency property maintenance on an annual basis. This responsibility is fulfilled through the property manager's input into and participation in developing the property's annual operating budget. For a discussion about proper budgeting for property maintenance, refer to Chapter 4, Multihousing Management Economics and Finances.

PLANNING THE MAINTENANCE OFFICE/GARAGE

Although the property manager's desk and base of operation is typically situated in the property or management office, the base of operation for the property's maintenance is typically its maintenance office/workshop/garage. This area, regardless of how small or large, must be well organized to allow maintenance workers to serve the property best. Figure 5–35 shows one desirable floor plan for a large property maintenance office and garage, including the recommended location of work desks and storage areas. Of course, this floor plan is just one of many, but it demonstrates the most efficient use of space to allow for the most effective delivery of maintenance service. (A discussion of considerations for laying out the maintenance office/garage is also included in Chapter 12, Management's Role During New Construction and Rent-up.)

MAINTENANCE STAFF COMMUNICATION

Much productive time is wasted when property managers are unable to contact maintenance managers/supervisors and/or workers during the course of a working day. In prior years, the beeper was considered a boon to this type of communication. But beepers require that the party being beeped has or locates a telephone to call the other party back.

Beepers are desirable when property managers and/or maintenance manager/supervisors are off-site and need to be contacted, but they do not provide instantaneous two-way communication. The most efficient technology that provides this important instantaneous communication, which is so vital especially in emergency situations, is a two-way radio or walkie-talkie system. It is therefore strongly recommended that all property managers and maintenance managers/supervisors and selected maintenance personnel be equipped with a two-way radio or walkie-talkie so that immediate communication can be facilitated. The one-time purchase and activation fees and the on-going operating fees (if there are any), of such technology pay for themselves over and over again in the convenience and immediacy of response time they provide. Of course, all personnel to whom two-way radios or walkie-talkies are assigned should be trained in the proper use and procedures of the instrument, which normally exclude personal conversations and communications.

MANAGEMENT AND MAINTENANCE DURING NEW CONSTRUCTION

For a complete discussion of management and maintenance concerns during new construction, refer to Chapter 12, Management's Role During New Construction and Rent-up.

THE MANAGEMENT MAINTENANCE PLAN (INCLUDING A RISK MANAGEMENT PLAN)

Throughout this text, reference has been made to the importance of the property manager codifying and documenting a property-wide management maintenance plan. As this management maintenance plan also should include a risk management plan, a comprehensive outline of the management maintenance plan (including a risk management plan) appears as an addendum to Chapter 6, Risk Management and Management Maintenance Plans.

CONCLUSION

Maintenance refers to the preservation of assets through the upkeep of a residential property's structural, physical, mechanical, and aesthetic elements. The maintenance goals of both conventional and federally assisted properties are the same: to maintain an attractive appearance and a safe, functioning living environment at a reasonable expense level. Regardless of its type or size, the maintenance of a multihousing property is the most visible indicator of how well the property is managed.

Although the property manager is accountable for the maintenance of the property, she/he is not expected to perform the maintenance tasks. Instead, more than any other aspect of multihousing management, property maintenance relies on the property manager's abilities to organize and delegate responsibility, motivate workers, and follow up on progress and results.

Supervising a maintenance team that may include a maintenance manager/supervisor (who should always be subordinate to the property manager), the property manager must recognize, schedule, plan for, and oversee each of the six categories of property maintenance: custodial or janitorial; corrective or service; preventive or planned; emergency or crisis; deferred; and vacant unit maintenance and preparation. The property manager also must carefully monitor deferred maintenance to ensure that it does not devolve into crisis maintenance.

During the execution of her/his maintenance-related duties, the property manager may find it necessary and/or desirable to

FIGURE 5–35. Sample Floor Plan for Property Maintenance Office and Garage

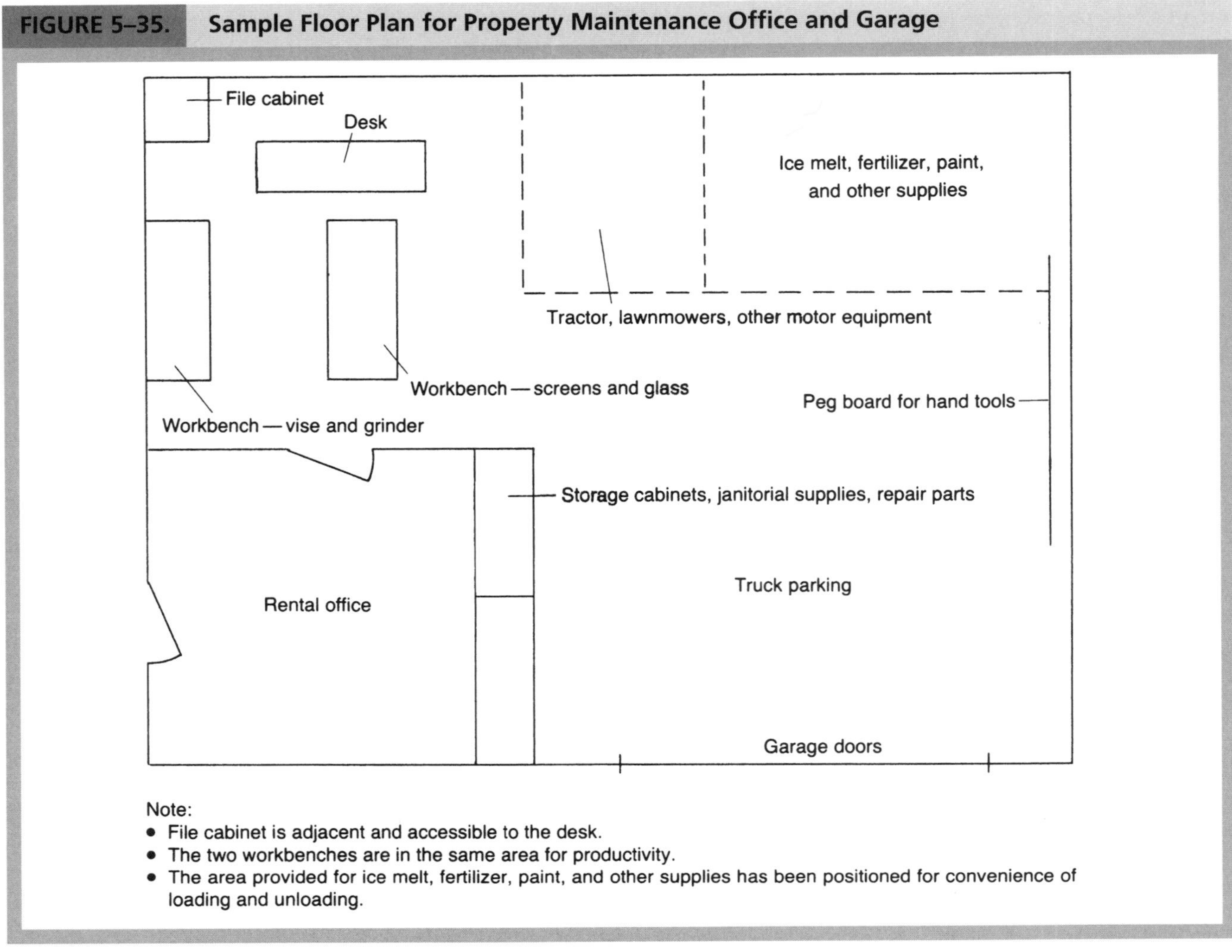

Note:

- File cabinet is adjacent and accessible to the desk.
- The two workbenches are in the same area for productivity.
- The area provided for ice melt, fertilizer, paint, and other supplies has been positioned for convenience of loading and unloading.

engage the services of outside contractors. Should this be the case, the property manager is responsible for conducting all appropriate and required inquiries into the candidate contractors, for issuing requests for bids and securing competitive bids to ensure the best price, and for seeing to it that the agreement between the selected contractor and the property is in order legally and favors the property to the greatest possible degree.

Energy and water conservation are included in the discussion of maintenance because most conservation work can be done simultaneously with maintenance work. Practicing property-wide energy and water conservation produces measurable benefits for the property as well as for the larger immediate and extended communities. It is the property manager's responsibility to create, implement, and enforce a workable energy and water conservation program for the property that everyone, from the management company decision makers to the property owner, maintenance staff, and residents, will respect, adhere to, and participate in.

Property-wide inspections are among the most effective instruments the property manager has to ensure a consistently high level of performance by maintenance staff. To this end, the property manager should conduct scheduled and unscheduled maintenance inspections on a regular basis, and "walking the property" on a daily basis should be the first habit a property manager develops.

In all maintenance-related efforts, it is critical for the property manager to maintain positive relations with residents and to encourage the maintenance staff to do likewise. The property manager must serve as the role model who informs all property staff members that the residents are the most important people in the property, that courteous and professional service must be rendered at all times, and that nothing less than this standard will be accepted.

With regard to maintenance-related finances, it is the property manager's responsibility to participate in the annual budget process so that sufficient funds will be allocated annually for on-going and emergency maintenance.

Finally, it is the property manager's responsibility to codify all maintenance-related programs, documents, and schedules in a property-wide management maintenance plan that includes a risk management plan and that will guide the manager and the property staff in the performance of their duties.

Of all management tasks, property maintenance is perhaps the least glamorous, but it is among the most vital. Without proper maintenance, a property cannot long stand, either physically or economically. With it, the property manager ensures the on-going viability of the property, the on-going satisfaction of both the owner and the residents, and the on-going success of her/his tenure as a property manager.

6

Risk Management and Management Maintenance Plans

THE IMPORTANCE OF A RISK MANAGEMENT PROGRAM

In Chapter 5, Property Maintenance and Energy and Water Conservation, much was said about the property manager's responsibility to provide a well-maintained living environment to all residents of the property being managed. No one would deny that safety and security are integral elements of a well-maintained living environment. In fact, it is the responsibility of every multihousing manager to ensure that the property she/he manages is a reasonably safe and secure environment for all residents, visitors, and employees and for the public in general. As emphasized throughout this text, it is also the property manager's responsibility to protect and preserve the owner's investment in the property. Failure to carry out either of these responsibilities—the responsibility to provide a safe and secure environment and the responsibility to protect and preserve the owner's investment—can result in significant costs to the owner and, in extreme cases, the loss of the owner's entire investment in the property.

This is true in large part because society has become increasingly litigious over the past several decades, with courts now looking more carefully at responsibility for causing and/or contributing to an injury or loss and damage awards in the many millions of dollars. Indeed, the size and frequency of awards have prompted insurance companies to limit coverage sharply or to eliminate it altogether for many policyholders with a history of losses. For others, insurance has become much more costly and difficult to obtain.

Moreover, the obligation of the landlord (a term that is used in many laws and regulations and which encompasses both the owner and the managing agent) to provide the resident with a safe and reasonably secure environment has increased significantly, and the regulations have become more stringent. Courts hold property owners and managers to a very high standard of accountability in providing safe and accident-free living environments and may award what many consider to be astronomical judgments for such claims as broken entry locks and hooligans being electrocuted after vandalizing electrical service transformers on the grounds of a property. In turn, conscientious residential property owners and managers must be acutely aware of, and take deliberate action to guard against, situations that could result in injury or loss to individuals and/or the property.

Moreover, the catastrophic events of September 11, 2001 introduced a risk not previously considered, but one that has placed additional concerns on multihousing owners and managers. Now, the possibilities of a terrorist attack and/or a major disaster within a residential community have become far less remote and in fact are possibilities that must be dealt with on an on-going basis.

The process of safeguarding people and property is known as risk management. Understanding risk at all levels and creating and implementing an effective risk management program that reduces or eliminates risk to the greatest possible extent are critical to the property manager's work.

THE RISK MANAGEMENT AUDIT

The property manager's first step in fulfilling the responsibilities of providing a safe and secure environment and protecting and preserving the owner's investment is to perform a property-wide risk management audit or review. This risk management inspection of every internal and external aspect of the property should be performed at least annually—ideally, quarterly—and should be updated as often as required by changes in and/or around the property or any aspect of the property.

Based on the results of the risk management audit, the property manager should generate a risk management plan and take immediate action pursuant to the plan to minimize or eliminate all of the risks. Aspects of risk management that merit a manager's close attention are discussed in this part of the text. A discussion and outline of a full management maintenance plan, including a risk management and a disaster plan, appear as an addendum to this chapter.

RESOURCES FOR RISK MANAGEMENT INFORMATION

The property manager in search of help devising a thorough risk management plan will want to contact the following resources for information and instructions:

- **The management company senior manager and/or executive property manager,** who has overseen the preparation of similar programs for other properties

- **The local police department,** which will send a representative to inspect the property and provide feedback on ways to increase safety and security and also will provide community relations experts who can present talks to residents on what they can do to increase their own safety and security

- **The local fire department,** which also will send a representative to inspect the property and provide feedback on ways to increase fire safety and security and also will provide community relations experts who can present talks to residents on what they can do to increase their own fire safety and security

- **The local weather bureau,** which can provide information on how to prepare for and what to do in the event of natural and weather-related emergencies

- **FEMA (Federal Emergency Management Agency), the local Red Cross chapter, and local hospitals,** all of which have a wealth of easily available information on measures that can be taken to prevent emergencies and what to do in the event of emergencies

- **Vendors and suppliers of equipment, machinery, and supplies,** who can work with the property manager and staff members to ensure the proper care and/or handling of their products and can provide knowledgeable information about what to do in the event of an emergency involving their product

THE FOUR RISK MANAGEMENT TOOLS

The multihousing manager has four risk management tools with which to work: avoidance, prevention, transfer, and retention. All four are commonly used in the operation of a multihousing property since any potential risk can be treated by one or a combination of these methods. Below, a discussion of each.

AVOIDANCE

As the name suggests, avoidance is the elimination of a risk altogether. For example, a manager can avoid the risks associated with a swimming pool, such as injury or drowning, by filling the pool with stone and converting it to a rock garden. This measure is clearly extreme, but it will avoid altogether any possibility of a problem arising because of the operation of the pool. Another example of avoidance would be replacing oil-fired heating equipment with gas furnaces, thus eliminating the risk of an environmental mishap created by an oil spill. Many risks associated with the operation of a multifamily housing property can be avoided through carefully thought-out design changes either during or after construction.

PREVENTION

As a risk management tool, prevention operates in the same general way as avoidance, but it is less extreme. Again using the example of the swimming pool, the manager can prevent risks by adopting a set of pool rules, removing the diving board, and hiring a lifeguard. The hazards associated with a pool are still there, but the lifeguard can minimize or help to prevent them by ensuring that the pool users follow the rules. The lifeguard also can intervene before an incident becomes severe, for example, by rescuing a small child who falls in the deep end of the pool and does not know how to swim. Another example of a preventive action would be the installation of sprinklers in all units in a building. The sprinklers will not stop a fire from occurring, but they will contain the damage and save lives if one does occur. Prevention is a commonly used tool encompassing both design changes and operational changes. It can be quite effective in reducing overall risks.

TRANSFER

The third risk management tool is to transfer the risk to someone else. Generally, such transfer involves legally contracting with someone to assume all or part of the risk. Purchasing insurance is a common method of transferring risk, in which the insurance company contracts with the owner and manager to assume some of the risks associated with operating a residential property in exchange for the owner's premium payments. Another common method of risk transfer is to require someone to sign a release-of-liability letter before performing work or using a facility, such as a clubhouse. Although some courts have declared release-of-liability letters void and unenforceable, many managers believe they are still useful, and they are still commonly used.

RETENTION

The final option in managing a risk is to recognize and assume—or retain—the risk. No matter how careful and thorough they are, all managers retain some risks. For example, virtually all types of building insurance have some deductible on losses. A deductible requires the manager to retain the risk of the first portion of the loss and transfers the risk after that point. In some situations, risk retention is prudent from both an operational and financial point of view. For instance, using the insurance example again, if increasing the deductible saves a percentage of the annual premium, then retaining that increased deductible risk will pay off in the first year—assuming, of course, that no loss occurs. But that is one of the risks that is taken.

DWELLING UNIT ACCESS: KEYS, LOCKS, WINDOWS, AND DOORS

Controlling access into the property, and especially into individual dwelling units, is a primary area of risk management. Without exception, each resident is entitled to security in her/his dwelling unit. The courts strictly interpret this right; no unauthorized parties should have access to any unit. This means that the property manager must enforce key control for residents at all times and must be ever-vigilant with regard to other access points, such as windows and doors other than the primary unit entrance door. To this end, locks to each unit should be changed or re-keyed every time a resident moves in or out. To accomplish this as cost effectively as possible, locks on units can be "traded" when a resident moves out. This way, the locks need not be re-keyed, just stored for a while. For example, a 300-unit property would have 312 lock sets, 300 on the units and 12 as spares. As a unit is vacated, one of the spare sets is put into the unit, and the locks in the unit are put in the spare carton. As the next unit is vacated, the same procedure is followed and so on. Over time, the distribution of locks in the property will be random, and the locks from the last 12 move-outs will not be in a unit. If a former resident were to keep a key to break into the new resident's home, she/he would have to figure out where the key fit. And it might not fit anywhere. This system is not as foolproof as re-keying everything on turnover, but it is much better than leaving the locks in place and it saves a considerable amount of money over re-keying.

There are systems available that allow a property manager to electronically alter the lock set/key system at any time. These systems usually include either a magnetic card or a computer chip embedded in the key. Either of these systems can be reprogrammed using the on-site management office computer. Systems such as these are useful in properties with high turnover rates because they save the cost and effort of physically re-keying locks.

Unit keys, mailbox keys, and common area access keys should be issued at the time of move-in, and the resident should sign a receipt acknowledging receipt of those keys (Fig. 6–1).

To the maximum extent possible, the keys issued to a resident should not permit duplication. All major lock manufacturers have restricted-distribution keyways available. Although they look like normal keys, these keys have additional ridges or grooves in them that make duplication in hardware stores or other locations much more difficult. The manager should switch to these restricted keys where feasible. Alternatives to metal keys include card, magnetic key, or computer chip access systems and palm or fingerprint readers, all of which offer the additional benefit of permitting access to multiple locks in addition to the apartment door lock, such as locks to garages, health facilities, and other common areas.

Residents who lose keys should sign an acknowledgment (Fig. 6–2) before being issued new keys.

The above measures should be documented as part of the property's operations manual and risk management plan and documented in the resident handbook as appropriate.

In addition to keeping careful control over unit keys, the manager should take precautions to ensure that the units themselves are relatively difficult to enter, even with a key. One way of adding to resident security and reducing the possibility of a claim is to add blind bolts to the doors. A blind bolt is a dead bolt lock with no cylinder on the outside of the door. It can only be used when the unit is occupied.

It is important to note here that double-cylinder locks (i.e., locks that require a key for both entry and exit) can themselves pose a serious risk in the event of a fire or other emergency. Because of this, some jurisdictions have codes prohibiting double-cylinder locks altogether. The use of double-cylinder locks should be avoided.

A secure means of locking all windows from the inside and limiting their opening to four inches or less also should be provided. Limiting the window opening to four inches or less will prevent someone from crawling in the window to gain access and also will prevent the possibility of a child

FIGURE 6–1. Key Receipt Acknowledgment

I/We have received the following keys for our residence. I/We agree to be responsible for these keys, and will obtain duplicates only from

____

(Name of property)

The number of keys received is as follows:

_____________ Unit keys

_____________ Lobby entrance keys

_____________ Garage entrance keys

_____________ Mailbox keys

I/We understand that, if I/we fail to return these keys when I/we vacate the apartment, I/we will be responsible for a re-keying charge of $ _____________per key.

Dated this _____________________ Day of _______________________ , 2________.

____

Lessee

____

Lessee

Acknowledged:

____

Authorized representative

____

(Name of property)

FIGURE 6–2. Lost/Stolen Key Acknowledgment

____
(Name of property)

I/We have hereby requested the replacement of the following keys which have been stolen from me/us or been lost or misplaced.

The number of keys received is as follows:

_____________ Unit keys

_____________ Lobby entrance keys

_____________ Garage entrance keys

_____________ Mailbox keys

I/We understand that the management of ___________(Name of property)__________ has advised me/us that in the case of lost unit keys, management recommends the replacement of the locks to prevent unauthorized entry to our unit, and possible theft or personal injury. I/we decline to have the locks changed and will hold the management and ownership of ________(Name of property)________ harmless from any damages resulting from this decision.

Dated this ______________________ Day of ________________________ , 2________.

____
Lessee:

____
Lessee:

Acknowledged:

____
Authorized representative:

____
(Name of property)

crawling or falling out the window. In the interest of child safety, window guards or window stops should be installed in all units above the first floor where young children are in residence. However, under all circumstances, windows should open readily from the inside in case of fire.

A manager should look carefully at how the windows and patio door walls are designed and have them modified, if necessary. As an example, one well-known type of aluminum window commonly used in apartments is designed to allow broken glass to be changed easily. However, someone familiar with the design can break into the unit by removing the glass pane, replacing the pane, and leaving virtually no trace of having been in the unit. Clearly, therefore, modifying these windows or replacing them entirely is in order. Certainly, they should not be ordered or reordered.

To the maximum extent the property's operating budget will permit, a property manager should review all possible means of access into units and make them as difficult to break into as possible. Quite often, unit security can be increased substantially with just a few inexpensive changes to make entry more difficult or time-consuming. Whatever unit security steps the property takes should be documented in the operations manual and risk management plan.

PROPERTY-WIDE KEY SECURITY

The property manager must be absolutely meticulous in managing the property's keys and keying system. Keys in the property's keying system include every key that offers access to any lock in the property, from individual dwelling units to the ignitions of property-owned vehicles to the file cabinets in the rental office. From a legal perspective, although the courts have provided no clear guidelines on keys, and case law and precedent govern the approach in most cases, in some jurisdictions the law allows for guilt by implication. That is to say that if a court holds that landlords (read owners and managers) have a duty to protect residents from criminal acts that are reasonably foreseeable, then a landlord would be held liable in an access-related incident if her/his building had a prior key problem.

Although master keys—single keys that open multiple locks—once served as the entry mechanism in virtually all multihousing communities, today they are fairly rare. The general rule on master keys is not to have them at all if they can be avoided. If a property has master keys, the manager must be extremely careful in designating who has access to them and what they use them for. This is true because master keys are quite dangerous if one becomes lost. If a master key is lost, especially if it is on the grounds of the community, the manager should give extremely serious consideration to rekeying the entire community. The expense is considerable, but so is a multimillion dollar judgment. Some general procedures regarding master keys appear in Figure 6–3.

The caveats against master keys notwithstanding, duplicate apartment keys may be retained by the property manager and the management office provided a system to track the usage of such keys is in place. Several key control systems are widely available. These systems may be as simple as keeping keys in sealed envelopes that must be opened to be used, to complex key tracking systems that use computer-controlled key draws.

In all cases, when it comes to keys the property manager must always remember and communicate to every member of the property staff that each and every property key should be treated as if it costs a million dollars because it could cost that much if it is lost or improperly handled. All key-related policies and procedures should be documented in the property's operations manual and risk management plan.

RISK MANAGEMENT IN THE PROPERTY'S COMMON AREAS

To provide the safest, most secure environment, the property manager must focus her/his risk management activities not only on individual dwelling units but also on the property's common exterior areas and commonly used interior areas. It is in these areas that the property manager must pay particular attention to reducing architectural and maintenance risks. The common areas risk management items that require particular attention are detailed below.

LIGHTING

It is the property manager's responsibility to periodically inspect all lighting throughout the common areas of the property, indoors and out, to determine that existing lighting provides sufficient light to ensure residents' safety during the dark hours. This survey becomes particularly important as a property ages because the plants used in landscaping will grow. After a time, if they are not properly trimmed, they will encroach on doorways and walkways. The property manager should pay particular attention to any place that could hide a mugger or rapist after dark or at any time. One of the most effective means of adding security in a potentially dangerous area is to increase the lighting in that area.

PEDESTRIAN TRAFFIC FLOW

Traffic flow deserves careful study. Property managers should review how residents and guests enter and leave the building(s), move through the parking areas, and enter and leave the property site. If an entrance area is hard to observe from a distance or if it is used infrequently, the property manager may want to close it off and limit its use to emergencies. Most buildings have multiple exits, which are required by fire codes. However, these exits need not all be accessible from the outside.

INTERIOR CORRIDORS AND STAIRS

The property manager also should review access to, and the safety of, all interior spaces, especially in buildings with no control over access. Specific attention should be paid to places where potential attackers or thieves could hide and to their escape routes. Most fire regulations require that all stairwells be accessible for leaving a building, but re-entry access to a residential floor from inside a stairwell may be re-

FIGURE 6-3. Procedures for Master Keys

- Restrict their distribution to only those staff members who must absolutely have them to function.
- To the maximum extent possible, all masters should be locked daily in a secure cabinet or safe that is accessible only to one or at most two persons during the hours the office is closed
- Make sure that master keys are never placed on key rings with identification that would connect them to the property if they are lost.
- Never mark a master key to distinguish it from other keys.
- Never entrust a master key to tradespeople or to residents to let themselves back into their units.
- Use non-duplicable blanks for master keys and stay away from single pin master keys if possible.
- Obtain a signed permission form to check the background and possible criminal record of potential employees who will have access to keys of any sort or to any part of the property. Do a thorough check.
- Bond all employees with access to any property keys either individually or under a master policy.

stricted in some localities. A manager might also place alarms on some doors that will go off if the door is used. The goal is to maximize the safety of residents.

FACILITIES AND AMENITIES, WITH EMPHASIS ON POOLS AND PLAYGROUNDS

Property managers should give particularly close scrutiny to the facilities and amenities on the property and how they may be used or misused. Swimming pools are particularly dangerous and have been the basis of much litigation pertaining to injuries and drownings. The injuries tend to result from diving or swimming without a lifeguard on duty, occasionally after pool hours. Of course, as required by law or the property's liability insurance company, a qualified lifeguard should be on duty at all times during pool operating hours. Diving boards are a significant source of claims and the best solution may be to remove them entirely. In fact, many insurers require their removal. At minimum, pool rules should require that all children under the age of 16 be accompanied by an adult or guardian when using the pool. Setting the age that high cuts down on the practice of parents sending their children to the pool alone so that management becomes a babysitter by default.

The pool should be fully equipped with the required emergency water safety equipment such as life rings with attached rope long enough to reach at least half of the pool's length, shepherd's hooks, and explanatory signs showing their use. A vividly marked and highly visible telephone marked "For Emergency Use Only" should be located no higher than 48 inches off the deck to be accessible even by small children. This phone should not require any coins but should be a direct connect to 911 or local emergency services. A written script, encased in waterproof casing, should be prominently adjacent to the phone and should provide the name and address of the community and the location of the pool within the community. As an additional safety feature and also as a likely requirement of the property's insurance underwriters, there should be only one entrance/exit gate for the pool and it should be self-locking.

Pool fences should be carefully checked to ensure that they are secure, that a child cannot crawl through them, and that they are high enough to discourage climbing. The pool entrance(s) should be locked at all times when the pool is not open for use. Keeping the pool area well lit at all times discourages fence jumping after hours.

Playgrounds are another source of risk management problems. Playground equipment should be commercial grade and installed in compliance with the manufacturers' specifications. Attention to design can keep the possibility of injury to a minimum. Should an injury occur and a lawsuit result, the property would probably be judged partly on whether the equipment involved is normal to the area. If the school districts around a property do not have a particular piece of equipment, the property probably should not have it either. Schools are quite careful to investigate the safety of their equipment and usually remove equipment that is considered dangerous. Watching their purchases for playgrounds provides a general guide to what is acceptable in the area.

ATTRACTIVE NUISANCE

An attractive nuisance is an unprotected or unsafe object, condition, or installation that tempts children to play in, on, or with it even though they risk injury to do so. Anything that could be considered an attractive nuisance requires the property manager's close attention. Attractive nuisances could include storm water run-off retention maintenance equipment, storage areas, sewage lift stations, and treatment plants. In reviewing the property for attractive nuisances, managers must consider how the hazardous object or area would appeal to youngsters; determine how best to keep youngsters out or, if that is not possible, how to reduce that appeal; examine the options for avoiding or preventing accidents; and minimize the danger.

In the case of a retention pond, for example, a manager should make sure the grade at the edge of the pond is gradual so that any child who fell in could get out easily. Playground areas should be far enough away from the pond to discourage toddlers from wandering there. If possible, the pond should be fully fenced off.

For reasons only a 6-year-old can explain, garbage handling areas are especially attractive. Therefore, the manager must review how dumpsters and compactors are positioned and what could happen if a child climbed into one. Compactors deserve special attention because of their potential for causing severe injuries. Key-controlled actuators should be used to prevent accidents, and regular checks should ensure that all safety systems are kept operational at all times.

Occasionally the solutions to these problems are aesthetically unattractive. If so, a manager needs to carefully weigh good looks against the potential for an accident followed by a claim.

In addition to performing the risk management audit described above, the property manager can contribute significantly to the effectiveness of a risk management program by being acutely aware of existing or potential risks during scheduled, unscheduled, and informal property-wide maintenance checks and taking action immediately to reduce or eliminate observed risks. All risk management actions that are taken should become part of the property's operations manual and should be included in the property's risk management plan. A partial list of potential risk hazards appears in Figure 6–4.

PROPERTY-WIDE FIRE AND EMERGENCY SAFETY

Fire prevention and occupant protection in the event of a fire or other natural disaster or emergency are of vital importance to the property manager, the management firm, and the owner. An effective fire and emergency safety plan is essential to the operation of any property.

FIRE PREVENTION

The key to an effective fire safety plan is to prevent a fire from happening in the first place. This task breaks down into three elements:

- Design
- Inspection and maintenance
- Resident education

Design

The design element of fire prevention is largely out of the property manager's control. The basic fire safety design provisions common to all multifamily buildings include partitions to slow flame spread, smoke detection devices, fire extinguishers, and fire hydrants. As the buildings get larger and more complex, additional fire safety features may include sprinklers, communications systems, special elevator controls, positive pressure stairwells, and a host of other specialized systems.

The property manager and the entire property staff should familiarize themselves with all of the fire safety design features of their particular property. In the course of their day-to-day work, they must guard against making changes or modifications that compromise the safety systems. The maintenance staff must be particularly careful because normal operations at the property can change the fire prevention systems designed into the building. For example, if a section

FIGURE 6-4. Potential Hazards

- Inoperative fire alarm systems or fire fighting equipment
- Improperly handled and stored flammable materials
- Improperly stored papers and rags
- Actual and potential gas leaks
- Sparking, damaged, or worn electrical connections
- Improperly protected plate glass, and plate glass that is not marked or poorly marked or not visible
- Loose or broken steps or disintegrating sidewalk or curbs
- Blocked exits and passageways
- Doors not removed or secured on stored refrigerator
- Hanging or dead limbs and dead trees
- Tree limbs rubbing on electrical wires
- Obstructed chimneys and vent stacks
- Missing or broken drain and catch basin covers
- Blocked storm drains
- Inadequate auto safety and speed signs
- Missing or faded crosswalks lines
- Cracks and potholes in streets, driveways, and parking lots
- Disintegrating speed bumps

of pipe between two units is replaced, the penetration must be properly sealed after the replacement or the fire protection provided by the partition may be significantly reduced.

Managers of aging properties should consider design changes that can be made to improve the safety of their buildings when major rehabilitation or maintenance work is undertaken.

Inspection and Maintenance

The property manager and staff have the primary responsibility for inspecting and maintaining a property's fire safety systems. During her/his routine safety inspections of the property, the property manager should look for conditions that are unsafe and pay particular attention to those that could become unsafe. Correcting conditions before they become dangerous is crucial to cost-effective risk management. However, safety consciousness should be practiced by the manager at all times. As previously indicated, during the regular weekly inspection and other movement around the property, the manager and staff should note, report, and take action to correct these situations so that little is left to record during the scheduled safety inspection.

Individual Units

For those properties with units equipped with individual smoke detectors and fire extinguishers, an annual inspection and tagging program should be undertaken and maintained. The fire extinguisher in each unit should be inspected and serviced annually. The work of recharging and certifying fire extinguishers must be done by someone trained in servicing them. Usually this is an outside contractor, but some large properties have an employee trained to service them for convenience and economy.

Likewise, all smoke detectors should be cleaned, tested, and tagged. using a tag of the type illustrated in Figure 6–5. Smoke detectors should be inspected at least quarterly and preferably monthly. The inspection date of each fire extinguisher also should be recorded in the unit file as well as on the tag.

In some buildings the smoke detection systems are especially sensitive and will yield false alarms fairly often. In those circumstances, residents occasionally disconnect the systems. As with many management situations, the property manager's goals in this one are to correct the immediate problem and to put the situation in writing in case the problem recurs. Therefore, any time an inspection discloses a disconnected unit, the property manager should:

- Direct the property maintenance supervisor or other maintenance technician to make sure the unit is reconnected immediately
- Make a note about the incident in the resident's file
- Issue a letter to the resident notifying her/him that disconnecting the alarm is a rule violation and that another violation is grounds for eviction

An increasing number of multifamily residences are now being built with sprinklers in the dwelling units and/or the common areas. Some state and local building codes require that certain types of structures or common areas be equipped with sprinkler heads or complete sprinkler systems. This is especially true in construction where units share common walls.

All sprinkler systems need to be serviced and tested annually to ensure that they will operate when needed. Sprinkler systems are quite complex, and servicing should be done by a properly trained contractor or staff member.

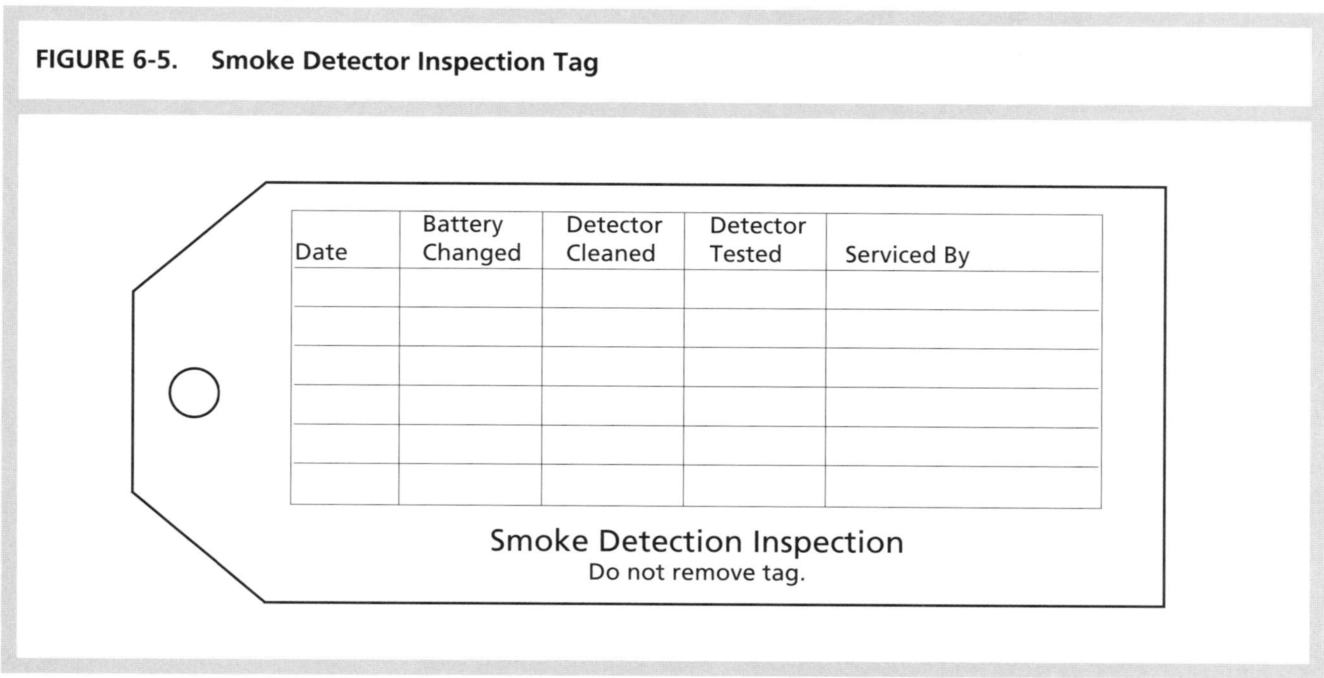

Date	Battery Changed	Detector Cleaned	Detector Tested	Serviced By

Smoke Detection Inspection
Do not remove tag.

FIGURE 6-5. Smoke Detector Inspection Tag

Storage Areas

Individual storage lockers and storage rooms in residential buildings are often overlooked by both managers and maintenance staff in checking for fire safety. A thorough inspection of the storage area will often yield an incredible quantity of dangerous material that should not be stored in the lockers. When they move in, residents should be given a storage list detailing what can and, more importantly, what cannot be kept in a storage area, and this information should be included in the resident handbook. Forbidden items that are commonly found in storage areas include:

- Gasoline
- Fuel oil
- Kerosene
- Lacquer thinner
- Paint thinners and reducers
- Alcohol
- All types of bottled gases
- Fireworks
- Ammunition

In addition, many residents have recreational equipment and vehicles that use liquid or gas fuels, and they often store these forbidden items in their storage lockers:

- Motorcycles
- Snowmobiles
- Outboard motors
- Gas barbecues
- Camping equipment

Residents will store fuel cans for these items without thinking of the potential consequences. Gas barbecue grills can pose a hazard because they generally use liquid petroleum gas, which is heavier than air and has no odor. One grill with a 20-pound LP bottle has enough gas in it to blow out the end of a building quite easily. The user instructions on many grills will note that they should not be stored in an enclosed area with the gas supply connected, but some residents do not follow the instructions.

In some residential properties, the manager may build exterior ventilated storage space so residents will not be tempted to store those dangerous items in interior storage rooms. But regardless of the storage facility itself, regular inspections of all storage rooms is a good practice. During these inspections, the manager can have dangerous items removed and also ensure that all aisles are clear.

All storage areas should be equipped with smoke detectors, and ABC-rated fire extinguishers, sized for the floor space involved, should be located at each door. Fire extinguishers are rated by the National Fire Prevention Association according to the type and size of fire for which they are effective. The types of fires are listed in Figure 6–6. A sprinkler system also can be a valuable risk-reducing measure in enclosed spaces that are seldom used and that contain combustible items.

Mechanical Rooms, Workshops, and Maintenance Storage

The manager should regularly inspect and review fire and safety precautions in all of the following rooms:

- Boiler and pump rooms
- Workshops
- Storage areas
- Stroller rooms
- Any other areas both accessible and not accessible to residents

All maintenance areas, machinery rooms, and related areas should be kept clean. They should contain the proper fire detection and firefighting equipment. Storage of dangerous materials should be kept to a minimum, and all flammable liquids should be stored in explosion-proof containers or cabinets. All oxidizers, such as pool chlorine, should be carefully stored away from other flammable materials because when they are wet some oxidizers can generate enough heat to ignite.

Fire and Emergency Equipment

Managers of mid- and high-rise buildings should consult a fire safety contractor to design an inspection and operation schedule that will keep the fire and emergency safety equipment in proper working order at all times. This equipment might include:

- Alarm annunciator systems
- Elevator controls
- Solenoid-actuated doors
- Wet or dry pipe sprinkler systems
- Fire pumps
- Smoke shafts
- Related items

Sound preventive maintenance programs are especially important for fire pumps and related water distribution sys-

FIGURE 6-6. Ratings for Fire Extinguishers

Class A — Combustibles, such as wood, paper, textiles, plastic, and rubber

Class B — Flammable liquids, such as cooking oil, paint thinner, gasoline, and kerosene

Class C — Electrical fires

tems to ensure that these systems will work reliably when called upon. The systems should be full-load tested at least at the manufacturers' recommended intervals, and more often if possible. Standby diesel pump and generator sets are prone to fuel system and bearing failure if they are not run at full load on a regular schedule. The same caution applies to standby or emergency lighting. Hose racks, extinguisher cabinets, and standpipes need to be cleaned, inspected, and serviced at recommended intervals as well.

Emergency Lighting, Exit Identification, and Fire Doors

Many types of buildings with interior corridors have emergency and exit lights that should be tested and inspected regularly. A schedule of preventive maintenance must be set up to ensure that the battery-powered emergency light systems are in working order at all times.

Exit lights must be kept operational at all times. Fire doors should either be equipped with alarm-actuated latches or kept in the closed position at all times.

The local fire marshal can be a valuable source of information for fire safety and inspection programs. If a fire marshal inspects the residents' storage areas and finds violations, a notice to desist from the marshal to the resident, possibly accompanied by a fine, may be more effective at achieving compliance than a note from management. Providing a map or layout of the property to the fire marshal can speed help to the property and its residents in an emergency. In addition, the fire marshal should receive a list of telephone numbers of staff persons to be contacted in an emergency.

Resident Education

One of the most important elements of a property's fire and emergency safety program is ensuring that residents know what to do in case a fire or emergency occurs. Some states and local jurisdictions have adopted statutes requiring building managers to establish emergency and evacuation plans for all buildings and to make sure that all residents know how to react in an emergency. For example, California has comprehensive statutes because of the threat of earthquakes, and similar statutes are becoming common in large metropolitan areas.

If the individual units do not open to the outside, an evacuation map with the fire exits clearly marked must be posted in each unit. Depending on the type of unit and its location in a building, the instructions can be simple or complex. An excellent location for the evacuation map is on the inside of the front door of the unit. Signs at all elevator call button locations should instruct residents to use the stairs in case of fire.

In elevator buildings, the manager should take special precautions for handicapped residents living above the first floor who cannot use stairs. The manager must ensure that the fire department knows their locations and that the handicapped residents know what to do in case of fire.

In some locales, fire departments ask that residents remain inside their units and wait to be escorted from the building. This practice is common in fire-resistive high-rise structures in which fire stairwells need to be kept clear for firefighters and equipment until the fire is contained.

The property manager should contact the local fire department to obtain the name, location, and contact information of the first response fire company. The manager should then visit the company and invite its members to visit the property to review and provide advice regarding the property's fire prevention plan.

The property's evacuation procedures should be detailed in the resident handbook, along with any special emergency procedures for hurricanes, tornados, or earthquakes if they are common in the area. The fire prevention bureau of the local fire department can help the manager develop evacuation plans and information for the resident handbook. Every aspect of the property's fire and emergency safety plan should be documented in the operations manual and the risk management plan.

SECURITY/MONITORING SYSTEMS, SECURITY PERSONNEL, AND PROPERTY MONITORING AS A SELLING FEATURE

SECURITY SYSTEMS

There are four types of security systems that deserve discussion relative to risk management: entry control systems such as lobby intercoms; surveillance systems that monitor comings and goings in common areas; individual dwelling unit security systems; and security systems that prevent tampering with the property's computer systems. The property manager must be familiar with all of these and their potential benefits to the property's risk management program.

Entry Control Systems

Many original entry control systems, most commonly found in high-rise buildings, require that visitors be "buzzed in" by residents before the lobby door or an outer door will open and admit them into the building. In these systems, a directory of residents is located in the outer lobby or vestibule. Each resident's name is listed and is attached to a buzzer that buzzes their apartment when pushed by a visitor. The buzzer activates an intercom that allows the visitor and the resident to converse. If the resident wishes to admit the visitor to the building, the resident pushes a button located on a panel in her/his unit. The button releases the solenoid latch and the visitor can open the door.

The primary problem with this type of entry control system is that it is especially prone to vandalism. A more modern system works basically the same way except that voice communication and latch release are activated through the resident's regular telephone.

In either case, in the interest of risk management, it is imperative that the manager ensure that the entry intercom device is operational at all times. It is equally important for the property manager to communicate to residents the importance of ascertaining the positive identity of a visitor before allowing access and the importance of closing entry doors behind oneself and not allowing entry into the building to anyone who does not belong there. These considerations must be included in the property's operations manual, risk management plan, and the resident handbook.

Surveillance Systems

Electronic surveillance systems are used by properties that wish to observe activity in one or more locations. Most surveillance systems include options for multiple displays and digital recordings. Wherever a surveillance system is installed and regardless of the reason, unless there is a video monitor to display what is being viewed and someone to watch the monitor, the surveillance system might as well not be there. The manner in which a property's surveillance system will be monitored and used should be included in the property's operations manual and risk management plan.

Individual Dwelling Unit Monitoring Systems

If the property offers individual dwelling unit monitoring systems as an amenity, then in the interest of risk management the property manager must ensure that every system in every unit is completely operational at all times. If the property does not provide this amenity and residents wish to install their own monitoring systems in their units, they should be allowed to do so with the understanding that the property is not responsible for the operation of the private system and that the system must be able to be removed, without permanent damage to the unit, when the resident moves out. These stipulations should be included in the property's operations manual, risk management plan, and resident handbook.

Computer Security

The management company and property manager must be careful to protect all computer equipment and files from such risks as viruses, worms, and "hacking." Viruses and worms are introduced into computer systems via external sources, such as the through an e-mail transmission or through the use of an infected disk. Should a virus or worm infect a computer system, it can destroy the entire database and those of all computers to which the infected computer is networked. It can also travel to other, distant computers that receive transmissions from the originally infected computer. Fortunately, there are many readily available and easy-to-install products that can protect computers from viruses and worms, and the property manager should ensure that they have been installed as a prudent risk management step.

"Hackers," or people who can break into computer systems either on-site or remotely, also present a risk. Both the rental and employment files of a multihousing property contain confidential information that should not be allowed to be made public or be in the possession of individuals who may wish to use that information for their own purposes. In addition, hackers can change rental, maintenance, and other records and wreak havoc on a management company's and/or property office's record-keeping system.

For these reasons, property managers who are responsible for the administration of one or more computer systems should take advantage of every computer-related security measure available, such as passwords, special codes, and firewalls, and should ensure to the greatest extent possible that only authorized individuals have access to the property's computer systems. All computer security-related measures should be included in the property's operations manual and its risk management plan.

SECURITY PERSONNEL

Residential properties that employ individuals whose sole responsibility is to patrol the premises and present the appearance of protection do so in one of two ways: they either employ these individuals directly or they contract out for their services through a security company. These individuals may patrol the property premises on a watch clock system, which requires that they "punch in" to time clocks located at various check points around the property to verify that they did their "rounds" or they may patrol using central station reporting, which requires them to call the central station at specified times for the same purpose. They may be assigned to walking patrols, motor patrols, even dog patrols, or they may be seated permanently at the entrance or in the lobby of a property building. However they are engaged and whatever type of service they provide, these individuals can be an important addition to the security of a property. They also can be another source of potential claims, particularly if they are armed.

In working with any security service, whether it is internal or subcontracted, the property manager must make certain that the service is operated in a professional manner, that it is adequately insured, and that the security personnel are properly trained and, if required, have retention and arrest authority from the local police jurisdiction. A poorly trained individual carrying a gun is an accident waiting to happen, and false arrest suits and claims of use of excessive force in dealing with trespassers are far too common to dismiss lightly. In some areas, proper insurance for security personnel can mean several million dollars, including false arrest coverage, and more if guns are carried.

Sometimes, well-trained, professional safety workers are scarce or unavailable. In those locales where hiring off-duty police officers is legal, a property manager may consider hiring them because police are well trained in both the law and the use of firearms. Also, a benefit of having police actually living in a residential property is that police vehicles discourage trespassers and other intruders from loitering there. However, the practice of properties providing a rent discount or rent-free dwelling unit to a police officer so that her/his patrol car is visible to residents and visitors may present its own type of risk because such "gifts" are illegal in many jurisdictions and may be interpreted as a bribe.

In any case, any individual hired to patrol the property premises must be directly accountable to the property manager, and the functions of these individuals must be clearly stated in the property's operations manual and risk management plan.

PROPERTY MONITORING AS A SELLING FEATURE

Although some multihousing professionals view the presence of a property monitoring system as a strong marketing tool, others believe that it should not be directly advertised because such advertisement could be misunderstood and utilized later in a legal proceeding against the property. If a property utilizes personnel for monitoring, such personnel should be hired as safety officers, compliance managers, lobby attendants, doormen, night managers, house officers, or resident aides.

The word "security" should not be in their titles, and their specific duties should be clearly spell out in their job descriptions.

In general, extreme care must be exercised in deciding how to market the safety features of a community without mentioning or implying security. To this end, the property manager may want to attach an addendum to the lease to be signed by each resident and stating that the property has made no representation concerning the safety of the community, no warranty or guarantee regarding the safety or security of the residents, and will not provide total reliance on security devices or measures that may fail for any number of reasons. A sample of such a lease addendum appears in Figure 6–7.

RISK MANAGEMENT AND PROPERTY STAFF

Throughout this text, the property manager's role as the decision maker and leader at the property has been emphasized. Nowhere is this more relevant than in a discussion of risk management. Here, the property manager must know exactly what to do and must have prepared the property staff in advance so that any situation that may arise will be handled as professionally and appropriately as possible.

It is the property manager's responsibility to keep the property's on-site staff well informed about fire, emergency, resident, and worker safety issues so that staff members will respond correctly in the event of a fire, an accident, or an emergency. This responsibility should be clearly defined in the property's operations manual and risk management plan.

Property staff members also should know how to handle hazards they may encounter in their normal workday. For example, multihousing properties commonly use hazardous substances in repair and maintenance of their facilities. All employees should be familiar with accepted standards for handling materials such as pesticides, herbicides, oxidizers (chlorine and related chemicals), naphtha and benzene products, urethanes, and other potentially dangerous materials. Use of these materials is governed by numerous regulations and requirements. The property manager should be familiar with all relevant local codes and requirements of the Occupational Safety and Health Administration (OSHA), National Institute of Occupational Safety and Health (NIOSH), National Fire Prevention Association (NFPA), National Electrical Code (NEC), and any others that may apply.

The OSHA Hazard Communication Standard (HazCom) requires all employers to:

- Train their employees on the hazards of the chemicals to which they are exposed in the course of their work and on the protective measures they need to take to protect themselves
- Maintain MSD sheets and labels for all hazardous materials
- Develop a written hazard communication program that describes how the property is meeting its obligations under HazCom and include this program in the property's operations manual and risk management plan

To help their members meet OSHA's hazard communications mandate, the National Association of Home Builders, the American Subcontractors Association, and the Associated Builders and Contractors, Inc., have copublished *Hazard Communication: A Compliance Kit for the Construction Industry* (Washington, DC: National Association of Home Builders). It is available from the NAHB Business Management Department. Co-sponsored by 22 additional industry organizations, this kit includes:

- Hazard Communication: A Guide for the Construction Industry, a 92-page book
- *Hazard Communication: An Employee Training Log*
- *Employee Rights Responsibilities Under the OSHA Hazard Communication Standard,* an employee handout that can also be used as a poster
- *Hazard Communication Management Training,* an audiocassette for employers and managers
- *Hazard Communication: Employee Training for the Construction Industry,* a videocassette for employees

The property manager should maintain the MSD sheets on the job site for all materials used on the site so that in the event of an accident the necessary information is available to emergency personnel treating the affected individuals. The manager also should ensure that the safety cautions called for in the use of hazardous substances are observed and that the needed protection is supplied. These protections include the use of eye protection, respirators, and gloves in many cases. For instance, properties using gas chlorine for treatment of the water in swimming pools or sewage will need appropriate gas masks, containment gear, and warning systems to deal with chlorine leaks. Appropriate safety gear should be kept near areas where materials are stored and used.

In addition to complying with the HazCom regulations, any property storing more than 10,000 pounds (approximately 1,250 gallons) of a hazardous substance would be subject to the Environmental Protection Agency's Community Right-To-Know Regulations. Properties would rarely have such large quantities on hand; however, managers of extremely large properties should be aware of these regulations in the event a major reroofing, remodeling, or redecoration involves exceptionally large quantities of tar, paint, or other toxic substance.

For all products used by property employees in maintenance, repair, and grounds keeping, a wise procedure is to use the least toxic product that will do the job. Having one or more employees trained in first aid and cardiopulmonary resuscitation (CPR) procedures is also a good idea. The American Red Cross regularly sponsors courses in local school districts, and similar courses are sometimes available through hospitals and other organizations. These courses are valuable as risk management tools.

In addition to the above, all property staff members, from maintenance workers to office staff, should be informed that they have another important role to play in keeping the property safe and secure. Specifically, they should be encouraged to inform the property manager immediately should they ob-

FIGURE 6–7. Lease Addendum for Resident and Occupant Acknowledgment of Property Security Policy

Addendum to Lease Dated ____ /____ /____

Resident and Occupant Acknowledgment of Property Security Policy

No Representation. Residents and Occupants acknowledge that neither Owner nor __(Name of Management Company)__ has made any representations written or oral concerning the safety of the community or the effectiveness or operability of any security devices or security measures installed within or attached to the rented premises.

No Warranty or Guarantee. Residents and Occupants acknowledge that neither Owner nor __(Name of Management Company)__ warrants or guarantees the safety or security of Residents, Occupants, or their guests or invitees against the criminal or wrongful acts of third parties. Each Resident, Occupant, guest, and invitee is responsible for protecting his or her own personal property.

No Reliance on Security Devices or Measures. Residents and Occupants acknowledge that security devices or measures may fail or be thwarted by criminals or by electrical or mechanical malfunction. Therefore, Residents and Occupants acknowledge that they should not rely on such devices or measures and should protect themselves and their property as if these devices or measures did not exist.

Signatures of all adult occupants

________________________________ Date ____________________

________________________________ Date ____________________

________________________________ Date ____________________

________________________________ Date ____________________

This addendum shall be attached to and made part of the lease dated ____ /____ /____ for the premises located at ____.

*This sample addendum provided by Patellis Property Management Co., Marietta, Georgia.

serve or experience anything that could put the property, its residents, workers, or property, at risk.

All employee risk management education, training, and procedures should be documented in the property's operations manual and risk management plan and should be shared with the property employees as appropriate.

THE PROPERTY MANAGER'S EMERGENCY HANDBOOK

The property manager is well advised to compile and maintain an emergency handbook, copies of which should be immediately available both in the management office and at the property manager's home for immediate reference. The emergency handbook should contain all of the items listed in Figure 6–8, along with any other information the property manager deems appropriate.

With this system, the property manager has only to grab one item to be prepared to function in an emergency. Having a well-prepared advance plan and a disaster handbook will make managing easier during the emergency. The entire text of the emergency handbook should be included in the property's operations manual and in its risk management plan so that anyone needing to refer to these documents will have all necessary information at a glance.

RESIDENT INVOLVEMENT IN RISK MANAGEMENT

As described above, it is the property manager's responsibility to provide all necessary security, fire, and emergency safety information to all residents and to do everything possible to ensure that residents will feel comfortable with and know how to use this information. Such information should be contained in the resident handbook and repeated frequently in the property newsletter. However, in the interest of risk management, the property manager must be careful to inform residents of only the safety and security measures the residents themselves can control and not those that only the owner, manager, or property employees control. In this way, the property manager fulfills her/his obligation to help secure the premises but makes no guarantees because guaranteeing security exposes the owner, the management company, and their employees to heavy liability.

WATCHFUL RESIDENTS AND COMMUNITY WATCH PROGRAMS

The caveat in the preceding paragraph notwithstanding, the property manager should encourage residents to be mindful of security at all times and to participate in, to the greatest extent possible, programs to improve security and safety in their own units and throughout the property. To this end, residents, like property staff members, should be encouraged to inform the property manager immediately should they observe or experience anything that could put the property, its residents, workers, visitors, or the general public at risk.

In addition, police departments in many, if not most, jurisdictions have an established community watch program that encourages civilians to participate in the patrolling of their neighborhoods and communities. Such programs, and the community watch signs and decals they provide, are effective security-improving measures. The property manager should contact the community affairs officer at the local police department for information about how to establish such a program in the property and how the residents of her/his property can participate in such a program. Residents who meet police officers in a nonthreatening setting, such as a discussion of the community watch program, often are more likely to view the police as friendly and helpful and call them if a suspicious situation occurs.

FIGURE 6-8. Recommended Contents of Property Manager's Emergency Handbook

- Emergency numbers for police, fire, ambulance besides 911
- Current emergency service numbers of the electric, gas, and water companies
- Updated emergency phone number list for all site staff and management executives as well as the insurance agent if appropriate
- Updated list of the phone numbers for all approved emergency contractors, electricians, plumbers, carpenters, boiler company, elevator company, locksmith, glass contractor, security personnel, and other vendors necessary to secure a site after a fire or other emergency
- Emergency numbers for the local Red Cross and other service agencies in the event that temporary emergency shelter, food, and clothing should be needed for residents
- Copy of the property evacuation plan
- Location and operation of all utility cutoffs, gas, water, and electricity
- Partial set of blueprints detailing major utility services, structural elements, and floor plans
- Keys necessary to access meter rooms, cutoffs, and equipment rooms
- Supply of incident/accident report forms and insurance claim notices

If the property participates in a community watch program, the program itself and the conditions of participation should be documented in the property's operations manual and in its risk management plan.

PROLONGED ABSENCES FROM THE DWELLING UNIT

Property residents are, of course, free to come and go as they please, and many go on vacations or business trips or leave for prolonged periods of time, without alerting the property manager. However, such prolonged absences from dwelling units can present several safety and security risks that both the property manager and residents should be aware of.

When residents are away from home for extended periods, there is often no way to contact them in the event of an emergency such as damage or potential damage to their unit from such sources as a gas or water leak or a fire. What's more, many residents also neglect to suspend mail and newspaper delivery when they go away. This is a security risk because accumulated mail and/or newspapers are sure signs to burglars that no one is home, making the unit an easy mark.

To avoid these potential risk situations, the property manager should communicate to residents the importance of letting an appropriate management office staff member know when the resident plans to be away and how the resident can be contacted. Residents also should be encouraged to suspend mail and newspaper delivery during an absence. If necessary, the property manager should instruct staff members to pick up day-old papers from in front of units during their daily walk of the property to make unoccupied units harder to identify. Information in the resident handbook and frequent reminders in the property newsletter about the use of lighting timers, stopping deliveries, and holding mail while residents are on vacation or business trips will help to increase resident safety and security.

RESIDENTS AND INSURANCE

Resident safety, security, property liability, and the importance of renters' insurance are topics most often contained and discussed in detail within the resident handbook. Additionally, these topics are usually included in the body of the resident lease. A discussion of insurance and risk management appears below.

INSURANCE AND RISK MANAGEMENT

WHO NEEDS TO BE INSURED AND COMMON TYPES OF INSURANCE

When it comes to professionally managed multihousing properties, both the property owner and the owner's managing agent must be insured. Without adequate and appropriate insurance, the owner could conceivably lose her/his/their ownership of the property and possibly even more, and the managing agent could conceivably lose the management company. It is imperative for both the owner and the management company to carry adequate and appropriate insurance coverage.

There are two primary types of insurance coverage in the multihousing industry: property loss insurance and liability insurance. Property loss insurance, which is generally referred to as first-party insurance, deals with loss or damage to the owner's property. Liability insurance (BIPD, or bodily injury and property damage insurance), which is generally referred to as third-party insurance, covers the property owner and the managing agent from claims arising from personal injuries or death or damage to the property of others. Comprehensive general property damage and general liability coverage protects the insureds against negligence resulting in damage to the property or personal injury. It does not, however, cover gross negligence (failing to act in a known risk situation) or fraud.

The major types of insurance coverage are as follows.

Property insurance covers all-risk policies and named peril policies. An all-risk policy covers everything that is not specifically excluded in the policy. Named peril policies cover only those things that are explicitly covered in the policy. Examples of property policy coverage include fire, extended coverage, vandalism and malicious mischief, earthquake coverage (which may be required in a separate policy depending on whether or not it is included), and damage from terrorism. This type of policy also covers the owner's stream of income in the event of a covered claim.

Liability insurance covers bodily injury and damage to the property of others.

Excess or umbrella liability coverage is generally bought in a separate policy to cover the excess over the limit of another policy.

Employee insurance includes such coverages as workers' compensation, disability, and unemployment insurance as required by law.

Other types of insurance coverage include:

- **Garage liability and garage legal liability,** which covers occurrences in the property's parking garage or parking area

- **Boiler and machinery coverage,** which is normally excluded from property policies and is therefore necessary as a separate policy to cover losses caused by a catastrophic occurrence due to machinery in the property

- **Employee dishonesty or fidelity,** which covers employee theft

- **Directors and officers coverage,** which covers claims against directors and officers of shared-interest associations

Both the property owner holding legal title to the property (regardless of whether the owner is an individual, more than one individual, or a corporate entity) and the owner's managing agent should be listed as insureds under the property's property and liability insurance policies. It is recommended that the owner and the management company also secure excess property and liability coverage and that they also carry errors and omissions coverage and catastrophe insurance. Shared-interest associations such as condominiums, cooperatives, and home owners associations also should carry directors and officers insurance.

THE PROPERTY MANAGER AND INSURANCE

With regard to the property's insurance, it is the property manager's responsibility to:

- Maintain the property's insurance records, including knowing what policies are currently in place, what is included in and excluded from existing policies, and what optional coverages are available, what are the premiums for existing policies, and when the existing policies expire
- Understand the principles of deductibles (the owner is liable for the first determined amount of risk before any insurance claim is collected) and coinsurance (the owner is responsible for the last determined amount of risk after the limit of the policy has been reached)
- Understand the possible benefits of an umbrella policy that will protect the property from a major liability claim that exceeds the basic liability coverage
- Understand the principles and ramifications of negligence (breaching a duty of care that results in damage), gross negligence (failing to act in a known risk situation), and fraud
- Factor policy premium payments into annual budgeting as an on-going operating expense and ensure timely payment of policy premiums to ensure uninterrupted coverage
- Ensure compliance with all terms and conditions of existing policies to ensure uninterrupted coverage (e.g., if the policy requires that certain actions be taken after inspections or at other times, the property manager must ensure that these actions are taken)
- Keep up to date with the many rapid changes that occur within the insurance industry and solicit competitive bids for comparable or better coverage prior to the expiration of existing policies to ensure the most comprehensive, most appropriate, and most cost-efficient coverage for the property
- Have at the ready all filing instructions and forms should it become necessary to file a claim
- Work with adjusters
- Maintain records of all required and up-to-date insurance coverages from all contractors and subcontractors engaged to work on the property
- Have a clear understanding with the owner of what the property can do for residents in the event of a major emergency or catastrophe before such an eventuality arises (i.e., the management company and property manager must have clear instructions from the owner relative to such questions as whether the property manager can offer a vacant apartment to a resident whose apartment has been damaged, and such questions must be considered in light of liability factors before the reasons to ask them actually arise)

REPORTING INCIDENTS AND CLAIM ADMINISTRATION

Even the best risk management program will not prevent instances of individuals being injured on the property site or damage to the property or its property. Whenever such an incident occurs, the property manager must document it immediately with whatever information she/he has, even if the information is incomplete, and pass that information on to the senior manager or insurance company as the policies dictate. Of course, the property manager should supplement any partial information provided with new information as it becomes available.

PERSONAL INJURIES

Residents, guests, and staff members may suffer accidents or injuries while on the property premises. Should such an incident occur, the property manager should follow the steps outlined in Figure 6–9 and complete an incident/accident report form as shown in Figure 6–10.

Personal injuries on the site are a serious matter no matter how insignificant they may seem at the time. The best rule of thumb is for the manager to document the incident carefully and to say nothing until she/he has had a chance to discuss the incident with her/his supervisor and, if necessary, with the property's insurance carrier.

In the majority of cases, the matter will end with the treatment of the injury. However, in a small number of cases the injury will result in a liability lawsuit against the property. In those cases, the documentation and lack of compromising statements will support a fair settlement of the case.

The property manager should not hesitate to call either the police or the fire department if a resident, guest, or worker is seriously injured. If a motor vehicle is involved, the police should always be called to file a report. Failure to call the appropriate authorities at the appropriate time could result in a judgment against the property. In addition, the insurance carrier may refuse to cover an incident if the insurance company is not notified, especially in a case in which a person with a minor injury refuses medical treatment but later seeks a jury trial. The property manager should develop guidelines for when to call the local police and fire departments, all staff members should be familiar with them, and the guidelines should be documented in the operations manual and the risk management plan.

Serious injuries and any criminal assaults should be treated with the utmost care by the property manager because in most cases, legal actions arise from such incidents. In the event of a criminal assault, serious injury, or death, the property manager would not only complete an incident/

FIGURE 6-9. Personal Injury Accident Procedures

- Obtain (or see that the injured party obtains) competent medical care immediately to treat the injury and document the physical condition of the injured party
- Fill out an incident/accident report completely (Fig. 6-11) and include all of the facts about the injured party, the circumstances of the injury, and the names, addresses, and phone numbers of all witnesses to the accident
- Notify the appropriate insurance carriers
- Where appropriate, take pictures of the accident scene and any automobiles or equipment involved in the accident
- Direct any questions or inquiries to the property management executive in charge

accident report, she/he also would obtain full copies of the relevant police and coroner's reports and immediately notify the executive to whom she/he reports and the insurance carrier.

In any event, the insurance carrier should be notified as soon as practicable after the incident or as soon as it is known to the manager. Even if the incident will not result in a claim being filed, it is good practice to send a copy of the incident report to the appropriate insurance carriers to put the carriers on notice should a claim later arise. When notification to carriers is made, the liability and excess/umbrella carriers both need to be notified.

All procedures relative to personal injuries at the property site should be documented in the property's operations manual and risk management plan.

PROPERTY DAMAGE TO THE OWNER'S PROPERTY ONLY

Over the life of a property, the property may be damaged from natural causes, from neglect, or as the result of an accident on the part of residents, visitors, or staff. In all cases, the property manager has two primary duties. First, she/he must fully document all damages to the structure and contents. Second, she/he must secure the structure so that further damage is minimized and residents, guests, and staff members are not endangered.

For incidents involving relatively small damages, the incident/accident report in Figure 6–11 would be used. For those situations in which considerable damage or a total loss is suffered, an official loss letter is more appropriate.

When property damage occurs, it must be carefully documented. The property manager should have access to a camera and/or video camera so that she/he can take pictures of and record the entire damaged area before clean-up begins. If photos are taken from all four walls looking into every room, the entire damaged area should be well documented. Keeping an inexpensive camera, a supply of film, and a video camera in the management office helps to reduce delays in documenting an incident.

In cases of fire or explosion, the property manager must obtain a copy of the fire marshal's report on the incident so that the document may be filed with the incident/accident report. In the event of a fire, after the fire trucks leave and the incident reports are filled out, the property manager must secure the building(s) to ensure that no subsequent damage occurs or that any subsequent damage is kept to a minimum. The senior management team must be notified immediately, and all unsafe areas must be closed to residents and visitors as soon as possible.

In some cases, either the owner or insurer may decide to take legal action against a former or current resident for negligence in causing damage. If a large natural disaster occurs, such as a tornado or a hurricane, the property manager will need to document all aspects of the loss carefully from the beginning.

All procedures relative to property damage at the property site should be documented in the property's operations manual and risk management plan.

FILING INSURANCE CLAIMS

Once a loss has occurred and the necessary incident reports have been filled out, the insurance claim should be filed with the insurance carrier. In most property loss situations, the property manager should work closely with the senior manager and the insurance agent who wrote the insurance policies on the property. The settlement of claims can be simple or complex, depending on the amount of damage and on the circumstances. The property manager will sometimes be involved in obtaining bids and estimates for repairs and reconstruction. The process must be managed carefully and should be done in close consultation with the senior manager and owner.

Depending on the type of insurance purchased by the owner, the loss may be fully covered or only partially covered. The manager should be careful to understand what items of repair or reconstruction she/he will be responsible for and follow all instructions carefully. The final settlement of the claim will require the signing of a statement usually called a proof of loss. This document is an agreement between the insured and the insurer that the matter has been fully and finally settled. The property manager should be careful to check with the owner or senior executives of the management company before signing a proof of loss because it legally ends all claims on the insurance carrier for that incident.

All procedures relative to filing insurance claims for the property should be documented in the property's operations manual and risk management plan.

FIGURE 6–10. Incident/Accident Report

Property ______________________ Date of Report ______________________

Date of Incident / Accident ______________________ Time __________ ☐ am ☐ pm

Site of Incident / Accident ______________________

Injured Person(s)

Name ______________________ Age ______ Home Phone ______________________

Business Phone ______________________

Home Address ______________________

Treating Physician ______________________ Hospital ______________________

☐ Tenant ☐ Visitor ☐ Employee ☐ Subcontractor ☐ Other ______________________

Description of Injury ______________________

☐ Tenant ☐ Visitor ☐ Employee ☐ Subcontractor ☐ Other ______________________

Description of Injury ______________________

Witnesses

Name ______________________ Home Phone ______________ Business Phone ______________

Address ______________________ City, State, Zipcode ______________________

☐ Tenant ☐ Visitor ☐ Employee ☐ Subcontractor ☐ Other ______________________

Name ______________________ Home Phone ______________ Business Phone ______________

Address ______________________ City, State, Zipcode ______________________

☐ Tenant ☐ Visitor ☐ Employee ☐ Subcontractor ☐ Other ______________________

Name ______________________ Home Phone ______________ Business Phone ______________

Address ______________________ City, State, Zipcode ______________________

☐ Tenant ☐ Visitor ☐ Employee ☐ Subcontractor ☐ Other ______________________

EMPLOYEE INSURANCE

Federal and state laws require certain types of insurance for employees who are direct employees of the property owner. However, in some jurisdictions, directors, officers, or other individuals who are not on the property payroll also can be deemed employees (depending on the definition in the federal, state, and local jurisdiction). Properties are required to carry Workers Compensation insurance to cover employees who are hurt while on the job. Workers Compensation covers medical costs and also, in most states, monetary damages and generally relieves the property owner of liability if the injured worker is covered under the Workers Compensation policy. Most states also require disability insurance, which covers employees who become disabled while not on the job but are not able to perform their work because of the injury sustained. Disability insurance can be temporary or permanent.

Workers Compensation, disability insurance, and other coverages are typically required, and it is the property manager's responsibility to ensure that the property's employees are appropriately covered.

MONITORING CONTRACTORS', SUBCONTRACTORS', AND VENDORS' INSURANCE COVERAGES

One aspect of risk management that is often overlooked by the property manager but should not be is the need to require contractors, subcontractors, and vendors to be properly insured and to maintain a file of their certificates of insurance. Simply put, if a contractor, subcontractor, or vendor who is not properly insured damages or destroys something while on the property site, the property owner or the owner's insurance carrier may have to cover the cost. Similarly, if a contractor, subcontractor, or vendor does not carry Workers Compensation insurance and one of her/his employees is injured or killed on the property site, the property owner will be responsible for covering that accident under the property's liability and umbrella/excess insurance. Both of these situations can constitute a considerable risk. It is one that the property should not have to bear.

For these reasons, a plan for monitoring contractors', subcontractors', and vendors' certificates of insurance is essential for effective risk management. As part of the contracting procedure, the property manager should require that a certificate of insurance be provided before a contractor, subcontractor, or vendor performs any work on the property site. The sample certificate in Figure 6–11 contains explanatory blocks noting where various policies, policy numbers, carriers, effective dates, and policy limits are shown. This form is widely but not exclusively used. Some insurance companies use certificates that vary somewhat in appearance but contain the same information.

The owner or management company will generally set the minimum limits and types of insurance to be required of all contractors, subcontractors, and vendors. The property manager ought to be familiar with these minimum requirements so that she/he can effectively review certificates that are presented. Contractors', subcontractors', and/or vendors' policies should always name the property as an additional insured party. Insurance companies seldom levy an additional charge for this inclusion, and it increases the protection for the property because it ensures that a notice would be mailed to the property in the event of cancellation of any of the policies.

Requiring that certificates of insurance be submitted in advance is the first part of an effective contractor/subcontractor/vendor insurance plan. The second part is an effective ongoing monitoring system. A simple but effective monitoring program can be implemented with a spreadsheet that indicates when contractors' and subcontractors' insurance policies expire. The manager can send out notices to remind contractors and subcontractors to obtain new certificates of insurance 30 to 60 days in advance of the expiration of their policies.

All insurance-related procedures for monitoring contractors, subcontractors, and vendors should be included in the property's operations manual and risk management plan.

THE MEDIA AND RISK MANAGEMENT

Any large accident or significant crime that occurs in or is connected with a multihousing property will attract the press nearly as soon as the ambulance or fire trucks arrive. Dealing with an emergency is difficult enough for a property manager without a television reporter and film crew following her/him around. On such occasions, the best course of action for a property manager is to be polite but firm. The best response is generally, "We have no comment at this time. We need to take care of our residents first. A statement will be issued later by [name the property management executive in charge of the property]."

The property manager and the community can well do without the sort of publicity that comes from an accident or crime on the property site. And the art of interviewing well is best practiced under less stressful circumstances. What's more, news tapes are increasingly being used in lawsuits. For these reasons, the property manager must be extra careful about making any sort of statement during or in the aftermath of an accident or incident at the property she/he manages.

The property's policies with regard to dealing with the media at all times, and especially in emergency situations, should be documented and included in the operations manual and the risk management plan.

CONCLUSION

Risk management—safeguarding people and property—is how the property manager fulfills her/his responsibilities to provide a reasonably safe and secure environment for the property's residents, visitors, employees, and the general public, and to protect the owner's investment in the property. In an increasingly litigious society with constantly evolving laws and regulations governing the obligations of the landlord (read owner and managing agent), understanding risk

FIGURE 6–11. Sample Certificate of Insurance

ACORD. CERTIFICATE OF INSURANCE

ISSUE DATE (MM/DD/YY)

PRODUCER

THIS CERTIFICATE IS ISSUED AS A MATTER OF INFORMATION ONLY AND CONFERS NO RIGHTS UPON THE CERTIFICATE HOLDER. THIS CERTIFICATE DOES NOT AMEND, EXTEND OR ALTER THE COVERAGE AFFORDED BY THE POLICIES BELOW

COMPANIES AFFORDING COVERAGE

CODE SUB-CODE

INSURED

COMPANY LETTER A

COMPANY LETTER B

COMPANY LETTER C

COMPANY LETTER D

COMPANY LETTER E

COVERAGES

THIS IS TO CERTIFY THAT THE POLICIES OF INSURANCE LISTED BELOW HAVE BEEN ISSUED TO THE INSURED NAMED ABOVE FOR THE POLICY PERIOD INDICATED, NOTWITHSTANDING ANY REQUIREMENT, TERM OR CONDITION OF ANY CONTRACT OR OTHER DOCUMENT WITH RESPECT TO WHICH THIS CERTIFICATE MAY BE ISSUED OR MAY PERTAIN, THE INSURANCE AFFORDED BY THE POLICIES DESCRIBED HEREIN IS SUBJECT TO ALL THE TERMS, EXCLUSIONS AND CONDITIONS OF SUCH POLICIES. LIMITS SHOWN MAY HAVE BEEN REDUCED BY PAID CLAIMS.

CO LTR	TYPE OF INSURANCE	POLICY NUMBER	POLICY EFFECTIVE DATE (MM/DD/YY)	POLICY EXPIRATION DATE (MM/DD/YY)	ALL LIMITS IN THOUSANDS
	GENERAL LIABILITY COMMERCIAL GENERAL LIABILITY CLAIMS MADE OCCUR. OWNER'S & CONTRACTOR'S PROT.				GENERAL AGGREGATE $ PRODUCTS-COMP/OPS AGGREGATE $ PERSONAL & ADVERTISING INJURY $ EACH OCCURRENCE $ FIRE DAMAGE (Any one fire) $ MEDICAL EXPENSE (Any one person) $
	AUTOMOBILE LIABILITY ANY AUTO ALL OWNED AUTOS SCHEDULED AUTOS HIRED AUTOS NON-OWNED AUTOS GARAGE LIABILITY				COMBINED SINGLE LIMIT $ BODILY INJURY (Per person) $ BODILY INJURY (Per accident) $ PROPERTY DAMAGE $
	EXCESS LIABILITY OTHER THAN UMBRELLA FORM				EACH OCCURRENCE $ AGGREGATE $
	WORKER'S COMPENSATION AND EMPLOYERS' LIABILITY				STATUTORY $ (EACH ACCIDENT) $ (DISEASE—POLICY LIMIT) $ (DISEASE—EACH EMPLOYEE)
	OTHER				

DESCRIPTION OF OPERATIONS/LOCATIONS/VEHICLES/RESTRICTIONS/SPECIAL ITEMS

CERTIFICATE HOLDER

CANCELLATION

SHOULD ANY OF THE ABOVE DESCRIBED POLICIES BE CANCELLED BEFORE THE EXPIRATION DATE THEREOF, THE ISSUING COMPANY WILL ENDEAVOR TO MAIL ____ DAYS WRITTEN NOTICE TO THE CERTIFICATE HOLDER NAMED TO THE LEFT, BUT FAILURE TO MAIL SUCH NOTICE SHALL IMPOSE NO OBLIGATION OR LIABILITY OF ANY KIND UPON THE COMPANY, ITS AGENTS OR REPRESENTATIVES.

AUTHORIZED REPRESENTATIVE

ACORD 25-S (3/88) ©ACORD CORPORATION 1988

* ACORD is a broad-based, nonprofit insurance association whose mission is to improve the operating costs and efficiency of the American agency system.

and creating and implementing an effective risk management program are critical to the property manager's work.

Reduced to its most elemental parts, risk management is simply a set of procedures that activate one or more of the four basic risk management tools: avoidance, prevention, transfer, and retention. But these procedures are imperative, and if they are not adhered to the result can be significant and even total loss for the property owner and the management company.

The property-wide risk management audit, ideally conducted quarterly, is the manager's first step and most powerful weapon in developing and implementing a risk management program. The ultimate program must address such considerations as dwelling unit access and property-wide key security; the safety and security of the property's common exterior and commonly used interior areas; property-wide fire and emergency safety; security systems; property staff safety issues and compliance with all employment-related safety regulations and codes; communication with residents regarding security, fire, and emergency safety; the full range of insurance issues; and how best to deal with the media in situations of accident, crime, and/or emergency at the property.

A variety of resources exist to help the property manager generate a practical and effective risk management plan. These resources include the management company senior manager and/or executive property manager, the local police and fire departments, the local weather bureau, the Federal Emergency Management Agency (FEMA), the local Red Cross chapter, and vendors and suppliers of equipment, machinery, and supplies.

In addition to formulating the property's risk management plan (which is a subplan of the property's management maintenance plan, which in turn is a subplan of the property's operations manual), the property manager also must have a complete and up-to-date emergency handbook immediately accessible at all times.

Despite the most competent manager's most superior efforts, a totally accident-free property is not really possible. But with an effective risk management plan and a manager dedicated to implementing it, any multihousing property can be made safer and more secure while keeping operating costs in check at the same time.

Following is a discussion and outline of a full management maintenance plan, including a risk management plan and a disaster plan.

ADDENDUM: THE MANAGEMENT MAINTENANCE PLAN (INCLUDING A RISK MANAGEMENT AND A DISASTER PLAN)

Maintenance refers to the upkeep of a property's structural, physical, mechanical, and aesthetic elements. Risk management refers to the obligation of the landlord (read owner and managing agent) to provide a reasonably safe and secure environment to all residents, guests, and employees of a property and the public in general and the managing agent's obligation to protect and preserve the owner's investment in the property. Both maintenance and risk management are topics so significant to the successful management of a property that each deserves a specific plan, customized to the unique characteristics of the property being managed. It is the property manager's responsibility to formulate these plans and to insert them into the overall operations manual as reference guidelines for the property's maintenance and risk management.

THE MANAGEMENT MAINTENANCE PLAN

To design and facilitate the most effective maintenance plan, the property manager must:

- Determine the property's immediate, medium-, and long-range maintenance needs and how the property's personnel and equipment can meet those needs
- Anticipate possible maintenance emergencies, how the property personnel and equipment can respond to each emergency, and what to do if the personnel and/or equipment are insufficient to respond to the emergency
- Be aware of, and know how to make the best use of, all resources and information necessary to ensure the maintenance of the property

To produce the most useful management maintenance plan, the property manager must be conversant with the necessary data and information, including:

- The market analysis for the property
- The income and expense analysis and rental projections for the property
- The long-term financial analysis for the property
- Management variables, including the type of housing property, the target market, and the property size and location

The property manager's maintenance program should contain clear descriptions of the tasks to be performed and clear assignments of which property personnel are to perform the tasks, when, and how they must document what they have done. The manager must distribute this program in the form of a written plan to every member of the property staff so there are no misunderstandings and everyone knows what is expected.

CONTENTS OF A MANAGEMENT MAINTENANCE PLAN

Although each property's management maintenance plan should be individually customized, the contents of a practical plan should include but may not be limited to:

- An organizational chart of the property staff
- A discussion of job positions and functions within the property staff

- Standard operating procedures for each job function
- Staff task scheduling
- The owner's and hence the manager's goals and plans for:
    - Cultivating property personnel
    - Addressing occupancy issues, including move-in, move-out, and eviction
    - Budget and record-keeping
    - Purchasing and disbursement
    - Security and risk management

Standard operating procedures (SOP) that should be discussed in detail and sample forms that should be inserted into the plan include but may not be limited to:

- Custodial/janitorial maintenance procedures and policies, including all task descriptions and staff scheduling instructions and forms
- Corrective and service maintenance procedures and policies (e.g., response within 24 hours), including all attendant forms and forms filing procedures (e.g., resident service request form, service request record form, part order control form, work completed form, smoke alarm test and energy and water conservation inspections forms, and housekeeping check forms)
- Procedures for monitoring staff service maintenance request handling
- Detailed outlines and procedures for year-round preventive maintenance programs
- Emergency maintenance procedures and protocols, including the arrangements for receiving after-hours emergency calls and all appropriate emergency contact information
- Deferred maintenance policies and procedures
- Unit turnaround procedures and control forms, including vacant unit maintenance and preparation procedures and forms, and resident and staff move-in and move-out instructions and forms
- Policies, procedures, and forms for the engagement of outside maintenance contractors
- Policies, procedures, and forms for property-wide maintenance inspections
- Policies, procedures, and forms for property-wide energy and water conservation
- Maintenance staff policies and procedures, including response to residents who request private work during off-duty hours; tips; and all other policies that the property has established for its staff members
- Policies, procedures, and forms for maintenance-related resident relations

THE RISK MANAGEMENT PLAN

The property manager who wishes to create an effective risk management program will understand and activate the four risk management tools of avoidance (eliminating risk), prevention (minimizing risk), transfer (transferring risk to someone else), and retention (recognizing and assuming the risk) and will take advantage of the various resources for risk management information, including:

- The management company senior manager and/or executive property manager
- The local police and fire departments
- The local weather bureau
- FEMA (the Federal Emergency Management Agency), the local Red Cross chapter, and local hospitals
- Vendors and suppliers of equipment, machinery, and supplies

Each property's risk management plan should be created based on the results of full-property risk management audits, ideally conducted quarterly and updated as required. The risk management plan should be appended to the management maintenance plan and included in the overall operations manual but also should be a standalone plan to provide specific risk management guidelines for the property.

CONTENTS OF A RISK MANAGEMENT PLAN

Although each property's management maintenance plan should be individually customized, the contents of a practical plan should include but may not be limited to:

- All dwelling unit security measures, policies, procedures, and forms, including but not limited to those involving keys, locks, windows, and doors
- All property-wide key policies, procedures, and forms
- All risk management policies, procedures, and forms for the property's common exterior and commonly use interior areas, including but not limited to lighting, pedestrian traffic flow, interior corridors and stairs, and facilities and amenities (with an emphasis on pools and playgrounds and attractive nuisances)
- Every aspect of the property's fire and emergency safety plan, including inspection and maintenance practices, resident education practices, evacuation procedures, and any special emergency procedures for hurricanes, tornadoes, or earthquakes (see the complete discussion

on disaster and emergency planning and procedures below)

- Discussions of the property's security and monitoring systems (including entry control systems, surveillance systems, individual dwelling unit security systems, and computer security systems)

- All employee risk management education, training, policies, procedures, and forms

- Instructions on hazardous materials handling for property staff, compliance with all relevant local codes and requirements, and a written hazard communication program

- All information regarding resident participation in risk management, including but not limited to a discussion of any community watch program that property residents participate in and the conditions of participation

- All insurance-related policies, procedures, and forms for engaging and monitoring contractors, subcontractors, and vendors

- Guidelines for when to call police and/or fire departments in cases of personal injury, property damage, or emergency at the property

- All insurance information, instructions, and documentation, including but not limited to policies, procedures, and forms for filing claims for the property

- The property's policies and procedures with regard to dealing with the media at all times, and especially in extraordinary and/or emergency situations

- The entire text of the property manager's emergency handbook

DISASTER AND EMERGENCY PLANNING AND PROCEDURES

Disasters of natural and human origin kill or injure hundreds of people and cause millions of dollars in property damage each year. The well-publicized disasters of recent years are all too familiar: the Northridge earthquake in California, Hurricane Iniko in Hawaii, flooding in the Midwest, the Oklahoma City bombing of the Alfred P. Murray Federal Building, and most recently at the time of the publication of this text, the devastating destruction of the World Trade Center in New York City and the Pentagon in Washington, D.C., on September 11, 2001 at the hands of terrorists. Add to these the thousands of other weather-related hazards, catastrophes of human origin, and medical traumas that result from emergencies in and around residential properties, and the scope of the tragedies is staggering.

No matter how new or advanced the building or how solid the construction, every property is vulnerable and any property can experience a disaster. In an effort to minimize both damage to the property and injury or loss of life to residents, the astute property manager must plan ahead and be prepared in the event that her/his property is affected by disaster. Careful planning can prevent an emergency altogether.

It is therefore critically important that every property have an emergency and disaster procedures plan. The plan should not stop short at procedures for responding to an emergency but should include prevention and preparedness as well. The greatest property management successes arguably are achieved in prevention rather than in response.

The emergency and disaster procedures plan also must include vital information and checklist forms that will facilitate both prevention and response. Assembling such forms requires careful and comprehensive preparation. Extensive research and teamwork are crucial. There must be an in-depth knowledge of the property and its residents, commercial and professional tenants, the neighborhood, and the community in which the property is located. A property manager cannot create this well-conceived plan alone; it must be formulated in cooperation with an emergency planning team that may be comprised of the property owner, police and fire department officials, disaster recovery contractors, outside service providers, the property's on-site management staff, and the management firm's internal office staff.

An emergency and disaster procedures plan also includes an emergency and disaster management team that actually sees the plan through to completion in an emergency or disaster situation. It is useful if members of this team have participated in the planning process.

Readiness is the key. Sound advance planning will almost always minimize the effects of a disaster on a residential property and may even prevent an emergency from occurring in the first place.

CONTENTS OF AN EMERGENCY AND DISASTER PLAN AND PROCEDURES MANUAL

Although each property's emergency and disaster plan and procedures manual should be individually customized, the contents of a practical plan should include but may not be limited to the following.

REFERENCE INFORMATION

This critical information should be used by those individuals involved in an emergency response, such as building staff and police or fire personnel. This reference information should include:

- Phone numbers of all residents and commercial and professional tenants, including emergency contact numbers

- Phone numbers of all property staff

- Phone numbers of all key management personnel

- Phone numbers of all emergency services, such as police, fire, bomb squad

- A general description of the property
- A list of the property's safety devices along with locations and operating features
- Building systems information (e.g., riser shut-off valve charts)
- Insurance information including the agent's name and emergency contact phone numbers, policy numbers, and carriers
- Key vendor information including 24-hour emergency service phone numbers (for plumbers, electricians, locksmiths)

EMERGENCY TYPES AND TEAM DUTIES

This section of the emergency and disaster plan and procedures manual should contain a general description of each type of emergency followed by a shift-by-shift customized form detailing how team members are dispatched in an actual emergency. This section has the dual purpose of providing crucial background and training information as well as information to be used during the first few critical moments of an emergency. Types of emergencies to be covered are:

- Elevator emergencies
- Crime
- Medical emergencies
- Earthquakes
- Hurricanes
- Fires
- Floods
- Bomb threats and bombs
- Nuclear accidents
- Nuclear attacks
- Biochemical events

EMERGENCY PREVENTION AND PREPAREDNESS

The emergency and disaster plan and procedures manual also should contain forms and checklists to be used by property staff for period inspection and updating of the:

- Sprinkler system
- Standpipe system
- Alarm systems
- Emergency lights
- Fire extinguishers
- Emergency supplies and equipment
- Evacuation routes
- Emergency procedures manual

7

Marketing Rental Housing and the Marketing Plan

THE RELATIONSHIP BETWEEN MARKETING AND SUCCESSFUL MANAGEMENT AND THE CERTIFIED LEASING PROFESSIONAL PROGRAM

Two concepts have been emphasized throughout this text. The first and main concept is the property manager's obligation to increase the property's net operating income (NOI) and produce a profit for the owner. The second—a supporting concept—is that the property manager must be at least familiar with, and ideally should be an expert in, the marketing, sales, and leasing of residential units. These two concepts go hand-in-hand because the most basic way to increase profit in a residential property is to increase income. And the best way to increase income is by increasing occupancy and/or rents. This is accomplished through effective marketing and leasing.

Depending on the size of the management company and/or the specifics of the agreement between the property owner and the management company, the property manager will be responsible to some greater or lesser degree for marketing and leasing the units within the property she/he manages. In larger management companies, an in-house marketing director or a marketing consultant may be responsible for seeing that the units in the properties managed by the firm are all rented. In such cases, the property manager must work closely with the marketing professional, the senior manager, and possibly the executive property manager and the owner to develop a marketing strategy, determine the marketing budget, implement the strategy, and evaluate the success of the strategy.

In other management companies or situations, the property manager may be directly responsible for overseeing the activities of a leasing or rental agent who works out of either the on-site management office or a separate on-site rental office. And in still other management companies or situations, the entire responsibility for developing, implementing, and evaluating a marketing strategy and for making the strategy work within a specified budget may fall to the property manager alone.

In all cases, the purpose of marketing and leasing is to maximize rental income. In most cases, it is beneficial to have the property occupied by long-term renters who pay on time and in full and who respect the property as their home and as the home of their fellow renters. The property manager should participate in marketing, sales, and leasing. After all, no one knows the property better than the person who, day in and day out, manages it and supervises its office workers and maintenance team, all of whom play a significant role in making the property a desirable place to live and thus a desirable "product" to market.

The property manager must understand that, far from being a one-time event, the marketing of a rental property is a constantly evolving series of interconnected actions that produce a successful, full, and profitable multihousing property. The principles of the marketing process that are presented here will stand the property manager in good stead whether she/he manages a conventional property or a HUD-assisted development and whether she/he is responsible for the rent-up of a new property or for the re-rental of units within an existing property. (See Chapter 12, Management's Role During New Construction and Rent-Up for more information on the property manager's participation during the construction and rent-up phases of a new property.)

THE CERTIFIED LEASING PROFESSIONAL PROGRAM

The certified leasing professional (CLP) program, sponsored by local Home Builders Associations and through corporate sponsorships, trains leasing professionals in multifamily leasing and sales skills. Topics covered by the CLP program include sales, communication skills, merchandising, customer satisfaction, Fair Housing, and ethics. The CLP program reviews and tests for competency in these areas and in other key areas that are vital to quality property leasing. To locate a local CLP school and/or to inquire regarding sponsorship of a CLP school, contact the Director of Professional Development, Multifamily Division, National Association of Home Builders, 1201 15th Street, NW, Washington, DC 20005, or call 1-800-368-8215.

THE RENTAL MARKETING PROCESS AND MARKETING STRATEGY

As indicated in Figure 7–1, the marketing of units in a residential rental property should proceed according to the following logical steps, all of which apply to both new construction and existing properties.

FIGURE 7–1. Rental Marketing Process

- Define and understand the characteristics of the property and why people would choose to live in the property.
- Define and understand the target market.
- Develop a marketing plan that addresses:
  - Logo and property identity
  - Off- and on-site signage system
  - Property brochure and informational materials
  - Advertising program
  - Public relations program
  - Referrals
  - Model units
  - Rental office design and staffing
- Convert the marketing strategy to a full budget and spending plan.
- Write a statement of the property's criteria for determining eligibility. (These criteria must be objective and nondiscriminatory, must be applied consistently to every applicant, and must comply with Equal Housing and all other federal, state, and local housing regulations.)
- Obtain prospects and show and lease the units.
- Periodically evaluate the results of the marketing plan by measuring them against established goals, reviewing both move-in and move-out paperwork, surveying existing residents, and conducting exit interviews with residents who move out.
- Revise and adjust the marketing plan based on the results of its periodic evaluation to produce the desired results.

MARKETING STRATEGY

The marketing strategy can be developed by the management company and/or an outside professional marketing firm whose primary business is developing marketing strategies for owners and managers of housing properties. But even when an outside firm is employed, the management firm and on-site management personnel should take an active role in both the analysis portion of the marketing study and in the development of the specific strategy that follows the analysis. The management company personnel can often perform some of the background work to enable the expensive time of the outside marketing experts to be used in the analysis and development of strategy. This combination of inside and outside expertise can be most effective, both in terms of the final strategy and from a cost standpoint.

Regardless of who devises the marketing strategy, its objective should be to attract the most desirable prospects and to convert them into long-term renters. All the marketing techniques available should be evaluated, and those that promise maximum appeal to the target market at a reasonable cost to the owner should be implemented and monitored for effectiveness.

IDENTIFYING MARKETABLE FEATURES AND BENEFITS AND DEFINING THE TARGET MARKET

Marketing equals selling, and everyone knows there's no point in trying to sell a product no one wants to buy. The key to effective marketing is to figure out what makes a product marketable and who would want to have it and then to compellingly communicate the product's features, benefits, and availability to the market most likely to want it and most able to afford it.

When marketing rental housing, the product is a lifestyle and a unit in the property. The challenges are identifying why people would want to live in the property and in the unit (the marketable features and benefits of the property and the unit), defining who those people are (the target market), and then communicating the availability of living in the property and the unit to the most desirable prospects (the marketing plan).

IDENTIFYING MARKETABLE FEATURES AND BENEFITS

As shown in Figure 7–2, there are seven primary reasons why people choose to rent in one property and not another: location, curb appeal and common areas, security, the specific unit, rent, the reputation of the management company and the image of the property itself, and property amenities.

Of these seven, location is universally accepted to be first. Depending on which study is consulted, the remaining six are ranked in a variety of priority orders; however, it is interesting to note that although rent is a critical factor in the decision-making process, it is often overshadowed by other considerations.

The fact that location is the primary consideration for renters reinforces the old real estate adage that the three most important considerations in selecting real estate are location, location, and location. Where a property is located matters very much to people. The property may be located in a neighborhood people particularly like or it may be near their place of employment, their friends, their family, schools, shopping, and/or houses of worship. Whatever the reason, location has traditionally been a fundamental deciding factor in residential decisions, and it continues to be so today.

After location, it is curb appeal, or the exterior appearance and condition of the property, that is one of the single most effective marketing tools. The landscaping; pedestrian and vehicular traffic surface design and maintenance; outdoor lighting; cleanliness and maintenance of the building exteriors and grounds; placement and maintenance of resident refuse handling equipment; appearance and maintenance of common outdoor facilities such as pools, ball courts, and playgrounds; and every aspect of the property that the eye can see represents a positive or negative impression. When the impression is positive, people are attracted enough to want to know more about what else the property has to offer. The fact is, a higher percentage of traffic into a rental office results from drive-by traffic than from signage or newspaper or broadcast advertising.

What's more, curb appeal not only helps to attract prospects but also maintains the goodwill of the existing residents. Goodwill minimizes turnover. As it is generally easier and less expensive to keep existing residents than it is to replace them, keeping people from moving out is an effective marketing strategy. In fact, many management companies have developed and implemented resident retention programs for this purpose.

The appearance and condition of the property's common interior areas, including but not limited to the common hallways, lobby, mailboxes, resident directory, elevators, floors, indoor lighting, and visible security measures, are also important to prospective renters. Moreover, it is reasonable to assume that prospects use their perceptions of the property's curb appeal and interior common areas appearance to draw inferences about the type and level of service that the property renders to its residents. All of these issues reinforce the assertion in Chapter 5, Property Maintenance and Energy and Water Conservation that creating and maintaining superior curb appeal assists in the marketing process because it attracts prospects—thus reducing the amount of money dedicated to advertising—and helps rental agents to close more deals faster.

FIGURE 7–2. Seven Primary Reasons Why People Choose to Rent in One Property and Not Another

- Location
- Curb appeal and common areas
- Security
- Specific unit, especially its floor plan and utilization of space
- Rent
- Reputation of the management company and image of the property itself
- Property amenities

People in search of a new home also evaluate properties and units within those properties according to how secure they will feel living there. As mentioned in Chapter 6, Risk Management and Management Maintenance Plans, the decision whether or not to advertise various aspects of a property's formal security/monitoring system must be made by the appropriate property decision makers. But regardless of whether security is an advertised feature, prospective renters will look to see how well the property has been dedicated to providing a safe and secure environment for residents.

Prospective renters also are interested in how intelligently and attractively the floor plans of specific units are arranged and in the special features of specific units that create a sense of uniqueness, such as a loft or bay windows. Renters are also more aware than the general population of the reputations of both management companies and/or individual properties, and they are understandably interested in the "added value" amenities that a property offers, such as health clubs.

When formulating a marketing plan, it is wise to list the features and benefits of the property relative to the seven factors discussed above and to exploit those features and benefits in the property's marketing and advertising campaigns.

DEFINING THE TARGET MARKET

As in most commodities, the rental market is subject to the law of supply and demand. Those units that respond to the demands of the market will be rented. It is therefore important to understand who the people in the market are and what they want from the rental experience. Demographic studies that define income levels and housing needs are particularly helpful in determining the "spin" that will be put on marketing to attract prospects who are most likely to want, and be able to afford, to live in the property. The property manager and all professionals involved with creating and implementing marketing strategy should make themselves intimately familiar with the demographic profile of the ideal renter for their property. Then they should construct and target all their marketing efforts to reach and influence those particular prospects.

MARKETING THROUGH MEDIA AND PUBLIC RELATIONS

If marketing is nothing more than selling, then advertising is the primary tool of marketing. Without advertising, even the best products can languish. But through advertising, the availability of a product and its features and benefits are exposed to the market. Marketing and advertising may be accomplished through the use of print media, such as signage, brochures, newspapers, and mailings; via broadcast media, such as radio and television; and via the Internet.

THE IMPORTANCE OF THE PROPERTY LOGO

In every advertising campaign that will include even just a single print element, the first step is to develop the visual element that identifies the product and makes it unique. This element is called the logo, the graphic representation of the product that generally includes both words and symbols.

When developing a logo for a residential property, care should be taken to ensure that the logo design makes a clean, attractive, and accurate graphic statement about the property. Without question, a professional graphic designer should be engaged for this creative project, which is usually undertaken when marketing is being conceived for a new or newly rehabilitated property or when it is necessary or desirable for a property to change its image.

Once a logo has been created, the property manager and marketing professionals should deliberately use it as the visual link that runs through all of the diverse elements in the marketing program. The logo should appear in or on all the property's business cards, stationery, signs, displays, brochures, advertisements, promotional materials, and web pages.

It should be painted or otherwise affixed on all property vehicles, awnings, and canopies and embroidered or otherwise displayed on all property uniforms. In short, it should be the identifying element of the property.

INSTITUTIONAL OR INDIVIDUAL GRAPHICS

The logo is part of a larger graphic campaign that identifies the property. In deciding how the property will be presented graphically, the decision must be made whether to use an institutional approach, in which a group of properties with different names use the same or similar logos, or the separate approach with an individual logo for each property.

A number of large property management firms use an institutional graphic approach. That is, all of their properties use a common logo design but with different names. This approach has the advantage of tying each property to an image of the company. It also permits each property to capitalize on the success of the other properties and the reputation of the management company.

A variation of this approach is to use similar names or similar subtitles with the property name. For example, a firm may name all its properties after different trees. A subtitle such as "Another XYZ Apartment Property" can also be used as a common thread.

The disadvantage of institutional graphics is that the consumer may become confused about which property is which. This confusion can result in additional marketing problems if one or more of a group of properties is performing poorly. This institutional approach requires substantial time and thought to execute well.

The more common approach is to use an individual logo for each property. In developing ideas for the logo, consideration should be given to the multiple uses it will have, how it will look when reproduced for each use, and how much it will cost to reproduce so that it makes as impressive a presentation as possible. Such questions as how a multicolored logo will look reproduced in black and white, how it will look on a computer screen, and how it will look when it is significantly increased or decreased in size must be considered in the decision-making process. How quickly an image downloads is also an important factor for web-based marketing strategies. Ultimately, the design should be executed so that the logo will look crisp in any size from 3/4 inch to 4 feet or more across. Figure 7–3 shows a logo that looks good in various sizes as well as in full color, in various individual colors, and in black and white.

OFF-SITE AND ON-SITE SIGNAGE

As discussed in Figure 7–4, a property's signage includes both off-site signs such as billboards, directionals, and trailblazers that advertise the property and help people to find it and on-site signs such as markers, directionals, features, traffic control signs, and informationals that work for both the property's residents and visitors. Whether off-site or on-site, all of a property's signs must be uniform in appearance and of the highest quality to attract and retain the most desirable residents.

Figure 7–3

FIGURE 7–4. Off-site and On-site Signs

Off-site Signs

Billboards—Large promotional signs ranging in size from 4×8 to 12×45 feet or larger.

Off-site directionals or trailblazers—Medium-size signs (from 2×3 to 4×8 feet) that indicate the distance and direction of travel to the site.

Bootlegs—Small temporary signs (18×24 inches or less) with the name of the site and a self-adhesive arrow. They are tacked to trees, telephone poles, or small stakes stuck in the ground.

On-site Signs

Marker or monument sign—Main sign at the entrance to the property.

On-site directionals or trailblazers—Signs directing visitors to the rental office or information center.

Features—Signs denoting marketing features of the property such as pools, tennis courts, dog walks, etc.

Traffic control signs—Street signs, stop signs, yield signs, speed limit signs, etc.

Informationals and pedestrian signage—Large or complex sites often will have a street and building directory as well as building labels to assist guests in finding specific locations. High-rise multifamily buildings will use informational and pedestrian signs within the building to identify various rooms and locations in the building, to identify elevator floors, to provide directions at elevator banks, and for other informational purposes.

TYPEFACE AND READABILITY

Selecting the typeface of a property's signage is an important task. The goal of the selection process is to create signs that are distinctive and exceptionally readable and that complement the logo. Ideally, the graphic artist who designs the logo will present one or more typefaces from which to choose. Choosing a typeface that is commonly accessible to typesetters, sign firms, sign painters, and manufacturers and found in most computer programs will help reduce production costs.

In addition to selecting the most readable and effective typeface, it is important to design signs that are easy to read from a car driving down a highway in poor weather, at twilight, and at night. Depending on the speed at which they are traveling, prospects may have as little as three seconds to read a sign when driving.

OFF-SITE SIGNAGE

Off-site signage is one of the most effective means of attracting interest in a multihousing property and often serves as the directional aid that assists people in getting to a property. The types of off-site signs are discussed below.

Billboards

These large promotional signs range in size from 4 × 8 to 12 × 45 feet or larger. Although they can be quite expensive, billboards can make a significant difference in the amount of traffic that comes into a site, particularly if the property is not located on a major thoroughfare and otherwise would not attract much drive-by traffic.

Billboards can be leased from an outdoor advertising firm or permission can be negotiated to erect a billboard on a particular site and you contract to have it erected and painted. If a billboard may be needed on a permanent basis, negotiating for a site and getting the necessary permits to erect a billboard is usually the most economical course of action. For rent-up situations in which wide exposure of the property is needed, leasing will prove to be a simpler and faster alternative. (See Chapter 12, Management's Role During New Construction and Rent-Up for more information on the property manager's participation during the construction and rent-up phases of a new property.)

The key to the effectiveness of a billboard is its location. A well-designed billboard in a poor location will not generate results. The density of traffic and the types of drivers passing a given location dictate placement. To use billboards successfully, the target market must be studied carefully and the billboard placed where it will be seen by the greatest number of people in the target market. Major thoroughfares within one to one-and-a-half miles of the property are usually sound locations for billboards.

The design of the billboard and its copy are critical. The goal is to generate as much curiosity as possible and to stimulate prospect traffic in the property. The essentials on any billboard are the name of the property, where it is located, and the rental office phone number. The essential considerations of a property billboard are listed in Figure 7–5.

A billboard should carry only the essential message and get prospects to the property. Figure 7–6 shows an excellent billboard juxtaposed against a poorly executed billboard (on which the name has been altered for the sake of confidentiality). The graphics on the bad billboard are awful, its maintenance is poor, and the sign detracts significantly from the appeal of the property.

For most purposes, a simple, easy-to-read billboard design will serve a multihousing property well, attract traffic, and be most cost effective.

Off-Site Directionals or Trailblazers

If a site is difficult to get to or quite some distance from a major thoroughfare, a directional sign (sometimes called a trailblazer or reassurance sign) of the type shown in Figure 7–7 will be appropriate. The sole function of these signs is to get people to the site, so sign information should be restricted to a name, directional arrow, and distance. For difficult-to-reach properties, the lettering should be done in reflective stock so the signs are more visible at night both to prospects and to residents' guests who may be unsure of how to get to the site.

The same questions and issues pertinent to the location of billboards apply to directionals.

FIGURE 7–5. Considerations in Billboard Design

- ***What size is the billboard?***
- ***What is the average speed of the traffic passing the location?***
  The higher the speed, the shorter the time a billboard can be read and the larger the lettering or type must be to be readable. Billboard copy should be short enough to read within 3 to 5 seconds.
- ***How does the billboard fit in with its location?***
  If it is in a forest of other signs, the design will have to be quite different from what it would be if it were the only billboard on the road for a mile.
- ***Will the board be lighted at night and, if so, with what types of lights?***
  To a limited extent, the light dictates the colors used and the amount of copy on the sign. Different types of lighting have different effects on various colors. A professional billboard manufacturer will be able to provide the necessary information to make an informed decision.
- ***How will the colors selected look during cloudy, overcast, or inclement weather and during the various seasons of the year?***
  These questions are particularly important in areas that have snow on the ground for long periods or that have seasons of rain and heavy cloud cover. In the snowbelt, for example, the billboard must be positioned so that it is not obscured by snow banks nor coated with slush and mud thrown off by highway-clearing equipment.
- ***What will the billboard's initial cost and ongoing maintenance costs be?***
  Complex designs executed in many colors are more prone to fading, bleeding, and peeling than a simple design that requires less frequent touch-ups.

FIGURE 7–6. Excellent Billboard and Poorly Executed Billboard

FIGURE 7–7. Directional Sign

Bootlegs

Bootlegs are inexpensive temporary signs, generally 18 × 24 inches or smaller, that are tacked to trees, telephone poles, or small stakes stuck in the ground. As shown in Figure 7–8, copy on the bootleg sign is usually limited to the name of the site and an arrow. Widely used to supplement traditional billboards and directionals, and especially helpful in rent-up situations, bootleg signs get their name from the fact that they are not legal in many locations.

ON-SITE SIGNAGE

On-site signage is the only element of a property's signage program that will be seen by 100 percent of the prospects. Once they become residents, they will see it every day. Therefore, considerable thought should be given to the design of all on-site signage, and the signs should be of the highest possible quality.

Most multihousing sites incorporate the five major types of on-site signs described in Figure 7–4: the marker or monument sign; directionals; features; traffic control signs; and informationals. All of these signs should be tied together by a harmonious common design that not only incorporates the property's logo and typeface but also complements the overall architectural treatment of the buildings. Where appropriate, all signs should indicate the phone number of the management and the rental offices along with their hours.

The Marker or Monument Sign

Of all the on-site signs, the marker or monument sign, sometimes also called the keystone entry sign, is the most important. It is the sign at the main entrance to the property and serves as the focal point for all other on-site signs.

The goal with the marker is to have a clean design that conveys a positive image of the property and invites people to turn in and see what it has to offer. People driving by comprise a significant percentage of the traffic that comes into a multihousing property, and the image projected by the market is often the only impression of the property they will have.

Location, durability, and good looks are the key considerations. If the marker is on a two-way street, it should be prominent when approached from either direction. It can be placed on an island in the drive, to the side, or two signs can be placed one on each side of the street. Deciding where to place the marker depends on a driver's line of sight when approaching the site and on the time needed to react to the sign once it is spotted. If the property is located on a high-speed street, the marker may have to be of considerable size to be visible enough to allow someone to slow down and turn in. In nearly all cases, the marker should be illuminated at night.

The marker must comply with any setback requirements and height restrictions. An increasing number of municipalities have strict ordinances that severely limit the height, type, and size of signs that may be erected. In some cases, it

FIGURE 7–8. "Bootleg" Sign

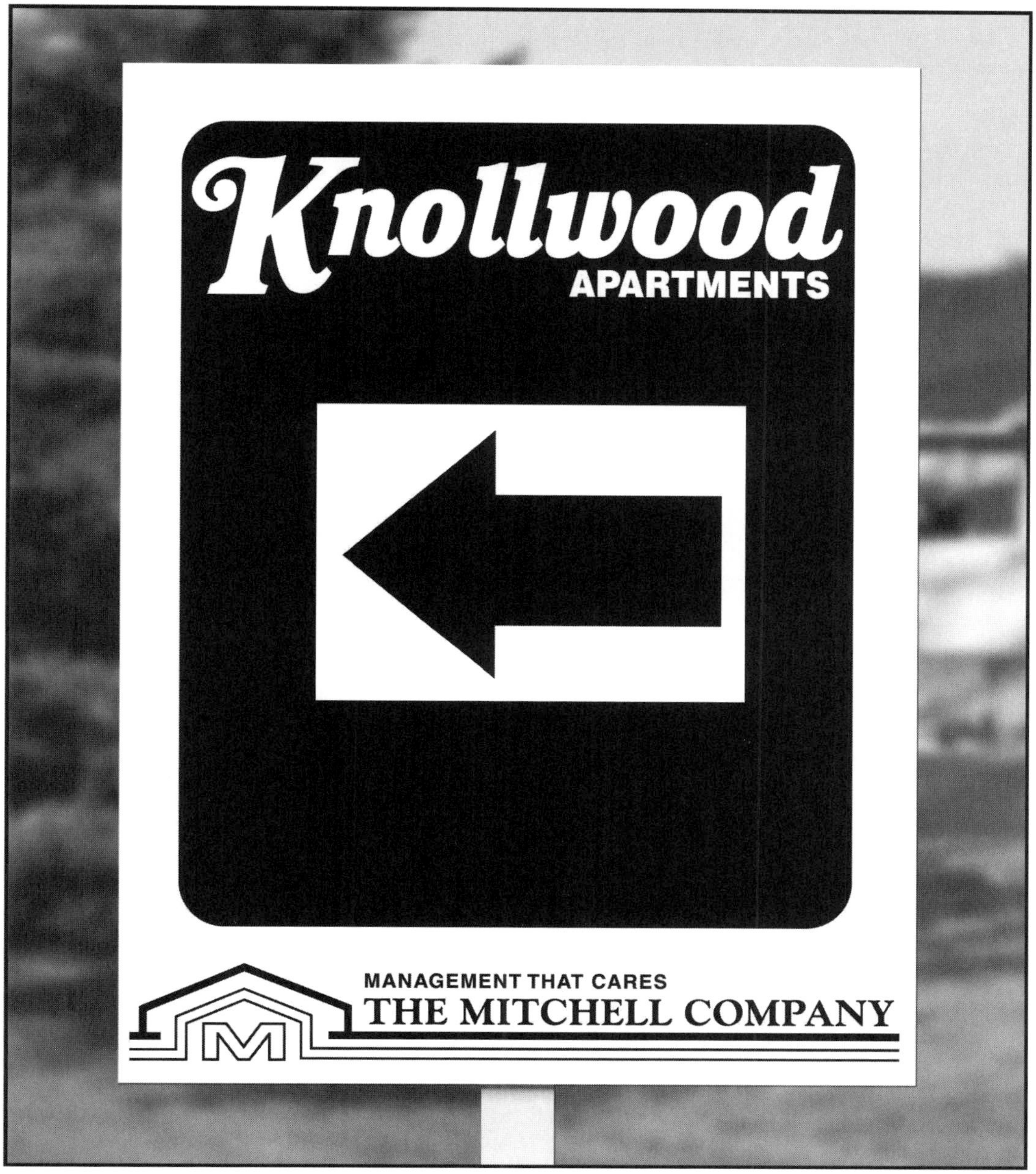

may be necessary to obtain a zoning variance to get an effective sign erected.

An additional consideration is any easement or right-of-way expansion rights that may exist. If possible, placement of the marker should allow for future expansion of the right-of-way work on the easement to prevent destruction of the sign at a later date.

Most markers are constructed of stone, masonry, or wood. The size will be dictated as much by budget considerations as by the site, but it should be of sufficient size to be readily seen.

Signs located on islands or near streets should also be of sufficient strength to withstand an occasional out-of-control automotive assault. Berms, brickwork borders, and high curbing contribute substantially to the life of the marker in such situations.

Easy maintenance is a major consideration. The sign should be cleaned and painted on a regular basis. When possible, the marker should be designed to allow the site staff to do as much of this work as possible. Figure 7–9 shows an effective marker that is attractive, highly visible, and easily maintained. It is sandblasted redwood, a popular material that is durable and accepts and holds paint well.

In selecting colors for the marker, the manager should consider carefully the overall environment in which the sign will be placed. Although earth tones and subtle colors may look good on the drawing board, they may blend so effectively into the background that the sign is not noticed. Usually this problem can be solved by selecting colors that are several shades closer to primary colors yet are the same general color as those used in the overall decoration of the property.

The myth that markers have to cost a lot to be effective is false. Figure 7–10 shows a marker cut from cedar lap siding with a band saw. It looks good and wears well.

On-Site Directionals or Trailblazers

Once prospects arrive at the site, a key task is to get them to the management or rental office. Directional signs perform this task. To determine how many and what size directionals to use, a plot plan of the property should be reviewed and all of the possible routes to the office should be mapped out, not just from the main entrance but also from any secondary or back entrances.

A directional will be needed at every turn or junction in the route to the office from every entrance. Figure 7–11 shows a typical directional sign. The directionals should match the marker in design whenever feasible. Normally about two feet square or two feet in diameter, they should be mounted so that they can be easily seen from a distance of up to 150 feet. If the rental office operates in the evening and/or doubles as a clubhouse that residents may use, the lettering on the directionals should be done in reflective stock so the signs will show up well at night.

Feature Signs

Feature signs can be an important addition and an effective silent salesperson for the property. They are used to identify marketing features of the property's image in a potential resident's mind before she/he gets to the office. An example of an innovative feature sign is shown in Figure 7–12, which identifies the dog walk in a property in an area where dogs frequently are not accepted.

FIGURE 7–9. Marker

FIGURE 7–10. Marker

FIGURE 7–11. Directional Sign

FIGURE 7–12. Feature Sign

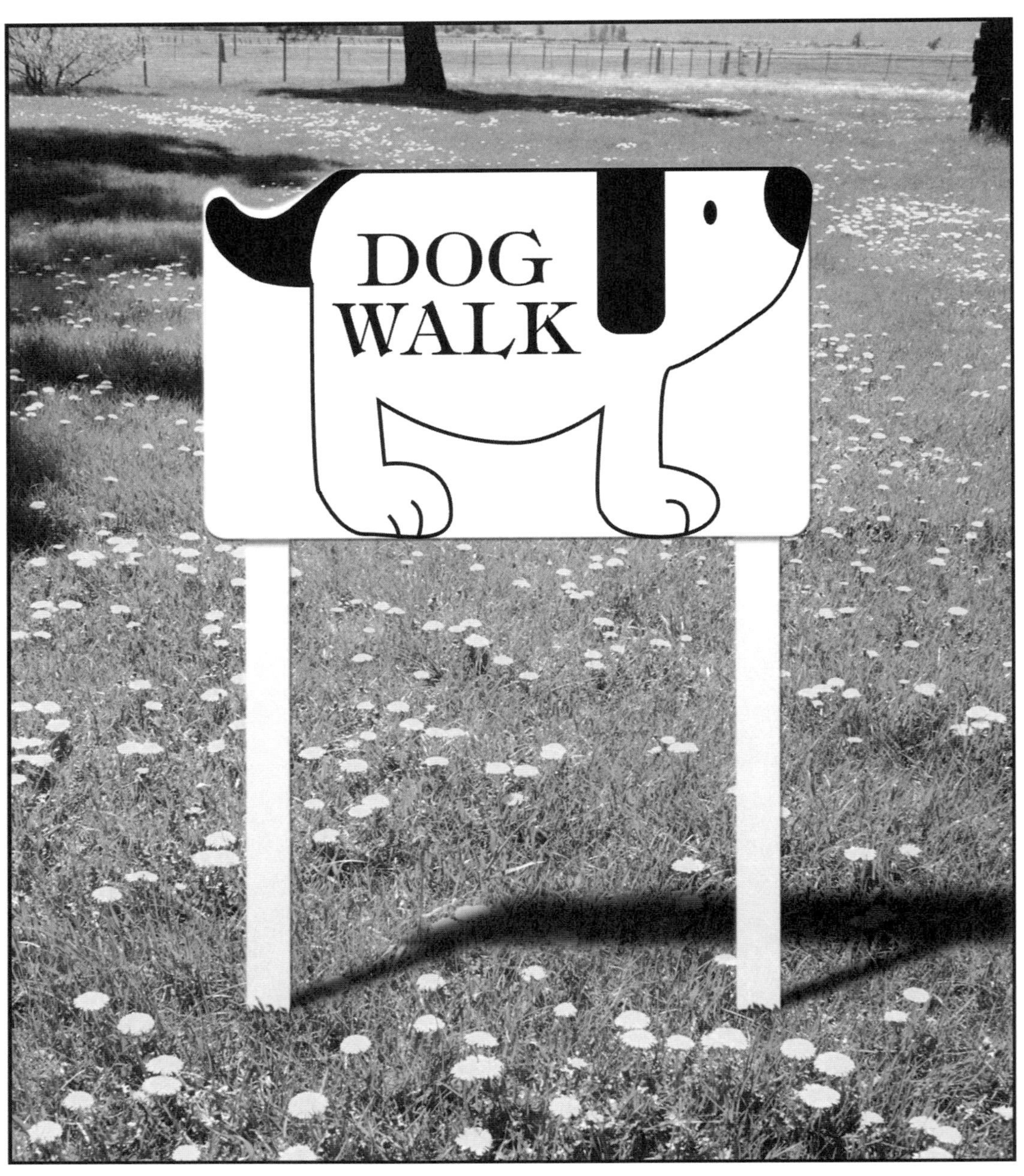

Traffic Control Sign

A multihousing property will often need speed limit, fire zone, no parking, and stop signs. These signs can be purchased ready-made in the usual reflective aluminum variety or custom-made as shown in Figure 7–13. Custom-made signs have the advantage of keeping sign treatment consistent and in character with the property; however, they are a more expensive alternative.

Informationals

Informational signs are a necessity in large or complex sites to direct residents and guests to their on-site destinations. For example, a large, easy-to-read informational site plan or map near the main entrances to the property will help visitors locate their destinations easily. Street signs should be well placed and visible, not obscured by trees or other high items. Building and unit number signs should never be ob-

FIGURE 7–13. Custom-made Sign

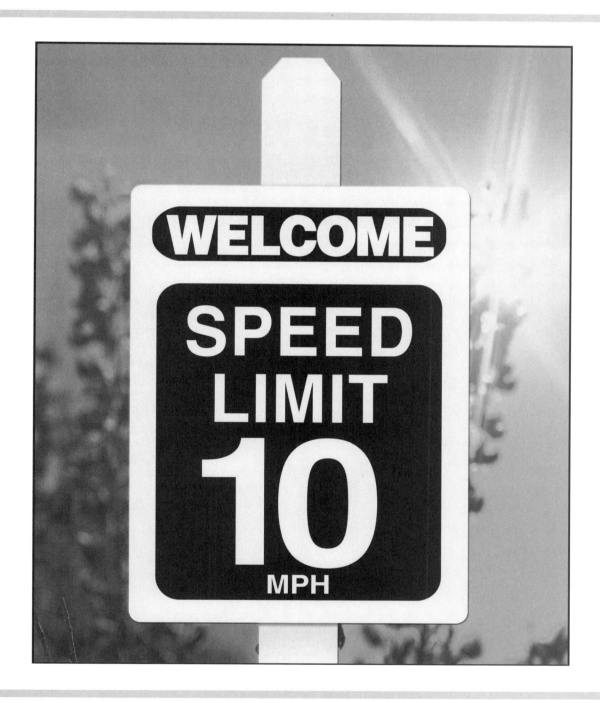

scured and must be easily readable at all times, especially at night when the overwhelming use of the signs occurs.

In high-rise multifamily buildings, informational and pedestrian signs within the building are used to identify various rooms and locations in the building, to identify elevator floors, to provide directions at elevator banks, and for other informational purposes. The design of these signs also should echo the overall design theme of the property.

Well-designed, properly maintained, on-site and off-site signs are a vital part of the property's overall on-going marketing program. The property manager therefore should devote considerable effort to getting the signs right initially and keeping them well maintained once they are erected or installed.

The graphics and design of property signage should be reexamined at least every 10 years because signs gradually become dated and may detract from the property's curb appeal. A complete redesign and reconstruction of the signs should be considered every decade or whenever the marketing plan of the multihousing property is changed significantly.

THE PROPERTY BROCHURE AND INFORMATIONAL MATERIALS

Prospects in serious search of a new home often visit several properties and see many different units in a short period of time. An informational brochure helps prospects remember what they have seen. For this reason, the informational brochure is a critical element of the marketing campaign at all stages of rent-up and re-rental.

The informational brochure should:

- Convey the central theme of the property
- Reflect the property's lifestyle and management's pride in the housing offered
- Reinforce the property's most marketable benefits, such as
  - Location
  - Amenities
  - Social activities
  - Unit floor plans

The brochure should contain these items:

- The name of the property
- The property logo
- Directions for reaching the property or a map
- Floor plans of each unit type
- A picture, architectural rendering, or drawing of one or more major amenities, such as a clubhouse, and a written list of all amenities
- The history and description of the management company
- The rental agent's contact information (the rental office phone number, mobile phone number, and e-mail address should always be included; sometimes the rental agent also includes her/his home phone number)
- Any other items that would help sell the property to prospects

Rental prices should not be shown in the brochure because they are subject to change.

The sample brochure shown in Figure 7–14 is actually a folder that contains separate inserts for each model and a fact sheet about the property's amenities. Basic information on the property is printed on the inside of the folder, and a map appears on the back. This is a particularly practical format for an informational brochure because the insert pages can be changed as needed without having to reprint the entire package and because the folder gives prospects extra "pockets" to carry any additional information they may receive about the property.

Although a folder-type brochure is effective, the type of brochure, its design, and its production costs will depend on the:

- Type of property
- Number or units that turn over each year
- Degree of competition in the marketplace
- Overall market vacancy rates
- Corporate marketing approach
- Price range of the units
- Other properties managed by the same firm using common marketing approaches

Under any circumstances, the rental agent should be trained in the effective use of an informational brochure. Specifically, the brochure should be given to visitors after they have viewed the model and also when making personal marketing contacts and in marketing mailings.

PRINT AND BROADCAST ADVERTISING PROGRAMS

Newspaper Advertising

Many people look in the classified section of the newspaper when they are interested in renting an apartment. So in most markets, the classified section of the daily newspaper is the major advertising medium for a multihousing property. The classified section may contain both classified and display advertising. A classified ad typically contains words without illustrations or pictures, is typeset by the newspaper, and appears only in the paper's classified section. Display ads are larger, often contain illustrations and graphics such as logos, may be designed and provided to the newspaper camera-ready by a graphic artist or advertising agency, and may appear either in the classified section or anywhere else in the paper.

For the purposes of marketing re-rental units, classified ads like the ones shown in Figure 7–15 are generally adequate to get the job done. However, when a property has a great number of vacancies and/or unassigned intents to vacate, display ads like the ones in Figure 7–16 should be considered. Display ads are also appropriate for a grand opening and during the rent-up phase. Display ads should be prepared by a professional such as a graphic designer or advertising agency because they have the required expertise in design, layout, and typesetting.

Although retailers often run ads in the lifestyle or sports sections of the newspaper, these sections may be cost prohibitive for multihousing rental properties. Large management companies occasionally use institutional display ads such as the one shown in Figure 7–17 to highlight a number of projects under their management, but this type of ad is designed to inform the community in general about the prop-

FIGURE 7–14. Brochure for a Medium Development*

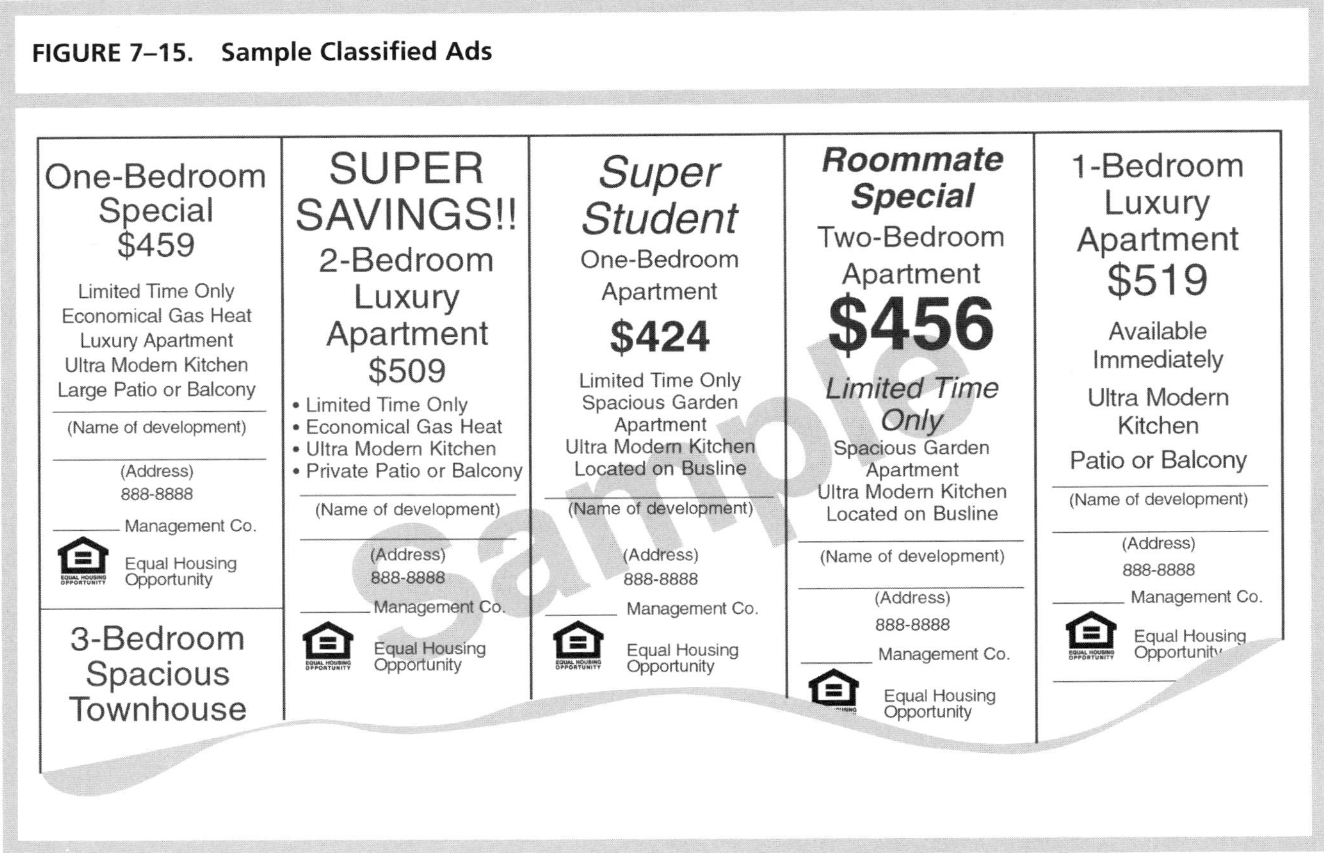

FIGURE 7–15. Sample Classified Ads

erty and/or the management company rather than to attract prospects.

In some properties, it is the senior manager or property manager who is responsible for placing ads in local newspapers; in others, it is the rental agent. In management situations wherein the property manager is not directly responsible for advertising the property, she/he should ask for the opportunity to provide input.

A classified ad often proves the most effective in getting a prospect to visit a residential property when it highlights a specific unit, creates a sense of urgency, and provides some type of magnet. Therefore, each classified ad should contain:

- A specific reason for visiting a specific unit
- The location of the property (with major crossroads or directions indicated if it is difficult to get to)
- The minimum price of the highlighted unit (the manager must be sure that the current rent appears in the ad and that the ad is changed whenever the rent changes)
- The property and/or management company website address

A sense of urgency is created with such expressions as "limited time only," "limited availability," and "only three two-bedroom specials left." Magnets include such expressions as "Fall special" and "two-bedroom special." Ads appealing to a specific target market are most effective, such as "student special."

Ads should highlight units currently vacant or those about to become available. Amenities, utilities, location of schools and shopping centers, and available bus service are other items that could be included. Seasonal amenities such as swimming pools, fireplaces, and nature walks also could be included at appropriate times depending on what will appeal most to the target market.

The ad should have a clean, crisp, sharp look. It could list the most attractive benefits immediately after the primary magnet statement. For example, mentioning a fireplace is appropriate for an ad placed in the winter months.

The ad's "sign off" can simply be the property's name, address, and phone number and, if there is one, the property's web address. If the management company is recognizable, the final sign-off can be the name of the company, its customary and most recognizable logo, and its website.

All ads should conform to Equal Housing Opportunity requirements and carry the Equal Housing Opportunity logo as required (Fig. 7–18).

Ad frequency and size should be determined by the number of vacancies and unassigned intents to vacate and the size of any waiting list. In most markets, ads are run on Fridays or Sundays. The best weekdays to run either type of ad varies with the market. The individual placing the ad should ask the newspaper for the circulation counts on a day-by-day

FIGURE 7–16. Display Ads

FIGURE 7–17. Institutional Display Ad

STRONG & SILENT

(Name of management firm) has developed a quiet reputation over the years. No phones ring off the hook in our Maintenance Offices. We don't set off fireworks to draw attention to our communities. They're spacious. They're built solidly. They last a long time. People seem to know it. The ones who continue to renew their leases and live in our communities year after year know it best. We are (Name of management firm)—your strong and silent partner in fair and decent housing.

(Name of development)
(Address)
(Phone number)
(TDD number)

(Name of development)
(Address)
(Phone number)
(TDD number)

(Name of development)
(Address)
(Phone number)
(TDD number)

(Name of development)
(Address)
(Phone number)
(TDD number)

(Name of development)
(Address)
(Phone number)
(TDD number)

(Name of development)
(Address)
(Phone number)
(TDD number)

(Name of development)
(Address)
(Phone number)
(TDD number)

(Name of development)
(Address)
(Phone number)
(TDD number)

EQUAL HOUSING OPPORTUNITY

FIGURE 7–18. Equal Housing Opportunity Logo

basis and for the various multiple- and single-day rates. Because classified ads are much less expensive than display ads, running them on days other than the ideal day also is often cost-effective. The Saturday rates may involve a weekend discount. Running ads on the day the weekly food section appears with the major grocery store ads also can increase circulation of the ad.

Classified ads can be used alone or in conjunction with display advertising. They can be placed on any day; however, Mondays and Fridays appear to be the least effective. An exception is a town or city with a dominant afternoon newspaper. In this case, the Friday ad would be more effective than a Saturday ad. Display and classified ads should be run on different days to achieve maximum coverage over time.

A multihousing management executive in South Carolina suggests that the minimum "capture rate" for a successful ad requires that 50 percent of the callers visit the property and 33 percent of the visitors sign leases. If sufficient traffic is not being generated by a classified ad, a quarter inch of white space around the ad will serve to call greater attention to it.

In summary, hard-hitting classified ads should convey the most appealing features of the property in the least number of words, and those words should help to create a sense of urgency for a specific prospect to visit a specific unit.

Ads and vacancies should be monitored on an on-going basis to check the need to continue advertising and to review its effectiveness. Obviously, an ad that is no longer necessary should be canceled immediately. When the project has a sufficient number of walk-in applicants to maintain full occupancy, frequent advertising is not necessary.

Prior to making an advertising decision, the senior manager and/or property manager should check the traffic control record that is maintained in the rental office. This record should show not only the daily traffic and weather conditions but also the source of traffic (for example, drive-by, newspaper advertising, or word of mouth). This record gives some clues about the best source of prospects, whether advertising has been effective for that particular property, and if so, which days are best and which newspapers generate the most traffic.

Usually a property's annual newspaper advertising costs should not exceed 25 percent of an average unit's monthly rate multiplied by the number of units. For example, for a 100-unit property with per-unit monthly rent of \$450, the annual newspaper ad cost usually should not be more that \$11,250, or \$216.35 per week.

$$\$450 \times 25\% = \$112.50 \times 100 = \$11,250$$

$$\$11,250 \div 52 = \$216.35 \text{ per week}$$

The property manager should monitor the quantity and quality of the traffic generated through print advertising. Effectiveness is best measured in terms of actual rentals rather than traffic. Of course, if the rental staff is losing rentals because they are not being properly trained and motivated to handle the traffic, the property has a renting problem and not an advertising problem. (To that end, a discussion of how rental agents should conduct themselves appears later in this chapter.) Managers can use the checklist in Figure 7–19 to evaluate their ads to ensure that they are as effective as possible and that they will provide maximum impact for every dollar spent.

Handbills and Flyers

Handbills and flyers bridge the gap between brochures and print advertising such as in a newspaper. In fact, newspaper ads can be reproduced to save on the cost of designing an effective flyer. Useful in target marketing, handbills or flyers might be placed on the bulletin board of a local company (with the company's permission, of course) or on car windshields in parking lots (where this is permitted).

Flyers should include the features and benefits of the property and all the appropriate information, including travel and contact information. They should be reproduced on colored paper or printed in colorful inks so that they stand out

FIGURE 7–19. Advertising Checklist

- Get attention. Use an interesting layout and make sure the headline conveys the product's promise to do something that people want done for them.
- Show an advantage. What can they save, gain, or accomplish with the product?
- Prove the ad's claims with facts, specifications, official recognition, and/or guarantees.
- Persuade people to grasp this advantage. Draw a word picture. Show the advantages of the product and how easy it is to get it.
- Ask for action. For an immediate response, give people something specific to do and put in an extra hook, inducement, or reason for doing it at once.

wherever they are, and as with all the property's print advertising, they should be of the highest possible quality.

Specialized Advertising

Advertising in community, civic, fraternal, and religious publications and in apartment guides that are given away free at the supermarket and other places can be an effective, inexpensive marketing tool. However, the publication's readership profile should be carefully compared with the property's typical resident profile to ensure that the marketing is appropriate. The initial neighborhood and regional analyses as well as the property analysis should be used when making this comparison.

Apartment locator guides, which are common in large metropolitan areas, can also provide effective results, but the high cost of such advertising must be carefully considered.

Specialized advertising materials can also be distributed to businesses and organizations in the general area of the property. Ideally, the brochures or special flyers would be left with an officer of the organization or posted on the bulletin boards to invite the organization's employees or constituents to visit the property and rent an apartment or townhouse near their place of employment or social activities.

Radio and Television Marketing

Broadcast marketing for residential properties continues to grow in popularity as technology expands and make it possible to reach wider numbers of people in more targeted markets.

In many markets, radio is an accepted means of advertising multihousing properties. The movement to radio is especially common in those markets in which classified advertising has become quite expensive. Radio is an especially useful way of targeting markets to a finer degree than can be done in newspapers because each radio station has a unique audience that defines a particular demographic group (i.e., rock music stations typically attract different listeners than do classical music stations).

Generally, for new properties in the rent-up stage, management hires an advertising agency to develop the initial radio spots, but an agency is not necessarily required. Once the property has been in operation awhile, or in smaller markets, the radio stations themselves can produce acceptable spots as part of the cost of the commercials. However, a benefit of advertising agencies is that they often can provide an analysis of the relative cost in terms of exposure and in terms of what stations are more appropriate for the property's resident profile. This type of specialized assistance from an advertising agency is worth the cost because of the expenditure involved in radio advertising and the complicated nature of the advertising medium.

Television is seldom used because its cost is exponentially higher when compared with radio. An advertising agency and production house are mandatory in the production of television commercials because of the considerable technical and production expertise necessary to produce a top-notch commercial. In a few markets, some properties are advertising on local cable channels, but the practice is still relatively rare.

Marketing Via the Internet

Websites that are proprietary to management companies and/or to individual properties are becoming more and more commonplace, especially in the rent-up stage. This is true because once a site is established the Internet can provide not only a completely interactive brochure experience at very low cost but also a virtual tour of the property and available units.

Websites can be configured to provide a wide menu of conveniences to advertisers and visitors. They can be made to be national or local; they can piggyback on existing sites or be hosted by "malls" that also host other sites or they can stand alone with their own proprietary domain name; they can provide links to other sites of interest and they can be a destination link from those sites; they can broadcast information about the management company only, about the property only, or about the management company, the property, and all of the management company's portfolio properties; and, perhaps most significant, they can provide immediate communication interaction via e-mail.

There are two specific caveats regarding websites. The first is quality. Just as curb appeal represents the first actual impression prospects get of the property, so a website represents the first virtual impression prospects get. A property website must therefore reflect the same high quality as all other marketing efforts. This requires the services of a professional who specializes in website design and hosting. Such services can be costly but may be worthwhile depending on the property owner's goals.

The second caveat is how traffic is drawn to the website. Many Internet marketers overlook the fact that people must first be made aware of a web presence before they will log on. Creating this awareness almost always requires advertising first in other media, such as print, to call attention to the website and get people to visit. Under any circumstances, if a property does have a website, the web address should be included in all print and broadcast advertising.

PUBLIC RELATIONS

The purpose of public relations is to create and promote a favorable image for the property in the local community and to attract potential residents. Public relations marketing techniques include social activities such as grand opening ceremonies and open houses; community, corporate, and organization contacts; news releases; and responding to media inquiries.

Grand Opening Ceremony

See Chapter 12, Management's Role During New Construction and Rent-Up for a discussion of grand opening ceremonies as effective public relations and marketing tools.

Open House

Although available units can be shown in an open house type of atmosphere, the number of prospects typically attracted by an open house may negatively impact the quality of life of existing residents. In general, unless there are a significant number of units available, open houses work best in the rent-up phase. (See Chapter 12, Management's Role During New Construction and Rent-Up for a discussion of open houses as effective public relations and marketing tools.)

Community, Corporate, and Organization Contacts

Newcomers and individuals looking to make a move often contact the local Chamber of Commerce, religious or fraternal organizations, and other trusted organizations for help locating a desirable place to live. For this reason, it is incumbent upon the property manager, either personally or through the property's rental agent, to ensure that all such local groups are acquainted with the property and its available housing. This can be achieved by regular mailings to these groups and by joining the groups as appropriate so that the property becomes part of their awareness. Such awareness will be made evident when the leaders of these groups make announcements about available units during a service or membership meeting or in the organizational newsletter and when representatives of these organizations contact the property to inquire if a vacancy exists when someone asks them. Clearly, making such contacts is invaluable for the property manager and/or rental agent responsible for renting in the property.

Corporate Contacts

Corporate contacts are also especially valuable. The property manager and/or rental agent should make appointments and visit selected local industries, companies, and businesses to inform the appropriate officers of the existence of the property and its many benefits, features, and advantages. Other suggested contacts include airports, hotels, social agencies, colleges and universities, hospitals, military bases, and, of course, real estate agents. The purposes of these visits are to inform key individuals about the availability of units in the property and to leave informational materials that can be posted on employee bulletin boards and the like. Because one contact is not usually sufficient to produce the desired results, follow-up contacts should be scheduled on a regular basis, ideally once each quarter.

Corporate Relocation Companies

In such a mobile workplace, corporate relocation companies are engaged constantly to assist in the relocation of employees from location to location. Cultivating these companies is a valuable tool for the multihousing marketer.

Community Contacts and Participation

Many marketing benefits accrue from the property's visibility in community-wide activities, especially community service projects. These benefits include a positive public image, more favorable press coverage, and increased application referrals.

By participating in community service projects, the property manager and/or rental agent becomes the property's "ambassador" to the community. Examples of participating in community service activity include working with a committee raising funds for a worthy cause or allowing use of the property clubhouse as a polling place, a blood donation center, a collection center for toys for underprivileged children, or for other nonprofit activity. (A caveat: The property should not become affiliated with any particular political party or cause. The manager should also not permit use of the clubhouse for such activities to the detriment of resident use.)

News Releases

An effective public relations campaign includes cultivating the local media so that they report favorably on the property. This can be achieved by writing news releases and submitting them to local papers on a regular basis; once a month is sufficient. Items that could be used in news releases include the property opening, the first resident to occupy a unit in the property, the achievement of 100 percent occupancy, children's activities such as a Halloween or Christmas party, special property activities held in the clubhouse or party room, the promotion of a maintenance technician to maintenance supervisor or the hiring of a new rental assistant, and any other newsworthy event.

The format of a news release is fairly straightforward. It should be written on property stationery, include contact information on the top, have a one-line heading, and respond to the questions who, what, when, where, why, and how. It does not have to be brilliantly written because that's the newspaper editor's job, but it may be advisable to engage a professional writer on a per-project basis to ensure that releases are issued on a regular basis as part of an overall public relations campaign.

REFERRALS

Resident Referrals

Positive word-of-mouth advertising by the existing resident population is the least expensive and most highly effective way to attract applicants. In fact, residents are the best source of leads for possible prospects. Presumably, residents who are pleased with the service and other aspects of the property where they live will tell their friends when a unit appropriate to them becomes available. And someone who is referred by an existing resident is virtually sold already. As previously mentioned in this text, this is why truly good management, maintenance, and service play such an integral role in the overall property marketing program.

From time to time as vacancies occur, the property manager can personally contact residents for referrals. The property manager might say, "We have a couple of vacancies at present in your building and because we think a lot of you as a resident, we would like to ask if you know of someone who would enjoy living in our property." Occasionally, in states where it is allowed, some property managers send a "birddog" letter to residents asking if they know someone who is interested in living in the property and offering an incentive for information about prospective residents who later rent. Because several states have laws forbidding paid referrals to anyone who is not a licensed real estate salesperson or real estate broker, property managers should check with a local attorney before beginning a paid referral program.

Some property managers have attracted new residents by sending special mailings to residents in competing properties. This approach is not recommended because it is unethical and because it can create a "raiding war" that can damage all the properties involved.

Referrals from Colleagues

Although "pirating" residents from competing properties is unethical and potentially damaging, the fact is that managers of neighboring properties can be an excellent source of referrals when relationships with them are cultivated properly. These contacts can be made easily at meetings of professional organizations for multihousing managers. In many cases, the managers of properties with long waiting lists or with different types of units are happy to refer potential residents not fitting their properties' resident profiles in exchange for similar referrals.

MODEL UNITS

If the purpose of an effective marketing and advertising campaign is to attract likely prospects to the property, then the purpose of the model unit is to whet prospects' appetites for the lifestyle they might enjoy at the property. The model unit is therefore an effective marketing tool, especially in properties with 150 or more units and properties with annual unit turnover rates in excess of 60 percent of the total units.

Models should be used when the property budget permits the existence of an empty unit. The closer a model is to the office, the shorter the time needed to show it. However, some management companies operate under the alternate practice of locating models at some distance from the office. The walk to the models provides an opportunity to learn something about the prospects' wants and needs and to show them the amenities such as the swimming pool, the tennis courts, and the playground.

The number and the types of models are determined by the number of different types of units in the property, the marketing needs, and the budget. For example, if the majority of the property consists of one-bedroom units, a one-bedroom model would be logical.

In most markets, the most cost-effective way to furnish a model apartment is by leasing furniture from a reputable leasing company. Leasing furniture is less costly and less time-consuming than purchasing furniture that must be sold later. In many cases, the leasing firm will provide the furniture either at no cost or at a substantial discount in exchange for furniture rental referrals. Naturally, the furniture should be appropriate to the property and its resident profile and should be attractively displayed and accessorized. Leasing companies often have decorating consultants who will place the furniture and accessories to show the unit to its maximum advantage.

Opinions differ about the desirability of signage in model apartments. Signs can be used as point-of-sale reinforcers and to point out otherwise obscure features of the apartment and thus can be an effective adjunct to the rental agent's presentation. In any case, the signage should not detract from the overall effect of the model.

RENTAL OFFICE CONSIDERATIONS

The following considerations should be taken into account when creating and staffing the ideal rental office.

APPEARANCE AND FUNCTIONALITY

After a prospect has experienced the exterior of the property, the next most important impression is the one made by the rental office. The office must be neat, attractive, and businesslike to attract the type of residents wanted in the property. Neat and attractive means that the office must be immaculate at all times. The property manager should set up a program to have the rental office cleaned at least once daily. The manager must inspect the office thoroughly upon arrival each morning to ensure that the mirrors are clean, all lights function and are turned on, and trash is removed from wastebaskets. Businesslike means that it must be clear that this is an office where important business is conducted. This means that the office has been equipped with the appropriate number and quality of desks, chairs, file cabinets, computer stations, tables, and lamps and that the furniture has been both attractively and functionally arranged to provide prospective residents with privacy while allowing staff to efficiently handle administrative tasks.

DISPLAYS

Any displays that are exhibited should literally display the property's pride in itself. For example, one display might be a plot plan showing the locations of the buildings, individual units, parking areas, carports, and the clubhouse and other amenities. Framed floor plans of each type of unit and a framed printed history of the management company could hang on the walls. A map with color-coded pins could show schools, houses of worship, major industry, shopping areas, and transportation in the area. Another display might outline the salient selling features of the property, such as a swimming pool, tennis courts, saunas, and an exercise room. A rendering of the clubhouse or other buildings could be displayed. All displays should be attractively and intelligently created and arranged.

CLOSING CORNER

Although it is the ideal arrangement, few properties have enough extra space to dedicate to a separate closing room. However, prospects appreciate the level of respect demonstrated by a private area where presentations, application completion, discussions about finances, and lease signings can take place in a confidential atmosphere without distractions. In the absence of a designated closing room, it is important to arrange the office so that a separate area has been set aside for this purpose.

VISITOR'S LOG

A visitor's log should be maintained to record information about prospects who come to the property. The log should include such information as the prospect's name and phone number (for re-contact), how the prospect learned about the property (for marketing feedback), and what the prospect was looking for (also for marketing feedback). The log can be an actual book, but individual prospect cards or forms are easier to work with.

OFFICE HOURS

The rental office hours of operation should accommodate the times of maximum expected traffic in the area. Someone should be in the office during the posted hours, especially the lunch hour, because prospects often look for housing during their lunch breaks. Staggered lunch periods eliminate the need to close the office during the posted hours. On those rare occasions when the office must be closed briefly during posted hours, a professionally prepared sign should be left on the door advising any prospects of the exact time when someone will be available to them. Then, of course, someone must return at or before that time.

STAFFING

How the rental office will be staffed depends on the budget and on how the owner and management wish to present the property to prospects. In some properties, a receptionist introduces the prospect to an in-take person who then introduces the prospect to the rental agent, while in other properties a single clerical person handles all the paperwork while the lone rental agent handles all rental functions. Some management companies employ part-time rental agents and clerical personnel for weekends and high traffic periods. In any case, the rental office must be adequately staffed so that whoever is interacting with prospects does not have to stop in the middle of a presentation to answer the phone or greet other prospects.

THE MARKETING BUDGET

A property's marketing budget is part of its larger operating budget, and a detailed marketing budget that itemizes costs serves as a source document for the overall property budget. All of the considerations discussed so far, including all modes of advertising, signage, model units, and appointing and staffing the rental office, must be taken into account when devising the property's marketing budget, and they must be monitored to ensure that they are producing the desired results. Marketing and advertising can be a considerable expense, so the marketing and promotion program and its associated costs must be carefully reviewed to determine that the anticipated expenses will be matched by the necessary and appropriate prospect traffic.

A marketing budget is necessary for a marketing strategy that produces maximum rents at a reasonable cost. The only way to ensure that the cost is reasonable is to price out certain elements of the marketing program. Sometimes, compromises will have to be made but only where viable less expensive alternatives exist.

STATEMENT OF ELIGIBILITY CRITERIA

THE AFFIRMATIVE MARKETING PROGRAM

Affirmative marketing programs assure the public that the property's dwelling units are available to anyone and everyone who can afford them. Title VIII of the Civil Rights Act of 1968 as amended by the Fair Housing Amendments Act of 1988, better known as the Fair Housing Act, requires that rental housing be made available to all persons without regard to race, color, religion, sex, handicap, familial status, or national origin.

Simply put, the affirmative marketing program is a plan that ensures that the owner and manager of multihousing properties make a conscious effort to let all potential applicants know housing is available. The U.S. Department of Housing and Urban Development (HUD) requires the establishment of an affirmative fair marketing plan prior to the approval of the loan to build any HUD-financed or HUD-insured multihousing developments.

All owners of housing need a full, affirmative, fair marketing plan and should have a full set of Fair Housing policies. All advertising, showing, and leasing activities should be conducted in accord with the plan and policies on a consistent basis. The Equal Opportunity logo (Fig. 7–18) should be used in all advertising and on major on-site and off-site signage.

The law also covers other elements of the advertising program that must conform to affirmative marketing policies. A management company should have an in-house compliance department or officer or access to such an expert who can advise regarding compliance with all federal, state, and local regulations regarding marketing and rental requirements.

TELECOMMUNICATION DEVICES FOR DEAF PERSONS

Under Section 504 of the Rehabilitation Act of 1973 (as amended), Section 8.6 (a)(2) states "where a recipient communicates with applicants and beneficiaries by telephone, telecommunication devices for deaf persons (TDDs) or equally effective communication systems shall be used." This requirement applies to subsidized properties. The TDD phone numbers should be listed in all advertisements and brochures of subsidized properties. The TDD telephone device that is used for the hearing impaired to communicate also should be considered for market rate properties but is not required at the time of the publication of this text.

MARKETING IN A SOFT MARKET

A soft or unresponsive market periodically occurs for a variety of reasons. The economy may be sluggish or the area where the property is located may be undergoing a demographic shift. Whatever the reason, a soft market presents a significant but not insurmountable challenge to a property's marketing program. Below is a discussion of some strategies and techniques that can be used to encourage prospects to visit and rent in a soft market.

SOFT MARKET INCENTIVES

Rent concessions, discounts, reductions, and free rent are common incentives used in soft markets. However, care should be given to the most effective use of "concession" dollars. The best use may not be to cut rent or give a first month's rent free, as many properties do. Instead, the property may do better to provide leasing incentives that more directly address the needs and desires of the individual prospect and simultaneously create the most residual value to the property. In other words, the dollars would go for desirable features that stay in the unit when the current resident moves out.

Such an option program should be among the marketing actions to be considered when unit availability reaches 20 percent. (Unit availability should include both vacant units not assigned and intents to vacate that are not assigned.) The 20 percent guideline applies to each unit type, such as two-bedroom walk-up, three-bedroom townhouse, and not to all units combined because each unit type represents an individual market.

An option program that adds features or benefits to a unit enables the rental agent to tailor her/his sales presentation to the individual prospect. The objective is to determine the prospect's "hot button" and offer the type of incentive that would most appeal to that person and be most likely to produce a rental. Adding items to a unit is often a most cost-effective way to rent units in soft markets and to avoid "giving the product away" with free rent or other incentives.

For instance, in lieu of an outright rent concession, the rental agent might offer certain "added value" items that could be installed in the resident's apartment at no additional charge to the prospect and at little or no additional cost to the property. Examples of such value-added features are listed in Figure 7–20.

The rationale for offering such value-added features is this: If a ceiling fan and a miniblind are provided with a one-bedroom and the actual value of the items is less than one month's rent, these items add value to the unit and the property and can later justify rent increases on these apartments, whereas free rent is lost forever and cannot be recouped. Even the tangible goods option is better than a rent concession because the item becomes a tangible reminder of the special deal and has some lasting favorable effect on goodwill.

Whenever a property considers offering such value-added features, no charge items, or tangible good items as incentives, the total cost of the incentive, including labor and materials, should be carefully calculated and normally should not exceed a month's rent (or whatever amount is approved by the owner and/or upper management). When the program is implemented for a particular type of unit, at least one of that type should be equipped with some of the items, such as a ceiling fan and miniblinds. Seeing the items helps the prospect to visualize the item with which she/he may not be familiar. A demonstration also helps to "sell" the item to the prospect.

FIGURE 7–20. Value-added Concessions in Lieu of Rent Concessions

Value-added unit feature
- Ceiling Fan
- Miniblinds
- Microwave oven (permanently installed so it cannot be removed)
- Wallpaper accent walls (kitchen only)
- Washer and dryer
- Painted accent wall (usually a dining room wall in a neutral tone)
- Vertical blinds
- Glass shower doors
- Track lighting system

No-charge items
- Fireplace
- Location with a premium view
- Carport (rent free for 2 weeks)

Tangible goods items
- Firewood for fireplace
- Videocassette recorder (VCR)
- Television
- Bicycle

Giving rent concessions also establishes a negative precedent that may be difficult to overcome. Therefore, rent concessions should be used as a last resort marketing strategy and only after approval from the owner and/or upper management, depending on the management agreement and the authority for taking such action. Conversely, an "added value" incentive program is flexible in that any combination of value-added, no charge, and/or tangible good items may be offered. Such a program is primarily a closing tool and, as such, should not be advertised. It allows the rental agent maximum latitude in how to use the available options. For this incentive program to succeed, therefore, all of the property's rental agents must be thoroughly trained in how to employ the flexible policy. In any case, incentive programs should not take the place of performing an up-to-date market analysis.

MULTIHOUSING MARKETING FIRMS

In soft markets and in some rent-up situations, the owner/ management company/ property manager may consider hiring a marketing firm to rent-up the property. (See Chapter 12, Management's Role During New Construction and Rent-Up for a discussion of using multihousing marketing firms during rent-up.) Marketing consulting firms can provide an "assault team" of rental agents along with marketing support. Not surprisingly, the cost of these firms can be considerable, but they do provide a valuable option in some cases. Therefore, the decision to engage an outside marketing firm must be made at the highest level.

REFERRALS

As previously mentioned, word-of-mouth referrals are often the best marketing tools. In soft markets, cultivating referrals from residents, industry colleagues, and local real estate agents may be an effective means of attracting prospects. When referral incentives are considered, the local laws governing such fees must be researched before a paid referral program is put in place.

THE EFFECTIVE PROFESSIONAL RENTAL AGENT

The rental agent—also called a leasing agent—is the salesperson for the units in the property. The best rental agents are skilled matchmakers, bringing the most desirable prospects together with their most desirable dwelling unit.

As previously mentioned, the position of rental agent may be filled by a number of individuals. It may be filled by a management company's marketing director or a member of the company's marketing staff, by an outside rental professional, or by the property manager herself/himself. But regardless of who the rental agent is, she/he must master the following techniques and characteristics to be most successful and do the greatest service for the property and for the prospects who visit.

MAKE A POSITIVE FIRST IMPRESSION

In any kind of selling, the first impression is critical. Studies have shown that people make up their minds about the people they meet within the first 30 seconds of being introduced, and usually in less time than that. And no one ever gets a second chance to make a positive first impression. Prospects who get as far as meeting the rental agent have already formed some sort of judgment about the property itself and have committed, to a greater or lesser degree, to entering the selling cycle. Typically, the rental agent is the first human being with whom they will have a prolonged interaction as a representative of the property. Clearly then the first impression that the rental agent makes is very important. This impression is based on appearance, personality, and knowledge. It is therefore the rental agent's responsibility to cultivate these three areas to the highest level of professionalism.

PROJECT PROFESSIONALISM

The neat, smartly dressed rental agent puts prospects in a positive frame of mind for the presentation. Suits and ties for men and tailored pants or skirt suits or dresses for women are classics that always project professionalism.

DEVELOP AN EFFECTIVE PRESENTATION

An effective presentation requires training, which can be provided in-house or through various industry organizations. Training also comes from making actual presentations and learning from mistakes. One of the most common mistakes rental agents make is in the selection of words they use. Rental agents should always use positive language when talking about the property, the neighborhood, the residents, the management company, and coworkers. For example, people do not want to think of themselves as "tenants" living in a "unit" in a "project" that has "rules and regulations." They prefer to perceive themselves as "residents" living in a "home" in a "community" governed by "policies."

KNOW THE PROPERTY AND THE UNIT

The rental agent must be able to speak knowledgeably about the features and benefits of the general area, the neighborhood, the property as a whole, and the specific units she/he is showing. These features and benefits should be emphasized during the presentation to give the prospect specific reasons for renting at the property. For example, the agent should know about the area's schools, libraries, houses of worship, public transportation, hospitals, shopping malls, banks, park, daycare centers, and their distances and drive times from the property. She/he should know the types of units, their square footage, and rental rates. The rental agent also should know and "shop" the competition so that she/he will know how the property measures up to what else is available in the area.

THE IMPORTANCE OF TELEPHONE SALES ETIQUETTE

The telephone is an essential sales tool. How calls are handled may determine whether or not the prospect will actually visit the property. A rental agent never gets a second chance to make that first impression on the telephone, so she/he must be prepared as follows. When the phone rings, the agent should stop whatever she/he is doing and:

- Smile (it will be heard in her/his voice)
- Answer the call on the second ring in a warm, enthusiastic voice
- Identify the property and herself/himself
- Get the prospect's name as soon as possible and use it to make the person feel comfortable (but not too often or the prospect will feel uncomfortable)
- Create a professional image in the mind of the prospect
- Qualify the prospect by asking specific questions in a conversational manner
- Show a genuine interest in the prospect's housing needs
- Set up a definite appointment (the objective in responding to a telephone inquiry is to make an appointment)
- Give accurate directions

A sample phone conversation between a prospect and a rental agent might go something like this:

Agent: Thank you for calling [name of property]. This is Mary Jones. How may I help you?
Prospect: I'm looking for an apartment.
Agent: I'll be happy to help you. May I have your name, please?
Prospect: Yes, it's Mrs. Smith.
Agent: Thank you for calling, Mrs. Smith. How many bedrooms will you need?
Prospect: I am interested in a two-bedroom apartment.
Agent: Do you have any pets?
Prospect: No pets.
Agent: When would you like to move in?
Prospect: June first.
Agent: *(At this point, the agent should interest the prospect in a specific unit.)* We have a two-bedroom garden apartment with 900 square feet and a two-bedroom townhouse with 1,000 square feet, and I have one in particular with a fireplace and mauve carpeting.
Prospect: Yes, I might be interested in the apartment with the fireplace. What is the rent on that particular apartment?
Agent: The location is great, and it rents for $750. I can show it to you this afternoon.
Prospect: Well, I have a few more calls to make.
Agent: Do you know where we are located, Mrs. Smith?
Prospect: Yes, but I'm not sure if I could find it again.
Agent: Would you be coming in from Route 405?
Prospect: Yes.
Agent: Take Exit 17 and turn right on Euclid Avenue. Continue about half a mile until you see our sign on the left. After you turn left into the property the office is straight ahead.
Prospect: Okay, I think I can find it. I will try to come out.
Agent: Would you prefer to visit at 4:00 this afternoon, or tomorrow at 10:00 in the morning?
Prospect: I believe 4:00 would be better. Yes, let's make it at 4:00.
Agent: All right, Mrs. Smith. You have the directions, and you will be here at 4:00 this afternoon to look at the two-bedroom townhouse with the fireplace and wall-to-wall mauve carpeting. You would like to move in about June 1. May I have your phone number, Mrs. Smith?
Prospect: Sure, it's 999–0000.
Agent: My name again is Mary Jones, and I look forward to meeting you in person, Mrs. Smith. Thank you again for calling. Goodbye.
Prospect: Goodbye.

GREET PROSPECTS ENTHUSIASTICALLY

All prospects who come into the sales office should be greeted enthusiastically and professionally. They should be made to feel welcome by a receptionist and/or rental agent who rises immediately when they enter, approaches them with a smile, and greets them by extending a hand, introducing herself/himself right away, and asking for the prospects' names. As a sign of respect, the rental agent should address prospects as Mr. and Mrs. or Ms.

QUALIFY PROSPECTS

The purpose of qualifying prospects as soon as possible is to ascertain whether or not they meet the financial and/or family composition requirements to rent the type of unit about which they have inquired or for which they have applied. Within the parameters of what is legal, the rental agent should ask open-ended questions that focus on the information needed. Such questions can determine where prospects currently live, the type of home they currently live in, the size and composition of their households, if they have pets, their income, and their place of employment. Asking the right questions as early as possible in the presentation helps to determine whether the prospects and the property are appropriate for one another. For prospects who are either overqualified or underqualified, the interview should be terminated as quickly and gently as possible. For prospects who are suited to the property, listening closely to answers allows the rental agent to tailor the sales approach to the prospect's needs and desires and helps the agent decide on the most suitable apartments or townhouses for showing.

SHOW A UNIT TO ITS BEST ADVANTAGE

Once prospects have been qualified, the rental agent should show the apartment or townhouse most appropriate to the prospects. The agent should demonstrate the benefits of each feature of the unit, especially those features in which the prospects seem most interested. By carefully observing the prospects' reactions to certain features as they look over the apartment or townhouse, the rental agent can emphasize those features that appear to have the greatest appeal.

Of course, the units being shown should be immaculately clean. The drapes should be open, lights on, cooling or heating system on, closet doors closed, and toilet lids down.

SHOW THE PROPERTY TO ITS BEST ADVANTAGE

After showing one or two units, the rental agent should focus on the overall property, pointing out the features and benefits of living there during the walk to and from the units being shown. These features might include the appearance and landscaping of the grounds and amenities such as a swimming pool, tennis court, and community building. If the rental agent qualifies the prospects well, she/he will know what features to emphasize during the tour.

"SELL" THE HIGH QUALITY MANAGEMENT

During the course of showing available units and at an appropriate time in the presentation, the rental agent should mention the qualifications and staffing of the property's management team. The rental agent should emphasize that the overall goal of the property's management is a well-managed living environment, one that residents are proud and happy to call home.

PRESENT THE PROPERTY BROCHURE

Because the rental agent needs the prospect's undivided attention when he/she first arrives and also because some prospects will not be appropriate to the property, it is best to present the property brochure after viewing the available unit(s). The brochure helps to recap the features and benefits covered during the presentation and the visit to the unit. If the prospect is shopping at a number of properties, the brochure will help to recall the property and some of its specific features. The rental agent should attach a business card to the brochure.

DISCUSS FINANCES

If the prospect returns to the sales office with the rental agent after viewing one or more available units, it probably means she/he is willing to move forward in the sales cycle. At this point, the rental agent must discuss finances. As a rule of thumb, rent should not exceed 28 to 38 percent of a person's gross income (although this figure may vary from market to market and with current economic conditions). In subsidized housing, the applicant must be within the income limits for the applicable program and be able to pay the adjusted rent.

Ineligible prospects include those whose incomes are not within the specified limits, those who have too many persons for the size units available, and those who otherwise do not meet the property's standards. These same factors apply to applicants for government-assisted or government-insured housing.

OVERCOME OBJECTIONS

Assuming the prospect is qualified to rent in the property, this phase of the rental cycle will probably involve overcoming any objections she/he might have. The real objections applicants may have to the property must be understood so that they can be effectively answered. Often, the first objection presented by a prospect is not her/his real objection but one that she/he thinks sounds good or intelligent. In reality, prospects' true objections are often articulated in remarks that begin, "besides that," or, "in addition." A rental agent must listen closely and observe the prospect to determine what objection(s) must be overcome to close the sale.

Although the rental agent must always be attentive and responsive to prospects, the agent need not respond to every objection that prospects raise. In most cases, an objection is not really a deal breaker but simply a request for additional information. The rental agent is in a position to provide that information and try to close the sale.

Prospects who raise the following objections should still be considered eligible prospects and should be recontacted if they do not choose to rent immediately:

- The rooms are too small
- The rent is too high
- The prospect wants two baths
- The unit is located in the wrong area (for instance, upstairs)

These objections are not reasons for ineligibility. In most cases, these persons can be converted to residents by personal follow-up.

In any case, objections are normal in any selling situation, and the rental agent should be prepared to respond to them. Most people want to be sold and shown that their objections are not valid. It is the rental agent's job to counteract objections diplomatically and to help prospects decide to rent.

HELP PROSPECTS DECIDE TO RENT, AND CLOSE THE SALE

Helping the prospect decide to rent and closing the sale is the most critical part of the rental agent's presentation. Helping the prospect decide to rent is done most effectively by responding to objections appropriately, creating a sense of urgency (e.g., telling the prospect that only one unit like the one she/he is interested in is left [assuming this is true], and transitioning into a closing mode). Closing can be accomplished by:

- Asking the prospect which of the apartments she/he saw that she/he prefers to rent
- Asking the prospect if she/he wants to move in on the first or the fifteenth of the month
- Citing an upcoming event for the prospect, such as vacation time, and asking the prospect if she/he wants to move in before, during, or after that event
- Assuming that the prospect will rent and starting to fill out the application by asking the prospect for the information requested on the application form

If the apartment the prospect wants is not immediately available, the rental agent should put the prospect's name on the waiting list. If the waiting list is very long, the rental agent might refer the prospect to another property either owned by the same owner and/or managed by the same management company. To retain the prospect's goodwill, while the prospect is still there the agent should phone one of the firm's other properties and make an appointment for the prospect to visit or, better yet, take the prospect to the other property.

MAINTAIN PROSPECT RECORDS AND TRAFFIC REPORTS AND USE THEM TO FOLLOW UP WITH PROSPECTS WHO DO NOT RENT

The most successful rental agents know that the prospect who did not rent today may be the prospect who does rent tomorrow. That is why these savvy salespeople maintain careful records, such as the prospect record and the walk-in traffic report (Figs. 7–21 and 7–22).

The purpose of these forms is to:

- Serve as a marketing tool to help determine the most effective advertising
- Record types of units requested and an accurate account of phone and walk-in traffic

FIGURE 7–21. Prospect Record

Lead # ____________________
Taken by ____________________
Date ____________________
Co-renter ____________________

Name ____________________
Address ____________________
Work Address ____________________
Home Phone ____________ Office Phone ____________ Co-renter ____________
Directions ____________________
____
____

Type of Unit

☐ Apartment
☐ 1-bedroom
☐ 2-bedroom
☐ 3-bedroom
☐ 4-bedroom

☐ Townhouse
☐ 1-bedroom
☐ 2-bedroom
☐ 3-bedroom
☐ 4-bedroom

Amenities

☐ Balcony
☐ Fireplace
☐ Ceiling fan
☐ Washer/Dryer
☐ Accent wall
☐ Miniblinds
☐ Other ____________

How did you learn about our development?

☐ Previous resident. Who? ____________________
☐ Other referral. Who? ____________________
☐ Employee referral. Who? ____________________
☐ Advertising
- ☐ Sign. Where? ____________________
- ☐ Driving by. ____________________
- ☐ Newspaper. Which? ____________________
- ☐ *Yellow Pages* ____________________
- ☐ Direct mail. Which piece? ____________________

☐ Home or mall show. Where? ____________________
☐ Other. ____________________

Is lead qualified? ☐ yes
☐ no

Follow-up
Leasing agent ____________________ Rent $ ____________
Date of appointment ____________________
If person rented from a competitor, which one? ____________________

*Adapted from Figure 18–1, Linda W. Case *Remodelers Business Basics* (Washington, D.C. National Assocation of Home Builders,1989) p.108.

Figure 7–22. Walk-in Traffic Report

Property Name: ____________ Date: ____________

Weather	Phone	Prospect Name	Agent Initials	Size Requested	Date Needed	Just Looking	Referred By	Rent	Other Special Options	Follow Up Call	Thank You Card Sent	Result of Recontact

(continued)

FIGURE 7–22. Walk-in Traffic Report (*Continued*)

Property Name:________________________ **Date:** ____________

A.

Total Number of Phone Calls
Total Prospective Traffic
Subtract "Be-Backs"
Equals Total New Traffic for the Week

B

Unit	*# Requested*	*Assigned*	*W/L*
1BR			
1BR Loft			
2BR			
2BR2B			
2TH			
3TH			
Total			

C **Prospect Recontact Summary**

Total New Traffic Minus Total Rented on Assigned or W/L	
Subtract Ineligibles	
Subtract Other	
Total to be Recontacted	
Actual Number Recontacted	
Rentals Resulting from Recontacts During the Week	

D. **Advertising Summary** **(obtain from ad log)**

Total Weekly Ad Costs	
Cost of Ad per Rental	
Cost of Ad per Walk-In	
Main Advertising Theme	

Type of Ad	Date Ad Ran	Day Ad Ran
Classified		
Display		
Magazines		

(*continued*)

FIGURE 7–22. Walk-in Traffic Report (*Continued*)

Development Name: ______________________ Date: ______________

E. Referred By

B

	Current	YTD
Billboards		
Newspaper		
Radio/TV		
Business		
Resident		
Apt. Guide		
Apt. Locater		
Drive By (Signs)		
Phone Directory		
City Map		
Realtor		
Other		
Totals		

F. Closing Ratios

Employee Name	# Rentals ÷ Prospects Current Week	%	Rentals ÷ Prospects YTD	%

Closing Ratio for Entire Staff = Total Rentals ÷ Total New Traffic ________

I Marketing Calls

Name of Organization	Date	Person Contacted	Results

- Pinpoint reasons why prospective residents do not rent
- Provide a summary of the week's activity by giving an accurate account of apartments and townhouses rented for the week, including a description of each unit
- Create another opportunity to rent to an interested prospect. If the prospect does not rent, the report provides marketing information as to where she/he rented and why she/he did not rent at this property

The rental agent should complete the prospect report and the walk-in traffic report daily and should submit it to the property manager, who should submit it to the senior manager. The reports keep the senior manager aware of what is happening and ensure that procedures are being followed.

For example, if the report contains a large number in the "just looking" category, prospects probably are not being qualified properly. And if the section "referred by" has a large number in the "other" category, the rental agent probably did not do an adequate job of finding out how the prospect heard about the property.

It is the rental agent's job to recontact prospects who are qualified, who meet the property's standards, and who have any degree of interest in the property within 48 hours of their visits. In addition to the follow-up phone call, a thank-you note should be sent to each prospect who left the rental office without renting. The rental agent should use these recontacts to invite the prospect to return to the property at a later date or, if they rented elsewhere, to find out where, the type of apartment they rented, the rental rate, and why they rented there. This recontact procedure provides another opportunity to rent to interested, qualified prospects and learn valuable marketing information about where the prospects rented and why they did not rent from the property. The rental agent benefits either way.

The ultimate goal of recontacting is to get an eligible prospect to pay a deposit and get on the waiting list for a suitable unit to become available. If the prospect is unwilling to do this, then the rental agent should create a tickler file to remind herself/himself to recontact the prospect again anyway when an appropriate unit does become available. In any case, the rental agent should maintain prospect files and walk-in traffic reports and regard them as an on-going source of new residents and as an on-going monitor of professional performance.

MONITORING THE EFFECTIVENESS OF MARKETING EFFORTS

Whether in a rent-up or re-rental situation, attracting prospects to a multihousing property through marketing is not without its costs. Expense items include advertising, rental office space, and rental staff salaries, to name but a few. The owner, property management executive, senior manager, property manager, and rental agent will therefore want to keep a close eye on the effectiveness of marketing efforts.

In addition to the prospect record and walk-in traffic report, the following instruments provide important data regarding the success of a property's marketing activities.

THE VACANT UNIT CONTROL FORM

The vacant unit control form (Fig. 7–23) provides an encapsulated view of a week's activity relative to the vacant units in a property. It identifies the unit and the reason it is vacant, provides information about when the unit was re-rented and to whom, and provides numerical evidence of the status of vacant units within the property. The vacant unit control form is a static document that captures data for one week in time.

THE TREND REPORT

The trend report (Fig. 7–24) is a useful tracking mechanism that analyzes property operations viz. a viz. rental, occupancy, and marketing over a period of weeks and months, allowing quick and easy comparison with prior periods.

The standard information on the trend report includes move-outs, cancellations, and move-ins for a given period, usually one week. At the end of each week, the report shows:

- The number of units occupied
- Units vacant and assigned
- Units vacant, not assigned by unit type
- Intents not assigned by unit type
- A combination of vacant not assigned and intents not assigned
- Total units rented
- Total waiting list
- Traffic for the period
- Display and classified advertising for the period
- Cost of advertising per rental

The column titled "Special Events" is for information such as:

- A special promotion
- "Birddog" letters (not advised)
- Changes in rental agent
- Rent increase or decrease
- Special rental personnel bonus or incentive
- Any unusual weather conditions

In other words, this column includes anything that can affect the result of operating the property during a given week.

The origin of this trend report is particularly telling. It was created by a management company that was analyzing the rent and unit mix for a property that had excessive vacancies. The company representatives suspected that the rent for the two-bedroom units was too high in relation to other units because of the greater percentage of vacancies in that category.

Figure 7–23. Vacant Unit Control

Development Name: ____________________ From: ______________ To: ______________

	Name	Address	Unit Type	Rent	Reason	Destination	Date Moved	New Resident Name	Date Re-Rented	Date Ready	Date of Move-In
1		6340 BR-LN-DR	3TH	$475			4/22		3/21		5/52
2		4639 Com. Dr	2TH FP	$395	Bought House		4/30	( )			(5/22)
3		4419 Br. Ct. HD	2 Up	$375	Moved in w. daughter		4/29		4/8	5/6	5/10
4		6342 Brooklyn Dr.	2TH	$375			4/29	( )	4/15		(5/13)
5		6222 Br. Dr.	2TH End	$390			4/30		4/30		5/6
6		6359 Br. Dr.	3TH	$475	Job Transfer		5/8	( )			(5/13)
7											
8		Intents									
9	( )	6264 Brook Dr.	2TH	$360	Bought House		(6/1)	( )		(6/8)	
10	( )	4509 Comm. Dr.	2Up	$350	Moving to Ivywood		(5/31)	( )			(6/7)
11	( )	6240 Br.Ln.Dr.	2TH	$360	Buying House		(5/28)	( )	3/22		(6/2)
12	( )	4424 Br. Ln.Pl.	1Dn	$275	Transfer to Another Apt	6240 Brin. Dr.	(6/2)	( )	4/20		(6/10)

Figure 7–23. **Vacant Unit Control (*Continued*)**

Over 5 working days to get apartment ready.

	Unit Address	Reason
1		
2		
3		
4		
5		
6		
7		
8		
9		
10		
11		
12		
13		
14		
15		

Over 10 days for new resident to move in.

	Unit Address	Reason
1		
2		
3		
4		
5		
6		
7		
8		
9		
10		
11		
12		
13		
14		
15		

Cancellations:

Name	Unit Address	Date	Reason

Figure 7–24. Trend Report

Property ______________________ Report Date ______________________

Total Units ______________________ Objectives ______________________

Week Ending	Rentals	Move Outs	Cancelled	Move Ins	Total Occ.	Vacant & Assigned	Vacant not assigned/Intents not assigned					Total VNA	VMA/INA Combine	Models and Other	Total Rented	Waiting List	Traffice	Display adv.	Class adv.	Advertising Cost	Cost per Rental	Special Events
							1BR	2BR	2TH	3TH	4tTH											
3/7	1	2	0	6	197	6	1/1	4/1	2/1	/	/	7/3	10	0	203	3	14	Sun.	7 Days	345.00	345.00	
3/14	3	3	0	2	196	7	/1	4/1	2/2	1/	/	7/4	11	0	203	3	0	"	"	470.00	156.66	Icy conditions/New Rental Manager
3/21	3	3	1	0	193	9	1/	4/1	1/2	2/	/	8/3	11	0	202	3	20	"	"	330.00	110.00	
3/28	4	1	2	2	194	9	1/	5/1	/1	1/	/	7/2	9	0	203	4	30	"	"	330.00	82.50	
4/4	4	6	2	3	191	8	2/	4/	3/	2/	/	11/0	11	0	199	4	28	"	"	330.00	82.50	Project shopped 4/4/78
4/11	2	1	0	3	193	7	1/	4/	3/	2/	/	10/0	10	0	200	4	16	—	"	105.00	52.50	
4/18	2	1	2	1	193	6	3/	4/2	2/1	2/	/	11/3	14	0	199	1	8	Sun.	"	330.00	66.00	
4/25	5	0	1	1	194	9	1/	3/2	1/1	2/	/	7/3	10	0	203	1	18	"	"	330.00	66.00	
5/2	6	5	1	9	198	5	/	6/2	1/	/	/	7/2	9	0	203	0	17	—	Daily	470.00	78.33	Project shopped 5/5
5/9	15	2	2	9	205	5	/	/	/1	/	/	0/2	2	0	210	0	22	—	Daily	470.00	31.33	205 occupied by 5/30; RM bonus of $300
						/	/	/	/	/	/											$300 pd to RM for fill up bonus 5/17
						/	/	/	/	/	/											Rent Increase
						/	/	/	/	/	/											
						/	/	/	/	/	/											
						/	/	/	/	/	/											

However, when all vacancies that had occurred during the preceding six months were reviewed, it was noted that the vacancies in the two-bedroom units were decreasing at a faster rate than the vacancies in other units. The trend indicated that the two-bedroom units would have fewer vacancies within a few weeks. If anything, the rents on these units should be increased. This fact became obvious only when the vacancy trends were examined over a period of time. Therefore the company made the trend report a routine procedure.

Unlike static reports such as the vacant unit control form, which only provide snapshots of moments in time, the trend report is a dynamic report that provides a clear view of trends that may signal impending problems or positive turns. For example, if the close rate is currently at 20 percent (normally a good rate), a review of the trend report could reveal that the close rate has been 40 percent, is gradually declining, and probably will go down toward 5 or 10 percent within the next few weeks. Alerted, action can be taken to reverse the trend.

RESIDENT SURVEYS

Earlier in this chapter the following features were listed as the reasons people decide to rent in a given property: location; curb appeal and common areas; security; the specific unit, especially its floor plan and utilization of space; rent; the reputation of the management company and the image of the property itself; and property amenities.

In marketing, it is just as important to understand why people choose to move out as it is to know why they have moved in. After all, as has already been emphasized, resident retention is the most effective marketing tool. So when residents do move out, a move-out follow-up (Figs. 7–25 and 7–26) helps to determine why.

The move-out follow-up involves calling residents who have moved out to determine if they moved for some reason other than the one they gave when they filled out the intent to vacate form. This information helps to pinpoint move-out reasons that are property-related, such as poor maintenance, so that the property manager can take action to ensure that maintenance does not become a reason for other moves out of the property.

The move-out calls form (Fig. 7–25) provides a place to list former residents to be called along with their telephone numbers. This form shows a comparison of the initial reason given for moving and the reason given at the time of the interview. The move-out telephone survey form (Fig. 7–26) provides standard questions to ask to help these interviews move faster.

RENTAL OFFICE "SHOPPING" SURVEYS

A "shopping" survey is done by a hired individual who poses as a rental prospect for the purpose of evaluating the professionalism and effectiveness of a property's rental personnel. Used properly, "shopping" surveys should not indicate a lack of trust in property employees but instead be used as a method for determining where additional training may be required.

The shopping survey questionnaire (Fig. 7–27) covers the basics of what rental agents are expected to do. During the first week of operation, a new property should be "shopped" to ensure that the anticipated heavy traffic will be handled by well-trained personnel. And newly hired rental agents in every property should be shopped soon after they are placed in the rental office to provide feedback on the effectiveness of their training.

To obtain the most accurate information from the shopping survey, the shopper must receive proper instructions. The senior manager must clearly communicate the purpose of the survey as well as any specific instructions. For example, the shopper should appear to be a typical prospective resident who qualifies for the property from all standpoints and should be instructed to ask for the type of unit that is available.

Once the shopping survey has been submitted to the senior manager, she/he should review the report in detail with the rental agent who was shopped as soon as possible. If the report reflects an unsatisfactory performance, the senior manager should schedule another survey after the rental agent has received additional training.

A valuable measurement tool, the shopping survey is also used by rental agents to shop other properties as a training device and as a method of obtaining competitive information.

CONCLUSION

As emphasized throughout this text, the property manager's primary obligation is to increase the property's net operating income (NOI) and produce a profit for the owner. Becoming an expert in the marketing and leasing of residential units will be of invaluable assistance to the property manager in fulfilling this obligation because, regardless of whether she/he is directly responsible for the rental of units or works with a rental professional, the property manager will be responsible to some greater or lesser degree for implementing a marketing plan.

The goals of maximizing rental income and populating the property with long-term renters who pay on time and in full and who respect the property as their home and as the home of their fellow renters are accomplished by defining and understanding the characteristics of the property and why people would choose to live there; defining and understanding the target market; developing a marketing plan; establishing a marketing budget; determining the property's criteria for rental eligibility; obtaining prospects and showing and leasing the units; evaluating the results of marketing efforts; and adjusting the marketing plan as needed to produce the desired results.

Whether in rent-up or re-rental, in a strong or soft market, the marketing of a multifamily property and the units within the property is accomplished through the design of a unique property logo and identity; the use of print media (such as off-site and on-site signage, brochures, newspapers, and mailings), broadcast media (such as radio and television), and the Internet; and through effective public relations efforts. Additional strategies, such as value-added concessions and other incentives, may apply in particularly soft markets. Under any circumstances, the services of a professional graphic designer, sign manufacturer, and web designer are recommended for the best results. The services of an advertising agency, public relations organization, and/or professional multihousing

FIGURE 7–25. Move-out Calls

Resident	Phone Number	Move-out Date	Reason of Intent	Information from Phone Contact

(Property)

(Property Manager or Senior Mananger Signature)

(Month of Report)

(Date)

FIGURE 7–26. Move-out Telephone Survey

Former Resident ____________________ Date ____________

New Address ____________________ ☐ Private home ☐ Apartment

Property Name/Address ____________________ Unit Type ____________ Length of Occupancy ____________

1 What did you like best about living at this property? ____________________

2 What were your main objections to living here? ____________________

3 Which of the following facilities influenced you to select this property?

	First Choice	Second Choice
Appearance of aparment community	☐	☐
Nearby schools	☐	☐
Neighborhood's income level	☐	☐
Proximity to business	☐	☐
Nearby shopping	☐	☐

4 How long had you planned to live here? ____________________

Did you remain a resident for this period of time? ☐ Yes ☐ No

If answer is no, please explain ____________________

5 First awareness of apartment community:

☐ Newspaper ☐ Billboards/signs
☐ Friend ☐ Neighborhood
☐ Driving around ☐ Resident

6 Maintenance

	Yes	No
Did you understand request for service procedures?	☐	☐
Did you have occasion to use this procedure?	☐	☐
Was service given within reasonable amount of time?	☐	☐
Were service problems corrected?	☐	☐
Was service person helpful and courteous?	☐	☐
Was the laundry facility adequate?	☐	☐

7 Was the manager available when needed? ☐ Yes ☐ No

8 Would you recommend these apartments to your friends? ☐ Yes ☐ No

FIGURE 7–27. Shopping Survey Questionnaire

The purpose of this Shopping Survey is to enable the (name of management firm) Marketing Committeeto monitor the effectiveness of the rental staff. It will be used as a training tool in renting units.

Telephone Interview	Yes	Somewhat	No
1. Was the property telephone number easily obtainable?	☐	☐	☐
2. Was the office easy to reach via telephone?	☐	☐	☐
3. Did the leasing agent identify him/herself?	☐	☐	☐
4. Was your name requested?	☐	☐	☐
5. Was the attitude of the leasing agent professional?	☐	☐	☐
6. Were you encouraged to visit this property?	☐	☐	☐
7. Did the leasing agent attempt to establish an appointment?	☐	☐	☐
8. Were you given all the information you requested?	☐	☐	☐
9. Were the directions to the property clear and easy to understand?	☐	☐	☐

Locating the Property	Yes	No	N/A
10. If signs were noted en route, were they helpful and fresh looking?	☐	☐	☐
11. Was your first impression of this residential property favorable?	☐	☐	☐

Comments

____

____

Rental Office and Rental Personnel	Yes	Somewhat	No
12. Was the office professional in appearance?	☐	☐	☐

13. Please rate the overall appearance of the rental office:

☐ Excellent ☐ Good

☐ Satisfactory ☐ Unsatisfactory

	Yes	Somewhat	No
14. Was the leasing agent's appearance professional?	☐	☐	☐

Approach

15. How were you greeted?

☐ Very friendly and enthusiastically

☐ Somewhat friendly, but not enthusiastically

☐ Neither friendly nor enthusiastically

16. How quickly were you greeted?

☐ Immediately upon entering

☐ The person was either on the telephone or speaking with another person, but he/she did acknowledgemy presence and immediately approached me when the conversation ended.

☐ The person was doing paperwork, filing, or other office work and greeted me when finished.

(continued)

FIGURE 7–27. Shopping Survey Questionnaire (*Continued*)

	Yes	No	N/A
17. Did the leasing agent stand up when extending the greeting?	☐	☐	☐
18. Did he/she ask for your name?	☐	☐	☐
19. Did the leasing agent give you his/her name?	☐	☐	☐

Marketing Efforts	Yes	No	N/A
20. Did the leasing agent ask where you live now, what type of housing it is, the size of your family, and related information?	☐	☐	☐
21. If a model or vacant unit was available, did he/she offer to show it to you?	☐	☐	☐
22. Was the model attractive and well maintained?	☐	☐	☐
23. Was the vacant unit clean and ready for occupancy?	☐	☐	☐

If no, please explain:____

	Yes	No	N/A
24. If a model or vacant unit was not available, did the leasing agent attempt to rent another size unit to you or refer to another multifamilyproperty managed by the company?	☐	☐	☐
25. What reasons did he/she give you for renting at the property?	☐	☐	☐
26. Were you asked how you heard about this property?	☐	☐	☐
27. Did the leasing agent give you a brochure?	☐	☐	☐
28. Were you asked to rent at this property?	☐	☐	☐
29. Were you asked to sign a guest card or guest book?	☐	☐	☐
30. Were you asked for your phone number?	☐	☐	☐
31. Were you given information about the management company?	☐	☐	☐

32. Please rate the leasing agent's overall efforts to close the sale, and his/her overall sales approach:

Efforts To Close the Scale

☐ Excellent

☐ Good

☐ Satisfactory, needs improvement

☐ Poor, no effort made

Overall Sales Approach

☐ Excellent

☐ Good

☐ Satisfactory, needs improvement

☐ Poor, no effort made

Comments

____

____

____

____

____

____

marketing firm also may be advisable, depending on certain variables attendant to the individual property.

Once prospects make the decision to visit the property, it is the property manager's responsibility to ensure that prospects have a favorable view of the property and the model units, that the rental office and rental personnel reflect favorably on the property, and that the property complies with all local, state, and federal requirements in its marketing efforts.

Because the rental/leasing agent is the most significant player in the marketing cycle, she/he must do everything right to help prospects decide to rent and close the deal. The agent must make a positive first impression; have an effective and professional presentation; understand and respect the importance of in-person and telephone sales etiquette; qualify prospects; discuss the unit, the property, and management knowledgeably and positively; overcome objections; close the sale; and maintain appropriate records to enable follow-up and tracking of marketing information. Instruments used in monitoring the effectiveness of marketing efforts include the vacant unit control form, the trend report, resident surveys, and rental office "shopping" surveys.

By understanding the role of marketing in the overall success of a property, it should be clear to the property manager that mastering multihousing marketing is critical to her/his own success. Property managers and others interested in multihousing marketing can explore the certified leasing professional (CLP) program sponsored by local Home Builders Associations. For information, contact the Director of Professional Development, Multifamily Division, National Association of Home Builders, 1-800-368-5242 Ext 8215.

A discussion and outline of a marketing plan begins on the next page of this text.

ADDENDUM: THE MARKETING PLAN

Because the cash flow and net operating income (NOI) of a property depend virtually exclusively on rental income, the marketing plan that aims to maximize rental income while populating the property with long-term renters who pay on time and in full and who respect the property as their home and as the home of their fellow renters is a critical instrument for the property's success. Depending on the structure of the property and the management organization, the property owner's instructions, and the stipulations regarding marketing contained in the management agreement, the property manager will be responsible to a greater or lesser degree for the creation, implementation, monitoring, and evaluation of the marketing plan. The marketing plan should therefore be inserted into the property's operations manual as a reference guide for the property's marketing program.

CONTENTS OF A MARKETING PLAN

Although each property's marketing plan should be individually customized, the contents of a practical marketing plan should include but may not be limited to:

- Market analysis, including competitive analysis
- Analysis and identification of current renter demographics; identification of ideal renter demographics; and comparison of current and ideal renter demographics
- Property income and expense analysis and rental projections
- Property long-term financial analysis and rental projections
- Identification and articulation of the marketable features and benefits of the property, its units, and its lifestyle
- Statement of eligibility criteria (which must be objective and nondiscriminatory, must be applied consistently to every applicant, and must comply with Equal Housing and all other local, state, and federal housing regulations)
- Compliance with the stipulations(s) contained in the management agreement regarding management's responsibility and authority to perform various marketing functions
- Specification of the titles, responsibilities, and reporting/accountability flow of those professionals responsible for fulfilling the management agreement with regard to marketing functions (including those professionals employed by management, those subcontracted to management, and those working for the property and/or the owner outside of management's purview)
- Specification of the protocol to be followed to maintain and most expeditiously prepare the property and available/vacant units for marketing and showing
- Design and incorporation of a property logo and distinct property identity
- Design and implementation of an off-site and on-site signage system
- Design and production of a property brochure and informational materials
- Design and implementation of a marketing advertising program, including print, broadcast media, and the Internet
- Design and implementation of a marketing public relations program
- Design and implementation of a marketing referral program
- Identification, furnishing, and maintenance of one or more model units

- Design, equipment, and staffing of a rental office
- Hiring, training, and supervision of rental/leasing agents and rental office personnel
- Calculation of a marketing budget and spending plan and integration into the property's overall operating budget
- Identification and implementation of instruments for monitoring, evaluating, and adjusting the effectiveness of the marketing plan

8

Processing Applications, Move-in and Move-out Procedures, and Resident Relations and the Resident Handbook

ESTABLISHING POSITIVE RESIDENT RELATIONS FROM THE START

As stated in Chapter 7, Marketing Rental Housing and the Marketing Plan, the goal of virtually every multifamily property is to maximize rental income and to be populated by long-term renters who pay on time and in full and who respect the property as their home and as the home of their fellow renters. Logic dictates that, with only rare exceptions, residents will be willing to pay higher rents, stay long-term, remit payment on time and in full, and demonstrate respect for the property in which they live when their residential needs are met and they are happy living in their units and in the property. Of course, many factors contribute to this sense of satisfaction among residents, including the appropriateness of the unit and the property to their personal requirements, the maintenance service provided to the unit and the property, and the value residents feel they are getting for their rental dollars. In the end, though, all of these factors can be grouped into one ultimate defining category: the relationship between the resident and the property. Through the services it provides, it is professional management that shapes and defines this relationship.

Contrary to the notion that resident relations begin on the day the resident moves in, the reality is that cultivating positive resident relations must begin the very first moment a prospect learns of the property. From the image of the property that is communicated via marketing and advertising instruments to the initial interpersonal contact with a property staff member over the phone, via e-mail, or in person, to the impression that is made by the property's curb appeal the first time a prospect visits to when the resident first sets foot in the rental-ready unit, all of these experiences can and should be used to foster positive resident relations right from the start.

The importance of creating a positive first impression and cultivating superior resident relations has been emphasized throughout this text. Now the discussion moves forward to the proper procedures for processing applications, effecting seamless moves into and out of the property, and the all-important resident handbook, all of which present on-going opportunities to establish and enhance positive resident relations.

PROCESSING APPLICATIONS

Applications will be submitted to the property and the property's designated rental agent by individuals who are interested in becoming residents. For their part, the property owner, management company, and manager are interested in renting to individuals who meet the criteria of the most desirable residents (i.e., renters who pay their rent on time, reside peaceably with their fellow residents, and remain desirable renters in the property for a long time). Managers of developments assisted by the U.S. Department of Housing and Urban Development (HUD) or those financed by tax-exempt bonds have the additional objective of selecting applicants who are eligible under program regulations. What follows is a discussion of how the application process can bring the most desirable residents together with the multifamily community where they most want to live.

THE APPLICATION PROCESS

The Application Form

Prospects who are serious about wanting to rent a unit in a property must be required to complete a residency application such as the one shown in Figure 8–1. Prospects should fill out the application in the presence of and with the assistance of the rental agent or property manager and must sign the application themselves; no adult can sign an application for another adult. Seniors applying for residency under Section 8 elderly or family programs also must fill out a personal history form.

Each adult (18 years of age and older) who will live in the unit must sign the application. These signatures make each person individually liable for the accuracy of the information contained on the application. Unrelated persons who will occupy a unit together should fill out separate applications in case the need for collection activity arises in the future. Signatures are especially critical when unrelated persons are renting together because without proper signatures the property manager is not legally authorized to inquire into the applicant's credit history. Under all circumstances, all persons of all ages who will live in a dwelling unit must be listed on the application.

Although the form in Figure 8–1 provides a sample, each property should devise its own application form so that all information necessary for proper processing, leasing of the apartment, and eligibility determination is requested and obtained. Asking for information such as race, marital status, age, familial status, handicap, and sexual preference on a residency application is illegal unless the information is required to verify eligibility for a federal or state housing program. In any case, each applicant should be required to answer every question on the application form.

Background and Credit Checking Including the Fair Credit Reporting Act

The residency application should include a statement, signed by the applicant, that authorizes the property, through its rental agent and/or manager, to obtain an investigative report on the applicant's background and credit history. The statement should say that the report is to include information about the applicant's character, general reputation, personal characteristics, style of living, and credit standing. The application should have a box or line near the statement for applicants to initial or sign to indicate that they understand the agreement in the event of a dispute or litigation later.

A full credit report should be obtained for all applicants prior to deciding to admit them to the property. The most convenient and comprehensive way to accomplish this goal is to install a computer link in the rental/management office directly connected or connected via Internet to one or more credit reporting bureaus. Having the ability to run a full credit report at all times can be invaluable, especially for those properties that operate on the weekends.

The real benefit of a credit report is contained in the written information it produces. A written document avoids the possibility of misinterpreting oral data and reduces dependency on credit "scores."

A person's credit payment record is critical to the application process because although people's habits do not change easily, their economic and personal situations often do. Their payment records also change accordingly. A person who has been and/or is currently delinquent in paying financial obligations elsewhere is almost certain to be late in paying rent anywhere else she/he might live.

The Fair Credit Reporting Act requires that all applicants who are rejected based on their credit receive an adverse action notice that includes the name and contact information of the consumer reporting agency that provided the credit information. The adverse action notice also must state that the credit reporting agency was not responsible for the adverse action and that the rejected applicant has the right to dispute the accuracy of the credit report and request a free report within 60 days. It is imperative that property managers provide this adverse action notice to all applicants who are rejected because failure to do so can result in legal action against the property, the owner, and the management company.

Employment and Income Verification

It is vitally important to verify an applicant's income to determine whether or not she/he can afford to make regular ongoing rent payments. In HUD-assisted developments or those financed by tax-exempt bonds, an applicant's income also must be verified to ascertain that the applicant is within the income limits of the applicable program. In either case, the manager should verify every applicant's place of employment, length of employment, and income.

Typically, income is verified by mailing, faxing, or e-mailing a form such as the one shown in Figure 8–2 directly to the applicant's employer and asking the employer to complete and return the form directly to the rental/management office. Either way, the applicant should not handle the form at any time after signing its authorization to be used.

For certain developments financed with tax-exempt bonds, applicants are required to submit either a W-2 or the most recent 1040 to establish income. At HUD-assisted de-

FIGURE 8–1. Application for Residency*

	(Property)
	(Program) (Unit size)
(Applicant)	(Soc. Sec. No.)
(Spouse or other applicant)	
(Address)	
( ) (Home Phone) ( ) (Business Phone)	( ) (Business Phone) ( ) (Total Housing Cost)
(Present Landlord)	( ) (Business Phone)
(Address)	(City) (State) (Zip Code)
(Previous Address)	(City) (State) (Zip Code)
(Previous Landlord)	( ) (Business Phone)
(Address)	(City) (State) (Zip Code)

All others who will occupy the dwelling:

(Legal Name)	(Relationship)
(Legal Name)	(Relationship)
(Legal Name)	(Relationship)
(Legal Name)	(Relationship)

Employment status (attach additional statement if more than two wage earners):

(Employer)	(Employer)
(Address)	(Address)
(City) (State) (Zip Code)	(City) (State) (Zip Code)
(Position) (How long?)	(Position) (How long?)
(Supervisor)	(Supervisor)
(Supervisor's Phone)	(Supervisor's Phone)

*Applications for seniors developments may include additional questions that do not appear on this one.

continued

FIGURE 8–1. Application for Residency* (*Continued*)

Income

Employment earnings	Hourly/ Weekly	Annual	All other income	Monthly	Annual
Base pay of applicant	________	________	Social Security	________	________
Overtime or other employment earnings	________	________	Pensions/disability	________	________
Base pay of Spouse or other applicant	________	________	Interest/dividends	________	________
Overtime or other employment earnings	________	________	Alimony	________	________
Earnings of any other occupant	________	________	Total income	________	________

Assets (value) ____________ (Securities) ____________ (Real Estate) ____________ (Other)

____________ (Bank) $ ____________ (Savings) $ ____________ (Checking)

____________ (Address) ____________ (City) (State) (Zip Code)

Credit references

____________ (Company) ____________ (Company)

____________ (Address) ____________ (Address)

____________ (City) (State) (Zip Code) ____________ (City) (State) (Zip Code)

Emergency notification

____________ (Name) ____________ (Phone) (Relationship)

____________ (Address) ____________ (City) (State) (Zip Code)

____________ (Physician) ____________ (Business Phone) (Home phone)

____________ (Address) ____________ (City) (State) (Zip Code)

Medical insurance ☐ Yes ☐ No If yes, specify. ____________ Total premiums $ ________

No. cars in family________ Year________ Model____________ Amount owed $ ________

No. cars in family________ Year________ Model____________ Amount owed $ ________

Do you have any pets? ☐ Yes ☐ No Describe:____________

I, ____________, hereby apply to lease apartment located at ____________

Apt. no.________, Building no.__________, Commencing 20_____, at the monthly rental of $__________.

continued

FIGURE 8–1. Application for Residency* (*Continued*)

I authorize you to obtain an investigative credit report in connection with this application. I understand that this report may include information about my character, general reputation, personal characteristics, and/or mode of living, and credit standing. I understand I can request the name of the reporting agency providing this information.

The sum of $__________________ ☐ cash, ☐ check , is deposited. If this application is approved, I agree that the money deposited shall apply toward my security deposit in the amount of $________________ , and that I will enter into a lease on your standard form. Should this application be cancelled by the applicant, deposit will be refunded. Refunds will be mailed from the home office within 30 days of written notice of cancellation.

I understand that the apartment will be ready for occupancy on or about ___________________ , 20______ , but I agree that the Lessor shall not be under any obligation to provide occupancy on that date because of approval of this application or for any other reason. Should the apartment not be ready for occupancy within 30 days from the above date, I may cancel this application and receive full refund of my deposit.

I have read this application and I hereby state and represent that the information provided by me in this application is complete and accurate, and I acknowledge and agree that in the event I enter into a lease with __________________________________ Apartments that lease may be cancelled by Lessor in the event that any of the information provided by me in this application, or any other document furnished by me is materially inaccurate or incomplete. I understand that the Rules and Regulations are adopted for the benefit of all tenants and proper operation of the property, and I agree that my tenancy will be subject to them.

I hereby give permission for the Social Security Administration to release my employment information to

____.
(Development manager)

____
(Development manager's signature)

____
(Applicant's signature)

____
(Date)

____
(Applicant's signature)

FIGURE 8–2. Employment Verification*

Employment Verification Release
This form authorizes the source listed below to release the information requested on this verification.

TO: ______________________ (Name of source)

______________________ (Address)

______________________ (City, state, zip)

RE: ______________________ (Name of applicant)

______________________ (Address)

______________________ (City, state, zip)

______________________ (Social security number)

______________________ (Signature of applicant)

To Whom It May Concern:

The individual/family listed above has applied for rental assistance at our development. According to federal law, all family income and assets must be verified in written form by the appropriate source. This information is used to determine the family's eligibility within the income limits set by the U.S. Department of Housing and Urban Development and in calculating the applicant's rent. We would appreciate your providing the information requested below.

______________________ (Date)

______________________ (Property manager signature)

Employment verification

Is the income received exempt under federal statute? (For definition, see back of page.) ☐ Yes ☐ No

1. Employment date ______________________
2. Present position ______________________
3. Probability of continued employment ______________________
4. Current base rate $__________ per:

   ☐ Hour (average hours/week) ☐ Annually

   ☐ Week ☐ Month

   ☐ Other, please explain ______________________
5. Probability of pay increase in the next 12 months? ☐ Yes ☐ No If yes, give date __________

   New pay rate $ ______________________
6. Probability of overtime hours in the next 12 months? ☐ Yes ☐ No
7. Is employee entitled to any other compensation (bonus, tips, commissions, etc.)? ☐ Yes ☐ No

   If yes, please specify. ______________________
8. If employee is covered by pension or profit sharing, how much can be withdrawn without retiring or terminating employment? $______________________

**Adapted from form used by the Glick Management Co., Indianapolis, Indiana.*

continued

FIGURE 8–2. Employment Verification* (*Continued*)

9. If no longer employed, give date and reason for termination of employment ____________________

10. Is employee on leave of absence? ☐ Yes ☐ No If yes, state reason ____________________

Date from ____________________ to ____________________

____________________ ____________________ ____________________
(Signature of representative) (Phone) (Date)

____
(Title)

Annual Income Exclusions

- Meals on Wheels or other programs that provide food for the needy: groceries provided by persons not living in the household.
- Grants or other amounts received specifically for –
  - Auxiliary apparatus for a handicapped person
  - Expenses for attendant care provided by other than a family member living in the household
  - Medical expenses
  - Out of pocket expenses for participation in publicly assisted programs and only to participation in these programs (These expenses include special equipment, clothing, transportation, child care, and similar items.)
- Income associated with persons who live in the unit but are not regular household members, including –
  - Payments received for care of foster children
  - Income of live-in attendants
- Annual rent credits or rebates paid to seniors by government agencies
- Income excluded by federal statute –
  - Relocation payments made under Title I of the Uniform Relocation Assistance and Real Property Acquisition Policies Act of 1977
  - Allotment value of coupons made under Food Stamp Act of 1977
  - Payments received under Domestic Volunteer Service Act of 1973 (employment through VISTA, Retired Senior Volunteer Program, Foster Grandparents Program, youthful offender incarceration alternatives, senior companions)
  - Payments received under Alaskan Native Claims Settlement Act
  - Payments from certain submarginal U.S. land held in trust for certain Indian tribes
  - Payments, rebates, or credits received under federal Low-Income Home Energy Assistance Programs (Includes any winter differentials given to the elderly)
  - Payments under the Job Training Partnership Act (employment and training programs for Native Americans and migrant and seasonal farmworkers, Job Corps, veterans employment programs, state job training programs, career intern programs)
  - Payments from disposal of funds of Grand River Band of Ottawa Indian
  - The first $2000 of per capita shares received from judgments awarded by the Indian Claims Commission or the Court of Claims or from funds the Secretary of Interior holds in trust for an Indian tribe
  - Scholarships from any source or veterans benefits used or tuition, fees, books, equipment, supplies, transportation, miscellaneous personal expenses, and materials
  - Student loans (regardless of how they are actually spent)
  - Payments received from Title V of the Older Americans Act (Green Thumb, Senior Aides, Older American Community Service Employment Program)
  - Rent rebates made by the development with Section 5 through 7 of Chapter 3
  - Payments received under training programs funded by U.S. Department of Housing and Urban Development (Comprehensive Improvement Assistance Program)

continued

FIGURE 8–2. Employment Verification* (*Continued*)

Credit Reference Release

This form authorizes the source listed below to release the information requested on this verification.

TO: ______________________________
(Name of source)

____
(Address)

____
(City, state, zip)

RE: ______________________________
(Name of applicant)

____
(Address)

____
(City, state, zip)

____
(Social security number)

____
(Signature of applicant)

To Whom It May Concern:

The individual/family listed above has applied for residency at our development. In each application we require a check on the prospective resident's credit record. The applicant has given you as a reference because he/she has done business with you in the past.

Please rate this applicant, write remarks below, and return this form in the self-addressed stamped envelope. Thank you in advance for your cooperation.

______________________________ ______________________________
(Property manager signature) (Date)

Credit Reference

(If the account has been closed, please indicate "closed" and rate if possible.)

Account number ______________________ Rating ______________________

Date account opened ______________________ High credit $ ______________________

Current balance $ ______________________ Monthly payment $ ______________________

Payment record ____

____

____

____

______________________ ______________ ______________
(Signature) (Phone) (Date)

____
(Title)

velopments and also those developments financed with tax-exempt bonds, there are also a number of specialized verification forms that must be completed to establish employment, income, normal overtime, and other employment-related issues. Some HUD programs also require verification of Social Security income. Applicants for this type of housing also must sign forms giving permission to their banks, welfare agencies, and other appropriate organizations to release information for income verification.

Should a question arise about the accuracy or validity of the information provided on the employment verification form, the rental agent or property manager should ask to see the applicant's most recent pay stub or W-2 form and should make every attempt to talk directly with the individual who completed the form in question.

Some conventional properties and developments also insist on copies of income tax returns to verify income.

Rental History Verification

People's past rental history is a clear predictor of their future as renters. The rental agent or property manager should therefore check with the managers and landlords of properties in which applicants have recently lived to determine rent-paying history, whether the applicant abided by policies, how the applicant treated the property, and whether the applicant has good housekeeping habits. Because an applicant's present landlord may have a vested interest in giving an inaccurate but favorable report to get rid of a problem resident, the rental agent or property manager should try to contact at least three previous landlords.

The rental agent or property manager can use a form similar to the one shown in Figure 8–3 to obtain information on an applicant from the applicant's previous property manager. However, a phone call is strongly recommended because people are afraid of lawsuits and other legal action when they commit themselves to writing and are more likely to state true feelings in a one-to-one conversation. In addition, valuable information that is not conveyed in writing can be picked up over the telephone from tone of voice and other innuendoes. Conversation also allows for immediate answers to follow-up questions whereas written responses do not.

When making a previous residence investigation, the rental agent or property manager should keep in mind that she/he can be guilty of invasion of privacy if certain questions are asked about an applicant's personal life. To avoid any impropriety and to gain the greatest insight into the likely disposition of the applicant as a resident, the most telling question that can be asked of a past landlord or manager is, "Would you be willing to rent to this applicant again?"

Under any circumstances, rental agents and property managers should be consistent in applying their selection criteria. Similarly, when providing references for current or former residents to other rental agents or property managers, the report should be based exclusively on factual, verifiable information.

Rental agents and property managers must be aware that the Fair Credit Reporting Act requires that notice be provided to an applicant whenever information is sought about that applicant from a tenant screening service, a reference checking service, and/or from other information providers that either use credit reports from a credit bureau or rely on information about the applicant's rental history. Notice is not required, however, when a property owner, management company, and/or property manager verifies the information provided on a rental application independently and without the help of an outside service.

The Application Fee

Without an application fee, many persons who are not seriously interested in the property or who are patently unqualified may waste everybody's time by filling out an application. Conversely, an up-front application fee tends to discourage this type of applicant, shows the applicant's good faith, and covers the cost of the credit check and other administrative expenses associated with processing applications. (Credit check fees must be reflective of the actual cost of obtaining the credit report and not "made up.") However, in some localities, an application fee cannot be collected at some developments that are HUD-assisted or financed by tax-exempt bonds. The rental agent or development manager should check with the appropriate authorities before instituting an application fee; in some instances, a rental deposit can be collected.

Should an application fee be allowable, the application form must state whether or not the fee is refundable and under what circumstances and whether or not the fee is applicable to rent.

APPLICATION PROCESSING CHECKLIST

Regardless of whether the property is conventional, HUD-assisted, or financed by tax-exempt bonds, a processing checklist such as the one in Figure 8–4 simplifies the work involved in moving applicants forward through move-in. The rental agent or property manager should use this checklist to walk the applicant through the application process, placing checkmarks and dates next to each item as the process proceeds. When the entire process is finished, and assuming the applicant has been approved as a resident, the checklist should be the first item placed in the resident's file folder. (See Chapter 9, Managing the Site Office and the Operations Manual for more on resident files.)

The checklist provides an overall control at all times during application processing and ensures that all the appropriate forms and procedures are completed. It is especially helpful when a file involves more than one person. This application checklist also serves as a summary for periodic audits of the file by the senior manager. In fact, the bottom portion of the sample checklist shown in this text contains blanks for audit purposes.

PROCESSING APPLICATIONS AT HUD-ASSISTED DEVELOPMENTS

Rental agents and development managers at HUD-assisted developments must be fully knowledgeable about the spe-

FIGURE 8–3. Request for Residency Information

____
Date

____
Name

____
Title

____
Address

____
City, State, ZipCode

(insert name of applicant)
____

has applied for an apartment/townhouse at

____

We would appreciate any information you can give regarding the kind of residnet he/she was while renting from you. The form below is provided for your convenience. Your cooperation in completing and returning it in the enclosed self-addressed envelope is greatly appreciated.

Sincerely,

____

- · - · - · - · - · - · - · - · - · - · - · - · - · - · - · - · -

Address of apartment/townhouse rented

____

Move-In Date: ________________________

Move-Out Date: ________________________

Please check appropriate answer:

Housekeeping: ☐ Excellent ☐ Good ☐ Poor

Rent Paid: ☐ On time ☐ Late ☐ Varied

I ☐ would ☐ would not rent to this person again.

Other comments: ________________________

____

____

____
Title

____
Date

FIGURE 8–4. Processing Checklist

Property Name: ______________________ Resident Name: ______________________

Program: ____________ Date of Move-in: ____________ Apt. Address: ______________________

This checklist must be placed on top of the certification paper in each resident folder. The purpose of this checklist is to ensure that all paperwork required by HUD and/or the management company is processed and available for audit. Check all forms that are applicable to the resident. As each is completed, date the appropriate blank.

1. Credit Information	Date Requested	Date Received
☐ Credit Report	________	________
☐ Landlord Check	________	________
☐ Individual		
1 ______________________	________	________
2 ______________________	________	________
3 ______________________	________	________
☐ Guaranty of Lease	________	________
☐ Credit Report for guarantor	________	________
☐ Individual Credit Checks for guarantor		
1 ______________________	________	________
2 ______________________	________	________
3 ______________________	________	________

2. Management Company forms required for this application

- ☐ Acknowledgement of instructions
- ☐ Resident information handbook
- ☐ Vial of life
- ☐ Mailbox tag
- ☐ Lease
- ☐ Pro-rata addendum to lease
- ☐ Move-In inspection
- ☐ Rent due agreement
- ☐ Security deposit agreement
- ☐ Utility service letter
- ☐ Pet addendum to lease
- ☐ Acknowledgement of information
- ☐ Code sheet
- ☐ Carport agreement

3. Verifications required for this application	Date to resid. for authoriz.	Date Returned	Date to Company	Date Returned
☐ Personal history record for seniors	________	________	________	________
☐ Verification of employment (head)	________	________	________	________
☐ Verfication of employment (spouse or other)	________	________	________	________

continued

FIGURE 8–4. Processing Checklist (*Continued*)

	Date to resid. for authoriz.	Date Returned	Date to Company	Date Returned
☐ Verfication of deposit	______	______	______	______
1 Bank:______________	______	______	______	______
2 Bank:______________	______	______	______	______
3 Bank:______________	______	______	______	______
☐ Request for Social Security verification	______	______	______	______
☐ Physician's statement	______	______	______	______
☐ Drug verification	______	______	______	______
☐ Certificate of marital separation	______	______	______	______
☐ Cerification of shareholdings	______	______	______	______
☐ Certification of disability/handicap	______	______	______	______
☐ Verfication of medical/health insurance	______	______	______	______
☐ Certificate of child care	______	______	______	______
☐ Certificate of non-support of dependent children	______	______	______	______
☐ Verification of pension	______	______	______	______
☐ Certificate of single parent	______	______	______	______
☐ Verification of student status	______	______	______	______
☐ Divorce decree	______	______	______	______
☐ Welfare (ADC)	______	______	______	______

4. The forms required by HUD and the states change so often and vary so much by program that they are not printed on this form, but they should be listed here for each applicant

______________________ ______________________

______________________ ______________________

______________________ ______________________

______________________ ______________________

This certification/lease file was audited by: ______________________ Date __________

All papers were processed according to procedures: ☐ Yes ☐ No

If no, follow up audit will be made: ______________________

Corrections acceptable: ☐ Yes ☐ No

cial requirements for processing residency applications, and the development's operations manual should clearly articulate these requirements. For example, because HUD-assisted developments are generally for low- and moderate-income families, specific income requirements must be met. In addition, preference is given to certain categories of persons, such as the displaced and the handicapped. The development manager must maintain detailed income determination records in each resident's file to verify that all legal requirements have been met and must perform income recertification on a scheduled basis, such as every year. HUD-assisted developments also are subject to periodic audits by the U.S. Department of Housing and Urban Development.

Specific application requirements are detailed in HUD handbook 4350.3 *Occupancy Requirements of Subsidized Multifamily Housing Programs* for the program under which the development operates. The information contained in this handbook includes admission requirements and criteria and the appropriate forms to be completed. Although it can be done manually, HUD occupancy certification and recertification is most commonly processed electronically.

A letter such as the one shown in Figure 8–5, with the appropriate forms attached, can be given to applicants at HUD-assisted developments. Only those forms that are to be handled by the resident and that are appropriate for that resident should be attached. All other forms, such as verification of employment and income, must be processed directly from the rental/development office to the source of response. The type and number of forms will vary with the type of program. For the most up-to-date information on forms and their use, the most recent HUD handbooks can be obtained from the nearest HUD area office and by logging on to the HUD website at www.hud.gov.

PROCESSING APPLICATIONS AT DEVELOPMENTS FINANCED WITH TAX-EXEMPT BONDS

Multihousing developments financed with tax-exempt bonds are subject to the regulations set forth in Section 103(b)(4)(A) of the Internal Revenue Code and the state and/or local regulations of the authority issuing the bonds. Usually, 20 percent of the units in the development must be occupied at all times by individuals who earn less than 80 percent of the median income of the area as set forth by the Secretary of the U.S. Department of Housing and Urban Development. In addition to the 20/80 percent rule, states may impose income caps on the remaining residents and such other restrictions as are included in the bond regulatory agreement. In addition to a normal application, the prospective resident also will have to fill out an income certification, which must be verified, and an affidavit of income.

The form of the income certifications and affidavits vary by state, as do the income limits and caps. The rental agent or development manager of a bond-financed property must read the bond documents carefully and consult with the state or local regulatory agency to determine the income certification and record-keeping requirements for that particular development.

EQUAL HOUSING OPPORTUNITY

A property manager is obligated both ethically and legally (under Title VIII of the Civil Rights Act of 1968, amended by the Fair Housing Amendments Act of 1988) to provide equal housing opportunity to all persons without regard to race, color, religion, sex, handicap, familial status, or national origin. An Equal Housing Opportunity (EHO) statement, such as the one shown in Figure 8–6, should be posted in the rental office along with a copy of the property's rental policy, such as the one shown in Figure 8–7. The EHO statement and the rental policy should also be included in the property's operations manual. HUD-assisted developments must post HUD's EHO notices (HUD-928.1A) and post the notice shown in Figure 8–8 in the appropriate languages where advisable.

In establishing a system for complying with the EHO regulations, the property manager also should devise procedures for handling EHO complaints. These procedures should include the steps to be followed by any person who believes that she/he has not been treated fairly. Having a complaint procedure in place helps to reduce the possibility of a housing discrimination complaint being successfully lodged against the property. The procedure for handling such complaints should be incorporated into the operations manual as well.

REVIEWING COMPLETED APPLICATIONS, DETERMINING ELIGIBILITY, NOTIFYING PROSPECTS OF RESULTS, AND MANAGING THE WAITING LIST

REVIEWING COMPLETED APPLICATIONS AND DETERMINING ELIGIBILITY

Each residency application should be reviewed for evidence of adequate financial capacity to meet monthly payments; good rent payment history and credit rating; responsible living habits; and family size versus the vacant unit size (HUD and Title VIII guidelines specify the number of persons eligible to occupy certain types of units).

Eligibility is thus determined based on a combination of thorough credit check, income verification, prior landlord contacts, and a personal interview by the property manager at application time. As previously stated, the Fair Credit Reporting Act requires that notice be provided to an applicant whenever information is sought about that applicant from a tenant screening service, a reference checking service, and/or from other information providers that either use credit reports from a credit bureau or rely on information about the applicant's rental history. No notice is required if the property manager and/or her/his staff perform these checks without any outside assistance.

FIGURE 8-5. Letter to Applicant

Date

Name
Address
City, State ZipCode

Dear Applicant:

Thank you for your interest in our development. The information on the forms listed below is required to qualify you for occupancy. Copies of those forms you are required to have completed are attached. Please return them no later than <u>(date)</u>. The other forms will be sent from our office directly to the sources listed on your application for residency.

____

____

____

____

____

____

____

____

____

____

____

____

Sincerely,

____
Development Manager

FIGURE 8-6. Equal Housing Opportunity Policy Statement

The ___(Name of development)___ believes that all persons are entitled to equal housing opportunity. We do not discriminate against any individual or individuals because of race, sex, color, religion, handicap, familial status, or national origin. The __(Name of development)__ complies with all laws prohibiting such discrimination, including Title VIII, which prohibits—

- Discrimination in the rental or sale of dwellings and in the financing of housing
- Blockbusting
- Discriminatory advertising

NOTIFYING PROSPECTS OF RESULTS AND MANAGING THE WAITING LIST

Applicants should be advised in writing as soon as a determination has been made whether or not to admit them to the property as residents.

Ineligible Applicants

Letters that are sent to applicants who have been determined to be ineligible should state the reason for that determination and the appeals process. If an applicant believes the determination of ineligibility to be unjust, the manager should have her/him submit a formal appeal stating the reasons for the objection in writing. Under all circumstances, the property manager should ensure that notice to ineligible/rejected applicants strictly follows all legal requirements, especially those of the Fair Credit Reporting Act as discussed above, because failure to do so can result in legal action against the property, the owner, and the management company.

Eligible Applicants

For applicants who have been determined eligible, phone contact in addition to written notification is especially important because it lets the rental agent or property manager inform the applicant of the unit that is available and provides immediate feedback regarding the applicant's interest or lack of interest in moving in.

If an eligible applicant wishes to move into an available unit that has been offered, a lease signing appointment should be arranged. If an eligible applicant does not wish to move in, it is important to find out why. Has she/he decided to remain in her/his current home? Has she/he found somewhere else to live? Would she/he prefer a different unit in the property that is currently unavailable? The applications of eligible individuals who choose not to move in at the time a vacant unit is offered should be filed for future re-contact. The application of eligible individuals who prefer a currently unavailable unit should be placed on the waiting list.

Managing the Waiting List

When the property manager receives an intent to vacate form from a current renter, or a unit otherwise becomes available, the rental agent or the manager should use this list to match the available unit with an eligible applicant. Any follow-up contacts with the applicant should be recorded on the application, including any offers of available units and the applicant's response.

Each applicant on the waiting list should be contacted every six months until a unit is assigned or the application is canceled/withdrawn. This procedure enables the rental agent and/or manager to maintain a valid, current waiting list.

FIGURE 8-7. Rental Policy*

To become a resident of this development:

- Select your apartment or townhouse
- Make your deposit by check or money order payable to (name of development)
- Be prepared to wait up to 7 days because credit checks and approvals take that long
- If your application is approved and you decide not to rent the apartment or townhouse, you must forfeit all monies deposited
- If your application is approved and you accept the apartment or townhouse, you will sign a lease in which you agree to abide by all policies of the development
- If your application is not approved, all monies you have deposited will be refunded to you

To be placed on the waiting list:

If the type of apartment or townhouse you want is not available and you want to be placed on the waiting list, do the following:

- Make a deposit by check or money order payable to (name of development)
- Complete your application
- Be prepared to wait up to 7 days because credit checks and approvals take that long
- When the apartment or townhouse becomes available, you must sign a lease within 3 days of notification that the apartment or townhouse is available, and rent will begin within 7 days from notification. Otherwise you will forfeit all monies you have deposited.
- If your application is not approved, all monies will be refunded to you

To register a complaint:

If you have been rejected as an applicant and if you believe that you qualify as a resident, you should do the following:

- Write to (name of development)
- Explain in the letter the circumstances surrounding your rejection as you know them
- Be prepared to wait 7 working days after the receipt of your letter for your application and other material to be reviewed. You will be notified of the outcome of the review

**Adapted with permission from a rental policy poster of ALCO Management, Inc., Memphis, TN.*

FIGURE 8-8. HUD's EHO Notice

U.S. Department of Housing and Urban Development

EQUAL HOUSING
OPPORTUNITY

We Do Business in Accordance With the Federal Fair Housing Law

(The Fair Housing Amendments Act of 1988)

It is Illegal to Discriminate Against Any Person Because of Race, Color, Religion, Sex, Handicap, Familial Status, or National Origin

- In the sale or rental of housing or residential lots
- In advertising the sale or rental of housing
- In the financing of housing
- In the provision of real estate brokerage services
- In the appraisal of housing
- Blockbusting is also illegal

Anyone who feels he or she has been discriminated against may file a complaint of housing discrimination with the:

U.S. Department of Housing and Urban Development
Assistant Secretary for Fair Housing and Equal Opportunity
Washington, D.C. 20410

Previous editions are obsolete

Form HUD-928.1 (3-89)

If payment of a deposit for holding a spot on the waiting list is allowed, the waiting list should contain only the names of eligible applicants who have paid a deposit. (HUD regulations prohibit deposits at all HUD-assisted developments.)

Generally, the waiting list policy should be to continue to accept applications under any circumstances. If the wait is likely to be long, the rental agent or property manager should clearly explain to prospective applicants the approximate anticipated length of the wait in terms of months and/or years. However, an owner may decide to refuse to take any more applications when the average wait for a unit will be a year or longer. Should this be the case, and to avoid potential discrimination charges, all applicants—not just some—should be refused after the decision is made not to accept any more applications.

To estimate the length of time eligible applicants are likely to be on the waiting list before moving into the property, the number of people on the waiting list should be divided by the number of move-outs that are likely to occur at the property during the year. The rental agent or property manager should make sure that applicants understand the length of time they may be on the waiting list and not let people be lulled into complacency about finding a place to live soon just because they are on the waiting list.

When a person on a long waiting list turns down a suitable unit for the first time, a good policy is to advise the applicant that her/his name will drop to the bottom of the waiting list. All property policies, including HUD and other governing polices as appropriate, regarding application processing, applicant notification, and the property waiting list should be included in the property's operations manual.

APPLICATION CONTROL

MASTER CONTROL OF APPLICATIONS

An application control form such as the one shown in Figure 8–9 helps the rental agent and/or property manager follow the status of each application until it is accepted, rejected, or withdrawn. This form is as important to the manager of a small property as it is to the manager of a large one because it represents efficient management practice. It lists in chronological order the name of each person who has applied, the date of the application, the type of unit in which the person is interested, the various follow-up dates, and the final disposition of the application.

Applications should be posted on the application control form on a daily basis and in the order received. An applicant's name should be removed from the control form for any of the following reasons:

- The applicant has been deemed eligible and has accepted a unit that has been offered
- The applicant has been deemed eligible and has been placed on the waiting list
- The applicant has been deemed ineligible
- The applicant has requested that her/his name be withdrawn (the prospect can be reinstated by submitting another application)

THE APPLICATIONS FILE

The property's rental and/or management office should maintain residency applications according to their status. Separate sections of the applications file should be kept for applications that are in process (i.e., applications that are being checked and/or await additional documentation), eligible applications, and ineligible or withdrawn applications.

Another recommended method for maintaining applications is to have a separate file for each unit size. If kept manually, a listing could be attached to the outside of the unit folder showing the date and name of each applicant. As an application is assigned or canceled, the name is marked off the list, and the date of assignment or cancellation is inserted. Ideally, however, the applications files should be computerized.

THE LEASE SIGNING

As soon as an eligible applicant is matched with and accepts the offer of a vacant or upcoming vacant unit, the rental agent or property manager should arrange for the applicant to come to the office to sign a lease and start move-in processing. Every effort should be made to schedule lease signing appointments during normal working days, preferably Monday through Friday, because weekends should be reserved to accommodate the typically heavy traffic of prospects who visit the property.

Once the date and time of the lease signing appointment have been established through a phone conversation with the applicant, information about the appointment should be confirmed in a letter to the applicant. The letter should state the date, time, and location of the lease signing; remind the applicant to bring one month's rent, a security deposit, and whatever other fees and moneys are required and should specify how payment is to be presented (e.g., certified check, money order, personal check); and remind the applicant to bring whatever identification and documentation are required. Confirming the lease signing appointment in this way helps to ensure that the appointment will be kept and that the process will not be delayed by the applicant's failure to bring required moneys and/or documents to the appointment. This process of lease signing confirmation should be documented in the property's operations manual.

As discussed in Chapter 5, Property Maintenance and Energy and Water Conservation, information about the upcoming lease signing and projected move-in should be provided to the property's maintenance team as soon as the lease signing appointment is made so they can prepare the unit for reoccupancy. Then, no fewer than two days before the actual lease signing, the property manager should thoroughly inspect the unit to ensure that it is ready to be seen again by the applicant, probably during the lease signing appointment but definitely in advance of moving in.

Figure 8–9. Application Control Form

Date of Application[1]	Application Number	Current Address	Phone Number	Location Preference or Special Requests[2]	Follow-up Contacts and Final Disposition[3]

1. List only applicants who have paid deposit.
2. Preference might include a first floor two-bedroom unit; special request might include a fireplace unit.
3. Include date and method, whether by phone or letter, of each contact to advise applicant of his/her status on the waiting list.

Also in advance of the lease signing appointment, the property manager should coordinate with the rental agent to ensure that all necessary paperwork has been assembled and completed and that whoever is conducting the lease signing (the rental agent, the property manager, or another professional) is prepared with all the information new residents are most likely to want to know. The items and procedures required for the lease signing appointment should be documented in the property's operations manual as well.

ITEMS TO BE ADDRESSED AT THE LEASE SIGNING APPOINTMENT

The actual lease signing appointment should take place in a separate part of the rental or management office where the rental agent and/or property manager and the new resident(s) can be alone together to conduct business uninterrupted. The rental agent and/or property manager conducting the lease signing should take the following steps to ensure a smooth transaction and to make the first official encounter between the new resident and the property representative a positive experience. These steps should be documented in the property's operations manual.

Meet new residents promptly when they arrive for the meeting and greet them warmly and enthusiastically. Escort them personally to the lease signing area and offer coffee, tea, or soft drinks.

Appear completely at ease and totally prepared so as to instill confidence and trust in the new residents.

Obtain whatever moneys are due from the new resident and issue receipts.

Present the lease documents to the new resident and go over all of its stipulations, responding completely, honestly, and patiently to all questions. The lease documents should then be signed by all adult individuals who will occupy the unit. The residents should be presented with a duplicate original or a copy of the executed documents while the original executed documents are retained in the resident's file at the property and, if required, one copy provided to the main management office.

If the new resident will be paying directly for gas and/or electric service, cable TV, or other utilities, explain how arrangements are to be made to transfer service and billing to the new resident's name prior to move-in.

Present the resident handbook and have the new resident sign an acknowledgment of receipt of the handbook. This acknowledgment receipt should be placed in the resident's folder. Explain to the new resident that the handbook is their guide to tenancy in the property; review its contents with special emphasis on tenancy expectations, requirements, policies, and procedures; and respond to all questions.

After all paperwork has been completed and signed and all pertinent information has been discussed, insert all copies of paperwork belonging to the new resident into a folder, binder, or packet and present it to the new resident with a smile.

Issue the keys to the unit. The new resident should be given at least one set of keys, but the exact number depends on property policy as stated in the operations manual. Inform the new resident that producing any additional sets of keys beyond those allowed by property policy is the resident's responsibility. The new resident should be required to sign a key receipt form, which should be placed in the resident's file. Keys should be issued only after the lease has been signed and all moneys have been collected.

Issue a mailbox key and nameplates to the new resident. (For privacy and security, some properties list only last names or first initials and last names on the nameplates.)

Assign parking space(s), storage lockers, and/or other applicable facilities if this is property policy. Parking spaces are normally assigned only at properties where they are in short supply. If this is the case, or if such assignments are property policy, then the new resident should receive the assignment(s), car sticker(s), and an explanation of the parking policies during the lease signing meeting.

Explain the services that management provides, the functions of the management staff and the maintenance staff, the management office hours, after-hours and emergency contact information, and the proper procedures for submitting maintenance service requests and inquiries and complaints for management attention.

Ask the new resident if she/he has any questions about what has been presented so far. Listen attentively and patiently, and respond completely.

Escort the new resident to the unit for a move-in inspection. The purpose of this inspection is to establish agreement on the condition of the unit prior to occupancy. (This is why it is so important to have the maintenance staff make the unit ready before the lease signing meeting.) After the new resident is satisfied with having inspected the unit, have the resident sign a move-in inspection form, which should also be signed by the property manager. A copy of this form should be given to the resident, and a copy should be placed in the resident's file. The rental agent or property manager should explain that the resident will also be asked to be present at the eventual move-out inspection so that any changes in the condition of the unit can be compared with this move-in inspection report. If deficiencies are noted during this move-in inspection, it is the property manager's responsibility to have them corrected within 24 hours or other agreed-upon time, but certainly prior to move-in if at all possible. If any deficiency cannot be corrected before move-in, the resident should be advised why and told when all items will be completed. It is the property manager's responsibility to ensure follow-up to the new resident's satisfaction. Once all the corrections have been made, the resident should be asked to initial each appropriate item on the move-in inspection form.

Return to the lease signing area, inform the new resident of any move-in requirements and/or restrictions according to property policy (such as hours or days [e.g., Sundays, holidays] when moves are prohibited), and schedule a move-in date. The rental agent or property manager can avoid an area of potential misunderstanding by informing the resident that rent charges begin from the lease commencement date regardless of the actual date of move-in and that unscheduled move-ins are disallowed because they inconvenience other residents and disturb the work schedules of the property staff. When scheduling the move-in, it is important to check that no other move-in is already scheduled for the same day if more than one move-in will be difficult for the property to accommodate in any way. To ensure the greatest possibility that the property manager or rental agent will be able to be in touch with the new resident in advance of the move-in to reconfirm arrangements, the new resident should be asked to provide a phone number where she/he can be reached as near to the move-in day as possible. If her/his phone will be disconnected in advance of move-in, the property manager or rental agent should request a working mobile phone number and/or an e-mail address where the resident can be reached.

Provide to the new resident all pertinent information about how moving vans need to navigate the property and about the property's insurance requirements for moving companies. This information can help to avoid extra delivery and/or carry-in charges for new residents as well as damage to the property structure. For example, in high-rise buildings, new residents will need to know the size of the loading dock, if there is one, and any overhead or other space limitations the moving van may encounter. (For instance, some moving vans may not fit in loading docks of older buildings.) This is important for the rental agent and property manager to know and to share with the new resident so that the new resident can pass this information on to the moving company.

Assure new residents that a parking space for their moving van (if appropriate) and the use of an elevator (also if appropriate) will be reserved for their use during allowed move-in hours on their move-in day.

Again ask if the new resident has any questions and assure her/him that the property manager will be available after she/he moves in should any additional questions arise. When all discussions have ended, cordially shake each new resident's hand, confirm the move-in date, and say good-bye graciously and warmly. The next time the resident and the property manager meet will probably be on move-in day.

Following the successful lease signing appointment, the rental agent or property manager should provide to bookkeeping all necessary information to get the new residents into the property's bookkeeping system as quickly as possible.

MOVE-IN PROCEDURES INCLUDING ON-SITE TRANSFERS

In terms of resident relations, the first time the prospect visits the property and the lease signing appointment are the two primary impression makers before move-in day arrives. But it is the move-in day itself that is remembered most clearly by residents as their most significant first experience at the property. From the perspective of the property manager, it is on move-in day that resident relations truly begin to equate to resident retention. To a great extent, a resident's decision to renew the lease after the initial term is influenced by what she/he finds on move-in day. A smooth and welcoming move into a well-prepared unit is therefore a critical element in initial resident satisfaction, later resident retention, and overall resident relations.

A SUCCESSFUL MOVE-IN BEGINS WITH A SATISFACTORY FINAL MAINTENANCE CHECK

As indicated above, it is the property manager's responsibility to ensure that the unit in question is in pristine move-in condition at the lease signing appointment. Especially if there were deficiencies that required remediation as a result of the new resident's inspection during the lease signing appointment, but even if there were no such deficiencies, it is also the property manager's responsibility to conduct a thorough final maintenance inspection and quality control check of the unit and its immediate surrounding areas (hallways, stairwells, front steps) before the new resident move-in. A sample pre–move-in inspection and quality control checklist is provided in Figure 8–10. Each property manager should adapt this checklist to the specific characteristics and features of her/his own property.

CONFIRM THE MOVE-IN WITH THE NEW RESIDENTS

Although it may not always be possible to be in contact with new residents who are scheduled to move in, it is always a good practice for the property manager to try to be in touch with them 24 hours before the scheduled move-in to confirm the move-in date and time again and to assure new residents that everything is in readiness for their arrival in their new homes. The inability to contact a new resident the day before move-in should have no impact on what happens on move-in day. However, if the property manager is able to make this contact, the benefit in terms of resident relations is immeasurably positive.

RESERVE A PARKING SPACE AND AN ELEVATOR FOR MOVE-IN DAY

As mentioned above, one of the best ways to demonstrate to new residents that their move-in needs have been taken into consideration is to reserve a parking space for their moving van and an elevator for their exclusive or semi-exclusive use on move-in day (where appropriate, of course).

Also as indicated, during the lease signing appointment, new residents should have received all pertinent information about how moving vans need to navigate the property and what the moving company insurance requirements are for the property. Obviously, the parking space reserved for the van should be in front of or as close as possible to the new residents' new front door. Typically, existing residents are happy to cooperate when asked to relinquish a spot on someone else's move-in day because they recall that the same courtesy was extended to them on their move-in day and they have witnessed the same courtesy extended to residents on their move-out day.

In addition, where appropriate, the property manager should reserve an elevator for the move-in. Ideally, it should be a service elevator, but regardless of whether it is a designated service elevator or a regular passenger elevator, notice should be posted a day before the move-in informing existing residents of which elevator will be used for the move on the following day and stating that this elevator therefore may not be available for general use during the move. The property manager also should have contacted the maintenance crew to install protective padding on the walls of the elevator to be used for the move-in to protect both the new resident's belongings and the elevator walls.

FIGURE 8-10. Pre-move-in Inspection and Quality Control Checklist

- ☐ The apartment is immaculately clean.
- ☐ Work has been completed on any defects found during the move-out inspection.
- ☐ Appliances are in good working order, fully cleaned, and all owner's manuals are with them.
- ☐ All light fixtures work, have bulbs of the proper size, and are clean.
- ☐ Faucets work easily and are not dripping or leaking.
- ☐ Heating and air-conditioning units work correctly, have fresh filters, and have been tested.
- ☐ All windows and doors operate smoothly, have screens in place, and all locks operate properly.
- ☐ If they are provided, all window coverings are in place and operate correctly.
- ☐ The apartment has been fully cleaned, and all repainting and carpet and floor cleaning are properly done.

To a large extent, the resident's decision to renew the lease after the initial term will be influenced by what he/she finds on move-in. Proper preparation and quality control are essential to a successful retention program. If at all possible, the manager should conduct the final pre-move-in inspection, and the inspection should be completed far enough in advance of move-in to allow for any final repairs that need to be completed prior to move-in.

WELCOME THE NEW ARRIVAL

It cannot be emphasized strongly enough how important the move-in experience is to resident relations. Specific actions the property manager can take to welcome new residents as they move in are listed in Figure 8–11. All of the items on this list will help the new resident feel welcome and establish a good relationship between management and the resident. This feeling of welcome is an incentive for the resident to pay rent on time and to cooperate with property policy in general.

FOLLOW-UP COURTESY VISIT

The property manager should pay a brief courtesy visit to the new resident 24 to 48 hours after the move-in. This visit reinforces the welcome and it provides an opportunity for the resident to ask any questions concerning service and other matters that might not be clear or that she/he may have forgotten to ask earlier.

During the move-in follow-up courtesy visit, the property manager should give the new resident a copy of the most current property newsletter and/or calendar (if they exist) and personally invite the new resident to any upcoming property activities. The property manager also should pick up the new resident's work orders or follow-up memo listing any persisting unit defects and assure the new resident that they will be attended to immediately.

Clearly, resident relations defines the difference between a long-term resident who will recommend the property to others and an unhappy, short-term resident. It is the property manager's responsibility to do everything possible to create happy, satisfied residents starting on the day each resident moves in.

ON-SITE TRANSFERS

An on-site transfer occurs when an existing resident moves from one unit within a property to another unit within the same property. Although on-site transfers require the preparation of two units for one rental (the one being vacated and the one being moved into) and are an inconvenience to property staff, they should be approved without hesitation when the resident's current unit is severely damaged by fire or water or is otherwise uninhabitable, when a change in household or family size makes the present unit no longer suitable, when the lease on the present unit is due for renewal and the opportunity to move into a different unit will keep a desirable resident in the property, or under other circumstances in which it is to the property's benefit to allow an on-site transfer and keep the resident in the property.

Figure 8–12 shows suggested steps for processing a resident's on-site transfer. If the transfer is approved, the same steps should be taken for an on-site transfer as are taken when a new resident moves in.

MOVE-OUT PROCEDURES INCLUDING RESIDENTS WHO VACATE WITHOUT GIVING NOTICE ("SKIPS")

REQUIRE 30-DAY WRITTEN NOTICE OF INTENT TO VACATE

Residents are normally required to notify management of their intention to leave the property by submitting a written notice of intent to vacate at least 30 days before they plan to

FIGURE 8-11. Move-in Day Actions for Welcoming New Residents

- Reconfirm that the residents has all of his/her documents, including the lease, resident handbook, policies, emergency numbers, and information about the development and the town or city.
- Provide either work orders, a memo, or a form for the resident to write up any defects or maintenance problems he/she discovers.
- Provide assistance in disposing of boxes and packing materials or instructions on where to dispose of them.
- Confirm that utility transfers have been made and that the Postal Service is notified to start mail delivery.
- Provide information on subscriptions to daily or weekly newspaper delivered in the area.
- Provide a contact person in the event of a move-in problem.
- Explain appropriate property facilities and systems again.
- Complete any unfinished business from the lease-signing meeting.
- Introduce the new residents to neighbors where doing so is appropriate.

move. This notice gives management time to re-rent the unit and complete plans for making the unit ready for re-occupancy. Residents who fail to give the proper move-out notice may be liable for the payment of an additional month's rent and possible forfeiture of their security deposit, depending on the lease provisions, property and management company policy, and any applicable state laws.

As soon as the property manager receives a notice of intent to vacate, the vacating resident's folder should be moved from the present resident file to the moving-out file, and the unit should be listed on the vacant unit control form (see Fig. 7–23 in Chapter 7, Marketing Rental Housing and the Marketing Plan).

These simple policies regarding notice of intent to vacate and identifying and moving the resident's folder should be clearly stated in the resident handbook and the property operations manual, respectively.

SCHEDULE THE MOVE-OUT INSPECTION

The move-out inspection should be scheduled as soon as possible after the intent notice is received and should be per-

FIGURE 8-12. Suggested Steps for Processing an On-site transfer

- Evaluate the reason the resident wants to move.
- Inspect the present apartment prior to approving a transfer.
- Assess the resident for any resident-caused damage to his/her current unit. (If the resident has caused extensive damages in the present apartment, asking the resident to move out might be desirable.)
- If the candidate for transfer meets qualifications, schedule move-in date.
- Sign new lease.
- Transfer security deposit.
- Conduct move-in inspection.
- Record information on vacant unit control form.
- Transfer resident file folder.
- Notify bookkeeper of resident move-outs and move-ins and of any damage charges.
- Exchange keys.

formed by the property manager as quickly as possible after all furnishings have been removed. Final settlement of the account cannot take place until after this inspection.

The first purpose of a move-out inspection is to determine whether the resident has damaged the unit or its appliances and to establish a basis for assessing any damage charges. The second purpose is to pinpoint any items needing correction prior to occupancy by a new resident.

The vacating resident should be present at the move-out inspection. The electricity should be on during this inspection because the appliances should be tested to be sure they work and the lights may be needed to be sure that the unit is clean. Any deficiency in the unit that the resident can easily correct, such as cleaning a dirty stove, should be pointed out to the resident, and she/he should be encouraged to correct it so that the security deposit can be returned. Returning security deposits creates goodwill and increases the chances of beneficial word-of-mouth advertising.

DETERMINE FINAL RESIDENT CHARGES INCLUDING FINAL MONTH'S RENT AND DAMAGE CHARGES

Sometimes, residents move out on the last day of the month and there is no need to calculate a pro-rated rent charge for the last month. More often, however, residents move out before the last day of the month and they will expect to pay their final rent check for only the part of the month during which they occupied the unit. In such cases, it is important for the property manager to understand how to calculate the pro-rated daily amount the resident owes.

Assuming a basic 30-day month, to calculate the daily rate of a unit simply divide the monthly rent by 30. To calculate how much a resident owes for the part of the month she/he occupied a unit, multiply 1/30 of the monthly rent by the number of days the resident occupied the apartment in that month. For example, if a resident was paying $900 per month rent and moved out on the 25th day of the month, based on a 30-day month that is $900 ÷ 30 = $30 per day × 25 = $750. So the resident's final month's rent due is $750.

The move-out inspection report (see Fig. 5–18 in Chapter 5, Property Maintenance and Energy and Water Conservation) can serve as a checklist for resident damage charges. This form, which should be signed by the resident at the conclusion of the move-out inspection, prevents many potential misunderstandings and disputes over the condition of the unit and the amount of the security deposit refund.

RESERVE A PARKING SPACE AND AN ELEVATOR FOR MOVE-OUT DAY

As with moves into the property, the move-out process can be expedited and made more pleasant when the property manager reserves a parking space for the departing resident's moving van and an elevator for move-out use and does everything reasonably possible to make the move-out a positive experience. Helping to ensure a smooth move-out is among the last actions a property manager can take in the area of resident relations. Just as resident relations begin in earnest on move-in day, so they must continue until the moment the vacating resident drives away from the property for the last time. This is true because a satisfied former resident can be a valuable source of referrals and also may move back into the property at a later date.

SECURE THE VACATED APARTMENT

On the day a resident moves out, the property manager should reclaim the keys to the unit from the departing resident and arrange to have the unit secured. The manager also should instruct maintenance to change or rotate the front door lock(s). If a resident vacates and fails to turn in the keys, the lock(s) should be changed and the cost added to that resident's damage charges. The resident bears the responsibility for returning all unit-related keys to management as a prerequisite for the return of the resident's security deposit. This key return policy should be clearly stated in the resident handbook and in the property's operations manual.

RESIDENTS WHO VACATE WITHOUT GIVING NOTICE ("SKIPS")

The importance of the property manager "walking the property" daily has been emphasized throughout this text. One piece of information that may be obtained through these daily walk-throughs is the fact that a resident has "skipped," or moved without giving notice. Other ways of learning that a resident has skipped include reports from property staff, a property neighbor, and mail or other delivery or utility people who visit the property regularly for their own purposes.

As soon as the property manager determines that a resident has skipped, the manager should notify the bookkeeping department; calculate rent and other moneys due, including charges for unit damages; and locate the person's new address if possible. Figure 8–13 lists potential sources of this information on skips.

Residents who vacate without giving notice frequently owe back rent and may have incurred other charges as well. If the unit is vacated with charges owing, the property manager should consult the stipulations contained in the Fair Credit Reporting Act and, after fulfilling those requirements, make a report of the resident's skip and charges owed to the credit reporting firm for the property. Many management firms maintain a policy of reporting all skips with balances and, in many cases, later recover some or all of the funds owed. The property manager should consult with the credit bureau, the Fair Credit Reporting Act, and legal counsel, if necessary, to determine the appropriate reporting methods.

UNIT RE-OCCUPANCY PREPARATIONS

Whether a unit has been vacated by a responsible resident who provided the proper intent to vacate or by an irresponsible resident who skipped, the vacated unit should be prepared for re-occupancy as quickly as possible, ideally within three days of its having been vacated. In certain instances, especially skips, it may be legally necessary to provide notice to the vacated resident that the property intends to re-rent the unit. The property manager should consult with le-

FIGURE 8-13. Potential Sources of Information on Skips

- Relatives in the area or elsewhere, especially those listed on the initial applications under "In case of emergency"
- Places of employment or former employment
- Other residents in the development
- Former neighbors
- The former resident's banks or savings and loans
- Postal Service
- Former spouses
- Churches they attended
- Their children's schools
- Organizations to which they belong
- Restaurants they frequented
- Local grocery and retail shops they frequented
- Local credit bureau
- Telephone company
- Motor vehicle administration (The vehicle registration number of the former resident's car might be needed in case of a judgment.)

gal counsel regarding this and also the appropriate and legal steps to take if a resident has vacated and left possessions behind in the unit.

Whenever possible, the property manager should notify the maintenance staff in advance regarding upcoming unit re-occupancy preparations. The communication about unit preparation that should take place between the property manager and the property maintenance staff, and the actions to be taken to prepare a unit for re-occupancy, are detailed in Chapter 5, Property Maintenance and Energy and Water Conservation and in Chapter 7, Marketing Rental Housing and the Marketing Plan.

ADMINISTRATIVE ACTIVITIES FOR VACATED UNITS

Once a unit has been vacated, the departing resident's files and information should be removed from the active resident file and moved into the vacated resident file.

The bookkeeper should be notified that the move-out has actually occurred and of the amounts due to or from the vacating resident. Normally, the bookkeeper sends the departing resident a final settlement letter that contains a check for any remaining security deposit amount owed to the resident or a bill for any amount owed to the property. Any amount due the vacated resident should be paid promptly within the legal time limits required by the jurisdiction. Typically, this payment should be issued between 7 and 30 days of the resident's move-out, but the property manager should check with legal counsel regarding how long the property has to return moneys due to the ex-resident because exceeding the time limit could prove costly to the property.

COLLECTING UNPAID RENT AND DAMAGE CHARGES

When a resident vacates owing rent and/or damage charges, the property manager should instruct bookkeeping to deduct that amount from the security deposit or, if the security deposit is not sufficient to cover moneys due, to attempt to collect any balance. The most common means for collecting unpaid rent and moneys due from a vacated resident is through a collection agency. These agencies are staffed by professionally trained bill collectors whose purpose is to conserve the time of the property manager and other rental personnel who are not experts in this field.

Collection agencies receive a percentage of the amount collected, sometimes as much as 50 percent, and typically do not charge if they cannot effect a successful collection. For many properties and management companies, the philosophy behind engaging a collection firm is that it is better to have part of what is owed than nothing at all. As with skips and evictions, the property manager should consult with legal counsel regarding the collection of unpaid rent and damage charges.

THE EXIT INTERVIEW

As indicated above, the vacating resident who has given appropriate notice generally will provide a forwarding address for return of the security deposit and any other final communications from the property. Having this forwarding information also allows the property manager to contact the vacated resident to conduct a phone or written exit interview.

The purpose of an exit interview is to learn why a resident chose to leave the property. Just asking why can provide important information about how the ex-resident perceived living in the property and can give important clues as to what current residents may be thinking about the property, its management, and its maintenance. To obtain the most honest answers, the exit interview should be conducted after the resident has vacated but no longer than a month after. If conducted by phone, the exit interview should not be a confrontational conversation but one in which the property manager sincerely requests the previous resident's assistance in making the property a better place for the residents who continue to live there. If the exit interview is conducted via a written questionnaire that the property manager sends to the vacated resident, it might be included with the returned security deposit and should certainly be stamped and self-addressed for the former resident's convenience.

Having the information obtained from a successful exit interview can prove invaluable to the property manager who wishes to retain as many desirable residents as possible.

RESIDENT RELATIONS AND RESIDENT POLICIES

RESIDENT RELATIONS, PROPERTY MANAGEMENT, AND TENANTS ASSOCIATIONS

As has been stated throughout this part of the text, establishing and retaining positive resident relations is a primary aspect of the property manager's responsibilities. It is an objective that is not attained through a single act or in one fell swoop but rather through unwavering respect, responsiveness, and professionalism on the part of the management and maintenance staff toward residents and on-going management and maintenance efforts to foster a residential environment where residents feel welcome and proud to live.

Communication is a vital element in maintaining positive resident relations. This means keeping residents informed about what's going on property-wide (to the extent they are entitled to know) through a regularly published, owner-sanctioned newsletter produced and distributed by management; through management memos; and/or through periodic official informational meetings called and conducted only by the manager or management company.

PROPERTY POLICIES FOR RESIDENTS

In addition to the relationship value of informational newsletters, memos, and meetings overseen by management, these instruments of communication also give management the opportunity to remind residents about the policies that apply to their tenancy in the property and which are codified in the resident handbook. All societies need policies to function smoothly, and a multifamily property is nothing more than a microcosmic society. Hence, it is reasonable to project that without policies to regulate the conduct and other actions of residents with regard to living in the property, chaos would ensue. However, in the presence of policies that have been designed to protect both the owner and the residents, to assist staff in the orderly management and maintenance of the property, and to encourage the peaceful coexistence of all residents as neighbors in the property, an outstanding quality of life can be achieved.

COMMUNICATING POLICIES TO RESIDENTS

The most effective way to communicate policies regarding residency in the property is to codify all the policies into a resident handbook and distribute the handbook to residents as they move in. When changes in policies occur, all residents should be so notified in writing via a memo from management that cites the previous policy, explains any changes to it, and instructs residents to insert the new policy into the resident handbook so that it supersedes the previous policy.

In addition to publishing the property's policies in the resident handbook, certain policies also should be physically posted in the property. These policies include those that apply to the laundry room, recreational facilities such as a swimming pool and tennis court, and a clubhouse or party room. Signs in these areas ensure that the person using the facilities is reminded of the policies at the time of use. These signs in the property's common areas should always be professionally prepared, never handmade.

WHEN RESIDENTS VIOLATE PROPERTY POLICY

It is the property manager's responsibility to handle resident violations of property policy. The first step a property manager should take when a resident violates a property policy is to document the information the manager has regarding the situation. Then the manager should meet with the resident in her/his unit to discuss the problem and firmly press for an acceptable solution, which must include resident compliance with the policy. Regardless of the outcome, the manager should document her/his interaction with the resident. If the resident refuses or persists in the unacceptable behavior, the property manager should continue her/his documentation and meet with the resident again to suggest that the property would be willing to allow the resident to break the lease without penalty if she/he agrees to move out without incident. If the resident again refuses and again persists in the unacceptable behavior, the property manager may have to turn to eviction proceedings as the ultimate enforcement action. But securing a voluntary move-out as a last resort is much better than eviction proceedings, which are lengthy, costly, and of uncertain outcome. Under any circumstances, it is imperative that the property manager maintain ongoing, accurate documentation of all incidents and interaction with the resident in case the matter becomes an issue for litigation.

In all cases and at all times, including but not only while the property manager is pursuing all means of ameliorating a situation in which a resident is violating property policy, it is critical for the manager to apply the property's policies in an unbiased and objective manner and to do nothing that might subject the manager and/or the property and/or the management and/or the owner to a lawsuit claiming discrimination.

A discussion of how a property manager might handle a resident's violation of property policy is contained in Chapter 3, On the Front Line: The Property Manager.

CONCLUSION

Positive resident relations is the best way to retain residents, and retaining residents is one of the most effective ways to increase net operating income. Hence, the property manager must recognize that cultivating positive resident relations should start with the resident's first exposure to the property and must continue throughout each resident's tenure at the property.

Prospective residents should be assisted in filling out residency applications that meet all informational requirements, including those established by the U.S. Department of Housing and Urban Development (HUD) and those for developments financed by tax-exempt bonds, as appropriate. The application process and the application itself should include authorization by the applicant for the property to obtain an investigative background and credit history report and must comply with the Fair Credit Reporting Act.

The property manager also should check on each applicant's rental history by contacting at least three prior landlords. As above, all such checks must comply with the Fair Credit Reporting Act as required by law.

An application fee helps to ensure that applicants are serious and covers the cost of the credit check and other administrative expenses associated with processing applications. However, it is not legal to collect application fees in some areas, and the rental agent and property manager must be aware of the laws governing deposits in both conventional and government-assisted developments. Any requirements for one applicant must be required of all applicants, and the property manager should have an application processing checklist to help the process along.

Applicants should be advised in writing as soon as a determination has been made. Letters that are sent to ineligible/rejected applicants should state the reason for that determination and the appeals process and, again, should comply with the Fair Credit Reporting Act if credit history was part of the decision to reject the applicant. Eligible applicants should be contacted in writing and also by phone to obtain immediate feedback regarding their interest or lack of interest in moving in. If the eligible applicant wishes to move into a unit that has been offered, a lease signing appointment should be arranged. If an eligible applicant does not wish to move in, the property manager should find out why and the application should be filed for future re-contact. Applicants who want to wait for a particular unit should be placed on the waiting list and contacted every six months until a unit is assigned or the application is canceled or withdrawn.

Although most properties continue to accept applications under any circumstances, the owner may refuse to take any more applications if the wait is longer than one year. Applications should be tracked using an application control form that allows the property manager to follow the status of each application until it is accepted, rejected, or withdrawn. All property policies, including HUD and other governing policies as appropriate, regarding application processing, applicant notification, and the property waiting list should be included in the property's operations manual.

The lease signing appointment should be arranged by phone and confirmed in writing. Information about the upcoming lease signing and projected move-in should be provided to the property's maintenance team so they can prepare the unit for re-occupancy. The property manager should thoroughly inspect the unit before the lease signing and should ensure that all necessary paperwork has been completed and that whoever is conducting the lease signing is prepared with all the information new residents are most likely to want. The items and procedures required for the lease signing appointment should be documented in the property's operations manual.

The property professional (rental agent, manager, or other) conducting the lease signing should do everything possible to make the experience a complete, professional, and positive one for the new resident. The process of lease signing should include another inspection of the unit with the new resident so that any deficiencies can be noted and remedied prior to move-in. The move-in date should be scheduled at the conclusion of the lease signing meeting, and the property manager should provide bookkeeping with all necessary information to get the new resident into the property's bookkeeping system.

It is on move-in day that resident relations truly begin to equate to resident retention. A smooth and welcoming move into a well-prepared unit is a critical element in initial resident satisfaction, later resident retention, and overall resident relations. It begins with a satisfactory final maintenance check. Each property manager should use a pre–move-in inspection and quality control checklist to make sure everything is in order.

If possible, the property manager should confirm the move-in appointment with the new resident the day before. The property manager should have reserved a parking space for the moving van and an elevator for the new resident's move-in use, as appropriate, and should greet the new resident on arrival. Then, 24 to 48 hours after move-in, the property manager should pay a follow-up courtesy visit to reinforce the welcome, answer any remaining questions, and retrieve the work request form for any deficiencies that had been missed. Approved on-site transfers should be handled in much the same way as new move-ins.

The requirement of 30 days written notice of intention to vacate from residents is standard. A move-out inspection should be scheduled as soon as possible after the intent notice is received and final settlement should then be made. As with move-ins, a parking space and elevator should be reserved for move-outs. It is then critical for the manager to secure the unit and change the locks.

Residents who skip (vacate without giving notice) may be liable for the payment of an additional month's rent and possible forfeiture of their security deposit. On identification of a skip, the manager should notify the bookkeeping department, calculate rent and other moneys due, and locate the person's new address if possible in order to send a collection notice.

Each vacated unit should be prepared for re-occupancy as quickly as possible. The vacated resident's files and other information should be moved from the active resident file into the vacated resident file, and the bookkeeper should be notified that the move-out has occurred and of the amount due to or from the vacating resident. Any amount due to the vacated resident should be paid promptly within the legal time limit required by the jurisdiction. Many management companies use collection agencies or reports to credit bureaus to effect collections. As always, the manager should ensure that such reporting conforms to the Fair Credit Reporting Act.

The property manager also may wish to conduct a brief phone or write-in exit interview with the vacated resident to learn why the resident chose to leave and how other residents may be perceiving life at the property.

Communication through regularly published property newsletters, memos, and periodic informational meetings is an effective way to keep residents happy.

Tenancy and residency policies are essential for any property to function smoothly. The best way to communicate the property's policies is to assemble them all into a resident handbook and distribute the handbook to residents as they move in. Where appropriate (e.g., the pool, tennis courts), property policies also should be visibly posted.

When residents violate policies, the property manager must get them to comply or leave, either by agreement or by eviction. All such procedures should be documented in the property's operations manual. A discussion and outline of a resident handbook begins on the next page of this text.

ADDENDUM: THE RESIDENT HANDBOOK

The well-organized, clearly written, and indexed resident handbook guides and assists residents in their relations with the property and its management and maintenance staff, with each other and with the units and buildings in which they live, and assists property staff in their relations with residents. The resident handbook relieves property staff of many calls requesting information because the answers can easily be found in the handbook. It precludes the argument from residents that they were unaware of certain policies, requirements, and/or restrictions because all property policies, requirements, and restrictions are clearly stated in the handbook. It improves relations between residents and management personnel because residents realize that the policies are in writing and are applied universally to everyone and that the staff does not have discretion in administering them. It encourages greater compliance with property policies because a policy in writing, especially in an official publication, carries more weight and is less likely to be contested or appealed for exceptions.

The resident handbook is useful from day one of a tenant's residency, setting the tone for the entire relationship between residents and the property at the most critical time of that relationship—move-in—when residents are presented with the handbook and sign a form acknowledging that they have received it. Presentation of the resident handbook at move-in also ensures that the property manager will remember to discuss and emphasize policies that should be covered at that time.

The resident handbook should be thorough and all-inclusive. It should cover every aspect of tenancy in the property, as demonstrated by the recommended outline below. It should be written in common, everyday language, not legalese, but it should be reviewed by the property's legal counsel prior to distribution to residents to ensure the accuracy and appropriateness of its contents. It may be compiled by a management company staff member, a property staff member, the property manager, by a professional who specializes in producing resident handbooks for multifamily properties* or by a freelance copywriter with superior organizational skills. It may be bound in any number of ways (e.g., stapled, spiral bound, three-ring binder), but in any case it should look impressive so that residents will respect it as the official resource guide it is meant to be. And finally, it should be updated regularly. When changes in policies occur, all residents should be so notified in writing via a memo from management that cites the previous policy, explains any changes to it, and instructs residents to insert the new policy into the resident handbook so that it supersedes the previous policy. The entire resident handbook should be updated, revised, and redistributed every three to five years, more often if necessary.

CONTENTS AND OUTLINE OF A RESIDENT HANDBOOK†

Note that the suggested contents and outline of a resident handbook that appear below should be adapted to the individual needs of each property.

FIRST PAGE

The first page of the resident handbook should be a quick guide to the contact information residents need most. It should include:

- Management office location and phone numbers (regular business hours, after hours, and emergency)
- Maintenance office location and phone numbers (regular business hours, after hours, and emergency)
- Addresses and phone numbers of the local police precinct and fire department (in addition to 911)
- Local post office address, phone number, and hours
- Local utility companies' addresses and phone numbers (regular business hours, after hours, and emergency)

- Property's voting precinct number and addresses of local polling place(s)
- All other addresses and phone numbers that residents might need

INTRODUCTORY POLICY STATEMENT

A general policy statement should introduce the handbook and provide residents with the rationale for the handbook. Specifically, the handbook should begin with the information that the policies contained in the handbook have been developed to allow each resident the ability to enjoy a safe and secure living environment while protecting the rights of all residents and that information is also provided about all obligations and responsibilities residents have accepted by renting in the property. The introductory statement also should state that the policies contained in the handbook are effective as of a given date and may be subject to change at any time with written notice from management.

ABOUT THE PROPERTY

Residents like to know about the place where they live, and a little background about the property goes a long way toward establishing pride of residency. Information contained in the resident handbook about the property might include:

- Year constructed
- Number of residential units
- Number of professional and other units
- Other pertinent information, including property-wide amenities and services
- Property staff information, including the names of management and maintenance staff, their titles and duties
- Name of developer and/or owner (if appropriate)
- Property management company information, including name, address, phone, fax, website, and e-mail contact information of management company and assigned management professionals
- Maintenance supervisor's contact information
- Other contacts and information pertinent to the property

FINANCIAL MATTERS

- The security deposit requirement, refund policy, and damage charges
- Rent remittance and collection procedures
- Rent payment delinquency policy and collection procedures
- Discussion of future changes in rent levels
- Other property fees (e.g., health club membership, party room rental)
- Other

PROPERTY AMENITIES, FACILITIES, AND SERVICES

Note that policies affecting common use areas, such as swimming pools and tennis courts, should also be posted as professionally produced signage in those areas.

- Bicycle room
- Bulletin board
- Cable and Internet access
- Common areas
- Delivery entrance
- Electricity
- Elevators (passenger, service, delivery, etc.)
- Exterminator
- Front door
- Health club/exercise room
- HVAC (heating, ventilation, and air conditioning)
- Intercom and resident directory (lobby and elsewhere)
- Laundry facilities
- Lobby and common hallways
- Luggage carts
- Mail handling (mailroom, mail distribution, etc.)
- Newsletter (property-wide as authorized and published by the owner/ management)
- Packages (package room, package handling, package distribution, etc.)
- Parking
- Resident relations with property staff (e.g., non–work-related communications, private work in individual units, etc.)

- Roof (use of roof area, roof deck, etc.)
- Service/delivery entrance
- Social hall/party room (use of social hall/party room, rental of social hall/party room, etc.)
- Storage (storage room, storage cages, rental of storage space, etc.)
- Suggestion box (as authorized by the owner and management)
- Swimming pool
- Telephone directories (when delivered to property)
- Tennis courts
- Other

GENERAL MAINTENANCE AND REPAIR POLICIES

- Maintenance and repair responsibilities of the property
- Maintenance and repair responsibilities of renters, including chargeback policy
- Service requests (procedure for submitting service requests, including a copy of the work order form, etc.)
- Other

UNIT DWELLING/TENANCY POLICIES

- Air conditioners in individual dwelling units
- Unit access/key policy (including all keys, keys provided, key reproduction, emergency access policy, convenience key policy, "safe key" policy, return of keys upon move-out, lost keys, etc.)
- Unit alterations (including major alterations, painting, floor scraping, etc., with requirements, restrictions, and forms)
- Unit damage
- Unit decorating (including outdoor decorating, front door decorating, interior decorating, etc.)
- Unit use (e.g., professional use policy)
- Cable/satellite dish access and use in individual dwelling units
- Clothes washing machines and dryers in individual dwelling units
- Complaints about property staff/complaints about management/complaints about neighbors
- Compliance with policies, including violations
- Deliveries (to property/to individual dwelling units)
- Dishwashers in individual dwelling units
- Disposal of household refuse/disposal of large items/recycling policy
- Energy conservation in individual dwelling units
- Floor covering requirements inside units
- Front doors of units
- Hallways and stairwells (tenancy policies)
- Heat in individual dwelling units
- Housekeeping, cleanliness, and maintenance of reasonable living conditions in individual dwelling units
- Installation of appliances in individual dwelling units
- Insurance (renter's insurance and other coverages for individual dwelling units)
- Internet access in individual dwelling units
- Lease expiration and re-rental policies
- Move-in/move-out procedures, including intent to vacate notification, all forms, etc.
- Noise and disturbance policies
- Pets
- Supervision of children in common areas and in individual dwelling units
- Terraces, balconies, patios adjacent/belonging to individual dwelling units
- Ventilation in individual dwelling units
- Water conservation in individual dwelling units
- Windows/window guards/window ledges in individual dwelling units
- Other

SECURITY AND SAFETY ISSUES

- Community watch programs
- Property access for residents, residents' visitors and

guests, delivery people, contractors and work people, domestic help, solicitors, etc.

- Individual dwelling unit access for residents, residents' visitors and guests, delivery people, contractors and work people, domestic help, solicitors, etc., including announcement of visitors, etc.; forms for access to individual dwelling units by visitors, guests, etc.; convenience key policy, "safe key" policy, lost key policy, etc., including all procedures and forms

- Property-wide and individual dwelling unit fire precautions/smoke and fire detectors/required fire safety plan, etc.

- Property-wide evacuation procedures

- Individual unit security systems

- Resident absence from property (prolonged absence policy)

- Roof security and safety policy

- Window guards

- Other

SUBLETTING

- Subletting a dwelling unit/subletting fees, including all policies, requirements, fees, and forms

- Other

APPENDICES

- Sample copies of all forms, policies, etc., to be reproduced and inserted as appropriate

- Other

OTHER

As appropriate

*The editor of this text, Barbara Dershowitz, is such an expert. Her company, Business Communications Workshop (516/938–0323), specializes in producing resident handbooks, property staff handbooks, residential property newsletters, and all manner of multi-housing communication vehicles.

†This list of suggested contents and outline for the resident handbook shown in this text is the property of and is reprinted with the permission of Barbara Dershowitz and Business Communications Workshop.

9

Managing the Site Office and the Operations Manual

THE IMPORTANCE OF MANAGING THE SITE OFFICE

The site office—the on-premises management office that also may house the maintenance and/or rental offices—is literally the nerve and brain center of any residential property. The property manager and all key on-site management personnel operate from the site office. Even if the maintenance supervisor and crew work in a separate office or garage, and even if the rental office is located away from it, all roads eventually lead to the site office for every property employee and resident.

In every center of operation, someone has to be the leader, the ultimate authority, the person to whom all other workers are accountable. In the site office, that individual is the property manager. So in addition to being an expert in property management, the property manager also must be competent at managing a functioning office, its organization and operations, and its workers.

Just as every residential property and every work environment has a character and rhythm all its own, so each site office also will have its own character and rhythm. Although the atmosphere in some site offices is relaxed and easy-going, in others it is more rigid and strict. The most important thing is that the office functions well.

No, not all site offices operate the same way. But the best-managed ones have a lot in common. This part of the text provides guidance in establishing an efficient and smoothly functioning site office.

SITE OFFICE LOGISTICS

WHERE SHOULD THE SITE OFFICE BE LOCATED?

In most cases, when the property manager arrives at a new assignment, the site office will be wherever it is, and that is where it usually stays. However, if it is possible to locate it ideally, and certainly when a new property is in the planning and construction phase or an existing property is being renovated, then the considerations of traffic flow, space availability, and budget should be taken into account and the site office should be situated as strategically as possible.

Some experts suggest that this strategic location means putting the site office in close proximity to the property's recreational facilities. Others recommend a location close to the model unit(s), if the property has any. Of course, still others recommend that the site office be located some distance from the models so that prospects will have to walk the grounds to get from one to the other. But all the experts agree that the most important consideration is that the site office be easily accessible to property employees and especially to residents. Easy access is particularly important if the site office houses the rental office as well.

WHAT SHOULD BE THE SITE OFFICE HOURS OF OPERATION?

Ideally, the site office should be open 24 hours a day, seven days a week, every day of the year. After all, residents live in their homes all the time. But if operating 24/7/365 is not possible, then the office should be open, staffed, and ready for business as much a possible, and especially on weekends when it is most convenient for residents to come in. This is particularly true if the site office also houses the rental office because prospects are most likely to visit on weekends.

Deciding when the site office will be open may or may not fall to the property manager. If it does, the manager is well advised to keep the office open every weekday at least during the standard business hours of 9:00 a.m. to 5:00 p.m. If possible, an earlier opening and later closing time are even better. The property manager also should arrange at least two weekday "late nights," say until 9:00 p.m. Although weekend hours may be shortened (for example, 10:00 a.m. to 3:00 p.m.), doing so depends on the rental office situation and on the level of attention and responsiveness the property wishes to provide to its residents and prospective residents. The bottom line is that the site office must be open and functioning a sufficient number of hours to provide adequate and appropriate service to residents and prospects.

HOW SHOULD THE SITE OFFICE BE ORGANIZED?

Physical Office Organization

From a physical perspective, the site office should be organized as efficiently as possible. This means that it should be furnished with enough workstations, chairs, telephones, computers, file cabinets, and all other equipment necessary to allow office staff to perform their daily administrative functions optimally. All equipment should be in good condition and situated in such a way as to facilitate a logical, comfortable traffic pattern.

Depending on the space available and on the structure of the office staff, the site office may be a single open area shared by the entire staff or it can be a space organized to reflect the hierarchy of positions. For example, in properties in which there is a receptionist and a waiting area, the receptionist's desk is usually located close to the entry door and in the waiting area. There may be some kind of partition between the waiting room and the back office to prevent residents from seeing and having access to all the mechanical and technical functions of the back office, but such a partition may not be necessary if the office is well organized and secure. Bookkeepers and clerical workers may be located behind the receptionist. The property manager may have her/his own private office at the back of the site office.

As indicated in Chapter 7, Marketing Rental Housing and the Marketing Plan, separation and a clear definition of functions are essential if the site office and the rental office share the same space. At the very least, a designated "private" space should be set aside for personal discussions between the property manager and residents and/or between the rental agent and prospects. Under no circumstances is it advisable for a prospect—or anyone, for that matter—to be able to overhear complaints from existing residents or unpleasant exchanges between the property staff and residents.

Regardless of how the site office is physically arranged, the most important thing is that it be well organized and orderly. There can be no question that the site office reflects the property's overall attitude. A messy, disorganized office bespeaks a messy, poorly maintained environment. Conversely, an orderly, well-organized, and smoothly functioning office makes a much more positive statement about the property as a whole.

Site Office Staff Organization

From a personnel perspective, the ideal site office would be staffed with an adequate number and the appropriate categories of workers to attend to all the property's requirements. In a perfect world, this would include a management assistant to help the property manager, separate administrative assistants for the manager and the management assistant, one or more bookkeepers as needed, a receptionist, and a full clerical support staff. In real life, however, space, budget, and other considerations tend to be balanced against actual need.

Depending on her/his involvement at the ultimate decision-making level at which the owner and management company executives operate, the property manager may or may not have a say in how the office is staffed. If she/he does have a say, then the request should be made for the categories of worker most necessary to ensure that the office can provide the maximum level of service to the property's residents and prospects. But regardless of whether or not the property manager has input into the staff structure, she/he will most certainly be held accountable for how the site office staff performs.

MANAGING THE SITE OFFICE STAFF

Although the property manager typically operates within the specific universe of the property(ies) she/he manages, it is assumed that she/he will have the support of the management company's main office in-house and contracted resources. These resources include management company line personnel such as other managers, the senior manager, division/district/regional managers and directors, and the company's executive echelon, (i.e., the executive property manager, the president, the chief operating office, the chief financial officer, the chief executive officer), as well as staff personnel in human resources, purchasing, marketing, accounting, legal services, and MIS/computer operations. Although the property manager must know how to access and work productively with all these people to be most successful, they are not a direct part of the site office staff and the property manager is not responsible for how they perform.

Conversely, at the property itself, the manager may communicate and coordinate on an on-going basis with a staff that includes as many workers as the property manager's management and/or administrative assistant(s); the maintenance supervisor; all members of the maintenance, grounds, housekeeping staff, and security personnel; one or more bookkeepers; the rental agent; clerical and office support staff; and part-time and/or seasonal employees of the property. These people compose the property manager's staff, and it is these people whom the manager must manage.

Chapter 2, Planning for Multihousing Management Success and Chapter 3, On the Front Line: The Property Manager provide a great deal of information about property staffing and staff management techniques. It is appropriate to reiterate here that the property manager must be adept not only at property management but also at staff management. To mold the most productive team, the manager must be familiar not only with all labor laws and unions as appropriate to the property but also with human resources procedures and effective staff management techniques.

Most significantly, the property manager must work constantly to ensure that all property office workers understand their purpose, which is to serve the property's residents. This can be achieved in two ways. First, the property manager must administer and adhere to the polices and procedures contained in the property's employee handbook (see Chapter 2, Planning for Multihousing Management Success and Chapter 3, On the Front Line: The Property Manager). Second, the property manager herself/himself must serve as a model of integrity, high morale, sensitivity to human needs, intelligence in business dealings, and the willingness to do the necessary work and then go the extra mile toward excellence. This is true because virtually without exception all workers take their cues from how their supervisors behave and perform on the job.

In the end, cultivating a productive, smoothly functioning property office is the property manager's most important staff management responsibility. Once this has been accomplished, all the other work will be completed as a matter of course.

SITE OFFICE TECHNOLOGY

It has been stated in earlier parts of this text that computer literacy is an essential property management skill and that up-to-date technology is an essential property management tool. A designated MIS (management of information services or systems) department and an MIS director have been included in the management company flow chart, and reference has been made to the wide and constantly expanding library of specialized multihousing management software programs for data entry and maintenance, computing, and producing reports.

It is not possible to emphasize strongly enough how important technology is to professional management. Fax machines, copiers, voice mail, and a carefully designed computer system should all be standard site office equipment.

The specific computer software to be used in the site office, especially the accounting and report formatting software, probably will be dictated by the management company to ensure uniformity and allow for company-wide tracking. These programs have a variety of applications, including reports such as market surveys; rent payment and delinquency tracking; rent analyses and occupancy reports; forms and spreadsheet formatting; what-if models and projections; and graphic representations, among many others. The management company also may support proprietary software that provides additional, customized services to the site office, maintenance office, and rental office, as well as online services and information that residents, prospects, and others can access via the Internet.

The site office computer system should be networked not only among all the property's computers, including those in the maintenance and rental offices, but also with the central management company. If the management company does not have an MIS expert on staff to oversee computer functions, then a professional should be consulted regarding the type of system most appropriate to the office, the configuration of the system, any other technology that could extend the system's functionality, and the installation of the system in the property.

Flexibility and ease of use should be the hallmarks of the property and site office computer system. The considerations for designing such a system and network are similar to those for designing a financial management system. Specifically,

- What members of the site office staff will be using the system and the products the system is to produce?
- What will the system's products be used for?
- What training is required to operate the system?
- What will the site office staff need to make the system work best?
- Where outside the site office will the data from the system be sent?
- Do any of the people outside the office who will be receiving the information need special formatting or other considerations?
- What will be the initial and on-going operating costs of the system?
- How complex is the system, and is it easy to maintain?
- How can the confidential information contained in the system be kept secure?

Although it is essential for the site office to maintain files of certain hard documents, such as leases, many files and records previously kept in hard copy can be scanned to the computer, saving considerable space and paper and making the research and retrieval of information immeasurably faster and easier. For example, resident maintenance requests and histories can be computerized, as can staff schedules, inventories, resident histories, and virtually every form required to operate the property. To this end, site office technology should include a scanner. The site office computer system also should support an Internet connection and e-mail for every site employee whose job involves use of the computer.

As discussed in Chapter 6, Risk Management and Management Maintenance Plans, computer security is critical to the site office and its records. The installation of a computer system of any magnitude should be followed immediately by steps to keep the computer, its equipment, and its files free of risk from viruses, hackers, and thieves.

HANDLING AND CONTROLLING MONEY IN THE SITE OFFICE

Tight control over the handling of money in the site office is important if the property manager wishes to maintain efficiency, control rent collection and follow-up, facilitate bookkeeping and auditing, reduce theft, and discourage robberies. The techniques listed in Figure 9–1 can help prevent mishandling of rent and other moneys received at the site office.

SITE OFFICE EMPLOYEE BONDING

Management company and property employees who handle money and/or approve purchases should be bonded to protect the company and the property against employee theft of funds. Bondability should be a condition of employment for employees who handle money and/or approve purchases.

RENT BILLING AND COLLECTION METHODS

Each property owner and management company must decide whether to bill for rent each month and whether to use a billing statement or coupon books. Some owners and managers believe that billing is unnecessary because the monthly rent and rent due date are always the same for the duration of each lease. However, billing is recommended, and statement billing is recommended over coupon books because it tends to increase collections and also because it allows communication with residents at least once a month.

As indicated in Chapter 4, Multihousing Management Economics and Finances, the common methods of collecting rent are at the site office, by mail to the management firm's central office, by mail to a bank lock box, via direct deposit (also called direct transfer or electronic transfer), and via credit card. Each of these methods has advantages and disadvantages.

Allowing residents to make rent payments at the site office via personal or bank check or money order gives residents convenience and an immediate receipt and gives the property manager better control of the rent collection process. However, collecting rent at the site office also may increase the chances of theft and reduce the office's efficiency. It also reduces the benefit of having all checks received in a central location because some residents may choose other methods of payment if available.

The central office mail method provides quicker use of the funds and reduces the chance of on-site theft. However,

FIGURE 9-1. Procedures for Controlling Money in the Site Office

- Use pre-numbered rent receipts for all payments received. Property personnel are responsible for all numbered receipts that are issued. This method also makes periodic audits easier.
- Date stamp incoming checks every day to ensure collection of late charges.
- Require daily bank deposits to reduce the chances of a problem, such as misplacing check. The temptation to anyone interested in theft increases with the amount of cash on hand. Daily deposits also make funds available to the property faster.
- Urge residents to pay their rents by personal or certified checks or money orders. Avoid accepting cash at the site office. This common management practice helps to minimize the possibility of robbery. It also decreases the chance that employees will mishandle or steal the money or make incorrect change. Personal checks, certified checks, money orders, and credit card payments are acceptable for rent payment. Cash is legal tender in payment of an obligation, and refusal could possibly cancel that obligation.
- Verify residents who are delinquent in paying their rent. Periodically, the senior manager or another central office representative should contact delinquent renters on a random basis to determine if any rent was collected but not reported and/or if the amount reported was the amount actually collected.
- Make periodic audits of the property files. This common business practice provides further assurance that the moneys collected have been deposited and properly recorded.

late mail delivery may delay crediting the resident's account and deposit of the funds into the property's account.

The lock box mail method falls in between these two, providing security but also the possibility of payments lost or delayed in the mail.

As more people do their banking and bill-paying electronically, direct transfer is becoming increasingly popular. It relieves the resident of having to write and deliver or mail a check each month by automatically transferring funds from the resident's designated account into the property's account. This ensures on-time payment, assuming the resident has sufficient funds to cover the transfer. The drawback of direct transfer is that the same amount must be debited each month, so it's difficult to achieve accurate accounting when resident payments include variable charges such as cable TV and electric.

Payment by credit card also allows for automatic debiting and has the added advantage of flexibility because each month's amount due can be billed each month. Assuming the amount does not exceed the card holder's credit limit, credit card payment assures monthly payments to the property and may also provide bonus perks, such as "points" to the resident who holds the credit card. The disadvantage of accepting credit card payments is the cost to the property from the credit card company.

The management company, which is generally responsible for this particular task, will take all factors into consideration before establishing a rent collection policy, which should then become part of the property's operations manual.

ANCILLARY INCOME

Although rent represents almost all of a typical rental property's income, many properties take in considerable sums of ancillary income generated through such methods as charging residents for storage bins, bicycle racks, use of an on-premises fully equipped health club, and making arrangements with telecommunications companies to rent the property rooftops for the placement of cellular antennas. Because it is the property manager's responsibility to manage these revenue producers from the site office, it is appropriate to understand how they work and what their relationship is to handling property funds. To that end, below is a discussion of how ancillary income is generated via on-premises laundry facilities, clubhouse or party room rental, and carport or indoor parking space rental. The property owner and manager may come up with other creative ways to generate ancillary income.

Laundry Facilities

Virtually all rental tenants want on-premises laundry facilities, and often the presence or absence of a property laundry room will play a role in a prospect's decision of whether or not to rent. Typically, a very high percentage of a property's ancillary income comes from the on-premises laundry facility.

This specialized service business requires expertise, capital, and trained manpower. More often than not, subcontracting the installation and maintenance of the laundry facility is more economical and practical than operating it with property staff. This is true because the subcontractor installs and maintains all of the necessary equipment to operate an efficient facility, thus saving the property the cost of buying the equipment, insuring it, repairing it, carrying an inventory of replacement parts, and risking pilferage or theft. The subcontractors who provide this service usually are also responsible for damage to the equipment in case of fire or theft, for furnishing liability insurance, and for updating obsolete equipment.

The laundry facility should contain a sink, one or more sorting tables, a suspended rod or hooks where clothes on hangers can be hung temporarily, some chairs, a trash receptacle, a bulletin board for residents to communicate with each other, and perhaps a second bulletin board for communications from management. Generally, the service contract will call for the laundry concessionaire to provide many if not all of these laundry room amenities.

For its part, the property furnishes the facility, pays for the utilities (i.e., electricity, gas, and water), and is responsible for the cleanliness of the laundry area and equipment. The subcontractor pays the property a percentage of the gross income from residents' use of the washers and dryers. In return, the subcontractor is given exclusive laundry concessionaire contracts that run for periods of several years, sometimes as many as seven years or longer. The contractual agreement between the laundry services provider and the property, which is usually negotiated by the management company, includes the payment of the license fees, the price for washing and for drying a load of clothes, and the profit-sharing percentage mentioned above.

Gross revenues per unit per month from the laundry facility will vary according to a number of factors, including resident profile, unit mix, number of machines, and number of locations. The ideal number of machines similarly depends on a variety of factors, including size of equipment, resident profile, unit mix, and number and layout of buildings.

Offering to make changes in the site office for properties with coin-operated laundry facilities and installing soap dispensers and change machines in laundry rooms are practices that are not recommended. Keeping a lot of change in the site office tempts thieves, and making change takes time away from actual site office work. Soap dispensers and change machines are subject to failure and pilferage, and most residents bring their own soap and change when they do laundry anyway. Nevertheless, some properties install change machines to ensure that residents do their laundry on-site. Many properties, however, have installed a debit-card system in their laundry facilities to eliminate the need for coins altogether, and an increasing number of properties also are installing laundry facilities with Internet connections that notify residents when their laundry cycles are done and when machines are available.

Under any circumstances, the laundry facility should be clean, well ventilated, well lighted, secure, and operated by a concessionaire that provides 24-hour local maintenance service. To provide maximum service and convenience to residents and to maximize revenue, the laundry facility should operate for the maximum number of hours consistent with security and minimal disturbances to nearby residents.

In all laundry facilities, the collection of money is an especially important task. Generally, the laundry concessionaire makes collections on a weekly basis. To ensure a proper count, a trustworthy property representative should witness the money collection and counting.

Clubhouse or Party Room Rental

If a property has a clubhouse or party room, it is common practice to allow residents to rent the facility for their own social use. When a resident wishes to do so, she/he typically goes to the site office to make the arrangements.

After determining that the clubhouse or party room is available at the time requested, the property manager or other site office worker responsible for administering clubhouse/party room rentals should review the clubhouse/party room rules with the resident and answer any questions about them. When it is clear that the resident understands the rules and the time limitations of the rental period, the resident should be required to complete a clubhouse/party room rental agreement form. The agreement should hold the resident responsible for any damage to the premises, define the beginning and end of the rental period, specify the fees and deposits required, and forbid serving alcoholic beverages at functions that include persons under 21 years of age. Figure 9–2 shows a sample clubhouse/party room rental contract. As with all similar documents, the property manager should consult with an attorney before putting this form into use.

The resident should then be required to make a refundable damage deposit, pay the rental fee, and sign the rental agreement along with the property representative. The original contract should be filed in the clubhouse/party room folder in the site office, and the resident should get a copy accompanied by the clubhouse/party room rules and regulations. The site office should then provide notification to the maintenance supervisor or crew of the upcoming social event so that maintenance staff can schedule set-up beforehand and clean-up afterwards.

Following the function, a maintenance representative should inspect the clubhouse/party room and note at the bottom of the agreement the cleaning that was necessary, any damage, and any appropriate charges. The agreement should then be dated and returned to the site office, where any charges due should be deducted from the resident's deposit before it is returned.

Rental of Carport or Indoor Parking Spaces

Although free outdoor parking spaces are usually part of life in rental properties where outdoor on-premises parking is available, some properties generate ancillary income by renting carports or indoor parking spaces to residents. Where this is done, these spaces should be actively marketed, and the maintenance staff should be designated to report to the site office whenever someone parks in a space she/he did not pay for. The site office must therefore notify the maintenance crew whenever a carport or garage space is either leased or becomes available.

Should the maintenance crew discover a rogue car in a space either rented by someone else or unrented, the car should be "ticketed" with a warning and then towed if it has not been removed after several days. The property manager should consult an attorney and make sure that any such procedures follow the local laws relating to such problems.

Fees for rental of carport or indoor parking spaces may be billed and collected on a monthly basis or according to a bimonthly, quarterly, semi-annual, or annual payment program. Whatever the program, residents will appreciate the value of having a protected parking space. For its part, the property need only ensure that no one but the resident who rented the space is allowed to park there.

RECORDING MONEY TRANSACTIONS IN THE SITE OFFICE

All payments received in the site office, regardless of source—rent, security deposit, clubhouse rental—should be recorded as they are received. The management company should communicate to the property manager the specific procedures for recording and transmitting moneys collected on a daily basis, and these procedures should be detailed in the property's operations manual. Figure 9–3 shows a sample deposit transmittal form that can be formatted for computer use or entered manually.

MANAGING THE PROPERTY'S BANK ACCOUNT AND MAKING BANK DEPOSITS

Because the management company is contracted to manage the property's finances, the management company is responsible for overseeing the property's bank accounts (e.g., operating account, reserve account, petty funds account). These accounts should be in the name of the property and for the account of the owner. Depending on the agreement between the owner and the management company, the accounts may also list the management company as agent for the owner. Also depending on the agreement between the owner and the management company, any number of people—including the owner, the property manager, the management company financial officer, and others—may be authorized as a signatory on one or more of the property's bank accounts.

Under no circumstances should management company accounts or funds be used for property operations, nor should any accounts for the property be carried in the name of the management company only. In addition, and perhaps more importantly, under no circumstances should the property's moneys be commingled with the accounts of other properties managed by the management company. These practices comply with the usual management agreements between property owners and management companies and reflect sound fiduciary policy. Of course, the contracting parties to the management agreement may modify or completely change the normal practices because they can contract to do anything that is legal.

In any case, all property receipts and disbursements should be made into and out of the appropriate property bank accounts. Deposits should be made on a daily basis, and the property manager or designated property bookkeeper should keep meticulous records of each deposit. For example, the deposit slip that accompanies each day's deposit should equal that day's total on the daily deposit transmittal form.

FIGURE 9–2. Sample Clubhouse Contract

This agreement, made this ___________ day of ___________ by and between ___________,_______________ hereinafter referred to as "Lessee" ___________, and ___________ hereinafter referred to as "Company."

WITNESSETH THAT: In consideration of $___________ and a security deposit of $___________ the Lessee does hereby lease the Clubhouse from the Company on ______________ from ______________ for approximately ___________ persons.

Lessee further attests and agrees to the following:

(1) Lessee is over 21 years of age.

(2) The Clubhouse will be used only for ______________________ and Lessee will personally attend the affair and be present at all times during the hours stated

(3) Lessee will comply, and obtain the compliance of all persons in attendance, with all applicable provisions of the Alcoholic Beverages Laws of the state and of the county in which the Clubhouse is located. Lessee also takes full responsibility for preventing and prohibiting consumption of alcoholic beverages by anyone who is under the legal age and attends the affair, and the Company reserves the right to prohibit alcoholic beverages from being served at any function where guests under the legal age will be in attendance unaccompanied by their parents or legal guardian.

(4) Lessee will be responsible for any damage to the property of the Company that occurs during the terms of this contract, and will pay for all cost of restoration, replacement, or repair of same.

(5) Lessee for himself, and on behalf of all persons who will be on the premises for the aforementioned affair, releases and forever discharges the Company and its agents and employees from any and all claims and/or damages from or arising out of the use of said premises.

(6) Lessee warrants that he has been discharged as authorized agent or representative to have complete authority to execute this contract, if the use of the Clubhouse is for a club, association, or corporation

(7) That authorized representatives of the Company may enter the Clubhouse at any time during the rental period.

(8) Music and noise that is part of the affair must be contained within the confines of the Clubhouse and not be so loud as to disturb other residents of the community. The Company reserves the right to terminate the affair if noise levels become and remain excessive after warning.

(9) The security deposit is to be applied toward the cleaning of the premises after the affair specified in this contract. If the premises have been cleaned to the satisfaction of the Company, said deposit will be refunded.

(10) Lessee agrees that his guests will comply with all the rules and regulations governing the use of the community and its facilities.

(11) Lessee will/will not be required to have in attendance at the affair and off-duty police officer/representative of the Company, whose services shall be prepaid by Lessee.

Lessee:_________________________________ Date: ______________

Lessee:_________________________________ Date: ______________

Lessee:_________________________________ Date: ______________

*Inspected by*_____________________________ *Date:*_________ *Time:* ______________

Conditions: ____

____

Charges: ____

Figure 9–3. Deposit Transmittal

Date of Deposit ______________

(Development) ______________ DTS Number ______________

(Please type or print)

					1	2	3	4			5	6	7
		Resident Name						Deposit of Nonresident Receipts					
Resident Number	Last	First	Initial	New	Paid on Accounts	Resident Security Deposits	Bad Checks Redeposited (chargeback)	Credit Acct. No.	Amount	Description	Cash	Checks	Receipt Number
44010203	Doe	John	A.	X	403.00	96.00						499.00	#133
44020104	Smith	James	Q.		348.50					*money order*	25.00	348.50	#134
44091002	James	Lyndia	V.				25.00						#135
44999998	Johnson	David	W.						10.00	*clubhouse rental*		10.00	#136
44999999	*Total Application fees (list on reverse side)*				//////	//////	//////	25610	75.00	Application Fees	25.00	50.00	
				Total	751.50	96.00	25.00	**Total Col. 4**	85.00	Total	50.00	907.50	
								Total Cols. 1,2,3,4	457.50	Total deposit		957.50	

Instructions on Reverse Side

Mary Smith
(prepared by)

*The total of columns 1, 2, 3, and 4 must equal the total of columns 5 and 6 and must also be the amount of the total deposit. Indicate the total only on the line provided in column 4. Column 2 is for security deposits collected at the time of move-in. If the payment is from a new resident moving in, place and X in the space provided after the name and attach the paperwork. Do not list applications deposits in Column 2. List the name and amount of application fess on page 2 of this form.

(continued)

Figure 9–3. Deposit Transmittal (*Continued*)

				Applications				
Name	Last	First	Middle Initial	Cash	Check	Unit Type	Application Redeposit	Receipt Number

The operations manual should contain detailed instructions on all procedures for handling money at the property and on all forms used for this purpose.

CHECK CASHING IN THE SITE OFFICE

It should be a firm policy of the site office not to provide check cashing services for property workers, residents, or anyone. As with making change for laundry facilities in the site office, cashing checks consumes time that can better be spent serving residents in other ways. Also, keeping enough money on hand to make change and cash checks is a dangerous policy because of possible robbery.

HOLDUPS AND ROBBERIES IN THE SITE OFFICE

Although various security devices and the practice of keeping as little cash as possible in the site office will help to lessen the possibility of holdups and robberies, holdups and robberies may happen. Addressing them should be a concern of the property manager, the management company, and the owner.

In the case of a holdup or robbery, the primary concern of the owner, the management company, and the property manager should not be to protect the money but instead minimize the chance of personal harm or injury. Therefore, the policy of the owner, the management company, and the property should be that all employees are to cooperate fully should they be confronted in a holdup or robbery situation on the property premises or in the execution of their duties on behalf of the property. This policy should be clearly communicated to property workers and articulated specifically in the property operations manual.

It should also be property policy that residents must secure their own insurance to cover theft of their personal items as well as other items of personal loss and liability. (In rental properties, renter's insurance is appropriate. In shared-interest associations, homeowner's insurance or co-op insurance is appropriate.) This fact should be made clear by the manager when the resident moves in. Although the owner is therefore not normally responsible for resident losses that result from a robbery, in nearly all cases when a holdup or robbery takes place in the site office, the funds stolen are under the jurisdiction of the property. In these cases, the owner is responsible and should carry adequate and appropriate insurance coverage for such eventualities. (See Chapter 6, Risk Management and Management Maintenance Plans for a discussion of insurance.)

SITE OFFICE AUDIT

Sound business practice calls for periodic (perhaps semi-annual or annual) audit of all property files, including rent collection, ancillary income collection, petty cash, and other money items. Certain red flags, such as excessive delinquencies or unusually slow collections, also can signify the need for an audit of the property records. The frequency, responsibility, and procedures for audits should be included in the property's operations manual.

Accountants who specialize in service to multifamily rental properties will know how to conduct this periodic audit. It should include ensuring that rent receipts correspond to entries on deposit transmittal forms and on bank deposit slips, that the property is collecting and depositing ancillary income appropriately, and that all financial transactions that take place in the site office on behalf of the property are done according to protocol. The results of the auditor's work should be provided to the owner, the management company executive, and the property manager.

The stealing of money, especially rent payments, can be a serious problem for an owner, a management company, and a property manager, and all precautions must be taken. The rent-collection and money-processing system must be designed to minimize any chance for mishandling funds. But no matter how efficient the system, it needs on-going monitoring and verification that it is being operated properly. Auditing the property from time to time protects the owner's investment, the reputation of the management company, and serves as a safeguard for the honest employee as well as against the dishonest one.

MANAGING PROPERTY INVENTORIES

Except for smaller properties, most multifamily properties need a proper and adequate inventory of supplies and equipment to run efficiently. Typically, the property manager is responsible for ensuring that the authorized quantities and types of supplies, equipment, and spare parts are on hand at all times to complete service requests, to perform property maintenance, and to operate the site office. The procedures for maintaining property inventories should be documented in the property operations manual.

MAINTENANCE SUPPLIES AND EQUIPMENT INVENTORY CONTROL SYSTEM

A maintenance supplies and equipment inventory control system should be used to achieve the goal of being neither overstocked nor understocked but adequately stocked. The system may consist of a numbered list of property equipment on a control form and stickers with corresponding numbers to place on the appropriate pieces of equipment. Many such systems are computerized and use bar-coded stickers for identification. In any case, this method provides easy and quick identification of the property's various pieces of equipment.

In consultation with the property manager and property maintenance supervisor (if there is one), the purchasing manager or other knowledgeable and authorized person at the management company should determine the inventory levels to be maintained at the property. The authorized quantity of each item should be based on the historical usage of the item and should be adequate to permit timely repairs when necessary. Figure 9–4 shows the first page of a sample inventory list for property maintenance supplies and equip-

FIGURE 9–4. Property Maintenance Supplies and Equipment

Property ____________________ Date ____________

Equipment	Number On Hand	Serial Number	Brand Name & Model	Number of Each Item Authorized
Truck, Plow				
Tractor w/mower deck				
Weight				
Chain				
Snow Blade				
Snow Blower				
Two Wheel Trailer				
Leaf Rake				
Lawn Trailer				
Lawn Mower				
Shovel				
Shovel				
Shovel				
Post Hole Diggers				
Saw, manual or electric				
Electronic Drill Mtr.				
(Spray Containers)				
Step Ladder				
Step Ladder				
Step Ladder				
Step Ladder				
Torch, propane gas				
Welder, electric				
Cutting Torch				
Cutting Gages				
Leak Detector				

**This first page of an 11-page inventory illustrates the way to list a property's maintenance equipment inventory.*

ment. Figure 9–5 is a maintenance supply inventory form that may be used for major components or high-dollar maintenance parts.

Obviously, careful judgment should be exercised in determining the quantities to be maintained in inventory. Consideration must be given to:

- The age and condition of the property
- Property finances
- Use of outside contractors for jobs such as apartment cleanings, painting, exterminating, landscaping, snow/leaf removal, etc.
- Storage space availability, including any centrally located warehouse storage
- Sources of supplies
- Speed of delivery of ordered items

The inventory procedure should call for the property manager to requisition a sufficient number of each item to replenish the supply up to the recommended amount. Many vendors provide web-based purchase order systems in return for purchasing supplies from them. This inventory requisitioning should be done on a biweekly or monthly basis and means that a property worker must review existing inventory according to the same schedule to alert the property manager as to which items must be reordered. This property worker may be the maintenance supervisor or a trusted maintenance worker, an office worker, or the property manager herself/himself. In any case, the individual who takes regular inventory must be completely trustworthy so as to ensure an honest count and appropriate ordering.

On a semi-annual basis and whenever the property has a change in property managers and/or in the person responsible for maintaining property inventory, the management company should send the purchasing manager, the senior manager, or another designated management company representative to take a physical inventory of the supplies and equipment on premises at the property. The same inventory form for maintenance supplies and equipment used by the property should be used by the management company to ensure that all line items have been addressed. These audits help the management company and property owner keep tabs on product usage and costs at the property and assures both outgoing and incoming personnel of a clean changeover so that accusations cannot be made later.

SITE OFFICE EQUIPMENT AND FURNITURE INVENTORY CONTROL SYSTEM

Procedures should call for the property manager to maintain a site office equipment and furniture list showing all office equipment, such as computers and calculators, as well as all office, clubhouse, and lounge furniture. Figure 9–6 shows a sample site office equipment and furniture inventory form. All appropriate columns for each piece of equipment and furniture should be completed, including brand name and description, model number, serial number, date of purchase, supplier's address and phone number, original cost, and warranty information. The property manager should keep this list in the site office.

The purpose of this list is to provide all necessary information in the case of equipment or furniture theft or breakdown. Warranty information, which prevents paying for repairs that may be covered by warranty, should include the supplier's name, address, and phone number. It should also include the period of time covering parts and/or labor and should indicate whether a "loaner" machine is available to the property when the property's machine has to be taken off-site for repair. This listing and the information it contains can also be helpful when determining whether to purchase a service contract for a piece of machinery after its warranty period has expired and when considering replacement of a machine because of age or condition. To this end, the property manager will also want to maintain an equipment service history such as the sample in Figure 9–7 for each piece of office equipment.

Depending on the policy established by the owner and management company, when equipment breaks down, the property manager may be required to contact the senior manager for approval for the repair expenditure as well as the method to be used. At that time a decision can be made whether to replace or repair the item, and if a repair is to be made, whether the repair is covered by warranty. If the decision is made to repair the equipment, the property manager can contact the supplier directly without any further involvement of the senior manager. If the decision is made to replace the equipment, the property manager will be bound by the management company's supplies and equipment purchase protocols as discussed below and specified in the property's operations manual.

PURCHASING PROPERTY SUPPLIES AND EQUIPMENT

METHODS OF PURCHASING

Management companies use a variety of methods to purchase supplies and equipment for the properties they manage. These methods are discussed below.

Property Purchase and Central Office Payment

Under this method of making purchases for the property, the property orders the goods or services directly from the vendor. The vendor submits an invoice to the property manager for approval. The property manager forwards the invoice to the central accounting department for payment to the vendor.

Property Purchase and Payment

Under this method of making purchases for the property, the property manager has the checkbook and the authority to purchase goods and services up to a predetermined amount.

FIGURE 9–5. **Maintenance Supply Inventory**

Item ______________________ Stock Number ______________________

Minimum Quantity ______________________ Manufacturer ______________________

Maximum Quantity ______________________ Supplier ______________________

Unit Cost ______________________ Delivery Time ______________________

Ordered			Received		Inventory	
Date	Purchase Order Number	Quantity	Quantity	Balance Due	Quantity Used	Balance On Hand

FIGURE 9–6. Site Office Equipment and Furniture Inventory

Brand Name & Description	Model Number	Serial Number	Date of Purchase	Supplier Address & Phone	Original Cost	Warranty or Other information

FIGURE 9–7. Equipment Service History

____
Development

Item	Date	Repair Cost	Repair Details

Control is generally exercised by having the property manager stay within budgetary and purchase limitations.

Petty Cash Purchasing

Under this method of making purchases for the property, a small amount of cash is kept in a petty cash fund at the site office for the cash purchase of small, preapproved items, such as stationery, printing, and postage and/or for minor emergencies. Some properties also maintain a petty cash fund for the maintenance staff.

Property Charge Accounts

Under this method of making purchases for the property, charge accounts are established in the property's name. When a purchase is made by the property manager, a copy of the receipt is sent to the central accounting department for matching with the account's monthly statement. Payment is made directly from the central office.

Central Office Purchasing

Under this method of making purchases for the property, the property manager or other employee sends purchase requisitions to the central purchasing department at the management company. (In many management companies, the use of purchase requisitions is limited to orders placed by employees who are field representatives, such as maintenance supervisors in charge of several properties.) Central purchasing issues a purchase order to the vendor, and the goods or services are supplied directly from the vendor to the property. Upon receipt of the goods or services, the signed delivery ticket is sent to the central accounting department to be matched with the invoice and the purchase order. When all three are matched, the accounting department pays the vendor directly.

Service Work Order

As discussed in Chapter 5, Property Maintenance and Energy and Water Conservation, this method of purchasing is generally handled by the property maintenance supervisor for work done by contractors. Usually payment is made by the central accounting department.

COMPETITIVE BIDDING

As discussed in Chapter 5, Property Maintenance and Energy and Water Conservation, competitive bidding is not a method of purchasing. It is a process used to select suppliers or contractors before the purchase is made. Competitive bidding can be utilized for large repair/improvement projects, as well as for repetitive purchasing of supplies. The competitive bidding process means soliciting bids from several suppliers or contractors using a standard bid form with detailed specifications (see Fig. 5–24 in Chapter 5, Property Maintenance and Energy and Water Conservation). The specifications should contain the minimum quality standards and should be prepared by a knowledgeable person. Bidding according to the specifications keeps all bids on an apple-to-apple basis. Normally, the lowest bid meeting the detailed specifications is accepted, assuming that all bidders possess the credentials to assure timely receipt of goods or services and consistent quality in line with specifications. (Refer to Chapter 5, Property Maintenance and Energy and Water Conservation for a complete discussion about the competitive bidding process.)

PURCHASING AND PAYMENT PROCEDURES

Purchasing and payment procedures ensure proper controls, minimize paperwork, maximize efficiency, and ensure payment on a timely basis. All purchasing and payment procedures should be clearly spelled out in the property's operations manual.

PURCHASING GUIDELINES

The following guidelines should be considered when devising a purchasing system.

The Purchasing Goal

The goal is to obtain the best price, quality, and service consistent with product or service requirements.

The Person Responsible for Purchasing

The person responsible for purchasing (the senior manager, the property manager, or the purchasing agent) should be able to negotiate and use whatever leverage exists to obtain the best price possible. For example, if the purchaser represents a large property or several properties, substantial cost savings may be realized through negotiating for volume purchasing (also called bulk purchasing).

THE ROLE OF THE PURCHASING AGENT

If this position exists in the management company, the guidelines may call for the purchasing agent to purchase all of the company's requirements for major appliances and bulk items. These items would be ordered by a purchase requisition submitted to the purchasing agent, who then issues a purchase order in accordance with the purchase and payment procedures outlined in the operations manual. The purchasing agent also designates and recommends a source and price range for other items. She/he may also recommend a specific type or certain minimum standards. These items can be purchased locally in accordance with the purchasing agent's guidelines or may be purchased directly through the purchasing agent with a purchase requisition.

Purchasing from an Undesignated Supplier

Except in an emergency, purchases from suppliers other than those designated by the purchasing agent should receive prior approval from the purchasing agent. This policy is required for two reasons. First, it helps to ensure that the property receives the best price available. Second, it serves to advise the purchasing agent of a possible better price and source that can be used for the entire management company.

Purchasing from a New Supplier

A property manager or senior manager who considers using a new supplier should discuss with the purchasing agent the type of item to be purchased along with the price, quality, and service. In some cases, the purchasing agent will talk to the supplier directly before approval is granted to ensure that everyone understands the arrangement or agreement and that any price savings is obtained on a company-wide basis. If the purchasing agent is to function effectively in getting the best available pricing, service, and quality, everyone in the company must cooperate by supplying useful information.

Locating the Best Price

Because the senior manager, property manager, and maintenance supervisor are responsible for controlling maintenance expenditures and remaining within budget, they must help locate the best values at the best prices for supplies and materials. Generally, the central purchasing department is assumed to provide the best price, but the senior manager, property manager, and maintenance supervisor are not relieved of the responsibility of being cost conscious and finding a better price if it is available. If any employee can get a better price than what is being procured centrally, she/he should notify the purchasing agent so that appropriate action may be taken.

Receipt of Supplies and Equipment Deliveries

Only authorized property personnel should be allowed to accept and sign for supplies and equipment received at the property. Authorized personnel typically include the property manager, maintenance supervisor, rental agent, and anyone so designated by these individuals.

PROCESSING INVOICES FOR PAYMENT

Unless directed to send their invoices to the site office, vendors usually send their invoices to the central accounting department of the management company for payment. Procedures may call for the accounts payable clerk at the management company to match the invoice with the purchase order and delivery receipt and make payment or to forward the invoice to the property manager for sign-off and return to either the senior manager for second review and sign-off or send it directly back to the accounts payable department for remittance. All policies and procedures for the purchase of and payment for supplies and equipment should be documented in the property's operations manual.

SITE OFFICE RECORDS, FILES, REPORTS, AND LOGS

The volume of information, records, files, and reports processed in the typical site office requires a systematized and efficient record-keeping system. Ideally, this system should be computerized. Otherwise, processing requires too much time and manpower, and retrieval is too difficult and slow. The procedures for maintaining all site office records, files, reports, and logs should be documented in the property's operations manual.

TYPES OF SITE OFFICE RECORDS AND FILES

The following items discussed throughout this text should be maintained in the site office records and files, either in the site office systems computer and/or as hard copy on file, as necessary and appropriate. In addition to the items listed below, the property manager must have immediate and total access to all rental office files, including all applications in process, all eligible applications, all withdrawn or ineligible applications, all credit report requests made to credit agencies (this information should be kept as a log to verify charges received from the credit agency(ies) used by the rental office and to verify that a credit report has been requested on every applicant), and all other files and records of rental office activity.

Unit File/Unit Maintenance File Folders

Each unit in the property should have a separate file folder filed by building and unit number. All records regarding the physical unit, such as service requests, appliance replacements, work orders, and move-in and move-out inspection forms, should be maintained in this file. A review of the unit folder should quickly tell the history of maintenance and service requests relating to that unit and any problems with, and replacement dates of, appliances in the unit. The unit file folder also should indicate the history of the unit's residents for easy cross-referencing with the resident file.

Resident File Folders

Each current resident in the property should have an individual file or be included in the property's resident directory that it cross-references with the unit file. Information on file about the resident should include copies of all property-related documents and correspondence related to that resident. Figure 9–8 suggests a convenient order in which to keep the various items in a resident's file. Following the list provides internal consistency so that anyone using the files can quickly locate a needed document.

For convenience, many properties also maintain a quick-check reference list of current residents. This file permits quick identification of where a resident lives and any emergency contact phone numbers. It is especially useful when only the resident's name is known and time is of the essence in locating the needed information. The information contained on the list should be cross-referenced to the unit and resident files.

With regard to vacated residents, although the law in most states does not specify a minimum length of time to maintain their files, property managers are well advised to keep vacated resident files for at least three years. If the management company has a good storage system, the files may be kept indefinitely. The primary reason for storing these files is in the event of future disputes and/or litigation. Wherever possible, files should be stored on disk in the interest of saving space and retrieval time.

FIGURE 9-8. Organization of Resident's File

Starting with the top form, place in order listed. Not all items will apply to all residents.

Right side of folder (from top to bottom)
- FHA form
- Lease with addendum and stipulations
- Amendment to lease
- Security deposit
- Rent due
- Gas and lights
- Acknowledgment of receipt of information
- Pet permit
- Guarantee of lease
- Credit letter for guarantor
- Move-in inspection
- All verifications
- Application

Left side of folder (from top to bottom)
(Attach with fasteners that can be opened and closed; do not staple.)
- Processing checklist
- Code sheet
- Copies of letters to and from resident
- Dwelling unit inspection book

Upon recertification or lease renewal
(The most recent packet of recertification information should be on top. Information in the packets should be in order listed.)
- FHA form
- New lease (if applicable)
- All verifications
- Recertification application (on top of last year's FHA form)

Consideration should be given to maintaining unit file folders and resident file folders separately, as resident file folders contain confidential and personal information that should not be available to overly inquisitive property personnel or anyone else with access to the files.

Rent Roll

In effect, the rent roll, which lists all renters, the units they are renting, and the amounts due from each renter on a monthly basis, is the accounts receivable of the property and represents the rents collected and to be collected during the month. It is the most important financial document maintained in the site office. It provides management with an auditable track of all rent-related income by unit and can be modified to suit the management company's accounting procedures. It is the primary document called for by auditors and supervisors when reviewing the anticipated monthly rental income of the property. The rent roll is closed out monthly in accordance with the month-end procedures of the management company.

Accounts Payable File

The accounts payable file consists of the invoices not yet paid for goods or services received by the property.

Contracts File

The contracts file should contain all contracts pertaining to the property (e.g., exterminating, trash removal services, landscaping service). Depending on management company policy, the original contract should be retained at either the property or in the accounts payable department of the management company and a copy retained at the other. Property contract files should be organized in alphabetical order. If separate files are kept for each contractor/vendor, both the contracts files and the contractor/vendor files should be coded to allow for easy cross-referencing.

Insurance File

All documents relating to the property's insurance coverage should be kept in a special file section. As with the property contracts file mentioned above, depending on management company policy, the original insurance papers should be retained either in the property or at the management company, and a copy retained at the other.

Supplies and Equipment Files

Also as mentioned earlier, all information relating to the property's supplies and equipment inventory should be recorded on standardized property forms, ideally computerized. In addition, each piece of major equipment (such as trucks, tractors, and major maintenance machinery) should have an individual file folder. Each folder should contain items such as the original invoice and any repair work orders. Depending on management company policy, the information contained in these files may also be kept at the management company and in the property maintenance office. In any case, the site office must have all of the information contained in these files.

Purchase Orders

As indicated above, depending on management company policy, purchase orders may wind up back at the site office after they have been honored or they may be retained by the management company accounting department. If the latter is true, a copy of the purchase order should be provided by the central accounting department to the site office for the property's on-site records. Also depending on management company policy, processed purchase orders may be filed by vendor name, by subject, or by maintenance item, or cross-referenced by all three. The property manager must maintain strict control over purchase order forms to ensure that they are used only for approved property-related purchases.

Compliance File

The compliance file should contain all required permits, licenses, and forms that are required for the property's operation.

Correspondence File

The correspondence file should contain folders with copies of all correspondence to and from the site office. Depending on management company policy, correspondence files may be organized chronologically, by correspondence recipient, or in any other way that allows for easy reference and retrieval.

Reports and Logs Files

As discussed in detail below, the property manager and other property personnel are often required to prepare many different reports on a wide range of property-related issues and to maintain on-going logs for verification of certain activities. These reports and logs should be computerized, and a separate file should be established to contain these reports and logs so that they can be referenced for future use.

Forms File

Master copies of each form used at the property should be kept in individual file folders and as computer templates.

Property Personnel File Folders

Each property worker should have an individual file folder that contains the entire history of her/his employment at the property from initial employment application to the present. Property personnel file folders should be organized alphabetically by employees' last names. Personnel records should be retained for at least five to seven years after an employee leaves, but if the management company has a good storage system, these files should never be destroyed. These files are usually secured and maintained by the property manager.

TYPES OF PERIODIC PROPERTY REPORTS

The purpose of most periodic reports is to provide information for management to use in making decisions. Typically, it is the property manager's responsibility to compile and present these reports to the senior manager or other individual at the management company, and possibly also to the owner. For example, the property's weekly traffic report can be used to help determine how effective the advertising is, whether additional or different advertising is required, and what type of advertising might yield better results. Other reports discussed throughout this text that would likely be helpful to management include the walk-in traffic report; the weekly vacancy summary; report of applications and rejections; summary of important operational events; report on significant incidents and accidents occurring at the property during a specified time period; maintenance contract work report covering maintenance work for a specified period of time; rent collection report; risk prevention review; and property status report (including analysis of the rental situation, occupancy, advertising, rent collection, and cash flow).

All property reports prepared by the property manager should reflect accurate information and be submitted on a timely basis. A copy of each report should be retained in the site office.

TYPES OF PROPERTY LOGS

Daily Log

This log, which should be maintained by the property manager, should be a kind of journal that records the daily goings-on at the property. It should include major happenings at the property; a list of daily visitors to the property (perhaps contained on an attached traffic control report); and descriptions/explanations of any property accidents and/or security incidents.

Payroll Register

The property manager is often required to review and consolidate the timecards of each property employee onto a payroll register like the one shown in Figure 9–9. Upon completing and authenticating the register by signature, the property manager should forward the register to the management company for further processing. In an attempt to reduce paperwork, the individual timecards of each property employee should be retained on-site with a copy of the pay-

Figure 9–9. **Payroll Register**

_______________________ Property

_______________________ Pay Period Ending

Employee Name	Regular Hours	Overtime Hours	Sick Hours	Personal Hours	Vacation Hours	Holiday Hours	Total Pay Hours	Date New Employee Started	Last Date Employee Worked

_______________________ Manager's Signature

_______________________ Date

roll register. Should there be a discrepancy in an employee paycheck, the property manager would then have all the documentation to effect a correction or to explain the concern to the employee. The payroll register also serves as a control for the property and property manager and lets management continuously monitor property payroll. Most payroll software programs include this type of reporting.

Long-Distance Calls Log

All long-distance calls made on any site office phone should be posted in a log such as the one shown in Figure 9–10. The information should include the name of the person making the call, the number called, the person or firm called, and the reason for the call. In addition to serving as a control for long-distance calls, this log assists in checking phone bills. Completed pages of the log should be maintained in the appropriate file folder and copies should be submitted to the central accounting department.

Reports and Activities Log and Calendar

To assist in planning and organizing for the timely submission of reports and the accomplishment of other required activities, the property manager should maintain a reports and activities log like the one shown in Figure 9–11. This log is easier to maintain if it is keyed to a calendar, like the one shown in Figure 9–12, that triggers starting each report or activity on a timely basis and makes sure it is not overlooked. In effect, the combination of a calendar and a log serves as a follow-up system. The property manager should maintain the log and calendar and keep them in a prominent location in the office where they can easily be used on a daily basis.

Each report or activity on the report log should be keyed to the specific page in the operations manual for quick reference. The log has places for the name of the report or activity, frequency, date of initiation or mailing, person responsible, and a brief explanation of that report or activity. The calendar contains the report or activity code number and shows at a glance which report or action must be initiated on that day. There are also many computer programs that include a task or to-do tracking component that can be used for this purpose.

MANAGING SITE OFFICE RECORDS, FILES, REPORTS, AND LOGS

Property records are considered legal records, so they must be legible and well-kept. Entries into a property record, file, report, or log should be notated with the date and the name or initials of the property employee who makes them.

The use of hard copy files should be monitored by a "File Out" notice affixed to the file drawer or the file folder. The notice should have a space for the name of the person who took out the file, when it was removed, and when it was returned.

In general, property and resident files should never leave the site office. If an authorized individual from the management company requests information from a property file, a photocopy should be sent. If the original is needed elsewhere, the property manager should make certain that the property retains a complete set of copies of everything in the file in case the file is lost or damaged.

KEEPING PROPERTY RECORDS, FILES, REPORTS, AND LOGS SAFE

Many of the records, files, reports, and logs maintained in the site office are critical to the property's operations, to the people who work there, and to the residents who live there. Many of these records, files, reports, and logs also would be time-consuming and sometimes costly to duplicate if they were lost or damaged.

The warning contained in Chapter 4, Multihousing Management Economics and Finances therefore bears repeating here: All property records, files, reports, and logs should be maintained in a lockable and secure environment that keeps them safe from fire, water damage, break-in, vandalism, and other possible damage. This is true whether the discussion is about hard copy documents stored in file cabinets or computer files stored on the hard drive or on disk or CD. All computerized files should also be backed-up at an off-site location via tape, CD, the Internet, et cetera to ensure their safety and also to provide another copy in case the first copy becomes corrupted.

This protection is essential not only to guard against destruction of the records, files, reports, and logs but also to guard against breaching confidentiality. For example, much information contained in resident and employee files is confidential, is protected by federal and state privacy statues, and should be made available only to the property owner, the owner's authorized employees, authorized management company staff, and federal agency inspectors.

In addition to protecting confidential documents inside the site office, management company and property policy should be that no records, files, reports, or logs should be released to anyone outside the management organization without the permission of the senior manager. This includes requests from the police, Federal Bureau of Investigation, or other law enforcement agencies. In this way, unintentional violations of privacy regulations will not occur. This policy should be clearly stated in the property's operations manual.

PERIODIC PURGING OF FILES, RECORDS, REPORTS, AND LOGS

From time to time, the property manager should purge the property's files, records, reports, and logs in accordance with the file destruct dates specified in the management company's/property's operations manual. For example, the procedure might require the destruction of former vendor folders that are five years old and property-specific reports that are three years old. If a predetermined destruct date does not exist, the property manager should check with the senior manager for dates for destroying specific files, records, reports, and logs.

Hard copy records, files, reports, and logs that are to be kept for more than one year should be moved to a secure storage location after the first year to conserve space. The records should be carefully boxed and labeled for possible

FIGURE 9–10. Long Distance Call Log

____
Property

Date of Call	Person Making Call	Number Called (including area code)	Person or Firm Called	Reason for Call	Remarks

Figure 9–11. Reports and Activities Log

Code	Manual Page	Report or Activity	Frequency	Date to Mail	Explanation of Report or Activity	Reviewed By
A	VIII-12-18	Rental and turnover report	Weekly	Tues.	Rentals-Move-Ins/Outs-Vacancy	P.M.-R.P.M.
B	VIII-19,20	Traffic control report	Weekly	Tues.	Record of Walk-Ins & Phone Calls	P.M.-R.P.M.
C	VIII-21-23	Property Inspection	Weekly	W	Condition of Grounds, Bldgs., Vacant Units	P.M.-R.P.M.
D	II-17,18	Prospect recontact report	On request	Tues.	Follow-up on Prospect	P.M.-R.P.M.
E	VII-1,p.6	Persons generally delinquent	10th	N/A	List of Delinquent & NSF Tenants	R.P.M.
F	VII-1,p.7	Persons generally delinquent	25th	N/A	Contact regarding next month's rent	R.P.M.
G	III,F-1 VIII-32	Lease renewal/recertification	Monthly	First	Lease Renewal & Recertification	P.M.-R.P.M.
H	VI-1 VIII-28,29	Resident contacts	Monthly	First Wed.	Resident comment. Include on Inspection Report	P.M.-R.P.M.
I	VI-1	Filter inspection	Monthly	First Wed.	Condition of present filter. Include on Inspection Report	P.M.-R.P.M.
J	VIII-21	Property comparison	Monthly	Last Wed.	Comparable communities. Include on Inspection Report	P.M.-R.P.M.
K	IX-42	Time cards	Weekly	Wed.	Accounting of hours worked.	P.M.
L	IX-47,49	Monthly newsletter	Monthly	10th	Monthly resident information	P.M.-R.P.M.
M	VIII-2,p.10	Late rent notices	Monthly	10th	Mail late notice to delinquents	R.P.M.
N	VII-2,p.16	21st delinquent report	Monthly	21st (phone)	Report of delinquents as of 21st.	R.P.M.
O	VII-2,p.14	Delinquents to attorney	Monthly	25th	Delinquents turned over to attorney	R.P.M.
P	VII-2,p.14	Eviction proceedings	Monthly	15th	Commence eviction process for selected delinquents	R.P.M.
Q	VIII-30,31	Credit reports log	Monthly	3rd	Verify credit checks against billing	Accounting
R	VIII-26,27	Telephone calls log	Monthly	25th	Verify long distance calls	Accounting

S	VII-2-6	Move-in/out schedules	Weekly	Mon., & Fri.	List of scheduled move-ins/outs to Maint. On Mon. - Return to R.M. on Fri.	M.S.
T U	VIII-42 VIII-36,37	Occupancy report 9801 Community contact report	Annually As required	Jul-02 Tues (if appl)	Report to HUD When VNA-INA exceeds 3%	HUD P.M.-R.P.M.
V	VIII-43	Carport report	12-3-6-9	Quarterly	Number of carports available and rented	P.M.-R.P.M.
W	VII-3,p.16b VII-33,35	E.O.M. delinquent record	Monthly	Last day	List of delinquents not paid & living in project. Record/status of collection effort	P.M.-R.P.M.
X	VII-1	Persons generally delinquent report	Twice Monthly	5th, 15th	Submitted if 2 or more in project with rent not paid in preceding month	R.P.M.

P.M. ***Property Manager***

R.P.M. ***Regional Property Manager***

M.S. ***Maintenance Superintendent***

Figure 9–12. Rental Reports and Activities Calendar

Sunday	Monday	Tuesday	Wednesday	Thursday	Friday	Saturday
	1 G S	2 A B D U	3 K Q C H I	4	5 S X	6
7	8 S	9 A B D	10 K L M C E	11	12 S	13
14	15 P S X	16 A B D	17 K C	18	19 S	20
21 N	22 S	23 A B D	24 K C	25 F O R	26 S	27
28	29 S	30 A B D	31 W J K C	Other T V		

future use, the labels on the boxes should clearly identify the destruct dates, and the boxes should be initialed by the property manager. Virtually all records, files, reports, and logs also can be transferred to computer disks, CDs, or Internet services, labeled, and stored indefinitely using little or no space.

The manager should dispose of old hard copy records, files, reports, and logs by using a professional-quality paper shredder or a professional disposal firm that shreds, burns, or acid reduces documents. Under no circumstances should old records merely be put in the trash. Much confidential material is contained in them, and the records, although outdated, still have to be treated in a confidential manner.

SITE OFFICE LEGAL OBLIGATIONS

It is the property manager's responsibility, supported by the management company and the management company's legal counsel, to ensure that the site office complies with all appropriate legal obligations. Compliance with individual local, state, and federal regulations; business- and real estate-related obligations; insurance carrier requirements; required grievance procedures; employment regulations; and all requirements specific to that particular type of property and work environment should be specified in the property's operations manual.

The listing of legal and other obligations discussed below is not necessarily complete. Each property manager should consult with the appropriate legal advisor(s) to ensure compliance with all appropriate legal obligations and requirements.

LOCAL, STATE, AND FEDERAL REGULATIONS

Compliance with local, state, and federal regulations implies compliance with all state and local codes and ordinances and all federal laws impacting the property as a residential property and as a place of business and employment (e.g., lead paint, safety, occupancy).

BUSINESS AND REAL ESTATE LICENSES

Some localities require the purchase and display of a business license in the site office. Some require the display of a real estate license for property management. Some require a salesperson's license for renting. The property management executive normally would be responsible for knowing which licenses, if any, are needed for the legal operation and management of the property and what management must do to comply. (Refer to Chapter 13, The Law and Multihousing Management for more information about professional requirements and certifications for residential managers throughout the United States.)

EQUAL HOUSING OPPORTUNITY REQUIREMENTS

All multihousing properties are required by federal law to comply with Equal Housing Opportunity (EHO) posting requirements. This requirement includes but is not limited to the EHO logo on the main property sign and on all marketing materials and is spelled out in detail in various publications of the U.S. Department of Housing and Urban Development (HUD) and other government agencies. The property manager is responsible for ensuring that these requirements are adhered to and that they are specified in the property's operations manual.

INSURANCE CARRIER REQUIREMENTS

Insurance carriers often make certain stipulations with which the insured must comply for the coverage to commence and remain active. The senior manager or other responsible management company representative should supply the property manager with the insurance carrier requirements, and the property manager, together with the appropriate management company decision makers and perhaps the owner, should design and implement a program of requirements compliance.

REGULATIONS AT FEDERALLY ASSISTED DEVELOPMENTS

The U.S. Department of Housing and Urban Development actively monitors the compliance of federally assisted developments with the requirements of affirmative marketing programs, resident selection policies, and grievance procedures.

Prior to being approved as the managing agent at an assisted development, a management company must submit an Affirmative Fair Housing Marketing Plan on HUD form 935.2 and must follow the plan to the letter during its entire tenure at the development. The management company must also provide the opportunity to all prospective residents to know the basis for resident selection by posting these policies in the rental office and/or by presenting them to prospects in a flyer. Likewise, all residents are entitled to know the grievance procedures in the event they have a problem or disagreement with development management. These procedures should include final appeal to HUD, if necessary.

CONCLUSION

The site office is the central command station of the property. The property manager is responsible for managing not only the operations of the property itself but also and especially everything that takes place in, and everyone who works in, the site office.

Although there are varying schools regarding where the site office should be situated, everyone agrees that it should be optimally accessible to property workers, residents, and prospects. The site office should be open and functioning a sufficient number of hours each day and each week to provide adequate and appropriate service to residents and prospects. The site office should be organized as efficiently as possible and furnished with enough workstations, chairs, telephones, computers, file cabinets, and other equipment to allow office staff to perform their functions optimally. Especially but not only if the site office and the rental office are in the same office, a designated "private" space should be set aside for personal discussions between the property manager and residents and/or between the rental agent and prospects. The bottom line is that the site office should be well organized and orderly.

Regardless of whether the property manager has input into the staffing of the site office, she/he will be held accountable for how the site office staff performs. In addition to managing property personnel such as the maintenance supervisor, the maintenance, grounds, and housekeeping staff, security personnel, part-time and season property workers, and the rental agent, this means that the property manager also must manage an office staff that may include one or more management assistants, one or more bookkeepers, and one or more clerical workers. The property manager must therefore be skilled in employee management techniques, must administer the polices and procedures of the property's employee handbook uniformly and consistently, and, most importantly, must ensure that the site office workers understand that their ultimate purpose is to serve the property's residents. To get the most out of the site office staff, the property manager must serve as a role model of a positive and productive work ethic.

The site office should be fully computerized and contain up-to-date technology for maximum efficiency. Ideally, the computer system at the site office should be networked with the computer system at the management company so that each can access the other's records and each can communicate with the other.

As manager of the site office, the property manager also must oversee the flow of money into and out of the property. To this end, all site office workers should be bonded and knowledgeable about the property's policies regarding rent billing, rent payment and collection, and banking procedures.

Under no circumstances should any management company accounts or funds be used for the property's operations, nor should any accounts for the property be carried in the name of the management company only. In addition, under no circumstances should the property's moneys be commingled with the accounts of other properties managed by the management company.

To minimize the chance of personal harm or injury, it should be management company and property policy to protect people and not money in the event of a holdup or robbery in the site office or during a property employee's execution of her/his duties for the property. The property owner should carry adequate and appropriate insurance coverage for such eventualities.

The site office should not offer change-making or check cashing service to anyone.

An audit of all property records and files should be conducted semi-annually or annually and also when the management company and/or owner notices red flags such as excessive delinquencies or unusually slow collections occurring. An independent accountant familiar with residential properties should know how to perform such an audit.

The property manager also is responsible for maintaining sufficient inventory of supplies and equipment for the property's maintenance and for its office operation. The management company should instruct the property manager in the procedures for requisitioning and maintaining inventories, and the management company should perform a physical inventory of supplies and equipment at the property whenever there is a change of property manager and/or the person responsible for maintaining the property inventory.

The management company also should inform the property manager regarding how to manage the repair and/or replacement of property equipment; the management company's purchasing and payment protocols for property purchases; the management company's competitive bidding policy; and who at the property may sign for and accept deliveries of property supplies and equipment. It is the property manager's responsibility to administer these policies from the site office.

The property manager also will be called on to prepare, present, and maintain a variety of records, files, reports, and logs. In addition to having immediate and total access to all rental office files, these items include but may not be limited to unit file folders, resident file folders, the rent roll, accounts payable file, contract file, insurance file, supplies and equipment files, purchase orders, compliance files, correspondence files, reports and logs files, forms file, property personnel file folders, all reports (e.g., weekly traffic reports, weekly vacancy summary, report of applications and rejections, summary of important operational events, reports on significant incidents and accidents during specified time periods, maintenance contract work report covering work for specified periods of time, rent collection reports, risk prevention review, property status reports), daily logs, recap of hours worked log, long-distance calls log, and reports and activities logs and calendars.

Property records are considered legal records, so they must be legible and well-kept. The property manager should have a system of knowing where each folder, file, record, report, and log is at all times. In general, property files should never leave the site office without prior approval from the senior manager or other appropriate management company decision maker. If an authorized individual from the management company requests information from a property file, a photocopy should be sent. If the original is needed elsewhere, the property manager should make certain that the property retains a complete set of everything in the file.

All property records, files, reports, and logs should be maintained in a lockable and secure environment that keeps them safe from fire, water damage, break-in, vandalism, and other possible damage. This is true whether the files are hard copy documents stored in file cabinets or computer files stored in the hard drive or on disk or CD. This protection is essential not only to guard against destruction of the records, files, reports, and logs but also to guard against breaching confidentiality.

From time to time the property manager should purge the property's files, records, reports, and logs. Hard copy records, files, reports, and logs that are to be kept for more than one year should be moved to a secure storage location after the first year to conserve space. Virtually all records, files, reports, and logs also can be transferred to computer disks or CDs, labeled, and stored indefinitely using little or no space.

The property manager should dispose of hard copy records, files, reports, and logs by using a professional-quality paper shredder or a professional disposal firm that shreds, burns, or acid reduces documents. Under no circumstances should old records simply be put in the trash.

It is the responsibility of the property manager, supported by the management company and the management company's legal counsel, to ensure that the site office complies with all appropriate local, state, and federal regulations; business- and real estate-related obligations; insurance carrier requirements; required grievance procedures; and all requirements specific to that particular type of property.

The role of the property manager is a comprehensive one indeed. Not only responsible for the day-to-day functioning of the physical property, she/he also is responsible for interacting with residents and, as this part of the text has discussed, also for managing and supervising the site office and the site office staff.

Throughout the text of this book, reference has been made to the operations manual, which should serve as the "bible" for all property operations. A discussion and outline of the operations manual begins on the next page of this text.

ADDENDUM: THE OPERATIONS MANUAL

The operations manual of a multifamily property should serve as the ultimate guidebook for property operations. Its purpose is to help both the management company and the individual property manager operate more effectively, more efficiently, and more fairly by:

- Explaining how the management company operates, how the property operates, and how the management company supports the management of its client portfolio in general and the specific property in particular
- Codifying policies, procedures, protocols, and forms unique to the management company and to the individual property
- Articulating exactly how things get done and what is expected of everyone involved in the management process
- Providing a how-to resource that anticipates issues and challenges and supplies the solutions and responses for dealing with them in advance

All management companies and professionally managed properties, regardless of size, should have an operations manual and should update the operations manual periodically as revisions and/or new information needs to be included. The operations manual should become part of the agreement between the property owner and the management company, and ensuring that the property is operated and maintained in accordance with the standards and procedures set forth in the operations manual should become the property manager's responsibility.

To be the most valuable and effective resource, the operations manual should be written in simple, concise, easy-to-understand language, and it should be bound in such a way as to allow it to be a living document that can most easily be updated and revised. This is achieved by binding the manual in a three-ring binder so that pages with revisions can be easily inserted and removed. All pages and entries should be dated to ensure the most recent information.

CONTENTS AND OUTLINE OF THE OPERATIONS MANUAL

The operations manual should be organized to include all of the management company's and property's policies, procedures, and forms. Policies are the rules governing action in a given situation. Procedures are the steps for implementing the policies. Forms are the tangible documentation used for demonstrating and evaluating policies and procedures and, if properly designed, are among the most efficient ways to transmit information.

The following topics should be included in the operations manual. Each topic should be given its own titled section for easiest reference. Note that this suggested outline should be adapted to the individual needs of each property.

- A history of the management company or management entity
- A statement of the management company's corporate philosophy
- An organizational chart of the management company
- All management company contact information
- A discussion of line and staff positions and functions within the management company
- The management company's internal personnel policies (which should be included in the management company's employee handbook separate from the property's employee handbook)
- A history of the property and its ownership
- An organizational chart of property staff
- A discussion of outside professionals, such as legal counsel and engineers, who are involved in the operations of the property
- A discussion of job positions and functions within the property (including the property manager and maintenance, rental, office, and all other property personnel)
- All property-related contact information
- Full copies of the property's employee handbook
- A management maintenance plan
- A risk management plan

- Marketing plans
- Resident handbooks
- An emergency handbook
- Policies, procedures, and forms including but not limited to the following:
    - Rent billing and collection, including collection of delinquent rent
    - Rent increases and decreases (for both conventional properties and subsidized developments)
    - Security deposit administration
    - Lease signing
    - Lease distribution
    - Move-in/move-out
    - Eviction (for both conventional properties and subsidized developments)
    - Purchasing and payment
    - Competitive bidding
    - Inventory maintenance
    - Inventory audits
    - Ancillary income
    - Property bank accounts
    - Financial audits of the property
    - All financial reporting
    - Property computers
    - Monitoring property maintenance service
    - Handling various types of resident problems and complaints
- Property records, files, reports, and logs maintenance, storage, and purging
- Compliance with all local, state, and federal and other legal obligations; business- and real estate-related obligations; insurance carrier requirements; grievance procedures; employment requirements; and all requirements specific to the property and its work environment (for both conventional properties and subsidized developments)

10

Management of Shared-Interest Associations

SHARED-INTEREST ASSOCIATIONS

According to the Community Associations Institute (CAI) Research Foundation, as of July 2002 there are more than 230,000 shared-interest associations (also called community associations) throughout the United States, housing more than 40 million residents. Furthermore, an estimated 60 percent of all new homes in major metropolitan areas are built within shared-interest associations. Clearly, shared-interest associations are a significant segment of the multifamily housing landscape. And as with all multifamily properties, they demand professional management.

UNDERSTANDING THE STRUCTURE OF SHARED-INTEREST ASSOCIATIONS

Shared-interest associations are multifamily communities that may consist of high-rise apartments, semi-attached townhouses, or detached single-family homes. Cooperative corporations, condominium associations, homeowners associations (HOAs), and property owner associations (POAs) are common types of shared-interest associations. They are called shared-interest associations because although each dwelling unit is individually owned, all the unit owners (who may be individuals or other entities such as corporations) share together in the ownership and the operational and financial obligations of the association's common land, amenities, property, and other elements. In return for fulfilling the obligations of shared-interest ownership, the association gives its owners certain services and the right of owners to avail themselves of the association's private amenities.

In general, shared-interest associations require that each owner accept and abide by a set of legal agreements, usually referred to as covenants, as a stipulation of ownership in the association. These legal agreements contain provisions for the operation and maintenance of the association and define the owners' obligations to the association, and vice versa. A board of directors, board of managers, board of trustees, or other governing body and its officers (president, vice president[s], treasurer, secretary, and other members) are elected by the owners of the shared-interest association, usually on an annual basis. Depending on the bylaws of the association, individuals elected to the governing body may or may not be required to be owners. In any case, it is the responsibility of this elected body to make decisions on behalf of the association and all its owners according to the stipulations contained in the association's bylaws and other governing documents. However, pursuant to the individual association's bylaws, some decisions impacting the association may be subject to approval by the full body of owners. These decisions by the governing body may, and typically do, run the gamut from whether or not to install a new roof to what color uniforms the association's maintenance staff will wear.

In all shared-interest associations except cooperative corporations, each owner owns the real title to her/his dwelling unit; is responsible for the real estate and other taxes attendant to the dwelling unit; and shares with all the other owners the right to use, and the obligation to maintain, the association's common elements. The cooperative corporation is only slightly different from other forms of shared-interest associations in that a corporation (generally nonprofit) owns the cooperative's real property and issues shares of stock to shareholders (also called stockholders), who then are entitled to enter into a proprietary lease that grants the right to reside in a dwelling unit in the cooperative building. Under the terms of this proprietary lease, the shareholder can live in the co-op as long as she/he owns stock in the corporation. As with other shared-interest associations, cooperative shareholders are entitled to use, and have the obligation to share in the maintenance of, the co-op's common elements and financial obligations. In co-ops in which there is an underlying mortgage for the co-op's land and/or building(s), shareholders also bear the communal responsibility for the mortgage debt service.

Owners' required monetary contributions to the shared-interest association may be called maintenance, common charges, assessments, fees, rent, or dues and may be made monthly, quarterly, annually, or according to another payment schedule. But whatever the payments are called and however often they are made, all of the owners of the shared-interest association are legally bound to pay what they owe to the association in full and on time. Failure to do so could result in legal action by the association against the owner that could bring about foreclosure on the unit and revocation of the owner's ownership stake in the association. This is more significant than eviction from a rental property because such an action against a shared-association owner may nullify her/his investment in the association.

HOW THE STRUCTURE OF SHARED-INTEREST ASSOCIATIONS AFFECTS THEIR MANAGEMENT

In many respects, the management requirements of shared-interest associations are the same as those of rental properties. Both demand meticulous financial oversight; physical, structural, mechanical, and aesthetic maintenance; deliberate risk management; effective marketing; practical policies and procedures for new owners and residents coming into the association and for owners and residents who relinquish residency in the association; and, above all, superior professional management. However, the differences in structure between rental properties and shared-interest associations do impact how shared-interest associations are managed.

The most significant differences between rental properties and shared-interest associations are defined by the number and objectives of the owners of each. Typically, rental properties have a limited number of owners, and those owners are investors interested in maximizing the net operating income of their investment. While in shared-interest associations virtually every resident is also an owner (except for those residents who rent or sublease from owners) and these owners are certainly interested in maintaining and enhancing the value of their investments, most are usually more concerned with the quality of life within the "homes" they own and live in.

Also, in rental properties when a resident becomes troublesome or an issue arises that requires an authoritative decision, management can and should turn to the owner for definitive instructions to resolve the situation. In shared-interest associations, although a board exists to set policy and oversee management performance, in reality management is at the beck and call of as many owners as there are dwelling units. In fact, on more than one occasion, blocks of shared-interest association owners have been responsible for bringing about a change in management even though the elected board may not have wanted the change.

Given the ownership rights of all owners in shared-interest associations, although the management of rental properties is challenging, the management of shared-interest associations is arguably more challenging indeed.

SHARED-INTEREST ASSOCIATION ECONOMICS AND FINANCES

Overwhelmingly, shared-interest associations are nonprofit by design. The moneys that owners pay to the association go directly to support the association's operating and capital costs and its reserve fund(s). In all shared-interest associations, the amount each owner pays to the association on a monthly, quarterly, or annual basis in the form of maintenance, common charges, assessments, fees, rent, or dues is determined by the association's governing body according to current and projected financial information and budgeting. This information and budgeting is provided by the association's treasurer and/or budget committee working in concert with management and the association's independently engaged financial professionals. Usually, the amount each owner of a shared-interest association pays into the association is calculated based on her/his percentage ownership in the association.

In almost all shared-interest associations, owners receive management-generated billing statements indicating the obligation amount and date due. This is different from some rental properties in which no billing is sent to renters as long as the rent level remains the same. However, such billing is necessary in shared-interest associations because owners are often liable for additional and individually varying payments for items such as special assessments or maintenance chargebacks to the association. (See the section below for more on maintenance chargebacks.)

The various means of collecting owner obligations in shared-interest associations are the same as rent collection procedures in rental properties (i.e., in-person at the management office, by mail to the central management office or a designated bank lock box, via direct or electronic transfer, personal checks, bank checks, third-party checks, money orders, or credit cards). However, the fact that an association may collect owner obligations on a schedule other than monthly is another difference between shared-interest associations and rental properties, in which rent is virtually always due and collected on a monthly basis.

Should the association's governing body determine that the current level of income from owners is insufficient to cover the association's costs, the governing body may vote for an increase in owner obligations and/or a special assessment, and all owners are legally bound to accept and comply with the increase or special assessment. Another option available to shared-interest associations to increase revenue is to raise ancillary income through such measures as charging owners for parking spaces, storage lockers, bicycle racks, on-premises fitness and health club memberships, social room rentals, and, in certain types of shared-interest associations, dwelling unit sublet/rental fees and transfer fees (also called "flip taxes" and collected by the association when an owner sells her/his unit). As with some rental properties, some shared-interest associations even raise money by renting rooftops to telecommunications companies that use them for the placement of their antennas or dishes and by inviting movie production companies to use their properties as shooting sites.

Although these are effective ways for shared-interest associations to raise additional funds, restrictions may apply relative to how much money can be raised through means other than owner contributions. Examples of such restrictions include Section 216 of the Internal Revenue Code applicable to cooperative corporations, also known as the 80/20 rule, and Section 528 of the Internal Revenue Code applicable to condominium associations. The governing bodies and management of shared-interest associations that are contemplating raising ancillary funds should therefore consult with the association's legal counsel before instituting any fundraising measures.

MANAGEMENT'S ROLE IN THE FINANCIAL MANAGEMENT OF SHARED-INTEREST ASSOCIATIONS

Although the financial management of shared-interest associations is similar to that of rental properties, a significant difference is the reporting element. Unlike rental properties in which the manager and/or management company makes financial reports to one or more owners of the property, the bylaws of most shared-interest associations require that annual audited financial statements and projected operating budgets be provided to all owners and that all owners have an opportunity to ask questions and receive answers from the association's accounting professionals. This distribution typically occurs in advance of the annual meeting of owners, the meeting of which is generally required pursuant to an association's bylaws. It is at the annual meeting that the association's accounting professionals review the financial statement and projected budget with all attending owners and respond to owners' inquiries, elections for the governing body are held, and the governing body and management make their annual reports to owners.

In addition to this reporting requirement, co-ops also must issue to each owner her/his individual association-related tax information in January of each year so that the owner can report this information on her/his tax return. Such information would include the amount the owner can deduct as a co-op shareholder. This reporting requirement, and the tax-related benefits of shared-interest association ownership, are finance-related aspects that differentiate shared-interest associations from rental properties, which offer no tax benefits to renters.

Almost all of the information contained in Chapter 4, Multihousing Management Economics and Finances is applicable to shared-interest associations. As alluded to in that part, in light of the fact that many multihousing management organizations manage a mix of both rental properties and shared-interest associations, and in the interest of streamlining management operations, it is incumbent upon the management company to design and maintain a sound financial management system that can accommodate a number of different properties, including rental and shared-interest associations, within the same overall design scheme. It is further incumbent upon the management company to employ finance-related experts who understand and can apply the similarities and differences between rental properties and shared-interest associations. The professional manager should make herself/himself an expert in this area of multifamily housing management as well.

MAINTENANCE, ENERGY, AND WATER CONSERVATION IN THE SHARED-INTEREST ASSOCIATION

The need to maintain the physical, structural, mechanical, and aesthetic elements of the property, and the need for the property to conserve energy and water, are the same in a shared-interest association as they are in a rental property. In fact, all of the overarching principles of maintenance and conservation articulated in Chapter 5, Property Maintenance and Energy and Water Conservation apply to shared-interest associations. Most significantly different, however, is who is responsible for effecting the maintenance of the property and the individual dwelling units.

In a rental property, it is ultimately the owner who is responsible for maintaining both the property's common areas and its dwelling units. The owner gives maintenance instructions to management and management communicates the owner's instructions to the property staff and oversees the staff's performance. In a shared-interest association, the maintenance of the association's common elements works in basically the same way. The association's governing body gives maintenance instructions to management, and management communicates the instructions to the association staff and oversees the staff's performance. It is in the maintenance of the individual dwelling unit that a major difference occurs.

To start, there is little in-unit maintenance performed by property staff in shared-interest associations. For example, unlike all of the maintenance considerations that go into preparing a vacated unit for re-rental in a rental property, when the owner of a shared-interest association unit sells the unit and vacates it is that owner's responsibility to prepare the unit for the next owner/resident. The association has nothing to do with it.

But more important is the definition of who is responsible for in-unit maintenance in an occupied unit within a shared-interest association. In rental properties, the owner typically is responsible for the overwhelming number of maintenance activities in occupied units (although there are some instances when chargebacks do apply). In a shared-interest association, however, the association's bylaws dictate which maintenance and repair items are the association's responsibility, which are the owner's, and which the association may perform at the owner's request and then charge back to the owner.

For example, many shared-association bylaws and other governing documents define the dwelling unit owned by the owner as the space contained within the interior walls of the surrounding structure. In other words, everything inside the unit from the inner wall into the unit is the owner's responsibility to maintain (such as a leaky water spigot), while everything actually inside the common walls (such as pipes, electrical wiring, etc.) and everything in the association's common areas are the responsibility of the association to maintain. It is the financial obligation that the owners pay to the association on a regular basis that pays for the maintenance of these common property elements.

A representative definition of cooperative shareholders' maintenance responsibilities and the cooperative corporation's maintenance responsibilities has been extrapolated from a standard cooperative corporation's offering plan and is shown in Figure 10–1.

RISK MANAGEMENT IN THE SHARED-INTEREST ASSOCIATION

Overall, the principles of risk management discussed in Chapter 6, Risk Management and Management Maintenance Plans apply to shared-interest association as well as to rental properties. Most, if not all, of the same elements must be taken into consideration, and most of the same insurance requirements apply. The most significant differences are as follows.

First and foremost, individuals who serve on the association's governing body, typically as volunteers, must be protected by insurance in case they unknowingly and/or unintentionally make a costly, dangerous, or otherwise injurious decision that negatively impacts the association and/or its owners. This type of insurance, called directors and officers liability coverage, is critical. Without it, no responsible person would volunteer to serve in any capacity in a shared-interest association. The majority of shared-interest associations carry directors and officers liability coverage for their governing bodies and also include their managing agent as an additional insured. Those that do not, should.

Two other risk management differences between rental properties and shared-interest associations apply to the individual dwelling unit. In rental units, the owner complies with effective risk management by changing the lock each time a rental tenant moves out. But because units in a shared-interest association are individually owned, the association has nothing to do with the locks of unit front doors.

Similarly, although renters may be encouraged to purchase renters insurance (and some rental properties require this), it is typically the owner who assumes the risk for the units in her/his rental property. In shared-interest associations, however, owners should and often are required to carry homeowners or co-op insurance, as appropriate. In this way, ownership in a shared-interest association is more similar to private home ownership.

MARKETING THE SHARED-INTEREST ASSOCIATION

Unlike with rental properties in which the marketing and leasing of the property's dwelling units are often an explicit part of the management agreement, marketing and sales are generally not part of the management agreement for shared-interest associations. However, marketing and sales may be included in the management contract for a shared-interest association in the case of new construction or the recent conversion of a pre-existing rental property to shared-interest association status. (See Chapter 12, Management's Role During New Construction and Rent-Up.) More often, though, if a management company does offer sales and brokerage services, it is to assist unit owners in the private sale or leasing/rental of their units and is based on the owner compensating the management company on an individual basis.

Under any circumstances, the other principles of multi-housing marketing discussed in Chapter 7, Marketing Rental Housing and the Marketing Plan, including creating and maintaining a positive image for the association, are also applicable to shared-interest associations.

ADMISSIONS, POLICIES AND PROCEDURES, AND THE HOUSE RULES HANDBOOK IN THE SHARED-INTEREST ASSOCIATION

A great many policies and procedures apply to the ownership, residency, and management of shared-interest associations. Many of an association's policies and procedures are explicitly articulated in the association's bylaws, which usually contains a subsection of house rules that define residency in the association. Depending on the stipulations contained in the association's bylaws, both the bylaws and house rules may be subject to amendment, revision, or deletion by the association's governing body.

Admissions is one particular area wherein shared-interest associations differ greatly from rental properties. In condominium and homeowners associations, for example, anyone who meets certain financial criteria may be allowed to purchase a unit in almost the same way as anyone who has the funds can purchase a private home; the unit owner need only

FIGURE 10-1. Sample Definition of a Cooperative Corporation Shareholders' Maintenance Responsibilities and the Co-op's Maintenance Responsibilities

The following sections are extrapolated from a boilerplate cooperative corporation offering plan and define the differences between shareholders' maintenance responsibilities and the cooperative corporation's maintenance responsibilities.

Maintenance and Repair Responsibilities of Shareholders

Each shareholder is responsible for the cost of interior repairs to her/his apartment, and for apartment decoration and painting, including the interior of window frames, sashes, and sills. The shareholder is required to keep the interior of the apartment, (including interior walls, floors, and ceilings, but excluding windows, window panes, window frames, sashes, sills, entrance and terrace doors, frames, and saddles), and terrace floor tiles, in good repair, and is solely responsible for the maintenance, repair, and replacement of plumbing, gas, and heating fixtures and equipment, and such refrigerators, dishwashers, air conditioners, washing machines, ranges, and other appliances, as may be in the apartment. (Plumbing, gas, and heating fixtures include exposed gas, steam, and water pipes attached to fixtures, appliances, and equipment, and the fixtures, appliances, and equipment to which they are attached, and any special pipes or equipment which the shareholder has installed within the wall or ceiling, or under the floor; but does not include gas, steam, water, or other pipes or conduits within the walls, ceilings, or floors, or air conditioning or heating equipment, which is part of the standard building equipment.)

The shareholder is solely responsible for the maintenance, repair, and replacement of all lighting and electrical fixtures, appliances, and equipment, and all meters, fuse boxes, or circuit breakers and electrical wiring and conduits from the junction box at the riser into and through the shareholder's apartment.

Maintenance and Repair Responsibilities of the Cooperative Corporation

The Cooperative Corporation is responsible for the maintenance of, and for the performance and cost of repairs to, the building's public and common areas (unless such maintenance and/or repairs is necessitated by the act of a shareholder or other person, in which case that person may be responsible for the cost of repairs).

Inside individual apartments, the Cooperative Corporation is responsible for the maintenance of, and for the performance and cost of repairs to, windows, window panes, window frames, sashes, sills, entrance and terrace doors, frames, and saddles. The Cooperative Corporation also is responsible for the maintenance of, and for the performance and cost of repairs to gas, steam, water, or other pipes or conduits within the walls, ceilings, or floors, or air conditioning or heating equipment, which is part of the standard building equipment.

The Cooperative Corporation and its agents and their authorized workmen are permitted to visit, examine, or enter any apartment and any storage space assigned to any shareholder, at any reasonable hours of the day upon notice, or at any time and without notice in case of emergency, to make or facilitate repairs in any part of the building or to cure any default by the shareholder, and to remove such portions of the walls, floors, and ceilings of the apartment and storage space as may be required for any such purpose. The Corporation shall thereafter restore the apartment or storage space to its proper and usual condition at the Corporation's expense if such repairs are the obligation of Corporation, or at the shareholder's expense if such repairs are the obligation of the shareholder or are caused by the act or omission of the shareholder or any of the shareholder's family, guests, agents, employees, or subtenants.

In order that the Cooperative Corporation shall at all times have access to the apartment or storage room for the purposes provided for in the Proprietary Lease (specifically for repair purposes in this context), the shareholder shall provide to the Cooperative Corporation a key to each lock providing access to the apartment or the storage room. (Shareholders must provide new keys when new locks are installed.) Should an emergency arise in the apartment or storage room and the shareholder or an agent of the shareholder is not present to provide access, the Cooperative Corporation has the right to enter the apartment or the storage room using the key provided to make such repairs as are required by the emergency. Should an emergency arise in the apartment or storage room and the shareholder or an agent of the shareholder not be present to provide access and the shareholder neglected to provide an access key to the Cooperative Corporation, then the Corporation has the right to forcibly enter the apartment or storage room to effect the necessary repairs without liability for the damages, which will be the shareholder's responsibility.

agree to sell to the prospect. Also in condominiums and homeowners associations, the association typically has the right of first refusal to purchase, meaning that the association must first decline to buy the unit from the unit owner before the unit can be put on the open market. (In the overwhelming majority of cases, the association does not exercise its right of first refusal and the unit owner is free to sell as she/he pleases.) Although the admissions procedure is slightly different in cooperative corporations in which the governing body or its designated admissions committee generally has the right to approve or reject prospective shareholders, nevertheless ownership in a cooperative has considerably more in common with private ownership than with renting.

With regard to these admissions procedures, each shared-interest association is at liberty to create its own policies and procedures within the parameters of the law (especially but not only Fair Housing and antidiscrimination laws) and the association's governing documents. It is management's job to administer those policies and procedures completely and uniformly.

Typically, once a prospective shared-interest association purchaser has been approved, the procedure progresses like the closing on a private home. Both the seller and purchaser may be represented by attorneys, while the association is generally represented by management. To assist in this process, many management companies that manage shared-interest associations also support in-house transfer and closing departments. In this way the management company has all of the paperwork attendant to the unit and the new unit owner, and the new owner becomes familiar with management even before the transaction is consummated.

With regard to welcoming the new owner, this is a policy decision of the association's governing body. If they wish to extend a welcome on behalf of the association, they can appoint a committee or individual as an emissary of the association or they can delegate management to serve this purpose. Regardless of who welcomes the new owner, it is not a single property owner doing the welcoming as it is in a rental property. Instead it is a group of co-owners welcoming the newest member of their association, an association that management serves but is not a member of. This difference is not lost on the property manager who grasps the fundamental structure of shared-interest associations.

The property manager who understands the structure of the shared-interest association also understands the function and importance of committees in the association. Committees composed of involved owners are vital in terms of shaping the policies and procedures of a shared-interest association. Such committees as the finance committee, the building and grounds/beautification committee, the admissions committee, and the communications committee, for example, report to the association's governing body and make valuable contributions to the association's operations and quality of life. Whereas management may view certain committees in rental properties as breeding grounds for troublemakers and insurrectionists, management must work productively hand-in-hand with the committees of a shared-interest association and must always remember that each committee member is an owner in the association and consequently another "boss."

A house rules handbook that articulates the association's policies, procedures, and residency guidelines based on the association's bylaws and the decisions of its governing body is as important in a shared-interest association as a resident handbook is in a rental property. A suggested outline for a shared-interest association house rules handbook appears in Figure 10–2.

OFF-SITE AND ON-SITE MANAGEMENT OF THE SHARED-INTEREST ASSOCIATION

As with rental properties, some shared-interest associations are managed by portfolio managers who operate out of the management company's central office and visit the properties they manage on a predetermined schedule, and some shared-interest associations support an on-site management office. When the latter is the case, the property manager should become familiar with all of the topics in Chapter 9, Managing the Site Office and the Operations Manual because they are substantially the same for both rental and shared-interest properties.

Regardless of whether the property manager works off-site or on-site, a major difference for the property manager is the meeting requirements of shared-interest associations. Specifically, the bylaws of the majority of shared-interest associations require regular (typically monthly) meetings of the governing body and annual meetings of all owners to review and discuss the association's current and projected financial, physical, mechanical, and operational aspects. The presence of the property manager is usually mandatory at these meetings, and it is expected that the manager will bring with her/him a clearly organized and well-written management report that summarizes management activity and informs the association's governing body and its owners of the items currently under consideration and/or recommended for consideration. Although similar meetings and reports may also be required by rental property owners, the property manager of a shared-interest association must accommodate the fact that everyone she/he reports to is an owner and probably also a layperson when it comes to residential real estate management. Therefore, management reports must be comprehensively and clearly written so that they can be easily understood by everyone who has a right to read them.

Another major difference between rental properties and shared-interest associations is the fact that the decision makers of shared-interest associations can change annually, and sometimes more often than that. Whereas the owner of a rental property tends to be the same person or entity for extended periods of time, the owners who populate the decision-making body of a shared-interest association can change with each annual election and/or through other eventualities, such as the resignation of one board member and the appointment by the board of another owner to fill the vacancy through the duration of the term. The point is that the shared-interest association manager must be able to work well with many different people and personalities and must be prepared for frequent turnover among the association's decision makers.

FIGURE 10-2. Suggested Outline of a House Rules Handbook for Shared-interest Associations

As with resident handbooks in rental properties, the well-organized, clearly written and indexed house rules handbook for a shared-interest association guides and assists owners in their relations with the association, its governing body, its management and maintenance staff, and with each other. It clearly states the association's house rules, policies, procedures, and residency requirements and restrictions, and encourages greater compliance on the parts of all owners.

The house rules handbook should be thorough and all-inclusive, as demonstrated by the recommended outline below. It should be written in common, everyday language, not legalese, but it should be reviewed by the property's legal counsel prior to distribution in order to ensure the accuracy and appropriateness of its contents. It may be compiled by a management company staff member, by a professional who specializes in producing house rules handbooks for multifamily properties*, or by a freelance copywriter with superior organizational skills. It may be bound in any number of ways (e.g., stapled, spiral bound, three-ring binder, etc.), but in any case it should look impressive so that owners will respect it as the official resource guide it is meant to be. And finally, it should be updated regularly. When changes in policies occur, all owners should be so notified in writing via a memo from the association's governing body that cites the previous policy, explains any changes to it, and instructs owners to insert the new policy into the handbook so that it supersedes the previous policy. The entire handbook should be updated, revised, and redistributed every three to five years, and more often, if necessary.

Contents and Outline of a House Rules Handbook for a Shared-interest Association†
Note that the suggested contents and outline of a house rules handbook that appear below should be adapted to the individual needs of each association.

- **First page**

The first page of the house rules handbook should be a quick guide to the contact information owners and residents need most. Included should be:

- The management office location and phone numbers (regular business hours, after hours, and emergency)
- The maintenance office location and phone numbers (regular business hours, after hours, and emergency)
- The addresses and phone numbers of the local police precinct and fire department (in addition to 911)
- The local Post Office address, phone number, and hours
- The local utility companies' addresses and phone numbers (regular business hours, after hours, and emergency)
- The property's voting precinct number and addresses of local polling place(s)
- All other addresses and phone numbers that residents might need.

- **Introductory policy statement**

A general policy statement should introduce the handbook and provide owners with its rationale. Specifically, the handbook should begin with the information that the policies contained in it are based on the association's by-laws and actions taken by the association's governing body in order to protect owners' investments and rights while allowing them to enjoy a safe and secure living environment. The introductory statement also should state that the house rules, policies, procedures, and residency guidelines contained in the handbook are effective as of a given date, and may be subject to change by the association's governing body at any time with written notice from the governing body.

- **About the association**

Owners like to know about the place they own and live in, and a little background about the association goes a long way toward establishing pride of ownership and pride of residency. Information contained in the house rules handbook about the association might include:

- Introduction to the type of shared-interest association (cooperative, condominium, home owners association, etc.)
- Year constructed
- Year converted to shared-association status (if applicable)
- Number of residential units
- Number of professional, commercial, and other units
- Other pertinent information, including association amenities and services
- Association staff information, including management and maintenance staff, their titles and duties, etc.
- Explanation of the structure and functions of the governing body
- List of standing and ad hoc committees, and how owners can serve
- Standard month/date of the annual meeting, election procedures, and other pertinent governance information

(*continued*)

FIGURE 10-2. Suggested Outline of a House Rules Handbook for Shared-interest Associations (*Continued*)

- Discussion of retained professional services (e.g., corporate counsel, accountant, insurance, engineer, etc.)
- Management company information, including name, address, phone fax, website, and e-mail contact information of management company and management professional(s)
- Maintenance supervisor's contact information
- Other contacts and information pertinent to the association
- Statement regarding compliance with house rules, violations, fines, etc.
- Other information as appropriate

- **Financial matters**
  - Maintenance/Common Charges/Dues/Fees, etc. (How levels are set, remittance procedures, collection procedures, etc.)
  - Assessments (How levels are set, remittance procedures, collection procedures, etc.)
  - Late Fees and violation fees (Fees, collection procedures, etc.)
  - Other

- **Association amenities, facilities, and services**

Note that policies affecting common use areas should also be posted in those areas.

  - Bicycle Room
  - Bulletin Board
  - Cable and Internet Access
  - Common Areas
  - Delivery Entrance
  - Electricity
  - Elevators (passenger, service, delivery, etc.)
  - Exterminator
  - Front Door
  - Health Club/Exercise Room
  - Garage/Parking Lot
  - HVAC (Heating, Ventilation, and Air Conditioning)
  - Intercom and Resident Directory (Lobby and elsewhere)
  - Internet Access
  - Laundry Facilities
  - Lobby and Common Hallways
  - Luggage Carts
  - Mail Handling (mailroom, mail distribution, etc.)
  - Newsletter
  - Packages (package room, package handling, package distribution, etc.)
  - Playground
  - Roof (use of roof area, roof deck, etc.)
  - Service/Delivery Entrance
  - Social Hall/Party Room (use and rental of social hall/party room, etc.)
  - Storage (storage room, storage cages, rental of storage space, etc.)
  - Suggestion Box
  - Swimming Pool
  - Telephone Directories
  - Tennis Courts
  - Other

- **General maintenance and repair policies**
  - Maintenance and Repair Responsibilities of the Association
  - Maintenance and Repair Responsibilities of Owners, including Chargeback Policy
  - Service Requests (procedure for submitting service request, including copy of work order form, etc.)
  - Other

- **Unit dwelling/residency policies**
  - Air Conditioners in Individual Dwelling Units
  - Unit Access/Key Policy (including Emergency Access Policy, Convenience Key Policy, etc.)

(*continued*)

FIGURE 10-2. Suggested Outline of a House Rules Handbook for Shared-interest Associations (*Continued*)

- Unit Alterations (including major alterations, painting, floor scraping, etc., with Alteration Agreement requirements and forms)
- Unit Use (e.g., professional use policy, etc.)
- Cable/Satellite Dish Access and Use in Individual Dwelling Units
- Clothes Washing Machines and Dryers in Individual Dwelling Units
- Complaints about Association Staff/Management/Neighbors
- Deliveries (to association /to individual dwelling units)
- Dishwashers in Individual Dwelling Units
- Disposal of Household Refuse/Disposal of Large Items/Recycling Policy
- Energy Conservation in Individual Dwelling Units
- Floor Covering Requirements Inside Units
- Hallways and Stairwells (residency policies)
- Heat in Individual Dwelling Units
- Housekeeping, Cleanliness, and Maintenance of Reasonable Living Conditions in Individual Dwelling Units
- Installation of Appliances in Individual Dwelling Units
- Insurance (requirements for home owners coverage, etc.)
- Internet Access in Individual Dwelling Units
- Move-in/Move-out Policies and Procedures
- Noise and Disturbance Policies
- Pets
- Supervision of Children in Common Areas and Individual Dwelling Units
- Terraces, Balconies, Patios, etc., Adjacent/Belonging to Individual Dwelling Units
- Ventilation in Individual Dwelling Units
- Water Conservation in Individual Dwelling Units
- Windows/Window Guards/Window Ledges in Individual Dwelling Units
- Other

- **Security and safety issues**
  - Access to the Association and Common Areas (For owners/residents; visitors and guests; delivery people; contractors and work people; domestic help; solicitors, etc.)
  - Access to Individual Dwelling Units (For owners/residents; visitors and guests; delivery people; contractors and work people; domestic help; solicitors, etc., including announcement of visitors, etc.; forms for access to individual dwelling units by visitors, guests, etc.; emergency and emergency key access policy; convenience key policy; including all procedures and forms)
  - Fire Safety (including association and individual dwelling unit fire precautions; smoke and fire detectors; required Fire Safety Plan, etc.)
  - Prolonged Owner/Resident Absence from Dwelling Unit (Prolonged Absence policy)
  - Roof Security and Safety Policy
  - Window Guards
  - Other

- **Selling, subletting/renting, and financing/refinancing**
  - Selling a Dwelling Unit/Transfer of Shares (for co-ops)/Transfer Fee (Flip Tax)/Sales Fees (including all policies, requirements, fees, and forms)
  - Subletting/Renting a Dwelling Unit/Subletting/Rental Fees (including all policies requirements, fees, and forms)
  - Financing/Refinancing a Dwelling Unit (including all policies, requirements, fees, and forms)
  - Other

- **Appendices**
  - Sample Copies of all Forms, Policies, etc., to be reproduced and inserted as appropriate

- **Other**
  - As required

---

* The editor of this text, Barbara Dershowitz, is such an expert. Her company, Business Communications Workshop, (516/938-0323), specializes in producing House Rules handbooks, property staff handbooks, residential property newsletters, and all manner of multihousing communication vehicles.

† This list of suggested House Rules handbook contents and outline is the property of, and is re-printed with the permission of, Barbara Dershowitz and Business Communications Workshop.

THE MANAGEMENT AGREEMENT FOR SHARED-INTEREST ASSOCIATIONS

Every owner in a shared-interest association pays her/his pro-rated share to support the association's operations and to ensure that the association will be able to meet its financial obligations. Among these obligations is the association's management fee, which is almost universally a flat monthly fee (as opposed to management fees in rental properties, which may be based on a percentage of rent collected). As with rental properties, how the management fee is to be collected, and all responsibilities of management, are articulated in the management agreement.

The management agreement between a shared-interest association and a management company should always be in writing and signed by the appropriate member(s) of the association's governing body and the appropriate management company representative. Typically, the management agreement for a shared-interest association includes the following:

- Legal title of the association, if any (e.g., Rolling Hills Condominium, Lake Ariel Estates, Oak Street Owners Corporation), and the address of the association and legal name and address of the management company
- Areas of management responsibility, including but not limited to financial, operational, maintenance, long-term planning, admissions processing, owner/resident relations, and attendance requirements at regularly scheduled meetings of the association
- Association personnel and staff supervision and compensation, including the chain of command for hiring and firing association employees and management company employees serving the association, and the maintenance of employee records
- Management spending limits and association reimbursements to management
- Performance indemnification and management company insurance, including a clearly stated management indemnification clause and the insurance coverage that management is required to carry
- Calendar and hours of operation of the management company
- Management emergency response procedures
- Transition considerations, including an outline of how management will effect a smooth management transition
- Term of the agreement (commencement and termination dates)
- Cancellation provisions
- The management fee and any additional/ancillary services and fees

A sample management agreement between a condominium association and a management company appears in Figure 10–3.

CONCLUSION

Shared-interest associations such as cooperative corporations, condominium associations, homeowners associations (HOAs), and property owner associations (POAs) represent a significant multifamily housing presence. They are called shared-interest associations because although each dwelling unit is individually owned, all the owners also share in the ownership and in the operational and financial obligations of the association's common land, amenities, property, and other common elements. Owners abide by a set of legal agreements, called covenants, as a stipulation of ownership in the association and elect, usually annually, a governing body of individuals (usually but not always owners) to make most of the decisions for the association and its owners.

Owners fulfill their obligations to the association by paying to the association a set monetary contribution (called maintenance, common charges, assessments, fees, rent, or dues) on a predetermined schedule (monthly, quarterly, annually, or other). Failure to honor this obligation can result in the association foreclosing on the owner's unit and nullifying the owner's investment in the association.

Shared-interest associations usually are nonprofit. The moneys owners pay to the association support the association's operating and capital costs and its reserve fund(s). The amount each owner pays is determined according to current and projected financial information and budgeting and is calculated based on each owner's percentage ownership in the association. Owners' payments are collected via the same means as rent payments in rental properties. Shared-interest associations may raise additional funds in any number of ways but must be careful to stay within the parameters of applicable tax regulations.

The bylaws of most shared-interest associations require that annual audited financial statements and projected operating budgets be provided to all owners and that all owners have an opportunity to ask questions and receive answers from the association's accounting professionals. This distribution typically occurs in advance of the annual meeting of owners at which the association's accounting professionals review the financial statement and projected budget with all attending owners and respond to owners' inquiries, elections for the governing body are held, and the governing body and management present their annual reports. Shared-interest associations also must issue to each owner her/his individual association-related tax information as appropriate so that the owner can report this information on her/his tax return.

The maintenance of the common property of a shared-interest association is similar to that of a rental property. However, there is little in-unit maintenance in a shared-interest association because each owner owns his/her unit individu-

FIGURE 10-3. Sample Management Agreement for a Shared-interest Association

THIS AGREEMENT, made as of the ________ day of _________________, 2 ______ between XYZ Condominium, having its principal office at XYZ Street, New York, New York hereinafter referred to as the "Owner", and ABC Management Company, a corporation organized and existing under the laws of the State of New York, having its principal office at 60-10 East 73rd Street, New York, New York 10017, referred to as the "Agent".

W I T N E S S E T H:

In consideration of the terms, conditions, and covenants hereinafter set forth, the parties hereto mutually agree with each other as follows:

FIRST: (a) The Owner hereby appoints the Agent, and the Agent hereby accepts appointment, on the terms and conditions hereinafter provided, as exclusive managing agent of the XYZ Street Condominium located at XYZ Street, located in the County of New York, State of New York, and consisting of approximately ______ Residential Units, and ______ Commercial spaces (hereinafter referred to collectively as the "Building"), together with the land on which it is erected.

(b) The Agent agrees, notwithstanding the authority given to the Agent in this agreement, to confer fully and freely with the Owner in the performance of its duties as herein set forth. The Agent agrees to keep itself informed on all policy matters and resolutions adopted by the Board of Managers to encourage whenever possible the principles of cooperative effort among the Unit Owners.

SECOND: In order to facilitate efficient operation, the Owner shall inform the Agent with regard to standards to be kept and furnish the Agent with a set of community or house rules and a complete set of the plans and specifications to the extent available. With the aid of these documents and inspection made by competent personnel, the Agent will inform itself with respect to the layout, construction, location, character, plan and operation of the lighting, heating, plumbing, and ventilating systems, as well as elevators and other mechanical equipment. Copies of guarantees and warranties in force at the time of the execution of this Agreement shall be furnished to the Agent.

THIRD: The Agent shall hire in its own name all managerial personnel for the efficient discharge of the duties of the Agent hereunder. Compensation for the services of such employees shall be the responsibility of the Agent. If requested by the Owner, in agreement with the Agent, the Agent will, within forty-five days after receipt of such request, replace the individual complained of who has primary responsibility for the management of the Building or is the District Manager responsible for the Building, with another member of the Agent's staff. The Agent represents that the Property Manager shall be ______________________________________ and that it shall not change such person without the Owner's prior written consent.

FOURTH: The Agent shall perform the following services with due diligence and care:

(a) Cause to be hired, paid and supervised, all persons necessary to be employed in order to properly maintain and operate the Building, who, in each instance shall be the Owner's and not the Agent's employees, and cause to be discharged all persons unnecessary or undesirable, except that no person presently employed at the Building shall be discharged, nor shall any new personnel be hired, without the prior consent of the Owner. It is expressly understood and agreed, however, that all employees are in the employ of the Owner, solely and not in the employ of Agent and that Agent is in no way liable to employees for their wages or compensation nor to the Owner, or others for any act or omission on the part of such employees.

(b) Cause the Building to be maintained in such condition as may be deemed advisable by the Owner, including interior and exterior cleaning, and cause repairs and alterations of the building to be made, including, but not limited to, electrical, plumbing, steamfitting, carpentry, masonry, elevator, decorating, and such other incidental alterations or changes therein as may be proper, subject only to the limitations contained in this agreement or in the Condominium Declaration or By-Laws. Ordinary repairs or alterations

(continued)

FIGURE 10-3. Sample Management Agreement for a Shared-interest Association (*Continued*)

involving an expenditure of over $______________ for any one item shall be made only with the approval of the Owner, but emergency repairs, i.e., those immediately necessary for the preservation of the Building or for the safety of the Units Owners, the occupants of the Building, or other persons, or required to avoid the suspension of any necessary service in the Building, may be made by the Agent irrespective of the cost thereof, without the prior approval of the Owner, after consultation, if feasible, with the president, vice president or treasurer of the Owner (in the order given). In the event that the Owner undertakes any capital improvement or major repair of the Building, the Agent shall be responsible for seeing that the work is done with as little interference or interruption of Building services as possible, and shall be responsible for seeing that all reasonable precautions are taken to preserve and protect the Building and the property of the Unit Owners and the occupants of the Building. In the event that the Owner undertakes such a capital improvement or repair involving an expenditure in excess of $______________, the Agent shall not be required to undertake supervisory responsibilities except under the provisions of a separate instrument setting forth the Agent's obligations and compensation relating thereto.

(c) Recommend and, with the approval of the Owner, cause all such acts and things to be done in or about the Building as shall be necessary or desirable to comply with any orders or violations affecting the Building, as a result of any action by any federal, state, or municipal authority having jurisdiction thereover, or any order of the New York Board of Fire Underwriters, the New York Fire Insurance Exchange or other similar body, except that if failure promptly to comply with any such order or violation would or might expose the Owner of the Agent to criminal liability, the Agent may cause such order or violation to be complied with after consultation, if feasible, with the president, vice-president or treasurer of the Owner (in the order given). The Agent shall notify the Owner promptly after receipt of any order or violation, as aforesaid. The Owner shall be responsible for the cost of complying with any order that may be issued in respect of the Building.

(d) Enter into contracts for electricity, gas, steam, air-conditioning, water treatment, elevator, telephone, window cleaning, rubbish removal, fuel oil, security services, vermin extermination, other essential services, or such of them as shall be advisable, but any such contract having a term longer than one (1) year or requiring annual payments in excess of $______________ must be authorized by an officer of the Owner.

(e) Purchase all supplies and engage all repair persons as shall be necessary to properly maintain and operate the Building; make all such contracts and purchases in either the Owner's or the Agent's name, as the Agent shall elect; and credit to the Owner any discounts or commissions obtained for purchases or otherwise. Purchases in excess of $______________ must be authorized by an officer of the Owner.

(f) Advise the Owner, in conjunction with an insurance broker, with respect to proper insurance coverage for the Building, its employees and occupants; if requested by the Owner, cause to be effected and/or maintained, in such amounts and through such carriers as the Owner shall designate or approve, fire, rent, plate glass, boiler, water damage, liability, workers' compensation, disability and any other insurance the Owner may elect to carry; and to cooperate with any independent insurance broker or consultant that the Owner may designate or approve and engage for the purpose of effecting insurance and protecting its interests with respect thereto. Agent, or its affiliates may receive commissions if duly licensed to do so.

(g) Check all bills received for services, work, and supplies ordered in connection with maintaining and operating the Building; pay or cause to be paid or forward to the Owner for payment as the Owner may direct, all such bills, as well as ground rent (if any), mortgage interest, mortgage amortization, water charges, sewer rent, assessments, real estate taxes, and corporate income and other taxes assessed against the Owner or the building as and when the same shall become due and payable, provided that Owner's operating account has sufficient funds to meet those obligations.

(h) Bill or cause to be billed, Unit Owners for common charges, rent or other charges; use its best efforts to collect such common charges, rent and other charges; and, when and if directed by the Owner, serve notice upon Unit Owners, tenants or sub-tenants to quit and surrender space occupied by them. Also, when directed by the Owner, and on its behalf, in the name of the Agent, or in the name of the Owner, cause liens for common charges to be filed, sue for common charges, rent and other charges which may at any time

(*continued*)

FIGURE 10-3. Sample Management Agreement for a Shared-interest Association (*Continued*)

be or become due to the Owner from any Unit Owner, tenant or sub-tenant in respect of space in the Building, and with Owner's consent, employ special counsel, if necessary, for the purposes of commencing foreclosure proceedings or other appropriate action, (subject to Owner's approval). For services rendered by Agent as a witness or expert witness on behalf of Owner and at Owner's request, or if subpoenaed in person by any litigant, in any arbitration or court proceeding, by reason of Agent's role as Managing Agent of the Building, a fee equal to $85.00 per hour for each hour expended in court or arbitration, in any discovery proceeding (deposition or document production). In connection with any court proceeding or arbitration, Agent shall be entitled to $85.00 per hour expended in document production.

(i) Consider and, when reasonable, attend to complaints of the Unit Owners. If the Agent shall deem any such complaint unreasonable, it shall advise the Owner of the complaint and the reason for its opinion that the complaint is unreasonable.

(j) Cause to be prepared and filed the necessary forms for unemployment insurance, withholding and social security taxes and all other tax and other forms relating to employment of Building employees and maintenance and operation of the Building required by any federal, state or municipal authority.

(k) Not later than the ___________ day of each month, render or cause to be rendered regular monthly statements, supported by disbursement vouchers, to the Owner, with remittance of amounts collected during the previous month less disbursements made on behalf of and for the account of the Owner, but only one such copy need be supported by disbursement vouchers. A copy of each such monthly statement shall be sent by the Agent to the President and Treasurer of the Owner.

(l) Set up and keep in good order a separate, accurate income and operating expense statement (other than books of account maintained by the Owner's accountants) and maintain orderly files containing rent records, insurance policies, correspondence, receipted bills and vouchers, and all other documents and papers pertaining to the Building or the operation thereof. In the event that Owner notifies Agent of any error in bookkeeping, billing or payment of expenses, Agent shall use its best efforts to correct such error immediately.

(m) Cooperate with the Owner's accountants in regard to the annual audit of the books of account of the Owner, including the annual report of the operations of the Owner for the year then ended. A copy of each such annual report after receipt from accountant shall be sent by the Agent to each Unit Owner.

(n) Cooperate with the Owner's accountants in regard to the preparation and filing on behalf of the Owner of federal, state, city and any other income and other tax returns required by any governmental authority.

(o) Assist Board of Managers in preparing an operating budget prior to the last meeting of the Board of Managers held in each calendar year, setting forth the anticipated income and expenses for the Owner for the ensuing year, a comparison of said budget to the income and expenses of the preceding and current years, and any required explanations with respect thereto.

(p) Provide a suitable meeting place for the Board of Managers, send notices to managers and Unit Owners, prepare agendas for, and cause a representative of its organization to attend, the annual meeting of the Unit Owners and meetings of the Board of Managers of the Owner. For attendance by Agent's representatives at any meetings called by Owner which extend after 8:30 p.m. (except in the case of an emergency, in which event the hourly fee shall not be payable), Owner shall pay Agent a fee of $50.00 per hour, per representative for each such hour, or part, that extends after 8:30 p.m.

(q) Prepare, type, and send out all letters, newsletters and reports as the Board of Managers of the Owner may request, and in that connection, make available reproduction facilities of the Agent at a reasonable charge.

(*continued*)

FIGURE 10-3. Sample Management Agreement for a Shared-interest Association (*Continued*)

(r) Accept applications and references from all prospective unit owners, prospective tenants of unit owners, obtain credit reports relating to such prospective unit owners and tenants; obtain from unit owners proposing to sell their units such record searches as the Owner may require, and submit same to the Owner; including the preparation of all necessary documents required for approval and the scheduling of interviews and assisting the Owner's committee in obtaining such other reasonable information it may require in respect of prospective owners, and make recommendations to the Owner respecting its exercise of a right of first refusal. Agent shall cooperate with Owner's counsel when required.

(s) When the books of tentatively assessed valuations of the City of New York are opened for public inspection in each year, ascertain the assessment of the land on which each Unit is located and the assessment of each Unit and report such assessments to the Owner. Should any Unit Owner consider such assessments excessive the Agent will, if requested by such Unit Owner, cooperate with the Owner's attorneys in the preparation of an application for correction of the assessed valuation to be filed with the Tax Commission of the City of New York and, if the Unit Owner shall not have any regular attorneys, retain special counsel (at Unit Owner's expense) to prepare such application (with the Agent's cooperation and to institute tax certiorari proceedings.

(t) If requested by Owner, coordinate and assist in the processing and negotiation of insurance claims for losses sustained by Owner to the Building. No additional fee shall be charged by Agent unless the damage to the Building exceeds $5,000.00. Agent shall cooperate in its role as Managing Agent, making all relevant records and information available to any party authorized by Owner to act on its behalf related to such insurance claims. When the damage to the Building exceeds $5,000.00 and Owner authorized Agent to negotiate with the insurance carrier, for services in connection with negotiating such claim, Owner will pay Agent 5% of any insurance recovery. Agent shall not settle any insurance claim without the consent of Owner.

(u) Generally, do all things reasonably deemed necessary or desirable by the Board of Managers of the Owner for the proper management of the Building. However, in the event any such other things are not within the services enumerated in paragraphs FOURTH (a) through FOURTH (u) above (e.g. without limitation, compliance with a new administrative or filing requirement), Agent shall be entitled to such additional compensation from Owner therefor as owner and Agent may mutually agree.

(v) Agent shall have the authority to prepare and secure signs to the Building with Agent's name thereon.

FIFTH: Everything done by the Agent under and in accordance with the provisions of this Agreement shall be done as Agent of the Owner, and all obligations or expenses incurred thereunder shall be for the account, on behalf, and at the expense of the Owner. Disbursements such as postage, messenger, photocopying, courier or overnight delivery expenses will be reimbursed to Agent by Owner. Any payments to be made by the Agent hereunder shall be made out of such sums as are available in the special account of the Owner, or as may be provided by the Owner. The Agent shall not be obliged to make any advance to or for the account of the Owner or to pay any sum, except out of funds held or provided as aforesaid, nor shall the Agent be obliged to incur any liability or obligation for the account of the Owner without assurance that the necessary funds for the discharge thereof will be provided. The Board shall reimburse Agent promptly for any moneys which Agent may elect to advance for the account of the Owner. Nothing herein contained, however, shall be construed to obligate Agent to make any such advances.

SIXTH: The Agent shall establish and maintain, in a manner to indicate the custodial nature thereof, a separate bank account as Agent of the Owner for the deposit of the moneys of the Owner, with authority to draw thereon for any payments to be made by the Agent to discharge any liabilities or obligations incurred pursuant to this Agreement, and for the payment of the Agent's fee. The Agent shall consult with the Owner to determine where surplus moneys are to be deposited or invested.

SEVENTH: The sole compensation which the Agent shall be entitled to receive for all services performed under this Agreement shall be $________________ per annum, payable in equal monthly installments of

(*continued*)

FIGURE 10-3. Sample Management Agreement for a Shared-interest Association (*Continued*)

$______________. If it becomes advisable or necessary to make extraordinary repairs or engage in extensive reconstruction or rehabilitation of the Building or any part thereof, or if Agent is called upon to perform any extraordinary services not customarily a part of the usual services performed by a managing agent, it is agreed by the parties hereto that Agent shall receive an additional fee therefor in an amount to be agreed upon between the parties, but in each instance, where Agent is to receive an additional fee, Agent shall give Owner prior written notice thereof.

Agent shall be entitled to the following additional fees.

(a) For selling property of the Owner or for leasing or subleasing space in the Building on behalf of the Owner, when engaged for such purposes by the Owner, in a prior writing, reasonable commissions to be computed in a manner and in such amounts are agreed upon between Owner and Agent, when Agent is engaged.

(b) For the processing of purchase or rental or sublease applications, Agent may charge unit owners who make application to rent or sell their unit, a processing fee in the sum of ________________________ Dollars, which fee may be increase in the event additional or special credit reports are required.

(c) For the coordination and assistance with financing or refinancing of residential mortgages, agent may charge unit owners who finance or refinance their unit, a fee in the sum of ________________________ Dollars.

(d) For the processing of rental or sublease renewals, Agent may charge unit owners who make application to renew their leases or subleases, a processing fee in the sum of $________________ which fee may be increased in the event additional or special credit reports are required.

(e) For processing of alteration applications for submission to the Owner, Agent may charge Unit Owners who apply for Board consent to alter their units a fee in the amount of $__________________.

EIGHTH: The Agent shall not be liable to the Owner for any loss or damage not caused by the Agent's own negligence or failure to comply with its obligations hereunder. The Owner will indemnify the Agent against and hold the Agent, its officers and employees harmless from (a) any liability, damages, costs and expenses (including reasonable attorneys' fees) sustained or incurred for injury to any person or property in, about and in connection with the Building, from any cause whatsoever, unless such injury shall be caused by the Agent's, its officers, agents or employees' own willful or gross negligence, or the Agent's failure to comply with its obligations hereunder, (b) any liability, damages, penalties, costs and expenses, statutory or otherwise, for all acts properly performed by the Agent pursuant to the instructions of the Owner, (c) any liability, damages, penalties, costs and expenses (including reasonable attorneys' fees) arising out of, resulting from, or being in any way connected with any liens filed by or on behalf of any architects, contractors, engineers, or others against the Condominium, the Board of Managers, or the party indemnified hereunder; provided, in each of the foregoing instances, that the Agent promptly advises the Owner of its receipt of information concerning any such injury and the amount of any such liability, damages, penalties, costs and expenses. The Owner further agrees to reimburse Agent upon demand for any moneys which the latter is required to pay out for any reason whatsoever, either in connection with, or as an expense in defense of, any claim, civil or criminal action, proceeding, charge or prosecution made, instituted or maintained against Agent or the Owner and Agent jointly or severally, affecting or due to the condition or use of the Building, or acts or omissions of Agent or employees of the Owner or Agent, or arising out of or based upon any law, regulation, requirement, contract or award relating to the hours of employment, working conditions, wages and/or compensation of employees or former employees of the Owner, or otherwise; and to defend promptly and diligently, at the Owner's sole expense, any claim, action or proceeding brought against Agent or Agent and the Owner jointly or severally arising out of or connected with any of the foregoing, and to hold harmless and fully indemnify Agent from any judgment,

(*continued*)

FIGURE 10-3. Sample Management Agreement for a Shared-interest Association (*Continued*)

loss or settlement on account thereof. It is expressly understood and agreed that the foregoing provisions of this article shall survive the termination of this Agreement, but this shall not be construed to mean that the Owner's liability does not survive as to other provisions of this Agreement. Nothing contained in this article shall relieve Agent from responsibility to the Owner for gross or willful negligence. The Owner will carry liability insurance, workers' compensation and employer's liability insurance, will include the Agent as an additional insured under the liability policy and will deliver a copy of such liability policy to the Agent or a certificate evidencing the same.

NINTH: The Agent, at the Owner's expense, if requested by Owner, shall procure a fidelity bond satisfactory in form to the Owner, and issued by a bonding, insurance or casualty company satisfactory to the Owner, pursuant to which the Owner will be held harmless by the surety in an amount up to a minimum of $100,000, which may be in the form of a blanket policy, from any loss of money or other personal property belonging to the Owner or for which the Owner is legally liable, caused by larceny, embezzlement, forgery, misappropriation, or any dishonest or fraudulent acts committed on or after the date of such bond, by the Agent, its directors, officers or employees. The Agent agrees to keep said bond in full force and effect throughout the term of this Agreement.

TENTH: This Agreement shall become effective as of ____________________ and shall continue in full force and effect until ____________________. Thereafter, it shall automatically renew for like one (1) year periods until terminated as hereinafter provided. At any time after the first year, this Agreement may be terminated at the option of either party at the end of any calendar month upon thirty (30) days' previous notice in writing from one party to the other. Upon termination, the parties shall account to each other with respect to all uncompleted business, and the Agent shall promptly deliver to the Owner all books and records and other instruments relating to the Building and the Owner that may be in the possession of the Agent.

ELEVENTH: Within sixty (60) days of commencement of the initial term of this agreement, Agent shall, at Owner's expense, cause to be issued a report, based upon a search of municipal records, detailing all outstanding liens, sidewalk notices, water and sewer charges, real estate taxes, municipal violations and orders. If the search reveals any outstanding items, Agent shall, at Owner's request and expense, take appropriate action necessary to cause open items to be discharged, if feasible.

TWELFTH: This Agreement shall be binding on the parties hereto, their heirs, executors, administrators, successors and assigns, and may not be changed orally but only by a writing signed by the party to be charged thereby.

IN WITNESS WHEREOF, the parties hereto have executed this Agreement as of the day and year first above written.

OWNER:
The Board of Managers of
XYZ Street Condominium

By: ______________________________

AGENT:
ABC Management Company

By: ______________________________
(Typed name of president)

ally. The association's bylaws dictate which maintenance and repair items are the association's responsibility, which are the owner's, and which the association may perform at the owner's request and then charge back to the owner.

Similarly, owners in shared-interest associations must assume individual risk for their units; for this reason, homeowners or co-op insurance is advised. However, shared-interest associations also should carry directors and officer liability insurance to cover those individuals who serve, usually voluntarily, on the association's governing body.

Except in certain cases of new construction and conversion, management companies are not generally engaged by shared-interest associations to perform the same level of marketing and brokerage they are engaged to perform for rental properties. If a management company does offer sales and brokerage services, it is to assist unit owners in the private sale or leasing/rental of their units and is based on the owner compensating the management company on an individual basis.

Many of an association's policies and procedures, including those governing admissions, are explicitly articulated in the association's bylaws, which usually contain a subsection of house rules that define residency in the association. Depending on the stipulations contained in the association's bylaws, both the bylaws and house rules may be subject to amendment, revision, or deletion by the association's governing body. A house rules handbook that articulates the association's policies, procedures, and residency guidelines based on the association's bylaws and the decisions of its governing body is as important in a shared-interest association as is a resident handbook in a rental property.

The on-site responsibilities of the shared-interest association property manager are virtually similar to those of the rental property manager. In addition, the shared-interest association property manager must attend all regularly scheduled meetings of the association's governing body and owners equipped with a management report that summarizes management activity and indicates items currently under consideration and/or recommended for consideration.

As with the management agreement for a rental property, the management agreement for a shared-interest association will stipulate all the salient points that define the management/property relationship.

The most significant difference between managing rental properties and managing shared-interest association is this: In rental properties, it is management's responsibility to introduce the property and its residency expectations to residents. It then falls to the resident (read rental tenant) to live up to those standards or face the consequences. In shared-interest associations, however, once management and the unit owners have made each other's acquaintance, it then falls to management to live up to the association's standards or face the consequences. Any professional manager will agree that recognizing this difference is critically important to the successful management of shared-interest associations.

11

Government-assisted and Government-insured Housing and Military Housing

GOVERNMENT PARTICIPATION IN MULTIFAMILY HOUSING

Residential shelter is among the most basic of human needs. Everyone needs an environment that is reasonably safe and sanitary in which to reside. The United States government has put in place a variety of programs designed to assist individuals and families who may not otherwise be able to afford suitable housing. The government also has established programs to assist members of the Armed Forces and their families in securing appropriate housing. The purpose of this chapter is two-fold. First, it explains how the government participates in meeting the housing needs of those who require assistance and those who serve the country. Second, it discusses the issues that impact the management of government-assisted and government-insured housing and military housing.

HISTORY AND OVERVIEW OF GOVERNMENT-ASSISTED AND GOVERNMENT-INSURED HOUSING

The earliest government housing subsidy programs in the United States began with the creation of the Federal Housing Administration (FHA) in 1934 and the Public Housing Administration. Using federal funding, the programs were run by local housing authorities that had to be created by city councils in accordance with state housing authority laws. The programs were intended to liberalize mortgage credit terms, stimulate a then-dormant housing industry, and improve economic conditions during and after the depression in the 1930s. Unlike present federal housing programs, which are much more narrowly focused, the original programs were intended for all segments of the population in need of housing and primarily served blue-collar workers who were having hard times because of the depression. It was only after World War II that the residents of public housing gradually changed from predominantly employed, blue-collar workers to the working poor and the unemployed.

During the late 1930s and 1940s, local housing authorities developed public housing with tax-exempt bonds issued by them and paid for with federal funds. To keep construction costs down, the housing developments typically lacked amenities and were generally unimaginative in design. In general, they remain so to this day.

FEDERAL HOUSING ADMINISTRATION

The FHA mortgage insurance program was created in 1934 to revive reluctant credit and mortgage markets. The FHA guarantee of payment if the homeowner defaulted on her/his house loan produced a strong, positive impact on the homebuilding industry in the 1930s by reducing the risk to private mortgage lenders. This stimulus increased the availability of credit and permitted more people to buy homes. In turn, increased demand prompted the housing industry to increase the housing supply. Whereas approximately 140,000 units were constructed in 1944, about 1,000,000 were built in 1946, and by 1950, the volume was 2,000,000 units.

The low level of housing construction during the depression and war years gave way to a pent-up demand for housing. Similar to the FHA insurance program, the post-war Veterans Administration Guarantee Program enabled returning veterans to borrow up to 100 percent of the cost of a home. The liberalized FHA insurance provisions (longer mortgages and higher loan-to-value ratios), combined with the Veterans Administration Guarantee Program, helped to stimulate a substantial amount of new housing construction during this period. Much of the federal effort was devoted to maintaining a stable mortgage market in the face of housing demand. But this effort served only the single-family home ownership market.

HOUSING ACT OF 1949

The Housing Act of 1949 expanded federal involvement in housing. Passed by Congress in response to the increasing recognition of the desperate housing conditions that existed for the urban and rural poor, the Act authorized a program of 135,000 new public housing units annually for six years. It also authorized slum clearance and the urban redevelopment program, later called urban renewal.

Under the Housing Act of 1949, local governments were required to build and/or provide low- and moderate-income housing as a relocation resource. This increased the supply of standard housing for these market segments. However, for many low-income families, urban renewal only resulted in a rearrangement of living quarters rather than the stated intention of improving housing.

PUBLIC HOUSING

Prior to 1933, the federal government's involvement in housing was limited to indirect assistance through the FHA mortgage insurance program and tax deductions for mortgage interest and real estate taxes for homeowners. The public housing program created by Congress in 1937 added a new feature to the government's involvement in housing and brought local government directly into housing for the first time. Under the public housing law, Congress authorized local government bodies, known as local housing authorities, to participate in the construction, ownership, and management functions of the public housing programs. The primary benefit was that housing authorities were provided with lower-cost sites for public housing.

Although the Housing Act of 1949 did not nearly satisfy the nation's low-income housing needs, it was notable for the goals it set for federal housing programs. Its policy statement is still germane today: to assure "a decent home and suitable living environment for every American family." Since 1949, every American president has quoted from this statement of policy in introducing major housing programs: "Private enterprise shall be encouraged to serve as large a part of the total market as it can" and "Governmental assistance shall be utilized where feasible to enable private enterprise to serve more of the total need." The Act's two housing goals continue to direct national housing policy to this date: a "home in a suitable living environment" and the use of a joint housing venture of the public and private sectors to achieve this objective

During the 1950s, federal policy gradually expanded from stimulating housing construction to solving the specific social housing problems of the residents of public housing through better development and environmental design. In addition, the increasing cost of housing directed public attention to families whose incomes were just above the incomes of families being served by public housing. The private sector began to find it increasingly difficult to produce affordable housing.

As a result, the federal government re-examined its role in housing. The mortgage insurance programs were working, but they were only serving predominantly middle-income families, many of whom were able to afford market-rate housing. At the time, housing for those with low incomes consisted primarily of high-rise, family-size units built on land cleared through the urban renewal process.

In many cases, both the public housing and urban renewal programs were deliberately manipulated by local politicians to segregate poorer, largely minority populations into high-rise ghettos in the large cities, where they were separated by barriers, such as highways and rail yards, from the more desirable middle-class housing. Much of the stock of urban public housing still suffers today from the problems generated by its placement and density.

HOUSING ACT OF 1959

The Housing Act of 1959 was significant in two ways. First, it extended the federal government's role in assisted housing for the moderate-income family. Second, it permitted developers other than local housing authorities to build and manage federally assisted housing.

The Section 202 program of the U.S. Department of Housing and Urban Development (HUD) provided federal funding for below-market interest rate (BMIR) direct loans to nonprofit developers of senior housing. As a condition of the lower interest rates, these developers were restricted in the amount of rent they could charge. The government also monitored the provision of services, maintenance of housing quality standards, occupancy standards, and the like. Income limits were established to assure that the benefit of the lower rents was limited to the seniors who could not afford market rents. The 202 program is one of the only surviving programs of this and later eras. Although it is no longer a BMIR program, it is still in operation today, one of the last direct assistance programs still building units.

This moderate-income private ownership concept was extended in 1961 by passage of Sections 221(d)(3) and (d)(4), amendments to the housing law. Under the (d)(3) program, nonprofit and limited dividend developers built housing for families at reduced rents (limited dividend means that the developer can make only a stipulated profit), and the federal government subsidized the interest rate on the mortgage via a one-time reduction of the interest rate from market rate to 3 percent. As with the 202 program, the government also monitored the project to ensure proper maintenance and the continued provision of services to the residents. Under the (d)(4) program, profit-motivated developers were provided FHA insurance on market rate housing developments to assist with the development of rental housing.

HOUSING ACT OF 1965

The Housing Act of 1965 expanded the 1959 Housing Act's use of subsidies for privately owned properties. Besides lowering the interest rate of the 221(d)(3) and 202 BMIR programs to as low as 3 percent, the Act created two new subsidy approaches: Rent Supplement and Section 23-Direct Leasing. The 1965 Act was one of the pillars of President Lyndon Johnson's Great Society. It marked a departure from previous government policy and the beginning of direct subsidy funding to private owners of housing. The Rent Supplement Program provided a graduated subsidy, depending on the income level of the tenant. The federal government paid the owner the difference between the market rent for the unit and the amount the resident could afford. As in other low-income rental programs, the resident was required to pay only 25 percent of her/his income for rent. (The percentage has since increased to 40 percent.) The rent supplement made up the difference. Initially, the subsidy could not be less than 10 percent nor more than 70 percent of the competitive/prevailing market rents of the area.

The original objective of Rent Supplement was to minimize the participation of the federal government and to achieve maximum private industry participation. It was intended to replace the 221(d)(3) BMIR program by substituting cash payments of varying amounts for below-market interest rate loans. However, Congress appropriated a limited amount of funds for its implementation and permitted the 221(d)(3) BMIR program to continue. As a result, instead of being replaced by the Rent Supplement Program, 221(d)(3) was frequently used for mortgage financing in conjunction with the Rent Supplement Program subsidies.

Section 23-Direct Leasing is an innovation that was developed within the public housing program financing structure. Under Section 23, local housing authorities can lease existing housing units for eligible residents. Leasing provides an alternative to the local housing authorities building new units to provide homes for low-income families. As in public housing units, the tenants only pay rent that they can afford. The difference between that amount and the rent for the leased unit is paid for by a federal subsidy. Under this program, the public housing subsidy helps to pay rent rather than being used for debt service.

The Housing Act of 1965 also elevated the Housing and Home Finance Agency to cabinet status as the U.S. Department of Housing and Urban Development. The new department greatly expanded the federal government's responsibilities and opportunities in housing and urban development. Creation of the new cabinet-level department consolidated national efforts dealing with the entire range of urban problems.

The Rent Supplement and Section 23 leasing provisions of the 1965 Act moved the federal government into the business of providing funding for low-income housing in a venture that expanded in scope until the middle 1970s. As funding became more limited, that role has diminished.

HOUSING AND URBAN DEVELOPMENT ACT OF 1968

The Section 235 and 236 programs were two new housing-finance tools authorized by the Housing Act of 1968. Section 235 enabled moderate-income families to obtain low-interest mortgage financing for the purchase of single-family homes. A federal subsidy supplemented the home buyer's mortgage payment to make housing affordable. The buyers were required to have incomes within 90 percent of the median income.

The Section 236 program provides mortgage insurance and interest subsidy for multifamily rental housing. It was enacted to substitute an expanded subsidy program for the existing seniors housing program under Section 202 and the below-market interest rate program under Section 221(d)(3).

The Section 236 program differed from the 221(d)(3) BMIR program by reducing the debt service that the rental payments had to cover because interest rates were subsidized to as low as 1 percent. The Sections 235 and 236 programs provided lower occupant costs than did other programs.

The Section 236 program permitted several variations and greater program flexibility. For instance, 20 percent of the units constructed under the 236 program could be used for low-income tenants who required help from the Rent Supplement Program to meet the basic rate charge. Thus, it opened the doors of otherwise moderate-income developments to a small number of low-income tenants. The program also provided for "exception income limits," whereby projects could, under certain circumstances (basically based on marketing considerations), rent to persons with incomes above the normal 236 income limits. Therefore, the Section 236 program permitted a greater mix of income levels associated with the Section 221(d)(3) and public housing programs. Enactment of this program was an all-out attempt at economic integration.

HOUSING ACT OF 1974

Dissatisfaction with the existing programs and a need to provide more flexibility in the approach to housing low-income families prompted the declaration of a moratorium on the Section 235 and 236 programs. In their stead, Congress enacted the Section 8 Housing Assistance Payments Program. (The moratorium on the Section 235 program was subsequently removed in 1976 as the result of a lawsuit, but construction under it is limited by lack of appropriations.)

The Section 8 program provides housing assistance payments to low-income families. The program has two basic types of assistance:

- Direct assistance to developers of new and substantially rehabilitated housing developments (similar to the Rent Supplements Program)
- Assistance through local housing authorities to low-income families who want to rent units in the existing housing market (commonly called Section 8, Existing, also called vouchers, similar to the Section 23 program)

Under the current Section 8 program, participants must pay up to 30 percent of their adjusted gross income for rent. The federal government pays the difference between the 30 percent and the actual rent. The total rent for any one unit cannot exceed the fair market rents that are established for each area by HUD. A participant's income must be within the income limits set for the area, and income must be re-certified every year.

The federal financing programs most commonly used for financing the construction of new developments under the Section 8 program include HUD Section 221(d)(3); HUD Section 221(d)(4); HUD Section 202; Farmers Home Administration Section 515; HUD 11(b), tax-exempt bond financing; state and local housing finance agencies' tax-exempt bonds; HUD Moderate Rehabilitation; HUD Section 223(f) Co-insured Mortgages; and the secondary mortgage market.

THE NEED FOR GOVERNMENT INVOLVEMENT IN HOUSING

The need for government involvement in housing exists for several reasons. First, housing has become increasingly unaffordable for a larger and larger segment of the population, especially those persons and families with low and moderate incomes. Second, construction costs have increased to the point that builders and developers are reluctant to build moderate- and low-income housing without some type of subsidy. Also, high interest rates, high construction and operating costs, and the inability to command rent levels sufficient to cover those costs have resulted in a slowing of construction of affordable rental housing, with a resulting decline in the vacancy rate. This low vacancy rate makes housing needs even more critical, especially for low- and moderate-income individuals and families.

Government involvement in housing is also necessary because with the Tax Reform Act of 1986, most of the tax incentives that investors had traditionally relied on to produce a cash flow and increase the yield on their investment were eliminated. The effect of these changes was to make many marginally profitable apartment developments permanently unprofitable. The changes included limitations on deduction of operating losses from other properties and lengthening of the depreciation period on apartments from 19 to 29 years, thereby reducing by a third the cash flow generated by depreciation.

An additional disincentive to investment was provided by political actions taken by Congress in 1987. Nearly all of the original 221(d)(3), 221(d)(4), and 236 mortgage loans had a provision allowing prepayment of the mortgages with no penalty after 20 years at the owner's option. This option allowed the owner to convert the property from subsidized to conventional if she/he wished or to demolish it and construct another development that would provide a higher yield on the same site (an office building, for example). In 1987, with the prospect of developers prepaying mortgages in substantial numbers, Congress passed an act prohibiting prepayment for two years. Hence, owners became leery and investors became reluctant to put funds into a development with no guarantee that the rules would be the same when they wanted to take those funds out.

Finally, in many instances, investors can achieve a better return through different types of investments that do not require management than they can investing in multifamily housing development. They earn more on their investments and fewer risks are involved.

With urbanization, inflation in land and construction costs, and changes in lifestyles, Americans increasingly live in multihousing developments. The federal government has come to play an important role in providing much of this multifamily housing, especially for low- and moderate-income families. This is true because although an average 15 to 30 percent of a family's income goes toward housing, poor families often spend up to 50 percent of their income on housing and are often relegated to the worst housing stock. This is the segment of the population that is addressed most through government housing programs.

GOVERNMENT HOUSING AGENCIES AND ONLINE HUD INFORMATION

FEDERAL AGENCIES

HUD is the primary housing agency on the federal level. HUD administers the federal government's participation in the low-rent housing program and protects the government's financial interests. This responsibility is carried out through HUD's offices in Washington, D.C., and regional and area offices throughout the country.

HUD programs fall into four categories: insured, assisted, direct loan, and public housing. The Government National Mortgage Association (Ginnie Mae) is responsible for administering the tandem Section 25 and 27 programs. The Farmers Home Administration (FmHA) administers its direct loan programs. The Federal National Mortgage Association (Fannie Mae) was created in 1938 to maintain a secondary market to buy and sell government-insured mortgages. In effect, Fannie Mae is the mortgagee for many government-assisted developments.

STATE AGENCIES

The state housing finance agencies are primarily responsible for securing tax-exempt bond financing for public housing developments. The majority of states have established state housing finance agencies with broad powers to finance multi- and single-family housing for a broad range of income groups. Usually located in the state capitals, these agencies often bear different names, such as the New Mexico Mortgage Finance Authority and the West Virginia Housing Development Fund. Although powers vary by state, most state agencies have the authority to raise funds by issuing tax-exempt revenue bonds. These state agencies use these funds to make direct loans available at favorable terms to developers for construction and permanent financing of low- and moderate-income housing.

State agency financing is one alternative for a Section 8 builder unable to obtain satisfactory conventional financing. HUD allocates a percentage of its annual Section 8 contract authority to state agencies.

LOCAL AGENCIES

The Housing Act of 1937 empowered the formation of public housing authorities for the construction, ownership, and operation of public housing. HUD provides technical, professional, and financial assistance to local housing authorities for building and operating low-rent housing.

HUD WEBSITE FOR LEGISLATIVE CHANGES, CERTIFICATION, RE-CERTIFICATION, AND SUBSIDY BILLING AND OTHER INFORMATION

Legislative changes continue to have a significant impact on HUD's policies and procedures for administering subsidized programs. In addition, HUD requires the owners and operators of developments operated under Section 236; Section 8, Housing Assistance Payments Program; Section 8, elderly; and FmHA Section 515, Rural Rentals with Section 8, among other programs, to automate reporting of forms.

For the most recent legislative and other information from HUD, log on to www.hud.gov. For the most recent forms from HUD, visit www.hudclips.org/sub_nonhud/html/forms.htm.

THE GOVERNMENT HOUSING PROGRAM PROCESS

LEGISLATIVE REQUIREMENTS

Every government housing program begins through legislation. For example, the Housing Act of 1974 established the Section 8 housing assistance payments program. Another act of Congress established the broad parameters or policy guidelines within which the program operates.

PROGRAM REGULATIONS

Following legislation, the next step in the process is the regulatory agency's establishment of regulations for implementing the program outlined by Congress. For example, the Regulatory Agreement is the basic contract between HUD and the owner. It is impossible to overemphasize the importance of the Regulatory Agreement. It is the primary agreement between the government and the owner of the project with a federally insured mortgage, and it sets forth the essentials of the agreement between the parties. It covers such issues as occupancy standards, maintenance requirements, distribution limitations, reporting requirements, and so forth. It should be noted that the Regulatory Agreement is only used when the mortgage is federally insured; projects that are assisted by HUD (e.g., project-based Section 8 contracts) but that do not have insured mortgages are controlled by the documents relevant to the type of subsidy (i.e., for Section 8, the Housing Assistance Payments contract). Figure 11–1 shows the obligations assumed by the owner under HUD programs. These are also the obligations that the manager of a HUD development must fulfill on behalf of the development owner.

APPROVAL OF DEVELOPER AND DEVELOPMENT PLANS

The next step in the government housing process is for HUD or another regulatory agency to approve the developer and the development plan for proposed construction under one of the federal programs. HUD follows detailed guidelines when reviewing the history, capability, and financial stability of the proposed developer. Plans for the development must be economically viable within the program guidelines. The developer must show that the development can be built within the cost constraints of the program and that it can be operated on an on-going basis with authorized rents sufficient to meet expected expenses, including repayment of the loan.

APPROVAL OF THE MANAGEMENT PROGRAM

The next steps are HUD approval of the management agreement between the managing agent and the owner and approval of the management plan, which is the agent's detailed statement concerning how the development is to be operated.

FIGURE 11-1. Owner's Obligations Under HUD Programs

- To maintain the property in good condition and provide for its management in a manner satisfactory to HUD
- To maintain a reserve fund for replacement of structural elements and mechanical equipment
- To obtain information from prospective and existing residents for certification of and recertification of income
- To prohibit residents from renting more than one unit at any given time without prior written approval from HUD
- To allow occupancy by families with children except in developments designed primarily for seniors (The HUD programs designed exclusively for persons over 62 years of age are exempt from the provisions of the Title VIII changes enacted in 1988. Also exempt are retirement or near-elderly housing. This housing is defined as intended for, and at least 80-percent occupied by, a minimum of one person aged 55 or over per unit and as providing significant social services beyond housing.)
- To establish a rent schedule with HUD approval and not to change the rent schedule without HUD approval
- To limit occupancy to families whose incomes are within the limits set by HUD, with the exception of residents who agree to pay fair market rental
- To limit occupancy to single persons whose incomes are within the limits set by HUD and who are handicapped, disabled, displaced, or at least 62 years of age. (In the Section 8 Program the surviving member of a household that is already receiving Section 8 funds would be eligible.)
- To comply with all federal, state, and local laws governing discrimination on the grounds of race, sex, color, creed, national origin, handicap, familial status, or age (As noted above, certain seniors developments are exempt.)
- To deny without HUD's written approval the use of dwelling accommodations for any purpose other than the originally intended use
- To incur no direct or contingent liability other than for current operating expense without HUD's prior written approval
- To make no distribution of development assets or income except from surplus cash and except when complying with all outstanding notices or requirements for proper maintenance of the development
- To keep the premises and books maintained in a reasonable condition for proper audit, subject to HUD inspection at any reasonable time
- To require no monetary condition or deposit as a condition of occupancy other than prepayment of the first month's rent plus a security deposit that does not exceed 1 month's rent or Total Tenant Payment, depending on the program.
- To keep security deposit funds separate from all other funds of the development in a trust account, the amount of which at all times equals or exceeds the aggregate of outstanding obligations under the account

* HUD Financed Senior Citizen, 202, and 811 *only*
HUD Insured - HUD will garentee the lendor all others

As with all management agreements, the rights and responsibilities of the owner and agent are set forth in the management agreement. The management plan must address most aspects of management responsibility, including:

- Orientation for residents
- Plans to carry our maintenance, repairs, security, and safety programs
- Collection procedures
- Policies and procedures for handling grievances
- Policies and procedures for servicing resident requests
- Leasing policies and procedures
- Working with tenant organizations
- Plans for evaluating support and participation of the residents
- Social service programs

The management plan is discussed in the section below.

ON-GOING MONITORING

Finally, HUD continuously monitors development management and financial activities. This monitoring involves periodic full-scale physical inspections through HUD's Real Estate Assessment Center (REAC), which centralizes the assessment of all HUD housing. If dissatisfied with conditions, the owner will be required to present to HUD a written plan of action, including a timetable for repairs, scope of work, and, in some cases, an explanation as to how the repairs will be funded. HUD also conducts periodic "comprehensive management reviews," which involve a detailed review of all of the development's physical, fiscal, and management operations, and other checks that might result from a red flag signal, including a spot check of the files to verify that the screening, selection, and processing of applicants is in accordance with regulations.

FEDERALLY INSURED AND FEDERALLY ASSISTED PROGRAMS

Although a number of the programs discussed in this section have been either curtailed or effectively discontinued, most are still active in the sense that they are authorized by regulation or statute. However, they are not being funded or are being funded at low levels of production. Nevertheless, all of the programs below still exist, as do the communities developed under these programs.

MORTGAGE PROGRAMS

Sections 221(d)(3) and 221(d)(4)

These mortgage insurance programs at market interest rate were designed to assist private industry in providing rental and cooperative housing for families of different income levels. The programs subsidized the financing of newly constructed and substantially rehabilitated residential developments that were built in accordance with HUD's minimum property standards.

Section 202

HUD Section 202, a direct mortgage loan program, assists private, nonprofit corporations and consumer cooperatives in the development of rental or cooperative multihousing for seniors and physically handicapped or developmentally disabled adults. The program allows HUD to make below-market interest rate loans directly to selected nonprofit mortgagors and to provide rental assistance to residents to strengthen the financial feasibility of the development.

Section 515

In small rural communities, the Section 8, New Construction Program utilized an FmHA Section 515, Direct Mortgage Loan Program rather than one of the HUD-insured loan programs. FmHA Section 515 aided new construction or substantial rehabilitation of rental or cooperative housing in rural areas. Occupancy was limited to low- and moderate-income families, persons aged 62 or older, and handicapped persons. Borrowers were required to conduct market surveys to determine the number of eligible occupants in the area who were willing and financially able to occupy the units. Interest credits were available to eligible borrowers to reduce the effective interest rate to as low as 1 percent. The FmHA 515 program was a major source of low- and moderate-income units in rural parts of the country. As of the writing of this text, no new applications are being accepted for this program.

MORTGAGE INSURANCE

As stated earlier, the FHA was established by the Housing Act of 1934. The Act included a provision for an insurance program designed to reduce financial risk for mortgage lenders and induce them to make credit available on more liberal terms. In return for a premium paid by the borrower, the FHA insures the lender against the risk that the borrower may default. FHA financing has placed home ownership within the reach of millions of families in the United States.

MORTGAGE SERVICING

Mortgage servicing consists of collecting the debt service (principal and interest) to amortize the loan and ensure that taxes, insurance, and other payments are made in accordance with the loan agreement. The mortgagee, either Ginnie Mae or a conventional lender, also performs periodic inspections to ensure that the loan is being safeguarded through proper operation and maintenance of the development.

RENTAL ASSISTANCE PROGRAMS

HUD Rent Supplement

The HUD rent supplement program provided a graduated rent subsidy depending on the income level of the resident. The federal government paid the owner and the difference between the market rent for the unit and the amount the resident could afford. As with other low-income rental programs, the resident was required to pay only 30 percent of her/his adjusted gross income for rent. The Rent Supplement Program was converted to Section 8 in the early 1980s and is subject to Section 8 guidelines.

Section 23, Leased Housing

Section 23 was developed within the public housing program financing structure as an alternative to building new units to provide homes for low-income families. A local housing authority leased existing housing units for eligible residents. As in conventional public housing, residents paid only the rent that they could afford. The difference between that amount and the rent for the private unit was paid by a federal subsidy. Under this program, the public housing subsidy helped to pay rent rather than a mortgage.

The rent supplement and Section 23 leasing provisions of the 1964 Housing Act strongly reaffirmed the emphasis begun in the 1959 Act toward subsidizing units in developments that are privately owned, constructed, and managed, but this program has been phased out and all units covered under the program have been converted to Section 8 throughout the country.

Section 8

The Section 8 program described above provides rental (and cooperative) housing assistance payments to low-income families. Congress appropriates Section 8 funds annually. HUD distributes Section 8 set-asides to state housing finance agencies for use in conjunction with the housing construction and rehabilitation financed by these agencies. There are two basic types of Section 8 assistance: project-based, in which HUD signs a contract with the owner and the subsidy is attached to the housing units, and certificates (vouchers) whereby HUD provides direct vouchers for distribution directly to residents by city or county housing authorities.

Figure 11–2 shows a compendium of major federal direct-assistance low- and moderate-income housing programs. HUD terminology frequently used in connection with the subsidized housing programs appears in Figure 11–3.

HUD MANAGEMENT REQUIREMENTS

HUD requires a comprehensive management plan from the developer during the planning stage of a HUD-insured multihousing development as the first step toward successful management. For best results, the program should be developed concurrently with the planning and construction of the physical plant. The detailed plan should include a full discussion of:

- The owner's relationship with the managing agent
- Personnel policies and staffing arrangements
- Publicizing and achieving early occupancy (Fair Market program)
- Certification and re-certification of resident eligibility
- Effective maintenance and repair
- Rent collection
- Accounting records and office procedures
- Management/resident relations
- Community services
- The management agreement

RESIDENT SELECTION, CERTIFICATION, AND RECERTIFICATION IN HUD DEVELOPMENTS

THE RESIDENT SELECTION PROGRAM

A well-planned resident selection program is vital to the success of low- and moderate-income housing developments. Ideally, the developer/sponsor and the future managing agent should put together the basic policies and criteria of the program at the time consideration is first given to building a development. Determining prospective resident eligibility according to applicable statutory limitations is the first step of a comprehensive selection policy formulated and planned in detail well in advance of initial occupancy. Although policies should be modified or changed if experience proves them to be in error, they should not be abandoned for what may be called "panic renting" to achieve faster rent-up. Figure 11–4 details the guidelines for developing a resident selection program.

RESIDENT ELIGIBILITY AND CERTIFICATION

Each subsidized program contains specific eligibility requirements based on income, family composition, and other criteria. The prospective resident must provide detailed information as proof of eligibility for occupancy. The development manager is responsible for verifying all eligibility requirements. The objective of certification and verification is to determine if the resident's gross annual income is within the prescribed income limits. The determination of anticipated income depends on the method of reimbursement or type of support pay received by the prospective tenant.

For the purpose of determining income verification and certification, gross annual income includes but is not limited to:

- Wages
- Pensions
- Social Security
- Interest and dividends from assets (or imputed income from assets in excess of $5,000, whichever is greater, including disposal of assets for less than fair market value in the last two years)
- Lump-sum additions to income that are received as a result of delayed payment of periodic income benefits (excluding lump-sum or delayed Social Security payments)
- Regular gifts and contributions

For audit purposes, management must retain evidence of eligibility, certification, and re-certification in the resident file for three years. Both the applicant and the manager must sign the application form and HUD 50059, *Owners Certification of Compliance with HUD's Tenant Eligibility and Rent Procedure.*

Discrimination against any applicant by owners or managing agents is prohibited. HUD policy is to provide a range of housing choices to families and individuals irrespective of race, color, sex, religion, national origin, familial status, or handicap. Therefore, when selecting and assigning eligible families and individuals in a specific development, managing agents must affirmatively consider minorities. A well-planned and implemented affirmative Fair Housing marketing plan can assist in attracting applicants from all groups, especially those least likely to apply.

FIGURE 11-2. Compendium of Major Federal Direct-assistance, Low- and Moderate-income Housing Programs*

Low-Income Public Housing

Year of Enactment: 1937
Nature of Assistance:
Full subsidy of capital costs and those operating costs of publicly owned housing that exceeds 30% of tenant income. Subsidy paid to local Public Housing Authority (PHA).

Tenant Eligibility:
Income lower than 50% of the area median, adjusted for family size. Local PHAs may apply further prioritizing criteria, such as family size or age.

Recent Issues:
Tenant rent contributions are being raised from 25% to 30% of income on a phased-in basis. These increases, and a reduction in eligible income limits from 80% to 50% of median, were enacted in 1981. Major outstanding issue is the need for rehabilitation of many older projects, as well as the perennial issue of how to best manage the projects and to restrain operating costs.

Section 202

Year of Enactment: 1949
Nature of Assistance:
Provides direct federal loans to non-profit sponsors to finance rental or cooperative housing for the elderly or handicapped. Interest rate set at the average rate on federal debt issued the preceding fiscal year. All new units also receive Section 8 New funds.

Tenant Eligibility:
Available only for households with head over 62 years old or handicapped. If Section 8 units, residents must be income eligible for Section 8.

Recent Issues:
This enjoys strong congressional support.

Section 221(d)(3) Below-Market Interest Rate (BMIR)

Year of Enactment: 1961
Nature of Assistance:
A relatively shallow interest rate subsidy to nonprofit or limited-dividend developers of low- and moderate-income rental housing. After 1965, the rate was 3%. Loans were made by private lenders at the reduced rate and then purchased at face value by the federal government.

Tenant Eligibility
Income eligibility was based originally based on a complex set of limits previously used in the urban renewal program. In general, the limits were about at local median income. However, many projects were built in neighborhoods where incomes were much lower than median. Because of this, some projects failed financially.

Recent Issues:
This program is only available for existing properties; not available for new properties. There is a 221(d)(3) for Market Rate Properties only.

(continued)

FIGURE 11-2. Compendium of Major Federal Direct-assistance, Low- and Moderate-income Housing Programs* (*Continued*)

Section 515 Rural Rental Program

Year of Enactment: 1968
Nature of Assistance:
Program was set up to provide the same type of interest rate subsidies to low-income rental housing in rural areas as under Section 236. Loans are made directly by the FmHA. Interest rate is reduced to 1%; if tenants can pay more than the subsidized base rent, excess is paid to government. Tenants are required to pay 30% of their income in rent.

Tenant Eligibility:
Income limits (relative to area median) have been somewhat higher than under Section 236. However, recent changes will bring them into conformity at 80% of local area median income. In addition, households with income below 50% of median may receive additional assistance through the HUD Section 8 program or the FmHA Section 521 program.

Recent Issues:
This program is available for existing properties only; no new applications are being accepted.

Section 236 Rental Program

Year of Enactment: 1968
Nature of Assistance:
An interest-rate subsidy to non-profit or limited-dividend developers of low- and moderate-income rental housing. The mortgage interest rate was subsidized down to 1% for loans made through private lenders and insured by FHA. Basic rents on the projects are calculated to cover the mortgage, operating cost, and a limited profit. New tenants are required to pay at least 30% of their income in rents. Rents in excess of basic rents remitted to the government.

Tenant Eligibility:
Eligibility was based originally on income being less than 135% of the maximum income eligibility for public housing. When the program was active, public housing caps were set by PHAs and generally were between 50% and 80% of median income. Today, tenants must have incomes lower than 80% of median.

Recent Issues:
This program only exists for existing units; not available for new units.

Section 8 Existing

Year of Enactment: 1974
Nature of Assistance:
Eligible individuals are given certificates that can be used to pay the owner of existing units the difference between 30% of the resident's income and the unit rent, up to the Fair Market Rent (FMR) for such a unit. Any unit meeting program housing quality standards and renting for no more than the FMR is eligible. Recipients are chosen by local PHAs from waiting lists for Public Housing or units under the other Section 8 programs. Recipient has the freedom and responsibility to find housing that meets program quality and rent standards. If recipient's pre-existing housing meets standards there is no need to move.

Tenant Eligibility:
Income lower than 50% of the area family median income, adjusted for family size.

Recent Issues:
Originally called the "Certificate Program" and has since been merged with the Choice Voucher Program".

(*continued*)

FIGURE 11-2. Compendium of Major Federal Direct-assistance, Low- and Moderate-income Housing Programs* (*Continued*)

Section 8 Moderate Rehabilitation

Year of Enactment: 1979
Nature of Assistance:
Similar to Section 8 Existing, except that the certificate is tied to the rehabilitated unit. Subsidy commitment to owner is 15 years. Rents are limited to 125% of the local Fair Market Rent for comparable existing units. Units rehabilitated under the program also benefit from the rapid amortization of rehabilitation expenses under the tax code.

Tenant Eligibility:
Income lower than 50% of the area family median income, adjusted for family size.

Recent Issues:
Many PHAs report great difficulty for potential participants finding qualifying units costing no more than the FMRs

Section 8 Loan Management, Property Disposition and Conversions

Year of Enactment: 1974
Nature of Assistance:
Program subsidizes financially distressed projects built under Section 221(d)(3) and Section 236. Section 8 Property Disposition contracts are provided to permit low-income tenants in a foreclosed property being sold by HUD to remain in the project. The Section 8 Conversion contracts replace Rent Supplement contracts. Commitment to owner is for 5-15 years.

Tenant Eligibility:
Income lower than 50% of the area family median income, adjusted for family size.

Recent Issues:
This program is available for existing properties only; no new applications are being accepted.

Choice Voucher System

Year of Enactment: 1983
Nature of Assistance:
Similar to the Section 8 Existing program. Major differences include (1) permitting recipients to supplement the voucher beyond Fair Market Rents or to keep the difference for lower rents, (2) permitting assistance payments to be adjusted only twice during a 5-year period, and (3) budget authority is provided for only 5 years at a time, rather than 15 years. Some units are tied to the Rental Rehabilitation Grant Program.

Eligibility:
Income below 50% of median for family of four (similar to Section 8 Existing).

Recent Issues:
Originally named the Housing Voucher Program.

(*continued*)

FIGURE 11-2. Compendium of Major Federal Direct-assistance, Low- and Moderate-income Housing Programss* (*Continued*)

Rental Housing Development Grant (HoDAG)

Year of Enactment: 1983

Nature of Assistance:
Funds are awarded to state or local governments to use in the manner of their choice to finance construction or substantial rehab of rental housing or cooperatives.

Tenant Eligibility:
At least 20% of the units must be reserved for households with incomes less than 80% of area median.

Developer Eligibility:
There is a national competition for these grants. Selection criteria include the availability of decent, affordable rental housing and the degree of private and local public funding.

Recent Issues:
This program is being phased out. HUD only considering existing backlog of applicants.

---

*For a complete listing of HUD programs, please visit www.HUD.org. Please note that a number of HUD programs are undergoing revisions. Such programs are in the midst of rewrites, major change, and/or elimination.

FIGURE 11-3. Glossary of HUD Terminology

actual income from assets—The interest produced by the household's savings and checking accounts, dividends earned by stocks and bonds, rents and royalties received from real property, and income derived from other capital investments.

adjusted income—The income amount used to calculate the resident's rent. It is obtained by subtracting total allowances from gross annual income. Adjusted income is calculated for all programs except BMIR.

allowance for dependents—A $480 deduction for each family member who is not the head of household, foster child, nor live-in attendant, nor the spouse of the head of household and who is under 18 years of age (17 years or less), a full-time student 18 years or older, handicapped, or disabled.

allowance for handicapped assistance—The amount of the handicapped assistance expenses for care attendants or auxiliary apparatus that exceeds 3 percent of annual income. To be eligible the care must be necessary to enable an adult family member to work. The allowance cannot exceed the amount earned.

allowance for medical expenses—The amount of total medical expenses that exceeds 3 percent of annual income. The allowance is for elderly households only [see *elderly households*].

annual income—The gross amount of income anticipated to be received by all adult members of a household during the 12 months following certification or recertification.

as-paid locality—A state, county, or city whose public assistance program specifies an amount for shelter and utilities a family will receive and adjusts the amount based upon the family's actual payment for shelter and utilities.

assets disposed of for less than fair market value—The cash value of net family assets that were disposed of for less than fair market value during the 2-year period preceding certification or recertification. Calculated as the difference between the cash value and the amount the family received. These assets are not counted for BMIR residents. They are not considered unless the total cash value of these assets exceeds $1,000.

assistance payment—The portion of the rent paid by HUD.

assisted tenant—A resident who pays less than the market rent (see definition of *market rent*), including residents receiving Rent Supplement, RAP, or Section 8 assistance, and all other 236 and BMIR residents except those paying the 236 market rent or 110 percent of the BMIR rent, respectively.

care attendant—An individual who is employed to care for elderly (seniors), handicapped, or other residents who are mentally or physically ill or incapacitated and need special assistance. A live-in attendant is not a party to the lease and his/her income is not considered in computing annual income, allowances, and assistance payments.

child care allowance—The amount paid for the care of household members under age 13 (12 or less to enable a family member to work, further his/her education, or seek employment after losing job. The amount allowed for employment cannot exceed the amount earned.

contract rent—The rent due the owner from both HUD and the resident. It includes the HUD-approved 236 Basic, BMIR, and Rent Supplement rents, and the Section 8 contract rent.

dependents—Family members who are younger than 18 years of age (17 years or less), a full-time student age 18, or over, or handicapped or disabled. Neither the head of the household co-head of household, spouse, foster child, nor live-in attendant are ever dependents.

Depository Institution Deregulatory Committee (DIDC) Rate—The passbook interest rate used to compute imputed income from assets. This rate is updated annually and obtained from federally insured banks or savings and loan institutions.

disabled person—A person is considered disabled if (a) the following Social Security disability definition is met or the individual has a developmental disability as described in paragraph (b).

(a) Section 223 of the Social Security act defines disability as an inability to engage in any substantial gainful activity because of any physical or mental impairment that is expected to result in death or has lasted or can be expected to last continuously for a least 12 months; or, for a blind person at least 55 years old, inability because of blindness to engage in any substantial gainful activities comparable to those in which the person was previously engaged with some regularity and over a substantial period.

(*continued*)

FIGURE 11-3. Glossary of HUD Terminology (*Continued*)

(b) A developmental disability is a severe, chronic disability that—

- Is attributable to a mental and/or physical impairment
- Was manifested before the age of 22
- Is likely to continue indefinitely
- Results in three or more substantial functional limitations in the capacities for independent living, self-care, receptive and expressive language, learning, mobility, self-direction, and economic self-sufficiency and requires special, interdisciplinary, or generic care, treatment or other services of lifelong or extended duration that are individually planned and coordinated.

For Section 202 projects, persons are considered disabled only if they meet the criteria in paragraph (b) printed above. For all other purposes, persons are considered disabled if they meet the criteria in either (a) or (b).

displaced—A person (a) who has been displaced by governmental action or (b) whose unit has been extensively damaged or destroyed as a result of a disaster, declared or otherwise formally recognized, pursuant to federal disaster relief laws.

elderly household—A household whose head, spouse of the head of household, or sole member is 62 years of age or older, handicapped or disabled (see *handicapped* and *disabled* in this glossary). Elderly households may be two or more persons living together who are 62 years old or older, handicapped, or disabled or one or more such persons living with another person who is essential to the elderly, handicapped or disabled person's care and well-being.

elderly household deduction—An allowance of $400 for each elderly household. Only one deduction is allowed per eligible household. A family may not designate a family member as head of household solely to qualify the family as an elderly household.

family—This term is not defined by HUD. Owners must define it in the resident selection plan. The commonly used definition is: "Two or more persons sharing residency whose income and resources are available to meet the family's needs and who are related by blood, marriage, or operation of law (or who give evidence of a stable relationship that has existed for a period of time)."

gross rent—The contract rent (see *contract rent*) plus any allowance for utilities (see *utility allowance*) and other services.

handicapped—A person having a physical or mental impairment that—

- Is expected to be of long duration
- Substantially impedes his/her ability to live independently
- And is of such a nature that the person's ability to live independently could be improved by more suitable housing conditions

handicap assistance expenses—Costs of care attendants and auxiliary apparatus for handicapped and disabled family members. Costs for both care attendants and auxiliary apparatus must directly enable the handicapped person or other family member to work.

imputed income from assets—The result of multiplying the total cash value of the family's assets by the current DIDC rate (see *Depository Institution Deregulatory rate*).

interest reduction subsidies—The monthly payments or discounts made by HUD to reduce the debt service payments and, hence, rents required on Section 236 and BMIR projects. It includes the monthly interest reduction payments made to mortgagees of Section 236 projects and front-end loan discounts paid on BMIR projects.

low-income family—A family whose income does not exceed 80 percent of the median income for the area as determined by HUD.

market rent—The unsubsidized rent the owner would collect if HUD did not make interest reduction or tenant assistance subsidies available to the development (see *interest reduction subsidies* and *tenant assistance payments*). It includes the HUD-approved market rent on a 236 or Rent Supplement development, 110 percent of the HUD-approved BMIR rent, and the contract rent on a Section 8 unit.

material noncompliance—One or more substantial violations of the lease (including nonpayment of rent) or repeated minor violations of the lease that—

- Disrupt the livability of the building or development
- Affect the health or safety of any person
- Abridge the right of any resident to the quiet enjoyment of the leased premises and related facilities

(*continued*)

FIGURE 11-3. Glossary of HUD Terminology (*Continued*)

- Interfere with the management of the building
- Or have an adverse financial effect on the building or development

net family assets—The cash value of the household's funds and equity including—

- Savings, checking, IRA and Keogh accounts
- Money market funds
- Certificates of deposit
- Equity in real property or other capital investments
- Cash in safe deposit boxes or at home

For all programs except BMIR, any asset disposed of at less than fair market value within the prior 2 years is also counted (see *assets disposed of for less than fair market value*).

post-1981 Universe—Section 8 units with contracts for housing assistance payments that are effective on or after October 1, 1981 (Section 8 units only).

pre-1981 Universe—Section 8 units with contracts for housing assistance payments effective before October 1, 1981.

project—Buildings that are located on adjacent sites and managed as one development, even if they have separate mortgages and/or project numbers.

single person—One person who lives alone or intends to live alone.

tenant assistance payment—The monthly amount HUD pays toward a resident's rent and utility costs. It includes the regular monthly payments under the Rent Supplement Program, the Rental Assistance Program, and Section 8.

tenant damages—Physical damage to the resident's unit caused by negligence or willful abuse on the part of the resident or resident's guests.

tenant rent—The portion of the contract rent payable by the family (the difference between the total tenant payment and the utility allowance)

third party—An employer, public agency, or physician or other individual or entity who can verify data provided by an applicant.

total medical expenses— Medical expenses that the resident anticipates incurring for the 12 months following the effective date of the certification and that are not covered by insurance.

total tenant payment—The portion of the gross rent payable by the family (the difference between the gross rent and the amount of the assistance payment payable on behalf of the family).

utility allowance—A HUD—approved amount determined as an allowance for the cost of utilities (except telephone) payable directly by the family.

utility reimbursement—Housing assistance payable by the owner to the family (the amount by which the utility allowance exceeds the total tenant payment).

very low-income family—A family whose income does not exceed 50 percent of the median income for the area, as determined by HUD.

welfare rent—The maximum amount (based on family size) a public assistance agency can pay for shelter and utilities for a family. Welfare rent is used only for welfare recipients in as-paid localities (see as-*paid localities*).

FIGURE 11-4. Guidelines for Developing a Resident-Selection Program

- All elements of the resident selection program must be in compliance with the Federal Preference Rules established by HUD as of March 4, 1988. These rules stipulate the order in which applications should be considered, and those who are entitled to preferential treatment for placement in units (homeless families, for example). The full preference rules and operating procedures are available in Handbook 4350.3 CHG-5.*

Under the Section 202 program, priorities for admission have been established (e.g., displaced persons).

- The primary purpose of subsidized housing programs is to provide a decent home and living environment for people with low- and moderate-incomes who have been living in substandard housing or have been forced to pay an excessively high percentage of their incomes for rent. A resident-selection program must not lose sight of these basic objectives by eliminating the very people who are supposed to be helped.
- Achieving a healthful and desirable social and economic mix of residents is another important objective. Experience has demonstrated that the concentration of low-income families with similar serious problems tends to create an unstable social environment that in turn may breed crime and violence and drive out the more stable families. Under such circumstances, maintaining a socially desirable environment or a financially sound development is virtually impossible. Therefore, While keeping in sight the basic objective of providing low-cost housing to those who need it, the tenant selection program should attempt to ensure that a substantial number of financially stable families at both the lowest and the highest-possible income levels are accepted as residents.
- The question of what constitutes the reasonable percentage of income a family should pay as rent is not answered easily. The general assumption is that 30 percent of adjusted income is reasonable. However, many families presently living in substandard housing are forced to pay much more. A family able to pay its rent with regularity under such circumstances should be given the chance to obtain better quality housing even though it must continue to pay more than 30 percent of its income as rent.
- Credit checks and references from former landlords and credit bureaus can be of value in screening applicants if the usefulness of these methods is kept in proper perspective. For example, references from former landlords may be of little value if the applicant has been living in substandard housing.
- Some managers have successfully used a rating system to help determine which applicants should be selected. Although not a HUD requirement, this system could be used in initial resident selection and also in continuing efforts to keep all units fully occupied. The form could be completed based on a preoccupancy interview.

*One criticism of the changes in preference is that they pushed other deserving applicants off the waiting lists for public housing and will eventually alter the mix in public housing.

Development managers must properly use size and design to avoid over-concentration of one group of tenants in any area of the development. In developments that include families of several income levels, managers should endeavor to achieve a balance of income groups throughout the development.

Managers also must be careful to assign residents to units no larger than necessary to accommodate current family needs. Unit occupancy is also subject to local housing codes. The minimum and maximum limits shown in Figure 11–5 apply. These limits are intended to provide for varying needs without overcrowding. For example, a family of four with one boy and one girl may need a three-bedroom unit.

When an owner believes that strict conformity to size requirements may cause undue hardship on residents or may place the development in financial jeopardy because of lack of market, she/he may apply to the area insuring office for a waiver of occupancy requirements. HUD recognizes that overcrowding can lead to substandard housing conditions. In general, a waiver of maximum limits is granted only under temporary emergency conditions.

When the composition of a family or household changes after initial occupancy, the manager must notify the head of household that, as soon as a unit is available, the family will be assigned a different unit to meet its new composition needs. Depending on the change in the family composition, the new unit may be one with more or fewer bedrooms. In any case, although the development owner must absorb the cost of making the vacated unit rent ready less any damages, this relocation is at the resident's expense. Failure of the resident to accept another unit could result in loss of the subsidy and being converted to a "market renter."

RESIDENT ELIGIBILITY, CERTIFICATION, AND RE-CERTIFICATION UNDER SECTION 221(D)(3) BMIR

Under Section 221(d)(3), management prepares HUD form 50059, *Owners Certification of Compliance with HUD's Tenant Eligibility and Rent Procedure*. The form must bear the signature of the applicant and be retained in the management files. The manager must verify the income and retain evidence of the verification in the files for three years.

In determining an applicant's eligibility, gross income cannot exceed the prescribed income limits for such housing in the community. After determining eligibility of applicants, preference should be given to persons displaced by local, state, or federal action or by natural disaster.

Units in a BMIR development may be assisted under the Rent Supplement Conversion, Section B Set-Aside, or the Section 23, Housing Assistance Program. When such options are used, the assisted residents must meet eligibility and occupancy requirements established under the specific assistance programs being used.

Applicants whose gross incomes exceed the maximum limit for resident's eligibility cannot be accepted. On recertification, if their gross annual incomes exceed the maximum income limit, they are eligible to remain in the development but they must pay the adjusted market rent: the BMIR rent plus 10 percent of the BMIR rent.

Development owners and their managers are responsible for selection of tenants and for maintaining the usual management/resident relationships. However, HUD periodically inspects and audits development operations to be certain that owners and managers are complying with program requirements.

Waivers of income limits may be requested by owners when full compliance with the income limits would place the development in financial jeopardy. The owner may apply to the area insuring office for a temporary increase or suspension of income limits for a period of six months or one year. A reasonable number of units should always be kept available for immediate occupancy by applicants within the income limits in effect at the time of the temporary increase or suspension. Because of the subsidized nature of the program, requests for waivers should be extremely rare.

The area insuring office will not approve a request for a waiver unless the housing owner can show that every effort was made to comply strictly with the income limits. In cases in which waivers are granted, the persons admitted who are over the income limits are required to pay the adjusted market rent. The rent is based on the gross annual income without any deductions.

FIGURE 11-5. Minimum and Maximum Limits to Subsidized Unit Occupancy

Number of Bedrooms	Minimum Number of Persons	Maximum Number of Persons
0	1	2
1	1	2
2	2	4
3	4	6
4	6	8

This U.S. housing subsidy program is the only one that will allow nonimmigrant student aliens as residents. Nonimmigrant student aliens have foreign residences and have no intention of abandoning them. These aliens must be qualified to pursue a full course of study at an established institution or other recognized place of study in the United States and will be admitted to the United States on a student visa for that purpose.

REQUIREMENTS OF SECTION 236

As required by the Regulatory Agreement, the development manager must prepare Forms HUD 50059 and HUD 50059e under the 236 Program. The manager must compute the applicant's contribution toward rent based on a percentage of adjusted monthly income minus the utility allowance, a percentage of adjusted monthly income, or basic rent (the rent needed to support the mortgage at 1 percent interest), whichever is greater.

THE LEASE IN HUD DEVELOPMENTS

As with leases in conventional multifamily properties, the lease in a HUD development is a contract between the tenant and management that assures the tenant quiet, peaceful enjoyment and exclusive possession of a specific dwelling unit in return for payment of rent and reasonable protection of the property. The lease must conform to the provisions of the HUD Regulatory Agreement. Prior to its use, the basic lease form developed by the owner's or the management company's attorney must be submitted to HUD for review and approval. No lease can be executed for a period of less than 30 days, and all leases expire on the last day of the last month of the lease period. On completion of a lease period of at least one year, the owner does not have to execute a new lease with the tenant. It becomes a month-to-month lease.

HUD has model lease forms for the guidance of owners and managers. Because these forms may require revision to comply with local law or practice, they are intended to be used only as models. Area insuring offices have been instructed to distribute them only in quantities consistent with the use of the forms as guides and not as actual leases.

HUD does not have to approve public housing dwelling leases prior to their adoption. However, field offices may provide technical assistance during the development of the leases. In addition, HUD may at any time require a local housing authority to modify its dwelling lease to conform to HUD requirements.

The comments in the paragraphs that follow are for guidance only and do not include all provisions of the appropriate model lease:

SECTION 221(D)(3) BMIR

A model lease form is available. The lease must contain clauses whereby the lessee (tenant):

- Certifies the accuracy of statements in the application and income certification
- Agrees that information regarding family income, family composition, and other eligibility requirements is an obligation of tenancy; that she/he will comply promptly with all requests from the owner or HUD for such information, and that failure or refusal to comply with such requests shall be a violation of her/his tenancy
- Agrees to furnish re-certification of current family income at the request of the owner or HUD

SECTION 236

A model lease form is available. The tenant agrees:

- That information regarding family income, family composition, and other eligibility requirements is an obligation of her/his tenancy with respect to the amount of rent owed and right of occupancy
- That a re-certification of income shall be made annually from the date of the lease and on 30 days notice the monthly rental payment is subject to adjustment to reflect income changes reported on any re-certification when required

SECTION 8

A model lease form is available. The lease requirements are the same as for Section 236 with the exceptions noted in this chapter.

RECERTIFICATION REQUIREMENTS IN HUD DEVELOPMENTS

All assisted tenants in HUD developments must be re-certified annually. Tenants paying market rent do not need to re-certify.

INCOME RE-CERTIFICATION

At least once per year, incomes of households living in public housing developments must be re-certified. If the head of the household is 62 years of age or older, the household is exempt from re-certification. The length of time from admission to the date of first re-certification may be extended to 18 months to fit a local authority's schedule.

INTERIM RE-CERTIFICATION

An owner must process an interim re-certification under certain conditions and needs to verify only those factors that have changed since the last certification or re-certification. If the tenant's income changes, the tenant is entitled to an interim re-certification as often as every 30 days if it would result in a change in the tenant's rent.

An owner may refuse to process an interim re-certification when the tenant reports a decrease in income if the decrease was caused by a deliberate action of the tenant to avoid paying rent (for example, the tenant quit a job to qualify for a lower rent) or the owner receives confirmation that the decrease will last less than one month (for example, an employer states that the tenant will be laid off for only two weeks).

ANNUAL RE-CERTIFICATION PROCEDURES

Owners must complete all of the steps listed below.

- Notify the tenant that the re-certification is due to occur
- Interview the tenant to obtain information on income, assets, family composition, and allowances
- Verify the tenant's income, assets, and allowances
- Complete form HUD-50050 and applicable HUD 50059 worksheet
- Have the tenant sign the HUD-50059
- Notify the tenant of any rent increase resulting from the re-certification

To implement the re-certification on time, the owner must:

- Give the tenant the initial request for re-certification information 75 to 90 days before the date the re-certification is scheduled to be effective
- Complete all steps at least 35 days before the effective date (early completion enables the owner to give the tenant 30 days advance notice of any increase in her/his rent)
- Send a second request if the tenant does not respond within 30 days after the first request for re-certification information
- Maintain a tracking system to facilitate timely completion of re-certification

Both the initial request and any follow-up request must meet these requirements.

PAST-DUE RE-CERTIFICATION

The HUD field office or contract administrator may suspend payments for units on which re-certifications are past due. A re-certification is past due when the scheduled effective date has passed and the re-certification steps outlined above have not been completed. A re-certification can also be considered past due when the effective date is past and a 30-day posting period for rent increase has not yet expired.

EFFECTIVE DATE OF CHANGE IN A TENANT'S RENT IN THE EVENT OF PAST-DUE RE-CERTIFICATION

In the case of past-due re-certification, the effective date of change in a tenant's rate will vary depending on whether the rent increases or decreases and on who delayed the re-certification (the tenant, the owner, or a third party).

GRIEVANCE PROCEDURES IN HUD DEVELOPMENTS

It is good management practice to have procedures that permit tenants to formally air grievances to the management company and/or owner. These procedures should be referred to and/or described in the resident handbook and posted in public areas of the development. The basic elements of these procedures should explain how and where to file a complaint in writing; how hearings will be conducted; how findings are made; how to appeal to a higher authority; and final determination of the grievance.

TENANT ORGANIZATIONS IN HUD DEVELOPMENTS

Although the actions suggested in this section are not required by law, they are advisory in nature and should prove helpful to owners and managers.

OBJECTIVES OF TENANT INVOLVEMENT IN DEVELOPMENT AFFAIRS

Management's goal for tenant involvement in development affairs should be the establishment of a well-organized, capable tenant organization. Tenant organizations may provide an effective channel of communication with management. In the operation of subsidized developments, lack of communication has been acknowledged as a significant hurdle for management. To be of value to both management and tenants, the tenant organization should increase its understanding, and inform management, of individual and collective tenant needs, problems, and desires; increase tenants' understanding of and cooperation in management concerns and responsibilities; assure that the tenants play a useful part in the management process by advising management of their concerns; and act to implement and promote services and programs of benefit to all tenants.

The owner and development manager continue to hold final authority and responsibility for compliance with all provisions of the Regulatory Agreement, the mortgage, and other pertinent requirements. However, occasions arise when management should consult the tenant organization.

The development manager's cooperation is often needed by tenants during their efforts to establish an organization or in working with one already established. The development manager should be neither afraid nor suspicious of the tenants, nor should she/he be negative about their rights and ability to organize and to assume responsibility for their own welfare and problems. She/he should be willing to work with them and, above all, to listen to them.

ESTABLISHING THE TENANT ORGANIZATION

In some cases, the development manager may need to take the initiative in the creation of a tenant organization. If so, she/he should never appear to be creating a house organization. The establishment of a formal tenant organization is not an end in itself. A spirit of cooperation can emerge as management and tenants work together and as they make visible progress in improving the social and physical conditions of the development.

Tenants organizing on their own is usually an indication that they are interested in creating a desirable living environment within the development and the community or that they have unresolved complaints. Management must be willing to discuss its own procedures, policies, and basic management philosophy and be prepared to consider revisions for the mutual benefit of tenants and owners.

If conflict develops among opposing tenant groups and the development manager takes sides with any group, that action usually aggravates the conflict. Instead, tenants might be encouraged to hold an election to establish one organization with one set of officers to represent all tenants in the development. In such a situation, tenants might consider obtaining the assistance of a neutral outside community group, agency, or institution to help monitor or conduct an election. A small voter turnout should not prevent those elected from being recognized as representatives of all tenants in the development, as long as all tenants have been informed of the issues and persons involved and given a chance to vote. Candidates should be nominated by petition or in meetings open to all tenants. The term of office and the provisions for future elections should be established at the outset. The adoption of a constitution and bylaws also is advisable.

PRODUCTIVE TENANT INVOLVEMENT

The goal of tenant participation should be mutual cooperation in preventing and solving problems. Management should be receptive to the views of tenant organizations and seek their active participation in preventing problems and in finding and implementing solutions to problems. A relationship of this type can be achieved only if tenants have an organization that effectively represents them and enables them to work with management. This capacity to prevent and to resolve mutual problems is applied best in stages.

In the first stage, management, community services staff, and tenants work together to identify problems adversely affecting the social and physical atmosphere of the development. Examples of types of problems that might emerge appear in Figure 11–6.

The identification of problems and issues is a continuing part of the process because as progress in solving problems is made, tenants gain new insight about what must be done and new ideas on how to accomplish goals through cooperation. Success keeps the process alive, including tenant involvement in the improvement of the living environment of the development.

The second stage consists of deciding which problems should be addressed first. In establishing priorities, both sides must be flexible enough to reach mutually satisfactory goals. The number of problems that can be handled at any given time is limited by a number of factors, including the quality of management, the establishment of tenant trust in management, and management's willingness to work with the tenants.

The final stage of the problem-solving process is devising and implementing solutions. Special tenant committees may be set up to study various problems and to recommend solutions. An efficient tenant organization might assist in or even conduct referral services for tenants with special problems. The owner may provide available community space and other development resources and help coordinate outside resources and support.

The measurement of cooperative progress made by tenants and management is a key element in an effective tenant organization. Reliable indicators of progress on problems is of great help to both, but most of all to management. Such indicators can be based on comparative monthly maintenance expenses for various items such as broken light bulbs or windows, vacancy rates, and rent delinquency rates. Data for the indicators could be gathered by management with the assistance of a tenant committee, and monthly figures could be posted on bulletin boards in public areas.

HANDLING COMPLAINTS

An effective and operating tenant organization can contribute materially to the settlement of tenant complaints. Complaints are expressions of dissatisfaction over specific or general conditions within the development. Initially, such complaints might be presented to a committee of the recognized tenant organization. This committee can frequently resolve the issue. If it cannot be resolved, the committee can present the matter to the manager or owner for further action.

HUD DEVELOPMENT FINANCES

RENT COLLECTION

Rent collection requires tact, diplomacy, and tenacity. In spite of any compassion the development manager might feel for people identified as disadvantaged, the rent must be collected. The rent schedule is computed on the assumption of meeting operating expenses, debt service, and the limited distribution where authorized. The rent schedule has no fat.

FIGURE 11-6. Types of Problems to Resolve Between Management and Tenant Organizations

Problems of Management
- How to attain and maintain financial stability
- How to maintain full occupancy with minimum turnover
- How to keep the development clean and in good repair
- How to obtain cooperation from residents

Problems of Residents as Residents
- How to get fast action to fix broken windows and to clear stopped up toilets
- How to get management to maintain the property at a high standard
- How to handle rent increases
- How to get an adequate response to problems at convenient times

Problems of Residents as Individuals
- How to obtain a better job and achieve long-range financial security
- How to keep the family together and progressing
- How to get the baby to the health clinic
- How to benefit from community services and facilities

Problems That Concern Management and Residents
- How to reduce vandalism and keep the development safe
- How to keep children in residence interested and occupied
- How to prevent and police littering
- How to improve community services

Success in rent collection is directly related to policies established and time spent on resident selection procedures. The operating practice for rent payment must be well known to the tenants. Management must establish and explain rental policy rules. Tenants must understand them and the development manager must apply them realistically.

A prenumbered rental receipt book in triplicate form should be obtained for cash-control purposes. The receipt should contain a block showing whether the type of payment received is cash, check, or money order. If a tenant uses more than one type of remittance to pay one month's rent, the amount of each type should be shown on each line, and the total should be equal to the total received. These copies are distributed as follows:

- The tenant always receives the original receipt
- The second copy is attached to the deposit slip to show that the total daily collections were deposited intact and then forwarded to the accounting department
- The third copy is retained in the receipt book for posting and as a cash control check

If voiding a receipt becomes necessary, the word "void" should be written on the original so that it shows on all three copies. The voided original and third copy should be retained in the book for audit purposes, and the duplicate should be attached to that day's deposit slip for accountability. Each deposit must equal the daily collections and be deposited into the development's bank account.

ACCOUNTS AND FINANCIAL RECORDS

Under provisions of the mortgagor's certificate and the Regulatory Agreement, as well as some noninsured Housing Assistance Payment (HAP) contracts, management must maintain the requirements set forth in HUD Handbook 4370.2, *Financial Operations and Accounting Procedures for Insured Multifamily Projects* and Handbook 4350.1, *Insured Project Servicing*. These handbooks outline in detail the prescribed accounts that must be established and maintained. The owner's accountant should review the handbooks and establish the necessary records to comply with HUD's prescribed accounting requirements before the development is ready for renting. If the system is established and running smoothly before rent-up begins, the development can avoid problems arising because basic data got lost before inputting and the development staff cannot remember the past financial transactions. Often, the knowledge of a transaction is needed to supplement basic documents in posting to the official records. Early establishment of the HUD required accounting system also saves the development a significant amount in audit fees for the annual financial statement.

Near the date of anticipated initial occupancy, HUD requests information concerning the fiscal year the owner has adopted, the month income commences, and the individual to whom fiscal correspondence should be addressed.

About 15 days prior to the end of each fiscal year, HUD issues a reminder memorandum to the owner to furnish the annual financial report within 60 days after the end of the fiscal year. For this and other reasons cited, the immediate establishment of an orderly set of records and accounts by the development accountant is essential.

MONTHLY BUDGET AND ACCOUNTING

The preparation of a budget is required by HUD. But irrespective of HUD requirements, a budget also can serve as a practical control device and useful evaluation and management tool. The effective development manager utilizes the monthly budget to highlight problems that might be corrected before becoming unmanageable. The development manager should submit the budget to the senior manager or owner for approval at least 30 days before the beginning of the new fiscal year. HUD Forms 92547a, 92547b, and 92466—"Budget Worksheet," "Rent Spreadsheet," and "Amendment to the Regulatory Agreement," —contain the necessary line-items for formulating a budget for a subsidized multihousing development.

The owner or manager should design monthly reports to provide a simple evaluation of the financial condition of the development and to give quick appraisal of any managerial actions needed to correct unsatisfactory financial conditions. For example, when the budget shows certain costs are escalating, a rental increase may be necessary and should be requested.

RESERVE FOR REPLACEMENT

Both the commitment for insurance and the Regulatory Agreement require the establishment of a reserve fund for replacements. The reserves are funded monthly along with mortgage payments, in an amount established by HUD. All projects with insured mortgages are required to establish and maintain a replacement reserve; some, but not all, noninsured Section 8 projects are required to do so as well. This fund assures the availability of funds to replace a variety of installed items in a development. The normal longevity of ranges, refrigerators, water heaters, air conditioners, floor tile, bathroom tile, and other items is based on experience with these items. HUD will periodically review the adequacy of the reserves and perhaps adjust the payment upward or downward. Owners should do so as well, most particularly when preparing requests for increases in rent, and request HUD approval for appropriate adjustments as needed. Housing management maintenance engineers in area insuring offices should be consulted in making this determination.

The monthly deposit to the reserve fund for replacements may be revised periodically to meet current requirements. Although the fund is held as a development asset, disbursements must be approved by HUD. In the event of a change in development ownership, the reserve fund for replacements is transferred to the new owner.

RESIDUAL RECEIPTS

A residual receipts account must be established for subsidized nonprofit developments and maintained by the mortgagee. When income exceeds the requirements as defined by a "surplus cash calculation" that the owner is required to include in the annual financial statement, the excess must be deposited in the residual receipts account within 60 days of the end of the fiscal year. Residual receipts may be accessed for project purposes with prior HUD approval. In all but the oldest Section 8 projects, the residual receipts belong to the federal government and go back to HUD at the end of the Section 8 contract.

LOW-RENT PUBLIC HOUSING PROGRAM

PUBLIC HOUSING AUTHORITIES

The public housing program was developed under the federal Housing Act of 1937. The statute provided funding for local authorities to build public housing units for low-income families. However, most state legislatures are required to pass enabling legislation to create public housing authorities. As the creation of both the federal and state governments, the authorities can receive federal funding to build public housing, and they can eventually gain full ownership of the housing from the federal government through HUD. HUD pays the debt service. In some cases, HUD provides guidelines and regulations for the public housing authorities' operations, and in others it provides operating subsidies. The most significant guidelines and regulations that affect housing managers are:

- Income definition
- Project maintenance
- Terms of the lease
- Evictions and grievances

LOCAL HOUSING AUTHORITY RESPONSIBILITIES

HUD can enter into a contract for financial assistance with any public housing agency or authority authorized to engage in the construction and administration of low-rent housing or slum clearance. A housing authority may be an entity of a state, county, municipal, or city government, or an autonomous public/corporate entity. It has the responsibility of planning, financing, constructing or purchasing, leasing, and managing the properties subject only to applicable laws and its contractual relationships with HUD and the local governing body. By virtue of its ownership or leasehold interest in the properties, the public or local authority performs all the functions of a private owner, including leasing units, collecting rents, maintaining the properties, and all other related duties. Similar functions may be performed by private management firms under formal agreements with housing authorities.

LOCAL HOUSING AUTHORITY OFFICIALS

The officials of a local housing authority, called commissioners, are appointed in accordance with the state or other enabling legislation and usually serve without pay. Generally, they serve in the same capacity as directors of a corporation by establishing policies under which the organization conducts the business, seeing that the policies are followed by the employees and ensuring that the enterprise is successful. Formal actions of the local authority are taken through written resolutions by the commissioners.

LOCAL HOUSING AUTHORITY STAFF

The executive director or administrator, the principal staff member of a local authority, is usually appointed by the commissioners. She/he carries out the policies established by the commissioners and has the authority to employ, train, and supervise the remainder of the staff.

LOCAL HOUSING AUTHORITY LEGAL POWERS

The legal powers of the local housing authority include all those necessary for development construction and management as well as the issuance of bonds.

MANAGEMENT OF LOW-RENT PUBLIC HOUSING

SPECIAL CHARACTERISTICS OF PUBLIC HOUSING

The following special characteristics of public housing affect its management and can add to the demands on the development manager:

- Public housing is often located in impacted areas

Frequently, it houses residents who are socially and economically limited

- Residents often require special social services
- It is subject to frequent political pressures
- It operates with limited management budgets
- It seldom needs to market for residents because these developments almost always have a waiting list
- The staff may be employees in a civil service program, such as the Federal Job Training Corps

ADMISSION REQUIREMENTS IN LOW-RENT PUBLIC HOUSING

The local authority is required to adopt and publicize regulations governing its admission policy. The regulations must be reasonable and give full consideration to the items listed in Figure 11–7.

For determining minimum and maximum rents in public housing, development managers must use the household's anticipated income. Although a household's current income is a valuable guide in determining anticipated income, the local authority must consider any circumstances that could affect the family's income or deductions over the next year. HUD's *Handbook 7465.1* contains detailed procedures for determining income.

The local authority can limit access to the program to those families living in the authority's jurisdiction at the time of application or it can establish a preference on a similar basis. Applicants who are working or who have been notified that they are hired to work in the jurisdiction must be treated as residents of the jurisdiction. The standards must be consistent with the objectives of Title VI and Title VII of the Civil Rights Act of 1964 and Title VIII of the Civil Rights Act of 1968. They also must not impede the local authority's attainment of its goals for housing families with a broad range of incomes. Without incurring vacancies, the local housing authority must make every effort to limit occupancy of developments built for a special purpose such as seniors or handicapped persons.

Although HUD has no specific requirements for the number of persons who may live in a public housing unit, the underutilization of space is inconsistent with an efficient and economical operation and a waste of scarce housing resources. At the same time, overcrowding is inconsistent with the local authority's obligations to provide decent, safe, and sanitary housing. Historically, local housing authorities have assigned families to units according to the table in Figure 11–8, subject to state and local laws.

The age, sex, and relationship of family members must be taken into consideration in assigning families within these ranges. The maximum number may be exceeded to permit an infant to share a bedroom with its parents. A family is defined as two or more persons sharing residency whose income and resources are available to meet the family's needs and who are either related by blood, marriage, operation of law, or have demonstrated a stable family relationship.

RESIDENT SELECTION POLICY IN LOW-RENT PUBLIC HOUSING

Title VI of the Civil Rights Act of 1964 and Title VIII of the Civil Rights Act of 1968 require a uniformly nondiscriminatory applicant selection policy for low-rent public housing. Applicants who meet these requirements are put on the waiting list and are chosen in sequence as vacancies occur. Eligible families should notify the public housing authority of any change in family composition, income, or other factors that could affect the family's status and eligibility for housing. Basically, the resident selection policy should be based on a first-come/first-served basis.

Title VI of the Civil Rights Act of 1964 and Title VIII of the Civil Rights Act of 1968 also require that low-rent public housing not discriminate in the treatment of residents. Businesses associated with the development's operation are also prohibited from acts of discrimination.

FIGURE 11-7. Considerations in Developing Resident Admission Policies in Low-Rent Public Housing

- Authority's public responsibility for re-housing displaced families
- Applicant's possible status as a member of the Armed Services or as a veteran
- Applicant's age, disability, present housing conditions, urgency of housing need (homelessness), and sources of income
- Local authority must adopt criteria to house families with the range of income representative of the low-income families in the area of operation
- Separate ranges of income must be developed for seniors
- System must be sufficiently flexible to ensure administrative feasibility and to keep units from remaining vacant while waiting for application from families falling within the appropriate income ranges
- Authority may not adopt policies that totally exclude households with the lowest income. At least 20 percent of the dwelling units in a development must be occupied by very low-income families, as defined by the HUD and published annually by census tract in October

RENT DETERMINATION IN LOW-RENT PUBLIC HOUSING

Except in specific cases, the gross rent charged to any family may not exceed 30 percent of family income. The rent for any family may not be less than 5 percent of total family income, unless a higher percentage is required by state and local laws. For a local housing authority to qualify for an operating subsidy in any fiscal year, the aggregate gross rents paid by the families in the development or group of developments may not be less than 20 percent of the aggregate income of all families.

The local housing authority is responsible for ensuring that its dwelling lease is consistent with state and local landlord/tenant laws and the authority's enabling legislation. The area council advises the local authority on the resolution of any apparent conflicts between state or local law and the HUD lease requirements. Any proposed dwelling lease or dwelling lease amendment submitted to the HUD field office for review must be accompanied by evidence that the local housing authority provided an opportunity for residents to comment on the proposed changes. Specific lease requirements are included in the detailed handbook procedures.

GRIEVANCE PROCEDURES IN LOW-RENT PUBLIC HOUSING

HUD requirements governing public housing grievance procedures assure that residents are afforded an opportunity for a hearing. The grievance procedure is incorporated in the dwelling leases.

FIGURE 11-8. Maximum and Minimum Persons in Public Housing Units

Number of Bedrooms	Minimum Number of Persons	Maximum Number of Persons
0	1	2
1	1	2
2	2	4
3	4	6
4	6	8
5	8	10

TENANT PARTICIPATION IN MANAGEMENT IN LOW-RENT PUBLIC HOUSING

The guidelines regarding tenant participation in management are similar to those for assisted developments as described above.

RECORD-KEEPING AND REPORTING REQUIREMENTS IN LOW-RENT PUBLIC HOUSING

The local authority must maintain complete and accurate books of accounts and records in connection with the construction and operation of these developments. The records must:

- Permit a speedy and effective audit
- Fully disclose the amount of the loan and annual contributions
- Track the construction cost of each development and the amount of any nonfederal funds used or grants-in-aid made in connection with each development
- Maintain accounts and other fiscal records prescribed by the government and operating records, including:
  - Applications for admission and occupancy
  - Evidence to verify information on the applications
  - Records of the development's personal property and an annual inventory of all equipment

The local authority must furnish to HUD the required financial, operating, and statistical reports, records, statements, documents, and supporting data.

Government officials, including local and federal as well as state civil rights and housing officials, have full and free access to the development and to all the books, documents, papers, and records of the local authority that are pertinent to its operations.

SITE INSPECTIONS OF LOW-RENT PUBLIC HOUSING BY HUD OFFICIALS

The areas of periodic site inspections of low-rent public housing by HUD officials include:

- Maintenance
- Determination of resident incomes
- Income reviews
- Resident selection
- Record-keeping
- Resident complaints and responses to them
- Fair Marketing and Equal Housing Opportunity Programs
- The entire management operation

HUD officials are guided by detailed forms and procedures in checking each of these items. Again, HUD handbook regulations detail the procedures to be taken by HUD officials during these inspections. The completed inspection report form, along with the cover letter, is sent to the housing authority for its information and response.

BUDGETS IN LOW-RENT PUBLIC HOUSING

The budget year is ordinarily the fiscal year established in contracts with HUD, but it may be any year mutually agreeable with the local authority and that assistant regional administrator for housing assistance.

These budgets are generally characterized by limited income, management subsidy requirements, and the absence of debt service requirements as a result of federal annual contributions.

The budget is prepared (usually by someone on the controller's staff of the local authority involved) no earlier than 150 days and no later than 90 days before the expiration of the first and each succeeding fiscal year. The local authority submits the proposed budget to the regional office for approval.

During the fiscal year or budget period, the local authority may not incur expenditures in excess of the approved budget for total administration expense, total routine expense, and/or total nonroutine expense. The limitations on spending do not apply to emergency expenditures necessary to eliminate an immediate hazard to the life, health, or safety of tenants.

UPDATED INFORMATION ON HUD PROGRAMS AND NAHB'S HOUSING CREDIT CERTIFICATION PROGRAM

INFORMATION ON HUD PROGRAMS

The information contained in this chapter regarding HUD and other programs was current at the time of writing. For immediate access to updated information on HUD programs, visit the HUD website at www.HUD.gov.

NAHB'S HOUSING CREDIT CERTIFICATION PROGRAM

The National Association of Home Builders-Multifamily offers the Housing Credit Certification (HCC) Program, a professional certification program that sets competency standards for housing credit professionals involved in developing, investing in, allocating, and managing housing credit properties. The credential is awarded by the Board of Governors of the HCC Board under the auspices of the National Association of Home Builders-Multifamily and the National Affordable Housing Management Association (NAHMA). Comprehensive course schedules, descriptions, and fees for the HCC Program are available by calling the NAHB University of Housing at (800) 368–5242, ext., 8338, or (202) 266–8338.

OVERVIEW OF AMERICAN MILITARY FAMILY HOUSING

Military family housing is an important benefit provided to active duty members of the American Armed Services. However, at the time of the writing of this text, military family housing in the continental United States (CONUS) faces significant challenges. The professional multihousing manager must be aware not only of how military family housing works but also of how the current challenges of military family housing might affect the civilian/private sector property(ies) she/he manages.

The annual cost of American military family housing is approximately $10.5 billion. The United States Office of the Under Secretary of Defense (Acquisition and Technology) administers military family housing, but broad authority is delegated to installation and base commanders to decide how best to accomplish their mission vis-a-vis utilization of military family housing. Although the Department of Defense (DOD) publication *DOD Housing Management 4165.63-M* (September 1993) is the basic housing management manual for the American military, various branches of the Armed Forces may issue supplemental instructions to provide for unique requirements within their respective commands.

MILITARY FAMILY HOUSING ON BASE OR "ON THE ECONOMY"

There are currently two categories of military family housing: housing that is owned and managed by the military and nonmilitary, private sector housing units in civilian communities. Housing that is owned and managed by the military is located on or near a military installation and is segregated by rank. When it is available, on-base family housing is provided to qualified service members and their families through their allotted "BAH" allowance.

When a service person resides in a civilian housing community near the military installation to which she/he is assigned, the DOD provides a monthly nontaxable monetary allowance for the military family to rent or purchase their home. This Basic Allowance for Housing (amusingly referred to as "BAH" by service personnel) varies by rank, duty location, and family composition and is adjusted in high-cost areas. Service persons who reside in civilian housing communities are said to be "living on the economy."

Military personnel seeking on-base family housing must submit an application to the housing office of the base to which they are currently assigned or are being newly assigned. In the case of service members who are being assigned to a new base, the application must include a copy of the service member's Permanent Change of Station (PCS) orders. Acknowledgment of the application will most likely include specific information about the availability and waiting time for on-base housing. If military family housing is not readily available, the acknowledgment will include information about off-base housing, and the service member will be assigned a waiting list sequence number for on-base family housing.

Under special and rare circumstances, service members may be moved ahead in the waiting sequence because of military necessity (for example, a job that requires on-base residency), financial distress, or special family needs such as an Exceptional Family Member (EFM) who needs access to medical facilities on or close to the base.

When the wait for on-base housing at a given base equals or exceeds the period of time the service member will be assigned to that base and the surrounding civilian community does not offer sufficient, affordable, or acceptable (by military standards) units to absorb the incoming service member and her/his family, the military base and its surrounding communities are classified as a critical housing area. Service members assigned to bases in critical housing areas are discouraged from relocating their families to those areas until suitable and affordable housing becomes available.

The possibility that on-base family housing may not be available is a very real one because the demand for on-base military housing at most military bases within the continental United States far exceeds the supply, and the majority of units that do exist are acknowledged to be substandard. For these reasons, approximately 75 percent of all military personnel assigned to any given base are currently "living on the economy."

THE MILITARY FAMILY HOUSING CHALLENGE

All branches of American military service are currently facing major housing challenges because the stock of military housing is old and, in most cases, in poor repair. The average age of the military housing stock is 33 years—close to, if not at or past, the end of its projected life. Many military housing units need major renovations or replacement, but maintenance and remodeling efforts have been inadequate and inconsistently funded. To make matters worse, military base housing offices have undergone major budget cuts over the past several years. Housing staffs, including managers, have been reduced by lack of funds, by attrition, and by the conversion of Civil Service positions to civilian contractor positions. In 1996, the General Accounting Office (GAO) stated that nearly half of the existing military family housing units did not meet suitability standards and that a remedy would cost in excess of $20 billion.

The Congressional Budget Office (CBO) has recommended that the DOD shift military families from on-base housing to housing in civilian communities as a more cost-effective housing alternative. The GAO concurs, and the current approach to the challenge is to meet the military's family housing needs through an increased reliance on the private sector.

For the multihousing property manager, this means that members of the United States military may become residents in the properties she/he manages.

THE MILITARY'S RENTAL PARTNERSHIP PROGRAM

As previously stated, approximately 75 percent of all military personnel assigned to bases within the continental United States "live on the economy." The Rental Partnership Program is an innovative method to assist military personnel in finding safe, suitable, affordable private sector housing within a reasonable commuting distance from their assigned base. Although each base's implementation of the Rental Partnership Program is customized to fit the special needs of the base, the service members who work there, and local property owners, the program's overall goal is always the same: to provide acceptable homes to service members and their families.

Under the Rental Partnership Program, a base's housing office and staff, supervised by the base commander, solicits participation in the program from apartment communities within a reasonable commuting distance from the base. The DOD defines a reasonable commuting distance to be no more than a 60-minute drive during rush hour. Although no property owner is obliged to participate in the Rental Partnership Program, the program does offer significant benefits to the military, to the service person and her/his family, and also to the owner. Once the agreement between the property owner and the military is signed, both are legally bound to abide by it.

RENTAL PARTNERSHIP PROGRAM BENEFITS FOR THE SERVICE PERSON

The Rental Partnership Program benefits military personnel who participate in it in the following ways:

- The base housing office will provide to the service member a list of local multifamily communities that participate in the program. Although the service member is not required to patronize those communities, doing so can greatly reduce the time it takes to find suitable housing.

- The service member cannot be turned down for poor credit (but may be turned down because of a poor rental history).

- Participating rental communities may waive all or a portion of the security deposit, application fees, and, in some instances, reduce the rent for service members (thus reducing or eliminating the amount the service member will have to pay beyond the allowance provided by the basic allowance for housing).

- Participating communities agree to accept direct deposit and payroll deduction payments, so the service member does not have to write a check.

- Participating property owners agree to accept and include a "Military Clause" as part of their lease. This clause allows the service member to break the lease without penalties provided the reason for breaking the lease is attributed to the service member having received Official Permanent Change of Station orders. (A copy of these orders must be attached to the written notice of intent to vacate.)

The Rental Partnership Program benefits property owners who participate in it in the following ways:

- The program reduces per-unit advertising costs because the service member is referred to the property by the base housing office. All the property owner/manager needs to do is enter into an agreement to participate in the program.

The program guarantees that rent is paid on time by an allotment deposited directly to the property on the first working day of each month.

- The program guarantees occupancy for at least one year because only service members with a minimum of one year remaining on their tour of duty at that base or one year remaining in military service are allowed to participate in this program.

- The program guarantees payment of vacating damages or rent owed by a presigned allotment signed by the service member in lieu of a security deposit.

- The program requires that both the owner/manager and a representative of the base housing office be present during the move-out inspection, thus eliminating move-out-related disputes.

- The military base's housing office will provide assistance to the property owner should problems arise with the program and/or with military residents who reside in the owner's property under the program.

WHAT THE PROPERTY MANAGER NEEDS TO KNOW ABOUT THE RENTAL PARTNERSHIP PROGRAM

Participation in the Rental Partnership Program requires no special management of the unit in question nor any special treatment of the service person or her/his family beyond those stipulations indicated above. All a property owner/

manager needs to do to participate in the program is enter into an agreement with the local military base and then keep the base's housing office aware of available units in the property.

Clearly, the military's Rental Partnership Program offers many desirable benefits to multifamily property owners and managers. Owners and managers of properties that would be appropriate for participation in the Rental Partnership Program should review the landlord/tenant laws of their state (some states have modified their laws in favor of the active-duty service member) and then contact the housing referral office of the nearest military base.

CONCLUSION

Government-assisted and government-insured housing and military housing have been presented together in this chapter of the text because they represent the government's attempts to ensure suitable housing for all Americans, including those in need and those who serve the country. It is likely that during her/his career, the professional multihousing manager will encounter the management issues that impact government-assisted and government-insured housing and military housing. It therefore behooves the professional manager to be familiar with the challenges these housing sectors present, and their solutions.

The legacy of government housing subsidy programs in the United States began in the early 1930s with the creation of the Federal Housing Administration (FHA) and the Public Housing Administration. The public housing program created by Congress in 1937 and the Housing Acts of 1949, 1959, 1965, and 1974 and amendments encouraged the combined participation of the government and the private sector in supplying suitable housing for low- and moderate-income individuals and families. Government rent subsidies for low-income families and direct assistance to developers of new and substantially rehabilitated housing developments represent significant instruments in this effort. The 1965 elevation of the Housing and Home Finance Agency to cabinet status as the U.S. Department of Housing and Urban Development (HUD) greatly expanded the federal government's responsibilities and opportunities in housing and urban development and consolidated national efforts dealing with the entire range of urban problems.

Today, HUD is the primary housing agency on the federal level. HUD administers the federal government's participation in the low-rent housing program and protects the government's financial interests. On the state level, state housing finance agencies are primarily responsible for securing tax-exempt bond financing for public housing developments. Most state agencies have the authority to raise funds by issuing tax-exempt revenue bonds and use these funds to make direct loans at favorable terms to developers for construction and permanent financing of low- and moderate-income housing. On the local level, the Housing Act of 1937 empowered the formation of public housing authorities for the construction, ownership, and operation of public housing. HUD provides technical, professional, and financial assistance to local housing authorities for building and operating low-rent housing.

For the most recent legislative and other information from HUD, log on to www.hud.gov. For the most recent forms from HUD, visit www.hudclips.org/sub_nonhud/html/forms.htm.

All government housing programs go through the same process. They begin with the legislation that creates them and then they issue regulations for implementing the program as outlined by Congress. Then, HUD or another regulatory agency must approve the developer and the development plans, as well as the management agreement between the managing agent and the owner and the management plan. As with all management agreements, the rights and responsibilities of the owner and agent are set forth in the management agreement. The management plan must address most aspects of management responsibility.

Under HUD regulations, specific resident certification and re-certification protocols must be followed to ensure that development residents conform with the required renter profile. Each subsidized program contains specific eligibility requirements based on income, family composition, and other criteria. The prospective resident must provide detailed information as proof of eligibility for occupancy, and the development manager is responsible for verifying all eligibility requirements. Discrimination against any applicant by owners or managing agents is prohibited.

When selecting and assigning eligible families and individuals in a specific development, managing agents must affirmatively consider minorities. A well-planned and implemented affirmative Fair Housing marketing plan can assist in attracting applicants for all groups. Managers also must properly use size and design to avoid over-concentration of one group of tenants in any area of the development and must be careful to assign residents to units no larger or smaller than necessary to accommodate family needs and subject to local housing codes.

Leases in HUD developments must conform to the provision of the HUD Regulatory Agreement. Prior to its use, and the basic lease form developed by the owner's or the management company's attorney must be submitted to HUD for review and approval. No lease can be executed for a period of less than 30 days, and all leases expire on the last day of the last month of the lease period. On completion of a lease period of at least one year, the owner does not have to execute a new lease with the tenant. HUD has model lease forms for the guidance of owners and managers.

All assisted tenants must be re-certified annually (tenants paying market rent do not need to re-certify). Specific procedures apply to the re-certification process. The manager must be familiar with these procedures. Specific procedures also exist to allow tenants to air grievances to the management company and/or the owner. The manager must be familiar with these procedures as well.

Although many of the tenants of low-income development are disadvantaged, the manager must not allow compassion to interfere with her/his job of collecting rent. Success in rent collection is directly related to policies established and time spent on resident selection procedures. The operating practice for rent payment must be well known to the tenants. Tenant must understand the development's rental policy rules and management must apply them uniformly and realistically.

Management must maintain the accounting and financial record-keeping requirements set forth by HUD. HUD requires a monthly budget, a reserve fund for replacements, and annual audits. The manager must expect that HUD will continuously monitor development management and financial activities to ensure that all aspects of the development are operated in accordance with regulations.

Low-rent public housing was developed under the federal Housing Act of 1937 and provides funding for local authorities to build public housing units for low-income families. In some case, HUD pays the debt service on the developments and provides guidelines and regulations for the public housing authorities' operations, and in others it provides operating subsidies. HUD can enter into a contract for financial assistance with any public housing agency or authority authorized to engage in the construction and administration of low-rent housing or slum clearance. The public housing authority has the responsibility of planning, financing, constructing or purchasing, leasing, and managing the properties, subject only to applicable laws and its contractual relationship with HUD and the local governing body. By virtue of its ownership or leasehold interest in the properties, the public or local authority performs all the functions of a private owner, including leasing units, collecting rents, maintaining the properties, and all other related duties. Similar functions maybe performed by private management firms under formal agreement with housing authorities. Specific admission requirements, resident selection procedures, rent determination procedures, grievance procedures, budgeting, record-keeping, and reporting requirements apply to low-rent public housing.

Specific management challenges are presented by the facts that low-rent public housing is often located in impacted areas; frequently houses residents who are socially and economically limited and who often require special social services; is subject to frequent political pressures; and operates with limited budgets and with staff who may be employees in a civil service program. To be successful, the manager must learn to master these challenges.

The National Association of Home Builders-Multifamily offers the Housing Credit Certification (HCC) Program, a certification program for housing credit professionals involved in developing, investing in, allocating, and managing housing credit properties. For information, call the NAHB University of Housing at (800) 368–5242, ext., 8302.

With regard to military family housing, this is an important benefit provided to active duty members of the American Armed Services. The United States Office of the Under Secretary of Defense (Acquisition and Technology) administers military family housing, and the Department of Defense (DOD) publication *DOD Housing Management 4165.63-M* (September 1993) is the basic housing management manual for the American military. The annual cost of American military family housing is approximately $10.5 billion.

Today, military family housing in the continental United States faces significant challenges. The stock of on-base military housing (which, when available, is provided to service members free of charge) is old and, in most cases, in poor repair; many military housing units need major renovations or replacement, but maintenance and remodeling efforts have been inadequate and inconsistently funded and military base housing offices have undergone major budget cuts over the past several years.

For these reasons, the Congressional Budget Office (CBO) has recommended that the DOD shift military families from on-base housing to housing in civilian communities as a more cost-effective housing alternative. The General Accounting Office (GAO) concurs, and the current approach to the challenge is to meet the military's family housing needs through an increased reliance on the private sector. Under this arrangement, the DOD provides a monthly nontaxable monetary Basic Allowance for Housing ("BAH") for the military family to rent or purchase their home. As a result, an estimated 75 percent of military families are living "on the economy" (the term used when military personnel reside in civilian communities off-base), and multihousing property managers are finding military personnel among the residents of the properties they manage.

The military's Rental Partnership Program is an innovative method to assist military personnel in finding safe, suitable, affordable private sector housing within a reasonable commuting distance from their assigned base. The Rental Partnership Program offers definite benefits and advantages to the military, to the service person and her/his family, and to the property owner.

No special or extraordinary demands are made on management under the Rental Partnership Program, and all a property owner or manager needs to do to participate in the program is enter into an agreement with the local military base and then keep the base's housing office aware of available units in the property. Owners and managers of properties that would be appropriate for participation in the Rental Partnership Program should review the landlord/tenant laws of their state and then contact the housing referral office of the nearest military base.

Understanding the structures and operations of government-assisted and government-insured housing and military housing is essential to the performance of multihousing property management. The manager who wishes to excel will master the specifics of these two areas of government involvement in the multihousing industry.

12

Management's Role During New Construction and Rent-Up

THE EXPANDED ROLE OF PROFESSIONAL MANAGEMENT DURING NEW CONSTRUCTION AND RENT-UP

The relationship between multihousing construction and rent-up and multihousing management has evolved simultaneously with the increased professionalization of the multihousing management field. In the early years of the industry, the assignment of a management entity to a soon-to-be-built or rehabilitated property was not a primary consideration for the property's builder/developer/sponsor/owner. Today, however, builders, developers, sponsors, and owners recognize the wide range of management issues that must be dealt with from the inception of a new multihousing project. As a result, in varying degrees depending on the relationship with the builder, developer, sponsor, or owner, multihousing management is often called on to make critical contributions during the construction and rent-up stages of an ever-increasing number of multifamily properties.

The principles of management participation in construction and rent-up that are discussed in this chapter are applicable not only to the construction and rent-up of new conventional and assisted rental properties but also to the rehabilitation and re-opening of existing conventional and assisted rental properties, to the construction and sales of new shared-interest associations, and to the conversion of rental and other properties to shared-interest association status (e.g., the conversion of a rental apartment building to a cooperative or condominium). And they apply to developers, builders, sponsors, and owners who intend to manage and market their own new or newly rehabilitated properties as well. For the purpose of expediency in writing, all of these scenarios will be referred to in this part as "new construction" and "rent-up."

MANAGEMENT INPUT DURING PLANNING AND NEW CONSTRUCTION

MANAGEMENT'S ROLE DURING PLANNING

Knowledgeable input from a qualified multihousing manager during the planning phase of a new multifamily property helps to ensure that the design of the property will be conducive to safe, efficient, and cost-effective operation. Appropriate management personnel are in excellent positions to give practical and productive input to architects, builders, and developers about items that present management challenges in a multifamily property and how to overcome those challenges. For example, the management professional can explain to the developer/owner why it would be more prudent from a maintenance standpoint to locate slop sinks in one area of a building than in another. It is during the planning phase that management can offer valuable risk management input as well.

Whether or not input from management is accepted and implemented depends on factors such as whether the builder/developer is the owner, what the owner's goals are for the property, and the way management conveys these recommendations. Nevertheless, assuming the multihousing management organization and/or professional has been engaged to offer such input, the input must be genuine, it must reflect expertise, and it must be of the highest quality to produce the most beneficial results for all concerned and to maintain and elevate the perception of management's participation in the property's earliest stages.

MANAGEMENT'S ROLE DURING CONSTRUCTION

Builders, developers, sponsors, and owners involved in new construction projects will have an entire corps of construction professionals on whom they will rely. It is not the purpose of management to serve as the construction manager or supervisor. In fact, management must be cautious about taking on construction-related responsibilities because of the legal, insurance, and other issues involved. Nevertheless, management should be present during the construction phase to become familiar with the property literally "from the ground up" and to offer management-related and maintenance-related input.

AREAS OF POSSIBLE MANAGEMENT INPUT DURING THE PRECONSTRUCTION AND CONSTRUCTION PHASES

The Maintenance Office/Garage

A well-designed, optimally functional maintenance office or garage is critically important to any multihousing property. It is during the planning and construction phases that management can make the best recommendations regarding the location and design of the property's maintenance office/garage. To do so, considerations should include the space available for the maintenance office/garage; the levels and numbers of maintenance personnel who will be working at the property and in the office/garage; the types and amount of equipment and supplies that must be maintained on-premises to best service the property; and the budget allocated to establish and operate the maintenance office/garage.

A sample plan for a maintenance garage appears in Figure 5–35. Of course, every property's maintenance set-up will differ according to the specifics of the property.

The Site Office

As discussed in Chapter 9, Managing the Site Office and the Operations Manual, management should take the opportunity afforded by participating in a property's planning and construction phases to recommend the design of a site office that will allow for optimal productivity. This means an office of adequate size to accommodate all personnel, equipment, records, and traffic flow; equipped with up-to-date technologies; budgeted to allow for adequate staffing and hours of operation; and located as accessibly as possible to property employees, residents, and prospective residents. During the planning and construction phases, management should do everything possible to convince the builder/developer/sponsor/owner of the wisdom of constructing a top-notch site office right from the start.

The Rental Office (Sales Office in Shared-Interest Associations)

Management that has been engaged to participate in a property's planning should take the opportunity to recommend the design of a rental office that will allow for maximum results as discussed in Chapter 7, Marketing Rental Housing and the Marketing Plan. Regardless of whether the rental office is located inside the site office or in a separate, independent office, the rental office should make the best possible first impression as it is often the first interior property facility new prospects see. Management's input should contribute to the establishment of a top-notch rental office right from the start.

Model Units

The model unit is one of the most important elements of an effective rent-up (or sales) campaign. As discussed in Chapter 7, Marketing Rental Housing and the Marketing Plan, models usually are used in existing properties when the property's budget permits the existence of an empty unit. However, one or more model units are essential during initial rent-up (or sales).

The number and the types of models should be determined by the number of different types of units in the property. A new property with a mix of studio, one-, two-, and three-bedroom units should have models of each type of unit to show prospects. These model units should be outstandingly furnished and decorated and should contain tasteful, effective signage that markets the features of both the individual unit and the property to prospects. They also should be located so that all prospects, including those who may be mobility challenged, can get to them easily.

LANDSCAPING

Landscaping is an important element of curb appeal everywhere, but especially in new properties. A management representative who is knowledgeable about landscaping could participate with the property's maintenance supervisor and landscape architect to select and verify the grass, trees, shrubs, plants, and other landscape elements to be installed at the property.

MANAGEMENT AND THE FINAL CONSTRUCTION PHASE

As mentioned above, management should not be involved in the construction of a new property in any construction supervisory or oversight capacity. Nevertheless, management should be kept apprised of construction progress and should walk the property often to become completely familiar with it.

At the end of the construction process, management should obtain the following items:

- Complete sets of as-built plans and specifications. (These plans—the original mechanical, structural, and other plans with changes made by the builder noted on each sheet—are necessary to understand what was built as opposed to what was originally designed. Management needs these as-built plans to know what was really installed, especially behind walls and in other areas that are not immediately apparent. The plans should be kept on file for locating water and sewer cutoffs and cleanouts and to provide crucial information in the event of an emergency such as a fire.)
- List of subcontractors and suppliers used in construction of the property, including:
  - Subcontractor/supplier name, address, and phone number
  - Work performed and items for which the subcontractor/supplier is responsible in the event that warranty work becomes necessary
  - Specific guarantee(s) with expiration date
  - The name, address, and phone number of the person to contact in case of a problem. (Upon final completion, the construction company representative should forward an updated subcontractor/supplier list to the management representative. Similar information should also be provided for each of the major sources of materials in the event of the subcontracting firm's dissolution or bankruptcy.)

Complete copies of all permits, licenses, and certificates of occupancy.

- Complete equipment lists (including band names and model numbers) and instruction manuals and warrantees.
- All keys to the property. (Because construction contractors often make duplicate keys for their own convenience during construction, there is no guarantee that all the keys to the property will be accounted for when the keys are given to management. For this reason, contractors should be encouraged to utilize a construction master key system at the outset. This system allows the contractor to give a construction master key to subcontractors and laborers. At acceptance of the property by the owner, the contractor or owner inserts and turns a special key in each lock, thereby making that lock unlockable by a construction master key and functional using only the key that came with the lock.)

Once the property has been accepted as "rent ready" and has been turned over to management, management should inspect each individual unit in advance of marketing and then again before the first resident moves in. A punchlist of items resulting from these inspections should be provided to the owner and/or the construction manager, and management should follow up to ensure that each unit and the property as a whole are indeed "rent ready."

In addition, on the owner's acceptance of the property as "rent ready," management should perform a security assessment of the property before the first resident moves in and should present the findings of the assessment to the owner (and/or the construction manager). Management should follow up here also to ensure that each unit and the property as a whole are as secure as possible.

Finally, as soon as the property has been turned over to the management, management must install all the necessary personnel to operate the property. This means that during the earlier stages management should have been interviewing and hiring all appropriate management, maintenance, and rental personnel according to management's agreement with the owner so that the property is able to begin functioning optimally as soon as it is ready.

FINANCIAL CONSIDERATIONS DURING PLANNING AND RENT-UP

Overwhelmingly, the builder/developer/sponsor/owner who invests in the construction of a new multihousing property or in the rehabilitation of an existing property does so to realize a profit. As with any such venture, careful financial planning as discussed in Chapter 4, Multihousing Management Economics and Finances is essential to achieve the goal of profitability.

BUDGETING FOR A NEW PROPERTY

The primary difference between budgeting for an existing property and budgeting for a new property is that a new property has no history. Hence, any budget must be zero-based. Once the property is up and running, however, it is possible to do variance analyses based on what was projected and what has actually transpired, and a historically based budget can evolve.

In new properties, first-year budgets should be prepared on a monthly basis to allow for close tracking of income and expenses. Such budgets should include a higher allocation for marketing while budgeting for repairs and other commonly recurring expenses may be lower during the rent-up budget period.

ESTABLISHING RENT LEVELS IN CONVENTIONAL PROPERTIES

In most cases, the preliminary establishment of rent level was done by the builder/developer/sponsor/owner in the very earliest stages of the project based on the rental target market profile (i.e., low, middle, or high income); the desirability and status appeal of the property; the individual unit being rented; the cost to operate the property; comparable or competitive rents; and market conditions and what the marketplace will bear. As the project progresses and begins to rent-up, rent levels will need to be fine-tuned to produce the greatest net operating income and profit.

For example, if, after two or three months the units of a new property are renting rapidly, it may be wise to reconsider the rents. They may be too low in the current marketplace and should be gradually increased for new prospects until a balance is struck between those eager to rent and those who show some resistance.

Conversely, if it is discovered that the initial rents are too high, it may be wise to consider providing signing incentives before lowering the rents, which could cause problems with renters who have already signed on. If a rent reduction proves the only way to go, then those renters already in place should enjoy the same reduction immediately and get refunds or credits for the overage they already have paid.

ESTABLISHING RENT LEVELS IN FEDERALLY ASSISTED AND PUBLIC HOUSING DEVELOPMENTS

In federally assisted and public housing developments, residents are required to pay a certain percent of their income for rent in accordance with the latest approved rent schedule for that particular type of development. These schedules are based on comparable market analyses and the individual development's needs. The amount of rent charged in these types of developments generally has little to do with the condition of the property or the size of the apartment being rented and is established by the government agency that owns the development.

MANAGING THE PROPERTY'S FINANCIAL ACCOUNTS FROM THE START IN CONVENTIONAL PROPERTIES

As discussed in Chapter 4, Multihousing Management Economics and Finances, management that is responsible for overseeing a property's bank accounts (e.g., operating account, reserve account, petty funds account) should establish these accounts in the name of the property and for the account of the owner. Depending on the agreement between the owner and the management company, the accounts may also list the management company as agent for the owner, and any number of people (e.g., the owner, property manager, management company financial officer) may be authorized as a signatory to one or more of the accounts.

MANAGING THE PROPERTY'S FINANCIAL ACCOUNTS FROM THE START IN FEDERALLY ASSISTED AND PUBLIC HOUSING DEVELOPMENTS

As discussed in Chapter 11, Government-assisted and Government-insured Housing and Military Housing, under provisions of the mortgager's certificate and the regulatory agreement, management must maintain the requirements set forth in HUD Handbook 4370.2, *Financial Operations and Accounting Procedures for Insured Multifamily Projects* and Handbook 4350.1, *Insured Project Servicing*.

These handbooks outline in detail the prescribed chart of accounts that must be established and maintained. The accountant for the project should review the handbook and establish the necessary records to comply with HUD's prescribed accounting requirements before the development is ready for renting. Often, the knowledge of a transaction is needed to supplement basic documents in posting to the official records. Early establishment of the HUD-required accounting system also saves the development a significant amount in audit fees for the annual financial statement.

Near the date of anticipated initial occupancy, HUD requests information concerning the fiscal year the project has adopted, the month income commences, and the individual to whom fiscal correspondence should be addressed. Management, or whoever is responsible for the property's finances, must be prepared to respond to this request.

WRITTEN MANAGEMENT PLANS FOR NEW PROPERTIES

The management company and professional manager intending to succeed in service to builders/developers/sponsors/owners of new properties will present to their clients written evidence of superior planning. The following documents should be prepared by management and customized to address the unique management requirements and expectations of each property in the management company's portfolio, including properties of new construction:

- An operations manual
- A management maintenance plan (including a risk management plan)
- A marketing plan
- An employee handbook
- A resident handbook

HUD MANAGEMENT REQUIREMENTS

HUD requires a comprehensive management plan from the developer during the planning stage of a HUD-insured multihousing development. For best results, the program should be developed concurrently with the planning and construction of the physical plant. The detailed plan should include a full discussion of:

- The owner's relationship with the managing agent
- Personnel policies and staffing arrangements
- Publicizing and achieving early occupancy (Fair Market program)

- Certification and re-certification of resident eligibility
- Effective maintenance and repair
- Rent collection
- Accounting records and office procedures
- Management/resident relations
- Community services
- The management agreement

MARKETING AND PUBLIC RELATIONS FOR NEW CONSTRUCTION AND RENT-UP

Depending on the nature of the new construction project, the competition, the marketplace, and other factors, it may be advisable to commence marketing activities well in advance of the projected occupancy date and sometimes even in advance of commencement of construction. Under any circumstances, the principles of marketing discussed in Chapter 7, Marketing Rental Housing and the Marketing Plan apply to all projected, new, and existing multifamily properties. These principles include:

- Creating and implementing a marketing strategy
- Exploring the wisdom and cost efficiency of hiring a professional marketing firm
- Establishing an identity for the property through a proprietary logo and incorporating the logo and property identity in all marketing materials, signage, and advertisements
- Implementing the advertising campaign through print and broadcast media, the Internet, direct mail, etc.
- Continually reviewing and adjusting the marketing strategy and activities to yield the most desirable results

PUBLIC RELATIONS FOR NEW CONSTRUCTION AND RENT-UP

As discussed in Chapter 7, Marketing Rental Housing and the Marketing Plan, the purpose of public relations is to create and promote a favorable image for the property in the local community and to attract prospective residents. Public relations marketing techniques for new properties in the rent-up phase include:

- Social activities
- Networking with local organizations
- Cultivating the local media
- Referrals

SOCIAL ACTIVITIES

Grand Opening Ceremony

A grand opening ceremony is a grand way to announce the presence of a new multihousing property in the community. The mayor, other municipal leaders, and media representatives should be invited to the ceremony, which might include a ribbon-cutting, brief speeches, and refreshments. The event can be as casual or as elaborate as the budget will allow but should be impressive. The media should be contacted well in advance, given the details about the property, and invited to participate in and write about and take photographs or videotapes at the ceremony. Newspaper, radio, and television news coverage may result. Press kits should be available for media representatives. These kits should contain a press release about the opening, photographs, a brochure, and a short narrative about the property suitable for publication.

Open House

An effective method of attracting prospects is to place a display ad announcing an open house on a Saturday or Sunday. The open house could include group and/or individual tours of the property, its amenities, and model units; informational sessions about the property held throughout the day; and nonstop refreshments. Personnel directors and senior executives of the major employers in the areas, representatives of local colleges and hospitals that require housing for their staff members, representatives of local civic groups, and representatives of the closest military bases' housing offices should also be invited. Coupling an open house with other promotional efforts, such as a radio station remote broadcast, can provide good results.

Of course, enough staff people should be present at the open house to handle the prospects who visit so that prospects can be properly oriented to the property and given an opportunity to rent/buy if they wish to do so. At the very least, staff people should record visitors' names and telephone numbers for later contact.

Needless to say, the property must be in first-class condition for an open house.

NETWORKING WITH LOCAL ORGANIZATIONS

The developer/sponsor/owner and/or the management representative should begin to network with local organizations during the early stages of a property's planning and construction. This is so that interest in the property can be piqued locally and to create a sense of excitement as the property nears completion. The groups to network with include the local Board of Trade and Chamber of Commerce, local apartment or multifamily councils, local real estate organizations, local welcome wagon organizations, local social and religious groups, and local corporate targets whose employees will always need housing in close proximity to work.

CULTIVATING THE LOCAL MEDIA

Getting free, positive exposure in the local press is the purpose of a public relations campaign that aims at cultivating the local media. During construction and rent-up, local media can be cultivated through simple press releases that follow the progress of construction, announce the opening of the property and availability of units in the property, and announce the grand opening and/or open house events. Then, of course, the news release campaign must continue with other announcements, such as the first resident to occupy a unit in the property.

Cultivating the media also means responding to media inquiries for information. This can be done by having press kits at the ready and identifying the best spokesperson for the property.

REFERRALS

Although referrals usually come after a property has been operating for a while, it is possible to get referrals for a new property from residents of other properties constructed by the same construction company as the new property, or owned by the same owner, or managed by the same management company. The idea is to inform satisfied residents of other properties who have a connection to the new property that the new property is open and ready for business. Industry colleagues and local real estate professionals also can be sources of referrals.

MARKETING IN A SOFT MARKET

Sometimes, even the best planned properties open in the midst of a soft market. When this happens, the owner and/or manager can offer incentives such as those discussed in Chapter 7, Marketing Rental Housing and the Marketing Plan and/or engage a professional marketing firm to get the ball rolling. It is important for real estate investors and managers to remember that the market is cyclic and that soft markets always turn around eventually.

THE ROLE OF THE RENTAL (SALES) AGENT IN RENT-UP (INITIAL SALES)

Whether she/he is an employee of the management company, the developer or owner, or a professional multihousing marketing firm, the rental (or sales) agent is arguably the most important player in the mix during the rent-up (sales) phase of a new multifamily property. For this reason, the property owner must be willing to make the appropriate investments to bring the best rental professionals on board right from the start. The qualities of the successful rental (sales) agent are outlined in Chapter 7, Marketing Rental Housing and the Marketing Plan.

MONITORING THE EFFECTIVENESS OF MARKETING EFFORTS

The new property rent-up checklist shown in Figure 12–1 can be used to ensure that the important marketing actions are planned and carried out in a timely way so that when the opening date arrives, all elements of a solid marketing program are in place. A project under construction status report form like the one shown in Figure 12–2 will help the manager and developer/owner keep track of the number and percentage of rentals during the rent-up stage. The vacant 12–2 unit control form and the trend report discussed in Chapter 7, Marketing Rental Housing and the Marketing Plan also should be used to evaluate the effectiveness of the new property's current marketing activities. Other instruments to measure marketing effectiveness include in-person, one-on-one interviews with prospects who decide to rent and those who decide not to; "shopping" the property's rental (sales) office to see how it is being marketed to prospects; and "shopping" competing properties' rental (sales) offices to see how they are being marketed.

THE PROPERTY'S FIRST RESIDENTS

The policies and procedures for processing applications and move-ins as discussed in Chapter 8, Processing Applications, Move-in and Move-Out Procedures, and Resident Relations all apply to the rent-up phase of a new property. The property developer/owner and management must comply from the start with all standard requirements for conventional and/or assisted properties and should take the same care in verifying the eligibility and desirability of initial residents as they do with subsequent residents. In fact, more care should be taken because the first people to move into a property often set the tone for the property as a whole.

The developer/owner and management also will want to maintain strict control over applications and waiting lists to ensure the fastest, most desirable initial rent-up. They also will want to make sure that everything is in order for lease signings and moves into the property so that all processes move forward smoothly.

From a more personal perspective, the developer/owner and management will want to help the property's original residents to acclimate and feel comfortable in their new homes as quickly as possible. A pleasant way to do this is to present special welcome baskets with information about the local area, including coupons and other items from local merchants (who may be willing to sponsor the welcome basket for the promise of distribution to all new residents). When a certain number of new residents have moved in, a welcome party is another good public relations idea.

Management also will want to keep in close communication with the property's first residents to ameliorate any inconveniences that may occur because of the property's newness. For instance, if construction is still going on when the first residents move in, management should anticipate that the new resident's car may get dusty and may provide an alternate parking space or a coupon for a free wash at the local carwash. Or, before scaffolding is dropped down the side of a building for window work, management should inform residents who have already moved in to keep their blinds closed for privacy during the hours the workmen will be on the scaffolding. New residents also should be encouraged to communicate with management regarding any incomplete punchlist items inside their apart-

FIGURE 12–1. New Development Rent Up Chart

Name of Development ______________________ Date ______________

Total Units	1BR	1BRL	2BR2B	2TH	3TH	Total
# Released as of ________	________	________	________	________	________	________
# Rented + % of total	________	________	________	________	________	________
#VNA* + % of released	________	________	________	________	________	________
______________________						
# Released as of ________	________	________	________	________	________	________
# Rented + % of total	________	________	________	________	________	________
#VNA* + % of released	________	________	________	________	________	________
______________________						
# Released as of ________	________	________	________	________	________	________
# Rented + % of total	________	________	________	________	________	________
#VNA* + % of released	________	________	________	________	________	________
______________________						
# Released as of ________	________	________	________	________	________	________
# Rented + % of total	________	________	________	________	________	________
#VNA* + % of released	________	________	________	________	________	________
______________________						
# Released as of ________	________	________	________	________	________	________
# Rented + % of total	________	________	________	________	________	________
# VNA* + % of released	________	________	________	________	________	________
______________________						
Initial Rents						
Adjusted On ________	________	________	________	________	________	________
________	________	________	________	________	________	________
________	________	________	________	________	________	________
________	________	________	________	________	________	________
________	________	________	________	________	________	________
________	________	________	________	________	________	________
________	________	________	________	________	________	________

**VNA=Vacant, not assigned*

Figure 12–2. Development Under Construction Status Report

Development ______________________ Date ______________

Unit Type	Number of Units	Released						Constr. Assigned	Occ. + V/A +constr. assigned	Total Percent Rented	Rents
		Number Released	Occupied	V/A*	Total Rented	Percent Rented	V/NA**				
Total											

Unit Type	Bldg. # ____ Rel. Date ____ Mix Assigned		Bldg. # ____ Rel. Date ____ Mix Assigned		Bldg. # ____ Rel. Date ____ Mix Assigned		Bldg. # ____ Rel. Date ____ Mix Assigned		Bldg. # ____ Rel. Date ____ Mix Assigned	
Total										

Prepared by: ______________

Distribution: *Development Manager*

Property Manager

Executive Property Manager

Initial Building Release Date: ______________

Absorption Rate: ______________

Number of Weeks: ______________

Number Rented: ______________

*Vacant/Assigned

**Vacant/Not Assigned

ments so that these items can be attended to satisfactorily. Taking care of new residents with actions such as these will reflect favorably on the property, on the owner, and on management and will produce the positive word-of-mouth promotion that is so critical to every property, both new and established.

Yet, even with the best care, some residents will choose to move out in the first year. The property owner and management must be prepared for a certain amount of turnover during the initial 12 months and should establish a system that includes exit interviews to learn how much of that turnover is due to the property versus other reasons. Pending the results that are discovered regarding move outs, both the owner and management should focus on ensuring that the property's quality of life is such that all desirable residents will want to continue living there.

CONCLUSION

Increasingly, builders, developers, sponsors, and owners are turning to professional management organizations for guidance and assistance during the construction and rent-up phase of new properties. This includes existing conventional and assisted properties undergoing rehabilitation and new shared-interest associations and rental properties undergoing conversion to shared-interest association status.

During the planning phase, knowledgeable management professionals can provide valuable input with regard to the management, maintenance, and risk management of the new property. Management input regarding such areas as the maintenance office/garage, site office, rental office, model units, and landscaping can be helpful. However, management should not serve as the construction manager or supervisor because of the legal, insurance, and other issues involved.

In the final construction phase when the property has been accepted as "rent ready" and has been turned over to management by the owner, management should obtain the property's as-built plans and specifications; a list of subcontractors and suppliers who participated in the property's construction; complete copies of all permits licenses and certificates of occupancy; complete equipment lists; and all keys to the property. Management also should perform inspections and security assessments of each unit and the property as a whole and should provide punchlists to the owner. Management should then follow up to ensure that each unit and property is indeed "rent ready."

Also during this phase, management should be interviewing and hiring the appropriate management, maintenance, and rental personnel so that the property can operate optimally right from the start.

A new property's rent-up year budget will necessarily be zero-based. A historically based budget will evolve once the property is up and running. First-year budgets should be prepared on a monthly basis to allow for close tracking of income and expenses. Typically, budget allocations will be higher for marketing and lower for repairs during the first year. Also during the first year, the owner and management will be working together to fine-tune rent levels so that rent-up can proceed most efficiently and profitably. Management will need to comply with all HUD-related requirements and regulations with regard to budgeting and setting rent levels.

HUD requires a comprehensive management plan from the developer during the planning of a HUD-insured multihousing development, but management should produce an operations manual, a management maintenance plan (including a risk management plan), a marketing plan, an employee handbook, and a resident handbook for all new properties.

Marketing and public relations efforts for a new property follow the same principles as for any property except that all marketing and public relations programs will have to be created from scratch for the new property. Such events as a grand opening and an open house are good public relations tools for new properties. The rental office and the professionals staffing should be of the highest caliber, and the effectiveness of marketing and rental efforts for a new property should be closely monitored to ensure the desired results.

Management should do everything possible to ensure a smooth move-in for the property's first residents and to make their first months in the new property as pleasant as possible. All apartment punchlist items should be attended to immediately, and special care should be taken to make these original residents comfortable and happy. Even so, a certain number will move out during the first year, and management should conduct exit interviews and perform other research to learn how to reduce that number effectively and how to keep existing residents in place.

Participation in the very beginning stages of development and construction is a major step forward for the multihousing management professional. The professional multihousing manager should become an expert in the planning, construction, and rent-up considerations of new multifamily properties to become as valuable as possible to clients, to the management organization that employs her/him, and to the multihousing management profession as a whole.

13

The Law and Multihousing Management

THE MULTIHOUSING MANAGER AND THE LAW

The wide range of areas in which the multihousing manager must be knowledgeable has been emphasized throughout this text. Certainly, the law in all its myriad applications is a significant area in the practice of multihousing management. Virtually everything a multihousing management company does, both as a legal entity and as fiduciary of its client properties, is governed by federal, state, and/or local laws, regulations, or codes.

Does this mean that the professional multihousing manager must earn a law degree and practice law to perform her/his job? The answer is decidedly no. Although the multihousing manager will assuredly absorb a great deal of legal knowledge and experience as she/he proceeds in her/his career, it is not necessary that the manager be a legal expert. Rather, what the manager must know about the law is two-fold.

First, the manager must realize the true gravity of the law in all aspects of multihousing management and must have at least a working understanding of all aspects of those multihousing laws that pertain to the property(ies) for which the manager is responsible. Second, the manager must recognize the obligation to seek definitive legal counsel whenever she/he has even the slightest question of law and know who to turn to to obtain the answers she/he seeks.

There are two broad categories of legal inquiry relative to multihousing management. The first relates to the operation of the management company as a legal entity. As with all businesses, the multihousing management company must comply with all applicable laws, regulations, and codes to remain viable.

The second category of legal activity relative to multihousing management involves the properties that have been entrusted to the management company. A countless catalogue of laws, regulations, and codes governs the operation of multihousing properties. What's more, these laws, regulations, and codes are in a constant state of flux, changing and evolving on an almost daily basis and thus it is virtually impossible for one person to have immediate knowledge of them all.

To fulfill their fiduciary responsibility to their clients, management organizations establish various levels of relationship with attorneys knowledgeable in laws governing property management. Smaller management concerns may seek the counsel of needed attorneys on a per-project/hourly basis and/or keep a consulting attorney on retainer, while larger organizations may support an entire in-house legal department. Similarly, property owners often have the same types of arrangements, with smaller operators seeking legal advice on an as-needed basis or retaining a legal generalist for most issues while larger operators with many properties may have a team of attorneys or even their own in-house legal staff. These relationships are necessary for both the management company and each individual property because the law impacts every aspect of the operations of both. (This is why legal expenses should always be factored into the operating budget of the management company and each property it manages.)

The most competent multihousing manager is not one who pours over law books in search of answers to law-related questions. The most competent multihousing manager uses the resources available to her/him to get the answers she/he needs by consulting with the appropriate legal expert in the immediate area of inquiry according to the policies and procedures of the management organization. The manager must fully and completely explain the circumstances of the inquiry to the legal advisor and must realize that the answer to one inquiry may not necessarily apply to any similar future situation. Hence, the manager must maintain on-going contact with the appropriate legal advisor(s) according to the protocol of the management company and must seek legal counsel whenever a law-related issue arises. Once the manager gets the answer she/he seeks, she/he should document the situation, the question, the response, and the source so as to maintain a record and to be able to make a complete report to the senior manager and/or the property owner, as appropriate.

Below is a list of categories in which even the most experienced multihousing professional may require the assistance of a knowledgeable legal resource. Because the practice of law relative to the fields of real estate and residential real estate management is so vast, it should not be difficult to locate an appropriate legal authority for a definitive response to any question.

TYPICAL AREAS OF LEGAL INQUIRY

- Accounting law
- Affirmative marketing and other multihousing marketing laws and regulations
- Business law
- Collective bargaining and union laws
- Credit and collections laws
- Employment law
- Energy and water conservation laws and regulations
- Environmental laws and regulations
- Fair Housing laws
- Federal regulations from such agencies as HUD and FmHA
- Immigration law
- Insurance law
- Investment law
- Labor laws
- Landlord/tenant law
- Laws governing the homebuilding industry
- Laws governing all ancillary service providers to the homebuilding industry
- Laws governing contracts, agreements, and covenants
- Laws governing discrimination in housing and employment
- Laws governing records, files, and documents of the multihousing management organization
- Laws governing the responsibilities of fiduciaries
- Laws governing safety, security, and risk management
- Laws governing shared-interest associations
- Public housing laws
- Real estate law
- Rent law
- Tax law
- Use of legal means to influence legislation and regulations
- Vehicular law

THE NATIONAL ASSOCIATION OF HOME BUILDERS RAM AND ADVANCED RAM PROGRAMS AND THE LAW

As discussed in Chapter 1, The Expanding Role of Professional Multihousing Management, the National Association of Home Builders (NAHB) offers the longest-established residential property management certification in the United States through its RAM and Advanced RAM credentialing programs. These programs train property managers of multifamily rental, shared-interest, subsidized, market-rate, and military housing throughout the country. An introduction to, and review of, the legal issues impacting multifamily management is part of the RAM and Advanced RAM courses of study. For more information, contact NAHB at (800) 368–5242, extension 8650.

LICENSING REQUIREMENTS FOR MULTIHOUSING MANAGERS

At the time of the writing of this text, the multihousing management industry has recognized the benefits of defining itself through nationally uniform standards. Those who have devoted their careers to the practice and advancement of multihousing management acknowledge that this effort is essential to elevating the industry to the station of professionalism it rightfully deserves.

The NAHB is in the forefront of this effort. In 1996, the RAM Board of Governors voted into existence the State Licensing of Property Managers Subcommittee. The purpose of the subcommittee was to investigate existing state licensing requirements and to determine how uniform and standardized RAM training and certification can be included in state licensing requirements.

The committee was chaired by David Kuperberg, CPM®, Adv. RAM, co-author of this text. Under Mr. Kuperberg, the subcommittee was charged with compiling data to determine the professional residential property management licensing requirements for fee-based management companies in all 50 states and the District of Columbia. (The survey did not include requirements for owner-managed properties.) The study was made in compliance with the RAM Strategic Plan expressed in the RAM Board of Governors Operational Handbook of May 1997, "to identify the standards of the industry."

STUDY PROTOCOL

On direction from the NAHB, a survey form was designed to solicit from each state and the District of Columbia responses to the following inquiries:

- Does the state require a separate and distinct license for property management companies to manage multifamily rentals, condominiums, cooperatives, and/or homeowners associations?
- Does the state require a separate and distinct license for individual employees of property management companies to manage multifamily rentals, condominiums, cooperatives, and/or homeowners associations?
- Does the state require property managers to have a real estate broker and/or salesperson license to manage multifamily rentals, condominiums, cooperatives, and/or homeowners associations?
- Does the state have any pending licensing requirements?

This survey was mailed to representatives of the state departments of all 50 states and the District of Columbia in November 1996. Responses were received and tabulated between November 1996 and September 1997, when the last response was received. No subsequent study has been made; hence, the information resulting from the survey as discussed below is the most current information available in a codified document.

GENERAL DISCUSSION OF SURVEY RESULTS AND FINDINGS

The results of the survey revealed the need for standard requirements for multifamily management throughout the District of Columbia and the 48 states that responded. (Alaska and Massachusetts did not respond.) As indicated in the study (*Licensing of Residential Property Managers: A Study of State Licensing Requirements,* National Association of Home Builders: 1997), the following findings of the survey are particularly salient:

- As of 1997, of the 48 responding states and the District of Columbia, only Montana had separate and distinct licensing requirements for both property management companies and individual employees of property management companies and also required a real estate broker and/or salesperson license to manage all types of residential properties.
- As of 1997, 46 of 48 responding states and the District of Columbia had no separate and distinct licensing requirements for property management companies.
- As of 1997, 41 of 48 responding states and the District of Columbia had no separate and distinct licensing requirements for individual employees of property management companies.
- As of 1997, 35 of 48 responding states and the District of Columbia had no separate and distinct licensing requirements for either property management companies or for individual employees of property management companies.
- As of 1997, 35 of 48 responding states and the District of Columbia required only a real estate broker and/or salesperson license for residential property management in most cases.
- As of 1997, 16 of 48 responding states and the District of Columbia did not require a real estate broker and/or salespersons license.
- As of 1997, 12 of 48 responding states and the District of Columbia had no separate and distinct licensing requirement for property management companies, no separate and distinct licensing requirements for individual employees of property management companies, and did not require a real estate broker and/or salesperson license.

The most significant finding of this study is that no uniform professional standard existed throughout the United States for the licensing of residential property management.

Figure 13–1 contains a state-by-state narrative of responses to the survey. Figure 13–2 contains a directory of real estate license law agencies and offices (by jurisdiction).

THE FUTURE OF PROFESSIONAL MULTIHOUSING MANAGEMENT

The multihousing sector is a stronghold of the American housing economy. The NAHB reports significant increases in the level of multifamily housing production while the length of time it takes for newly built rental and shared-interest association units to be rent or sold is declining. In 2002, the most recent study of the U.S. Department of the Census, Decennial Censuses and American Housing Survey, reported more than 15 million apartment residents in the United States. In the same year, according to the Community Associations Institute (CAI) Research Foundation, there were more than 231,000 shared-interest associations throughout the United States, housing more than 40 million residents. And it was estimated that 60 percent of all new homes in major metropolitan areas are built within shared-interest associations.

This is all good news for you, the multihousing management professional.

FIGURE 13-1. State-by-State Narrative of Licensing Requirements for Multifamily Management Companies and Managers

The information below is taken directly from, *Licensing of Residential Property Managers: A Study of State Licensing Requirements,* a study prepared by David Kuperberg, CPM®, Adv. RAM, Chair of the RAM State Licensing of Property Managers Subcommittee, and published in 1997 by the National Association of Home Builders. (Alaska and Massachusetts did not respond to the survey for this study.)

Narrative of Responses by State

Alabama
No separate and distinct state licensing requirements for property management companies or individual employees of property management companies. Requires property managers to have real estate broker and/or salesperson license for management of condominiums only.

Alaska
Did not respond.

Arizona
No separate and distinct state licensing requirements for property management companies or individual employees of property management companies. Does not requires real estate broker and/or salesperson license. ***New proposed licensing requirements were contained in the State Department's 1997 proposed legislation. Result unknown.***

Arkansas
No separate and distinct state licensing requirements for property management companies. Has separate and distinct state licensing requirements for individual employees of property management companies under certain circumstances. Requires real estate broker and/or salesperson license under certain circumstances.

California
No separate and distinct state licensing requirements for property management companies or individual employees of property management companies; a real estate broker's license permits all licensed activity. Requires a separate and distinct license for individual employees of property management companies to manage multifamily rentals, condominiums, and cooperatives, with exceptions. Requires real estate brokers and/or salesperson license.

Colorado
No separate and distinct licensing requirements for property management companies or individual employees of property management companies. Requires real estate broker and/or salesperson, with exceptions. "Licensure enables broker to engage in any aspect of industry of which they are competent."

Connecticut
No separate and distinct license for property management companies to manage multifamily rentals, cooperatives, or home owners association; a separate and distinct license is required for property management companies to manage condominiums. Property management companies managing multifamily rentals, cooperatives, and home owners association must hold a brokers license. No separate and distinct license requirement for individual employees of property management company to manage multifamily rentals, cooperatives, or home owners associations. A separate and distinct license is required for individual employees to manage condominiums. Requires brokers and/or salesperson license to manage multifamily rentals, cooperatives, and home owner associations. Does not requires real estate and/or salesperson license to manage condominiums.

(*continued*)

FIGURE 13-1. State-by-State Narrative of Licensing Requirements for Multifamily Management Companies and Managers (*Continued*)

Delaware
No separate and distinct licensing requirements for property management companies or individual employees of property management companies. Requires real estate brokers and/or salesperson license to manage multifamily rentals, condominiums, and cooperatives, unless the properties are owner-managed. Requirement of real estate brokers and/or salesperson license to manage home owners associations depends on extent and nature of activities.

District of Columbia
No separate and distinct licensing requirements for property management companies or individual employees of property management companies to manage multifamily rentals, condominiums, or cooperatives. Separate and distinct license requirements for both property management companies and individual employees of property management companies to manage home owners associations. Does not require real estate brokers and/or salesperson license.

Florida
No separate and distinct license for property management companies to manage multifamily rentals, condominiums, or cooperatives. Requires a separate and distinct license for property management companies to manage home owners associations/community associations under certain circumstances. Requires a separate and distinct license for individual employees of property management companies to manage multifamily rentals, condominiums, cooperatives, and home owners associations under certain circumstances and with exemptions. Requires real estate brokers and/or salesperson license to manage multifamily rentals, condominiums, and cooperatives, but not home owners associations.

Georgia
No separate and distinct license requirement for property management companies or individual employees of property management companies. Requires real estate brokers and/or salesperson license.

Hawaii
No separate and distinct license requirements for property management companies to manage multifamily rentals, cooperatives, or home owners associations. Condominium Managing Agent Registration requirement for the management of condominiums. No separate and distinct license requirements for individual employees of management companies. Requires real estate brokers and/or salesperson license to manage multifamily rentals and condominiums.

Idaho
No separate and distinct licensing requirements for property management companies or individual employees of property management companies. Does not require real estate brokers and/or salesperson license.

Illinois
No separate and distinct license requirement for property management companies. Requires a real estate brokers, salesperson, or leasing license for individual employees of property management companies. "Any broker or sponsored salesperson or sponsored leasing agent many manage property." ***At the time of response to the survey, rules for the administration of the leasing license were awaiting approval of the State Legislature. Result unknown.***

Indiana
No separate and distinct license requirements for property management companies or for individual employees of property management companies. Requires a real estate brokers and/or salesperson license. "Anyone who manages a property that he does not own must have a real estate license."

(*continued*)

FIGURE 13-1. State-by-State Narrative of Licensing Requirements for Multifamily Management Companies and Managers (*Continued*)

Iowa
No separate and distinct license requirements for property management companies or for individual employees of property management companies. Requires real estate brokers and/or salesperson license except for cooperatives where leases are for one year or less.

Kansas
No separate and distinct license requirements for property management companies or for individual employees of property management companies. Does not require real estate brokers and/or salesperson license.

Kentucky
No separate and distinct license requirement for property management companies or for individual employees of property management companies. Requires real estate brokers and/or salesperson license. "A real estate license is not required for 'A person engaged in property management if that person (a) is a regular employee of the owner or principal broker of the company engaged in property management; (b) receives as his primary compensation use of a rental unit.'" Also, "A license is not required for any person who as owner or lessor performs brokerage activity with reference to property owned or leased by him or to his regular employees with respect to the proper so owned or leased, if the acts are performed in the regular course of, or as an incident to, the management of the property and the investment in it."

Louisiana
No separate and distinct license requirement for property management companies or for individual employees of property management companies. Requires real estate broker and/or salesperson license.

Maine
No separate and distinct license requirement for property management companies or for individual employees of property management companies. Does not require real estate broker and/or salesperson license.

Maryland
No separate and distinct license requirement for property management companies or for individual employees of property management companies. Does not require real estate broker and/or salesperson license.

Massachusetts
Did not respond.

Michigan
No separate and distinct license requirement for property management companies or for individual employees of property management companies. Does not require real estate broker and/or salesperson license.

Minnesota
No separate and distinct license requirement for property management companies or for individual employees of property management companies. Requires real estate broker and/or salesperson license.

Mississippi
No separate and distinct license requirement for property management companies or for individual employees of property management companies. Requires real estate broker and/or salesperson license to manage all residential properties except home owners associations.

(*continued*)

FIGURE 13-1. State-by-State Narrative of Licensing Requirements for Multifamily Management Companies and Managers (*Continued*)

Missouri
No separate and distinct license requirement for property management companies or for individual employees of property management companies. Requires real estate broker and/or salesperson license to manage all residential properties except those that fall under exemption categories.

Montana
Requires either a real estate license or separate license for property management companies to manage all types of residential properties. Requires that all individual employees of property management companies who perform licensed activity be licensed.

Nebraska
No separate and distinct license requirement for property management companies or for individual employees of property management companies. Requires real estate broker and/or salesperson license.

Nevada
No separate and distinct license requirement for property management companies. Requires separate and distinct license for individual employees of property management companies to management multifamily rentals, condominiums, and cooperatives, except under certain exceptions. Requires real estate broker and/or salesperson license. ***At the time of response to the survey, legislation was pending in the 1997 Legislative Session to require a Property Management Permit to engage inn the business of property management, which would include management of home owners associations. The proposed legislation was sponsored by the Nevada Association of Realtors. The Community Association institute also submitted a bill draft request to certify home owners association managers. The bill draft request was not available at the time of response to the survey. Result unknown.***

New Hampshire
No separate and distinct license requirement for property management companies. Separate and distinct license required only for individual employees of property management companies managing home owners associations. Requires real estate broker and/or salesperson license to manage multifamily rentals, condominiums, and cooperatives but not home owners associations.

New Jersey
No separate and distinct license requirement for property management companies or for individual employees of property management companies. Requires real estate broker and/or salesperson license.

New Mexico
No separate and distinct license requirement for property management companies or for individual employees of property management companies. Requires real estate broker and/or salesperson license.

New York
No separate and distinct license requirement for property management companies or for individual employees of property management companies. Requires real estate broker and/or salesperson license to manage multifamily rentals and cooperatives.

North Carolina
No separate and distinct license requirement for property management companies or for individual employees of property management companies. Does not require real estate broker and/or salesperson license.

(*continued*)

FIGURE 13-1. State-by-State Narrative of Licensing Requirements for Multifamily Management Companies and Managers (*Continued*)

North Dakota
No separate and distinct license requirement for property management companies or for individual employees of property management companies. Does not require real estate broker and/or salesperson license.

Ohio
No separate and distinct license requirement for property management companies or for individual employees of property management companies. Requires real estate broker and/or salesperson license.

Oklahoma
No separate and distinct license requirement for property management companies or for individual employees of property management companies. Requires real estate broker and/or salesperson license for management of multifamily rentals and condominiums.

Oregon
No separate and distinct license requirement for property management companies or for individual employees of property management companies. However, there is a separate, alternative license for property managers in addition to the real estate broker and/or sales person license required to manage multifamily rentals, condominiums, and cooperatives (where the living units are managed as rental units). Requires real estate broker and/or salesperson license.

Pennsylvania
No separate and distinct license requirement for property management companies or for individual employees of property management companies. Does not requires real estate broker and/or salesperson license.

Rhode Island
No separate and distinct license requirement for property management companies. Separate and distinct license requirements for individual employees of property management companies to manage multifamily rentals, condominiums, and cooperatives, depending on duties. Requires real estate broker and/or salesperson license for management of multifamily rentals, condominiums, and cooperatives depending on duties.

South Carolina
No separate and distinct license requirement for property management companies; does not license companies, only individuals. Separate and distinct license requirements for individual employees of property management companies to manage multifamily rentals, condominiums, and cooperatives. Does not require real estate broker and/or salesperson license.

South Dakota
Requires either a Property Manager or brokers license for property management companies. No separate and distinct license requirements for individual employees of property management companies. Requires a real estate broker and/or salesperson license.

Tennessee
No separate and distinct license requirement for property management companies. Separate and distinct license requirement for individual employees of property management companies except resident managers. Requires real estate broker and/or salesperson license.

(*continued*)

FIGURE 13-1. State-by-State Narrative of Licensing Requirements for Multifamily Management Companies and Managers (*Continued*)

Texas
No separate and distinct license requirement for property management companies. Real estate brokers and/or salesperson license required if property manager negotiates the rentals or leasing of real property. Individuals, corporations, and limited liability companies are subject to the license requirement if these services are provided as part of the management services.

Utah
Requires a separate and distinct license for property management companies that manage multifamily rentals, condominiums (only if rentals), and cooperatives (only if rentals). Real estate agent's or brokers license required for property management unless an exemption applies. Separate and distinct license for individual employees of property management companies to manage multifamily rentals, condominiums, and cooperatives unless the employee provides property management monies on real estate owned entirely by the employer. Requires real estate and/or brokers license. ***At the time of response to the survey, Utah was considering the issuance of a specialized brokers license for individuals who engage only in property management. Result unknown.***

Vermont
No separate and distinct license requirement for property management companies or for individual employees of property management companies. Does not require real estate broker and/or salesperson license.

Virginia
No separate and distinct license requirement for property management companies. Separate and distinct license requirement for individual employees of property management companies for multifamily rentals only. Requires real estate broker and/or salespersons license only for management of multifamily rentals.

Washington State
No separate and distinct license requirement for property management companies or for individual employees of property management companies. Requires real estate broker and/or salesperson license with exemption for incidental management by members of the owner's family, and management by resident managers. ***At the time of response to the survey, the Washington State Real Estate Commission had a standing committee involved in the study of property management licensing, which committee anticipated drafting amendments to define property management and the tasks and duties that would not require licensure. The earliest opportunity for legislative consideration of any draft amendment is the upcoming 1998 Session.***

West Virginia
No separate and distinct license requirement for property management companies or for individual employees of property management companies. Requires real estate broker and/or salesperson license.

Wisconsin
No separate and distinct license requirement for property management companies or for individual employees of property management companies. Requires real estate broker and/or salesperson license only for management of multifamily rentals.

Wyoming
No separate and distinct license requirement for property management companies or for individual employees of property management companies. Does not require real estate broker and/or salesperson license.

FIGURE 13-2. Directory of Real Estate License Law Agencies and Offices (by Jurisdiction)

Alabama
Real Estate Commission
1201 Carmichael Way
Montgomery, Alabama 36016
334-242-5544

Alaska
Division of Occupational Licensing
Real Estate Commission
3601 'C' Street, Suite 722
Anchorage, Alaska 99503
907-563-2169

Arizona
Department of Real Estate
2910 North 44th Street, Suite 100
Phoenix, Arizona 85018
602-468-1414

Arkansas
Real Estate Commission
612 South Summit Street
Little Rock, Arkansas 72201-4740
501-682-2732

California
Department of Real Estate
2201 Broadway
Sacramento, California 95818
916-227-0782

Colorado
Department of Regulatory Agencies
Division of Real Estate
1900 Grant Street, Suite 600
Denver, Colorado 80203
303-894-2166

Connecticut
Department of Consumer Protection
Real Estate & Professional Trades Div.
165 Capitol Avenue
Hartford, Connecticut 06106
860-566-5130

Delaware
Real Estate Commission
PO Box 1401
Dover, Delaware 19901
302-739-4522, ext. 219

District of Columbia
Dept. of Consumer &
Regulatory Affairs
614 H Street N.W., Room 921
PO Box 37200
Washington, D.C. 20013-7200
202-727-7450

Florida
Division of Real Estate
400 W. Robinson Street
Orlando, Florida 32801
407-423-6053

Georgia
Real Estate Commission
Suite 1000-Cain Tower
229 Peachtree St., N.W.
Atlanta, Georgia 30303-1605
404-656-3916

Hawaii
Real Estate Commission
250 S. King St., Room 702
Honolulu, Hawaii 96813
808-586-2643

Idaho
Real Estate Commission
PO Box 83720
Boise, Idaho 83720-0077
208-334-3285

Illinois
Office of the Commissioner
of Savings & Residential Finance
500 East Monroe Street, 2nd Fl.
Springfield, Illinois 62701
217-782-9300

Indiana
Professional Licensing Agency
IGCS, 302 W. Washington St.
E034
Indianapolis, Indiana 46204-2700
317-232-2980

Iowa
Professional Licensing &
Regulation Division
Real Estate Commission
1918 SE Hulsizer Avenue
Ankeny, Iowa 50021
515-281-3183

(*continued*)

FIGURE 13-2. Directory of Real Estate License Law Agencies and Offices (by Jurisdiction) (*Continued*)

Kansas
Real Estate Commission
Three Townsite Plaza, Suite 200
120 SE 6th Avenue
Topeka, Kansas 66603-3511
913-296-3411

Kentucky
Real Estate Commission
10200 Linn Station Rd., Ste. 201
Louisville, Kentucky 40223
502-425-4273

Louisiana
Real Estate Commission
PO Box 14785
Baton Rouge, Louisiana 70898-4785
504-925-4771

Maine
Real Estate Commission
35 State House Station
Augusta, Maine 04333
207-624-8516

Maryland
Dept. Of Labor, Licensing & Regulation
Real Estate Commission
501 St. Paul Place, 8th Fl.
Baltimore, Maryland 21202-2272
410-333-8124

Massachusetts
Board of Registration of Real Estate Brokers & Salespersons
Real Estate Board
100 Cambridge Street, Rm. 1313
Boston, Massachusetts 02202
617-727-2373

Michigan
Dept. of Commerce - BOPR
Office of Commercial Services, Licensing Division
PO Box 30243
Lansing, Michigan 48909
517-373-0490

Minnesota
Department of Commerce
133 East 7th Street
St. Paul, Minnesota 55101
612-296-2488

Mississippi
Real Estate Commission
1920 Dunbarton Drive
Jackson, Mississippi 39216-5087
601-987-3969

Missouri
Real Estate Commission
PO Box 1339
Jefferson City, Missouri 65102
314-751-2628

Montana
Dept. of Commerce
Board of Realty Regulation
111 N. Jackson
PO Box 200513
Helena, Montana 59620-0513
406-444-2961

Nebraska
Real Estate Commission
1200 'N' Street, Ste. 402
Lincoln, Nebraska 68508
402-471-2004

Nevada
Dept. of Business & Industry
Real Estate Division
2501 E. Sahara Avenue
Las Vegas, Nevada 89158
702-486-4033

New Hampshire
Real Estate Commission
State House Annex, Rm. 437
25 Capitol Street
Concord, New Hampshire 03301
603-271-2701

New Jersey
Real Estate Commission
20 West State Street
CN-328
Trenton, New Jersey 08625
609-292-8280

New Mexico
Real Estate Commission
1650 University Blvd, NE
Suite 490
Albuquerque, New Mexico 87102
505-841-9120

(*continued*)

FIGURE 13-2. Directory of Real Estate License Law Agencies and Offices (by Jurisdiction) (*Continued*)

New York
Department of State
Division of Licensing
84 Holland Avenue
Albany, New York 12208
518-473-2728

North Carolina
Real Estate Commission
PO Box 17100
Raleigh, North Carolina 27619-7100
919-733-9580

North Dakota
Real Estate Commission
314 East Thayer Avenue
PO Box 727
Bismarck, North Dakota 58502-0727
701-328-9749

Ohio
Division of Real Estate
77 South High Street, 20th Fl.
Columbus, Ohio 43266-0547
614-466-4100

Oklahoma
Real Estate Commission
4040 N. Lincoln Boulevard
Suite 100
Oklahoma City, Oklahoma 73105
405-521-3387

Oregon
Real Estate Agency
1177 Center St., NE
Salem, Oregon 97310-2503
503-378-4170

Pennsylvania
Real Estate Commission
PO Box 2649
Harrisburg, Pennsylvania 17105-2649
717-783-3658

Rhode Island
Real Estate Administrator
Dept. of Business Regulation
233 Richmond Street
Suite 230
Providence, Rhode Island 02903
401-277-2255

South Carolina
Dept. of Labor Licensing &
Regulation
Real Estate Commission
1201 Main Street, Suite 1500
Columbia, South Carolina 29201
803-737-0700

South Dakota
Real Estate Commission
PO Box 490
Pierre, South Dakota 57501-0490
605-773-3600

Tennessee
Real Estate Commission
500 James Robertson Parkway
Suite 180, Volunteer Plaza
Nashville, Tennessee 37243-1151
615-741-2273

Texas
Real Estate Commission
PO Box 12188
Austin, Texas 78711-2188
512-459-6544

Utah
Division of Real Estate
PO Box 45806
Salt Lake City, Utah 84145-0806
801-530-6747

Vermont
109 State Street
Montpelier, Vermont 05609-1106
802-828-3228

Virginia
Dept. of Professional &
Occupational Regulation
3600 West Broad Street
Richmond, Virginia 23230
804-367-8552

Washington State
Department of Licensing
Business & Professions Div.
Real Estate Program
PO Box 9015
Olympia, Washington 98507
360-586-6101

(*continued*)

FIGURE 13-2. Directory of Real Estate License Law Agencies and Offices (by Jurisdiction) (*Continued*)

West Virginia
Real Estate Commission
1033 Quarrier Street, Suite 400
Charleston, West Virginia 25301-2315
304-558-3555

Wisconsin
Director
Bureau of Direct Licensing &
Real Estate
PO Box 8935
Madison, Wisconsin 53716
608-266-5439

Wyoming
Real Estate Commission
2020 Carey Avenue, Suite 100
Cheyenne, Wyoming 82002-0180
307-777-7141

As has been shown throughout this text, the field of multihousing management offers a wide variety of challenges and opportunities. Few other professions provide such constant interaction with such areas as law, finance, insurance, construction, structural and mechanical engineering, plant maintenance, leasing and sales, purchasing, marketing, computer technology, human resources and personnel management, and interpersonal relations. And few other professions require a greater commitment to personal and professional advancement and service to others.

No day in the career of a multihousing manager is like any other day. Exciting, demanding, and rewarding, each day represents the chance to protect and enhance an owner's investment while ensuring a certain quality of life for people right where they live.

CONCLUSION

Multihousing management is a noble profession and a wise career choice. The professional perception of the industry, along with industry salaries, is on a steady increase as the value of the service multihousing managers provide is more widely recognized and appreciated. Led by the National Association of Home Builders (NAHB), the field of multihousing management is working to define itself through uniform standards that will carry the industry forward.

The future holds great promise for the well-trained multihousing manager. The NAHB welcomes you into the field and pledges to provide the resources and support you need to become an outstanding multihousing management professional.

14

Text Glossary and Multihousing Lexicon

Most of the entries below appear in this text. All entries are pertinent to the field of multifamily management.

The definitions of all words identified by an asterisk (*) were provided by, and are used with permission from, Mortgage Bankers Association of America, 1919 Pennsylvania Avenue, NW, Washington, DC 20006, phone (202) 557–2785, www.campusmba.org.

The definitions of all words identified by a caret (^) were extrapolated from this text.

Unless otherwise indicated, all other definitions are from *Webster's Unabridged Dictionary of the English Language* (Random House, Inc.: 2001).

A and D loan
See *Acquisition and development loan.*

Abatement (rental)*
A reduction or elimination of rent payments for a specified period of time, usually granted by the landlord as an inducement to the tenant to enter into or to renew a lease.

Absentee ownership*
Ownership of property (usually income producing) by a nonoccupant who employs others to manage and maintain the property.

Absorption rate*
The rate at which vacant space is either leased or sold to users in the marketplace. Absorption rate is usually expressed in square feet per year or, in the case of multifamily housing, number of units per year.

Accrual basis of accounting*
An accounting method under which income and expenses are charged to the periods for which they are applicable, rather than when payment is made or received. (See also *Cash basis of accounting*.)

Acquisition and development loan (A and D loan)*
A loan for the purchase and preparation of raw land for development. Usually a construction loan or land sale is the source of repayment.

Acquisition cost*
In a HUD/FHA transaction, the price the borrower paid for the property plus any of the following costs: closing, repairs, or financing (except discounts in other than a refinance transaction). Does not include prepaid discounts in a purchase transaction, mortgage insurance premiums, or similar add-ons.

ADA
See *Americans with Disabilities Act.*

Adjustable rate mortgage (ARM)*
A mortgage loan or deed of trust that allows the lender to adjust the interest rate in accordance with a specified index periodically and as agreed to at the inception of the loan. Also called variable rate mortgages (VRM).

Advanced RAM^
The advanced multihousing management credential conferred by the National Association of Home Builders (see also *Registered in Apartment Management Program*).

Affirmative action
The encouragement of increased representation of women and minority group members in employment (and housing, education, etc.).

Agent*
One who legally represents another, called a principal, from whom express or implied authority has been derived.

AHS
See *Annual housing survey.*

Amenity*
A feature that enhances property value. Examples are off-street reserved parking within a condominium community, tennis courts, a swimming pool, or the proximity of public transportation.

Americans with Disabilities Act (ADA)^
Signed into law on July 26, 1990, and effective as of July 26, 1992, the ADA guarantees fair and equitable access to employment opportunities (and housing, public accommodations, transportation, state and local government services, and telecommunications) for qualified disabled individuals.

Amortization*
Repayment of a mortgage debt with periodic payments of both principal and interest, calculated to retire the obligation at the end of a fixed period of time.

Amortization schedule*
A table showing the amounts of principal and interest due at regular intervals and the unpaid mortgage balance after each payment is made.

Annual housing survey (AHS)*
A yearly HUD/Census Bureau study of housing units and trends in the movement of owners and renters.

Annual percentage rate (APR)*
A term defined in section 106 of the Federal Truth in Lending Act (15 USC 1606), which expresses on an annualized basis the charges imposed on the borrower to obtain a loan (defined in the Act as "finance charges"), including interest, discount, and other costs.

Apartment*
A complete and separate living unit in a building containing at least one other like unit.

Apartment hotel*
An apartment complex that provides some hotel services, such as a restaurant or cleaning and linen services. Units are furnished and tenants may stay for extended periods.

Appraisal*
An opinion or estimate of value. Also refers to the process by which a value estimate is obtained.

Appreciation*
An increase in value for any reason except inflation.

Appurtenance*
Anything belonging to or attached to land such as a barn, garage, or easement that is part of the property and is therefore included in a sale or transfer.

APR
See *Annual percentage rate.*

ARM
See *Adjustable rate mortgage.*

Arrears*
The situation in which mortgage interest and real estate taxes are paid at or after the end of the period for which they are levied. Late payment is also described as being in arrears.

As-built plans^
The original mechanical, structural, and other construction plans with changes made by the builder noted on each sheet.

Assessed valuation*
The value that a taxing authority places on real property that becomes the base for computing local property taxes. May also refer to a levy against property for a special purpose, such as a sewer assessment.

Assessment*
A value factor assigned to real property and used to determine real property taxes. The process of reaching the assessed valuation. Also, an add-on tax to raise money for a special purpose.

Assignment of rents*
A transfer to the mortgagee of the right to collect rents from tenants in the event of default by the property owner.

Assisted housing^
Federal housing based on grants that reduce the cost of housing and allow for lower rent levels.

Assumption*
The act of taking over the previous borrower's obligation of a mortgage note. Assumptions may be advantageous if the terms of the mortgage are advantageous and they are not changed by the lender when the mortgage is assumed.

Assumption fee*
The amount paid to a lender for the paperwork and processing of records necessary to approve and document a new debtor.

Assumption of mortgage*
A buyer's acceptance of primary liability for payment of an existing note secured by a mortgage or deed of trust. The seller remains secondarily liable, unless specifically released by the lender.

Attractive nuisance^
An unprotected or unsafe object, condition, or installation that tempts children to play in, on, or with it even though they risk injury to do so.

Audit^
Sometimes mistakenly referred to as a certified audit, an audit is a financial examination that looks at how the records are kept, the way in which accounting duties are divided, the internal controls, the accuracy of the books, the possibilities of fraud, and the on-going viability of the property.

Average life of a mortgage*
A statistic used to estimate the yield on mortgages. Most mortgages written for long terms pay off earlier, either voluntarily or by foreclosure after default. For example, 30-year mortgages traditionally have been considered to have approximately a 12-year average life. Investors base impact of discounts or premiums on the yield of a mortgage on the average life, as opposed to the written term.

Average rate of return*
The return on an investment, as calculated by averaging the total cash flows over the years during which the cash flows are received by the investor.

BAH
See *Basic Allowance for Housing.*

Balance sheet^
A financial report showing assets, liabilities, and equity.

Balloon mortgage*
A mortgage with periodic installments of principal and interest that do not fully amortize the loan. The balance of the mortgage is due in a lump sum at a specified date, usually at the end of the term.

Basic Allowance for Housing (BAH)^
The monthly nontaxable monetary allowance provided by the Department of Defense (DOD) to a military service person who rents or buys a home near the military installation to which she/he is assigned.

Basic rent*
The rent charged in a subsidized housing project and computed on the basis of a maximum subsidy.

Bedroom community*
A suburban residential area where most residents commute to neighboring metropolitan areas to work.

Below market interest rate (BMIR)*
Describes mortgage insurance programs in which the interest rates on the mortgages are below those ordinarily charged for similar conventional financing; used to assist low- and moderate-income families to rent or buy dwelling units.

Betterment*
An improvement, replacement, or maintenance that results in a higher asset valuation.

Birddog letter^
In slang, a "birddog" is someone who tries to steal someone else's date. In multifamily language, a birddog letter is sent to residents asking if they know someone who is interested in living in the property and offering an incentive for information about prospects who later rent. Birddog letters are illegal in some states.

Blanket mortgage*
A mortgage that covers more than one parcel of real estate owned by the mortgagor.

BMIR
See *Below market interest rate.*

Bodily injury liability insurance*
Protection against loss arising out of the liability imposed on the insured by law for damages due to bodily injury, sickness, or disease sustained by third parties. See also *Personal injury.*

Boiler and machinery insurance*
Coverage for the loss to boilers and machinery caused by explosion or mechanical breakdown. The policy may cover damage to the boilers, machinery, other property, and business interruption.

Boilerplate
The detailed standard wording of a contract, warranty, etc.

Bonding
Binding security; firm assurance. (Individuals who are bonded are deemed to be trustworthy.)

Breakeven point*
The figure at which occupancy income is equal to all required expenses and debt service. Used to determine the amount of cash flow necessary to operate a residential or commercial property.

Bridge loan*
A loan that enables a buyer to get financing to make a down payment and pay closing costs before selling the present property. Also called "gap financing."

Broker*
An individual employed on a fee or commission basis as an agent to bring buyers and sellers together and assist in negotiating contracts between them.

BSPRA
See *Builder's and sponsor's profit and risk allowance.*

Builder's and sponsor's profit and risk allowance (BSPRA)*
A credit against the required equity contribution in HUD/FHA insurance programs granted the developer for its services in sponsoring and building the project.

Builder-seller sponsor*
A project sponsor specifically organized to build or rehabilitate and sell a project immediately on completion to a private, nonprofit organization at the certified cost of the project. The nonprofit sponsor buys a total package. (See also *Investor sponsor* and *Nonprofit sponsor.*)

Building code*
Regulations based on safety and health standards that govern design, construction, and materials used in construction.

Building efficiency*
A ratio of net rentable area to gross building area.

Building permit*
Written authorization from a local government for the construction of a new building or for extensive repairs or improvements on an existing structure.

Built-ins*
Permanent, immovable appliances or similar features.

Capital appreciation
An increase or rise in the value of property.

Capital budget^
A budget that anticipates the property's financial needs over time, usually the upcoming three to five years.

Capital expenditure*
The cost of a capital asset or a property improvement made to add value to or extend the useful life of an existing capital asset.

Capitalization (Cap) rate*
The rate of return on net operating income considered acceptable for an investor and used to determine the capitalized value. This rate should provide a return on, as well as a return of, capital. Also known as "cap rate."

Cash basis of accounting*
An accounting method under which income is reported when actually received and expenses are deducted when paid. (See also *Accrual basis of accounting*.)

Cash flow (after taxes)*
Cash received less cash paid out, including income taxes paid.

Cash flow (before taxes)*
Cash received less cash paid out, before any consideration for income taxes.

Cash-on-cash return*
The rate of return on an investment as measured by cash returned to the investor, based on the investor's cash investment and without regard to income tax savings or the use of borrowed funds.

Cash reserve*
Reserves normally kept by the owner of the property to fund any operating shortfall or capital improvements that are required for the property. (See also *Contingency reserve* and *Reserve account/Reserve fund*.)

CDBG
See *Community Development Block Grant*.

Certificate of completion*
A document issued by an architect or engineer stating that construction is completed in accordance with the terms, conditions, and approved plans and specifications.

Certificates of insurance*
A form that evidences policy coverage, limits, etc., which is generally used as proof of insurance. These forms have no legal status and cannot be used in lieu of actual insurance policies.

Certificate of occupancy*
Written authorization given by a local municipality that allows a newly completed or substantially renovated structure to be inhabited.

Change order*
A document evidencing a change in the original plan of construction by a building owner or general contractor.

Chart of accounts*
For accounting purposes, a numerical designation assigned to each asset, liability, and capital account of a business.

Closed-end mortgage*
A mortgage under which the mortgagor is prohibited from borrowing additional funds under the same mortgage.

Closing*
In real estate, the delivery of a deed, the signing of a note, and the disbursement of funds necessary to consummate a sale or loan transaction.

CMO
See *Collateralized mortgage obligation*.

Co-borrower*
Second or additional person equally responsible for payments on a mortgage. A co-borrower does not have to take title to the property but usually has to sign the mortgage note.

Co-insurance^
The condition of insurance under which the owner is responsible for the last determined amount of risk after the limit of the policy has been reached.

Collateral*
Property pledged as security for a debt, for example, mortgaged real estate.

Collateralized mortgage obligation (CMO)*
Mortgage-backed security in which payments on the underlying collateral are partitioned to provide for different maturity classes, called "tranches." Investors choose to buy one or more tranches, with each tranche representing a different maturity. Investors receive payments of interest or principal prioritized according to tranche.

Combined loan-to-value*
The principal balance of all mortgages on the property (including second and third trusts), divided by the value of the property.

Commingling*
Combining funds (such as escrows) into one account that should be accounted for and deposited into separate accounts.

Common area*
An area owned by the owners or tenants of a complex or subdivision for the common use of residents.

Common area maintenance expenses*
Expenses associated with the maintenance of the common areas.

Community apartment project*
Multiple ownership of an apartment in which each owner is a tenant-in-common.

Community association*
A group composed of property owners that serves to protect and maintain a neighborhood or commonly owned properties.

Community Development Block Grant (CDBG)*
Under Title 1 of the Housing and Community Development Act of 1974, eight former categorical grant and loan programs were replaced by a system of unified block grants, under which communities of over 50,000 people are entitled to receive funding while other communities may apply for discretionary funding. Its purpose is to encourage more broadly conceived community development projects and to expand housing opportunities for low- and moderate-income persons.

Community Reinvestment Act (CRA)*
Federal legislation that requires every financial institution to help meet the credit needs of its entire community, including low- and moderate-income neighborhoods.

Co-mortgagor*
A second borrower who signs a mortgage loan with a mortgagor. The co-mortgagor's income, assets, and debts are combined with the mortgagor's for underwriting and ratio analysis purposes. The co-mortgagor's name must appear on the FHA Certificate of Commitment and on the mortgage or deed of trust.

Comparables*
Properties used for comparative purposes in the appraisal process that have similar characteristics to the subject property. Also called "comps."

Compilation^
A financial report in which the auditor assembles a balance sheet, income statement, and statement of changes in financial position for the property from the records maintained by the management company and does not test or verify any of the transactions nor give an opinion as to the accuracy of the statements. This is the most limited type of financial examination.

Component depreciation*
A method of depreciation involving the separation of the cost of various elements of a building (such as roofing, plumbing, and mechanical components) to take advantage of the shorter useful lives of such elements and, thereby, increase the depreciation deductions in the early years of a project. (See also *Curable depreciation, Depreciation, Economic depreciation, Functional depreciation, Incurable depreciation, Physical depreciation,* and *Straight-line depreciation.*)

Component financing*
A method to achieve maximum financing by splitting a real estate parcel into separate fee and leasehold interests and financing each component separately. Also called "split financing."

Concessions*
A discount or other inducement given by a landlord or seller to a prospective tenant or buyer to induce them to sign a lease or purchase property.

Condominium*
A form of property ownership whereby the purchaser receives title to a unit in a multiunit structure and a proportionate interest in common areas. (Condominiums fall under the category of shared-interest associations.) (See also *Home (or condominium) owners association [HOA].*)

Condominium conversion*
The process of changing rental units into a condominium form of ownership.

Condominium declarations*
The basic condominium documents that must be registered by the originating property owner prior to the conveyance of the first unit sold. The declaration thoroughly describes the entire condominium entity, including each unit and all common areas, and specifies essential elements of ownership that permanently govern its operation. Also known as a "master deed."

Construction loan*
A short-term, interim loan for financing the cost of construction. The lender advances funds to the builder at periodic intervals as work progresses.

Contingency reserve*
A reserve account in which funds are held until certain specified conditions are satisfied. (See also *Cash reserve* and *Reserve account/Reserve fund.*)

Conventional financing*
Mortgage financing that is not insured or guaranteed by a government agency.

Convertible mortgage*
A type of adjustable-rate mortgage that may be converted to a fixed rate mortgage at specified intervals during a predetermined time period. In income property lending, a mortgage in which lender-provided funds convert to equity ownership after a predetermined period of time.

Cooperative*
In real estate, a form of multiple ownership in which a corporation or business trust entity holds title to a property (usually an apartment complex) and grants occupancy rights to shareholder tenants through proprietary leases. (Cooperatives fall under the category of shared-interest associations.)

Cost approach to value^
The cost approach calculates the value of a property relative to what it cost to construct. (See also *Income/economic analysis approach to value, Market approach to value,* and *Physical approach to value.*)

Covenant
An agreement, usually formal, between two or more persons to do or not do something specified.

Credit*
Financial status—ability of borrowers to meet the terms of their obligations.

Credit rating*
A rating given to a person or company that establishes credit worthiness based on present financial condition, experience, and past credit history.

Critical Housing Area^
The military term referring to an area where the wait for on-base housing at a given military base equals or exceeds the period of time a service member will be assigned to that base and the surrounding civilian community does not offer sufficient, affordable, or acceptable units to absorb incoming service members and their families. Service members assigned to bases in critical housing areas are discouraged from relocating their families to those areas until suitable and affordable housing becomes available.

Curable depreciation
See *Deferred maintenance*.

Curb appeal^
The visual attractiveness of a property based on what one can see from the curb.

Debt/equity ratio*
The proportion of capital borrowed to the amount of capital invested out-of-pocket or obtained through the sale of common stock. Also called "leverage ratio."

Debt service*
A borrower's periodic mortgage payments comprised of principal and/or interest on the unpaid mortgage balance.

Debt service coverage ratio*
A ratio of effective annual net operating income to annual principal and/or interest payments. Also called "debt service coverage."

Deductible^
In insurance, the amount the owner is liable for as the first determined amount of risk before any insurance claim is collected.

Deed of trust*
A type of security instrument in which the borrower conveys title to real property to a third party (trustee) to be held in trust as a security for the lender, with the provision that the trustee shall reconvey the title on the payment of the debt and, conversely, will sell the land and pay the debt in the event of a default by the borrower.

Default*
The nonpayment of a mortgage or other loan in accordance with the terms as specified in the note.

Default ratio*
The occupancy level at which the effective gross income from an income-producing property is insufficient to pay operating expenses and debt service, thus creating the risk of default. The ratio is calculated by dividing the effective gross income into operating expenses plus debt service.

Defeasance*
A provision in a mortgage that allows the debtor to reclaim property that has been foreclosed, if certain conditions are met.

Deferred maintenance*
Postponed, infrequent, or inadequate maintenance practices on a building or property, often resulting in physical depreciation and loss of value. Deferred maintenance can be an indicator of inadequate cash flow or lack of pride in the property. Also called "curable depreciation."

Demand letter*
Correspondence sent to the borrower indicating that unless the loan is made current within a certain time frame, the lender can, by virtue of a default, declare the entire principal balance outstanding, as well as all interest due under the note, to be due and payable.

Department of Housing and Urban Development (HUD)
According to the HUD website at www.hud.gov., the government's Department of Housing and Urban Development was created in 1965, but its history extends back to the National Housing Act of 1934. The mission of HUD is to ensure a decent, safe, and sanitary home and suitable living environment for every American by creating opportunities for home ownership; providing housing assistance for low-income persons; working to create, rehabilitate, and maintain the nation's affordable housing; enforcing the nation's Fair Housing laws; helping the homeless; spurring economic growth in distressed neighborhoods; and helping local communities meet their development needs.

Depreciation*
A decline in value of a building or other real estate improvement, resulting from age, physical wear, and economic or functional obsolescence. This figure is deducted annually from net income. (See also *Curable depreciation, Component depreciation, Economic depreciation, Functional depreciation, Incurable depreciation, Physical depreciation,* and *Straight-line depreciation.*)

Developer*
A person or entity who prepares raw land for building sites or rehabilitates existing buildings.

Development loan*
A short-term loan advanced before a construction loan, used by developers to acquire land and install basic utilities such as roads, sewers, and water supply systems.

Directors and Officers (D & O) Liability Insurance^
Insurance that covers claims against directors and officers of shared-interest associations.

Discount point*
Amount payable to the lending institution by the borrower or seller to increase the lender's effective yield. One point is equal to 1 percent of the loan.

Down unit^
A unit identified as being unrentable as a result of a physical deficiency. Also called "off line" unit.

Draw*
Disbursement of a portion of the loan proceeds, usually at a predetermined point in the construction or rehabilitation schedule, to pay for work already completed. The balance of the proceeds is retained until the next scheduled draw, or until completion of the construction or rehabilitation work, to protect the lender against the contractor's failure to complete the work as scheduled.

Due diligence review*
An examination by a purchaser of a servicing portfolio. Generally, the reviewer will look at credit quality and underwriting of the loan collateral underlying the servicing rights, correctness and completeness of the loan documents, the seller's servicing practices and methodologies, and the accuracy of the portfolio-offering document. As used here, a re-underwriting of the loan in line with the borrower's request to determine the feasibility of the request by the lender.

Dwelling unit*
Living quarters occupied, or intended for occupancy, by a household.

Economic depreciation*
The loss of the value of real estate caused by changes outside the particular property affected, for example, a decline in the neighborhood or a change in zoning. (See also *Component depreciation, Curable depreciation, Depreciation, Functional depreciation, Incurable depreciation, Straight-line depreciation,* and *Physical depreciation*.)

Economic value*
The condition of the property based on its earning potential.

EEOC
See *Equal Employment Opportunity Commission.*

Effective gross income*
Stabilized income after vacancy and bad debt allowances that a property is expected to generate.

Effective yield*
The annual return expressed as the face interest rate divided by the amount invested, used when a mortgage or other debt instrument is bought at a discount or premium.

Equal Employment Opportunity Commission (EEOC/EEO)
An independent federal agency created under the Civil Rights Act of 1964, as amended, to police a program (Equal Employment Opportunity) to eliminate discrimination in employment based on race, color, age, sex, national origin, religion, or mental or physical handicap.

Equity*
The net value of an asset. In the case of real estate, it would be the difference between the present value of the property and the mortgage amount on that property.

Equity participation*
The right of a lender to a share in the gross profits, net profits, or net proceeds in the event of sale or refinance of a property on which the lender has made a loan. Also known as an "equity kicker."

Escrow*
An item of value, money, or documents deposited with a third party to be delivered upon the fulfillment of a condition. For example, the deposit by a borrower with the lender of funds to pay taxes and insurance premiums when they become due or the deposit of funds or documents with an attorney or escrow agent to be disbursed upon the closing of a sale of real estate. In some parts of the country, escrows of taxes and insurance premiums are called impounds or reserves.

Eviction*
The lawful expulsion of an occupant from real property.

Fair Housing Act^
Title VIII of the Civil Rights Act of 1968 as amended by the Fair Housing Amendments Act of 1988, better known as the Fair Housing Act, requires that rental housing be made available to all persons without regard to race, color, religion, sex, handicap, familial status, or national origin.

Fair market rent*
An amount determined by HUD to be the cost of modest, nonluxury rental units in a specific market area.

Fair market value*
The price at which property is transferred between a willing buyer and a willing seller, each of whom has a reasonable knowledge of all pertinent facts and neither being under any compulsion to buy or sell.

Family and Medical Leave Act (FMLA)^
The Family and Medical Leave Act of 1993 (FMLA) was enacted to provide workers with time off to adjust to a new child in the home or to deal with a serious illness in the family unit without fear of losing their jobs.

Fannie Mae (Federal National Mortgage Association-FNMA)*
The nation's largest mortgage investor created in 1968 by an amendment to Title III of the National Housing Act (12 USC 1716 et seq.). This stockholder-owner corporation, a portion of whose board of directors is appointed by the president of the United States, supports the secondary market in mortgages on residential property with mortgage purchase and securitization programs.

Fannie Mae DUS lender*
A lender designated by Fannie Mae who originates, underwrites, closes, and services Fannie Mae-approved multifamily mortgage loans.

Farmers Home Administration (FmHA)*
A former government agency within the Department of Agriculture that operated under the Consolidated Farm and Rural Development Act of 1921 and Title V of the Housing Act of 1949. This agency provided financing to farmers and other qualified borrowers who were unable to obtain loans elsewhere.

Federal Emergency Management Agency (FEMA)
According to the FEMA website at www.fema.gov, the Federal Emergency Management Agency is an independent federal agency reporting to the president and tasked with responding to, planning for, recovering from, and mitigating against disaster. FEMA can trace its beginnings to the Congressional Act of 1803, generally considered the first piece of disaster legislation, which provided assistance to a New Hampshire town following an extensive fire.

Federal Housing Administration (FHA)*
A federal agency within the Department of Housing and Urban Development (HUD) that provides mortgage insurance for residential mortgages and sets standards for construction and underwriting. The FHA does not lend money nor does it plan or construct housing.

FEMA
See *Federal Emergency Management Agency.*

FHA
See *Federal Housing Administration.*

FHA loan*
A loan made through an approved lender and insured by the Federal Housing Administration. Although there are limits to the size of FHA loans, they are intended to finance moderately priced homes.

Fiduciary*
One who acts in a capacity of trust and confidence for another.

Final closing*
The date upon which the permanent mortgage lender funds the mortgage loan.

Financial accounting^
The term used when records and reports are prepared for the use of outside accounting professionals, attorneys, or anyone else.

Financial statement*
A financial report including a balance sheet and an income statement.

Financial statement analysis*
Evaluation of the existing and potential income stream of the real estate to determine prospective cash flow and debt service capacity.

First mortgage*
A mortgage that gives the mortgagee a security right over all other mortgages of the mortgaged property.

Fixed rate mortgage (FRM)*
A mortgage in which the interest rate and payments remain the same for the life of the loan.

Flat rental*
Rental payments under a lease that are fixed and unchanged throughout the term of the lease.

Float*
A loan application in which the lender has not committed to lend at a particular interest rate (the rate is not locked in). In mortgage servicing, the period of time between the receipt of borrower's principal and interest payments, and remittance of those funds to investors.

Floating rate loan*
A loan originated without a firm commitment to the borrower, thereby closing at the market rate.

Floor plan*
Scale architectural drawings showing details of floor design and layout.

FmHA
See *Farmer's Home Administration.*

FMLA
See *Family and Medical Leave Act.*

Forbearance*
The act of refraining from taking legal action despite the fact that the mortgage is in arrears. It is usually granted only when a mortgagor makes satisfactory arrangements to pay the amount owed at a future date.

Foreclosure*
A legal procedure in which a mortgaged property is sold in a legal process to pay the outstanding debt in case of default.

Freddie Mac (Federal Home Loan Mortgage Corporation)*
Created by Congress in Title III of the Emergency Home Finance Act of 1970 (12 USC 1451 et seq.). This stockholder-owned corporation, a portion of whose board of directors is appointed by the president of the United States, supports the secondary market in mortgages on residential and multifamily properties with mortgage purchase and securitization programs.

Free and clear return*
Net operating income divided by total capital investment. Also called "rate of return" or "overall rate."

FRM
See *Fixed rate mortgage.*

Frontage*
The property line abutting the most important adjacent property, usually a street, lake, river, or ocean.

Fully amortized*
A mortgage that has a zero balance at the end of the mortgage term.

Functional depreciation*
In real estate, loss of value as a result of advancements in technology or design that make the features of the current facility obsolete. Also called "functional obsolescence." (See also *Component depreciation, Curable depreciation, Depreciation, Economic depreciation, Incurable depreciation, Physical depreciation,* and *Straight-line depreciation.*)

Functional obsolescence
See *Functional depreciation.*

Gap financing*
An interim loan given to finance the difference between the floor loan and the maximum permanent loan as committed. Also called "bridge financing."

Garden apartment
An apartment on the ground floor of an apartment building having direct access to a backyard or garden; a low-level apartment building or building complex surrounded by lawns and trees, shrubbery, or gardens.

Ginnie Mae (Governmental National Mortgage Association-GNMA)*
Created in 1968 by an amendment to Title III of the National Housing Act (12 USC 1716 et seq.). This federal government corporation is a constituent part of the Department of Housing and Urban Development (HUD). Among other governmental functions, it guarantees securities backed by mortgages that are insured or guaranteed by other government agencies. Also called Government National Mortgage Association (GNMA).

GMC
See *Guaranteed mortgage certificate.*

GPI
See *Gross potential income.*

GPM
See *Graduated payment mortgage.*

Grace period*
A period of time (usually 15 days) after a mortgage payment is due in which the lender will not charge a late penalty or report the payment as late.

Graduated lease
See *Step-up lease.*

Graduated payment mortgage (GPM)*
A type of flexible payment mortgage in which the payments increase for a specified period of time and then level off. Usually results in negative amortization.

Gross area*
The total floor area of a building measured from the outside of the exterior walls.

Gross income*
Total income produced by a property before any expenses are deducted.

Gross possible income^
The total income possible for a property before any deductions or allowances.

Gross potential rent^
Gross potential rent is calculated by adding the current rent of all apartments in a property. The gross potential rent informs the owner and the manager of the maximum potential rent if the property were 100 percent occupied and every resident paid on time and in full.

Gross rent multiplier*
A figure derived from the relationship between gross rental income and sales price. Used to compare rental properties.

Guaranteed loan*
A loan guaranteed by a government agency or any other interested party.

Guaranteed mortgage certificate (GMC)*
A bond-like instrument issued by Freddie Mac that represents ownership in a large pool of residential mortgages. Principal is returned annually and interest is paid semiannually.

Guarantor*
A party who is secondarily liable for another's debt or performance (in contrast to a surety who is primarily liable with the principal debtor).

Guaranty*
A promise by one party to pay a debt or perform an obligation contracted for or by another in the event that the obligor fails to pay or perform as contracted. For VA loans, the amount of money VA will reimburse a lender on default of a VA mortgage. Also referred to as the amount of entitlement or eligibility.

Guaranty fee*
Price for guaranteeing to an investor the timely payment of principal and interest from all the mortgages underlying a mortgage-backed security.

HazCom^
The Office of Safety and Health Administration Hazard Communication Standard (HazCom) that requires all employers to train employees about the hazards they are exposed to in the course of their work; maintain material safety data (MSD) for all hazardous materials; and develop a written hazard communication program that describes how the property is meeting its obligations under HazCom.

Historically based budget^
A historically based budget uses assumptions about the property's existing history of costs to project expenses into the future.

HOA
See *Home (or condominium) owners association.*

Home (or condominium) owners association (HOA)*
A nonprofit corporation or association that manages the common areas and services of a planned unit development or condominium project. In a condominium project, it has no ownership interest in the common areas; in a planned unit development, it holds title to common areas.

HUD
See *Department of Housing and Urban Development.*

HVAC*
The heating, ventilating, and air conditioning system.

Hybrid investment*
An investment that is a mix of debt and equity.

Income and expense statement*
The actual or estimated schedule of income and expense items reflecting net gain or loss during a specified period.

Income/economic analysis approach to value^
The income/economic analysis approach values a property based on the financial return the property provides to the owner. (See also *Cost approach to value, Market approach to value,* and *Physical approach to value.*)

Income/expense ratio*
A qualifying ratio used in underwriting a residential loan that computes the percentage of monthly income required to meet the monthly housing expense.

Income property*
Real estate developed or improved to produce income.

Income property loan*
A loan secured by commercial real estate.

Incurable depreciation*
A loss in the value of improvements that is not economically feasible to correct. (See also *Component depreciation, Curable depreciation, Depreciation, Economic depreciation, Functional depreciation, Physical depreciation,* and *Straight-line depreciation.*)

Installment debt*
Borrowed money that is repaid in several successive payments, usually at regular intervals, for a specific amount and for a specified term.

Interest rate cap*
A limit on interest rate increases and/or decreases during each interest rate adjustment (adjustment period cap) or over the term (life cap) of the mortgage.

Interim financing*
Financing used from the beginning of a project to the closing of a permanent loan, usually a construction or development loan.

Internal rate of return (IRR)*
A method of determining investment yield over time, assuming a set of income, expense, and property value conditions.

Investor*
Any person or institution that invests in mortgages or mortgage-backed securities.

Investor sponsor*
An investor sponsor in cooperative housing programs is a private, profit-making organization that undertakes the development of housing projects for sale at a profit to nonprofit cooperative corporations. (See also *Builder-seller sponsor* and *Nonprofit sponsor.*)

IRR
See *Internal rate of return.*

Joint tenancy*
Form of co-ownership giving each tenant equal interest and equal rights in the property, including the right of survivorship.

Joint venture*
An association formed for a specific purpose and duration between two or more parties to own and/or develop real estate. A joint venture may take a variety of legal forms including partnership, tenancy in common, or corporation.

Jointly owned property*
Property held in the name of more than one person.

Jumbo mortgage*
A mortgage that is larger than the legislated purchase limits of Fannie Mae and Freddie Mac.

Land sale-leaseback*
A transaction whereby an entity purchases land, leases it back to the developer, and extends a leasehold mortgage loan secured by the improvements on that land.

Landlord*
Owner or lessor of real property.

Lease*
A written document containing the conditions under which the possession and use of real and/or personal property are given by the owner to another for a stated period and consideration. (Also called an Occupancy agreement.)

Lender liability*
An area of legal findings that would hold the lender financially responsible for damages and costs based on the lender's activities (especially in the management of real estate securing any of the lender's mortgage loans, as this relates to environmental cleanup liability).

Lessee*
One holding rights of possession and use of property under the terms of a lease. (See also *Tenant.*)

Lessor*
One who leases property to a lessee. Also called a "landlord."

Letter of credit*
A letter authorizing a person or company to draw on a bank or stating that the bank will honor their credit up to the stated amount.

Leveraged buyout*
The acquisition of a company, financed primarily with borrowed money, using the acquired company's assets to collateralize the loan.

Lien*
A legal hold or claim of a creditor on the property of another as security for a debt. Liens may be against real or personal property.

Limited partnership*
A form of business ownership that consists of one or more general partners who are fully liable and one or more limited partners who are liable only for the amount of their investment.

Living on the economy^
The term used when military service persons reside in civilian housing communities.

Loan administration*
A mortgage banking function that includes the receipt of payments, customer service, escrow administration, investor accounting, collections, and foreclosures. Also called servicing.

Loan fee*
A fee charged to a borrower by a lender for negotiating a loan, sometimes used in reference to an additional fee over and above the origination fee.

Loan guaranty certificate*
A VA document that states the portion of a loan that is guaranteed.

Loan-producing cycle*
The period from loan application through funding of a mortgage loan.

Loan-to-value ratio (LTV)*
The ratio of the amount of the loan to the appraised value or sale price of real property (expressed as a percentage).

Loan transfer*
The assumption of existing financing by a new owner when a property is sold.

Local housing authority*
A government agency that monitors and implements programs to satisfy community housing development needs.

Lock box*
A postal address, maintained by the firm's bank, that is used solely for the purpose of collecting checks. A major goal of a lock box is to reduce collection float because the receipts are immediately credited to the firm's bank account.

Lot*
A measured parcel of land having fixed boundaries as shown on the recorded plat.

LTV
See *Loan-to-value ratio.*

Managerial accounting^
The term used when financial records and reports are prepared for the use of the owner and the manager.

Margin*
In an adjustable rate mortgage, the spread between the index and the mortgage interest rate.

Market approach to value^
The market approach to valuation compares the value of the owner's property with the current value of other substantially similar properties. (See also *Cost approach to value, Income/economic analysis approach to value,* and *Physical approach to value.*)

Master deed
See *Condominium declarations.*

Material safety data (MSD)
The Office of Safety and Health Administration Hazard Communication Standard (HazCom) requires employers to maintain material safety data for all hazardous materials in the workplace.

Maximum loan amount*
Highest loan dollar amount allowed under federal or conventional guidelines. In commercial real estate, the highest loan dollar amount that a property can support, based on projected income.

MBS
See *Mortgage-backed security.*

Millage
The tax rate, as for property, assessed in mills per dollar (one-tenth of a cent).

Mortgage*
A pledge of property, usually real property, as security for a debt. By extension, the document evidencing the pledge. In many states this document is a deed of trust. The document may contain the terms of repayment of the debt. By further extension, "mortgage" may be used to describe both the mortgage proper and the separate promissory note evidencing the debt and providing the terms of the debt's repayment.

Mortgage-backed security (MBS)*
An investment instrument backed by mortgage loans as security. Ownership is evidenced by an undivided interest in a pool of mortgages or trust deeds. Income from the underlying mortgages is used to pay interest and principal on the securities.

Mortgage banker*
An individual, firm, or corporation that originates, sells, and/or services loans secured by mortgages on real property.

Mortgage broker*
A firm or individual who, for a commission, matches borrowers and lenders. A mortgage broker takes applications and sometimes processes loans but generally does not use its own funds for closing.

Mortgage discount*
The percentage difference between the principal amount of a mortgage and the selling price.

Mother Hubbard clause*
A provision in a mortgage that allows the lender, in the event of a default, to foreclose not only that mortgage but also any other mortgages that have been executed by the borrower and which are held by the lender.

MSD
See *Material safety data.*

Multifamily development*
A complex consisting of two or more residential buildings as a part of a single development. Generally associated with garden apartments, townhouses, and high-rise apartment complexes.

Multifamily housing*
A building with more than four residential units.

NAHB
See *National Association of Home Builders.*

National Association of Home Builders (NAHB)^
The National Association of Home Builders (NAHB), parent organization of the Registered in Apartment Management (RAM) Program, is a national trade association representing the housing industry. The multifamily housing industry is represented by the NAHB Multifamily Council. NAHB established the Multifamily Council in 1982 to direct programs and services to its increasingly diverse multifamily membership and to serve as the voice of the multifamily builder-owner.

National Institute for Occupational Safety and Health (NIOSH)
According to the NIOSH website at www.cdc.gov/niosh, the National Institute for Occupational Safety and Health (NIOSH) is the Federal agency responsible for conducting research and making recommendations for the prevention of work-related disease and injury. The Institute is part of the Centers for Disease Control and Prevention (CDC).

Negative amortization*
The unpaid interest that is added to the mortgage principal in a loan wherein the principal balance increases rather than decreases because the mortgage payments do not cover the full amount of interest due.

Negative cash flow*
The deficit that is created when expenditures required to maintain an investment exceed income received on the property.

Net operating income (NOI)^
Net operating income (NOI) is the difference between all of a property's operating revenue for a given period of time (such as rent received, late fees, NSF [insufficient funds] charges, ancillary income from laundry and vending, cable TV, parking or storage charges, and any other revenue that the property might have) and the property's operating expenses for the same period of time (such as office expenses, property staff payroll, management fees, utility expenses, and all maintenance and upkeep expenses that don't involve capital expenditures) before subtracting income taxes, debt service, capital items, and interest. Basically, it is the money remaining in the property's operating account at the end of the subject time period. Most property owners wish to maximize their NOI.

NIOSH
See *National Institute for Occupational Safety and Health.*

NOFA
See *Notice of funding availability.*

NOI
See *Net operating income.*

Nonperforming loan*
A loan that has not fulfilled one or more of the terms, covenants, conditions, or obligations required under the mortgage.

Nonprofit sponsor*
A group not motivated by profit that backs a housing project. Units can be rented on a nonprofit basis or the sponsor can allow individual, cooperative, or condominium ownership. (See also *Builder-seller sponsor* and *Investor sponsor.*)

Nonrecourse loan*
Type of loan that prohibits the lender from attempting to recover against the borrower (personally) if the security value for the loan falls below the amount required to repay the loan.

Notice of funding availability (NOFA)*
Notice by HUD-area offices to inform potential project sponsors of contract authority available under federal programs.

Occupancy agreement
See *Lease.*

Occupancy rate*
The percentage of space or units that are leased or occupied.

Occupational Safety and Health Administration (OSHA)
The division of the Department of Labor that sets and enforces occupational health and safety rules.

Off line unit
See *Down unit.*

Off-site improvements*
Improvements outside the boundaries of a property that enhance its value, such as sidewalks, streets, curbs, and gutters.

On-site improvements*
Any construction of buildings or other improvements within the boundaries of a property that increase its value.

Open-end mortgage*
A mortgage with a provision that the outstanding loan amount may be increased by mutual agreement of the lender and the borrower.

Operating budget^
The basic document for planning the financial operation of a property for the coming year.

Operating expense ratio*
The percentage relationship between operating expenses and effective gross income.

Origination*
Securing a completed mortgage application from a commercial or residential borrower.

OSHA
See *Occupational Safety and Health Administration.*

Overall rate
See *Free and clear return.*

Over-improvement*
Renovation or remodeling inappropriate to a site because of its excess size or cost or inadequate return.

Owner-occupied purchase*
The purchase of a property for the purpose of the primary residence of the owner.

Performing loan*
A loan that has fulfilled and continues to fulfill all of the terms, covenants, conditions, or obligations required under the mortgage.

Permanent financing*
A mortgage loan, usually covering development costs, interim loans, construction loans, financing expenses, and marketing, administrative, legal, and other cost. This loan differs from the construction loans, financing expenses, and marketing, administrative, legal, and other costs. This loan differs from the construction loan in that financing goes into place after the project is constructed and open for occupancy. It is a long-term obligation, generally for a period of 10 years or longer.

Personal injury*
Injury other than those arising out of bodily injury such as false arrest, malicious prosecution, wrongful entry or eviction, libel or slander, or violation of privacy. The extent of such coverage may vary from policy to policy. (See also *Bodily injury liability insurance.*)

PHA
See *Public housing authority.*

Physical approach to value*
An appraisal method whereby property value is derived by estimating the replacement cost of improvements, less estimated depreciation, plus the estimated land value. Synonymous with cost approach. (See also *Cost approach to value, Income/economic analysis approach to value,* and *Market approach to value.*)

Physical depreciation*
Decline in the value of a physical asset or real property resulting from normal usage, age, wear and tear, disintegration, or action of the elements. Depreciation can be curable or incurable. (See also *Component depreciation, Curable depreciation, Depreciation, Economic depreciation, Functional depreciation, Incurable depreciation,* and *Straight-line depreciation.*)

Piggyback financing*
A loan made jointly by two or more lenders on the same property under one mortgage or trust deed.

Planned unit development (PUD)*
A comprehensive development plan for a large land area. A PUD usually includes residences, roads, schools, recreational facilities, commercial, office, and industrial areas. Also, a subdivision having lots or areas owned in common and reserved for the use of or all of the owners of the separately owned lots.

Plat*
A map representing a piece of land subdivided into lots with streets, boundaries, easements, and dimensions shown thereon.

PMI
See *Private mortgage insurance.*

PMSR
See *Purchased mortgage servicing rights.*

Point*
An amount equal to 1 percent of the principal amount of a mortgage. Loan discount points are a one-time charge assessed at closing by the lender to increase the yield on the mortgage loan to a competitive position with other types of investments.

Preferred debt*
Any debt obligation that has precedence over others, as in a senior or first mortgage.

Primary residence*
Residence that the owner physically occupies and uses as his or her home.

Private conduit*
A private market entity (without ties to the federal government) that increases the availability of real estate financing by purchasing and selling mortgages and mortgage-backed securities. Private conduits match lender and investor needs, allowing for the sale or securitization of loans by mortgage bankers to a national market.

Private mortgage insurance (PMI)*
Insurance written by a private company protecting the mortgage lender against financial loss occasioned by a borrower defaulting on the mortgage.

Pro forma statement*
A financial or accounting statement using estimates and assumptions to project income and the performance of real property over a period of time.

Proprietary lease^
The lease held by shareholders of a residential cooperative corporation granting them the right to reside in a dwelling unit of the cooperative property for as long as they own stock in the corporation.

Public housing/Public Housing Administration^
Housing owned or operated by a government and usually offered at low rent to the needy. The public housing program, created by Congress in 1937 and administered by the Public Housing Administration, authorized local government bodies, known as local housing authorities, to participate in the construction, ownership, and management functions of the public housing programs.

Public housing authority (PHA)*
A public agency created by state or local governments to finance or operate low-income housing.

PUD
See *Planned unit development*.

Purchased mortgage servicing rights (PMSR)*
Aggregate value of a servicing portfolio obtained from a source outside the purchasing company. It is classified as an intangible asset for both financial accounting and regulatory reporting purposes.

Quiet enjoyment*
The right of an owner to the use of property without disturbance.

RAM
The Registered in Apartment Management credential conferred by the National Association of Home Builders. (See also *Registered in Apartment Management*.)

Rate of return
See *Free and clear return*.

Real estate
See *Real property*.

Real estate investment trust (REIT)*
An investment vehicle in which title to real estate assets is held and managed by one or more trustees who control acquisitions and investments much like a mutual fund.

Real estate syndicate*
A group of investors who pool funds for investment in real property.

Real estate taxes*
Local government taxes levied on the ownership of real estate. Also known as "real estate property taxes."

Real property*
Land and improvements permanently attached to it, such as buildings. In some states, this term is synonymous with the term "real estate."

Recourse loan*
A type of mortgage loan in which the lender's remedies in the event of a borrower's default are unlimited, extending beyond the property to the borrower's personal assets. In secondary marketing, a loan that the lender must repurchase in the case of loan default or other defect.

REIT
See *Real estate investment trust*.

Registered in Apartment Management (RAM) Program^
The Registered in Apartment Management (RAM) Program was developed in 1971 by the National Association of Home Builders and is the oldest residential property management certification in the United States. The RAM program provides training to property managers of multifamily rental, condominium, cooperative, subsidized, market-rate, and military housing throughout the country.

Rehabilitation*
The process of reconstructing or improving property that is in a state of disrepair and bringing it back to its full potential or use. A mortgage for such purpose would be referred to as a rehab mortgage.

Rent
A payment made periodically by a tenant to landlord in return for the use of land, a building, an apartment, an office, or other property.

Rentable area*
The area of a property, measured in square feet, upon which rent can be collected.

Rental concession*
A landlord's agreement to forego part of the advertised rent in an effort to attract tenants.

Rental Partnership Program^
An innovative method to assist military personnel in finding safe, suitable, affordable private sector housing within a reasonable commuting distance from their assigned base. The program offers significant benefits to both the owners of the private sector properties and the miliary service personnel who participate in it.

Rent control*
Legal limitation of rent increases.

Rent roll*
A list of tenants leasing a property, which details terms of lease, area leased, and the amount of rent being paid.

Rent stabilized
Housing regulated by law so that rent increases may not exceed a specified amount.

Rent-up period*
The period after construction that a rental property requires to achieve projected stabilized income and occupancy levels.

Reserve account/Reserve fund^
In rental and shared-interest association properties, a contingency fund earmarked for capital replacements, repairs, improvements, and emergencies. (See also *Cash reserve* and *Contingency reserve.*)

Retirement community*
A planned community for those of retirement age, providing attractively sized and priced dwelling units and offering construction features, amenities, and locations for aging residents.

Return of investment (ROI)*
The percentage of profit returned in relation to the original capital invested in a project. Equity divided by cash flow.

Return on equity (ROE)*
The ratio of cash flow to the equity investment.

Review^
A financial examination in which the auditor examines a property's financial records, the way in which the records are kept, the internal controls in use, and occasionally tests the accuracy of financial statements in a limited way. The auditor will not render an opinion on the statements but will assemble them into the balance sheet, income statement, and statement of changes in financial position.

RHS
See *Rural Housing Service.*

Right of survivorship*
The survivor's right to the property of a deceased person. In the case of joint tenancy or tenancy by entirety (husband and wife), the undivided property passes to the survivor.

ROE
See *Return on equity.*

ROI
See *Return of investment.*

Rural Housing Service (RHS)*
A government agency within the U.S. Department of Agriculture that offers various financing programs available to aid in the development of rural America. These rural housing programs are divided into three categories; community facilities (CF), single family housing (SFH), and multi-family housing (MFH). These programs were formerly operated by the Rural Development Administration and the Farmers Home Administration.

Sale-leaseback*
A sales arrangement in which a seller deeds a property to a buyer for consideration. The seller then leases the same property back from its new owner.

Secondary financing*
A funding method using a loan secured by a second mortgage on a property. Sometimes used to refer to any financing technique other than equity and first mortgage debt.

Secondary mortgage market*
The market in which lenders and investors buy and sell existing mortgages or mortgage-backed securities, thereby providing greater availability of funds for additional mortgage lending.

Section*
A division or parcel of land on a government survey comprising one square or 640 acres.

Servicing spread*
That portion of the interest rate added by the lender to cover the cost of administering the mortgage asset.

Setback lines*
Lines that define the required distances for the location of a structure in relation to the perimeter of the property. They are in accordance with building codes, deed restrictions, and zoning requirements.

Shared-interest association^
A multifamily community in which each dwelling unit is individually owned and all the unit owners (who may be individuals or other entities such as corporations, etc.) share together in the ownership and the operational and financial obligations of the association's common land, amenities, property, and other common elements. In return for fulfilling the obligations of shared-interest ownership, the association gives its owners certain services and the right of owners to avail themselves of the association's private amenities. Cooperative corporations, condominium associations, home (or condominium) owner associations (HOAs), and property owner associations (POAs) are common types of shared-interest associations.

Skip^
The term used to refer to tenants who vacate a property without giving notice.

Soft costs*
Architectural, engineering, and legal fees associated with building construction, as distinguished from land and other costs.

Split financing
See *Component financing.*

Sponsor
See *Builder-seller sponsor, Investor sponsor,* and *Nonprofit sponsor.*

Spread*
The difference between the rate at which money can be borrowed and the rate at which it is loaned. Also, the difference between the ask and bid prices on a security.

Step-down leas*
A lease that provides for decreases in rent at set intervals.

Step-up lease*
A lease that provides for increases in rent at set intervals. Increases are sometimes based on appraisals. Also called a "graduated lease."

Straight-line depreciation*
A method of depreciation in which an equal amount of depreciation is taken annually over an asset's economic life. (See also *Component depreciation, Curable depreciation, Depreciation, Economic depreciation, Functional depreciation, Incurable depreciation,* and *Physical depreciation.*)

Subdivision*
Improved or unimproved land divided into a number of parcels for sale, lease financing, or development.

Sublease*
A lease executed by a lessee to a third person for a term no longer than the remaining portion of the original lease.

Subsidize*
A term for aid. Federally subsidized mortgages typically have an interest rate lower than market because of government assistance. Temporary buydowns are considered subsidized mortgages because there is money placed in an escrow fund to supplement the regular payment for a certain period of time.

Surety bond*
Written evidence of a third party, called the surety, that will be primarily liable for a debt in the case of default.

Survey*
A measurement of land, prepared by a registered land surveyor, showing the location of the land with reference to known points, its dimensions, and the location and dimensions of any improvements.

Syndication*
The sale of equity interests in real state projects to investors other than the original developer.

Tax-exempt bond*
A bond partly or wholly exempt from federal and/or state income tax.

Tax shelter*
A reduction of taxable income through the reinvestment of earnings on capital; any investment that postpones or avoids tax payments.

TDD
See *Telecommunications Device for the Deaf.*

Telecommunications Device for the Deaf (TDD)^
Under Section 504 of the Rehabilitation Act of 1973 (as amended), Section 8.6 (a)(2) states "where a recipient communicates with applicants and beneficiaries by telephone, telecommunication devices for deaf persons (TDDs) or equally effective communication systems shall be used." This requirement applies to subsidized properties. The TDD phone numbers should be listed in all advertisements and brochures of subsidized properties.

Tenancy*
The use of real estate under any kind of right of title.

Tenancy in common*
A form of undivided ownership interest by two or more persons that provides for no right of survivorship. The interest need not be of equal percentage.

Tenant*
One who is not the owner but occupies real property under consent of the owner and in subordination to the owner's title. The tenant is entitled to exclusive possession, use, and enjoyment of the property, usually for a time and amount specified in the lease. (See also *Lessee.*)

Term*
The period of time between the commencement date and termination date of a note, mortgage, legal document, or other contract.

Townhouse*
A rowhouse on a small lot that has exterior limits common to other similar units. Title to the unit and its lot is vested in the individual buyer with a fractional interest in common areas, if any.

Turnkey project*
A project in which a builder, contractor, or developer contracts to construct and deliver a completed facility, ready for occupancy and operation.

Usable area*
The actual number of square feet contained within a tenant's demised space.

Vacancy factor*
The percentage of gross rental income that represents vacant units.

Vacancy rate*
The ratio between the number of vacant units and the total number of units in a multi-tenant building or development.

VA loan*
Mortgage made by an approved lender and guaranteed by the Department of Veterans Affairs. VA loans are made to eligible veterans and those currently serving in the military and have a lower downpayment than other types of loans.

Valuation*
The estimation of a property's price through appraisal.

Variable rate mortgage (VRM)
See *Adjustable rate mortgage.*

Vendor*
The seller of personal or real property.

Working capital*
The excess of current assets over current liabilities.

Zero-base budget^
A budget created exclusively by researching projected income and costs without any historical data.

INDEX

Page numbers in *italics* denote figures

S

T

U

V